# MARKETING MANAGEMENT

## A STRATEGIC DECISION-MAKING APPROACH

# MARKETING MANAGEMENT
## A STRATEGIC DECISION-MAKING APPROACH

### EIGHTH EDITION

**JOHN W. MULLINS**
Associate Professor of Management Practice in Marketing
and Entrepreneurship
London Business School

**ORVILLE C. WALKER, JR.**
James D. Watkins Professor of Marketing, Emeritus
University of Minnesota

McGraw Hill
Connect
Learn
Succeed™

Connect
Learn
Succeed™

MARKETING MANAGEMENT: A STRATEGIC DECISION-MAKING APPROACH, EIGHTH EDITION
International Edition 2013

Exclusive rights by McGraw-Hill Education (Asia), for manufacture and export. This book cannot be re-exported from the country to which it is sold by McGraw-Hill.  This International Edition is not to be sold or purchased in North America and contains content that is different from its North American version.

10  09  08  07  06  05  04  03  02  01
20  15  14  13  12
CTP  COS

**When ordering this title, use ISBN 978-007-132637-7 or MHID 007-132637-5**

Printed in Singapore

www.mhhe.com

# ABOUT THE AUTHORS

## John W. Mullins

**John W. Mullins** is Associate Professor of Management Practice in Marketing and Entrepreneurship at London Business School. He earned his MBA at the Stanford Graduate School of Business and, considerably later in life, his PhD in marketing from the University of Minnesota. An award-winning teacher, John brings to his teaching and research 20 years of executive experience in high-growth firms, including two ventures he founded, one of which he took public.

Since becoming a business school professor in 1992, John has published more than 40 articles in a variety of outlets, including *Harvard Business Review, MIT Sloan Management Review,* and *The Wall Street Journal,* as well as in numerous scholarly journals in marketing and in entrepreneurship. His research has won national and international awards from the Marketing Science Institute, the American Marketing Association, and the Richard D. Irwin Foundation. He is also coauthor of *Marketing Strategy: A Decision-Focused Approach,* 7th edition.

John's consulting, executive education, and prolific case-writing regularly take him to destinations in Africa, India, and Latin America. His best-selling trade book, *The New Business Road Test: What Entrepreneurs and Executives Should Do Before Writing a Business Plan,* is the definitive work on the assessment and shaping of market opportunities. John's newest trade book, *Getting to Plan B: Breaking Through to a Better Business Model* with noted venture capital investor Randy Komisar, has won widespread critical acclaim. It is reshaping the approach entrepreneurs and other innovators are taking to starting their ventures.

## Orville C. Walker, Jr.

**Orville C. Walker, Jr.** is Professor Emeritus in the University of Minnesota's Carlson School of Management, where he served until recently as the James D. Watkins Professor of Marketing and Director of the PhD Program. He holds a master's degree in social psychology from Ohio State University and a PhD in marketing from the University of Wisconsin–Madison.

Orville is the coauthor of three books and has published more than 50 research articles in scholarly and business journals. He has won several awards for his research, including the O'Dell award from the *Journal of Marketing Research,* the Maynard award from the *Journal of Marketing,* and a lifetime achievement award from the Sales Management Interest Group of the American Marketing Association.

Orville has been a consultant to a number of business firms and not-for-profit organizations, and he has taught in executive development programs around the world, including programs in Poland, Switzerland, Scotland, and Hong Kong. Perhaps his biggest business challenge, however, has been his attempt to turn a profit as the owner-manager of a small vineyard in western Wisconsin.

# BRIEF CONTENTS

# CONTENTS

# PREFACE

## WHY THIS BOOK?

WHY DID YOUR INSTRUCTOR CHOOSE THIS BOOK? Chances are, it was for one or more of the following reasons:

- Your instructor has designed his or her course around the use of cases, a real-world project, or a marketing simulation such as Markstrat, to bring marketing decision-making to life. This book has been written with exactly these kinds of instructors in mind. Thus, one of your instructor's key objectives is to give you the necessary tools and frameworks to enable you to be an effective contributor to marketing decision-making—regardless of whether you follow a career in marketing positions *per se,* in another functional area, or as an entrepreneur or in other general management roles. This book's focus on **strategic decision-making** sets it apart from other texts that place greater emphasis on *description* of marketing phenomena than on the strategic and tactical marketing *decisions* that managers and entrepreneurs must make each and every day.

- Your instructor wants to use the most current and most **internet-savvy** book available. We integrate the latest web and social networking developments, from Aprimo to Zynga and more, throughout the book, and we devote an entire chapter, Chapter 14, to the development of marketing strategies for today's digitally networked world. In addition, we supplement the book with an interactive website to help you self-test what you learn and to help your instructor choose the best cases and other materials and in-class activities.

  Our goal—and probably that of your instructor as well—is to make both the latest internet-based tools as well as time-tested marketing principles relevant to those of you who will work in companies of all kinds, dot-com and otherwise.

- Your instructor appreciates and believes you will benefit from the **real-world, global perspectives** offered by the authors of this book. Our combined entrepreneurial, marketing management, and consulting experience spans a broad variety of manufacturing, service, software, and distribution industries and has taken us—and thereby you, the reader—around the world many times. Simply put, we've actually done what we teach, as well as what we write about in this book.

As the reader will see from the outset in Chapter 1, marketing decision-making is a critical activity in every firm, from start-ups to big companies with traditional marketing departments. Further, it is not just marketing managers who make marketing decisions. People in nearly every role in every company can have powerful influence on how happy customers are, or are not, with the goods and services the company provides. Stockbrokers must attract new customers. Accounting and consulting firms must find ways to differentiate their services from other providers so their customers have reasons to give them their business. Software engineers must understand how their technology can benefit the intended customer, for without such benefits, customers will not buy. Thus, we have written this book to meet the marketing needs of readers who hope to make a difference in the long-term strategic success of their organizations—whether their principal roles are in marketing or otherwise.

In this brief preface, we want to say a bit more about each of the three distinctive benefits, listed above, that this book offers its readers. We also point out the key changes in this edition compared to previous ones; and we thank our many students, colleagues, and others from whom we have learned so much and without whom this book would not have been possible.

## A FOCUS ON STRATEGIC DECISION-MAKING

Previous editions of this book have been known for their strategic approach, an approach that helps clarify the relationships among corporate, business-level, and marketing strategies for firms large and small; the relationships between marketing strategies and the marketing environment; and the relationships between marketing and other functional areas in the firm. This eighth edition retains this strategic perspective while providing the reader with specific tools and frameworks for making marketing decisions that take best advantage of the conditions in which the firm finds itself—both internally, in terms of the firm's mission and competencies, and externally, in terms of the market and competitive context in which it operates.

By focusing on decision-making, we believe we've written the best textbook available for instructors who incorporate case-based teaching, marketing simulations, and/or course-long projects like the development of a marketing plan in their course design. And, by keeping each chapter—and the book in total—concise and readable, we allow space in students' busy schedules for instructors to add supplemental readings to highlight the latest in marketing thinking.

Our decision-focused approach is also important to students and executives who are our readers, because, in most well-designed marketing management classes and executive courses, the students or participants will be asked to make numerous decisions—decisions in case studies about what the protagonist in the case should do; decisions in a course project, such as those entailed in developing a marketing plan; or decisions in a marketing simulation.

Our decision-focused approach is also important to employers, who tell us they want today's graduates to be prepared to "hit the ground running" and contribute to the firm's decision-making from day one. The ability to bring thoughtful and disciplined tools and frameworks—as opposed to seat-of-the-pants hunches or blind intuition—to marketing decision-making is one of the key assets today's business school graduates offer their employers. This book puts the tools in the tool box to make this happen. In the end, employers want to know what their new hires can *do,* not just what they *know.*

## WEB-SAVVY INSIGHTS

This book brings a realistic and informed perspective to an important question many students have been asking in recent years: "Has the advent of the internet changed all the rules?" Our answer is, "Well, yes and no." On the one hand, the internet has made available a host of new marketing tools, from Facebook to e-mail marketing to delivery of digital goods and services over the internet, many of which are available to companies in every industry. On the other hand, time-tested marketing fundamentals, such as understanding one's customers and competitors and meeting customer needs in ways that are differentiated from the offerings of those competitors, have become even more important in the fast-moving digital world, as the many dot-com failures attest.

Thus, throughout the book, we integrate examples of dot-com companies—both successful and not—to show how both yesterday's and today's marketing tools and decision frameworks can most effectively be applied. Because the advent of social networking and other new technologies is so important in its own right, however, we also devote Chapter 14 to this fast-growing arena. This chapter provides for marketers in all kinds of companies a road map for decisions about where, when, and how to deploy the tools now available in today's digitally networked world.

## A REAL-WORLD, GLOBAL PERSPECTIVE

Theory is important, because it enhances our understanding of business phenomena and helps managers think about what they should do. It is in the *application* of theory—the world of marketing practice—where we believe this book excels. Our decision focus is all about application. But we don't just bring an academic perspective to the party, important as that perspective is.

One of us, John Mullins, brings to this book 20 years of executive experience in the retailing industry in the United States, including three entrepreneurial companies. John now works in Europe at the London Business School, where he draws on the perspectives of MBA students and executive education participants from more than 120 countries to inform this book with the realities of building vibrant businesses in today's global economy. John's work in executive education regularly takes him not only to North America and Europe, but to Africa, Asia, and Latin America as well. His first-hand vantage point into these fast-growing regions will be evident to readers of this book.

Orv Walker spent most of his career at the Carlson School of Management at the University of Minnesota, where he worked with some of the world's leading consumer goods marketers and won the marketing discipline's most prestigious awards for his research. Orv also enjoyed a number of years running a business as a vintner in the rolling hills of western Wisconsin.

Both of us have contributed the fruits of our research to the growing body of knowledge in the marketing management, marketing strategy, new product development, and entrepreneurship arenas. The result of our collective experience and expertise is a book filled with examples of real people from around the world making real decisions, examples of start-ups and high-growth companies as well as examples of larger, more established firms.

## WHAT'S NEW IN THIS EDITION?

In this eighth edition of *Marketing Management*, we've done significant updating to reflect four key trends that are sweeping the world of marketing theory and practice and changing the aspirations of graduates everywhere:

- The growing interest of many of today's students in all things entrepreneurial and in learning what it will take to run their own companies, whether now—upon, or even before graduation—or at some later point in their careers.
- The growing importance of fast-growing emerging markets like India and China on the global economic stage and the growing realization in companies everywhere that business today is a global game.
- The changing nature of marketing research. These changes are being brought about by two factors: the power of the internet to make many kinds of research both less expensive and faster to carry out, and by a growing recognition that understanding customer needs in today's increasingly complex world requires more than a consumer survey administered now and again.
- The growing ubiquity and power of social networks—Facebook, LinkedIn, Twitter, and the like—which offer numerous opportunities for marketers of all kinds, whether companies with goods of services to market or political uprisings seeking to change the world.

We've addressed the first of these issues, the growing interest of students in **entrepreneurship** by continuing to add new examples throughout the book about how entrepreneurial companies—not just large, established ones—are applying the tools and concepts that this book brings to life. The author team knows from experience that the entrepreneurial path makes for a challenging—and always exciting—career path. As increasing numbers of today's graduates are taking the entrepreneurial plunge, we'd like our readers who choose such a path to be well-equipped for the journey.

Recent editions of this book have been known for their real-world global perspective and this edition is no exception. We've continued to work hard in this revision to add examples from **fast-growing emerging economies** like India, China, and elsewhere. Four new globally focused case vignettes—on the emerging middle class in the developing world (Chapter 7) on marketing Coca-Cola in China (Chapter 12): on the marketing of the Tata Nano, the world's least expensive automobile (Chapter 13): and on the strategy and global organizational structure that Swedish appliance-maker Electrolux employs (Chapter 17)—will provide our readers with new insight into marketing on today's global stage. For almost every company, it seems, India or China—or Brazil, Russia, or another developing country—is important as a source of supply or labor, as a market for what the company produces, or both.

To address the **changing nature of marketing research,** we've done a significant updating of Chapter 6. We now open the chapter with a case vignette on Intel's secret weapon, an anthropologist and ethnographer named Genevieve Bell, whose team's consumer insights—along with those of other technology-driven companies that are ramping up their qualitative and ethnographic research efforts—are changing the way high-tech products are conceived and developed. Throughout the chapter, we address the many changes in marketing research—and in forecasting, too—that these and other changes, including the growing clout of social networks and other web-based phenomena, are bringing about.

Perhaps nothing, however, provides a greater opportunity for today's marketing graduates than the **growing ubiquity and power of social networks** and their applicability for marketers of all kinds. Thus, we've done a major updating of Chapter 14 to accomplish two things. First, we've removed much of the earlier material that described many of the marketing possibilities of the internet, since many of today's internet marketing tools are well understood by today's web-savvy readers. Second, we've refocused the chapter on the reality that today we live and work in a digitally networked world. A new case vignette opens the chapter with a look at the burgeoning array of opportunities in the market for apps. In addition, throughout the chapter, dozens of new examples address the social networking phenomenon, mobile and location-based advertising, and other digital world developments from a variety of perspectives.

As today's digitally networked world continues its rapid evolution, keeping students (the easy part, since many of the most important changes are being led by members of their generation) and instructors (the harder part!) current on such developments is essential and, in our view, well worth the entire chapter we dedicate to it.

In addition to the major changes we've noted above, every chapter has undergone rigorous scrutiny, with materials refreshed and updated, new examples added, outdated ones deleted, and some of the latest empirical evidence incorporated so readers know what works and what doesn't. Instructors will be pleased to know, however, that the structure and flow of this eighth edition remains unchanged. Our purpose in each and every change we have made is to better prepare the reader to "hit the ground running" and contribute to marketing decision-making from whatever vantage point in the organization he or she sits. **Our focus on strategic decision-making** remains, as always, the key strength of this book.

## ADDITIONAL RESOURCES

Supplemental materials for instructors and students are available on the book website at **www.mhhe.com/ mullins8e**. Instructor resources include an instructor's manual, PowerPoints, and a test bank. A list of recommended cases and supplementary readings is also available. These materials range from both classical and recent practitioner-focused articles from *Harvard Business Review and MIT Sloan Management Review to carefully selected, classroom-ready, knock-your-socks-off teaching cases set all over the world (all

*with teaching notes available), in companies large and small, old and new. They'll help any instructor keep his or her course bang up to date and pragmatically focused.*

## THANKS!

Simply put, this book is not solely our work—far from it. Many of our students, colleagues, and those we work with in industry have made contributions that have significantly shaped our perspectives on marketing decision-making. We are grateful to all of them. We wish to give thanks to the individuals who reviewed the previous edition of this text and provided useful feedback: Catharine Curran, University of Massachusetts–Dartmouth; Anna Andriasova, University of Maryland University College; Sanjay S. Mehta, Sam Houston State University; Prema Nakra, Marist College.

We also thank a small army of talented people at McGraw-Hill/Irwin for their work that has turned our rough manuscript into an attractive and readable book. In particular, our editors, Laura Spell and Lori Bradshaw, have been instrumental in giving birth to this edition. Without them, we'd probably still be writing!

Finally, we thank Harper Boyd, without whom this book would not exist, and our parents, without whom, of course, neither of us would be here. To all of you we extend our love, our respect, and our gratitude for passing on to us your curiosity and your passion for learning. We therefore dedicate this book to Harper Boyd, to Jeannette and Orville Walker, Sr., and to Alice and Jack Mullins.

**John W. Mullins**
**Orville C. Walker, Jr.**
**London, U.K.; Madison, Wisconsin**
**Summer 2011**

# Walkthrough

## Case Vignette

These vignettes have been chosen to increase the book's global focus and international perspective.

---

# CHAPTER SIX

## Measuring Market Opportunities: Forecasting and Market Knowledge

### Intel's Secret Weapon[1]

GENEVIEVE BELL HAS A RADICAL IDEA. Bell, the only female among Intel's roster of top technical talent dubbed Intel Fellows, and Director of Intel's User Experience Group, thinks the world would be a better place if we can better understand how people would like to use technology, rather than tossing technology that people don't really want into the market at an alarming pace. Bell was given her own lab at Intel in 2010, an event that may change Intel, or even the future of technology itself.

"Imagine," says Bell, "If we were willing to take on board the ways in which PCs don't work and applied that to other technologies such as our refrigerators or televisions. If your fridge said, "I'm terribly sorry, you cannot have that cold milk until I've rebooted myself
~~wnloaded new drivers!" or your TV said, "You~~
~~watch the end of the cricket match because I am~~
~~ing my hard drive," we would all go insane."~~

directions, leading new product strategy and definition, and driving consumer-centric product innovation and thinking across the company. All this is everyday work for this wiry-haired woman who as a very small girl used to kill things—frogs and the like—growing up in an aboriginal community in Australia's outback.

Why is there a role like Bell's at Intel today? "I joined Intel in 1998," she recalls, "There was a collective sense in Intel's senior management that they didn't know what was going to happen when PCs became mass market. They knew they had market research, they knew they had the skills to size markets and how to survey people, and a little bit of usability work was going on even then, but I think the sense of what was missing was this notion about what was motivating people, what did they care about and was there an opportunity if you understood the things to drive new uses of technology."

"For many years thereafter, a part of every presentation I gave, every class I taught, every meeting I attended was explaining what an anthropologist was, what ethnography was, what was user centered design and why it was going to be a useful tool at Intel." In her 13 years at Intel, Bell has fundamentally changed how the company envisions, plans, and develops its product platforms.

### ~~s~~ Charter at Intel

~~s~~ view, her charter at Intel is straightforward, ~~...~~vide insights and inspire innovation." Her team ~~...~~l scientists, interaction designers and human ~~...~~ engineers is charged with setting research

---

gives his or her permission to be sent marketing messages. Were this not the case, the system would be inundated with unwanted messages to the point that it would come to a screeching halt![19] The growth of unwelcome e-mails, or spam, is a customer problem that software makers are working hard to address.

**Blogging** is another fast-growing internet application. Given the ease with which anyone can now post material on the web, companies large and small are developing blogs with which they can, sometimes anonymously, promote their products or ideas or even disparage competition. There are even sites (for example, *www.betterbusinessblogging.com*) to help businesses develop their blogs!

**Podcasting,** a technology that provides a way for consumers to receive audio via the internet, is another growing web-based application. Advertisers and other providers such as CNN, the Cable News Network, provide short audio feeds that can be downloaded and listened to on a PC or on a portable MP3 player.

While the new media seem, on the surface, to be radically different from their more traditional counterparts—radio, television, and print—the logic entailed in planning their roles in promotional programs is no different than for other media. Considerations of reach, frequency, and cost—measured in cost per thousand impressions (or "hits" or "click-throughs" on the web)—provide a means of comparing their value to one another and to traditional media. **Cost per acquisition,** another measure, is useful for web advertising that results directly in actual customer purchases, a model familiar in the direct-marketing industry. To the extent that new media performance can be measured (How many extra customers does a restaurant get for weekday lunches as a result of its ad, and at what cost per customer?), marketers will be encouraged to use them to their full economic potential.

The rapid growth of these and other new media has led to a variety of ethical issues marketers must address, including the implications of location-based services discussed in Ethical Perspective 13.2.

**International Media** Global advertising has been aided by the rise of globally oriented television media like CNN, MTV, and ESPN, all of which originate primarily in the United States, and a variety of other media like STAR-TV and Al Jazeera, which originate in Asia and the Middle East, respectively. The ability of media like these to deliver to

### ETHICAL PERSPECTIVE 13.2
#### Do You Really Want Burglars to Know Where You Are?

The creators of PleaseRobMe.com, a simple website that publishes a live feed of location-based posts that appear on Twitter, points out that the tweeters are somewhere other than at home. The site's creators want to highlight the fact that tweeters on the likes of Foursquare and other location-based services give away information that burglars would love to have.

But the founders of location-based services and the venture capitalists backing them will have to deal with growing concerns that collecting information about people's movements may have unintended consequences.

The Centre for Democracy and Technology, a privacy advocate, argues that the privacy policies of companies that are collecting and using location-based data are "uneven at best and inadequate at worst."

Some companies are better, of course, and some worse. Loopt includes software that monitors its service for suspicious patterns of behaviour, it says. But politicians are getting into the act, holding a congressional hearing in Washington to examine the implications of such services and their rapid growth. If web-savvy burglars want to take advantage of all this data, it would appear that they'd better do so soon.

Source: "Follow Me," *The Economist*, March 6, 2010, p. 81. For more on Foursquare and Loopt, see *www.foursquare.com* and *www.loopt.com*.

---

## Ethical Perspectives

These minicases highlight ethical issues that commonly arise in marketing management.

**STRATEGIC ISSUE**

*Statistical methods generally assume that the future will look very much like the past. Sometimes this is not the case.*

much like t
CenturyLin
Mountain a
when its sta
failed to allo

## Strategic Issue

Highlight critical information and crucial questions throughout each chapter.

cal data that *are* available. Whe
to introduce a new flavor, its
to forecast the sales for the nev
high-technology products, for
extremely expensive to produce

## Global Perspective and Internet Icons

Identify global examples as well as effective internet marketing for both new and economic marketers.

which to play them. First, Nap
rage with consumers (though
convinced the courts that Naps
than 300 million units, proving
use of analogs like these, as w
*not* to copy—is a crucial appro

## Take-aways

End-of-chapter points review the most important "lessons learned" from each chapter.

## TAKE-AWAYS

1. Every forecast and estimate of market potential is wrong! *Evidence-based* forecasts and estimates, prepared using the tools provided in this chapter, are far more credible—and generally more accurate—than

3. Superior market knowledge is not only an important source of competitive advantage, but it also results in happier, higher volume of, and more loyal customers. Thus, the systematic development of market knowledge

# SECTION ONE

# THE ROLE OF MARKETING IN DEVELOPING SUCCESSFUL BUSINESS STRATEGIES

# CHAPTER ONE

# The Marketing Management Process

## Samsung—Building a Global Brand[1]

SAMSUNG ELECTRONICS is the largest component of South Korea's largest *chaebol*—one of the giant family-controlled conglomerates that have been instrumental in building the country's economy over the last half century. Samsung's electronics unit started out in 1970 making cheap TV sets for the Sanyo label. Over time it morphed into a technically innovative company that was one of the pioneers in developing flat-screen displays, plasma TVs, multifunction cell phones, and other digital devices. But until the mid-1990s, the unit competed primarily by (a) producing technical components or low-cost manufactured products for firms with better-known brands, such as Dell, Hewlett-Packard, and General Electric; and (b) selling me-too consumer products—like TVs and microwave ovens—under the Samsung brand through discount chains like Walmart at very low prices.

Samsung's cost-driven competitive strategy worked well until 1996, but then several shocks in its market and competitive environments forced a major reevaluation. First, the global market for memory chips and other components Samsun supplied for other electronics brands softened because of increased competition and excess capacity. At about the same time, sales of Samsung's own branded products were also declining. As Yun Jong-yong—a company veteran who was brought in as CEO of the electronics unit—complained, Samsung could build a TV that was technically as good as a Sony, but because of the down-market image of the Samsung brand its sets sat at the back of the store or piled up in discount chains. Finally, the Asian financial crisis of 1997 made a major strategic shift essential for the unit's survival.

## New Competitive and Marketing Strategies

Mr. Yun initiated an ambitious new competitive strategy aimed at developing and marketing technically superior products while building an image of Samsung as a stylish, high-quality brand commanding a premium price. The objective was to establish a unique competitive position using technical innovation and design to appeal to younger and relatively upscale customers around the world. "If we were to continue competing only on price," Mr. Yun argued, "the Chinese would slaughter us."

**Technical Innovation and R&D**  In order to implement its new competitive strategy, Samsung had to become a pioneer in developing new digital technologies. While Sony and other rivals had a substantial lead in consumer electronics, that lead was rooted in the analog world. The digital world required new technical innovations. Consequently, the firm shifted substantial resources into R&D focused on technologies such as large-area LCDs, display drivers and chip sets, and mobile telephony. In the 2009 fiscal year, it spent 7.6 trillion won (over $7 billion)—nearly 6 percent of the unit's revenue—on R&D. More than one-quarter of the company's workforce—some 44,000 people—are engaged in R&D activities in about 40 research centers around the world.

### New Product Development and Design

But cutting-edge technology does not guarantee market success. It must be incorporated into products that deliver benefits that at least some segment of consumers will consider to be worth the price. And some of those benefits may be subjective—attractive styling, say, or a cool image. Therefore, new product development at Samsung usually involves a team of designers who collaborate closely with the firm's engineers, manufacturing people, and marketers. To ensure they stay in touch with consumer tastes in different countries, the firm's 450 designers are assigned to design centers in cities like London, Tokyo, Shanghai, and San Francisco, and the company's market researchers run focus groups and user surveys in many markets around the world.

### Marketing Programs to Build the Samsung Brand

Revamping Samsung's marketing efforts was also critical to the success of its new competitive strategy because even the most technically sophisticated and well-designed products are likely to fail unless potential customers know they exist, can acquire them easily, and think they're worth the money. Therefore, Eric Kim was recruited from outside the firm to head a global marketing effort. One of his first moves was to reorganize the firm's distribution channels. Consistent with the strategic objective of establishing Samsung as a high-quality brand worthy of a premium price, many of the company's products were pulled out of low-priced discount chains and distributed through service-oriented electronics specialty stores and web retailers—like Best Buy and Amazon.com—instead.

To ensure consistency in Samsung's marketing communications across world markets, Mr. Kim consolidated the firm's roster of advertising agencies from 55 down to a single global advertising group, British-based WPP. He then launched the firm's first brand-building campaign with fashion-forward TV commercials showing off the company's cool sense of style as well as the technical sophistication of its products.

The firm also makes extensive use of more contemporary promotional tools such as product placements, sponsorships, and internet advertising to strengthen its brand. For instance, Samsung provides both financial and technical support for a variety of sporting and cultural events in every major region of the world. It is a sponsor of the Olympics, Asian games, and other international events, but it also supports regional and local events—such as the Montreal Jazz Festival and the Chelsea Football Club in the UK—as a means of staying close to local customers.

## The Results

Samsung Electronics' revamped competitive strategy and the marketing programs designed to implement it have been a smashing success. According to studies by Interbrand (a brand consultancy), the global value of Samsung's brand increased by more than 200 percent from 2000 through 2008, and it overtook Sony as the most valuable consumer electronics brand. As a result, the unit's sales grew to 139 trillion won (about $119 billion) in the 2009 fiscal year, and operating profit reached 11.6 trillion won.

## Marketing Challenges Addressed in Chapter 1

The activities of Samsung's managers as they worked to redefine the company's brand image and supporting marketing plan demonstrate that marketing involves decisions crucial to the success of every organization, whether large or small, profit or nonprofit, manufacturer, retailer, or service firm. The CEO of a high-tech firm like Samsung must decide what technologies to pursue, what goods or services to sell, to whom, with what features and benefits, at what price, and so on. A chief financial officer for a large multinational corporation must market the merits of the company to the capital markets to obtain the resources needed for continued growth. The executive director of a nonprofit community agency must pursue the resources necessary for the agency to achieve its mission, whether those resources come from fees for the services it delivers or from grants and contributions. And all of those managers must market their ideas for improving their organizations' prospects and performance to their colleagues inside the firm as well as to customers, suppliers, strategic partners, and prospective employees. Thus, most managers engage in tasks involving marketing decisions virtually every day.

This book provides prospective managers and entrepreneurs with the marketing tools, perspectives, and analytical frameworks they'll need to play an effective role in the marketing life and overall strategic development of their organizations, regardless of whether or not they occupy formal marketing jobs. Chapter 1 addresses a number of broad but important questions all managers must resolve in their own minds: Are marketing decisions important? Does marketing create value for customers and shareholders? What constitutes effective marketing practice? Who does what in marketing and how much does it cost? And finally, what decisions go into the development of a strategic marketing program for a particular good or service and how can those decisions be summarized in an action plan?

# Why Are Marketing Decisions Important?

The improved performance of Samsung Electronics following the retooling of its strategic marketing plan illustrates the importance of good marketing decisions in today's business organizations. And according to many managers and expert observers around the world, a strong customer focus and well-conceived and executed marketing strategies will be even more crucial for the success of most organizations as the global marketplace becomes more crowded and competitive.[2]

The importance of marketing in a company's ongoing success can be better appreciated when you consider the activities marketing embraces. Marketing attempts to measure and anticipate the needs and wants of a group of customers and respond with a flow of need-satisfying goods and services. Accomplishing this requires the firm to

- Target those customer groups whose needs are most consistent with the firm's resources and capabilities.
- Develop products and/or services that meet the needs of the target market better than competitors.
- Make its products and services readily available to potential customers.
- Develop customer awareness and appreciation of the value provided by the company's offerings.
- Obtain feedback from the market as a basis for continuing improvement in the firm's offerings.
- Work to build long-term relationships with satisfied and loyal customers.

The most important characteristic of marketing as a business function is its focus on customers and their needs. This is a focus that all managers—not just marketers—need to adopt to ensure their organizations can build and sustain a healthy "top line."

# The Importance of the Top Line

In the financial markets it is a company's bottom line—its profitability—that is most important. In the long run, all firms must make a profit to survive. But as the managers at Samsung are well aware, there can never be a positive bottom line—nor financing, employees, or anything else—without the ability to build and sustain a healthy top line: sales revenue. As a wise observer once said, nothing happens until somebody sells something. Or to paraphrase management guru Peter Drucker, everything a company does internally is a cost center. The only *profit* center is a customer whose check doesn't bounce.

**STRATEGIC ISSUE**

*A customer focus enables firms to enjoy success by exploiting changes in the marketplace, by developing products and services that have superiority over what is currently available, and by taking a more focused and integrated cross-functional approach to their overall operations.*

That is why the customer focus inherent in the marketing function is important. When properly implemented, a customer focus enables firms to enjoy success by exploiting changes in the marketplace, by developing products and services that have superiority over what is currently available, and by taking a more focused and integrated cross-functional approach to their overall operations, as Samsung has done in its product-development process.

# Marketing Creates Value by Facilitating Exchange Relationships

While we have described marketing activities from an individual organization's perspective, marketing also plays an important role in the broader context of the global economy. It helps facilitate exchange relationships among people, organizations, and nations.

> **Marketing** is a social process involving the activities necessary to enable individuals and organizations to obtain what they need and want through exchanges with others and to develop ongoing exchange relationships.[3]

Increased division and specialization of labor are some of the most important changes that occur as societies move from a primitive economy toward higher levels of economic development. But while increased specialization helps improve a society's overall standard of living, it leads to a different problem: Specialists are no longer self-sufficient. Artisans who specialize in making pots become very skilled and efficient at pot making, producing a surplus of pots, but they do not make any of the many other goods and services they need to survive and to improve their lifestyle. A society cannot reap the full benefits of specialization until it develops the means to facilitate the trade and exchange of surpluses among its members. Similarly, a nation cannot partake of the full range of goods and services available around the world or penetrate all potential markets for the economic output of its citizens unless exchanges can occur across national boundaries.

# What Factors Are Necessary for a Successful Exchange Relationship?

Many exchanges are necessary for people and organizations to reap the benefits of the increased specialization and productivity that accompany economic development. But such exchanges do not happen automatically, nor does every exchange necessarily lead to a mutually satisfying long-term relationship. The conditions for a successful exchange transaction can be met only after the parties themselves—or marketing intermediaries such as a wholesale distributor or a retailer—have performed several tasks. These include identifying potential exchange partners, developing offerings, communicating information, delivering products, and collecting payments. This is what marketing is all about. Before we take a closer look at specific marketing activities and how they are planned and implemented by marketing managers, we will discuss some terms and concepts in our definition of marketing and the conditions necessary for exchange. Let's examine the following questions:

1. Who are the *parties* involved in exchange relationships? Which organizations and people market things, and who are their customers?
2. Which *needs and wants* do parties try to satisfy through exchange, and what is the difference between the two?
3. *What* is exchanged?
4. How does exchange create *value?* Why is a buyer better off and more satisfied following an exchange?
5. How do potential exchange partners become a *market* for a particular good or service?

# 1. Who Markets and Who Buys? The Parties in an Exchange

Virtually every organization and individual with a surplus of *anything* engages in marketing activities to identify, communicate, and negotiate with potential exchange partners. Some are more aggressive—and perhaps more effective—in their efforts than others. When considering extensive marketing efforts aimed at stimulating and facilitating exchange, we think first of the activities of goods manufacturers (Intel, BMW, Samsung), service producers (Air France, McDonald's, 20th Century Fox), and large retailers (Zara, Marks & Spencer, Wal-Mart).

However, museums, hospitals, theaters, universities, and other social institutions—whether for profit or nonprofit—also carry out marketing activities to attract customers, students, and donors. In the past, their marketing efforts were not very extensive or well organized. Now, increasing competition, changing customer attitudes and demographics, and rising costs have caused many nonprofit organizations to look to more extensive marketing efforts to solve their problems.[4] For example, some U. S. churches are using marketing techniques to address social problems, as well as to increase church attendance. But as discussed in Ethical Perspective 1.1, such efforts can also raise ethical questions.

**Customers**   Both individuals and organizations seek goods and services obtained through exchange transactions. **Ultimate customers** buy goods and services for their own personal use or the use of others in their immediate household. These are called **consumer goods and services. Organizational customers** buy goods and services (1) for resale (as when TESCO buys several gross of Jeans for resale to individual consumers); (2) as inputs to the production of other goods or services (as when Toyota buys sheet steel to be stamped into car body parts); or (3) for use in the day-to-day operations of the organization (as when a university buys paper and printer cartridges). These are called **industrial goods and services.** Throughout this book we examine differences in the buying behavior of these two types of customers and the marketing strategies and programs relevant for each.[5]

## ETHICAL PERSPECTIVE 1.1
### Marketing Goes to Church in the United States

What's old-time religion to do? At a time when the search for spiritual guidance is on the rise, angels, crystals, and shamans are more engaging to some people than organized religion.

Amid the competition for a piece of America's soul, denominations such as the Southern Baptists, Lutherans, and Roman Catholics are searching for ways to reach baby boomers—without seeming too evangelical. Those religions, along with the Mormon Church, which is starting its 50th advertising campaign, have introduced national public-service campaigns focused on children and families. They are also producing cable and network television specials that incorporate Christian themes in their story lines, and studying how best to use the internet to get their spiritual message across.

The Lutheran Hour Ministries, which spends about half of its $20 million budget on marketing, produced an advertising campaign with themes about family, instead of specific religious messages. A print, radio, and TV campaign that appeared in Chicago shows two children with the words "Drugs. Violence. Peer Pressure. The world is tough. Being a kid shouldn't be." The rest of the text includes a toll-free number to call to receive a free audio cassette and booklet on how to "talk with your kids about today's issues and the Christian values they need in today's world."

Some observers have expressed doubts about the ethics of the Lutheran Hour approach, fearing that it may be just a well-disguised attempt to identify prospects for recruiting new church members. It is true that a person who calls the toll-free number can request a visit from members of a local Lutheran church. But "there's no hit made [to recruit]. It's not a bait-and-switch," says Dr. Dale Meyer, speaker for the Lutheran Hour Ministries.

However, other denominations—particularly evangelical congregations like California's Saddleback Valley Community Church, one of the biggest religious institutions in America—have recently been much more aggressive in using marketing techniques to recruit new converts as well as raise money for social projects like fighting poverty in Africa. Those techniques focus not only on media advertising, but also on internet ads, blogs, websites, and a variety of "product enhancements" such as the formation of interest and lifestyle groups within the congregation and the addition of church coffee shops and cafeterias. But these techniques can also provoke some negative reactions among segments of the churchgoing population. For instance, a recent study suggests that while baby boomers largely approve of these contemporary approaches to religion, "the younger generation sees the megachurches as too production-oriented, too precise. . . . They want a more traditional understanding of religion and faith."

*Sources:* Fara Warner, "Churches Develop Marketing Campaigns," *The Wall Street Journal,* April 17, 1995, p. B4; William C. Symonds, "Earthly Empires," *BusinessWeek,* May 23, 2005, pp. 78–88; Fara Warner, "Prepare Thee for Some Serious Marketing," *The New York Times,* October 22, 2006, Section 3, pp. 1–4; and Brett McCracken, "The Perils of 'Wannabe Cool' Christianity," *The Wall Street Journal,* August 13, 2010, archived at *www.online.wsj.com.*

# 2. Customer Needs and Wants

Needs are the basic forces that drive customers to take action and engage in exchanges. An unsatisfied **need** is a gap between a person's actual and desired states on some physical or psychological dimension. We all have *basic physical needs* critical to our survival, such as food, drink, warmth, shelter, and sleep. We also have *social and emotional needs* critical to our psychological well-being, such as *security, belonging, love, esteem,* and *self-fulfillment.* Those needs that motivate the consumption behavior of individuals are few and basic. They are not created by marketers or other social forces; they flow from our basic biological and psychological makeup as human beings.

Organizations also must satisfy needs to assure their survival and well-being. Shaped by the organization's strategic objectives, these needs relate to the resource inputs, capital equipment, supplies, and services necessary to meet those objectives.

**Wants** reflect a person's desires or preferences for specific ways of satisfying a basic need. Thus, a person wants particular products, brands, or services to satisfy a need.

A person is thirsty and wants a Coke. A company needs office space and its top executives want an office at a prestigious address in midtown Manhattan.

Basic needs are relatively few, but people's many wants are shaped by social influences, their past history, and consumption experiences. Different people may have very different wants to satisfy the same need. Everyone needs to keep warm on cold winter nights, for instance. But some people want electric blankets, while others prefer old-fashioned down comforters.

This distinction between needs and wants helps put into perspective the charge that "marketers create needs," or that "marketers make people want things they don't need." Neither marketers nor any other single social force can create needs deriving from the biological and emotional imperatives of human nature. On the other hand, marketers—and many other social forces—influence people's wants. A major part of a marketer's job is to develop a new product or service and then to stimulate customer wants for it by convincing people it can help them better satisfy one or more of their needs.

**Do Customers Always Know What They Want?**   Some managers—particularly in high-tech firms—question whether a strong focus on customer needs and wants is always a good thing. They argue that customers cannot always articulate their needs and wants, in part because they do not know what kinds of products or services are technically possible. As Akio Morita, the late visionary CEO of Sony, once said:

> Our plan is to lead the public with new products rather than ask them what kind of products they want. The public does not know what is possible, but we do. So instead of doing a lot of marketing research, we refine our thinking on a product and its use and try to create a market for it by educating and communicating with the public.[6]

Others have pointed out that some very successful new products, such as the Chrysler mini-van and Compaq's pioneering PC network server, were developed with little or no market research. On the other hand, some famous duds, like Ford's Edsel, New Coke, and McDonald's McLean low-fat hamburger, were developed with a great deal of customer input.[7]

The laws of probability dictate that some new products will succeed and more will fail regardless of how much is spent on marketing research. But the critics of a strong customer focus argue that paying too much attention to customer needs and wants can stifle innovation and lead firms to produce nothing but marginal improvements or line extensions of products and services that already exist. How do marketers respond to this charge?

While many consumers may lack the technical sophistication necessary to articulate their needs or wants for cutting-edge technical innovations, the same is not true for industrial purchasers. About half of all manufactured goods in most countries are sold to other organizations rather than individual consumers. Many high-tech industrial products are initiated at the urging of one or more major customers, developed with their cooperation (perhaps in the form of an alliance or partnership), and refined at customer beta sites.

As for consumer markets, one way to resolve the conflict between the views of technologists and marketers is to consider the two components of R&D. First there is basic research and then there is development—the conversion of technical concepts into actual salable products or services. Most consumers have little knowledge of scientific advancements and emerging technologies. Therefore, they usually don't—and probably shouldn't—play a role in influencing how firms like Samsung allocate their basic research dollars.

However, a customer focus is critical to development. Someone—or some development team—within the organization must have either the insight and market experience or the substantial customer input necessary to decide what product to develop from a new technology, what benefits it will offer to customers, and whether customers will value those benefits sufficiently to make the product a commercial success. The importance of a customer focus often becomes clear when a firm attempts to develop a variety of successful new product offerings from a single well-established technology as illustrated by the travails of LEGO, the Swedish toy company, described in Exhibit 1.1.

In the case of an innovative new technology, it often must be developed into a concrete product concept before consumers can react to it and its commercial potential can be assessed. In other cases, consumers can express their needs or wants for specific benefits even though they do not know what is technically feasible. They can tell you what problems they are having with current products and services and what additional benefits they would like from new ones. For instance, before Apple introduced the i-Pod, few consumers would have asked for such a product because they were unfamiliar with the possibilities of digitization and miniaturization in the electronics industry. But if someone had asked whether they would buy a product smaller than a Sony Walkman that could store and play thousands of songs they could download from their computer without messing with cassette tapes or CDs, many probably would have said, "Sure!"

A strong customer focus is not inconsistent with the development of technically innovative products, nor does it condemn a firm to concentrate on satisfying only current, articulated customer wants. More important, while firms can sometimes succeed in the short run even though they ignore customer desires, a strong customer focus usually pays

## Exhibit 1.1  HOW LEGO REVIVED ITS BRAND

Not many toy companies in the world have as much brand recognition as LEGO. Three generations of kids around the world have built cars, fire trucks, even entire cities, with the Swedish company's plastic bricks. But despite its widely known and respected brand, the firm's profits declined dramatically in the early to mid-2000s.

One reason for the decline was a loss of strategic focus. LEGO launched a kid's TV series, a set of action figures drawn from that series, and other products in highly competitive categories which were largely unrelated to the firm's popular bricks and where the firm had no experience or special expertise.

More critically, LEGO began foundering within its core product line as well. Top management had given free reign to the firm's designers to develop more imaginative creations for kids to build with LEGO bricks. The designers happily embraced their new freedom and developed many increasingly complex and artistic designs. Unfortunately, those complex designs incorporated thousands of new components, many of which were not interchangeable with those of other products in the line. As a result, parts inventories exploded and supply costs went through the roof. To make matters worse, many of the new designs did not appeal to the kids who are the firm's

ultimate consumers, and sales of the company's core products went down hill.

Paradoxically, the solution to LEGO's product design and profitability problems involved *reducing* the creative freedom of the firm's designers. Top executives decreed that new product development projects should be managed by *teams* involving marketing managers familiar with tastes, preferences, and purchase behaviors in different countries; manufacturing managers who could help control production and supply costs; market researchers who could test kids reactions to various product prototypes; as well as designers.

While innovative product design is LEGO's primary competitive strength, the company has found that designers function most successfully when placed under some constraints; namely that the products being designed appeal to the customers who will use them. As Mads Nipper, LEGO's VP of Products and Markets points out, "Children are . . . very demanding about what they want to buy. If your offer does not stack up, they will go somewhere else."

*Source:* Jay Greene, "How LEGO Revised Its Brand," *www.businessweek/design.com*, July 23, 2010. See also, Jay Greene, *Design Is How It Works* (New York: Portfolio/Penguin Group, 2010), and *www.LEGO.com*.

big dividends in terms of market share and profit over the long haul,[8] as we'll see in the next chapter.

## 3. What Gets Exchanged? Products and Services

Products and services help satisfy a customer's need when they are acquired, used, or consumed. **Products** are essentially tangible physical objects (such as cars, watches, and computers) that provide a benefit. For example, a car provides transportation; a watch tells the time. **Services** are less tangible and, in addition to being provided by physical objects, can be provided by *people* (doctors, lawyers, architects), *institutions* (the Roman Catholic Church, the United Way), *places* (Walt Disney World, Paris), and *activities* (a contest or a stop-smoking program).

## 4. How Exchanges Create Value

**Customers Buy Benefits, Not Products**    As argued earlier, when people buy products to satisfy their needs, they are really buying the **benefits** they believe the products provide, rather than the products per se. For instance, you buy headache relief, not aspirin. The specific benefits sought vary among customers depending on the needs to be satisfied and the situations where products are used. Because different customers seek different benefits, they use different choice criteria and attach different importance to product features when choosing models and brands within a product category. (This is diagrammed in Exhibit 1.2.) For example, a car buyer with strong needs for social acceptance and esteem might seek a socially prestigious automobile. Such a buyer would be likely to attach great importance to criteria relating to social image and engineering sophistication such as a high-powered motor, European-road-car styling, all-leather interior, and a state-of-the-art sound system.

Keep in mind, too, that services offered by the seller can also create benefits for customers by helping them reduce their costs, obtain desired products more quickly, or use those products more effectively. Such services are particularly important for satisfying

## Exhibit 1.2

CUSTOMERS BUY BENEFITS, NOT PRODUCTS

organizational buyers. For example, a few years ago the Massachusetts Institute of Technology discovered that it was doing business with about 20,000 vendors of office and laboratory supplies each year. To improve the efficiency of its purchasing system, MIT developed a computerized catalog that staff members can access via the school's intranet. It then formed alliances with two main suppliers—Office Depot Inc. and VWR Corp.— who won the bulk of MIT's business by promising to deliver superior service. Both firms deliver purchases within a day or two right to the purchaser's desk rather than to a building's stockroom.[9]

**Product Benefits, Service, and Price Determine Value**   A customer's estimate of a product's or service's benefits and capacity to satisfy specific needs and wants determines the value he or she will attach to it. Generally, after comparing alternative products, brands, or suppliers, customers choose those they think provide the most need-satisfying benefits per dollar. Thus, **value** is a function of intrinsic product features, service, and price, and it means different things to different people.[10]

Customers' estimates of products' benefits and value are not always accurate. For example, after buying an air-conditioning installation for its premises, a company may find that the product's cost of operation is higher than expected, its response time to changes in the outside temperature is slow, and the blower is not strong enough to heat or cool remote areas in the building.

A customer's ultimate *satisfaction* with a purchase, then, depends on whether the product actually lives up to expectations and delivers the anticipated benefits. This is why customer services—particularly those occurring *after* a sale, such as delivery, installation, operating instruction, and repair—are often critical for maintaining satisfied customers.

Also, it is essential that companies handle customer complaints effectively. The average business never hears from 96 percent of its dissatisfied customers. This is unfortunate, for 50 percent of those who complain would do business with the company again if their complaints were handled satisfactorily—95 percent if the complaints were resolved quickly.[11]

**The Value of Long-Term Customer Relationships**   Firms have traditionally focused on the individual transaction with a customer as the fruition of their marketing efforts. But as global markets have become increasingly competitive and volatile, many firms have turned their attention to building a continuing long-term *relationship* between the organization and the customer as the ultimate objective of a successful marketing strategy. They are taking action to increase **lifetime customer value**—the present value of a stream of revenue that can be produced by a customer over time. For an automobile manufacturer, for instance, the lifetime value of a first-time car buyer who can be kept satisfied and loyal to the manufacturer— buying all future new cars from the same company—is well over a million dollars.

Throughout this book we will discuss marketing decisions and activities geared to increasing the satisfaction and loyalty—and therefore the lifetime value—of customers. While such activities can add to a company's marketing costs, they can also produce big dividends, not only in terms of long-term revenues and market share, but also in terms of profitability. The reason is simple: It costs more to attract a new customer than to keep an existing one.[12] To persuade a customer to leave a competitor and buy your product or service instead usually takes either a financial inducement (a lower price or special promotional deal) or an extensive and convincing communication program (advertising or sales force effort), all of which are costly. Consequently, the increased loyalty that comes through developing long-term customer relationship translates into higher profits.

**Brand Equity**   The assets—including customers' perceptions of a product's benefits and value, their positive past experiences, and their loyalty over time—linked to a brand's name and symbol constitute the brand's *equity*.[13] Brand equity reflects the value of the brand name and logo as promotional tools for attracting future buyers and building market share and profitability. That is why Samsung's recent marketing efforts have concentrated on building the equity of the Samsung brand in global markets by incorporating innovative technologies and stylish design in the firm's offerings and advertising them as appropriate products for modern lifestyles. Ultimately, in other words, a brand's value to the company depends on how much value customers think the brand provides for them; value creation cuts both ways.

## 5. Defining a Market

A **market** consists of (*a*) *individuals and organizations* who (*b*) are *interested and willing* to buy a particular product to obtain benefits that will satisfy a specific need or want, and who (*c*) have the *resources* (*time, money*) to engage in such a transaction. Some markets are sufficiently homogeneous that a company can practice undifferentiated marketing in them. That is, the company attempts to market a line of products using a single marketing program. But because people have different needs, wants, and resources, the entire population of a society is seldom a viable market for a single product or service. Also, people or organizations often seek different benefits to satisfy needs and wants from the same type of product (e.g., one car buyer may seek social status and prestige while someone else wants economical basic transportation).

The total market for a given product category thus is often fragmented into several distinct **market segments.** Each *segment* contains people who are relatively homogeneous in their needs, their wants, and the product benefits they seek. Also, each segment seeks a different set of benefits from the same product category.

Strategic marketing management involves a seller trying to determine the following points in an effort to define the target market:

1. Which customer needs and wants are currently not being satisfied by competitive product offerings.
2. How desired benefits and choice criteria vary among potential customers and how to identify the resulting segments by demographic variables such as age, sex, lifestyle, or some other characteristics.

---

**Exhibit 1.3**   **HAIER—A CHINESE MANUFACTURER PURSUES SEGMENTS OF THE APPLIANCE MARKET**

Haier, the rapidly growing Chinese manufacturer of washing machines, refrigerators, and other household appliances, uses extensive market research to modify product designs and marketing programs to fit the unique needs and preferences of a variety of geographic, socioeconomic, and lifestyle segments. For instance, customer surveys discovered that people in Saudi Arabia desired extra-large washing machines to hold the flowing robes that are commonly worn there. Consequently, Haier developed a machine with a 26-pound capacity—more than double that of the average washer. The product was a hit, selling more than 10,000 units in its first year. At the other extreme, the firm also offers a miniwasher, aimed at developing economies, that costs only $38. Another washing machine, designed to handle fluctuations in voltage and pick up where it left off if the power goes out, is marketed in rural areas of Asia where the power supply is not always reliable.

*Source:* David Rocks, "China Design," *BusinessWeek,* November 21, 2005, pp. 56–62.

3. Which segments to target, and which product offerings and marketing programs appeal most to customers in those segments.

4. How to position the product to differentiate it from competitors' offerings and give the firm a sustainable competitive advantage.

Exhibit 1.3 provides an example of a Chinese firm that has been very successful in segmenting the household appliances market, targeting precisely defined niches within that market, and positioning its products and services to appeal to the customers in these target segments.

## What Does Effective Marketing Practice Look Like?

Exchange transactions—and particularly long-term relationships—do not happen automatically. They are the result of many decisions that must be planned and carried out by somebody. Sometimes a single organization has the necessary resources to plan and execute an entire marketing strategy by itself. Usually, though, a firm's marketing program involves cooperative efforts from a network of more specialized institutions: suppliers, wholesalers, retailers, advertising agencies, and the like. In some cases, major customers may be involved in shaping and executing parts of a firm's marketing program, such as new product development and testing.

Regardless of who is involved, we refer to the entire sequence of analyses, decisions, and activities involved in planning, carrying out, and evaluating a strategic marketing program as the marketing management process. We take a more detailed look at this process— and at the roles of different functional managers and marketing institutions in planning and executing the activities involved—next.

### Marketing Management—A Definition

Our discussion suggests that marketing management occurs whenever one party has something it would like to exchange with another. Marketing management is the process that helps make such exchanges happen. More specifically,

> **marketing management** is the process of analyzing, planning, implementing, coordinating, and controlling programs involving the conception, pricing, promotion, and distribution of products, services, and ideas designed to create and maintain beneficial exchanges with target markets for the purpose of achieving organizational objectives.

Exhibit 1.4 diagrams the major decisions and activities involved in the marketing management process, and it also serves as the organizational framework for the rest of this book. For that reason, it is important to note the basic focus of this framework and the sequence of events within it.

**A Decision-Making Focus**   The framework has a distinct decision-making focus. Planning and executing an effective marketing program involves many interrelated decisions about what to do, when to do it, and how. Those decisions are the major focus of the rest of this book. Every chapter details decisions that must be made and actions taken with respect to a specific piece of a strategic marketing program and provides the analytical tools and frameworks you'll need to make those decisions intelligently.

**Analyzing the 4Cs**   A substantial amount of analysis of customers, competitors, and the company itself occurs *before* decisions are made concerning specific components of the marketing program. This reflects our view that successful marketing

## Exhibit 1.4

THE MARKETING MANAGEMENT PROCESS

management decisions usually rest on an objective, detailed, and evidence-based understanding of the market and the environmental context. Of course, most marketing strategies never get implemented in quite the same way as they were drawn on paper. Adjustments are made and new activities undertaken in response to rapid changes in customer demands, competitive actions, or shifting economic conditions. But a thorough and ongoing analysis of the market and the broader environment enables managers to make such adjustments in a well-reasoned and consistent way rather than by the seat of the pants.

The analysis necessary to provide the foundation for a good strategic marketing plan should focus on four elements of the overall environment that may influence a given strategy's appropriateness and ultimate success: (1) the *company's* internal resources, capabilities, and strategies; (2) the environmental *context*—such as broad social, economic, and technology trends—in which the firm will compete; (3) the needs, wants, and characteristics of current and potential *customers;* and (4) the relative strengths and weaknesses of *competitors* and trends in the competitive environment. Marketers refer to these elements as **the 4Cs,** and they are described in more detail below.

## Integrating Marketing Plans with the Company's Strategies and Resources

Many firms—particularly larger organizations with multiple divisions or business units—develop a hierarchy of interdependent strategies. Each strategy is formulated at varying levels within the firm and deals with a different set of issues. For example, as we'll see in the next chapter, IBM has reduced its focus and the proportion of resources it devotes to its traditional computer hardware businesses. Instead, it is seeking future growth and profits by investing heavily in developing information engineering, software, and business consulting services. This change in emphasis reflects IBM's new **corporate strategy.** This level of strategy reflects the company's mission and provides direction for decisions about what businesses it should pursue, how it should allocate its available resources, and its growth policies.

Samsung's heavy investment in R&D, consumer research, and product design to develop a new generation of technically superior, attractively designed digital electronics products represents part of a **business-level (or competitive) strategy** that addresses how the business intends to compete in its industry. Samsung seeks to gain a competitive advantage by offering cutting-edge technology, innovative design, and superior customer value.

Finally, interrelated decisions about market segments, product line, advertising appeals and media, prices, and partnerships with suppliers, distributors, retailers, and other agencies all reflect a firm's **marketing strategy.** This is the company's plan for pursuing its objectives within a particular product-market. In the case of smaller companies or start-ups with only a single product line, however, business-level competitive strategy and marketing strategy substantially overlap.

A major part of the marketing manager's job is to monitor and analyze customers' needs and wants and the emerging opportunities and threats posed by competitors and trends in the external environment. Therefore, because all levels of strategy must consider such factors, marketers often play a major role in providing inputs to—and influencing the development of—corporate and business strategies. Conversely, general managers and senior managers in other functions need a solid understanding of marketing in order to craft effective organizational strategies.

Marketing managers also bear the primary responsibility for formulating and implementing strategic marketing plans for individual product-market entries or product lines.

**STRATEGIC ISSUE**

*The marketing objectives and strategy for a particular product-market entry must be achievable with the company's available resources and capabilities and consistent with the direction and allocation of resources inherent in the firm's corporate and business-level strategies.*

But as the above discussion suggests, such strategic marketing programs are not created in a vacuum. Instead, the marketing objectives and strategy for a particular product-market entry must be achievable with the company's available resources and capabilities and consistent with the direction and allocation of resources inherent in the firm's corporate and business-level strategies. In other words, there should be a good fit—or internal consistency—among the elements of all three levels of strategy. Chapter 2 describes in more detail the components of corporate and business strategies and the roles marketers and other functional managers play in shaping the strategic direction of their organizations and business units.

# Market Opportunity Analysis

A major factor in the success or failure of strategies at all three levels is whether the strategy elements are consistent with the realities of the firm's external environment. Thus, the next step in developing a strategic marketing plan is to monitor and analyze the opportunities and threats posed by factors outside the organization. This is an ongoing responsibility for marketing managers.

**Understanding Market Opportunities**   Understanding the nature and attractiveness of any opportunity requires an examination of the external environment, including the markets to be served and the industry of which the firm is a part. In turn, this examination involves a look at broad macro issues like environmental trends that are driving or constraining market demand and the structural characteristics of the industry as a whole, as well as specific aspects of the firm and what it brings to the party. It is also necessary to examine the management team that will be charged with implementing whatever marketing strategy is developed to determine if they have what it takes to get the job done. Chapter 3 provides a framework for examining these issues, and dramatizes how different the attractiveness of one's market and one's industry can be; an insight that is easily (and often) overlooked.

**Customer Analysis**   The primary purpose of marketing activities is to facilitate and encourage exchange transactions with potential customers. One of a marketing manager's major responsibilities is to analyze the motivations and behavior of present and potential customers. What are their needs and wants? How do those needs and wants affect the product benefits they seek and the criteria they use in choosing products and brands? Where do they shop? How are they likely to react to specific price, promotion, and service policies? To answer such questions, a marketing manager must have some notion of the mental processes customers go through when making purchase decisions and of the psychological and social factors that influence those processes. Chapter 4 discusses the processes and influences that shape consumers' buying behavior. Because some aspects of the purchase process differ for organizations, Chapter 5 examines the buying behavior of institutional customers.

**Marketing Research and Forecasting**   Marketing managers must obtain objective information about potential customers, the satisfaction and loyalty of current customers, the firm's wholesale and retail partners, and the strengths and weaknesses of competitors. Consequently, even relatively small organizations often expend substantial financial and personnel resources studying the needs and preferences of potential customers, developing new products, and tracking the sales patterns and satisfaction of existing customers and channel members.

If managers are to make informed decisions, however, research information must be converted into estimates of the sales volume and profit the firm might reasonably expect a particular marketing program to generate within a given market segment. Chapter 6 discusses techniques and methods for collecting and analyzing marketing research information and for forecasting the market potential and likely sales volumes of particular market segments. The specific research methods that marketing managers use to make decisions about elements of a marketing program—such as what price to charge or which advertising media to use—will be examined in more detail in chapters dealing with each of these program decisions.

**Market Segmentation, Targeting, and Positioning Decisions**   Not all customers with similar needs seek the same products or services to satisfy those needs. Their purchase decisions may be influenced by individual preferences, personal characteristics, social circumstances, and so forth. On the other hand, customers who do purchase the same product may be motivated by different needs, seek different benefits from the product, rely on different sources of information about products, and obtain the product from different distribution channels. Thus, one of the manager's most crucial tasks is to divide customers into **market segments**—distinct subsets of people with similar needs, circumstances, and characteristics that lead them to respond in a similar way to a particular product or service offering or to a particular strategic marketing program. Chapter 7 examines dimensions for measurement and analytical techniques that can help managers identify and define market segments in both consumer and organizational markets.

After defining market segments and exploring customer needs and the firm's competitive strengths and weaknesses within segments, the manager must decide which segments represent attractive and viable opportunities for the company; that is, on which segments to focus a strategic marketing program. Chapter 7 discusses some of the considerations in *selecting a target segment.*

Finally, the manager must decide how to **position** the product or service offering and its brand within a target segment; that is, to design the product and its marketing program so as to emphasize attributes and benefits that appeal to customers in the target segment and at once distinguish the company's brand from those of competitors. Issues and analytical techniques involved in marketing positioning decisions are discussed in Chapter 8.

## Formulating Strategic Marketing Programs

Designing an effective strategic marketing program for a product-market entry involves three interrelated sets of decisions:

1. The manager must set specific objectives to be accomplished within the target market, such as sales volume, market share, and profitability goals. Those objectives must be consistent with the firm's corporate and business-unit strategic objectives, yet specific enough to enable management to monitor and evaluate the product-market entry's performance over time.

2. The manager must decide on an overall marketing strategy to appeal to customers—and to gain a competitive advantage—in the target market. The strategy must be consistent with the firm's capabilities, its corporate and business-unit strategies, and the product-market objectives.

3. The manager must then make decisions about each element of the tactical marketing program used to carry out the strategy. These decisions must be internally consistent and integrated across all elements of the marketing program.

**Specifying Marketing Objectives and Strategies**   The first step in developing a strategic marketing program is to specify the objectives and the overall marketing strategy of each target market. As we've mentioned, these are partly dictated by corporate and business-level objectives, strategies, and resources. For instance, the nature of Samsung's product line, its pricing and distribution policies, and its advertising appeals and promotion efforts are all influenced by the firm's competitive strategy of offering technically innovative and stylish electronics products at premium prices. Chapter 9 describes a number of generic business-level competitive strategies and examines the way such strategies influence decisions about marketing objectives and programs, as well as the role other functional managers play in implementing those marketing programs.

**Marketing Program Components**   Dozens of specific tactical decisions must be made in designing a strategic marketing program for a product-market entry. These decisions fall into four categories of major marketing variables that a manager has some ability to control over the short term. Often called **the 4 Ps,** the controllable elements of a marketing program are the **product offering** (including the breadth of the product line,

## Exhibit 1.5

DECISIONS WITHIN THE FOUR ELEMENTS OF THE MARKETING MIX

**Product**
- Quality
- Features
- Style
- Options
- Brand name
- Packaging
- Guarantees/ warranties
- Services

**Place**
- Numbers and types of middlemen
- Locations/ availability
- Inventory levels

**The target market**

**Price**
- List price
- Discounts
- Allowances
- Credit terms
- Payment period
- Rental/lease

**Promotion**
- Advertising
- Personal selling
- Sales promotion
- Point-of-purchase materials
- Publicity

quality levels, and customer services); **price; promotion** (advertising, sales promotion, and salesforce decisions); and **place** (or distribution). Because decisions about each element should be consistent and integrated with decisions concerning the other three, the four components are often referred to as the *marketing mix.*

> The **marketing mix** is the combination of controllable marketing variables that a manager uses to carry out a marketing strategy in pursuit of the firm's objectives in a given target market.

Exhibit 1.5 outlines some of the decisions that must be made within each of the four elements of the marketing mix. Chapters 10 through 13 discuss in more detail the various methods and criteria for making decisions about each of these program components.

# Formulating Strategic Marketing Programs for Specific Situations

The strategic marketing program for a product should reflect market demand and the competitive situation within the target market. But demand and competitive conditions change over time as a product moves through its life cycle. Therefore, different marketing strategies are typically more appropriate and successful for different market conditions and at different life-cycle stages. Chapter 14 explores marketing strategies for the rapidly evolving conditions being created by e-commerce and the digitally networked world. Chapter 15 examines marketing strategies for introducing new entries and for strengthening a product's competitive position as its market grows. Chapter 16 then discusses the marketing strategies a firm might adopt in mature and declining product-markets.

# Implementation and Control of the Marketing Program

A final critical determinant of a strategy's success is the firm's ability to implement it effectively. And this depends on whether the strategy is consistent with the resources, the organizational structure, the coordination and control systems, and the skills and experience of company personnel.[14] Managers must design a strategy to fit the company's existing resources, competencies, and procedures—or try to construct new structures and systems to fit the chosen strategy. For example, Samsung's brand building program would not be so successful without its substantial investments in R&D, marketing research, and product design, and a team structure that encourages communication and cooperation across functional areas throughout the development process. Chapter 17 discusses the structural variables, planning and coordination processes, and personnel and corporate culture characteristics related to the successful implementation of various marketing strategies.

The final tasks in the marketing management process are determining whether the strategic marketing program is meeting objectives and adjusting the program when performance is disappointing. This measurement and control process provides feedback to managers and serves as a basis for a market opportunity analysis in the next planning period. Chapter 18 examines ways to evaluate marketing performance and develop contingency plans when things go wrong.

# The Marketing Plan—A Blueprint for Action

The results of the various analyses and marketing program decisions discussed above should be summarized periodically in a detailed formal marketing plan.[15]

> A **marketing plan** is a written document detailing the current situation with respect to customers, competitors, and the external environment and providing guidelines for objectives, marketing actions, and resource allocations over the planning period for either an existing or a proposed product or service.

While some firms—particularly smaller ones—do not bother to write their marketing plans, most organizations believe that "unless all the key elements of a plan are written down . . . there will always be loopholes for ambiguity or misunderstanding of strategies and objectives, or of assigned responsibilities for taking action."[16] This suggests that even small organizations with limited resources can benefit from preparing a written plan, however brief. Written plans also provide a concrete history of a product's strategies and performance over time, which aids institutional memory and helps educate new managers assigned to the product. Written plans are necessary in most larger organizations because a marketing manager's proposals must usually be reviewed and approved at higher levels of management and because the approved plan provides the benchmark against which the manager's performance will be judged. Finally, the discipline involved in producing a formal plan helps ensure that the proposed objectives, strategy, and marketing actions are based on rigorous analysis of the 4Cs and sound reasoning.

Because a written marketing plan is such an important tool for communicating and coordinating expectations and responsibilities throughout the firm, we will say more about it in Chapter 17 when we discuss the implementation of marketing programs in detail. But

## Exhibit 1.6

CONTENTS OF A MARKETING PLAN

| Section | Content |
|---------|---------|
| I. Executive summary | Presents a short overview of the issues, objectives, strategy, and actions incorporated in the plan and their expected outcomes for quick management review. |
| II. Current situation and trends | Summarizes relevant background information on the market, competition, and the macroenvironment, and trends therein, including size and growth rates for the overall market and key segments. |
| III. Performance review (for an existing product or service only) | Examines the past performance of the product and the elements of its marketing program (e.g., distribution, promotions). |
| IV. Key issues | Identifies the main opportunities and threats to the product that the plan must deal with in the coming year, and the relative strengths and weaknesses of the product and business unit that must be taken into account in facing those issues. |
| V. Objectives | Specifies the goals to be accomplished in terms of sales volume, market share, and profit. |
| VI. Marketing strategy | Summarizes the overall strategic approach that will be used to meet the plan's objectives. |
| VII. Action plans | This is the most critical section of the annual plan for helping to ensure effective implementation and coordination of activities across functional departments. It specifies<br><br>• The **target market** to be pursued.<br>• **What** specific actions are to be taken with respect to each of the 4 Ps.<br>• **Who** is responsible for each action.<br>• **When** the action will be engaged in.<br>• **How** much will be budgeted for each action. |
| VIII. Projected profit-and-loss statement | Presents the expected financial payoff from the plan. |
| IX. Controls | Discusses how the plan's progress will be monitored; may present contingency plans to be used if performance falls below expectations or the situation changes. |
| X. Contingency plans | Describes actions to be taken if specific threats or opportunities materialize during the planning period. |

because the written plan attempts to summarize and communicate an overview of the marketing management process we have been examining, it is worthwhile to briefly examine the contents of such plans here.

Marketing plans vary in timing, content, and organization across companies. In general, marketing plans are developed annually; though planning periods for some big-ticket industrial products, such as commercial aircraft, may be longer, and in some highly volatile industries, such as telecommunications or electronics, they can be shorter. Plans typically follow a format similar to that outlined in Exhibit 1.6.

There are three major parts to the plan. First, the marketing manager details his or her assessment of the current situation. This is the homework portion of the plan where the manager summarizes the results of his or her analysis of current and potential customers, the company's relative strengths and weaknesses, the competitive situation, the major trends in the broader environment that may affect the product and, for existing products, past performance outcomes. This section typically also includes forecasts, estimates of sales potential, and other assumptions underlying the plan, which are especially important for proposed new products or services. Based on these analyses, the manager may also call attention to several key issues—major opportunities or threats that should be dealt with during the planning period.

The second part of the plan details the strategy for the coming period. This part usually starts by specifying the objectives (e.g., sales volume, market share, profits, customer satisfaction levels) to be achieved by the product or service during the planning period. It then outlines the overall marketing strategy, the actions associated with each of the 4 Ps necessary to implement the strategy, and the timing and locus of responsibility for each action.

Finally, the plan details the financial and resource implications of the strategy and the controls to be employed to monitor the plan's implementation and progress over the period. Some plans also specify some contingencies: how the plan will be modified if certain changes occur in the market, competitive, or external environments.

## Who Does What?

## Marketing Institutions

A strategic marketing program involves a large number of activities aimed at encouraging and facilitating exchanges and building relationships with customers. And all of those activities must be performed by somebody for exchanges to happen. One of the few eternal truths in marketing is that "you can eliminate the middlemen, but you can't eliminate their functions." Somebody has to gather information or feedback from customers concerning their needs and wants; use that information to design product or service offerings that will provide valued benefits; communicate the existence and benefits of the offering to the market; perform the storage, order fulfillment, and transportation activities necessary to make the product conveniently available to customers; finance purchases; collect payment; and resolve customer problems or complaints after the sale. The major flows of the physical product, payment, and information that occur during an exchange are summarized in Exhibit 1.7.

In a few cases, nearly all these activities are performed by a single organization and its employees. Such internal control of the full range of marketing functions and activities is referred to as **vertical integration.** Dell Computer's reliance on the internet to attract customers and process orders together with a flexible manufacturing system that produces computers to order and minimizes finished inventories, and Canon's reliance on its own

## Exhibit 1.7

WHAT MUST CHANGE HANDS TO COMPLETE AN EXCHANGE BETWEEN A BUYER AND A SELLER?

factories, salesforce, and distribution facilities to produce and market its copiers and printers are examples of highly integrated marketing organizations.

The majority of goods and services in most developed economies, however, are marketed through alliances or networks involving multiple institutions or middlemen. These networks are commonly referred to as **marketing channels** or **channels of distribution.** Each institution within the channel specializes in performing only a part of the activities or functions necessary to conduct exchanges with the end user. We will examine these institutions and the nature of their interactions with one another in more detail in Chapter 12. Marketing institutions fall into one of the following categories:

- **Merchant wholesalers** take title to the goods they sell and sell primarily to other resellers (retailers), industrial, and commercial customers, rather than to individual consumers.
- **Agent middlemen,** such as manufacturers' representatives and brokers, also sell to other resellers and industrial or commercial customers, but they do not take title to the goods they sell. They usually specialize in the selling function and represent client manufacturers on a commission basis.
- **Retailers** sell goods and services directly to final consumers for their personal, nonbusiness use.
- **Facilitating agencies,** such as advertising agencies, marketing research firms, collection agencies, railroads, and web portals, specialize in one or more marketing functions on a fee-for-service basis to help their clients perform those functions more effectively and efficiently.

## Who Pays the Cost of Marketing Activities—And Are They Worth It?

The final selling price of the product reflects the costs of performing the activities necessary for exchange transactions. Those costs vary widely across different products and customers. They account for a relatively high proportion of the price of frequently purchased consumer package goods such as cereals and cosmetics. Extensive transportation, storage, and promotion activities facilitate the millions of consumer purchases that occur every year. In developed economies, on average, roughly 50 percent of the retail price of such products is made up of marketing and distribution costs; one-half represents retailer margins, and the other half the marketing expenses of the manufacturer and wholesale middlemen.[17] On the other hand, marketing costs for nontechnical industrial goods, such as sheet steel or basic chemicals, are much lower because they are sold in large quantities directly to a small number of regular customers.

Though both individual and organizational customers pay for the marketing activities of manufacturers and their middlemen, they are still usually better off than if they were to undertake all the functions themselves. This is true for two reasons: First, the purchasing, storage, promotion, and selling activities of wholesalers and retailers allow customers to buy a wide variety of goods from a single source in one transaction, thereby increasing **transactional efficiency.** For example, a consumer may buy a week's groceries on a single trip to the supermarket (or perhaps even over the internet from a home-delivery service) rather than engage in separate transactions with a butcher, a baker, and a variety of farmers or food processors. Thus, the number of exchanges necessary for a consumer to acquire a desired assortment of goods and services is reduced and efficiency is increased when middlemen are added to an economic system.

A second benefit of an extensive marketing system is that specialization of labor and economies of scale lead to **functional efficiency.** Manufacturers and their agents can perform the exchange activities more cheaply than can individual customers. A railroad, for instance, can ship a load of new tires from a plant in Akron to a wholesaler in Tucson more cheaply than an individual consumer in Arizona could transport them in the family minivan.

From the customer's viewpoint, then, the increased transactional and functional efficiency of exchange produced by members of the marketing system increases the value—the **utility/price** relationship—of goods and services. A product has greater utility for a potential customer when it can be purchased with a minimum of risk and shopping time (**possession utility**), at a convenient location (**place utility**), and at the time the customer is ready to use the product (**time utility**).

## Room for Improvement in Marketing Efficiency

While the existence of specialized institutions in our economy's marketing system has greatly increased the efficiency and value of most exchange transactions from the customer's point of view, that does not mean the current system is nearly as efficient as it could be. Marketing is one of the few functional areas of business whose efficiency has not substantially improved in recent years. Two authorities estimate that, on average, manufacturing costs have declined from about 50 percent of total corporate costs after World War II to about 30 percent today through automation, flexible manufacturing systems, product redesign for manufacturing, just-in-time approaches, and so on. Similarly, they argue that the average costs of "management"—defined to include finance, accounting, human resources, and support functions like R&D—have fallen from about 30 percent to 20 percent as the result of downsizing, outsourcing, and process reengineering. On the other hand, they estimate that the percentage of corporate costs accounted for by marketing activities actually went up over the same period.[18]

Of course, there are some good reasons why marketing costs have increased in recent years, including the greater intensity of global competition, the rapid pace of technological change, the fragmentation of the communications media, and many other factors. However, at least part of the problem can be attributed to marketers themselves. Marketing managers have been slow to develop accurate measures and metrics of marketing performance and, therefore, slow to understand the effectiveness of various marketing actions relative to their costs, and thus their impact on a firm's bottom line. In a recent survey of over 100 marketing executives in global companies in the United States, United Kingdom, and Germany, for instance, nearly all respondents agreed that improving the effectiveness of their marketing investments was one of their corporation's top three business priorities. But 84 percent of those respondents admitted that marketing return on investment (MROI) is not well understood in their businesses, and only 54 percent said they measured *any* of their marketing activities consistently.[19]

We will focus throughout this book on ways marketers are attempting to improve operational efficiency through (1) more effective use of telecommunications and information technologies, such as internet ads, product placements, event sponsorships, company blogs, and the like; (2) the development of cooperative alliances with suppliers, middlemen, and ultimate customers; and (3) the search for new measurement and budgeting methods that are more clearly focused on improving cash flows and adding economic value.[20]

## The Role of the Marketing Decision Maker

The title *marketing manager* is necessarily and intentionally vague because many people are directly involved with an organization's marketing activities. This can include people not formally located in a marketing or sales department or even within the company. The exact nature of the marketing manager's job will vary widely depending on the industry involved, the organization's structure, and its position in the managerial hierarchy.

While the marketing manager bears the primary responsibility for formulating and implementing a strategic marketing program for a product or service, a single marketing manager (1) seldom does all the analysis or makes all the decisions involved in such plans all alone and (2) almost never has the formal authority to demand that all the activities specified in the plan be carried out by subordinates exactly as they are written down.

Many marketing activities are usually contracted out to independent middlemen or facilitating agencies or are performed in concert with a firm's suppliers, major customers, or other organizational partners. A marketing manager has no formal authority over these outsiders. Thus, the development and nurturing of long-term relationships with suppliers, channel members, and major customers can do more than simply improve marketing efficiency; they can provide the information, advice, and cooperation necessary to devise and carry out successful marketing strategies.[21]

Even those marketing activities that are performed in-house are seldom all within the domain of the marketing department or under the authority of a single marketing execu-

**STRATEGIC ISSUE**

*Creating value is a cross-functional endeavor, and marketing and nonmarketing executives alike must operate with a clear customer focus to make it happen.*

tive. Implementing a marketing plan requires cooperation and coordination across many specialized functional areas. Marketing is—or should be—everybody's business. After all, delivering superior value to customers is the key to business success, and that superior value flows from a combination of well-designed products or services, produced with high quality; efficient operations that enable low costs and competitive prices; and reliable customer service. Creating value is a cross-functional endeavor, and marketing and nonmarketing executives alike must operate with a clear customer focus to make it happen.

## Some Recent Developments Affecting Marketing Management

While many of the basic tasks involved in developing and implementing strategic marketing programs have remained unchanged for decades, recent developments in our economy and around the world have greatly changed the context in which those tasks are carried out and the information and tools that marketers have at their disposal. These developments include (1) the increased globalization of markets and competition, (2) the growth of the service sector of the economy and the importance of service in maintaining customer satisfaction and loyalty, (3) the rapid development of new information and communications technologies, and (4) the growing importance of relationships for improved coordination and increased efficiency of marketing programs and for capturing a larger portion of customers' lifetime value. Some recent impacts of these four developments on marketing management are briefly summarized below and will be continuing themes throughout this book.

### Globalization

International markets account for a large and growing portion of the sales of many organizations. But while global markets represent promising opportunities for additional sales growth and profits, differences in market and competitive conditions across country boundaries can require firms to adapt their competitive strategies and marketing programs to be successful. Even when similar marketing strategies are appropriate for multiple countries, international differences in infrastructure, culture, legal systems, and the like, often mean that one or more elements of the marketing program—such as product features, promotional appeals, or distribution channels—must be tailored to local conditions for the strategy to be effective.

## Increased Importance of Service

A service can be defined as "any activity or benefit that one party can offer another that is essentially intangible and that does not result in the ownership of anything. Its production may or may not be tied to a physical product."[22] Service businesses such as airlines, hotels, restaurants, and consulting firms account for roughly two-thirds of all economic activity in the United States, and services are the fastest-growing sector of most other developed economies around the world. While many of the decisions and activities involved in marketing services are essentially the same as those for marketing physical goods, the intangible nature of many services can create unique challenges for marketers. We will discuss these challenges—and the tools and techniques firms have developed to deal with them—throughout this book.

As the definition suggests, services such as financing, delivery, installation, user training and assistance, and maintenance are often provided in conjunction with a physical product. Such ancillary services have become more critical to firms' continued sales and financial success in many product-markets. As markets have become crowded with global competitors offering similar products at ever-lower prices, the creative design and effective delivery of supplemental services has become a crucial means by which a company may differentiate its offering and generate additional benefits and value for customers. Those additional benefits, in turn, can justify higher prices and margins in the short term and help improve customer satisfaction, retention, and loyalty over the long term.[23]

Of course, lousy customer service can have the opposite effect. This is especially a danger when intense price competition pushes a firm to cut costs by reducing or outsourcing customer service and support. For instance, a few years ago Dell attempted to maintain its long-standing low-cost position in the personal computer industry by—among other things—reducing the number of technicians in its customer call centers and limiting each technician's training to only a few specialized problem areas. As a result, increasing numbers of customers spent 30 minutes or more on hold when they called Dell for help, and 45 percent were transferred at least once before they found a technician with the expertise to solve their problem. Consequently, Dell's customer satisfaction rating in the United States plummeted, and despite expensive attempts to improve service—including the use of independent retail outlets to sell and service Dell equipment—the firm's market share, profits, and stock prices have still not fully recovered.[24]

## Information Technology

The computer revolution and related technological developments are changing the nature of marketing management in two important ways. First, new technologies are making it possible for firms to collect and analyze more detailed information about potential customers and their needs, preferences, and buying habits. Thus, it is now possible for many firms to identify and target smaller and more precisely defined market segments—sometimes segments consisting of only one or a few customers—and to customize product features, promotional appeals, prices, and financing arrangements to fit such segments.[25]

A second impact of information technology has been to open new channels for communications and transactions between suppliers and customers. As Exhibit 1.8 suggests, one simple way of categorizing these new channels is based on whether the suppliers and customers involved are organizations or individual consumers.

## Exhibit 1.8

CATEGORIES OF E-COMMERCE

| | | BUSINESS | CONSUMER |
|---|---|---|---|
| **Business** | | **Business-to-Business (B2B)**<br><br>Examples:<br>• Purchasing sites of Ford, Oracle, Cisco<br>• Supply chain networks linking producers and distribution channel members, such as 3M and Walmart | **Business-to-Consumer (B2C)**<br><br>Examples:<br>• E-tailers, such as E*Trade, Amazon<br>• Producers' direct sales sites, such as Dell, Ryanair, Sofitel Hotels<br>• Websites of traditional retailers, such as Sears, Lands' End, Marks & Spencer |
| **Consumer** | | **Consumer-to-Business (C2B)**<br><br>Examples:<br>• Sites that enable consumers to bid on unsold airline tickets and other goods and services, such as Priceline | **Consumer-to-Consumer (C2C)**<br><br>Examples:<br>• Auction sites, such as eBay, QXL |

*Source:* Adapted from "A Survey of E-Commerce: Shopping Around the web," *The Economist,* February 26, 2000, p. 11.

Global sales over the internet are growing so fast that solid estimates of their volume are hard to come by. However, internet revenues of manufacturers, wholesalers, retailers, and selected service firms (not including travel) amounted to nearly $3.5 trillion in the United States in 2008 (the most recent census data available at the time of this writing) and worldwide volume of $5.5 to $6.5 trillion seems a reasonable guess.[26] Growth in both the global and U.S. markets has averaged about 18 to 25 percent annually for the past several years, and is likely to continue at about the same pace.

Roughly 90 percent of those sales were business-to-business transactions, such as those in the upper-left quadrant of Exhibit 1.8. Many high-tech firms like Oracle Corp. and Cisco Systems, and even some more traditional companies such as Toyota and Xerox conduct all or a large portion of their purchasing activities over the web. And many firms rely on their websites to communicate product information to potential customers, make sales, and deal with customer problems.

Perhaps even more important, though, new information and communications technologies are enabling firms to forge more cooperative and efficient relationships with their suppliers and distribution channel partners. For example, Procter & Gamble and 3M have formed alliances with major retailers—such as Kroger and Walmart—to develop automatic restocking systems. Sales information from the retailer's checkout scanners is sent directly to the supplier's computers, which figure out automatically when to replenish each product and schedule deliveries direct to each of the retailer's stores. Such paperless exchanges reduce mistakes and billbacks, minimize inventory levels, improve cash flow, and increase customer satisfaction and loyalty.

In contrast, internet sales from businesses to consumers (the upper-right quadrant in Exhibit 1.8) accounted for only about $288 billion (excluding travel) in the United States in 2008, less than 3.6 percent of the country's total retail sales.[27] However, sales volumes of firms such as Amazon, Dell Computer, and iTunes are expanding rapidly, and many traditional retailers are expanding their marketing efforts on the web as well. And information available over the internet is affecting consumer purchase patterns even when the purchases are made in traditional retail outlets. For instance, a recent survey found that nearly 6-in-10 adults in the United States (58 percent) have researched a product or service online before making a purchase and 24 percent have posted comments or reviews about things they have bought.[28] The proportion of consumers gathering information online grew to 78 percent among people with internet accesss.

Clearly, the web is presenting marketers with new strategic options—as well as new competitive threats and opportunities—regardless of what or to whom they are selling. Therefore, we will devote all of Chapter 14 to marketing strategies for e-commerce, and discuss specific examples and their implications in every chapter.

## Relationships across Functions and Firms

New information technologies and the ongoing search for greater marketing efficiency and customer value in the face of increasing competition are changing the nature of exchange between companies. Instead of engaging in a discrete series of arm's-length, adversarial exchanges with customers, channel members, and suppliers on the open market, more firms are trying to develop and nurture long-term relationships and alliances, such as the one between 3M and Wal-Mart. Such cooperative relationships are thought to improve each partner's ability to adapt quickly to environmental changes or threats, to gain greater benefits at lower costs from its exchanges, and to increase the lifetime value of its customers.[29]

Similar kinds of cooperative relationships are emerging inside companies as firms seek mechanisms for more effectively and efficiently coordinating across functional departments the various activities necessary to identify, attract, service, and satisfy customers. In many firms, the planning and execution that used to be the responsibility of a product or marketing manager are now coordinated and carried out by cross-functional teams. Thus, the boundaries between functional areas are beginning to blur, and marketing programs are increasingly a group activity. Regardless of who is responsible or who carries out the work, however, the decisions and activities involved in such marketing programs remain the same. They are the focus of the rest of this book.

## TAKE-AWAYS

1. Marketing is pervasive. It is a social process involving the activities that facilitate exchanges of goods and services among individuals and organizations.

2. Customers buy benefits, not products. The benefits a customer receives from a firm's offering, less the costs he or she must bear to receive those benefits, determine the offering's value to that customer.

3. Delivering superior value to one's customers is the essence of business success. Because delivering superior value is a multifunctional endeavor, both marketing and nonmarketing managers must adopt a strong focus on the customer and coordinate their efforts to make it happen.

4. A focus on satisfying customer needs and wants is not inconsistent with being technologically innovative.

5. The marketing management process requires an understanding of the 4Cs: the company and its mission, strategies, and resources; the macroenvironmental context in which it operates; customers and their needs and wants; and competitors. Obtaining an objective, detailed, evidence-based understanding of these factors is critical to effective marketing decision making.

6. Marketing decisions—such as choices about what goods or services to sell, to whom, and with what strategy—are made or approved at the highest levels in most firms, whether large or small. Therefore, managers who occupy or aspire to strategic positions in their organizations need marketing perspectives and analytical skills.

# ENDNOTES

**1.** This case example is based on information found in "Samsung's Lessons in Design," issue: The Journal of Business and Design, Volume 9, No.1 (Fall 2003), pp. 25–31; "As Good as It Gets? Special Report: Samsung Electronics," The Economist, January 15, 2005, pp. 64–66; Moon Ihlwan, "Samsung's Rise in Digital TV," *BusinessWeek Online,* October 4, 2007; "Losing Its Shine," *The Economist,* February 9, 2008, p. 71; Cliff Edwards, "Samsung: Rethinking the Printer Business," *www.businessweek.com/innovation,* January 5, 2009; and the company's 2009–2010 Sustainability Report at *www.samsung.com.*

**2.** For example, see Christine Moorman and Roland T. Rust, "The Role of Marketing," *Journal of Marketing* 63 (Special Issue 1999), pp. 180–97; Frederick E. Webster, Jr., "Marketing Management in Changing Times," *Marketing Management,* January–February 2002, pp. 18–23; and David Kiley and Burt Helm, "The Short Life of the Chief Marketing Officer," *BusinessWeek,* December 10, 2007, pp. 63–65.

**3.** The American Marketing Association offers a similar, though more detailed, definition of marketing, as follows: "Marketing is the process of planning and executing the conception, pricing, promotion, and distributing of ideas, goods, and services to create exchanges that satisfy individual and organizational objectives."

**4.** For more examples, see Philip Kotler and Alan R. Andreasen, *Strategic Marketing for Nonprofit Organizations,* 7th ed. (Englewood Cliffs, NJ: Prentice Hall, 2008).

**5.** Some evidence indicates that differences between organizational and individual consumers account for more of the variation in the performance of a given business strategy across firms than any other environmental or organizational variable. See Donald C. Hambrick and David Lei, "Toward an Empirical Prioritization of Contingency Variables for Business Strategy," *Academy of Management Journal* 28 (1985), pp. 763–88.

**6.** Quoted in Gary Hamel and C. K. Prahalad, *Competing for the Future* (Cambridge, MA: Harvard Business School Press, 1994).

**7.** Justin Martin, "Ignore Your Customer," *Fortune,* May 1, 1995, pp. 121–26.

**8.** For empirical evidence, see John C. Narver and Stanley F. Slater, "The Effect of a Market Orientation on Business Profitability," *Journal of Marketing* 54 (April 1990), pp. 1–18; Stanley F. Slater and John C. Narver, "Market Orientation, Performance, and the Moderating Influence of Competitive Environment," *Journal of Marketing* 58 (January 1994), pp. 46–55; and Ahmet H. Kirca, Satish Jayachandran, and William O. Bearden, "Market Orientation: A Meta-Analytic Review and Assessment of Its Antecedents and Impact on Performance, *Journal of Marketing* 69 (April 2005), pp. 24–41.

**9.** John W. Verity, "Revolution in the Supply Closet," *BusinessWeek,* June 10, 1996, p. 112.

**10.** Rahul Jacob, "Beyond Quality and Value," *Fortune,* Special Issue, Autumn–Winter 1993, p. 10.

**11.** Patricia Sellers, "How to Handle Customers' Gripes," *Fortune,* October 24, 1988, p. 88.

**12.** Patricia Sellers, "Keeping the Customers You Already Have," *Fortune,* Special Issue, Autumn–Winter 1993, p. 57. See also, Frederick F. Reicheld, "Loyalty and the Renaissance of Marketing," *Marketing Management* 2 (1994), pp. 10–21.

**13.** For a more detailed discussion of brand equity, see David A. Aaker, *Brand Equity* (New York: Free Press, 1991); and David A. Aaker, *Building Strong Brands* (New York: Free Press, 1996).

**14.** C. K. Prahalad and Gary Hamel, "The Core Competence of the Corporation," *Harvard Business Review* 68 (May–June 1990), pp. 79–91; George S. Day, "The Capabilities of Market-Driven Organizations," *Journal of Marketing* 58 (October 1994), pp. 37–52; and Stanley F. Slater, Eric M. Olson, and G. Tomas M. Hult, "Worried About Strategy Implementation? Don't Overlook Marketing's Role," *Business Horizons* 53 (2010), pp. 469–79 (archived online at *www.sciencedirect.com.*)

**15.** For a more detailed discussion of formal marketing plans, see Donald R. Lehmann and Russell S. Winer, *Analysis for Marketing Planning,* 4th ed. (New York: Irwin/McGraw-Hill, 1997); and Marian Burk Wood, *The Marketing Plan: A Handbook* 3rd ed. (Upper Saddle River, NJ: Prentice-Hall, 2008).

**16.** David S. Hopkins, *The Marketing Plan* (New York: The Conference Board, 1981), p. 2.

**17.** Jagdish N. Sheth and Rajendra S. Sisodia, "Feeling the Heat," *Marketing Management* 4 (Fall 1995), p. 10.

**18.** Ibid.

**19.** "Prophet's 'State of Marketing' Study Finds Marketers Challenged to Measure Up," *www.prophet.com/newsevents,* February 28, 2008.

**20.** Rajendra K. Srivastava, Tasadduq A. Shervani, and Liam Fahey, "Marketing, Business Processes, and Shareholder Value: An Organizationally Embedded View of Marketing Activities and the Discipline of Marketing," *Journal of Marketing* 63 (Special Issue 1999), pp. 168–79; Roland T. Rust, Katherine N. Lemon, and Valarie Zeithaml, "Return on Marketing: Using Customer Equity to Focus Marketing Strategy," *Journal of Marketing* 68 (January 2004), pp. 109–27; Roland T. Rust, T. Ambler, G. Carpenter, V. Kumar, and R. Srivastava, "Measuring Marketing Productivity: Current Knowledge and Future Directions," *Journal of Marketing* 68 (October 2004), pp. 76–89; and Paul W. Farris, Neil T. Bendle, Phillip E. Pfeifer, and David J. Reibstein, *Marketing Metrics,* 2nd ed. (Upper Saddle River, NJ: Pearson Publishing Inc., 2010).

**21.** Ravi S. Achrol and Philip Kotler, "Marketing in the Network Economy," *Journal of Marketing* 63 (Special Issue 1999), pp. 146–63.

**22.** Philip Kotler and Gary Armstrong, *Principles of Marketing* (Englewood Cliffs, NJ: Prentice Hall, 1989), p. 575.

**23.** For examples, see Terry G. Vavra, *Aftermarketing* (Burr Ridge, IL: Richard D. Irwin, 1995).

**24.** Brian Hindo, "Satisfaction Not Guaranteed," *BusinessWeek,* June 19, 2006, pp. 32–36; Arik Hesseldahl, "Dell's Disappointing Quarter," *www.businessweek.com/technology,* February 28, 2008; and Aaron Ricadela, "Dell: Scant Signs of Recovery," *www.businessweek.com/technology,* July 14, 2009.

**25.** For examples, see Faith Keenan, Stanley Holmes, Jay Greene, and Roger O. Crockett, "A Mass Market of One," *BusinessWeek,* December 2, 2002, pp. 68–72; and Anthony Bianco, "The Vanishing Mass Market," *BusinessWeek,* July 12, 2004, pp. 61–72.

**26.** "U.S. Census Bureau E-Stats Report," *www.census.gov/estats,* May 27, 2010.

**27.** "U.S. Census Bureau E-Stats Report," May 27, 2010.

**28.** Jim Jansen, "Online Product Research," Pew Research Center's Internet and American Life Project, *www.pewinternet.org/reports/2010* (September 29, 2010). See also Nanette Byrnes, "More Clicks at the Bricks," *Business Week,* December 17, 2007, pp. 50–52.

**29.** Achrol and Kotler, "Marketing in the Network Economy."

# CHAPTER TWO

# The Marketing Implications of Corporate and Business Strategies

## IBM Switches Strategies[1]

FOR DECADES International Business Machines focused most of its efforts on the hardware side of the computer industry: first on large mainframe computers, then on personal computers (PCs), and then, as the internet began to take off in the mid–1990s, on servers and related equipment. Its target customers for that hardware were typically organizations rather than individual consumers and usually large organizations that needed lots of data processing capacity and had the financial resources to afford it.

IBM's competitive strategy was also quite consistent over the years. Given that the firm was never the lowest-cost producer in the industry, it did not try to compete with low prices. Instead, the firm pursued a quality differentiation strategy by offering superior products backed up by excellent technical service and selling them at premium prices.

To implement its strategy, the company tried to ensure a steady stream of cutting-edge products by allocating vast resources to R&D and product development. On the marketing side, the firm maintained substantial advertising and promotion budgets to keep potential customers informed about its constantly evolving product lines and to burnish the identity of the IBM brand. More important, though, were the millions spent recruiting, training, and compensating one of the world's largest and most technically competent salesforces.

## Technology Changes and Competitor Actions Require a Shift in Strategy

For decades IBM's corporate, business, and marketing strategies were all very successful. By the mid-1990s, however, several of IBM's traditional businesses were in trouble. The company's share of the worldwide PC market fell to about 8 percent in 1999, third behind Dell and Compaq. Similarly, while server sales, made up mostly of UNIX-based computers, were growing rapidly around the world, IBM was able to capture only a small share of that business. Even its venerable mainframe business, which had been a low-growth but highly profitable market throughout the 1980s and early 1990s, suffered a profit squeeze due to falling prices and declining demand.

IBM's performance problems can be traced to a variety of factors, which all worked to make the firm's tried-and-true corporate, competitive, and marketing strategies less effective than they once were.

For one thing, major technological changes in the macroenvironment—such as the rapid increase in power of desktop PCs, the emergence of the internet, and the development of internal, organizationwide computer networks—greatly contributed to the declining demand for large mainframe computers and centralized data processing systems.

Also, IBM's quality differentiation strategy became less effective as some of its product-markets began to mature and customers' purchase criteria changed. Technical and performance differences among competing brands became less pronounced as the PC industry matured, for example, and later buyers tended to be less technically sophisticated, more price-conscious, and more interested in buying equipment that was easy to use. IBM's premium price position put it at a disadvantage in attracting such customers.

Even IBM's traditional focus on large organizational customers contributed to the firm's problems in the newly emerging markets for servers and related equipment and software. It was slow to pursue the many small start-up businesses at the forefront of the dot-com revolution, leaving an open field for Sun, Cisco Systems, and other competitors.

## A New Corporate Strategy

In view of the changing environment and IBM's lackluster performance, top executives began to refocus the corporate mission, de-emphasizing the development and manufacture of high-tech hardware—even to the extreme of selling the firm's PC business to China's Lenovo Group Ltd.—while increasing the emphasis on providing customers with business consulting, software, and outsourcing services. To leverage the firm's existing competencies and its long-term relationships with its traditional customers, some of the new services the firm developed concentrated on helping large, bricks-and-mortar firms hook old corporate databases (often on mainframes) into new online systems. A broader strategic thrust involved the development of

"enterprise solutions on demand"—packages of networked and modularized technologies, software, and consulting services aimed at helping organizations in a variety of business and service sectors rethink, redesign, and manage large chunks of their operations; everything from accounting and customer service to human resources and procurement. For instance, an IBM-designed system and software helped the Bank of Russia reduce its transaction processing costs by 95 percent.

Recently, another strategic thrust focused on business analytics; designing systems to size up and organize the vast streams of data companies collect in order to identify opportunities for cutting costs or increasing revenues and customer satisfaction. The French retailer Carrefour, for example, recently used IBM analytics to dig through purchase patterns, figure out what each customer was likely to buy next, and offer targeted coupons that drew customers back into the stores.

## New Business and Marketing Strategies

IBM's new corporate emphasis on business services and software as its primary paths toward future growth also forced some changes in the firm's competitive and marketing strategies. At the business level, the firm still seeks to differentiate itself from competitors on the basis of superior quality and to charge premium prices for that quality. But in its new service businesses, competitive superiority depends on the knowledge, experience, and expertise of its consultants—and their familiarity with a customer's operations that comes from continuing interaction—rather than the technical quality of its products. Therefore, to implement its new service-based strategy effectively, the company reorganized and reallocated many of its internal resources.

Given that the success of IBM's new competitive strategy depends heavily on the knowledge and expertise of its personnel and their ability to forge beneficial relationships with customers, the firm's salesforce is more crucial than ever. But many salespeople who used to sell the company's hardware have been retrained and turned into business consultants. The company also acquired PriceWaterhouseCoopers consulting, a move that helped IBM focus more on executive-level business consulting in addition to traditional technology consulting.

The firm also found that in order to tailor systems to a customer's business problems, industry-specific knowledge and experience are useful. Consequently, its enterprise solutions and analytics services are focused on six broad sectors, including banking and financial markets, health care, government, telecommunications, and consumer products. Also, in order to develop innovative solutions, each customer is serviced by a team that includes representatives from consulting/sales, software, systems/technology, and sometimes R&D. A team's members may reside in different IBM offices around the world, but each team specializes in only one customer sector.

A majority of the firm's $6 billion R&D budget is now focused on solving business problems rather than on improving the technical performance of its hardware. More than 70 percent of the 4,900 U. S. patents granted to IBM in 2009 were for software and services.

Finally the superior expertise and experience of IBM's people—and the firm's ability to satisfy the service needs of customers in a variety of industries—was communicated via an advertising campaign featuring a series of ads that stress the firm's extensive consulting resources and capabilities and were placed in a variety of media directed at managers and entrepreneurs.

## The Bottom Line

While IBM's new strategies are bringing it face-to-face with new competitors in the business consulting and outsourcing industries, such as Accenture, SAS, and India's Tata Consultancy Services Ltd., early results are encouraging. Due in part to the global financial crisis, total revenues were down about 5 percent in 2009, but income from continuing operations was up 9 percent to a record $18 billion. And since the firm began refocusing its strategy in 2002 it has increased its pretax margin by 2 ½ times, quadrupled earnings per share, and more than doubled free cash flow.

## Marketing Challenges Addressed in Chapter 2

IBM's experiences in the information technology industry illustrate some important points about the nature of business strategy and the interrelationships among different levels of strategy in an organization. They also demonstrate the importance of timely and accurate insights into customer desires, environmental trends, and competitors' actions in formulating successful strategies at every level.

As we discussed in Chapter 1, marketing managers' familiarity with customers, competitors, and environmental trends often means they play a crucial role in influencing strategies formulated at higher levels in the firm. While the need for new corporate and competitive strategies at IBM became obvious because of stagnating sales and declining profits in some of the firm's most venerable businesses, decisions about the content of those new strategies were influenced by information and analyses supplied by the firm's marketing and sales personnel. Marketing executives were key members of the task force appointed to analyze the firm's strengths and weaknesses and develop new directions for growth and profitability.

Some firms systematically incorporate such market and competitive analyses into their planning processes. They also coordinate their activities around the primary goal of satisfying unmet customer needs. Such firms are *market-oriented* and follow a business philosophy commonly called the *marketing concept.* Market-oriented firms have been shown to be among the more profitable and successful at maintaining strong competitive positions in their industries over time. As we shall see later in this chapter, however, companies do not always embrace a market orientation—nor rely as heavily on inputs from their marketing and sales personnel—in developing their strategies. Some firm's strategies are driven more by technology, production, or cost concerns.

Regardless of their participation or influence in formulating corporate and business-level strategies, marketing managers' freedom of action is ultimately constrained by those higher-level strategies. The objectives, strategies, and action plans for a specific product-market are but one part of a hierarchy of strategies within the firm. Each level of strategy must be consistent with—and therefore influenced and constrained by—higher levels within the hierarchy. For example, not only the new services developed by IBM, but also their advertising appeals, prices, and other aspects of their marketing plans were shaped by the shift in corporate strategy toward emphasizing software, services, and business consulting as the primary avenues for future growth.

**STRATEGIC ISSUE**

*Each level of strategy must be consistent with—and therefore influenced and constrained by—higher levels within the hierarchy.*

These interrelationships among the various levels of strategy raise several questions of importance to marketing managers as well as managers in other functional areas and top executives. While marketing managers clearly bear the primary responsibility for developing strategic marketing plans for individual product or service offerings, what role does marketing play in formulating strategies at the corporate and divisional or business-unit level? Why do some organizations pay much more attention to customers and competitors when formulating their strategies (i.e., why are some firms more market-oriented) than others, and does it make any difference in their performance? What do strategies consist of, and are they similar or different at the corporate, business, and functional levels? What specific decisions underlie effective corporate and business-level strategies, and what are their implications for marketing?

## What Is Marketing's Role in Formulating and Implementing Strategies?

The essence of strategic planning at all levels is identifying threats to avoid and opportunities to pursue. The primary strategic responsibility of any manager is to look outward continuously to keep the firm or business in step with changes in the environment. Because they occupy positions at the boundary between the firm and its customers, distributors, and competitors, marketing managers are usually most familiar with conditions and trends in the market environment. Consequently, they not only are responsible for developing strategic plans for their own product-market entries, but also are often primary participants and contributors to the planning process at the business and corporate level as well.

The wide-ranging influence of marketing managers on higher-level strategic decisions is clearly shown in a survey of managers in 280 U.S. and 234 German business units of firms in the electrical equipment, mechanical machinery, and consumer package goods industries.[2] The study examined perceptions of marketing managers' influence relative to managers from sales, R&D, operations, and finance on a variety of strategic and tactical decisions within their businesses. Exhibit 2.1 summarizes the results.

The study found that, on average, marketing and sales executives exerted significantly more influence than managers from other functions on strategic decisions concerning traditional marketing activities, such as advertising messages, pricing, distribution, customer service and support, and measurement and improvement of customer satisfaction. Interestingly, though, the influence of sales executives was perceived to be even greater than that of marketing managers on some of these decisions. One reason—particularly in the industrial-goods firms selling electronic equipment and machinery—may be that sales managers have more detailed information about customer needs and desires because they have direct and continuing contact with existing and potential buyers.

## Exhibit 2.1

INFLUENCE OF FUNCTIONAL UNITS OVER VARIOUS BUSINESS DECISIONS

| Decisions | Marketing | Sales | R&D | Operations | Finance |
|---|---|---|---|---|---|
| **Business strategy decisions** | | | | | |
| Strategic direction of the business | 38 | 29** | 11** | 9** | 14** |
| Expansion into new geographic markets | 39 | 45** | 3** | 3** | 10** |
| Choices of strategic partners | 33 | 38* | 7** | 9** | 12** |
| New product development | 32 | 23* | 29** | 9** | 7** |
| Major capital expenditures | 13 | 11** | 13 | 29** | 35** |
| **Marketing strategy decisions** | | | | | |
| Advertising messages | 65 | 29** | 3** | 1** | 2** |
| Customer satisfaction measurement | 48 | 35** | 5** | 8** | 4** |
| Customer satisfaction improvement | 40 | 37** | 7** | 10** | 6** |
| Distribution strategy | 34 | 52** | 1** | 6** | 6** |
| Customer service and support | 31 | 47** | 5** | 10** | 7** |
| Pricing | 30 | 41** | 4** | 9** | 16** |

The number in each cell is the mean of the amount of points given by responding managers to each function, using a constant-sum scale of 100. A t-test was performed to compare column 2 (mean of relative influence of marketing) with columns 3 through 6 (relative influence of sales, R&D, operations, and finance). Statistically significant differences with marketing are indicated by asterisks, where: * $p<.05$; ** $p<.01$.

*Source:* Adapted from "Marketing's Influence within the Firm," by Christian Homburg, John P. Workman, Jr., and Harley Krohmer, *Journal of Marketing.* Copyright 1999 by the American Marketing Association. Reproduced with permission of the American Marketing Association in the format textbook via Copyright Clearance Center.

More surprisingly, marketing managers were also perceived to wield significantly more influence than managers from other functional areas on cross-functional, business-level strategic decisions. While the views of finance and operations executives carry more weight in approving major capital expenditures, marketing and sales managers exert more influence on decisions concerning the strategic direction of the business unit, expansion into new geographic markets, the selection of strategic business partners, and new product development.

Might the relative influence of the different functions become more similar as firms adopt more integrative organizational forms, such as cross-functional work teams? The study's results suggest not. Marketing's influence was not significantly reduced in companies that had instituted cross-functional structures and processes.

But marketing managers may not play as pervasive a strategic role in other cultures as they do in the United States. The study found that marketers' influence on both tactical and strategic issues was significantly lower in German firms. As one of the study's authors points out, "Germany has traditionally stressed technology and operations more than the softer, customer-oriented aspects central to marketing. So even when the environment changes, a signal to top-level German managers that marketing should be playing a greater role, they are reluctant to give it that role."[3]

# Market-Oriented Management

No matter where companies are located however, marketing managers do not play an equally extensive strategic role in every firm because not all firms are equally market-oriented. Not surprisingly, marketers tend to have a greater influence on all levels of strategy in organizations that embrace a market-oriented philosophy of business. More critically, managers in other functional areas of market-oriented firms incorporate more customer and competitor information into their decision-making processes as well.

Market-oriented organizations tend to operate according to the business philosophy known as the marketing concept. As originally stated by General Electric six decades ago, the **marketing concept** holds that the planning and coordination of all company activities around the primary goal of satisfying customer needs is the most effective means to attain and sustain a competitive advantage and achieve company objectives over time.

Thus, market-oriented firms are characterized by a consistent focus by personnel in all departments and at all levels on customers' needs and competitive circumstances in the market environment. They are also willing and able to quickly adapt products and functional programs to fit changes in that environment. Such firms pay a great deal of attention to customer research *before* products are designed and produced. They embrace the concept of market segmentation by adapting product offerings and marketing programs to the special needs of different target markets.

Market-oriented firms also adopt a variety of organizational procedures and structures to improve the responsiveness of their decision making, including using more detailed environmental scanning and continuous, real-time information systems; seeking frequent feedback from and coordinating plans with key customers and major suppliers; decentralizing strategic decisions; encouraging entrepreneurial thinking among lower-level managers; and using interfunctional management teams to analyze issues and initiate strategic actions outside the formal planning process.[4] For example, IBM formed a high-level cross-functional task force to reevaluate its market environment, develop a new strategic focus, and map new avenues toward future growth. And it has formed cross-functional teams to help individual customers identify and resolve their business problems and to sustain long-term relationships. These and other actions recommended to make an organization more market-driven and responsive to environmental changes are summarized in Exhibit 2.2.

# Does Being Market-Oriented Pay?

Since an organization's success over time hinges on its ability to provide benefits of value to its customers—and to do that better than its competitors—it seems likely that market-oriented firms should perform better than others. By paying careful attention to customer needs and competitive threats—and by focusing activities across all functional departments on meeting those needs and threats effectively—organizations should be able to enhance, accelerate, and reduce the volatility and vulnerability of their cash flows.[5] And that should enhance their economic performance and shareholder value. Indeed, profitability is the third leg, together with a customer focus and cross-functional coordination, of the three-legged stool known as the marketing concept.

Sometimes the marketing concept is interpreted as a philosophy of trying to satisfy all customers' needs regardless of the cost. That would be a prescription for financial disaster. Instead, the marketing concept is consistent with the notion of focusing on only those segments of the customer population that the firm can satisfy both effectively *and* profitably.

## Exhibit 2.2

GUIDELINES FOR MARKET-ORIENTED MANAGEMENT

1. Create customer focus throughout the business.
2. Listen to the customer.
3. Define and nurture your distinctive competence.
4. Define marketing as market intelligence.
5. Target customers precisely.
6. Manage for profitability, not sales volume.
7. Make customer value the guiding star.
8. Let the customer define quality.

9. Measure and manage customer expectations.
10. Build customer relationships and loyalty.
11. Define the business as a service business.
12. Commit to continuous improvement and innovation.
13. Manage culture along with strategy and structure.
14. Grow with partners and alliances.
15. Destroy marketing bureaucracy.

*Source:* "Executing the New Marketing Concept," by Frederick E. Webster, Jr., *Marketing Management.* Copyright 1994, by the American Marketing Association. Reproduced by permission of the American Marketing Association in the format textbook via Copyright Clearance Center.

Firms might offer less extensive or costly goods and services to unprofitable segments or avoid them altogether.

Substantial evidence supports the idea that being market-oriented pays dividends, at least in a highly developed economy such as the United States. A number of studies involving more than 500 firms or business units across a variety of industries indicate that a market orientation has a significant positive effect on various dimensions of performance, including return on assets, sales growth, and new product success.[6] Even entrepreneurial start-ups appear to benefit from a strong customer orientation. One recent study of start-ups in Japan and the United States found that new firms that focused on marketing first, rather than lowering costs or advancing technology, were less likely to be brought down by competitors as their product-markets developed.[7]

**STRATEGIC ISSUE**

*A market orientation has a significant positive effect on various dimensions of performance, including return on assets, sales growth, and new product success.*

## Factors That Mediate Marketing's Strategic Role

Despite the evidence that a market-orientation boosts performance, many companies around the world are not very focused on their customers or competitors. Among the reasons firms are not always in close touch with their market environments are these:

- Competitive conditions may enable a company to be successful in the short run without being particularly sensitive to customer desires.
- Different levels of economic development across industries or countries may favor different business philosophies.
- Firms can suffer from strategic inertia—the automatic continuation of strategies successful in the past, even though current market conditions are changing.

### Competitive Factors Affecting a Firm's Market Orientation
The competitive conditions some firms face enable them to be successful in the short term without paying much attention to their customers, suppliers, distributors, or other organizations in their market environment. Early entrants into newly emerging industries, particularly industries based on new technologies, are especially likely to be internally focused and not very market-oriented. This is because there are likely to be relatively few strong competitors during the formative years of a new industry, customer demand for the new product is likely to grow rapidly and outstrip available supply, and production problems

and resource constraints tend to represent more immediate threats to the survival of such new businesses.

Businesses facing such market and competitive conditions are often **product-oriented** or **production-oriented.** They focus most of their attention and resources on such functions as product and process engineering, production, and finance in order to acquire and manage the resources necessary to keep pace with growing demand. The business is primarily concerned with producing more of what it wants to make, and marketing generally plays a secondary role in formulating and implementing strategy. Other functional differences between production-oriented and market-oriented firms are summarized in Exhibit 2.3.

As industries grow, they become more competitive. New entrants are attracted and existing producers attempt to differentiate themselves through improved products and more-efficient production processes. As a result, industry capacity often grows faster than demand and the environment shifts from a seller's market to a buyer's market. Firms often respond to such changes with aggressive promotional activities—such as hiring more salespeople, increasing advertising budgets, or offering frequent price promotions—to maintain market share and hold down unit costs.

Unfortunately, this kind of **sales-oriented** response to increasing competition still focuses on selling what the firm wants to make rather than on customer needs. Worse, competitors can easily match such aggressive sales tactics. Simply spending more on selling efforts usually does not create a sustainable competitive advantage.

As industries mature, sales volume levels off and technological differences among brands tend to shrink as manufacturers copy the best features of each other's products. Consequently, a firm must seek new market segments or steal share from competitors by offering lower prices, superior services, or intangible benefits other firms cannot match. At this stage, managers can most readily appreciate the benefits of a market orientation, and marketers are often given a bigger role in developing competitive strategies.[8] Of course, a given industry's characteristics may make some components of a market orientation more crucial for good performance than others. For example,

## Exhibit 2.3

DIFFERENCES BETWEEN PRODUCTION-ORIENTED AND MARKET-ORIENTED ORGANIZATIONS

| Business activity or function | Production orientation | Marketing orientation |
| --- | --- | --- |
| Product offering | Company sells what it can make; primary focus on functional performance and cost. | Company makes what it can sell; primary focus on customers' needs and market opportunities. |
| Product line | Narrow. | Broad. |
| Pricing | Based on production and distribution costs. | Based on perceived benefits provided. |
| Research | Technical research; focus on product improvement and cost cutting in the production process. | Market research; focus on identifying new opportunities and applying new technology to satisfy customer needs. |
| Packaging | Protection for the product; minimize costs. | Designed for customer convenience; a promotional tool. |
| Credit | A necessary evil; minimize bad debt losses. | A customer service; a tool to attract customers. |
| Promotion | Emphasis on product features, quality, and price. | Emphasis on product benefits and ability to satisfy customers' needs or solve problems. |

in an industry dominated by large, dynamic competitors—as in the global automobile industry—being responsive to competitor moves may be even more important than a strong customer focus.[9] But the bottom line is that an orientation toward the *market*—competitors, customers, and potential customers—is usually crucial for continued success in global markets.

### The Influence of Different Stages of Development across Industries and Global Markets

The previous discussion suggests that the degree of adoption of a market orientation varies not only across firms but also across entire industries. Industries that are in earlier stages of their life cycles, or that benefit from barriers to entry or other factors reducing the intensity of competition, are likely to have relatively fewer market-oriented firms. For instance, in part because of governmental regulations that restricted competition, many service industries—including banks, airlines, physicians, lawyers, accountants, and insurance companies—were slow to adopt the marketing concept. But with the trend toward deregulation and the increasingly intense global competition in such industries, many service organizations are working much harder to understand and satisfy their customers.[10]

Given that entire economies are in different stages of development around the world, the popularity—and even the appropriateness—of different business philosophies may also vary across countries. A production orientation was the dominant business philosophy in the United States, for instance, during the industrialization that occurred from the mid-1800s through World War I.[11] Similarly, a primary focus on developing product and production technology may still be appropriate in developing nations that are in the midst of industrialization.

International differences in business philosophies can cause some problems for the globalization of a firm's strategic marketing programs, but it can create some opportunities as well, especially for alliances or joint ventures. Consider, for example, the partnership between French automaker Renault-Nissan and the Russian car manufacturer AvtoVAZ discussed in Exhibit 2.4.

---

### Exhibit 2.4  RENAULT'S PARTNERSHIP WITH RUSSIAN AUTOMAKER AvtoVAZ BENEFITS BOTH PARTIES

The AvtoVAZ car factory in the central Russian city of Togliatti is a decrepit, mile-long building where the company's Lada sedans are turned out by 40-year-old equipment. Nevertheless, the French carmaker Renault-Nissan recently paid $1 billion for a 25 percent stake in AvtoVAZ. Even after investing more millions to modernize the plant, Renault figures that Russia's low labor and energy costs will make the plant ideal for producing the Logan lineup of cars that the firm introduced in 2004. The no-frills Logan, starting at about $9,000, has become the world's most successful cheap car. Its partnership with AvtoVAZ should also help Renault appeal to Russian car buyers and capture a larger share of that country's rapidly growing market.

But AvtoVAZ will also benefit from the partnership, especially on the production side. A key reason the firm agreed to the deal with Renault was "the modern technology and know-how that the company will provide us," according to Chairman Sergei Chemezov. The partnership may also encourage global auto parts suppliers to build new, more-efficient plants near the AvtoVAZ factory.

*Sources:* Based on material in Carol Matlack, "Renault's Ghosn Takes On a Russian Relic," *www.businessweek.com*, February 29, 2008; and Carol Matlack, "Carlos Ghosn's Russian Gambit," *BusinessWeek*, March 17, 2008, pp. 57–58. For more information about Renault's acquisitions and alliances, see the company's website at *www.renault.com*.

**Strategic Inertia**   In some cases, a firm that achieved success by being in tune with its environment loses touch with its market because managers become reluctant to tamper with strategies and marketing programs that worked in the past. They begin to believe there is one best way to satisfy their customers. Such strategic inertia is dangerous because customers' needs and competitive offerings change over time. IBM's traditional focus on large organizational customers, for instance, caused the company to devote too little effort to the much faster-growing segment of small technology start-ups. And its emphasis on computer technology and hardware made it slow to respond to the explosive growth in demand for applications software and consulting services. Thus, in environments where such changes happen frequently, the strategic planning process needs to be ongoing and adaptive. All the participants, whether from marketing or other functional departments, need to pay constant attention to what is happening with their customers and competitors.

## Three Levels of Strategy: Similar Components, but Different Issues

We have argued that marketing managers have primary responsibility for the marketing strategies associated with individual product or service offerings, and that their perspectives and inputs often have a major influence on the decisions that shape corporate and business-level strategies. But we haven't said much about what those strategic decisions are. Consequently, it's time to define what strategies are and how they vary across different levels of an organization.

### Strategy: A Definition

Although *strategy* first became a popular business buzzword during the 1960s, it continues to be the subject of widely differing definitions and interpretations. The following definition, however, captures the essence of the term:

> A **strategy** is a fundamental pattern of present and planned objectives, resource deployments, and interactions of an organization with markets, competitors, and other environmental factors.[12]

Our definition suggests that a strategy should specify (1) *what* (objectives to be accomplished), (2) *where* (on which industries and product-markets to focus), and (3) *how* (which resources and activities to allocate to each product-market to meet environmental opportunities and threats and to gain a competitive advantage).

### The Components of Strategy

A well-developed strategy contains five components, or sets of issues:

1. *Scope.* The scope of an organization refers to the breadth of its strategic domain—the number and types of industries, product lines, and market segments it competes in or plans to enter. Decisions about an organization's strategic scope should reflect management's view of the firm's purpose, or *mission.* This common thread among its various activities and product-markets defines the essential nature of what its business is and what it should be.

2. *Goals and objectives.* Strategies should also detail desired levels of accomplishment on one or more dimensions of performance—such as volume growth, profit contribution, or return

on investment—over specified time periods for each of those businesses and product-markets and for the organization as a whole.

**3.** *Resource deployments.* Every organization has limited financial and human resources. Formulating a strategy also involves deciding how those resources are to be obtained and allocated, across businesses, product-markets, functional departments, and activities within each business or product-market.

**4.** *Identification of a sustainable competitive advantage.* One important part of any strategy is a specification of *how the organization will compete* in each business and product-market within its domain. How can it position itself to develop and sustain a differential advantage over current and potential competitors? To answer such questions, managers must examine the market opportunities in each business and product-market and the company's distinctive competencies or strengths relative to its competitors.

**5.** *Synergy.* Synergy exists when the firm's businesses, product-markets, resource deployments, and competencies complement and reinforce one another. Synergy enables the total performance of the related businesses to be greater than it would otherwise be: The whole becomes greater than the sum of its parts.

## The Hierarchy of Strategies

Explicitly or implicitly, these five basic dimensions are part of all strategies. However, rather than a single comprehensive strategy, most organizations have a hierarchy of interrelated strategies, each formulated at a different level of the firm. The three major levels of strategy in most large, multiproduct organizations are (1) **corporate strategy,** (2) **business-level strategy,** and (3) **functional strategies** focused on a particular product-market entry. In small, single-product-line companies or entrepreneurial start-ups, however, corporate and business-level strategic issues merge.

Our primary focus is on the development of marketing strategies and programs for individual product-market entries, but other functional departments, such as R&D and production, also have strategies and plans for each of the firm's product-markets. Throughout this book, therefore, we examine the interfunctional implications of product-market strategies, conflicts across functional areas, and the mechanisms that firms use to resolve those conflicts.

Strategies at all three levels contain the five components mentioned earlier, but because each strategy serves a different purpose within the organization, each emphasizes a different set of issues. Exhibit 2.5 summarizes the specific focus and issues dealt with at each level of strategy; we discuss them in the next sections.

## Corporate Strategy

At the corporate level, managers must coordinate the activities of multiple business units and, in the case of conglomerates, even separate legal business entities. Decisions about the organization's scope and resource deployments across its divisions or businesses are the primary focus of corporate strategy. The essential questions at this level include, What business(es) are we in? What business(es) *should* we be in? and What portion of our total resources should we devote to each of these businesses to achieve the organization's overall goals and objectives? Thus, top-level managers at IBM decided to pursue future growth primarily through the development of consulting services and software rather than computer hardware. They shifted substantial corporate resources—including R&D expenditures, marketing and advertising budgets, and vast numbers of salespeople— into the corporation's service and software businesses to support the new strategic direction.

## Exhibit 2.5

KEY COMPONENTS OF CORPORATE, BUSINESS, AND MARKETING STRATEGIES

| Strategy components | Corporate strategy | Business strategy | Marketing strategy |
|---|---|---|---|
| Scope | • Corporate domain—"Which businesses should we be in?"<br>• Corporate development strategy<br>  Conglomerate diversification (expansion into unrelated businesses)<br>  Vertical integration<br>  Acquisition and divestiture policies | • Business domain—"Which product-markets should we be in within this business or industry?<br>• Business development strategy<br>  Concentric diversification (new products for existing customers or new customers for existing products) | • Target market definition<br>• Product-line depth and breadth<br>• Branding policies<br>• Product-market development plan<br>• Line extension and product elimination plans |
| Goals and objectives | • Overall corporate objectives aggregated across businesses<br>  Revenue growth<br>  Profitability<br>  ROI (return on investment)<br>  Earnings per share<br>  Contributions to other stakeholders | • Constrained by corporate goals<br>• Objectives aggregated across product-market entries in the business unit<br>  Sales growth<br>  New product or market growth<br>  Profitability<br>  ROI<br>  Cash flow<br>  Strengthening bases of competitive advantage | • Constrained by corporate and business goals<br>• Objectives for a specific product-market entry<br>  Sales<br>  Market share<br>  Contribution margin<br>  Customer satisfaction |
| Allocation of resources | • Allocation among businesses in the corporate portfolio<br>• Allocation across functions shared by multiple businesses (corporate R&D, MIS) | • Allocation among product-market entries in the business unit<br>• Allocation across functional departments within the business unit | • Allocation across components of the marketing plan (elements of the marketing mix) for a specific product-market entry |
| Sources of competitive advantage | • Primarily through superior corporate financial or human resources; more corporate R&D; better organizational processes or synergies relative to competitors across all industries in which the firm operates | • Primarily through competitive strategy, business unit's competencies relative to competitors in its industry | • Primarily through effective product positioning; superiority on one or more components of the marketing mix relative to competitors within a specific product-market |
| Sources of synergy | • Shared resources, technologies, or functional competencies across businesses within the firm | • Shared resources (including favorable customer image) or functional competencies across product-markets within an industry | • Shared marketing resources, competencies, or activities across product-market entries |

Attempts to develop and maintain distinctive competencies at the corporate level focus on generating superior human, financial, and technological resources; designing effective organization structures and processes; and seeking synergy among the firm's various businesses. Synergy can provide a major competitive advantage for firms where related businesses share R&D investments, product or production technologies, distribution channels, a common salesforce and/or promotional themes—as in the case of IBM.[13]

## Business-Level Strategy

How a business unit competes within its industry is the critical focus of business-level strategy. A major issue in a business strategy is that of sustainable competitive advantage. What distinctive competencies can give the business unit a competitive advantage? And which of those competencies best match the needs and wants of the customers in the business's target segment(s)? For example, a business with low-cost sources of supply and efficient, modern plants might adopt a low-cost competitive strategy. One with a strong marketing department and a competent salesforce may compete by offering superior customer service.[14]

Another important issue a business-level strategy must address is appropriate scope: how many and which market segments to compete in, and the overall breadth of product offerings and marketing programs to appeal to these segments. Finally, synergy should be sought across product-markets and across functional departments within the business.

## Marketing Strategy

The primary focus of marketing strategy is to effectively allocate and coordinate marketing resources and activities to accomplish the firm's objectives within a specific product-market. Therefore, the critical issue concerning the scope of a marketing strategy is specifying the target market(s) for a particular product or product line. Next, firms seek competitive advantage and synergy through a well-integrated program of marketing mix elements (the 4 Ps of product, price, place, promotion) tailored to the needs and wants of potential customers in that target market.

# The Marketing Implications of Corporate Strategy Decisions

To formulate a useful corporate strategy, management must address six interrelated decisions: (1) the overall scope and mission of the organization, (2) company goals and objectives, (3) a source of competitive advantage, (4) a development strategy for future growth, (5) the allocation of corporate resources across the firm's various businesses, and (6) the search for synergy via the sharing of corporate resources, intangibles, or programs across businesses or product lines. While a market orientation—and the analytical tools that marketing managers use to examine customer desires and competitors' strengths and weaknesses—can provide useful insights to guide all six of these strategic decisions, they are particularly germane for revealing the most attractive avenues for future growth and for determining which businesses or product-markets are likely to produce the greatest returns on the company's resources.

In turn, all of these corporate decisions have major implications for the strategic marketing plans of the firm's various products or services. Together, they define the general strategic direction, objectives, and resource constraints within which those marketing plans must operate. We next examine the marketing implications involved in both formulating and implementing these components of corporate strategy.

## Corporate Scope—Defining the Firm's Mission

A well-thought-out mission statement guides an organization's managers as to which market opportunities to pursue and which fall outside the firm's strategic domain. A clearly stated mission can help instill a shared sense of direction, relevance, and achievement among employees, as well as a positive image of the firm among customers, investors, and other stakeholders.

To provide a useful sense of direction, a corporate mission statement should clearly define the organization's strategic scope. It should answer such fundamental questions as: What is our business? Who are our customers? What kinds of value can we provide to these customers? and What should our business be in the future? For example, 25 years ago PepsiCo, the manufacturer of Pepsi-Cola, broadened its mission to focus on "marketing superior quality food and beverage products for households and consumers dining out." That clearly defined mission guided the firm's managers toward the acquisition of several related companies, such as Frito-Lay, Taco Bell, and Pizza Hut.

More recently, in response to a changing global competitive environment, PepsiCo narrowed its scope to focus primarily on *packaged* foods (particularly salty snacks) and beverages distributed through supermarket and convenience store channels. This new, narrower mission led the firm to (1) divest all of its fast-food restaurant chains; (2) acquire complementary beverage businesses, such as Tropicana juices, Lipton's iced teas, and Gatorade sports drinks; and develop new brands targeted at rapidly growing beverage segments, such as Aquafina bottled water.

PepsiCo's most recent mission continues to focus on packaged snacks and beverages sold through food retailers, but also seeks "Performance with purpose." That phrase essentially boils down to balancing the profit motive with the development of healthier, more nutritious snacks and drinks, and striving for a net-zero impact on the environment. Consequently, PepsiCo has either acquired or partnered with a Bulgarian nut packager, an Israeli hummus maker, and Naked Juice—a California company that makes nutritional beverages like smoothies.[15]

**Market Influences on the Corporate Mission**   Like any other strategy component, an organization's mission should fit both its internal characteristics and the opportunities and threats in its external environment. Obviously, the firm's mission should be compatible with its established values, resources, and distinctive competencies. But it should also focus the firm's efforts on markets where those resources and competencies will generate value for customers, an advantage over competitors, and synergy across its products. Thus, PepsiCo's new mission reflects (1) the firm's package goods marketing, sales, and distribution competencies, (2) its perception that substantial synergies can be realized across snack foods and beverages within supermarket channels via shared logistics, joint displays and sales promotions, cross-couponing, and the like, and (3) a corporate culture that believes the company should be an active player in solving some of the social problems—such as obesity and global warming—the world faces.

**Criteria for Defining the Corporate Mission**   Several criteria can be used to define an organization's strategic mission. Many firms specify their domain in *physical* terms, focusing on *products* or *services* or the *technology* used. The problem is that such statements can lead to slow reactions to technological or customer-demand changes. For example, Theodore Levitt once argued that Penn Central's view of its mission as being "the railroad business" helped cause the firm's failure. Penn Central did not respond to major changes in transportation technology, such as the rapid growth of air travel and the increased efficiency of long-haul trucking. Nor did it respond to consumers' growing willingness to pay higher prices for the increased speed and convenience of air travel. Levitt argued that it is better to define a firm's mission as *what customer needs are to be satisfied and the functions the firm must perform to satisfy them.*[16] Products and technologies change over time, but basic customer needs tend to endure. Thus, if Penn Central had defined its mission as satisfying the transportation needs of its customers rather than simply being a railroad, it might have been more willing to expand its domain to incorporate newer technologies.

One problem with Levitt's advice, though, is that a mission statement focusing only on basic customer needs can be too broad to provide clear guidance and can fail to take into account the firm's specific competencies. If Penn Central had defined itself as a transportation company, should it have diversified into the trucking business? Started an airline? As the upper-right quadrant of Exhibit 2.6 suggests, the most useful mission statements focus on the customer need to be satisfied and the functions that must be performed to satisfy that need. They are *specific* as to the customer groups and the products or technologies on which to concentrate. Thus, instead of seeing itself as being in the railroad business or as satisfying the transportation needs of all potential customers, Burlington Northern Santa Fe Railroad's mission is to provide long-distance transportation for large-volume producers of low-value, low-density products, such as coal and grain.

**Social Values and Ethical Principles**   An increasing number of organizations are developing mission statements that also attempt to define the social and ethical boundaries of their strategic domain. Some firms are actively pursuing social programs they believe to be intertwined with their economic objectives, while others simply seek to manage their businesses according to the principles of *sustainability*—meeting humanity's needs without harming future generations. For example, Unilever has launched a variety of programs to help developing nations wrestle with poverty, water scarcity, and the effects of climate change. The firm's motives are at least as much economic as moral. Some 40 percent of the Dutch–British giant's sales and most of its growth now take place in developing nations, and Unilever food products account for about 10 percent of the world's tea, 30 percent of all spinach, and a large portion of all processed fish. As environmental regulations grow stricter around the world, the firm must invest in green technologies or its leadership in packaged foods, soaps, and other products could be imperiled. "You can't ignore the impact your company has on the community and the environment," points out CEO Patrick Cescau. These days, "it's also about growth and innovation. In the future, it will be the only way to do business."[17]

Unfortunately, many top managers are unsure about what kinds of social programs and principles best fit their organization's resources, competencies, and economic goals. In a recent McKinsey & Co. survey of more than 1,100 top global executives, 79 percent predicted at least some responsibility for dealing with future social and political issues would fall on corporations, but only 3 percent said they currently do a good job dealing with social pressures.[18] Thus, crafting mission statements that specify explicit social

## Exhibit 2.6

CHARACTERISTICS OF EFFECTIVE CORPORATE MISSION STATEMENTS

|  | Broad | Specific |
|---|---|---|
| **Functional**<br>Based on customer needs | Transportation business | Long-distance transportation for large-volume producers of low-value, low-density products |
| **Physical**<br>Based on existing products or technology | Railroad business | Long-haul, coal-carrying railroad |

values, goals, and programs—with inputs from employees, customers, social interest groups, and other stakeholders—is becoming an important part of corporate strategic planning.

The ethical principles a firm hopes to abide by in its dealings with customers, suppliers, and employees tend to be more straightforward and specific than the broader issues of social responsibility discussed above. Consequently, roughly two-thirds of U.S. firms have formal codes of ethics, and a growing number have established formal departments dedicated to encouraging compliance with company ethical standards.[19]

Outside America, fewer firms have formal ethics bureaucracies. To some extent, this reflects the fact that in other countries governments and organized labor both play a bigger role in corporate life. In Germany, for instance, workers' councils often deal with issues such as sexual equality, race relations, and workers' rights.[20]

**Ethics** is concerned with the development of moral standards by which actions and situations can be judged. It focuses on those actions that may result in actual or potential harm of some kind (e.g., economic, mental, physical) to an individual, group, or organization.

Particular actions may be legal but not ethical. For instance, extreme and unsubstantiated advertising claims, such as "Our product is far superior to Brand X," might be viewed as simply legal puffery engaged in to make a sale, but many marketers (and their customers) view such little white lies as unethical. Thus, ethics is more proactive than the law. Ethical standards attempt to anticipate and avoid social problems, whereas most laws and regulations emerge only after the negative consequences of an action become apparent.[21]

### Why Are Ethics Important? The Marketing Implications of Ethical Standards

One might ask why a corporation should take responsibility for providing moral guidance to its managers and employees. While such a question may be a good topic for philosophical debate, there is a compelling, practical reason for a firm to impose ethical standards to guide employees. Unethical practices can damage the trust between a firm and its suppliers or customers, thereby disrupting the development of long-term exchange relationships and resulting in the likely loss of sales and profits over time. For example, one survey of 135 purchasing managers from a variety of industries found that the more unethical a supplier's sales and marketing practices were perceived to be, the less eager were the purchasing managers to buy from that supplier.[22]

**STRATEGIC ISSUE**

*Unethical practices can damage the trust between a firm and its suppliers or customers, thereby disrupting the development of long-term exchange relationships and resulting in the likely loss of sales and profits over time.*

Unfortunately, not all customers or competing suppliers adhere to the same ethical standards. As a result, marketers sometimes feel pressure to engage in actions that are inconsistent with what they believe to be right, such as paying bribes to win a sale from a potential customer or to ensure needed resources or services from suppliers and government agencies. Such dilemmas are particularly likely to arise as a company moves into global markets involving different cultures and levels of economic development where economic exigencies and ethical standards may be quite different. For example, in a recent survey of over 90,000 businesspeople in 68 different countries, more than one-quarter of respondents reported paying a bribe in the past year. Bribes were most common in Sub-Saharan Africa, where more than half of respondents had paid at least one, compared to 23 percent in Latin America, 19 percent in the western Balkans and Turkey, 5 percent in the European Union and North America, and less than 1 percent in Denmark and Norway.[23]

Such inconsistencies in external expectations and demands across countries and markets can lead to job stress and inconsistent behavior among marketing and sales personnel, which in turn can risk damaging long-term relationships with suppliers, channel partners, and customers. A company can reduce such problems by spelling out formal social policies and ethical standards in its corporate mission statement and communicating and enforcing those standards. For instance, Fluor—a multinational construction firm that earns more than half its $17 billion revenue overseas—has a strict ethical policy against paying any bribes or kickbacks to win new projects. The firm puts all employees through online anti-corruption training and provides advice to help them deal with sticky situations, but they then receive zero tolerance and face tough penalties for any infractions. This dedication to high ethical standards and transparency helped make Fluor the world's most admired engineering firm in *Fortune* magazine's survey in 2009.[24]

Unfortunately, it is not always easy to decide what a firm's ethical policies and standards should be. There are multiple philosophical traditions or frameworks that managers might use to evaluate the ethics of a given action. Consequently, different firms or managers can pursue somewhat different ethical standards, particularly across national cultures. Exhibit 2.7 displays a comparison (across three geographic regions) of the proportion of company ethical statements that address a set of specific issues. Note that a larger number of companies in the United States and Europe appear to be more concerned with the ethics of their purchasing practices than those of their marketing activities.

A general code of ethics prescribed for members of the American Marketing Association (the largest association of marketing professionals) is shown in Appendix 2.1 at the end of this chapter. Since many ethical issues in marketing are open to interpretation and debate, however, we will examine such issues and their implications individually as they arise throughout the remainder of this book.

## Exhibit 2.7

ISSUES ADDRESSED BY COMPANY ETHICS STATEMENTS

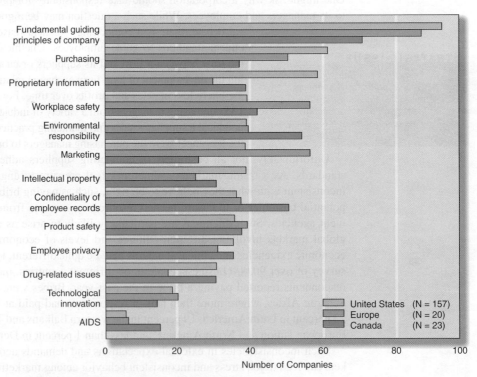

*Source:* Ronald E. Berenbeim, *Corporate Ethics Practices* (New York: The Conference Board, 1992). Used by permission.

## Corporate Objectives

Confucius said, "For one who has no objective, nothing is relevant." Formal objectives provide decision criteria that guide an organization's business units and employees toward specific dimensions and performance levels. Those same objectives provide the benchmarks against which actual performance can be evaluated.

To be useful as decision criteria and evaluative benchmarks, corporate objectives must be specific and measurable. Therefore, each objective contains four components:

- A *performance dimension* or attribute sought.
- A *measure or index* for evaluating progress.
- A *target or hurdle* level to be achieved.
- A *time frame* within which the target is to be accomplished.

Exhibit 2.8 lists some common performance dimensions and measures used in specifying corporate as well as business-unit and marketing objectives. When specifying short-term business-level and marketing goals, however, two additional dimensions become important: their relevance to higher-level strategies and goals and their attainability. Thus, we find it useful to follow the SMART acronym when specifying objectives at all levels: specific, measurable, attainable, relevant, and time-bound.

### The Marketing Implications of Corporate Objectives

Most organizations pursue multiple objectives. This is clearly demonstrated by a study of the stated objectives of 82 large corporations. The largest percentage of respondents (89 percent) had explicit profitability objectives; 82 percent reported growth objectives; 66 percent had specific market share goals. More than 60 percent mentioned social responsibility, employee welfare, and customer service objectives, and 54 percent of the companies had R&D/new product development goals.[25] These percentages add up to more than 100 percent because most firms had several objectives.

Trying to achieve many objectives at once leads to conflicts and trade-offs. For example, the investment and expenditure necessary to pursue growth in the long term is likely to reduce profitability and ROI in the short term.[26] Managers can reconcile conflicting goals by prioritizing them. Another approach is to state one of the conflicting goals as a constraint or **hurdle**. Thus, a firm attempts to maximize growth subject to meeting some minimum ROI hurdle.

In firms with multiple business units or product lines, however, the most common way to pursue a set of conflicting objectives is to first break them down into subobjectives, then assign subobjectives to different business units or products. Thus, subobjectives often vary across business units and product offerings depending on the attractiveness and potential of their industries, the strength of their competitive positions, and the resource allocation decisions made by corporate managers. For example, PepsiCo's managers likely set relatively high volume and share-growth objectives but lower ROI goals for the firm's Aquafina brand, which is battling for prominence in the rapidly growing bottled water category, than for Lay's potato chips, which hold a commanding 40 percent share of a mature product category. Therefore, two marketing managers responsible for different products may face very different goals and expectations—requiring different marketing strategies to accomplish—even though they work for the same organization.

As firms emphasize developing and maintaining long-term customer relationships, *customer-focused objectives*—such as satisfaction, retention, and loyalty—are being given greater importance. Such market-oriented objectives are more likely to be consistently pursued across business units and product offerings. There are several reasons for this.

## Exhibit 2.8

COMMON PERFORMANCE CRITERIA AND MEASURES THAT SPECIFY CORPORATE, BUSINESS-UNIT, AND MARKETING OBJECTIVES

| Performance criteria | Possible measures or indexes |
| --- | --- |
| • Growth | $ sales <br> Unit sales <br> Percent change in sales |
| • Competitive strength | Market share <br> Brand awareness <br> Brand preference |
| • Innovativeness | $ sales from new products <br> Percentage of sales from product-market entries introduced within past five years <br> Percentage cost savings from new processes |
| • Profitability | $ profits <br> Profit as percentage of sales <br> Contribution margin* <br> Return on investment (ROI) <br> Return on net assets (RONA) <br> Return on equity (ROE) |
| • Utilization of resources | Percent capacity utilization <br> Fixed assets as percentage of sales |
| • Contribution to owners | Earnings per share <br> Price/earnings ratio |
| • Contribution to customers | Price relative to competitors <br> Product quality <br> Customer satisfaction <br> Customer retention <br> Customer loyalty <br> Customer lifetime value |
| • Contribution to employees | Wage rates, benefits <br> Personnel development, promotions <br> Employment stability, turnover |
| • Contribution to society | $ contributions to charities or community institutions <br> Growth in employment |

*Business-unit managers and marketing managers responsible for a product-market entry often have little control over costs associated with corporate overhead, such as the costs of corporate staff or R&D. It can be difficult to allocate those costs to specific strategic business units (SBUs) or products. Consequently, profit objectives at the SBU and product-market level are often stated as a desired *contribution margin* (the gross profit prior to allocating such overhead costs).

First, given the huge profit implications of a customer's lifetime value, maximizing satisfaction and loyalty tends to make good sense no matter what other financial objectives are being pursued in the short term. Second, satisfied, loyal customers of one product can be leveraged to provide synergies for other company products or services. Finally, customer satisfaction and loyalty are determined by factors other than the product itself or the activities of the marketing department. A study of one industrial paper company, for example, found that about 80 percent of customers' satisfaction scores were accounted for by nonproduct factors, such as order processing, delivery, and postsale services.[27] Since such factors are influenced by many functional departments within the corporation, they are likely to have a similar impact across a firm's various businesses and products.

## Corporate Sources of Competitive Advantage

There are many ways a company might attempt to gain an advantage within the scope of its competitive domain. In most cases, though, a *sustainable* competitive advantage at the corporate level is based on company resources: resources that other firms do not have, that take a long time to develop, and that are hard to acquire.[28] Many such unique resources are marketing related. For example, some businesses have highly developed market information systems, extensive market research operations, and/or cooperative long-term relationships with customers that give them a superior ability to identify and respond to emerging customers' needs and desires. Others have a brand name that customers recognize and trust, cooperative alliances with suppliers or distributors that enhance efficiency, or a body of satisfied and loyal customers who are predisposed to buy related products or services.[29]

But the fact that a company possesses resources that its competitors do not have is not sufficient to guarantee superior performance. The trick is to develop a competitive strategy for each business unit within the firm, and a strategic marketing program for each of its product lines, that convert one or more of the company's unique resources into something of value to customers. Therefore, we will have more to say about converting corporate strengths into effective business-level competitive strategies later in this chapter.

## Corporate Growth Strategies

Often, the projected future sales and profits of a corporation's business units and product-markets fall short of the firm's long-run growth and profitability objectives. There is a gap between what the firm expects to become if it continues on its present course and what it would like to become. This is not surprising because some of its high-growth markets are likely to slip into maturity over time and some of its high-profit mature businesses may decline to insignificance as they get older. Thus, to determine where future growth is coming from, management must decide on a strategy to guide corporate development.

Essentially, a firm can go in two major directions in seeking future growth: **expansion** of its current businesses and activities, or **diversification** into new businesses, either through internal business development or acquisition. Exhibit 2.9 outlines some specific options a firm might pursue while seeking growth in either of these directions.

### Expansion by Increasing Penetration of Current Product-Markets
One way for a company to expand is by increasing its share of existing markets. This typically requires actions such as making product or service improvements, cutting costs and prices, or outspending competitors on advertising or promotions. Amazon.com pursued a combination of all these actions—as well as forming alliances with web portals, affinity groups, and the like—to expand its share of web shoppers, even though the expense of such activities postponed the firm's ability to become profitable.

Even when a firm holds a commanding share of an existing product-market, additional growth may be possible by encouraging current customers to become more loyal and concentrate their purchases, use more of the product or service, use it more often, or use it in new ways. Examples include museums that sponsor special exhibitions to encourage patrons to make repeat visits and the recipes that Quaker Oats includes on the package to tempt buyers to include oatmeal as an ingredient in other foods, such as cookies and desserts.

### Expansion by Developing New Products for Current Customers
A second avenue to future growth is through a product-development strategy emphasizing the introduction of product-line extensions or new product or service offerings aimed at existing

## Exhibit 2.9

ALTERNATIVE CORPORATE GROWTH STRATEGIES

|  | Current products | New products |
|---|---|---|
| **Current markets** | **Market penetration strategies**<br><br>• Increase market share<br>• Increase product usage<br>  Increase frequency of use<br>  Increase quantity used<br>  New applications | **Product development strategies**<br><br>• Product improvements<br>• Product-line extensions<br>• New products for same market |
| **New markets** | **Market development strategies**<br><br>• Expand markets for existing<br>  products<br>  Geographic expansion<br>  Target new segment | **Diversification strategies**<br><br>• Vertical integration<br>  Forward integration<br>  Backward integration<br>• Diversification into related<br>  businesses<br>  (concentric diversification)<br>• Diversification into unrelated<br>  businesses<br>  (conglomerate diversification) |

customers. For example, Arm & Hammer successfully introduced a laundry detergent, an oven cleaner, and a carpet cleaner. Each capitalized on baking soda's image as an effective deodorizer and on a high level of recognition of the Arm & Hammer brand.

### Expansion by Selling Existing Products to New Segments or Countries

Perhaps the growth strategy with the greatest potential for many companies is the development of new markets for their existing goods or services. This may involve the creation of marketing programs aimed at nonuser or occasional-user segments of existing markets. Thus, theaters, orchestras, and other performing arts organizations often sponsor touring companies to reach audiences outside major metropolitan areas and promote matinee performances with lower prices and free public transportation to attract senior citizens and students.

Expansion into new geographic markets, particularly new countries, is also a primary growth strategy for many firms. For example, the strategic plan of Degussa, the large German specialty chemicals manufacturer, calls for greatly increased resources and marketing efforts to be directed toward China over the next few years. As Utz-Hellmuth Felcht—the chairman of the firm's management board—points out, the vast number of untapped potential customers for the firm's products means China offers greater promise for future sales growth than Western Europe and North America combined.[30]

While developing nations represent attractive growth markets for basic industrial and infrastructure goods and services, growing personal incomes and falling trade barriers are making them attractive potential markets for many consumer goods and services as well. Market research firm DisplaySearch, for instance, predicts that China will become the world's largest market for flat-panel TVs by 2012, although price will be a more critical competitive factor than in more-developed economies.[31]

### Expansion by Diversifying   Firms also seek growth by diversifying their operations. This is typically riskier than the various expansion strategies because it often involves

learning new operations and dealing with unfamiliar customer groups. Nevertheless, the majority of large global firms are diversified to one degree or another.

**Vertical integration** is one way for companies to diversify. **Forward vertical integration** occurs when a firm moves downstream in terms of the product flow, as when a manufacturer integrates by acquiring or launching a wholesale distributor or retail outlet. For example, most of Europe's fashion houses—like Ermenegeldo Zegna and Georgio Armani—own at least some of their own retail outlets in major cities in order to gain better control over their companies' merchandising programs and more direct feedback from customers. In recent years such integrated retail outlets have also been important for establishing a foothold in developing markets such as China where independent retailers with a prestige image can be in short supply. Indeed, Zegna now earns 40 percent of its revenues from China.[32] **Backward integration** occurs when a firm moves upstream by acquiring a supplier.

Integration can give a firm access to scarce or volatile sources of supply or tighter control over the marketing, distribution, or servicing of its products. But it increases the risks inherent in committing substantial resources to a single industry. Also, the investment required to vertically integrate often offsets the additional profitability generated by the integrated operations, resulting in little improvement in return on investment.[33]

**Related** (or **concentric**) **diversification** occurs when a firm internally develops or acquires another business that does not have products or customers in common with its current businesses but that might contribute to internal synergy through the sharing of production facilities, brand names, R&D know-how, or marketing and distribution skills. Thus, PepsiCo acquired Cracker Jack to complement its salty snack brands and leverage its distribution strengths in grocery stores.

The motivations for **unrelated** (or **conglomerate**) **diversification** are primarily financial rather than operational. By definition, an unrelated diversification involves two businesses that have no commonalities in products, customers, production facilities, or functional areas of expertise. Such diversification mostly occurs when a disproportionate number of a firm's current businesses face decline because of decreasing demand, increased competition, or product obsolescence. The firm must seek new avenues of growth. Other, more fortunate, firms may move into unrelated businesses because they have more cash than they need in order to expand their current businesses, or because they wish to discourage takeover attempts.

Unrelated diversification tends to be the riskiest growth strategy in terms of financial outcomes. Most empirical studies report that related diversification is more conducive to capital productivity and other dimensions of performance than is unrelated diversification.[34] This suggests that the ultimate goal of a corporation's strategy for growth should be to develop a compatible portfolio of businesses to which the firm can add value through the application of its unique core competencies. The corporation's marketing competencies can be particularly important in this regard.

### Expansion by Diversifying through Organizational Relationships or Networks   Recently, firms have attempted to gain some benefits of market expansion or diversification while simultaneously focusing more intensely on a few core competencies. They try to accomplish this feat by forming relationships or organizational networks with other firms instead of acquiring ownership.[35]

Perhaps the best models of such organizational networks are the Japanese *keiretsu* and the Korean *chaebol*—coalitions of financial institutions, distributors, and manufacturing firms in a variety of industries that are often grouped around a large trading company that helps coordinate the activities of the various coalition members and markets their goods and services around the world. As we have seen, many Western firms, like IBM, are also forming alliances with suppliers, resellers, and even customers to expand their product and service offerings without making major new investments or neglecting their core competencies.

# Allocating Corporate Resources

Diversified organizations have several advantages over more narrowly focused firms. They have a broader range of areas in which they can knowledgeably invest, and their growth and profitability rates may be more stable because they can offset declines in one business with gains in another. To exploit the advantages of diversification, though, corporate managers must make intelligent decisions about how to allocate financial and human resources across the firm's various businesses and product-markets. Two sets of analytical tools have proven useful in making such decisions: **portfolio models** and **value-based planning.**

**Portfolio Models**     One of the most significant developments in strategic management during the 1970s and 1980s was the widespread adoption of portfolio models to help managers allocate corporate resources across multiple businesses. These models enable managers to classify and review their current and prospective businesses by viewing them as portfolios of investment opportunities and then evaluating each business's competitive strength and the attractiveness of the markets it serves.

**The Boston Consulting Group's (BCG) Growth-Share Matrix**     One of the first—and best known—of the portfolio models is the growth-share matrix developed by the Boston Consulting Group. It analyzes the impact of investing resources in different businesses on the corporation's future earnings and cash flows. Each business is positioned within a matrix, as shown in Exhibit 2.10. The vertical axis indicates the industry's growth rate and the horizontal axis shows the business's relative market share.

## Exhibit 2.10

BCG's MARKET GROWTH RELATIVE SHARE MATRIX

*Source:* Reprinted from Barry Hedley, "Strategy and the Business Portfolio," *Long Range Planning* 10. © 1977 with permission from Elsevier.

The growth-share matrix assumes that a firm must generate cash from businesses with strong competitive positions in mature markets. Then it can fund investments and expenditures in industries that represent attractive future opportunities. Thus, the **market growth rate** on the vertical axis is a proxy measure for the maturity and attractiveness of an industry. This model represents businesses in rapidly growing industries as more attractive investment opportunities for future growth and profitability.

Similarly, a business's **relative market share** is a proxy for its competitive strength within its industry. It is computed by dividing the business's absolute market share in dollars or units by that of the leading competitor in the industry. Thus, in Exhibit 2.10 a business is in a strong competitive position if its share is equal to, or larger than, that of the next leading competitor (i.e., a relative share of 1.0 or larger). Finally, in the exhibit, the size of the circle representing each business is proportional to that unit's sales volume. Thus, businesses 7 and 9 are the largest-volume businesses in this hypothetical company, while business 11 is the smallest.

### Resource Allocation and Strategy Implications

Each of the four cells in the growth-share matrix represents a different type of business with different strategy and resource requirements. The implications of each are discussed below and summarized in Exhibit 2.11.

- *Question marks.* Businesses in high-growth industries with low relative market shares (those in the upper-right quadrant of Exhibit 2.11) are called *question marks* or *problem children.* Such businesses require large amounts of cash, not only for expansion to keep up with the rapidly growing market, but also for marketing activities (or reduced margins) to build market share and catch the industry leader. If management can successfully increase the share of a question mark business, it becomes a star. But if managers fail, it eventually turns into a dog as the industry matures and the market growth rate slows.

- *Stars.* A *star* is the market leader in a high-growth industry. Stars are critical to the continued success of the firm. As their industries mature, they move into the bottom-left quadrant and become cash cows. Paradoxically, while stars are critically important, they often are net users rather than suppliers of cash in the short run (as indicated by the possibility of a negative cash

## Exhibit 2.11

CASH FLOWS ACROSS BUSINESSES IN THE BCG PORTFOLIO MODEL

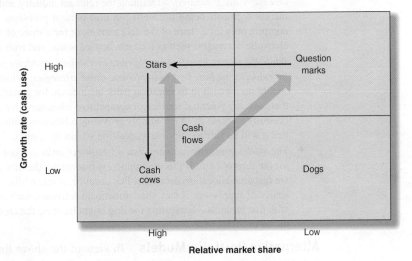

flow shown in Exhibit 2.11). This is because the firm must continue to invest in such businesses to keep up with rapid market growth and to support the R&D and marketing activities necessary to maintain a leading market share.

- *Cash cows.* Businesses with a high relative share of low-growth markets are called *cash cows* because they are the primary generators of profits and cash in a corporation. Such businesses do not require much additional capital investment. Their markets are stable, and their share leadership position usually means they enjoy economies of scale and relatively high profit margins. Consequently, the corporation can use the cash from these businesses to support its question marks and stars (as shown in Exhibit 2.11). However, this does not mean the firm should necessarily maximize the business's short-term cash flow by cutting R&D and marketing expenditures to the bone—particularly not in industries where the business might continue to generate substantial future sales.

- *Dogs.* Low-share businesses in low-growth markets are called *dogs* because although they may throw off some cash, they typically generate low profits or losses. Divestiture is one option for such businesses, although it can be difficult to find an interested buyer. Another common strategy is to harvest dog businesses. This involves maximizing short-term cash flow by paring investments and expenditures until the business is gradually phased out.

## Limitations of the Growth-Share Matrix

Because the growth-share matrix uses only two variables as a basis for categorizing and analyzing a firm's businesses, it is relatively easy to understand. But while this simplicity helps explain its popularity, it also means the model has limitations:

- *Market growth rate is an inadequate descriptor of overall industry attractiveness.* Market growth is not always directly related to profitability or cash flow. Some high-growth industries have never been very profitable because low entry barriers and capital intensity have enabled supply to grow even faster, resulting in intense price competition. Also, rapid growth in one year is no guarantee that growth will continue in the following year.

- *Relative market share is inadequate as a description of overall competitive strength.* Market share is more properly viewed as an outcome of past efforts to formulate and implement effective business-level and marketing strategies than as an indicator of enduring competitive strength.[36] If the external environment changes, or the SBU's managers change their strategy, the business's relative market share can shift dramatically.

- *The outcomes of a growth-share analysis are highly sensitive to variations in how growth and share are measured.*[37] Defining the relevant industry and served market (i.e., the target-market segments being pursued) can also present problems. For example, does Pepsi-Cola compete only for a share of the cola market, or for a share of the much larger market for non-alcoholic beverages, such as iced tea, bottled water, and fruit juices?

- *While the matrix specifies appropriate investment strategies for each business, it provides little guidance on how best to implement those strategies.* While the model suggests that a firm should invest cash in its question mark businesses, for instance, it does not consider whether there are any potential sources of competitive advantage that the business can exploit to successfully increase its share. Simply providing a business with more money does not guarantee that it will be able to improve its position within the matrix.

- *The model implicitly assumes that all business units are independent of one another except for the flow of cash.* If this assumption is inaccurate, the model can suggest some inappropriate resource allocation decisions. For instance, if other SBUs depend on a dog business as a source of supply—or if they share functional activities, such as a common plant or salesforce, with that business—harvesting the dog might increase the costs or reduce the effectiveness of the other SBUs.

**Alternative Portfolio Models**   In view of the above limitations, a number of firms have attempted to improve the basic portfolio model. Such improvements have focused primarily on developing more detailed, multifactor measures of industry attractiveness and a business's competitive strength and on making the analysis more future-oriented. Corporate managers must first select factors most appropriate for their firm and weight them according to their relative importance. They then rate each business and its industry on the two sets of factors.

These multifactor models are more detailed than the simple growth-share model and consequently provide more strategic guidance concerning the appropriate allocation of resources across businesses. They are also more useful for evaluating potential new-product-markets. However, the multifactor measures in these models can be subjective and ambiguous, especially when managers must evaluate different industries on the same set of factors. Also, the conclusions drawn from these models still depend on the way industries and product-markets are defined.[38]

**Value-Based Planning**   As mentioned, one limitation of portfolio analysis is that it specifies how firms should allocate financial resources across their businesses without considering the competitive strategies those businesses are, or should be, pursuing. Portfolio analysis provides little guidance, for instance, in choosing which of several competitive strategies a particular business unit should pursue.

**Value-based planning** is a resource allocation tool that attempts to address such questions by assessing the shareholder value a given strategy is likely to create. Thus, value-based planning provides a basis for comparing the economic returns to be gained from investing in different businesses pursuing different strategies or from alternative strategies that might be adopted by a given business unit.

A number of value-based planning methods are currently in use, but all share three basic features.[39] First, they assess the economic value a strategy is likely to produce by examining the cash flows it will generate, rather than relying on distorted accounting measures, such as return on investment.[40] Second, they estimate the shareholder value that a strategy will produce by discounting its forecasted cash flows by the business's risk-adjusted cost of capital. Finally, they evaluate strategies based on the likelihood that the investments required by a strategy will deliver returns greater than the cost of capital. The amount of return a strategy or operating program generates in excess of the cost of capital is commonly referred to as its **economic value added,** or EVA.[41] This approach to evaluating alternative strategies is particularly appropriate for use in allocating resources across business units because most capital investments are made at the business-unit level, and different business units typically face different risks and therefore have different costs of capital.

**Discounted Cash Flow Model**   Perhaps the best-known and most widely used approach to value-based planning is the discounted cash flow model. In this model, as Exhibit 2.12 indicates, shareholder value created by a strategy is determined by the cash flow it generates, the business's cost of capital (which is used to discount future cash flows back to their present value), and the market value of the debt assigned to the business. The future cash flows generated by the strategy are, in turn, affected by six "value drivers": the rate of sales growth the strategy will produce, the operating profit margin, the income tax rate, investment in working capital, fixed capital investment required by the strategy, and the duration of value growth.

The first five value drivers are self-explanatory, but the sixth requires some elaboration. The duration of value growth represents management's estimate of the number of years over which the strategy can be expected to produce rates of return that exceed the cost of capital. This estimate, in turn, is tied to two other management judgments. First, the manager must decide on the length of the planning period (typically three to five years); he or

# Exhibit 2.12

FACTORS AFFECTING THE CREATION OF SHAREHOLDER VALUE

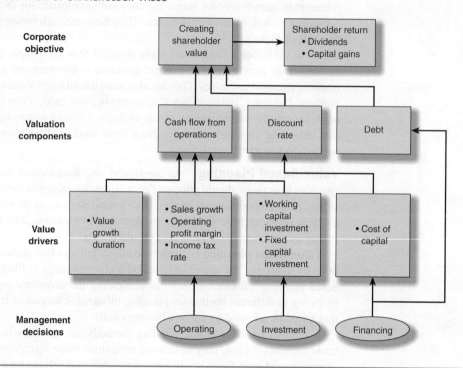

she must then estimate the residual value the strategy will continue to produce after the planning period is over. Such decisions are tricky, for they involve predictions of what will happen in the relatively distant future.[42]

## Some Limitations of Value-Based Planning

Value-based planning is not a substitute for strategic planning; it is only one tool for evaluating strategy alternatives identified and developed through managers' judgments. It does so by relying on forecasts of many kinds to put a financial value on the hopes, fears, and expectations managers associate with each alternative. Projections of cash inflows rest on forecasts of sales volume, product mix, unit prices, and competitors' actions. Expected cash outflows depend on projections of various cost elements, working capital, and investment requirements.

While good forecasts are notoriously difficult to make, they are critical to the validity of value-based planning. Unfortunately, there are natural human tendencies to overvalue the financial projections associated with some strategy alternatives and to undervalue others. For instance, managers are likely to overestimate the future returns from a currently successful strategy. Evidence of past success tends to carry more weight than qualitative assessments of future threats.

**STRATEGIC ISSUE**

*Some kinds of strategy alternatives are consistently undervalued. Particularly worrisome from a marketing viewpoint is the tendency to underestimate the value of keeping current customers.*

Some kinds of strategy alternatives are consistently undervalued. Particularly worrisome from a marketing viewpoint is the tendency to underestimate the value of keeping current customers. Putting a figure on the damage to a firm's competitive advantage from not making a strategic investment necessary to maintain the status quo is harder than documenting potential cost savings or profit improvements that an investment might generate. And, finally, value-based planning can evaluate alternatives, but it cannot create them. The best strategy will never emerge from the evaluation process if management fails to identify it.[43]

**Using Customer Equity to Estimate the Value of Alternative Marketing Actions** A recent variation of value-based planning attempts to overcome some of the above limitations—particularly the inaccuracy of subjective forecasts and managers' tendency to over- or underestimate the value of particular actions—and is proving useful for evaluating alternative marketing strategies. This approach calculates the economic return for a prospective marketing initiative based on its likely impact on the firm's customer equity, which is the sum of the lifetime values of its current and future customers.[44] Each customer's lifetime value is estimated from data about the frequency of their purchases in the category, the average quantity purchased, and historical brand-switching patterns, combined with the firm's contribution margin. The necessary purchase data can be gotten from the firm's sales records, while brand-switching patterns can be estimated either from longitudinal panel data or survey data similar to that collected in customer satisfaction studies. Because market and competitive conditions, and therefore customer perceptions and behaviors, change over time, however, the underlying data needs to be updated on a regular basis—perhaps once or twice a year.

The impact of a firm's or business unit's past marketing actions on customer equity can be statistically estimated from historical data. This enables managers to identify the financial impact of alternative marketing "value drivers" of customer equity, such as brand advertising, quality or service improvements, loyalty programs, and the like. And once a manager calculates the implementation costs and capital requirements involved, it is then possible to estimate the financial return for any similar marketing initiative in the near future.

# Sources of Synergy

A final strategic concern at the corporate level is to increase synergy across the firm's various businesses and product-markets. As mentioned, synergy exists when two or more businesses or product-markets, and their resources and competencies, complement and reinforce one another so that the total performance of the related businesses is greater than it would be otherwise.

**Knowledge-Based Synergies** Some potential synergies at the corporate level are knowledge-based. The performance of one business can be enhanced by the transfer of competencies, knowledge, or customer-related intangibles—such as brand-name recognition and reputation—from other units within the firm. For instance, the technical knowledge concerning image processing and the quality reputation that Canon developed in the camera business helped ease the firm's entry into the office copier business.

In part, such knowledge-based synergies are a function of the corporation's scope and mission—or how its managers answer the question, What businesses should we be in? When a firm's portfolio of businesses and product-markets reflects a common mission based on well-defined customer needs, market segments, or technologies, the company is more likely to develop core competencies, customer knowledge, and strong brand franchises that can be shared across businesses. However, the firm's organizational structure and allocation of resources also may enhance knowledge-based synergy. A centralized corporate R&D department, for example, is often more efficient and effective at discovering new technologies with potential applications across multiple businesses than if each business unit bore the burden of funding its own R&D efforts. Similarly, some argue that strong corporate-level coordination and support are necessary to maximize the strength of a firm's brand franchise, and to glean full benefit from accumulated market knowledge, when the firm is competing in global markets.

### Corporate Identity and the Corporate Brand as a Source of Synergy

Corporate identity—together with a strong corporate brand that embodies that identity—can help a firm stand out from its competitors and give it a sustainable advantage in the market. *Corporate identity* flows from the communications, impressions, and personality projected by an organization. It is shaped by the firm's mission and values, its functional competencies, the quality and design of its goods and services, its marketing communications, the actions of its personnel, the image generated by various corporate activities, and other factors.[45]

In order to project a positive, strong, and consistent identity, firms as diverse as Caterpillar, Walt Disney, and The Body Shop have established formal policies, criteria, and guidelines to help ensure that all the messages and sensory images they communicate reflect their unique values, personality, and competencies. One rationale for such corporate identity programs is that they can generate synergies that enhance the effectiveness and efficiency of the firm's marketing efforts for its individual product offerings. By focusing on a common core of corporate values and competencies, every impression generated by each product's design, packaging, advertising, and promotional materials can help reinforce and strengthen the impact of all the other impressions the firm communicates to its customers, employees, shareholders, and other audiences, and thereby generate a bigger bang for its limited marketing bucks. For example, by consistently focusing on values and competencies associated with providing high-quality family entertainment, Disney has created an identity that helps stimulate customer demand across a wide range of product offerings—from movies to TV programs to licensed merchandise to theme parks and cruise ships.

## The Marketing Implications of Business-Unit Strategy Decisions

The components of a firm engaged in multiple industries or businesses are typically called **strategic business units,** or **SBUs.** Managers within each of these business units decide which objectives, markets, and competitive strategies to pursue. Top-level corporate managers typically reserve the right to review and approve such decisions to ensure their overall consistency with the company's mission, objectives, and the allocation of resources across SBUs in its portfolio. However, SBU-level managers, particularly those in marketing and sales, bear the primary responsibility for collecting and analyzing relevant information and generating appropriate strategies for their businesses. Those managers are more familiar with a given SBU's products, customers, and competitors and are responsible for successfully implementing the strategy. The rationale for breaking larger firms into semi-autonomous SBUs usually stems from a market-oriented desire to move strategic decision making closer to the customers the business is trying to reach.

The first step in developing business-level strategies, then, is for the firm to decide how to divide itself into SBUs. The managers in each SBU must then make recommendations about (*a*) the unit's objectives, (*b*) the scope of its target customers and offerings, (*c*) which broad competitive strategy to pursue to build a competitive advantage in its product-markets, and (*d*) how resources should be allocated across its product-market entries and functional departments.

## How Should Strategic Business Units Be Designed?

Ideally, strategic business units have the following characteristics:

- *A homogeneous set of markets to serve with a limited number of related technologies.* Minimizing diversity across an SBU's product-market entries enables the unit's manager to better formulate and implement a coherent and internally consistent business strategy.
- *A unique set of product-markets,* in the sense that no other SBU within the firm competes for the same customers with similar products. Thus, the firm avoids duplication of effort and maximizes economies of scale within its SBUs.
- *Control over those factors necessary for successful performance,* such as production, R&D and engineering, marketing, and distribution. This does not mean an SBU should not share resources, such as a manufacturing plant or a salesforce, with one or more other business units. But the SBU should determine how its share of the joint resource is used to effectively carry out its strategy.
- *Responsibility for their own profitability.*

As you might expect, firms do not always meet all of these ideals when designing business units. There are usually trade-offs between having many small homogeneous SBUs versus large but fewer SBUs that top managers can more easily supervise.

What criteria should managers use to decide how product-markets should be clustered into a business unit? The three dimensions that define the scope and mission of the entire corporation can also define individual SBUs:

1. *Technical compatibility,* particularly with respect to product technologies and operational requirements, such as the use of similar production facilities and engineering skills.
2. Similarity in the *customer needs* or the product benefits sought by customers in the target markets.
3. Similarity in the *personal characteristics* or behavior patterns of customers in the target markets.

In practice, the choice is often between technical/operational compatibility on the one hand and customer homogeneity on the other. Frequently management defines SBUs by product-markets requiring similar technologies, production facilities, and employee skills. This minimizes the coordination problems involved in administering the unit and increases its ability to focus on one or a few critical competencies.

In some cases, however, the marketing synergies gained from coordinating technically different products aimed at the same customer need or market segment outweigh operational considerations. In these firms, managers cluster product-market entries into SBUs based on similarities across customers or distribution systems. General Foods Corporation, for instance, includes Cool Whip and Jell-O in the same SBU even though they require different production technologies because they are marketed as dessert products.

## The Business Unit's Objectives

As we discussed earlier, corporate objectives are typically broken down into subobjectives for each SBU. Those subobjectives often vary according to the attractiveness of the SBU's industry, the strength of its competitive position, and the like.

Similarly, breaking down an SBU's objectives into subobjectives for each of its product-market entries is often a major part of developing business-level strategy. Those subobjectives need to add up to the accomplishment of the SBU's overall goals; yet they should vary across product-market entries to reflect differences in the attractiveness and growth potential of individual market segments and the competitive strengths of the SBU's product in each market.

# The Business Unit's Competitive Strategy

The essential question in formulating a business strategy is, How will the business unit compete to gain a sustainable competitive advantage within its industry? Achieving a competitive advantage requires a business unit to make two choices:

- What is the SBU's competitive domain or scope? Which market segments can it target, and which customer needs can it satisfy? These are stated in more general terms than is the case with marketing strategy. They serve as guidelines for the formulation of strategies for the individual product-market entries.
- How can the business unit distinguish itself from competitors in its target market(s)? What distinctive competencies can it rely on to achieve a unique position relative to its competitors?

**Decisions about an SBU's Scope**   A business's strategic scope can be defined either broadly or narrowly. It can pursue a range of market segments within its industry or focus on only one or a few target segments. The decision about how many customer segments to serve usually hinges on a combination of factors, including the business's objectives and available resources, characteristics of the market (e.g., the number and size of different customer segments), and the SBU's strengths and weaknesses relative to its competitors. We will examine these decisions about strategic scope and the variables that influence them in more detail in Chapters 15 and 16 where we discuss strategies for different kinds of industries at varying stages in their life cycles.

For now, the important point to recognize is that the scope of a business's strategic focus has ramifications for nearly every component of its marketing program, including the breadth of its product line; the audience for its advertising, promotion, and personal selling efforts; the design of its distribution system; and the range of prices that are viable. For example, when IBM decided to expand the target market for its services to include a wider range of small business and dot-com start-ups, it had to develop many new service offerings to meet the needs of such customers. But it also had to abandon its strategy of charging only premium prices, change the content of its advertising, and redirect a significant portion of its personal selling and promotional efforts toward its new customer segments.

**Allocating Resources within the Business Unit**   Once SBU managers decide on the scope of market segments and product-market entries to pursue, they allocate the financial and human resources provided by corporate management across those product-markets. Because this process is similar to allocating corporate resources across SBUs, many firms use similar portfolio analysis or customer equity tools for both.

**Gaining a Competitive Advantage**   There are many ways in which a business unit might attempt to gain an advantage over its competitors within the scope of its strategic domain. To be successful over the long haul, however, a competitive strategy should have three characteristics.[46]

- It should generate customer value. It should give potential customers a good reason to purchase from the SBU instead of its competitors. The strategy should be predicated on providing one or more superior benefits at a price similar to what competitors charge or delivering comparable benefits at lower cost.

- The superior value must be perceived by the customer. Even if an SBU's product or service is better than the competition, if the customer is not aware of that—or doesn't attach much value to the additional benefits—it does not gain a competitive advantage. For example, as the technical and performance differences among PCs narrowed, IBM's competitive strategy of charging premium prices for technically superior products became untenable.
- The advantage should be difficult for competitors to copy. The easier it is for competitors to copy a successful strategy, the more short-lived the SBU's competitive advantage. For instance, Minnetonka, Inc., gained an advantage by introducing Check-Up, the first plaque-fighting toothpaste. But because its unique ingredients could not be patented, more than two dozen competing brands reached the market within a year; many from much bigger companies such as Procter & Gamble and Colgate-Palmolive.

**Marketing Resources and Competitive Advantage**    The trick, then, is for the business unit to develop a competitive strategy that converts one or more of its unique resources or competencies into something of value to customers. While one can conceive of a nearly infinite assortment of such strategies, most can be classified into a few "generic" types. For example, Treacy and Wiersema argue that market leaders tend to pursue one of three categories of competitive strategy. They either stress operational excellence, which typically translates into lower costs and prices, or differentiate themselves through product leadership or customer intimacy and superior service.[47] These generic strategies are summarized in Exhibit 2.13, together with some traits and competencies of businesses that are able to implement each strategy effectively. Note how many of the core business processes underlying all three strategy types are related to the marketing function.

Other authors suggest additional ways to categorize business strategies.[48] No matter how such strategies are defined, though, the key points are (a) that competitive strategies are built—at least in part—on marketing resources and competencies and (b) the competitive strategy pursued by an SBU, in turn, helps determine what strategic marketing programs are viable for its various product-market entries. We examine this symbiotic relationship between marketing resources and competencies, business-level competitive strategies, and marketing programs for individual products and services in more detail in Chapter 9.

## Exhibit 2.13

THREE COMPETITIVE STRATEGIES AND THE TRAITS AND COMPETENCIES OF BUSINESSES THAT IMPLEMENT THEM EFFECTIVELY

| | DISCIPLINES | | |
|---|---|---|---|
| Company traits | Operational excellence | Product leadership | Customer intimacy |
| Core business processes | Sharpen distribution systems and provide no-hassle service | Nurture ideas, translate them into products, and market them skillfully | Provide solutions and help customers run their businesses |
| Structure | Has strong, central authority and a finite level of empowerment | Acts in an ad hoc, organic, loosely knit, and ever-changing way | Pushes empowerment close to customer contact |
| Management systems | Maintain standard operating procedures | Reward individuals' innovative capacity and new product success | Measure the cost of providing service and of maintaining customer loyalty |
| Culture | Acts predictably and believes "one size fits all" | Experiments and thinks "out-of-the-box" | Is flexible and thinks "have it your way" |

# TAKE-AWAYS

1. Marketing perspectives lie at the heart of strategic decision making, whether at the corporate, business-unit, or product-market levels. All managers who aspire to general management roles need marketing concepts and tools in their repertoire.

2. Market-oriented firms—those that plan and coordinate company activities around the primary goal of satisfying customer needs—tend to outperform other firms on a variety of dimensions, including sales growth, return on assets, and new product success.

3. Unethical behavior by a firm's employees can damage the trust between a firm and its suppliers and customers, thereby disrupting the development of long-term relationships and reducing sales and profits over time.

4. The four major paths to corporate growth—market penetration, market development, product development, and diversification strategies—imply differences in a firm's strategic scope, require different competencies and marketing actions, and involve different types and amounts of risk. Decisions about which path(s) to pursue should consider all of these factors.

5. A strong corporate brand makes sense when company-level competencies are primarily responsible for generating the benefits and value customers receive from its various product offerings.

6. The ultimate goal in formulating business-unit strategies is to establish a basis for a sustainable competitive advantage that provides superior value to customers. Doing so requires the development of resources—often marketing resources, such as brand names, marketing information systems and databases, long-term customer relationships, and so on—that other firms do not have and that are hard to acquire.

7. Successful new firm formation typically requires a competitive strategy that delivers superior value to a narrowly defined target segment in a way that either avoids direct confrontation with established competitors or is difficult for them to emulate. Therefore, market sensing and analysis, market segmentation and targeting, and market positioning skills are usually crucial in helping new firms surmount the long odds against survival.

# ENDNOTES

**1.** This opening example is based on material found in Steve Hamm, "Big Blue Goes for the Big Win," *BusinessWeek*, March 10, 2008, pp. 63–65; Steve Hamm, "International Isn't Just IBM's First Name," *www.*businessweek.com, January 17, 2008; Steve Hamm, "Beyond Blue," *BusinessWeek*, April 18, 2005, pp. 68–76; Steve Lohr, "Big Blue's Big Bet: Less Tech, More Touch," *The New York Times*, Money & Business Section, Sunday, January 25, 2004, pp. 1, 10; Spencer E. Ante, "The New Blue," *BusinessWeek*, March 17, 2003; Jon Fortt, "How IBM's Analytics Software Saves Lives," *www.fortune.com*, March 15, 2010; and IBM's 2009 Annual Report at *www.*ibm.com.

**2.** Christian Homburg, John P. Workman, Jr., and Harley Krohmer, "Marketing's Influence within the Firm," *Journal of Marketing* 63 (April 1999), pp. 1–17. Also see Peter C. Verhoef and Peter S. H. Leeflang, "Understanding the Marketing Department's Influence within the Firm," *Journal of Marketing* 73 (March 2009), pp. 14–37.

**3.** Quoted in Katherine Z. Andrews, "Still a Major Player: Marketing's Role in Today's Firms," *Insights from MSI*, Winter 1999, p. 2.

**4.** Frederick E. Webster, Jr., "Executing the New Marketing Concept," *Marketing Management* 3 (1994), pp. 9–16.

**5.** Rajendra K. Srivastava, Tasadduq A. Shervani, and Liam Fahey, "Marketing, Business Processes, and Shareholder Value: An Organizationally Embedded View of Marketing Activities and the Discipline of Marketing," *Journal of Marketing* 63 (Special Issue 1999), pp. 168–79.

**6.** For example, see John C. Narver and Stanley F. Slater, "The Effect of a Market Orientation on Business Profitability," *Journal of Marketing* 54 (April 1990), pp. 1–18; Bernard J. Jaworski and Ajay Kohli, "Market Orientation: Antecedents and Consequences," *Journal of Marketing* 57 (July 1993); Stanley F. Slater and John C. Narver, "Market Orientation, Performance, and the Moderating Influence of Competitive Environment," *Journal of Marketing* 58 (January 1994), pp. 46–55; and Ahmet H. Kirca, Satish Jayachandran, and William O. Bearden, "Market Orientation: A Meta-Analytic Review and Assessment of Its Antecedents and Impact on Performance," *Journal of Marketing* 69 (April 2005), pp. 24–41.

**7.** Rohit Deshpande, Elie Ofek, and Sang-Hoon Kim, "Preempting Competitive Risk via Customer Focus: Entrepreneurial Firms in Japan and the U.S." Report #03-114, (Cambridge, MA: Marketing Science Institute, 2003).

**8.** Slater and Narver, "Market Orientation"; and John P. Workman, Jr., "When Marketing Should Follow instead of Lead," *Marketing Management* 2 (1993), pp. 8–19.

**9.** Charles H. Noble, Rajiv K. Sinha, and Ajith Kumar, "Market Orientation and Alternative Strategic Orientations: A Longitudinal Assessment of Performance Implications," *Journal of Marketing* 66 (October 2002), pp. 25–39.

**10.** For many examples, see Valarie Zeithaml, Mary Jo Bitner, and Dwayne Gremler, *Services Marketing*, 5th ed. (New York: McGraw-Hill, 2009).

**11.** E. Jerome McCarthy and William D. Perreault, Jr., *Basic Marketing: A Global Managerial Approach*, 11th ed. (Burr Ridge, IL: Richard D. Irwin, 1993), chap. 2.

**12.** This is a slightly modified form of the definition in Charles W. Hofer and Dan Schendel, *Strategy Formulation: Analytical Concepts* (St. Paul, MN: West, 1978), p. 25. However, our definition differs in that we view the setting of objectives as an integral part of strategy formulation, whereas they see objective setting as a separate process. Because a firm or business unit's objectives are influenced and constrained by many of the same environmental and competitive factors as the other elements of strategy, however, it seems logical to treat both the determination of objectives and the resource allocations aimed at reaching those objectives as two parts of the same strategic planning process.

**13.** However, while such corporate-level synergies are often used to justify mergers, acquisitions, and forays into new businesses, they sometimes prove elusive. For example, see Laura Landro, "Giants Talk Synergy but Few Make It Work," *The Wall Street Journal*, September 25, 1995, p. B1.

**14.** C. K. Prahalad and Gary Hamel, "The Core Competence of the Corporation," *Harvard Business Review* 68 (May–June 1990), pp. 79–91.

**15.** Katrina Brooker, "The Pepsi Machine," *Fortune*, February 6, 2006, pp. 68–72; Betsy Morris, "The Pepsi Challenge: Can This Snack and Soda Giant Go Healthy?" *Fortune*, March 3, 2008, pp. 55–66; and Beth Kowitt, "PepsiCo's Indra Nooyi: Niche Brands Are the Future," *www*.fortune.cnn.com, October 5, 2010.

**16.** Theodore Levitt, "Marketing Myopia," *Harvard Business Review* (July–August 1960), pp. 455–56.

**17.** Pete Engardio, "Beyond the Green Corporation," *BusinessWeek*, January 29, 2007, p. 52. For additional examples, see Daniel Franklin, "Just Good Business," A Special Report on Corporate Social Responsibility, *The Economist*, January 19, 2008, pp. SR3–SR22.

**18.** Pete Engardio, "Beyond the Green Corporation."

**19.** "Good Grief," *The Economist*, April 8, 1995, p. 57; "Doing Well by Doing Good," *The Economist*, April 22, 2000, pp. 65–67; and Joseph Weber, "The New Ethics Enforcers," *BusinessWeek*, February 13, 2006, pp. 76–77.

**20.** "Doing Well by Doing Good," p. 66.

**21.** Robert A. Cooke, *Ethics in Business: A Perspective* (Chicago: Arthur Andersen, 1988).

**22.** I. Fredrick Trawick, John E. Swan, Gail W. McGee, and David R. Rink, "Influence of Buyer Ethics and Salesperson Behavior on Intention to Choose a Supplier," *Journal of the Academy of Marketing Science* 19 (Winter 1991), pp. 17–23.

**23.** Maria Ermakova and Chris Spillane, "Corruption Rises over Three Years, More People Paid Bribes," *www*.bloomberg.com/news, December 10, 2010.

**24.** Mina Kimes, "Fluor's Corporate Crime Fighter," *Fortune*, February 16, 2009. p. 26. See also Eamon Javers, "Steering Clear of Foreign Snafus," *Business week*, November 12, 2007, p. 76.

**25.** Y. K. Shetty, "New Look at Corporate Goals," *California Management Review* 12 (Winter 1979), pp. 71–79; see also Robert S. Kaplan and David P. Norton, "Using the Balanced Scorecard as a Strategic Management System," *Harvard Business Review* 74 (January–February 1996), pp. 75–85.

**26.** Gordon Donaldson, *Managing Corporate Wealth* (New York: Praeger, 1984). See also, Kaplan and Norton, "Using the Balanced Scorecard," and Srivastava, Shervani, and Fahey, "Marketing, Business Processes, and Shareholder Value."

**27.** Daniel P. Finkelman, "Crossing the 'Zone of Indifference," *Marketing Management* 2, no. 3 (1993), pp. 22–31. See also, Jena McGregor, "Would You Recommend Us?" *BusinessWeek*, January 30, 2006, pp. 94–95; and Paul E. Farris, Neil T. Bendle, Phillip E. Pfeifer, and David J. Reibstein, *Marketing Metrics: 50 + Metrics Every Executive Should Master* (Philadelphia: Wharton School Publishing, 2006).

**28.** Jay B. Barney, "Firm Resources and Sustained Competitive Advantage," *Journal of Management* 17 (1991), pp. 99–120; and Margaret A. Peteraf, "The Cornerstone of Competitive Advantage: A Resource-Based View," *Strategic Management Journal* 14 (1993), pp. 179–92.

**29.** George S. Day, "The Capabilities of Market-Driven Organizations," *Journal of Marketing* 58 (October 1994), pp. 37–52; George S. Day and Prakash Nedungadi, "Managerial Representations of Competitive Advantage," *Journal of Marketing* 58 (April 1994), pp. 31–44; and George S.

**Day,** *Creating a Superior Customer-Relating Capability,* Report No. 03-101 (Cambridge, MA: Marketing Science Institute, 2003).

**30.** Interview with Mr. Utz-Hellmuth Felcht transcribed on *Knowledge@Wharton, www*.knowledge.wharton.upenn.edu, September 7, 2005.

**31.** Mariko Yasu, "Foreign Makers Tune In to China's TV Market," *www*. businessweek.com, August 12, 2010.

**32.** Clay Chandler, "China Deluxe: Armani, Mercedes, Dior, Cartier—Luxury Brands Are Rushing into China's Red-Hot Market," *Fortune,* July 26, 2004, pp. 148–156; and Carol Matlack and Eugene Tang, "Luxury Clothier Zegna's Macro Polo Moment," *Bloomberg BusinessWeek*, June 14, 2010, pp. 18–19.

**33.** Robert D. Buzzell and Bradley T. Gale, *The PIMS Principles: Linking Strategy to Performance* (New York: Free Press, 1987), chap. 8.

**34.** For a more comprehensive review of the evidence concerning the effects of diversification on firm performance, see Roger A. Kerin, Vijay Mahajan, and P. Rajan Varadarajan, *Contemporary Perspectives on Strategic Market Planning* (Boston: Allyn and Bacon, 1990), chap. 6.

**35.** For example, see Ravi S. Achrol and Philip Kotler, "Marketing in the Network Economy," *Journal of Marketing* 63 (Special Issue 1999), pp. 146–63.

**36.** Robert Jacobson argues that market share and profitability are joint outcomes from successful strategies and, further, that management skills likely have the greatest impact on profitability. See "Distinguishing among Competing Theories of the Market Share Effect," *Journal of Marketing* 52 (October 1988), pp. 68–80.

**37.** Yoram Wind, Vijay Mahajan, and Donald J. Swire, "An Empirical Comparison of Standardized Portfolio Models," *Journal of Marketing* 47 (Spring 1983), pp. 89–99.

**38.** For a more detailed discussion of the uses and limitations of multifactor portfolio models, see Kerin, Mahajan, and Varadarajan, *Contemporary Perspectives on Strategic Market Planning*, chap. 3.

**39.** The discounted cash flow model is the approach focused on in this chapter. It is detailed in Alfred Rappaport, *Creating Shareholder Value: A New Standard for Business Performance* (New York: Free Press, 1986).

**40.** For a detailed discussion of the shortcomings of accounting data for determining the value created by a strategy, see Rappaport, Creating Shareholder Value, chap. 2.

**41.** For a more detailed discussion of EVA and some practical examples, see Shawn Tully, "The Real Key to Creating Wealth," *Fortune*, September 20, 1993, pp. 38–50; and Terrence P. Pare, "The New Champ of Wealth Creation," *Fortune*, September 18, 1995, pp. 131–32.

**42.** A more in-depth discussion of the forecasts and other procedures used in value-based planning can be found in Rappaport, *Creating Shareholder Value*, or Kerin, Mahajan, and Varadarajan, *Contemporary Perspectives on Strategic Market Planning*, chap. 9.

**43.** The limitations of value-based planning are discussed in more detail in George S. Day and Liam Fahey, "Putting Strategy into Shareholder Value Analysis," *Harvard Business Review,* March–April, 1990, pp. 156–62.

**44.** Roland T. Rust, Katherine N. Lemon, and Valarie Zeithaml, "Return on Marketing: Using Customer Equity to Focus Marketing Strategy," *Journal of Marketing* 68 (January 2004), pp. 109–27. Also see Verena Vogel, Heiner Evanschitzky, and B. Ramaseshan, "Customer Enquity Drivers and Future Sales," *Journal of Marketing* 72 (November 2008), pp. 98–108; and Robert W. Palmatier, "Interfirm Relational Drivers of Customer Value," *Journal of Marketing* 72 (July 2008), pp. 76–89.

**45.** Wally Olins, *Corporate Identity* (Cambridge, MA: Harvard Business School Press, 1993).

**46.** David A. Aaker, *Strategic Market Management,* 5th ed. (New York: Wiley, 1998), chap. 8.

**47.** Michael Treacy and Fred Wiersema, *The Discipline of Market Leaders* (Reading, MA: Addison-Wesley, 1995).

**48.** For example, see Michael E. Porter, *Competitive Advantage* (New York: Free Press, 1985); and Robert E. Miles and Charles C. Snow, *Organizational Strategy, Structure, and Process* (New York: McGraw-Hill, 1978).

# APPENDIX 2.1

## THE AMERICAN MARKETING ASSOCIATION'S CODE OF ETHICS

### CODE OF ETHICS

Members of the American Marketing Association (AMA) are committed to ethical professional conduct. They have joined together in subscribing to this Code of Ethics embracing the following topics:

#### Responsibilities of the Marketer

Marketers must accept responsibility for the consequences of their activities and make every effort to ensure that their decisions, recommendations, and actions function to identify, serve, and satisfy all relevant publics: customers, organizations, and society.

Marketers' professional conduct must be guided by:

1. The basic rule of professional ethics: not knowingly to do harm.
2. The adherence to all applicable laws and regulations.
3. The accurate representation of their education, training, and experience.
4. The active support, practice, and promotion of this Code of Ethics.

#### Honesty and Fairness

Marketers shall uphold and advance the integrity, honor, and dignity of the marketing profession by:

1. Being honest in serving consumers, clients, employees, suppliers, distributors, and the public.
2. Not knowingly participating in a conflict of interest without prior notice to all parties involved.
3. Establishing equitable fee schedules including the payment or receipt of usual, customary, and/or legal compensation for marketing exchanges.

#### Rights and Duties of Parties in the Marketing Exchange Process

Participants in the marketing exchange process should be able to expect that:

1. Products and services offered are safe and fit for their intended uses.
2. Communications about offered products and services are not deceptive.
3. All parties intend to discharge their obligations, financial and otherwise, in good faith.

4. Appropriate internal methods exist for equitable adjustment and/or redress of grievances concerning purchases.

It is understood that the above would include, *but is not limited to,* the following responsibilities of the marketer.

#### In the area of product development and management:

- Disclosure of all substantial risks associated with product or service usage.
- Identification of any product component substitution that might materially change the product or impact on the buyer's purchase decision.
- Identification of extra-cost added features.

#### In the area of promotions:

- Avoidance of false and misleading advertising.
- Rejection of high-pressure manipulations or misleading sales tactics.
- Avoidance of sales promotions that use deception or manipulation.

#### In the area of distribution:

- Not manipulating the availability of a product for purpose of exploitation.
- Not using coercion in the marketing channel.
- Not exerting undue influence over the reseller's choice to handle a product.

#### In the area of pricing:

- Not engaging in price-fixing.
- Not practicing predatory pricing.
- Disclosing the full price associated with any purchase.

#### In the area of marketing research:

- Prohibiting selling or fund-raising under the guise of conducting research.
- Maintaining research integrity by avoiding misrepresentation and omission of pertinent research data.
- Treating outside clients and suppliers fairly.

#### Organizational Relationships

Marketers should be aware of how their behavior may influence or impact on the behavior of others in organizational relationships. They should not demand, encourage, or apply coercion to obtain unethical behavior in their relationships with others, such as employees, suppliers, or customers.

1. Apply confidentiality and anonymity in professional relationships with regard to privileged information.

2. Meet their obligations and responsibilities in contracts and mutual agreements in a timely manner.

3. Avoid taking the work of others, in whole, or in part, and representing this work as their own or directly benefiting

from it without compensation or consent of the originator or owner.

4. Avoid manipulation to take advantage of situations to maximize personal welfare in a way that unfairly deprives or damages the organization or others.

Any AMA members found to be in violation of any provision of this Code of Ethics may have his or her Association membership suspended or revoked.

# SECTION TWO

# MARKET OPPORTUNITY ANALYSIS

# CHAPTER THREE

# Understanding Market Opportunities

## The Cellular Telephone Business: Increasing Competition in a Growing Market[1]

FROM LONDON TO TOKYO to Nairobi to Chicago, cell phones have become a "can't do without it" tool of time-pressed businesspeople, hip teenagers, rural farmers, fishermen in Africa, and just about anyone else who wants to stay in touch. The market for mobile telephone service is growing rapidly. In 1983, when the first cellular phone system began operations, it was projected that by 2000, fewer than 1 million people would subscribe. As a result of dramatic growth among both business and household users, however, by 2005, the number of cell phone users had reached more than 2 billion worldwide! By 2007, there were more cell phone subscriptions than people in the world's developed economies and by 2011, three-quarters of the world's 5 billion people had cell phone subscriptions.

The continuing growth in demand for mobile voice and data services generates numerous opportunities in the cell phone manufacturing and cell phone service industries, among others. Prospective entrants and current players considering additional investments should consider, however, just how attractive these markets and industries really are.

### The Mobile Telephony Market

By all accounts, the *market* for mobile telephony has been an attractive one. New features such as color

screens, built-in cameras, and web browsers have attracted new users and encouraged existing users to upgrade their phones. As a result, the penetration of the newest third and fourth generation (3G and 4G) smartphones has risen sharply, especially in Asia. Users of 3G services represented 30 percent of all mobile phone users in Japan and a whopping 93 percent in Korea in 2005, compared to only 5 percent in Italy and the United Kingdom.

In the developing world, with plummeting prices that have made basic cell phones affordable to almost everyone, cell phone penetration passed the 50 percent mark in 2006. Not to be outdone, in the business world, a growing legion of businesspeople of all kinds began using their new smartphones to stay in touch and online, no matter where they went.

Given torrid growth on all fronts, most observers agree that the *market* for cell phone service and cell phones themselves has been and continues to be attractive indeed. But how attractive are the *industries* that serve this market?

### Cell Phone Manufacturing

Rapid-fire technological advances from Nokia, BlackBerry, and many others brought countless new features to the market, including software to access the internet the ability to send and receive photographic images, and various location-based services that take advantage of global positioning technology. Nokia rocketed to world leadership in cell phones, leaving early and longtime leader Motorola in the dust. Nokia saw its global market share grow to 40 percent by 2007, based on its continuing strength in developed markets and its growing dominance of the market for low-priced handsets in the developing world. As industry analyst Neal Mawston noted, "Nokia has a world-class product portfolio and very few rivals can compete with that. They are now enjoying huge economies of scale that success conveys. Anybody who tries to get in a handset war with them is going to get hurt."

But in the turbulent mayhem that has characterized the global cell phone industry since its inception, Nokia's success did not last. The coming of Apple's touch-screen iPhone in 2007 took traditional competitors like Nokia and Motorola as well as other smartphone makers like BlackBerry's Research in Motion by storm. In 2010, amid a slowdown in overall unit sales globally, Apple's 30 percent share of global operating profits among cell phone makers nearly matched Nokia's 40 percent share. Nokia's stock dropped to €8, off by two-thirds from €25 in 2008, as its worldwide cell phone market share fell to 25 percent. Motorola and Sony Ericsson fell into loss-making territory.

In June 2011, Nokia warned analysts that it would earn no profit at all in that quarter and its stock slipped below €5. Nokia's phones were simply no longer competitive with the likes of Apple, nor with other smartphones running Google's Android operating system. And with low-cost Chinese cell phone makers growing in clout in the low-priced markets, the chances for a quick turnaround for Nokia looked slim.

This recent history in the hotly competitive cell phone manufacturing industry suggests that a rapidly growing market does not necessarily provide a smooth path to success. Growing markets are one thing, but turbulent industries serving those markets are quite another.

## Cell Phone Service Providers

In 2007, European leader Vodaphone bought into India's rapidly growing market by acquiring 67 percent of India's third-largest operator, Hutchinson Essar. CEO Arun Sarin was delighted. "We are going to learn as much from India as we are going to take from India," he crowed. "Prices there are two-and-a-half cents a minute, and they make a 35 percent margin. How do you do that?"

Just two and a half years later, the price of a cell phone minute in India had collapsed to 1 U.S. cent per minute. Sarin moved on and in came cost-cutter Vittorio Collao as Vodaphone's new CEO. Despite (or as a result of) the fact that India's cell phone operators installed in one year as much network capacity as Germany had built in the last 15 years, the pressure on prices and profits was relentless. Newcomer Uninor, a unit of Norway's Telenor, introduced a plan that offered calls for as little as 0.20 rupees per minute, about half of 1 U.S. cent.

## Network Equipment Down, Too

Another industry that had raced to keep pace with the growing cell phone market—makers of network equipment like switches, towers, and more—also hit the skids. Longtime stalwarts Alcatel-Lucent and Nokia Siemens Networks were both running losses in 2010, in the face of waning demand for 3G technology and stiff competition from Ericsson and China's Huawei. They were hoping that orders for new 4G equipment would bail them out.

Thus, while the rapidly growing *market* for mobile telephone service has been an attractive one, the *industries* that serve this market face significant challenges.

# Marketing Challenges Addressed in Chapter 3

As the examples of the cellular phone manufacturing and service industries show, serving a growing market hardly guarantees smooth sailing. Equally or more important are industry conditions and the degree to which specific players in the industry can, like Nokia or Apple, establish and sustain competitive advantage at least for a while. Thus, as entrepreneurs and marketing decision makers ponder an *opportunity* to enter or attempt to increase their share of a growing market like that for mobile phones, they also must carefully examine a host of other issues, including the conditions that are currently prevailing in the industry in which they would compete and the likelihood that favorable conditions will prevail in the future. Similarly, such decisions require a thorough examination of trends that are influencing market demand and are likely to do so in the future, whether favorably or otherwise.

Thus, in this chapter, we address the 4 Cs that were identified in Chapter 1 as the analytical foundation of the marketing management process. We provide a framework to help managers, entrepreneurs, and investors comprehensively assess the attractiveness of opportunities they encounter, in terms of the *company* and its people, the environmental *context* in which it operates, the *competition* it faces, and the wants and needs of the *customer* it seeks to serve. We do so by addressing the three questions crucial to the assessment of any market opportunity: How attractive is the market we serve or propose to serve? How attractive is the industry in which we would compete? Are the right human resources—in terms of people and their capabilities and connections—in place to effectively pursue the opportunity at hand?

**STRATEGIC ISSUE**

*How attractive is the market we serve or propose to serve? How attractive is the industry in which we would compete? Are the right resources—in terms of people and their capabilities and connections—in place to effectively pursue the opportunity at hand?*

We frame our discussion of opportunity assessment using the seven domains shown in Exhibit 3.1. As the seven domains framework suggests and the cellular telephony story shows, in today's rapidly changing and hotly competitive world it's not enough to have a large and growing market. The attractiveness of the industry and the company's or entrepreneurial team's resources are equally important. Before digging more deeply into the framework, however, we clarify the difference between two oft-confused terms: *market* and *industry.*

# Markets and Industries: What's the Difference?

We define a *market* as being composed of individuals or organizations who are interested in and willing to buy a good or service to obtain benefits that will satisfy a particular want or need and have the resources to engage in such a transaction. One such market consists of college students who get hungry in the middle of the afternoon and have a few minutes and enough spare change to buy a snack between classes.

An *industry* is a group of firms that offer a product or class of products that are similar and are close substitutes for one another. What industries serve the student snack market? At the producer level, there are the salty-snack industry (makers of potato and corn chips and similar products); the candy industry; the fresh produce industry (growers of apples, oranges, bananas, and other easy-to-eat fruits); and others too numerous to mention. Distribution channels for these products include the supermarket industry, food service industry, coin-operated vending industry, and so on. Clearly, these industries differ and offer varying bundles of benefits to hungry students.

## Exhibit 3.1

THE SEVEN DOMAINS OF ATTRACTIVE OPPORTUNITIES

Source: John Mullins, *The New Business Road Test: What Entrepreneurs and Executives Should Do Before Writing a Business Plan* (London: FT/Prentice Hall, 2010).

Thus, markets are comprised of buyers; industries are comprised of sellers. The distinction, often overlooked, is an important one because both markets and industries can vary substantially in their attractiveness, as we've seen in the cellular arena.

Further, sellers who look only to others in their own industry as competitors are likely to overlook other very real rivals and risk having their markets undercut by innovators from other industries. Should Kodak have been more concerned with Fuji, Agfa, and other longtime players in the film and photoprocessing industries, or should it have worried about Hewlett-Packard, Sony, and various online players whose digital technologies are making photography's century-old silver halide chemistry go the way of the buggy whip? With unit sales of digital cameras now far outstripping sales of cameras that use film, Kodak's competitive landscape has certainly changed.[2]

## Assessing Market and Industry Attractiveness

The seven domains framework, among other things, enables marketers to answer two important questions in an evidence-based manner: How attractive is the market? How attractive is the industry? For a comparison of this approach to an older way of assessing the 4 Cs, see Exhibit 3.2.

For many years, strategy textbooks have taught students to conduct a SWOT analysis that enumerates the strengths, weaknesses, opportunities, and threats faced by the firm in a particular market and industry setting. Doing so is useful, of course, but it fails to organize the output into answers to important strategic questions, such as those of market or industry attractiveness or the ability of the firm or its offering to achieve sustainable competitive advantage. The seven domains framework organizes similar information as a SWOT, and more, and does so in a manner that addresses such questions explicitly.

As Exhibit 3.1 shows, markets and industries must be assessed at both the macro and micro levels of analysis. But what do these levels really mean? On both the market and industry sides, the macro-level analyses are based on environmental conditions that affect the market or industry, respectively, as a whole, without regard to a particular company's strategy, target market, or its role in its industry. These external and largely uncontrollable forces or conditions must be reckoned with in assessing and shaping any opportunity and, indeed, in developing any coherent marketing strategy.

At the micro level, the analyses look not at the market or the industry overall but at *individuals* in that market or industry, that is, specific target customers and companies themselves, respectively. We develop and apply the relevant analytical frameworks for the macro-level analyses first; then we address the micro-level analyses.

## Macro Trend Analysis: A Framework for Assessing Market Attractiveness, Macro Level

Assessing market attractiveness requires that important *macroenvironmental* trends— or *macro trends* for short—be noticed and understood. The macroenvironment can be divided into six major components: demographic, sociocultural, economic, regulatory, technological, and natural environments. The key question marketing managers and strategists must ask in each of these arenas is what trends are out there that are influencing demand in the market of interest, whether favorably or unfavorably.

## The Demographic Environment

As the saying goes, demography is destiny. All kinds of things—from sales of music CDs to the state of public finances to society's costs of health care to the financing of pensions—are governed to a significant extent by demographic changes. While the number of specific demographic trends that might influence one marketer or another is without limit, there are currently five major global demographic trends that are likely to influence the fortunes of many companies, for better or worse: the aging of the world's population, the effect of the AIDS plague on demography, a rapidly growing middle class in emerging a countries, increased levels of immigration, and the decline in married households in developed countries.

**STRATEGIC ISSUE**

*Demography is destiny. All kinds of things are governed to a significant extent by demographic changes.*

**Aging**　Exhibit 3.3 shows the projected increase in the portion of the population aged over 60 in several of the world's most developed countries. The chart shows that in Italy,

## Exhibit 3.3

AGING POPULATIONS: % OF THE POPULATION AGED OVER 60

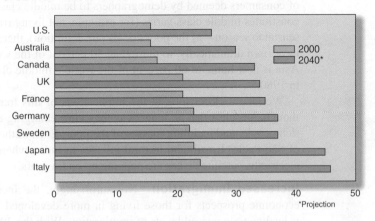

*Source:* Norma Cohen and Clive Cookson, "The Planet Is Ever Greyer: But as Longevity Rises Faster than Forecast, the Elderly Are Also Becoming Healthier," *Financial Times,* January 19, 2004, p. 15.

for example, about half the population will be over 60 by the year 2040, according to current projections. Providers of health care, vacation homes, life insurance, and other goods and services have taken note of the graying of the world's population and are taking steps to develop marketing strategies to serve this fast-growing market.

Doing so, however, isn't always easy. Many people do not wish to be pigeonholed as elderly, and some who are getting older may not be very attracted to goods or services that remind them of their age. One marketer dealing with this challenge is Ferrari, whose average customer is nearing 50 and getting older with each passing year. "The profile of our customers means we have to pay attention to practicality and functionality without compromising the sportiness," says Giuseppe Bonollo, Ferrari's strategic marketing director. "The way the doors open on the Enzo, for example, allows part of the roof and part of the door undermolding to come away as well, making it easier to enter the car."[3]

The implications of the aging trend are not as clear-cut as they might appear. Surprisingly, perhaps, some 25 percent of the early buyers of Apple's hot new iPhones—a "cool," cutting-edge product if there ever was one—were people over 50.[4] Further, there is evidence that today's elderly generation is both healthier and fitter than its predecessors. Thus, fears that health and other facilities will be swamped by hordes of ailing pensioners may be misplaced. "New data demolish such concerns," reports Raymond Tillis, professor of geriatric medicine at Manchester University in the United Kingdom. "There is a lot of evidence that disability among old people is declining rapidly."[5]

**AIDS**   The death toll due to HIV/AIDS in Africa, the hardest hit region, was some 8 million from 1995 to 2000,[6] and the pandemic continues. In 2005, an estimated 24 million adults and children died from AIDS in sub-Saharan Africa.[7] Across Africa, grandparents are raising an entire generation of children, since the parents have died.

Pharmaceutical companies and world health organizations are struggling to develop strategies to deal with the AIDS challenge, one that presents a huge and rapidly growing market, but one in which there is little ability to pay for the advanced drug therapies that offer hope to AIDS victims. But progress is being made, and the pandemic may soon be contained.

**Growing Middle Class**   In the emerging economies of Asia and Latin America, the pace of economic development in recent years has led to a rapid increase in the number of consumers deemed by demographers to be middle class. Though the definition of what constitutes middle class varies (for example, not living from hand to mouth, job to job, or season to season—as the poor do—is one definition), there is no dispute that their numbers have risen dramatically, to more than 50 percent of the world's total population by 2006.[8] Asia is now home to 60 percent of the world's middle class, compared to just 20 percent in 1980.[9]

We take a closer look at the implications of this trend in Chapter 6. For marketers, though, it is clear that no longer can they view emerging economies as consisting of a few rich people, and huddling masses of the poor. Even in the crowded, impoverished *favelas* of São Paolo, Brazil, and in rural villages in India, where there is little running water or electricity, satellite dishes are popping up on tin roofs.

**Increased Immigration**   Not surprisingly, the increasing imbalance between the economic prospects for those living in more developed versus less developed countries is leading to increased levels of immigration. With the 2004 enlargement of the European Union from 15 to 25 countries, fears have grown that some countries in the "old EU" will be swamped with immigrants from the accession countries in Eastern Europe, where per capita GDP is only 46 percent of the EU 15 average.[10]

In one sense, this wave of immigration is nothing new, for melting pot countries such as the United States and the United Kingdom have for centuries welcomed immigrants to their shores (see Exhibit 3.4). In the United States, many years of immigration from Mexico and Latin America have made the Sun Belt a bilingual region, and many now view Miami as the crossroads of Latin America. The implications for marketers seeking to gain market share among Hispanic Americans are obvious.

## Exhibit 3.4

MELTING POT BRITAIN: PAST, PRESENT, AND FUTURE

- **1600s:** About 50,000 French Protestants, known as Huguenots, admitted after religious persecution in France. The Huguenots give the word "refugee" to the English language.
- **1840s:** An estimated 1m Irish flee famine and flock to Britain's new industrial centres.
- **1890s:** About 100,000 Jews arrive in Britain from central and eastern Europe.
- **1930s:** 56,000 Jews fleeing from Nazi persecution join the earlier group.
- **1955–62:** 472,000 Commonwealth citizens, primarily from the Caribbean and southern Asia move to Britain. Many were actively recruited abroad by big employers including the London Underground.
- **1970s:** 30,000 Asians forced out of Uganda by General Idi Amin allowed to settle in UK by Edward Heath.

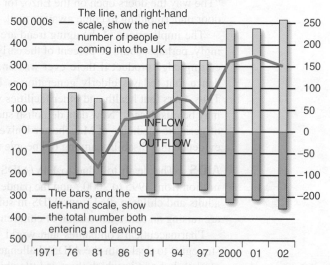

*Source:* Chart: "Melting Pot Britain: Past, Present, and Future," *The Sunday Times* (London), November 16, 2003, Focus, p. 16. Original source: National Statistics.

**Declining Marriage Rates**    A generation ago, a single, 30-something professional woman out with her single friends for a night on the town would have been considered an aberration. No more. Marriage in much of the Western world is on the wane. In the United States, married couples, 80 percent of households in the 1950s, now account for just 50.7 percent.[11] Young couples are delaying marriage, cohabitating in greater numbers, forming same-sex partnerships, and are remarrying less after a wedding leads to divorce. Later in life, they are living longer, which is increasing the number of widows.

Implications for marketers? For one, consider the implications of marrying in one's 30s, well into one's career, rather than in one's 20s. It's less likely that the parents of the bride will handle the wedding arrangements—not to mention the hefty bills that must be paid—so couples are planning and managing their weddings themselves. In the United Kingdom a new magazine, *Stag & Groom,* hit the market in 2004 to take the fear out of the wedding process for the clueless grooms who must now play a more important role. But would anyone really buy a wedding magazine for men? Despite the hilarious publicity its launch generated, *Stag & Groom* suffered an early demise. Macro trends alone don't guarantee the success of a new venture.

## The Sociocultural Environment

Sociocultural trends are those that have to do with the values, attitudes, and behavior of individuals in a given society. Cultures tend to evolve slowly, however, so some sociocultural trends can take a generation or more to have significant impact, as people tend to carry for a lifetime the values with which they grow up. Within this broadly stable pattern, however, sociocultural trends can and do exert powerful effects on markets for a great variety of goods and services. Two trends of particular relevance today are greater interest in ethical behavior by businesses and trends toward fitness and nutrition.

**Business Ethics**    For years, the world's leading coffee marketers, including Kraft and Nestlé, resisted calls to pay premium prices for coffee grown in a sustainable manner, on farms that pay their workers a living wage and that respect the environment. In 2003, Kraft, running neck and neck with Nestlé for the number one spot in market share globally, reached agreement with the Rainforest Alliance, a nonprofit organization that seeks to improve the working, social, and environmental conditions in agriculture in the third world. The agreement called for Kraft to buy £5 million of Rainforest Alliance–certified coffee from Brazil, Colombia, Mexico, and Central America in 2004, paying a 20 percent premium to the farmers.

Why did Kraft take this step? "This is not about philanthropy," says Kraft's Annemieke Wijn. "This is about incorporating sustainable coffee into our mainstream brands as a way to have a more efficient and competitive way of doing business."[12] In short, Kraft made the jump because consumers demanded it.

**Fitness and Nutrition**    Running. Working out. Fitness clubs. The South Beach and Atkins diets. These days, natural and organic foods are in (see Exhibit 3.5). Sugar and cholesterol—at least the bad LDL cholesterol—are out.[13] The implications of these sociocultural trends are playing out in grocery store produce departments, where entire sections are now devoted to organic produce; in the farming communities of North America and Europe, where fields formerly farmed with fertilizers are being transformed into organic ones; and on restaurant menus, where selections are being revamped to make them appeal to customers who have adopted new eating habits. The 20-ounce T-bone steak is a thing of the past, at least in some circles.

## Exhibit 3.5    HEALTH TRENDS GIVE KRAFT A STOMACH ACHE

Tracey Daugherty, a 33-year-old mother from Pittsburgh, grew up eating Kraft macaroni and cheese. Today, though, Kraft's marketing strategists have queasy stomachs because Daugherty and others won't feed it to their own children. "Kraft's products definitely have a childhood nostalgia," she says, "so it's hard to completely give up on them, but they're not on my shopping list." When she's pressed for time, Daugherty is more likely to pull an organic frozen dinner out of the freezer than boil up a batch of Kraft Mac and Cheese. On most nights, what's on her family's dinner table includes fresh produce and chicken or fish from Whole Foods, the fast-growing American grocery chain that built its reputation on natural and organic foods.

To cope with Americans' growing preference for fresh and natural foods rather than prepackaged and processed ones, the big food companies are having to rethink their businesses, find new suppliers, and augment their product lines with new, healthier versions of their longstanding best-sellers. Kraft, which owns brands such as Oscar Mayer (hot dogs,

with their high animal fat content, are not exactly known as a health food), Jell-O gelatin (mostly sugar, a no-no on today's low carbohydrate diets), and Nabisco (whose cookies and crackers are laden with both carbs and trans-fats, the latest addition to health experts' "avoid" lists), has struggled to meet their double-digit growth targets, as consumers increasingly shift their food dollars to healthier fare.

As Wharton Marketing Professor Patricia Williams points out, the question for the food giants is: "To what extent is the Atkins diet and the whole low-carb thing a fad, and to what extent is it a genuine shift in consumption patterns that will remain with us for a significant period of time?" It's a question that Kraft and others in the food industry cannot afford to take lightly.

*Sources:* Sarah Ellison, "Finicky Shoppers Pose Problems for Kraft Foods," *The Wall Street Journal Europe,* May 24, 2004, p. A7; and Knowledge@Wharton, "Low-Carb, High-Carb: What's a Baker/Pasta Maker to Do?" http://knowledge.wharton.upenn.edu/index.cfm?fa=printArticle&ID=994. For more on Kraft, see *www.kraftfoodscompany.com/welcome.aspx.*

These trends are driving more than just the food business, however. Attendance at health and fitness clubs is booming. Sales of home exercise equipment are up, along with advice on how to purchase and use it to best advantage.[14]

## The Economic Environment

Among the most far-reaching of the six macro trend components is the economic environment. When people's incomes rise or fall, when interest rates rise or fall, when the fiscal policy of governments results in increased or decreased government spending, entire sectors of economies are influenced deeply, and sometimes suddenly. As we write, with some Western economies struggling to bounce back from recession, the near-term future of the developed economies appears to lie in the factories of exporters or in the purses and wallets of their—or China's or India's—shoppers.

The implications of trends like these in consumer spending can be dramatic for marketers, to be sure, but they can be far subtler than one might imagine. Take robust economic health, for example. It's good for everyone, right? Not if you're the operator of a chain of check-cashing outlets or pawn shops, which thrive when times are tough and people need to turn unwanted assets into cash quickly. Or what about discount airlines? Shouldn't they be thriving in the recently troubled economic environment? Ryanair, Europe's largest airline by passenger count, announced that it would cut its capacity—grounding 80 of its 300 jets—for its winter season beginning in October 2011. "It's the first time ever that we'll go negative on traffic," CEO Michael O'Leary said in an interview. "We take

**STRATEGIC ISSUE**

*Take robust economic health, for example. It's good for everyone, right?*

delivery of 50 aircraft this winter so instead of running around trying to open up new bases and routes in November and December we'll sit them on the ground. There will still be strong growth next summer but trying to open up new routes with high oil prices is stupid in the winter"[15] The hundred-dollar price per barrel of oil has forced even the discounters like Ryanair and Southwest to raise prices, and cash-strapped travelers are finding other ways to get around (see Exhibit 3.6).

Economic trends often work, to pronounced effect, in concert with other macro trends. For example, the move of the baby-boomer generation into middle age in the 1990s, a demographic trend, combined with a strong global economy and low interest rates, both economic trends, led to booming demand for condominiums and vacation homes in resort areas such as the Rocky Mountains of Colorado and the south of Spain and Portugal. But prices in many resort areas have plummeted in the downturn.

## The Regulatory Environment

In every country and across some countries—those that are members of the EU, for example— there is a *regulatory environment* within which local and multinational firms operate. As with the other macro trend components, political and legal trends, especially those that result in *regulation* or *deregulation,* can have powerful impact on market attractiveness.

In September 2003, voters in Sweden resoundingly rejected the euro, preferring to maintain their own Swedish currency and thereby retain independent domestic control of their country's fiscal and monetary policy and remain freer than those in the euro-zone of what some see as stifling overregulation from Brussels.[16] For marketers involved in Swedish import or export businesses, the implications may prove significant, as uncertainties inherent in predicting foreign exchange rates make trade and investment decisions more tenuous.

The power of deregulation to influence market attractiveness is now well-known. Government, business, and the general public throughout much of the world have become increasingly aware that overregulation protects inefficiencies, restricts entry by new competitors, and creates inflationary pressures. In the United States, airlines, trucking, railroads, telecommunications, and banking have been deregulated. Markets also are being liberated in western and eastern Europe, Asia, and many developing countries. Trade barriers are crumbling due to political unrest and technological innovation.

Deregulation has typically changed the structure of the affected industries as well as lowered prices, creating rapid growth in some markets as a result. For example, the period following deregulation of the U.S. airline industry (1978–1985) gave rise to a new airline category—the budget airline. The rise of Southwest and other budget airlines led to lower

## Exhibit 3.6   NO PAT-DOWNS ON MEGABUS

Long distance discount bus operators like Megabus and BoltBus, with their easy internet booking, free WiFi, and power outlets on board, are winning customers like Chicago's Bobbie Joe Crail. "The bus can be inconvenient," says Crail, "but it's so much cheaper to string bus trips together than to fly."

Professor of transportation Joseph Schwieterman at DePaul University is not surprised. "It's not just high fuel prices—it's the hassle factor at the airports that has left many fliers disenchanted." On Megabus, passengers don't have to take their shoes off unless they want to, and there's no security pat-down either!

*Source:* Brian Burnsed, "Suddenly It's Cool to Take the Bus," *BusinessWeek* European Edition, September 29, 2008, p 64. For more on Megabus or Boltbus, see *www.megabus.com* or *www.boltbus.com/default.aspx*.

fares across all routes and forced the major carriers to streamline operations and phase out underperforming routes. A similar story has followed in the European market, where discount airlines Ryanair, easyJet, and others have made vacation destinations places to fly to rather than drive to.

As regulatory practices wax and wane, the attractiveness of markets often follows suit. For example, the deregulation of telecommunications in Europe, following earlier deregulation in the United States, opened markets to firms seeking to offer new services and take market share from the established monopolies. The rise of internet retailing and internet telephony has policy-makers arguing over the degree to which these internet activities should be subject to state and federal tax in the United States. The outcome of these arguments may have considerable effect on consumers' interest in buying and calling on the web.

## The Technological Environment

In the past three decades, an amazing number of new technologies has created new markets for such products as video recorders, compact disks, ever-more-powerful and ever-smaller computers, smartphones, new lightweight materials, and genetically engineered drugs. Technological progress is unlikely to abate.

Technology can also change how businesses operate (banks, airlines, retail stores, and marketing research firms), how goods and services as well as ideas are exchanged, how crops are grown, and how individuals learn and earn as well as interact with one another. Consumers today enjoy check-free banking, the death of the invoice, and ticketless air travel.

Many of these innovations are the result not only of changes in computing systems, but also of reduced costs in communicating (voice or data). For example, the cost of processing an additional telephone call is so small it might as well be free. Distance is no longer a factor—it costs about the same to make a trans-Atlantic call as one to your next-door neighbor. If you place the call on Skype, it can cost nothing at all!

At the dawn of the new millennium, developments in telecommunications and computing have led to the rapid convergence of the telecommunications, computing, and entertainment industries. Music-hungry consumers have been downloading music from legal and illegal sites thereby hammering the music industry (see Exhibit 3.7) and have forced the industry to change the way it distributes music. Apple's iPod led the way with an

**Exhibit 3.7    THE MUSIC INDUSTRY SINGS THE BLUES**

For seven years running, sales of compact discs have fallen due to the seismic shift in the way consumers obtain their music. Though CDs still account for most of all music sold, the sharp decline in their sales as a consequence of digital downloads has dramatically outweighed increases in CD revenues. Even the hits aren't what they used to be. Norah Jones's "Not Too Late" sold 1.1 million copies in its first six weeks in early 2007, compared to twice that figure for her "Feels Like Home" CD over its same postrelease period in 2004.

Music retailers are also feeling the pain, with more than 200 music stores closing in the United States in 2006 alone. Tower Records closed its 89 stores following a bankruptcy filing, and Musicland Holding Corp., owner of the Sam Goody chain, has shuttered more than half of its 900 locations in recent years.

Pali Research analyst Richard Greenfield is not optimistic that industry conditions will get better. "Even when you have a good release like Norah Jones," he says, "maybe the environment is so bad you can't turn it around."

*Source:* Ethan Smith, "For the Music World, the Tune Gets Sadder," *The Wall Street Journal European Edition,* March 22, 2007, p. 16.

estimated 83 percent share of legal music downloads in the fourth quarter of 2005,[17] and its music revenues have continued to grow rapidly.

Smartphone users check their e-mail, sports scores, breaking news, stock quotes, and more. Savvy marketers and entrepreneurs who follow technological trends are able to foresee new and previously unheard of applications such as these and thereby place themselves and their firms at the forefront of the innovation curve, sometimes earning entrepreneurial fortunes in the process. For others, though, like the music industry, the challenges brought on by these winds of change can be daunting.

**STRATEGIC ISSUE**

*Savvy marketers and entrepreneurs who follow technological trends are able to foresee new and previously unheard of applications, sometimes earning entrepreneurial fortunes in the process.*

In addition to creating attractive new markets, technological developments are having a profound impact on all aspects of marketing practice, including marketing communication (ads on the web or via e-mail), distribution (books and other consumer and industrial goods bought and sold via the web), packaging (use of new materials), and marketing research (monitoring supermarket purchases with scanners or internet activity with digital "cookies"). We explore the most important of these changes in the ensuing chapters in this book.

## The Natural Environment

Everything ultimately depends on the natural environment, including marketing. Changes in the earth's resources and climate can have significant and far-reaching effects. The world's supply of oil is finite, for example, leading automakers to develop new hot-selling hybrid gas-electric vehicles such as the Toyota Prius, which can go more than 50 miles on a gallon of gas. The skyrocketing price of oil has caused demand for gas-guzzling sport utility vehicles to plummet.[18]

In general, discussion of the problems in the natural environment has stressed the threats and penalties facing business throughout the world. But business can do a number of things to turn problems into opportunities. One is to invest in research to find ways to save energy in heating and lighting. Another is to find new energy sources such as wind farms and hydroelectric projects. In virtually every corner of the clean-tech and green-tech arenas, entrepreneurs and marketers are looking for ways to save the planet and deliver shareholder returns at the same time. There is a growing recognition that creating a more sustainable natural environment is an important job, one to which newly educated marketers can contribute (see Exhibit 3.8).

### Exhibit 3.8 CLEAN-TECH, GREEN-TECH SUSTAINABILITY AND *You*

Fuel-efficient cars are once again in favor, Tesla's electric cars are cool (*www.teslamotors.com*) and solar energy is hot. Clean-tech and green-tech investment funds have sprung up in Silicon Valley, London, Mumbai, and seemingly everywhere else to invest in companies that hope to create a more sustainable future. Green-tech outfits like Spain's T-Solar (*www.tsolar.com*), U.S. green energy producer Ameresco (*www.amerescosolar.com*); and the renewable unit of the Italian utility Enel (*www.enel.com*) have recently raised capital in hot IPOs.

Business school students, too, are getting in on the sustainability game. Business plan competitions for socially and environmentally friendly ventures, like the Global Social Venture Competition (*www.gsvc.org*) held annually at the Haas School of Business at the University of California, Berkeley, and fed from a network of business schools around the world, now motivate students to think in triple bottom-line terms, rather than solely about profit. Social returns, environmental returns, and economic returns: Wouldn't the world be a better place if we had more of all three?

*Sources:* Mark Scott and Alex Morales, "A Gold Rush in Green Technology," *Bloomberg Businessweek* European Edition, April 25, 2010, p. 24; the Global Social Venture Competition website at *www.gsvc.com*.

Businesses have seen opportunities in developing thousands of *green products* (those that are environmentally friendly) such as phosphate-free detergents, tuna caught without netting dolphins, organic fertilizers, high-efficiency LED lighting, recycled paper, and clothes made from 100 percent organic cotton and colored with nontoxic dyes. DuPont, long synonymous with petrochemicals, is reinventing itself as an eco-conscious company. More than $5 billion of its $29 billion in revenue now comes from sustainable products, including a new corn-based fiber called Sorona, which can be used to make clothing, carpet, and other products.[19]

Trends in the natural environment are creating opportunities for companies like DuPont. On the other hand, if global warming continues, it may play havoc with markets for winter vacationers, snowmobiles, and other products and services whose demand depends on the reliable coming of Old Man Winter. Other natural trends, such as the depletion of natural resources and fresh groundwater, may significantly impact firms in many industries serving a vast array of markets. Tracking such trends and understanding their effects is an important task.

## Your Market Is Attractive: What about Your Industry?

As we saw at the outset of this chapter, consumers and businesspeople have become hooked on cell phones, and the market for mobile communication has grown rapidly. By most measures, this is a large, growing, and attractive *market.* But are cell phone manufacturing and cellular services attractive *industries?* An industry's attractiveness at a point in time can best be judged by analyzing the five major competitive forces, which we address in this section.

## Porter's Five Competitive Forces[20]

Five competitive forces collectively determine an industry's long-term attractiveness—rivalry among present competitors, threat of new entrants into the industry, the bargaining power of suppliers, the bargaining power of buyers, and the threat of substitute products (see Exhibit 3.9). This mix of forces explains why some industries are consistently more profitable than others and provides further insights into which resources are required and which strategies should be adopted to be successful. A useful way to conduct a five forces analysis of an industry's attractiveness is to construct a checklist based on Porter's seminal work.[21]

The strength of the individual forces varies from industry to industry and, over time, within the same industry. In the fast-food industry, the key forces are rivalry among present competitors (for example, Wendy's versus Burger King versus McDonald's) and substitute products (neighborhood delis, salad bars, all-you-can-eat buffet restaurants, and frozen meals). The growing popularity of healthier fast-food alternatives has brought new entrants like Prêt A Manger in the United Kingdom and Chipotle and Panera in the United States, making rivalry even more fierce.

**Rivalry among Present Competitors**    Rivalry occurs among firms that produce products that are close substitutes for each other, especially when one competitor acts to improve its standing or protect its position. Thus, firms are mutually dependent: What one firm does affects others and vice versa. Ordinarily, profitability decreases as rivalry increases. Rivalry is greater under the following conditions:

## Exhibit 3.9

THE MAJOR FORCES THAT DETERMINE INDUSTRY ATTRACTIVENESS

- *There is high investment intensity; that is, the amount of fixed and working capital required to produce a dollar of sales is large.* High intensity requires firms to operate at or near capacity, thereby putting strong downward pressure on prices when demand slackens. Thus, high-investment–intensity businesses are, on average, much less profitable than those with a lower level of investment. More than 15 years ago, Bob Crandall, the then CEO of American Airlines, described the airline industry as being "intensely, vigorously, bitterly, savagely competitive."[22] The number of U.S. airlines going into bankruptcy over the past decade suggests that the industry's challenges are even more difficult today. As the noted investor Warren Buffett observed, the entire airline industry has not made a dime for investors in its century of existence.[23]

- *There are many small firms in an industry or no dominant firms exist.* The restaurant industry is a good example.

- *There is little product differentiation*—for example, gasoline, major appliances, TV sets, and passenger-car tires.

- *It's easy for customers to switch from one seller's products to those of others* (low switching cost for buyers).

The greater the competitive rivalry in an industry, the less attractive it is to current players or would-be entrants. Consider cell phone service. The cellular service industry is capital intensive. Though there are several dominant firms whose products are differentiated through rapid technological change, consumers' switching costs to change cell phone service providers or handsets are low. Thus, rivalry among service providers, as well as for cell phone manufacturers, is brutal (see Exhibit 3.10).

**Threat of New Entrants**    A second force affecting industry attractiveness is the threat of new entrants. New competitors add capacity to the industry and bring with them the need to gain market share, thereby making competition more intense. For cellular telephone operators, license requirements and the huge cost of obtaining bandwidth in government auctions make threat of entry into the cellular service industry relatively low. The greater the threat of new entrants, the less will be an industry's attractiveness, so this is good news for cellular operators. Entry is more difficult under the following conditions:

- *When strong economies of scale and learning effects are present,* since it takes time to obtain the volume and learning required to yield a low relative cost per unit. If existing firms are vertically

## Exhibit 3.10   SHAKEOUT IN CELL PHONES

A brutal price war for 3G subscribers in Japan led to market leader NTT DoCoMo's first-ever drop in annual revenue and operating profit in its year ended March 2005. Japanese cell phone carriers had introduced new fixed-price data plans that undercut earlier 3G offerings. With talking now more expensive than sending an e-mail or text message, some consumers changed their behavior. "Using the phone to talk seems like a waste because e-mailing and Web browsing are so much easier," said Hiroki Wakabayashi, a 27-year-old computer engineer whose high-speed mobile service from DoCoMo cost him $100 or more each month, a sum he was happy to spend. In March 2006, Britain's Vodafone threw in the towel, agreeing to sell its Japanese cell phone unit. Its exit after six years in Japan, following customer losses and falling profits, attests to the hotly competitive environment that it was unable to conquer.

On the manufacturing side, average selling prices of cell phones have fallen sharply, reflecting the growing importance of emerging markets where simpler handsets are all that consumers can afford. Some 42 percent of market leader Nokia's handsets in 2007 sold for less than €50, compared to 23 percent a year earlier. The story is no better at Motorola, Sony Ericsson, Samsung, or LG, where operating margins are being eroded.

Attractive markets? Perhaps. Attractive industries? Think again.

*Sources:* Ken Belson, "Advances in Phones No Panacea for Firms," *International Herald Tribune,* June 6, 2005, p. 9; Martin Fackler, "Vodafone Bruised, Hangs Up on Japan," *International Herald Tribune,* March 18–19, 2006, p. 1; The Lex Column, "Nokia Bucks the Trend," *Financial Times,* January 26, 2007, p. 18.

integrated, entry becomes even more expensive. Also, if the existing firms share their output with their related businesses, the problem of overcoming the cost disadvantage is made even more difficult.

- *If the industry has strong capital requirements at the outset.*
- *When strong product differentiation exists among current players.*
- *If gaining distribution is particularly difficult.*

A recent study suggests, however, that establishing entry barriers may be overrated as a mechanism for sustaining one's competitive advantage.[24] Entry barriers may well deter me-too entries, but they are less likely to deter more innovative entries. The results of this study suggest that a combination of effectively managing innovation cycles while building entry barriers through cost advantages or proprietary technologies can enhance incumbents' ability to sustain competitive advantage over time.

### Bargaining Power of Suppliers

The bargaining power of suppliers over firms in an industry is the third major determinant of industry attractiveness. It is exercised largely through increased prices or more onerous terms and conditions of sale. Its impact can be significant, particularly when there is a limited number of suppliers serving an industry. Their power is increased under the following conditions:

- *If the cost of switching suppliers is high.*
- *If prices of substitutes are high.*
- *If suppliers can realistically threaten forward integration.*
- *When the supplier's product is a large part of the buyer's value added*—as is the case with metal cans, where the cost of tin plate is over 60 percent of the value added.

In recent years, the bargaining power of suppliers in many industries has changed dramatically as more companies seek a partnership relationship with their suppliers. What was once an arm's-length adversarial relationship has turned into a cooperative one resulting in lower transaction costs, improved quality derived primarily from using a supplier's technological skills to design and manufacture parts, and decreased transaction time in terms of inventory replenishments through just-in-time procurement systems.

The greater the bargaining power of the key suppliers to an industry, the less will be the overall attractiveness of the industry. The newly discovered power that governments worldwide have exerted by auctioning bandwidth for new cellular services has raised their bargaining power as suppliers of bandwidth to the cellular industry, thereby reducing the attractiveness of this industry.

### Bargaining Power of Buyers

An industry's customers constantly look for reduced prices, improved product quality, and added services and thus can affect competition within an industry. Buyers play individual suppliers against one another in their efforts to obtain these and other concessions. This is certainly the case with some large retailers such as Walmart and Carrefour in their dealings with many of their suppliers.

The extent to which buyers succeed in their bargaining efforts depends on several factors, including these:

- *The extent of buyer concentration,* as when a few large buyers that account for a large portion of industry sales can gain concessions. Automakers' power over suppliers of tires is a good example.

- *Switching costs that reduce the buyer's bargaining power.*

- *The threat of backward integration,* thereby alleviating the need for the supplier.

- *The product's importance to the performance of the buyer's product*—the greater the importance, the lower the buyer's bargaining power.

- *Buyer profitability*—if buyers earn low profits and the product involved is an important part of their costs, then bargaining will be more aggressive.

The greater the power of the high-volume customers served by an industry, the less attractive will be that industry. One attractive dimension of the cellular phone service industry is that its customers have relatively little power to set terms and conditions for cellular phone service. Buyers are numerous and not very concentrated, and their cell phone costs are typically not of great importance or expense, relatively speaking.

### Threat of Substitute Products

Substitutes are alternative product types (not brands) that perform essentially the same functions, as plastic bottles versus aluminum cans, digital photography over silver-halide film, and the faxing or e-mailing of documents versus overnight express delivery. Substitute products put a ceiling on the profitability of an industry by limiting the price that can be charged, especially when supply exceeds demand. Thus, in food-packaging, aluminum cans are substitutes for plastic bottles and conversely, and each constrains the prices that can be charged by the other.

## A Five Forces Analysis of the Cellular Phone Service Industry

A useful way to summarize a five forces industry analysis is to construct a chart like that shown in Exhibit 3.11. There, we summarize one analyst's judgment of the favorability of the five forces for the European cellular phone service industry in the year 2011. This

## Exhibit 3.11

FIVE FORCES ANALYSIS OF THE EUROPEAN CELL PHONE SERVICE INDUSTRY IN 2011

| Five Forces | Score | Rationale |
| --- | --- | --- |
| Rivalry among present competitors | Rivalry is high leading to high customer churn: unfavourable | Products are differentiated through new features and services; customer switching costs are low. |
| Threat of new entrants | Threat of new entrants is low: moderately favorable | While rapid pace of technological change may bring new entrants based on new technologies (e.g., packet switching, satellites), new service providers must purchase a bandwidth license by spending billions. |
| Supplier power | Supplier power is high: moderately unfavorable | Governments in developed markets have raised the price of additional bandwidth through auctions. |
| Buyer power | Buyer power is low: very favorable | Even large customers have little power to set terms and conditions in this industry. |
| Threat of substitutes | Threat of substitutes is high: moderately unfavorable | PDAs and laptops using Wi-Fi networks to access the web could cannibalize sales of 3G wireless network cell phones. |

Overall conclusion: Only two of the five forces are favorable, while three are unfavorable. Thus, the cellular phone service industry, at least in the European market, is not very attractive at this time. In emerging markets, supplier power and threat of substitutes are more favorable, since governments are more welcoming of telecom development, and substitutes are not likely to enter anytime soon. Thus industry attractiveness is regarded as brighter therein.

analysis indicates that, consistent with the preceding discussion, compared to earlier in the industry's history when there were fewer players (thus, less rivalry), no threatening substitutes on the horizon, and a cozier relationship with governments to provide bandwidth, the industry in 2011 was probably less attractive than some industries, for which four or five of the forces might be favorable.

Thus, marketers who must decide whether to enter or continue to invest in this industry must make a judgment as to whether the rapid growth of the *market*—a *favorable **environmental context***—is sufficient to offset the deteriorating attractiveness of the *industry*—the *not-so-favorable **competitive situation***. Given this mixed outlook, strategists would consider other factors, including the degree to which they believe they are likely to be able to establish and sustain competitive advantage. We further develop this theme later in this chapter.

## Challenges in Macro-Level Market and Industry Analysis

**STRATEGIC ISSUE**

*Markets can be measured in various ways—in numbers of qualified potential customers or in terms of value.*

In order to analyze the attractiveness of one's market or industry, one must first identify, of course, exactly which market or industry is to be analyzed. On the market side and recalling that markets consist of customers—whether individual consumers, trade customers like retailers, or business users in B2B markets—the challenge often lies in sizing the relevant market. Markets can be measured in various ways—in numbers of qualified potential customers (those that are potentially willing and able to buy), in units consumed of a class of goods or services, in terms of value (their aggregate spending on a class of goods or services) and so on. It is informative to measure market size and growth rates in customer numbers and in unit and value terms.

On the industry side, there's the question of how narrowly or broadly to define one's industry. Are Ball, a maker of aluminum beverage cans, and AMCOR, a maker of plastic beverage bottles, in the same industry (the packaging industry) or different industries (aluminum containers and plastic packaging)? Are Ford and Mack truck in the same industry (automotive) or different industries (autos and trucks)? There are no simple answers here, but a good way to identify the most suitable definition of the industry you are in is to consider whether the kinds of key suppliers, the processes by which value is added, and the kinds of buyers are the same for your company and other companies whose industry you may consider yourself a part of. If two or all three of these value chain elements are similar, it's probably appropriate to say you are all in the same industry. If two or more of them are different, you probably are in different industries, as is the case for Ball and AMCOR, where many of the customers are the same, but key suppliers (aluminum versus petroleum-based plastics) and value-adding processes (aluminum cans and plastic bottles are made very differently) differ. Thus, a five forces analysis of the aluminum can industry would consider the threat of substitutes from the plastic, glass, and paper packaging industries. For an approach to strategic thinking that avoids the constraints of traditional industry definitions, see Exhibit 3.12.

## Information Sources for Macro-Level Analyses

In the developed economies, there is an endless supply of information about macro trends and industry forces, including the popular and business press, the internet, supplier and customer contacts, and so on. In emerging economies, however, such information is more difficult to find and can, in many cases, be misleading (see Exhibit 3.13). Thus,

---

### Exhibit 3.12    COMPETING IN BLUE OCEANS

Chan Kim and Renée Mauborgne argue that one way out of today's hotly contested industry spaces defined by conventional boundaries is to develop what they call blue oceans, previously unknown market spaces as yet undiscovered by existing competition. Rather than focusing on "beating the competition," they argue, managers should focus more of their strategic efforts on finding markets where there is little competition—blue oceans—and then take steps to exploit and protect these oceans.

Their research found that companies that were effective in creating blue oceans never used the competition as a benchmark. Instead, they made competition irrelevant by creating a huge leap in value for both the company and for the new buyers it served. Henry Ford's Model T automobile created a blue ocean, an automotive industry that barely existed at the time. So, too, did Federal Express in overnight package delivery, Cirque du Soleil in circus (or is it theater?), and CNN in news broadcasting.

A key tenet of all these companies is that they rejected the notion that there must be a trade-off between value and cost, an inherent assumption that's all too frequent in strategic circles. Rejecting the tired strategic logic of red oceans—overcrowded industries where companies seek ways of beating one another—can lead, they found, to rapid, profitable, and often uncontested growth for a decade or more.

*Source:* W. Chan Kim and Renée Mauborgne, "Blue Ocean Strategy," *Harvard Business Review*, October 2004. For more on Blue Ocean Strategy, see *www.blueoceanstrategy.com*.

## Exhibit 3.13    SAFARICOM OUTRUNS THE DATA

In October 2000, Michael Joseph, the newly arrived CEO of Safaricom, was pondering how best to relaunch Safaricom's mobile phone service in Kenya. Safaricom had taken over the formerly government-owned cell phone operation, which had only 15,000 high-priced cell phone lines serving the business and government elite. Joseph wondered if there was enough buying power to enable his company to target the mass market in Kenya. The secondary data were not encouraging, since there were only 10 land-based telephone lines per 1,000 people in Kenya and only 26 televisions per 1,000. GDP per capita was a paltry $360, according to government figures. He gambled that the data were wrong and there was more buying power in Kenya than the figures foretold. Joseph's gamble paid off. Safaricom's launch was a hit from the start, and by 2006, more than 5 million Kenyans had cell phones, nearly one in every six Kenyans.

*Source:* Charles Mayaka, "Safaricom (A)," United States International University, 2005. For more on Safaricom, see *www.safaricom.co.ke.*

gathering relevant data is not difficult, but it does take time and effort. A good place to start is with trade associations and trade magazines, both of which typically track and report on trends relevant to the industries they serve. Most local, state, and federal governments provide demographic data easily accessible at their websites, such as *www.census.gov* in the United States. Government sources and the business press are good places to look for economic trends and data from Eurostat, the statistical office of the European Union (*www.europa.eu.int/comm/eurostat*). Almost all sources of information are now readily available on the Web. Search engines such as Google are a powerful tool in the quest for information. A list of some of the most useful sources of secondary data for macro-level market and industry analyses is provided in Exhibit 3.14.

The key outputs of a competent macro trend analysis for any market should include both quantitative and qualitative data. Quantitative data should provide evidence of the market's size and growth rate, for the overall market as well as for key segments. Qualitative data should include factors that will likely influence these figures in the future, whether favorably or unfavorably.

## Understanding Markets at the Micro Level

A market may be large and growing, but that does not mean customers will buy whatever it is that is proposed to be offered if a particular opportunity is pursued. Most new products, including those targeted at large and growing markets, fail because not enough customers buy them. A clear version of Pepsi-Cola—without the caramel coloring—test-marketed unsuccessfully by Pepsi in the 1990s is but one of thousands of examples that capable marketers have brought to market with little success.

Thus, in assessing market opportunities at the micro level, one looks individually at customers—whether trade customers or end consumers or business users—to understand the attractiveness of the target segment itself. While we devote an entire later chapter to market segmentation and targeting (Chapter 7), it's worthwhile to take a brief look at the relevant issues for opportunity attractiveness here.

Opportunities are attractive at the micro level on the market side (see Exhibit 3.1) when the market offering meets most or all of the following tests.[25]

- *There's a clearly identified source of customer pain, for some clearly identifiable set of target customers, which the offering resolves.* Thus, customer need is established.

# Exhibit 3.14

## SOME INFORMATION SOURCES FOR MARKET AND INDUSTRY ANALYSIS

| Type of Information | Library Sources | Internet Sources |
|---|---|---|
| To find trade associations and trade magazines | *Gale Directory of Publications; Encyclopedia of Associations; UK Trade Association Forum; European Trade Associations* | www.gale.com<br>www.taforum.org |
| Information on specific companies | *Hoover's Online Business; Ward's Business Directory; Dun and Bradstreet Million Dollar Directory; Moody's Industrial Manual* | www.hoovers.com<br>www.sec.gov/edgarhp.htm<br>www.dnbmdd.com/mddi |
| U.S. demographic and lifestyle data | *Lifestyle Market Analyst* | www.census.gov |
| Demographic data on a specific region or local trade area in the United States | *Sourcebook of County Demographics; Sourcebook of Zip Code Demographics; Survey of Buying Power in Sales and Marketing Management; Claritas,* 1-800-234-5973 (fee) | |
| International demographics and world trade | *Predicasts F&S Index* United States, Europe, and International | www.instat.com<br>www.stat-usa.gov<br>www.cia.gov/cia/publications/<br>factbook/index.html<br>www.i-trade.com ec.europa.eu/<br>eurostat |
| Macro trends | *Statistical Abstract of the United States; Business Periodicals Index* | www.unescap.org/stat/ (Asia)<br>www.stat-usa.gov |
| E-commerce | *Red Herring magazine* | www.thestandard.com<br>www.ecommercetimes.com<br>www.comscore.com<br>www.emarketer.com |
| Proprietary providers of research reports | | www.forrester.com<br>www.gartner.com |
| Market share information | *Market Share Reporter* | www.scarborough.com |
| Average financial statements by industry | *Annual Statement Studies,* Risk Management Association, formerly, Robert Morris and Associates | www.rmahq.org/RMA/Rmauniverse/<br>productsandservices/RMAbookstore/<br>statementstudies/default.htm |

Given the rate of change on the web, some of the preceding internet addresses may change, and some print sources may add websites.

*Source:* Adapted from pp. 27, 63, 124, and 158 of *Find It Fast,* Fourth Edition, by Robert I. Berkman. Updated July 2009.

- *The offering provides customer benefits that other solutions do not.* Thus, customers are likely to buy *your* solution!
- *The target segment is likely to grow.*
- *There are other segments for which the currently targeted segment may provide a springboard for subsequent entry.*

For most companies and most goods or services, meeting the first two of these tests is all about delivering what Patrick Barwise and Seán Meehan call ***generic category benefits***—the basics that customers expect a good marketer to provide in a particular product category.[26] Often, doing so involves effective implementation—something some companies are not very good at—rather than a fancy strategy.

So, can an opportunity in a market that's stagnant or declining at the macro level be an attractive one? The answer is an emphatic yes! Starbucks transformed a boring and stagnant American market for coffee into a growth machine. Nike did likewise in athletic shoes. Deliver what the customer wants and needs—that others don't deliver effectively—and promote it successfully, and the world will beat a path to your door.

On the flip side, what about me-too products, mere knock-offs of others that are already successful? While there's often room for imitators and followers in fast-growing markets, as we'll see in Chapter 15, even they typically need to do something different—better, faster, or cheaper—in order to win a meaningful share of the market.

## Understanding Industries at the Micro Level

We've seen that, on the market side (see Exhibit 3.1), a particular opportunity may look attractive at the macro level but quite unattractive at the micro level—or vice versa, of course. Does the same pattern hold on the industry side of the picture?

On the industry side, the key micro-level question to ask is whether whatever competitive advantage there might be as a result of the benefits offered to the target market—the market side, micro-level assessment, as we've just seen—can be sustained over a significant period of time. Who wants to enter a market with something new, only to have competitors quickly follow and steal your thunder? Entering a market without a source of sustainable competitive advantage is a trap!

In Chapter 15, we address strategies for new and growing markets. Here, though, let's examine how one should determine whether to get into such a situation in the first place. To do so, we'll look, at the micro level, at the company itself rather than the broader industry of which it is a part, which we examined earlier at the macro level. Opportunities are attractive at the micro level on the industry side when the company itself meets most or all of the following tests.[27]

- *It possesses something proprietary that other companies cannot easily duplicate or imitate.*[28] Patents, at least defensible ones, can provide this, as can a well-known brand.

- *The business has or can develop superior organizational processes, capabilities, or resources that others would find it difficult to imitate or duplicate.* In the 1970s, before the Gap stores became a fashion brand in their own right, they sold only Levi-Strauss merchandise, most of which was also available in department stores. Gap's competitive advantage was that its systems ensured that virtually every item in its huge assortment of Levi's was in stock in every size every day, something other stores simply found too difficult to match in the days prior to bar codes and point-of-sale cash registers. Other stores had piles of Levi's, but often seemed to be out of the customer's size. As Gap's early advertising proclaimed, "Four tons of Levi's, in just your size!"

- *The company's business model is economically viable*—unlike the many dot-com businesses that went bust at the dawn of the millennium!

For an example of a situation in which there appeared to be—but was not—a sustainable competitive advantage, based on proprietary recipes for micro-brewed beer, see Exhibit 3.15.

## Exhibit 3.15   THE CRAFT BEER INDUSTRY LOSES ITS FIZZ

A good example of the "no sustainable advantage" problem is that encountered by American micro-brewers in the late 1990s. In the early 1990s, craft brewing was all the rage in the United States, and beer-loving entrepreneurs everywhere opened craft breweries and brew-pubs where they brewed hoppy ales and porters that consumers loved. Alas, recipes for great-tasting beers may be proprietary, but they are easily imitated, and a plethora of followers entered the fast-growing craft beer industry in pursuit of their share of the fast-growing micro-brew market. When growth in this segment came to a screeching halt in 1997, a shakeout ensued, and many craft brewers went out of business. Their customer benefits—great tasting beer—had been imitated and did not deliver *sustainable* competitive advantage.

*Source:* Carol Brown and John W. Mullins, "Challenges Brewing at Breckenridge Brewery," *Case Research Journal*, Spring 2003.

## The Team Domains: The Key to the Pursuit of Attractive Opportunities

Opportunities are only as good as the people who will pursue them. Thus, even if some combination of market and industry factors renders an opportunity attractive at first blush, there remain some crucial questions:

- *Does the opportunity fit what we want to do?*
- *Do we have the people who can execute on whatever it takes to be successful in this particular industry?*
- *Do we have the right connections?* As the saying goes, "It's not what you know, it's who you know."

These three questions address the remaining three of the seven domains in our opportunity assessment framework.

## Mission, Aspirations, and Risk Propensity

These days, every company has a mission statement, and every entrepreneur has a pretty good idea of what she wants to do—software, business process outsourcing, running a retail shop, or whatever. Similarly, everyone has some idea about what size opportunity is deemed attractive. For some companies, if an opportunity lacks the potential to reach, say, $100 million in sales, it's too small. For some entrepreneurs who wish to run lifestyle businesses, if an opportunity will require more than 20 people to pursue it, it's too big. Finally, everyone and every company has views on how much risk is acceptable. Are we prepared to bet the ranch, mortgage the house, or risk a shortfall in the progression of our ever-increasing quarterly earnings that we deliver to Wall Street?

Notwithstanding the merits of a particular opportunity in market and industry terms, it must also measure up to the expectations of the people who will pursue it, or they'll say, "No, this one's not for us." Most airline caterers probably will not pursue opportunities in fast-food retailing, despite their ability to source meals in a consistent—if not the tastiest—manner. Most large companies will not pursue opportunities to serve very small niche markets. It's not worth their time and attention to do so. Many entrepreneurs—or at least their spouses—are unwilling to mortgage the house. Whatever the tests for a given individual or company, they must be met if an opportunity is to be deemed attractive.

## Ability to Execute on the Industry's Critical Success Factors

In every industry, there's variation in performance. Some firms outperform others in their industry year after year. In most industries, in addition to hard-to-imitate elements that are firm specific, there are also a small number of critical factors that tend to separate the winners from the also-rans. These few factors are that industry's critical success factors, or CSFs for short. As the saying goes in retailing, there are three such factors in that industry: location, location, and location.

How might one's CSFs be identified? There are two key questions to ask:

- *Which few decisions or activities are the ones that, if gotten wrong, will almost always have severely negative effects on company performance?* In retailing, location is such a factor. Good customer service, for example, while important, is not a CSF, since there are many retailers whose customer service is nothing special—or downright nonexistent—but whose performance in financial terms is quite good.

- *Which decisions or activities, done right, will almost always deliver disproportionately positive effects on performance?* Again, in retailing, location qualifies. Certain high-traffic locations can be licenses to print money, no matter how well or poorly the business is run.

Thus, to assess opportunities, one must identify the industry's few CSFs, which generally do not include money, either (see Exhibit 3.16). Then one must ask a simple question: Do we have on our team—or can we attract—the competencies and capabilities necessary to deliver what's called for by our industry's CSFs?[29]

## It's *Who* You Know, Not *What* You Know

The familiar saying holds true in assessing opportunities, as well as in other arenas, but for a different reason. Despite the insights to be gleaned from the seven domains, reality dictates that there will remain considerable uncertainty about just how attractive a particular

**Exhibit 3.16    IS CASH A CRITICAL SUCCESS FACTOR?**

What about money, the reader may ask? Aren't the financial resources needed to pursue the opportunity just as important as the people? Most entrepreneurs and most venture capital investors would argue that the money is actually the easy part. If you have an opportunity to serve an attractive market, in an attractive industry, that's consistent with the kinds of things the people involved want to do, and with a team that can show they've done it before with the same CSFs, finding the money is not very difficult. The same holds true for prying money loose from the corporate coffers in established organizations.

*Source:* John W. Mullins, *The New Business Road Test: What Entrepreneurs and Executives Should Do Before Writing a Business Plan* (London: Prentice Hall/FT, 2011). For more on John Mullins and his books, see *http://faculty.london.edu/jmullins/*.

opportunity really is. Can we really deliver what we promise? Will customers really buy? Will macro trends change course, for better or worse? Will the structural characteristics of the industry change, favorably or otherwise? Will an unanticipated competitor arrive on our doorstep, or will a new market suddenly open up?

Any or all of these things can happen, and the people who are the best connected—up the value chain, to insightful suppliers with a broad view of what's happening in their customer markets; down the value chain, to customers who can tell you about their changing needs; and across the value chain, among fellow players in your own industry who face the same challenges you do—are the ones who will first see the winds of change shifting direction. In turn, they'll be the ones who are best placed to change strategy before others know the winds have changed. Put simply, networks count! Having a well-connected team in place enhances the attractiveness of the opportunity itself because the team is more likely to be able to ride out the inevitable winds of change.

## Putting the Seven Domains to Work

In the words of noted investor Warren Buffett, "When a management with a reputation for brilliance takes on a business with a reputation for bad economics, it's the reputation of the business that remains intact."[30] If you or your company choose unattractive opportunities to pursue, you'll face tough sledding, no matter what you learn from the rest of this book. Thus, it's worth keeping the lessons of this chapter in mind as you learn about the rest of the task of developing compelling marketing strategies in succeeding chapters.

It's also worth noting that the seven domains are not additive. A simple checklist on which you score each domain and sum the scores won't do, for an opportunity's strength on some domains—especially at the micro level—can outweigh weaknesses on others. Starbucks has done quite nicely in what was a boring and stagnant coffee market when it got started.

Finally, it's worth noting that opportunities don't just sit there; they change and may be further developed. Damaging flaws found in the opportunity assessment process are there to be mitigated or remedied by various means.[31] Thus, the seven domains provide a useful and integrative lens through which to examine the fundamental health of a business and the opportunities it has chosen to pursue at any stage in its products' life cycles, a topic to which we devote considerable attention in Chapters 15 and 16, where we explore the various strategies that are best suited to different stages in the development of markets.

To close this chapter, we wrap up with a brief look at a tool for coping with the reality of the changing world around us, and we consider the perils of swimming against the changing tide.

## Anticipating and Responding to Environmental Change

Critical changes in macroenvironmental conditions often call for changes in the firm's strategy. Such changes can be proactive or reactive, or both. To the extent that a firm identifies and effectively deals with key trends before its competitors do, it is more likely to win and retain competitive advantage. In any case, management needs systems to help identify, evaluate, and respond to environmental events that may affect the firm's longer-term profitability and position. One such approach uses an opportunity/threat matrix to better assess the impact and the timing of an event, followed by the development of an appropriate response strategy. This approach is discussed as follows.

## Impact and Timing of Event

In any given period, many environmental events that could have an impact on the firm—either positively or negatively—may be detected. Somehow, management must determine the probability of their occurrence and the degree of impact (on profitability and/or market share) of each event. One relatively simple way to accomplish these tasks is to use a 2 × 2 dimensional *opportunity/threat matrix* such as that shown in Exhibit 3.17. This example contains four potential environmental events that the high-speed access division of a large UK telecommunications company might have identified as worthy of concern in 2011. The probability of each occurring by the year 2016 was rated, as was the impact on the company in terms of profitability or market share. The event likely both to occur by 2016 and to have the greatest impact appears in the upper left-hand box. At the very least, such an event should be examined closely, including estimating with as much precision as possible its impact on profitability and market share.

The opportunity/threat matrix enables the examination of a large number of events in such a way that management can focus on the most important ones. Thus, events such as number 4 in the exhibit with a high probability of occurring and having a high impact should be closely monitored. Those with a low probability of occurrence and low impact, such as number 3 in the exhibit, should probably be dropped, at least for the moment. Events with a low probability/high impact (number 1) should be reexamined less frequently to determine whether the impact rating remains sound.

## Exhibit 3.17

OPPORTUNITY/THREAT MATRIX FOR A TELECOMMUNICATIONS COMPANY IN THE UK IN 2011

| Level of Impact on Company* | Probability of Occurrence (2016) | |
| --- | --- | --- |
| | High | Low |
| High | 4 | 1 |
| Low | 2 | 3 |

1. Wireless communications technology will make networks based on fiber and copper wires redundant.
2. Technology will provide for the storage and accessing of vast quantities of data at affordable costs.
3. Consumers will move most of their TV viewing from televisions to personal computers.
4. Voice-over-Internet Protocol (VoIP) will become the dominant force in the telecommunications industry.

*Profits or market share or both

# Swimming Upstream or Downstream:
# An Important Strategic Choice

Fitness is a social trend. The graying of the world population is a demographic one. Global warming and increased attention to sustainability are trends related to our natural environment. All these trends influence the fortunes of some companies, but not others. As we have seen, the influence of macro trends like these can be pervasive and powerful. In general, life is better swimming downstream, accompanied by favorable trends, than upstream, running counter to such trends.

Like mosquitoes or cooling breezes on a humid summer evening, trends will always be present, whether marketing managers like them or not. The question is what managers can do about them. For some trends, marketers and other managers can do little but react and adapt. In the 1990s, manufacturers of products sold in spray containers were required to find new propellants less harmful to the ozone layer. Governments concerned about global warming mandated this change. For other trends, such as the shift toward or away from casual dress in the workplace, favorable moves can be reinforced through effective marketing. Similarly, sometimes, unfavorable ones can be mitigated. But doing these things requires that important trends be noticed and understood.

The seven domains framework introduced in this chapter sets the market and competitive context—the 4 Cs—for the marketing decisions to be addressed in the remainder of this book. Such decisions cannot be made in a vacuum; for without a deep understanding of the context in which one goes to market, one simply cannot develop effective strategies that take into account the market and competitive realities. Gaining such an understanding requires information, of course. We deal with the challenges in gathering such information through marketing research and its use in forecasting in Chapter 6. But first in Chapters 4 and 5, we examine how to better understand buyer behavior.

**STRATEGIC ISSUE**

*Like mosquitoes or cooling breezes on a humid summer evening, trends will always be present, whether marketing managers like them or not. The question is what managers can do about them.*

# TAKE-AWAYS

1. Macro trends can and will profoundly influence the success of any business. Serving attractive markets, where trends are favorable—swimming with the tide—is likely to bring more success than serving markets where trends are unfavorable.

2. Similarly, competing in structurally attractive industries—those where the five forces are, on balance, favorable—is likely to generate better returns than in less attractive industries.

3. Notwithstanding the first two points above, the degree to which a company's goods or services resolve genuine customer needs of a clearly defined target market and the

degree to which its competitive advantage is sustainable over time are probably even more crucial to long-term success.

4. Understanding market opportunities is about more than understanding customers, competitors, and the environmental context. The capabilities and resources brought by the company itself are also important and are often overlooked.

5. The seven domains are not additive—simply scoring each domain and summing the scores won't do. Strong scores, especially at the micro level or on the team domains, can outweigh the effects of flat or declining markets or structurally unattractive industries.

# ENDNOTES

**1.** Information on the cellular telephone business in the 21st century comes from the following sources: Moon Ihlwan, "Asia Gets Hooked on Wireless," *BusinessWeek*, June 19, 2000, p. 109; Stephen Baker, "The Race to Rule Mobile," *BusinessWeek* International Edition, February 21, 2000; Stephen Baker, "Smart Phones," *BusinessWeek* International Edition, October 18, 1999; "Online Overseas," *New York Times*, June 7, 2000, p. H8; Steve Frank, "Darling to Dog to. . . ," *The Wall Street Journal Sunday*, June 18, 2000; Bea Hunt, "Basking in 3G's Rays," *Financial Times*, February 14, 2005, FTIT Review, p. 1; Andy Reinhardt, "Cell Phones for the People," *BusinessWeek*, November 14, 2005, p. 65; Andrew Parker and Paul Taylor, "Mobile Businesses Send out Differing Signal," *Financial Times*, February 15, 2010, p. 18; Joe Leahy, "A Tough Call," *Financial Times*, May 25, 2010, p. 13; "The Lex Column," *Financial Times*, September 19, 2010, p. 18; "Not Just Talk," *The Economist*, January 29, 2011, pp. 65–66; Christopher Lawton, "Nokia Warns as Margins Take a Big Hit," *The Walt Street Journal* European Edition, June 1, 2011, p. 1; and Hester Plumridge, "Nokia Chief Faces an Uphill Battle," *The Wall Street Journal* European Edition, June 1, 2011, p. 32.

**2.** Amy Yee, "Banishing the Negative: How Kodak Is Developing Its Blueprint for a Digital Transformation," *Financial Times*, January 26, 2006, p. 15.

**3.** Dan Roberts, "The Ageing Business: Companies and Marketers Wrestle with Adapting Their Products to Older Consumers' Demands," *Financial Times*, January 20, 2004, p. 19.

**4.** Francesco Guerrera and Jonathan Birchall, "Boom Time," *Financial Times*, December 6, 2007, p. 13.

**5.** Norma Cohen and Clive Cookson, "The Planet Is Ever Greyer: But as Longevity Rises Faster Than Forecast, the Elderly Are Also Becoming Healthier," *Financial Times*, January 19, 2004, p. 15.

**6.** Martin Wolf, "People, Plagues, and Prosperity: Five Trends that Promise to Transform the World's Population within 50 Years," *Financial Times*, February 27, 2003, p. 17.

**7.** "AIDS Epidemic Update," December 2005, p. 17, UNAIDS, *www.unaids. org*.

**8.** John Parker, "Burgeoning Bourgeoisie," *The Economist*, February 14, 2009, p. 5.

**9.** ibid.

**10.** *The Economist*, "A Club in Need of a New Vision," April 29, 2004.

**11.** Michelle Conlin, "Unmarried America," *BusinessWeek* European Edition, October 20, 2003, p. 106.

**12.** Sara Silver, "Kraft Blends Ethics with Coffee Beans," *Financial Times*, October 7, 2003, p.106.

**13.** Arthur Agatson, *The South Beach Diet* (Rodale, 2003).

**14.** Liz Neporent and Michele Bibbey, "The Ten Tricks of Buying Home Exercise Equipment," *www.ivillage.co.uk/dietandfitness/getfit/cardio/articles/0,,254_157720.00.html*.

**15.** Steve Rothwell, "Ryanair's First-Ever Capacity Reduction Marks End of Discount-Airline Boom," Bloomberg, at *http://www.bloomberg.com/news/2011-05-23/23/ryanair-expects-similar-profit-this-year-on-fuel-slower-traffic-growth-html*.

**16.** Stanley Reed, "The Euro: How Damaging a Hit?" *BusinessWeek* European Edition, September 29, 2003, p. 63.

**17.** Kevin Allison and Richard Waters, "Demand for iPods Puts Apple Shares at New High," *Financial Times*, January 11, 2006, p. 21.

**18.** David Welch, "GM: Live Green or Die," *BusinessWeek* European Edition, May 26, 2008, pp. 36–41.

**19.** Nicholas Varchaver, "Chemical Reaction," *Fortune* European Edition, April 2, 2007, pp. 41–44.

**20.** Michael Porter, *Competitive Strategy* (New York: Free Press, 1980).

**21.** For an example of such a checklist, see John W. Mullins, *The New Business Road Test*, chap. 13 (London: Prentice Hall/FT, 2010).

**22.** Wendy Zellner, Andrea Rothman, and Eric Schine, "The Airlines Mess," *BusinessWeek*, July 6, 1992.

**23.** "Airlines and the Canine Features of Unprofitable Industries," *Financial Times*, September 27, 2005, p. 23.

**24.** Jin K. Han, Namwoon Kim, and Hong-Bumm Kim, "Entry Barriers: A Dull-, One-, or Two-Edged Sword for Incumbents? Unraveling the Paradox from a Contingency Perspective," *Journal of Marketing* 65 (January 2001), pp. 1–14.

**25.** For more detail on micro-market attractiveness, see Mullins, *The New Business Road Test*, chap. 2.

**26.** Patrick Barwise and Seán Meehan, *Simply Better: Winning and Keeping Customers by Delivering What Matters Most* (Cambridge, MA: Harvard Business School Press, 2004).

**27.** Mullins, *The New Business Road Test*, chap. 5.

**28.** Ibid.

**29.** For the classic articles on competencies and capabilities, see George S. Day, "The Capabilities of Market-Driven Organizations," *Journal of Marketing* 58 (October 1994), pp. 37–52; and C. K. Prahalad and Gary Hamel, "The Core Competence of the Corporation," *Harvard Business Review* 68 (May–June 1990), pp. 79–91.

**30.** Quoted in Herb Greenburg, "How to Avoid the Value Trap," *Fortune*, June 10, 2002, p. 194.

**31.** For more on how crucial flaws may be mitigated or resolved, see Mullins, *The New Business Road Test*, chap. 9.

# CHAPTER FOUR

# Understanding Consumer Buying Behavior

## Cruise Ships—Not Just for Grandma and Grandpa Anymore[1]

NOT TOO LONG AGO, a sea cruise was widely viewed as a rather dull and sedate vacation alternative, appealing mostly to well-to-do elderly people who enjoyed playing shuffleboard, sipping tea, and dressing for dinner. But that perception began to change in the 1980s. As a result, the global cruise industry experienced rapid growth in both revenues and profits during the 1990s and into the new century. Due to concerns about terrorism, rising energy costs, increased pollution of harbors, and the like, industry growth slowed a bit after 2002. And the global financial crisis also took a bite out of sales. Nevertheless, Carnival Corporation, the industry's market share leader and parent of several lines—including Carnival, Princess, Holland America, and Seabourn in North America, P&O Cruises, Cunard and Ocean Village in the United Kingdom, AIDA Cruises in Germany, and Costa Cruises in Asia and South America—served over 8.5 million passengers in 2009. The firm made $1.8 billion in net income on revenues of 13.1 billion. Nearly half the firm's revenues, and over one-third of its passengers, came from outside the United States.

## Savvy Marketing Helped Fuel Industry Growth

A number of factors helped change consumer perceptions and build demand for cruise vacations. Perhaps most important, the major players in the industry strengthened all aspects of their marketing programs to appeal to a wider variety of customer segments.

First, firms invested heavily in improving their physical facilities. Many new ships were built that were not only much bigger and steadier than their predecessors, but also incorporated amenities such as casinos, shopping arcades, theaters, health spas, internet access in every stateroom, suites with private balconies, and even a skating rink and a water park. Shorter and cheaper cruises were added to attract more price-sensitive customers. Ships were located in more ports around the world—from Southampton in the United Kingdom to Hong Kong, Majorca, Australia, Dubai, and even Galveston, Texas—to draw passengers from a wider geographic area. And major sums were devoted to advertising and promotion programs.

Perhaps the biggest factor underlying the industry's growth, however, was the ability of the major competitors to understand and cater to the differing needs, desires, and purchase criteria of different customer segments. Ship designs, onboard amenities and activities, food and beverage options, itineraries, and prices were all tailored to specific demographic, social, and lifestyle groups. For instance, P&O Princess launched "Ocean Village" cruises in the Mediterranean. They are targeted at younger couples who enjoy sports and educational activities and offer passengers the chance to participate in such things as scuba diving,

## Exhibit 4.1

TYPES OF CRUISES, BENEFITS OFFERED, AND MAJOR COMPETITORS

| TYPE OF CRUISE | RATES | AMENITIES/BENEFITS | MAJOR COMPETITORS |
|---|---|---|---|
| Contemporary/ Resort class | $100 to $300 (per person per day) | Value-oriented cruises of 3–7 days; casual environment; newer or recently renovated ships; lots of open deck and pool space; organized activities, sports, etc.; "Vegas"- or "Broadway"-style productions, dancing, etc.; both sit-down and buffet-style meals. | Carnival, Royal Caribbean, Norwegian Cruise Line |
| Premium | $200 to $600 | Semiformal, premium-quality cruises of 7 days or longer; ships designed to offer more space per passenger; more attentive service; theme lounges, theaters, cigar bars, etc.; supervised activities, games, fitness facilities; premium food and beverage offerings. | Holland America, P&O Princess |
| Luxury | $600 to $1,500 | Cruises emphasize greater choice of food, beverage, and entertainment options in a more formal atmosphere; more spacious and luxurious accommodations; more exotic itineraries. | Cunard Line; Crystal Cruises |
| Exclusive | $1,000 plus | Exclusive, yacht-like environment with only 100–200 passengers; high staff-to-customer ratio allows highly individualized service | Seabourn Cruise Line, Silversea Cruises, Swan Hellenic |

*Sources:* "Cruises by Cruise Line," The Cruise Company, *www.cruisecompany.net*; and *www.carnival.com*.

gourmet cooking, and wine tasting. Some lines offer "romantic" cruises targeted at honeymooners; others appeal to the singles crowd; and many lines, including the ships launched by Disney focus on families with young children by offering multiroom suites and lots of supervised activities for various age groups. Even within the traditional target audience for cruises—relatively upscale retirees in their 50s and 60s—lines offer cruises with unique benefits to appeal to subsegments with different interests and preferences. At one extreme, for instance, Hapag-Lloyd Cruises offers a 165-day excursion that leaves Dubai in November, visits islands in the Indian ocean and South Pacific, South Africa, Patagonia, Australia and Asia, and returns to Dubai in April. Rates start at $86,570. Some categories

of cruises, the benefits they promise, and major lines that offer them, are summarized in Exhibit 4.1.

# Future Challenges

Political unrest around the world poses a threat for some popular destinations, and rising energy costs are likely to squeeze industry profits. And since cruises are discretionary purchases, economic conditions can have a major impact on revenues. For instance, Carnival's net income declined by $600 million from 2007 through 2009 due largely to the global financial crisis.

One of the industry's biggest potential challenges, though, is over-capacity. You might think that the extensive capital investment required to launch a new cruise ship would raise substantial barriers to entry and restrain industry competitiveness, but the substantial growth and profits cruise lines have enjoyed spurred them to build more and bigger ships at an increasing rate. Carnival alone is scheduled to bring 10 new ships into service by 2014, raising its total to 108. And two of those ships will be behemoths capable of accommodating more than 6,300 passengers each.

The primary challenge, then, is for firms in the industry to increase the growth in passenger bookings to fill the growing capacity and recoup the huge investment in new ships. One way to do this is to develop long-term relationships with past customers in the hopes of generating more repeat business. Carnival, for instance, offers substantial discounts to past customers. Given that the vast majority of vacationers around the world have never gone on a cruise, however, the greatest potential for growth involves converting nonusers into new customers. As Micky Arison—Carnival's CEO—points out, "In Germany they sell 80 million packaged holidays a year, but only 250,000 of them are cruises." But attracting new customers will require an even better understanding of what those people want from a vacation and how they make their leisure purchase decisions.

## Marketing Challenges Addressed in Chapter 4

The ability of the global cruise industry to generate substantial new and profitable growth in a market that had been stagnant for years illustrates why examining the needs, desires, and purchasing behavior of existing and potential customers is a critical step in analyzing market opportunities. Consumers buy goods and services as means to an end, as potential solutions to their unsatisfied needs and wants. And they select particular brands or deal with a specific supplier (Carnival Cruise Line) because they perceive them to offer desirable benefits (an interesting itinerary, great food, attentive service, romantic atmosphere, programs for the kids, etc.) and superior value.

Consumer decision making is essentially a problem-solving process. Most customers, whether individual consumers or organizational buyers, go through similar mental processes in deciding which products and brands to buy. Despite this similarity, different customers often end up buying different things. Some vacationers take two-week luxury cruises, some take four-day "contemporary" cruises, while many others go to Disney World or visit Paris instead. These differences reflect variations in consumers' *personal characteristics*—their needs, benefits sought, attitudes, values, past experiences, and lifestyles—and their *social influences*—their social class, reference groups, and family situations.

The more marketers know about the factors affecting their customers' buying behavior, the greater their ability to design attractive product or service offerings, to define and target meaningful market segments, and to develop marketing programs to fit the concerns and desires of those segments. This chapter provides a framework to help organize an analysis of the mental processes individual consumers go through when making purchase decisions and the individual and environmental factors affecting those decisions.

Not all purchase decisions are equally important or psychologically involved. The decision to spend several thousand dollars on a cruise is a bigger deal for most people than the decision to add bananas to their shopping cart. The first question we explore, then, is whether consumers' mental processes are different when they purchase high-involvement goods or services than when they buy more mundane, low-involvement products. If so, what are the implications of those decision-making differences for the marketing manager or entrepreneur charged with developing the strategic marketing plan for a particular product or service?

Regardless of their involvement with a particular purchase decision, different people often choose different products or brands. This fact raises two important questions that we'll explore later in the chapter. How do a person's psychological processes and traits—such as perception, memory, attitudes, personality, and lifestyle—affect his or her buying behavior? And what impact do social influences—like culture, social class, reference groups, and the family—have on purchase decisions?

## The Psychological Importance of the Purchase Affects the Decision-Making Process

From an individual consumer's point of view, some purchase decisions are more important, and therefore more psychologically involving, than others. *High-involvement* purchases involve goods or services that are psychologically important to the buyer because they address social or ego needs and therefore carry social and psychological risks (e.g., the risk of looking foolish to one's family or friends). They may also involve a lot of money and therefore financial risk. Because a consumer's level of involvement with a particular purchase depends on the needs to be satisfied and the resources available, however, a high-involvement product for one buyer may be a low-involvement product for another.

The decision processes involved in purchasing high- and low-involvement products and services are quite different. As Exhibit 4.2 indicates, the decision process pursued by a given consumer can be classified into one of four categories depending on whether (1) the consumer has a high or low level of product involvement, and (2) he or she engages in an extensive search for information and evaluation of alternative brands or makes the decision routinely.[2]

**STRATEGIC ISSUE**

*The decision processes involved in purchasing high- and low-involvement products and services are quite different.*

## How Do Consumers Make High-Involvement Purchase Decisions?

When purchasing high-involvement products or services, consumers go through a problem-solving process involving five mental steps: (1) problem identification, (2) information search, (3) evaluation of alternatives, (4) purchase, and (5) postpurchase evaluation. These five steps are diagrammed in Exhibit 4.3 and discussed in the context of buying a

## Exhibit 4.2

TYPES OF CONSUMER DECISION MAKING

| EXTENT OF ANALYSIS | EXTENT OF INVOLVEMENT | |
| --- | --- | --- |
| | HIGH | LOW |
| Extended (information search; consideration of brand alternatives) | Complex decision making (cars, homes, vacations) | Limited decision making, including variety seeking and impulse purchasing (adult cereals and snack foods) |
| Habit/routine (little or no information search; focus on one brand) | Brand loyalty (athletic shoes, cologne, deodorant) | Inertia (frozen vegetables, paper towels) |

## Exhibit 4.3

STEPS IN THE HIGH-INVOLVEMENT, COMPLEX DECISION-MAKING PROCESS

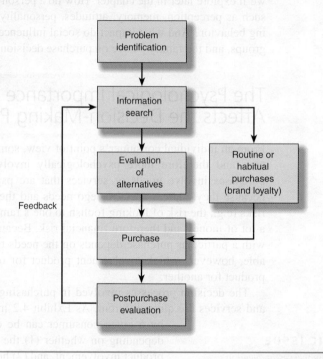

Caribbean cruise by a hypothetical person—Paul MacDonald, who is 33 years old and single.

**Problem Identification**　Consumers' purchase-decision processes are triggered by unsatisfied needs or wants. Individuals perceive differences between ideal and actual states on some physical or sociopsychological dimension. This motivates them to seek products or services to help bring their current state more into balance with the ideal.

Given that most of us have limited time and financial resources, it is impossible for us to satisfy all our needs at once. Instead, we tend to focus on those that are strongest. The size of the gap between our current and our desired state largely determines the strength of a particular need. A need can become stronger and be brought to our attention by a deterioration of our actual state or an upward revision of our ideal state.

A change in a consumer's actual state can occur for several reasons:

- For physical needs, a natural deterioration of the actual state occurs all the time. A person's body burns energy and nutrients. Thus, periodically we get hungry and tired and are motivated to find something to eat and some place to go to sleep.
- A person's actual state may change as the result of the depletion of the current solution to a need. Our hypothetical consumer might be motivated to buy a cruise package because the condo in Florida he usually rents for his winter vacation is not available this year.
- In some cases consumers can anticipate a decline in their actual state. If Paul MacDonald knew that the condo owner was trying to find someone to lease the condo for the entire season, he would likely investigate alternatives for his winter vacation.

Similarly, a change in a consumer's desired state may occur for several reasons:

- The desired state may be revised upward because of new information. Thus, MacDonald may have seen an ad showing how much fun a person can have on a cruise or received such information from a friend.
- As one need is satisfied, the desired state on other need dimensions increases and becomes more demanding.

**Information Search**   Having recognized that a problem exists and might be satisfied by the purchase and consumption of a product or service, the consumer's next step is to refer to information gained from past experience and stored in memory for possible later use. To continue with our example, MacDonald's knowledge about cruises derives primarily from advertising, his mother and father who recently took a cruise, and friends—most of whom are married. Since he has no firsthand knowledge of cruises, he will need to seek additional information, especially regarding accommodations, schedules, and fares. For a listing of the factors that are likely to increase information search, see Exhibit 4.4.

Because services are intangible, difficult to standardize, and their production and consumption inseparable, they are more difficult to evaluate than products. Thus, most services are hard to assess until they are being consumed after purchase (cruises and restaurant meals). Some services are difficult to assess even after they have been consumed (legal services, medical diagnosis, etc.). These assessment difficulties can force consumers to rely on different cues, such as the provider's credentials or reputation, when evaluating services.[3]

**How Much Information Will a Consumer Seek?**   People seek additional information about alternative brands until they perceive that the *costs* of obtaining more information are equal to the additional *value* or *benefit* derived from the information. Information is

## Exhibit 4.4

FACTORS THAT ARE LIKELY TO INCREASE PREPURCHASE SEARCH

**Product factors**

Long interpurchase time (a long-lasting or infrequently used product); frequent changes in product styling; frequent price changes, volume purchasing (large number of units); high price; many alternative brands; much variation in features.

**Situational factors**

*Experience:*
First-time purchase; no past experience because the product is new; unsatisfactory past experience within the product category.

*Social acceptability:*
The purchase is for a gift; the product is socially visible.

*Value-related considerations:*
Purchase is discretionary rather than necessary; all alternatives have both desirable and undesirable consequences; family members disagree on product requirements or evaluation of alternatives; product usage deviates from important reference group; the purchase involves ecological considerations; many sources of conflicting information.

**Personal factors**

*Demographic characteristics of consumer:*
Well-educated; high income; white-collar occupation; under 35 years of age.

*Personality:*
Low dogmatic (open-minded); low-risk perceiver (broad categorizer); other personal factors, such as high product involvement and enjoyment of shopping and search.

valuable to consumers to the extent that it helps make a more satisfying purchase and avoids the negative consequences associated with a poor choice. Thus, consumers are likely to place a higher value on—and seek more—information when the purchase is important. This importance derives from (*a*) the strength of a person's need for the product; (*b*) the person's ego-involvement with the product; and (*c*) the severity of the social and financial consequences of making a poor choice. This is why people tend to seek more information about high-priced, socially visible products that reflect their self-image (cars, home, clothing, and, for some, cruises) than for lower-priced products that other people seldom notice, such as furnace filters or paper towels.

Even when products are very expensive and ego-involving, some consumers are unlikely to conduct an exhaustive search for information before making a decision because of the costs involved. Perhaps the biggest cost for most people is the *opportunity cost* of the time involved in seeking information. They give up the opportunity to use that time for other, more important or interesting activities, such as working or taking trips. For some people, however, the opportunity costs of shopping are low because they enjoy wandering through stores or scanning newspaper ads or websites for bargains. Also, as we'll see later, the internet is reducing the opportunity costs of obtaining at least some kinds of product information.

There are also *psychological costs* involved in searching for information. Collecting information can be a frustrating task, often involving crowded stores, rude salespeople, or slow websites. Also, some consumers become frustrated and confused when they have a lot of complex information to evaluate before making a choice. And paradoxically, the more brands, models, and styles that are available in a product category, the more likely the consumer will experience information overload. In other words, increasing the choices available can make it harder for people to make a choice, and thereby increase the likelihood they will postpone a decision and not buy anything.[4]

Because services, more than products, are associated with greater perceived risk, the individual involved is likely to use more information sources in the attempt to better cope with the risk. This often leads to an extended information-acquisition process, which may include purchase postponement.

**Sources of Information**   Assume that switching from renting a condo to a cruise is important and costly enough for Paul MacDonald to seek additional information before doing so. Which sources can he use? The three broad categories of information sources are personal, commercial, and public. *Personal sources* include family members, friends, and members of the consumer's reference group.

*Commercial sources* refer to various information disseminated by service providers, marketers, and manufacturers and their dealers. They include media advertising, promotional brochures, package and label information, salespersons, and various in-store information, such as price markings and displays. *Public sources* include noncommercial and professional organizations and individuals who provide advice for consumers, such as doctors, lawyers, governmental agencies, travel agencies, consumer-interest groups and web blogs.

Consumers are usually exposed to more information from commercial sources than from personal or public sources. However, many consumers are influenced more by personal sources when deciding which service, product, or brand to buy. Consumers use information from different sources for different purposes and at different stages within the decision process. In general, commercial sources perform an *informing function* for consumers. Personal and public sources serve an *evaluating and legitimizing function.* Thus, MacDonald might rely on advertising and discussions with his travel agent to learn what cruises are available, what the schedules are for each, the kind and size ship used, how much each cruise costs, and the details concerning the various types of entertainment offered. It is highly likely that MacDonald would also seek the opinions of friends in deciding whether to take a cruise and in selecting a particular one. In doing so, he is consistent with the general proposition that consumers choose more personal sources for services than for goods because service consumption is highly personal and must be experienced to be understood.[5]

### How Is the Web Affecting Consumers' Search for Information?

The internet is reducing the opportunity costs of information gathering, thus making it easier for people to make informed decisions. As we saw in Chapter 1, nearly 60 percent of American consumers report searching for product information online. And a recent survey of people shopping for consumer electronics products—which are high-involvement purchases for most people—found that more than 80 percent searched for information online even though a majority went to a conventional retail store to make the purchase.[6] And while the internet may reduce the opportunity costs of information search, most consumers still spend a great deal of time researching their electronics purchases: 15 hours for televisions, 12 for digital cameras, and so on.[7]

Many manufacturers and service providers have established their own sites. Some of these sites not only provide information about product options and characteristics, but also offer tutorials about how to use the product, help lines, and other information geared to helping customers obtain full value from their purchases. For instance, the outdoor gear retailer REI provides hundreds of "how-to" articles and videos, as well as iPhone and Android apps for such things as finding out about snow conditions at ski areas around the world, on its site at *www.rei.com*.

**STRATEGIC ISSUE**

*Many new sites have taken over much of the search for information about alternative offerings in a product category in exchange for a small fee from the consumer or advertising from manufacturers or dealers in the category.*

More important, many new sites have taken over much of the search for information about alternative offerings in a product category in exchange for a small fee from the consumer or advertising from manufacturers or dealers in the category. For example, *www.cruisecompany.net* provides detailed information on cruises organized by type of cruise, itinerary, or cruise line, in exchange for a commission on any cruise a consumer books through the site.

While such sites facilitate the consumer's search for information about high-involvement products and services, they do not solve all the consumer's problems. Most of the information provided by such sites is obtained from commercial and public, rather than personal, sources. Therefore, some consumers may not consider it very useful for evaluating alternative choices, particularly when it comes to choosing intangible services. Also, sensory information such as touch and smell, which can be important for evaluating foods, fashion items, and similar products, cannot be displayed on the web. These shortcomings help explain why some sites, such as Expedia.com, and amazon.com, publish product reviews and evaluations submitted by individual customers.

A more recent development has blurred the distinction between public and personal information sources. Personal web logs—or blogs—provide a way for individuals to share their own experiences and opinions with a large public audience, and for potential customers to obtain personal insights from a vast number of product users.

The potential impact of blogs on buyer behavior is illustrated by the experience of the Kryptonite division of Ingersoll-Rand. On September 12, 2004, someone with the moniker "unaesthetic" posted in a group discussion site for bicycle enthusiasts the observation that the ubiquitous, U-shaped Kryptonite bike lock could be easily picked with a ballpoint pen. Within days, a number of blogs posted a video demonstrating the problem. Kryptonite responded with a bland statement arguing that the locks remained a "deterrent to theft," but more and more bloggers began writing about the issue and their experiences. By September 19, according to one internet measurement firm, about 1.8 million people saw postings about the lock's shortcomings in a single day. Finally, on September 22, Kryptonite was forced to announce it would exchange a new, redesigned product for any affected lock for free, a move that was estimated to cost the firm 100,000 new locks and more than $10 million (about 40 percent of the division's annual revenue).[8]

The impact of blogs on buyer behavior and firms' marketing programs is growing rapidly since an estimated 23,000 new web logs are started around the world every day. And other disgruntled consumers are posting videos to YouTube and similar sites illustrating their problems and frustrations with products or service providers. For instance, more than 340,000 people have watched Michael Whitford smash his nonfunctioning Apple Macbook with a sledgehammer. It is important to note, though, that even very dissatisfied customers can be salvaged if the company takes quick and positive action. After Apple replaced his laptop, for example, Mr. Whitford wrote on his blog "I'm very happy now. Apple has regained my loyalty."[9]

Consequently, one authority advises that "there should be somebody at every company whose job is to put into Google and blog search engines the name of the company [or one of its brands], followed by the word 'sucks,' just to see what customers are saying."[10] Of course, firms might also try to take advantage of the growing influence of blogs by creating one of their own, but this can raise some ethical issues, as discussed in Ethical Perspective 4.1.

### Evaluation of Alternatives[11]

Consumers find it difficult to make overall comparisons of many alternative brands because each brand might be better in some ways but worse in others. Instead, consumers simplify their evaluation in several ways. First, they seldom consider all possible brands; rather, they focus on their *evoked set*—a limited number they are familiar with that are likely to satisfy their needs.

Second, consumers evaluate each of the brands in the evoked set on a limited number of *product dimensions or attributes*. They also judge the *relative importance* of these

---

### ETHICAL PERSPECTIVE 4.1
#### Company Blogs—Honesty Is the Best Policy

Given the growing popularity and influence of consumer blogs in many industries, firms are trying to get in on the act by sponsoring company blogs or encouraging employees to start their own. Most companies that want to blog try to walk a fine line: telling employee bloggers to be honest but also encouraging evangelism for the firm's products or services. Unvarnished corporate propaganda almost always drives readers away, but honest people with real opinions keep them coming back.

One ethical no-no that can have severe economic consequences is trying to hide the identity of the company behind the blog. For instance, Mazda—hoping to reach young potential car buyers—crafted a blog supposedly run by a 22-year-old hipster named Kid Halloween. He posted links to three videos he said a friend had recorded off-public-access TV. One showed a Mazda 3 attempting to break dance, and another had it driving off a ramp like a skateboard. Inevitably, the cars were totaled. Other bloggers quickly sensed a phony in their midst—the expensive videos were a tip-off—and began criticizing Mazda on a number of widely read blogs addressed to auto enthusiasts. Consequently, the firm was forced to pull the site after only three days. The lesson, according to Steve Hayden, who helps create blogs for clients of advertising giant Ogilvy & Mather, is that "if you fudge or lie on a blog you are biting the karmic weenie. The negative reaction will be so great that, whatever your intention was, it will be overwhelmed. . . . You're fighting with very powerful forces because it's real people's opinions."

*Source:* David Kirkpatrick and Daniel Roth, "Why There's No Escaping the Blog," *Fortune*, January 10, 2005, pp. 44–50.

attributes, or the minimum acceptable performance of each. The set of attributes used by a particular consumer and the relative importance of each represent the consumer's *choice criteria.* In the case of our cruise example, the dates of the cruise, the ports of call, the entertainment offered, and the costs are examples of MacDonald's choice criteria for selecting a specific cruise.

Third, consumers combine evaluations of each brand across attributes, taking into account the relative importance of those attributes. This multiattribute assessment of a brand results in an overall *attitude* toward that brand. The brand toward which consumers have the most favorable attitude is the one they are most likely to buy.

**Product Attributes and Their Relative Importance**  Consumers use many dimensions or attributes when evaluating alternative products and services. Thus, in addition to the above service attributes, MacDonald might also use the newness and size of ship, types of food served, availability of an exercise room, and kinds of gambling as additional ways of comparing his options. Usually, however, consumers base their evaluations on half a dozen dimensions or less. Exhibit 4.5 contains a general list of product attributes consumers might use to evaluate alternatives.

Different consumers may use different sets of attributes to evaluate brands within the same product category. But even when two people use the same set of attributes, they may arrive at different decisions because they attach varying degrees of importance to the attributes. Paul MacDonald is primarily interested in entertainment, demographics of those taking the cruise, and cost, whereas another traveler might attach greater importance to gambling, ports of call, and food.

A consumer's personal characteristics and social influences—needs, values, personality, social class, and reference groups, among other things—help determine which attributes are considered and their relative importance. Environmental factors and the usage situation can also affect the perceived importance of various product benefits. For instance, some people buy more prestigious and expensive brands of beer or wine for their party guests than for their own everyday consumption.

**Forming Attitudes toward Alternative Brands**  Even if two consumers use the same attributes and attach the same relative importance to them when evaluating product offerings, they may not necessarily prefer the same brand. They might rate the various brands differently on specific attributes. Differences in brand perceptions are based on past experience, the information collected, and how that information is perceived and processed. And as we shall see later, technology is making it increasingly possible for consumers to interact with manufacturers and suppliers during the production process so that product and service offerings can be customized to meet a customer's preferences on

# Exhibit 4.5

| SELECTED ATTRIBUTES CONSUMERS USE TO EVALUATE ALTERNATIVE PRODUCTS OR SERVICES | |
| --- | --- |
| Category | Specific attributes |
| Cost attributes | Purchase price, operating costs, repair costs, cost of extras or options, cost of installation, trade-in allowance, likely resale value. |
| Performance attributes | Durability, quality of materials, construction, dependability, functional performance (acceleration, nutrition, taste), efficiency, safety. |
| Social attributes | Reputation of brand, brand personality, status image, popularity with friends, popularity with family members, design, style, fashion. |
| Availability attributes | Carried by local stores, credit terms, quality of service available from local dealer, delivery time. |

important attributes.[12] Consequently, brand attitudes may also depend on which manufacturer can be most flexible in customizing its product.

**Purchase**   Even after a consumer has collected information about alternative brands, evaluated them, and decided which is the most desirable, the decision process still is not complete. The consumer must now decide where to buy the product. Choosing a source from which to buy the product involves essentially the same mental processes as does a product-purchase decision. The source is usually a retail store but may also be a mail-order catalog such as L. L. Bean or a website like RedEnvelope.com. Consumers obtain information about alternative sources from personal experience, advertising, comments of friends, and the like. Then they use this information to evaluate sources on such attributes as lines of merchandise carried, services rendered, price, convenience, personnel, and physical characteristics. Consumers usually select the source they perceive to be best on those attributes most important to them. If their experiences with a source are positive over time, they may develop patronage loyalty and routinely shop that source—similar to the way consumers develop brand loyalties.

Consumers shopping in a retail store intent on purchasing one brand sometimes end up buying something different. MacDonald, for example, could be switched from one cruise to another by the travel agent. This happens because the consumer's ultimate purchase can be influenced by such factors as out-of-stocks (no outside cabins on a particular cruise), a special display, or a message from a salesperson ("I can get you a better deal on a similar cruise if you can go two weeks later").

**Postpurchase Evaluation**   Whether a particular consumer feels adequately rewarded following a purchase depends on two things: (1) the person's *aspiration or expectation level*—how well the product was expected to perform (delivery of a quality pizza while it is hot)—and (2) the consumer's evaluation of how well the product actually did perform (the pizza arrived cold).

Consumers' expectations about a product's performance are influenced by several factors. These include the strength and importance of each person's need and the information collected during the decision-making process. In the case of MacDonald, a persuasive ad or an enthusiastic endorsement of a given cruise by a friend who is a frequent cruise-goer may have caused him to expect more from his cruise than he would have otherwise. He may, however, attribute part of any dissatisfaction to his own actions—an unwillingness to participate in some of the entertainment. The fact that consumers are part of the service production process makes self-blame a real possibility.[13] Nevertheless, even with services there is a danger for marketers in using exaggerated claims in product advertising. Such claims can produce inflated expectations the product cannot live up to—resulting in dissatisfied customers.

It is important to note that, as the diagram in Exhibit 4.3 indicates, the consumer's evaluation of a purchase feeds back into memory where the information can be recalled for a similar purchase decision. Stored information about one or more negative past experiences with a brand or supplier will reduce the odds that the consumer will make the same purchase again. Consistent positive experiences can ultimately lead to *brand loyalty*—the routine repurchase of the same brand with little consideration of any alternatives.

Some experts argue that consumers more often develop loyalty to service providers than to physical products because of the difficulty of evaluating alternatives before actually experiencing the service. Also, repeated patronage can bring additional benefits, such as discounts, or more customized service as the provider gains more insights into the customer's preferences.[14] This helps explain why about 25 percent of all cruise passengers are repeat customers.

## Low-Involvement Purchase Decisions

Because low-involvement products are not very important to consumers, the search for information to evaluate alternative brands is likely to be minimal. As a result, decisions to buy products such as cookies or cereals often are made within the store, either *impulsively* on the basis of brand familiarity, or as a result of comparisons of the brands on the shelf. The consumers' involvement and their risks associated with making poor decisions are low for such products. Therefore, consumers are less likely to stay with the same brand over time. They have little to lose by switching brands in a search for variety. Even so, many consumers develop loyalty to a given brand, as in the continued popularity of such low-involvement products as Wrigley Doublemint chewing gum and Gold Medal flour, which have been around for years.

Most purchase decisions are low in consumer involvement—the consumer thinks the product or service is insufficiently important to identify with it. Thus, the consumer does not engage in an extensive search for information for such a purchase. Information involving such products is received passively as in, for example, seeing an ad for Green Giant frozen vegetables, which is neither interpreted nor evaluated, but simply noticed and filed away in memory.

Later, the consumer identifies a need to buy some frozen vegetables. On the next trip to the supermarket, the consumer sees the Green Giant brand in the frozen-foods section and buys several packages. The familiarity generated by exposure to earlier advertising (and/or word-of-mouth information) was sufficient to stimulate the purchase of Green Giant though the consumer does not have a strong, positive brand association.

After buying and using the product, the consumer may decide Green Giant vegetables are either good or bad. This attitude will be likely to affect future purchases of frozen vegetables. However, such brand evaluations occur only *after* an initial purchase has been made. This is the opposite of complex decision making.

**Inertia**   As Exhibit 4.2 indicated, there are two low-involvement buying decisions. When there are few differences between brands and little risk associated with making a poor choice, consumers either buy brands at random or buy the same brand repetitively to avoid making a choice. Marketers must be careful not to confuse such repeat *inertial-purchasing* with brand loyalty because it is relatively easy for competitors to entice such customers to switch brands by offering cents-off coupons, special promotions, or in-store displays. Highly brand-loyal customers, on the other hand, resist such efforts on account of their strong brand preference.

**Impulse Purchasing and Variety Seeking**   The second low-involvement purchase process is *impulse buying,* when consumers impulsively decide to buy a different brand from their customary choice or some new variety of a product. The new brand is probably one they are familiar with through passive exposure to advertising or other information, however. Their motivation for switching usually is not dissatisfaction but a desire for change and variety.

## Understanding the Target Consumer's Level of Involvement Enables Better Marketing Decisions

The preceding discussion clearly indicates that consumers employ different decision-making processes and may be influenced by different psychological, social, and situational factors, depending on their level of involvement with the product or service they are buying. These differences between high- and low-involvement consumer behavior are summarized in Exhibit 4.6.

Such behavioral differences have a major implication for marketers. A given marketing strategy, or decisions concerning any of the 4 Ps in a marketing plan, will not be equally effective for both high- and low-involvement products. Even though consumers may have differing degrees of psychological involvement with a given product category, the marketer needs to determine whether the majority of potential customers in his or her target segment are likely to be highly involved with the purchase decision or not. The various elements of the strategic marketing plan can then be tailored to the overall level of involvement of people in the target market. Exhibit 4.7 summarizes some major differences in marketing actions appropriate for high- versus low-involvement product or service offerings. These differences are briefly discussed in the following sections.

**STRATEGIC ISSUE**

*A given marketing strategy, or decisions concerning any of the 4 Ps in a marketing plan, will not be equally effective for both high- and low-involvement products.*

**Product Design and Positioning Decisions**   Consumers evaluate both high- and low-involvement products on criteria that reflect the *benefits* they seek. Both types of products and services must offer at least one compelling and valued benefit to continue to win acceptance in the market. Because consumers tend to evaluate high-involvement products and services *before* purchasing, however, it is particularly important that such offerings be designed to provide at least some benefits that are demonstrably superior to those offered by major competitors, and that marketing communications are effective in making potential customers aware of those benefits.

For low-involvement goods and services, on the other hand, much brand evaluation occurs *after* the purchase is made. Consumers tend to be most positive about—and more likely to repurchase—brands that don't disappoint them or cause unexpected problems. Consequently, firms that market low-involvement products or services need to pay

## Exhibit 4.6

HIGH-INVOLVEMENT VERSUS LOW-INVOLVEMENT CONSUMER BEHAVIOR

| High-involvement consumer behavior | Low-involvement consumer behavior |
| --- | --- |
| • Consumers are information processors. | • Consumers learn information at random. |
| • Consumers are information seekers. | • Consumers are information gatherers. |
| • Consumers represent an active audience for advertising. | • Consumers represent a passive audience for advertising. |
| • Consumers evaluate brands before buying. | • Consumers buy first. If they do evaluate brands, it is done after the purchase. |
| • Consumers seek to maximize expected satisfaction. They compare brands to see which provides the most benefits related to their needs and buy based on a multiattribute comparison of brands. | • Consumers seek an acceptable level of satisfaction. They buy the brand least likely to give them problems and buy based on a few attributes. Familiarity is the key. |
| • Personality and lifestyle characteristics are related to consumer behavior because the product is closely tied to the person's self-identity and belief system. | • Personality and lifestyle are not related to consumer behavior because the product is not closely tied to the person's self-identity and beliefs. |
| • Reference groups influence consumer behavior because of the importance of the product to group norms and values. | • Reference groups exert little influence on consumer behavior because products are not strongly related to their norms and values. |

*Source:* Adapted from *Consumer Behavior and Marketing Action*, 5th edition by ASSAEL, 1995.

## Exhibit 4.7

MARKETING DECISIONS FOR HIGH-INVOLVEMENT VERSUS LOW-INVOLVEMENT PRODUCTS OR SERVICES

| Marketing mix element | Marketing decisions where the consumer exhibits high involvement | Marketing decisions where the consumer exhibits low involvement |
| --- | --- | --- |
| Product decisions | For long-term success, one or more compelling product benefits are necessary, regardless of the level of consumer involvement. | For long-term success, one or more compelling product benefits are necessary, regardless of the level of consumer involvement. |
| Pricing decisions | Price, unless substantially lower, is likely to be of secondary importance to performance criteria. High price may suggest high quality or status, to the seller's benefit. Demonstrable consumer benefits are more likely than price to drive consumer choice. | Price offers can be effective in gaining trial. A sustained low price, compared to competitors (such as for private-label goods in supermarkets), may provide sufficient inertia for repeat purchase. |
| Promotional decisions | Consumers are interested in the information that sellers provide. Promotional vehicles that communicate in greater detail (e.g., print advertising, internet, infomercials, personal selling) are likely to be effective. | Consumers *are not* interested in the information that sellers provide. Large advertising budgets and a clear focus on a single demonstrable consumer benefit are probably necessary to get the message across. |
| Distribution decisions | Consumers will be relatively *less* concerned with convenience in purchasing. Relatively less extensive distribution is necessary. | Consumers will be relatively *more* concerned with convenience in purchasing. Relatively more extensive distribution is necessary. |

particular attention to basic use-related attributes, such as consistent product quality, reliability, convenient packaging, and user-friendliness.

### Pricing Decisions

Highly involved consumers generally buy the brand they believe will deliver the greatest value. They are willing to pay a higher price for a brand if they believe it will deliver enough superior benefits relative to cheaper competitors to justify the difference. They may even use high price as an indicator of a brand's superior quality or prestige, particularly in categories where quality is hard to evaluate objectively before purchase, such as professional services.

Many consumers buy low-involvement products largely or solely on the basis of low price. Therefore, special sales or coupon offers can be effective in gaining trial of such goods and services. If no problems are experienced during consumption, consumers may continue to buy the brand out of inertia, at least until a competitor offers an attractive price promotion.

### Advertising and Promotion Decisions

Highly involved consumers typically seek at least some information about alternative brands, retail outlets, and so on, before making a purchase decision. Therefore, promotional vehicles that communicate in greater detail—such as print advertising, company websites, infomercials, or a salesperson—are more likely to be attended to and be effective in marketing high-involvement goods and services.

On the other hand, because low-involvement customers are usually passive information gatherers, advertising needs to focus on only a few main points and to deliver the message frequently in order to make it easy for consumers to gain familiarity and positive associations with a brand. Television is often the primary medium for low-involvement products because it facilitates passive learning. Distinctive package design is also important for such products since it helps consumers recognize brands they've seen advertised.

**STRATEGIC ISSUE**

*Because low-involvement customers are usually passive information gatherers, advertising needs to focus on only a few main points and to deliver the message frequently.*

**Distribution Decisions**   Extensive retail distribution is particularly important for low-involvement products because most consumers are unwilling to search for, or expend extra effort to obtain, a particular brand. Thus, the larger the proportion of available retail outlets, including websites, vending machines, and the like, a marketer can induce to carry a brand, the larger that brand's market share is likely to be.

Because consumers are more willing to spend some time and effort to acquire their favorite brand in a high-involvement category, extensive retail coverage is less critical for such products. The marketer may be better off being relatively choosy in selecting retailers to carry a brand, particularly if those retailers will play an important role in promoting the product or servicing it after the sale. The value of some exclusive, prestigious brands is clearly enhanced by the fact they are *not* available from every mass merchandiser in town.

**Strategies to Increase Consumer Involvement**   In some cases, a firm may try to increase consumers' involvement with its brand as a way to increase revenues. Increased customer involvement can be attempted in several ways. *The product might be linked to some involving issue,* as when makers of bran cereals associate their products with a high-fiber diet that may reduce the incidence of colon cancer. Of course, the involving issue might be social rather than personal. Thus, *cause-related marketing* is the practice of designating a portion of a brand's sales or profits to a nonprofit cause—such as the Special Olympics or breast cancer research—and aggressively publicizing it.[15] However, as cause-related marketing has become more popular, its effectiveness as a tool for increasing consumer involvement and brand preference may be declining, as discussed in Exhibit 4.8. Or *the product can be tied to a personally involving situation,* such as advertising a sleeping aid late in the evening when insomniacs are interested in finding something to help them sleep. Finally, *an important new feature might be added to an unimportant product* as when Revlon introduced its ColorStay Lipcolor, which promised a miracle for women—unsmeared lipstick all day long. Despite being double the price of other lipsticks, women responded to the claim that it "won't smear off on your teeth, your glass, or him" so well that ColorStay became the number-one-selling brand in drugstores and other mass merchandisers.[16]

## Exhibit 4.8   IS CAUSE-RELATED MARKETING LOSING ITS IMPACT?

In recent years, many consumer products manufacturers and retail chains have sponsored marketing campaigns linking their brands or stores to a social issue. These caused-related campaigns include multicompany programs—such as (product) Red for the benefit of African AIDS Victims—as well as efforts by individual firms, like Avon's breast cancer crusade. The popularity of such programs has grown partly because they often fit well with the social objectives detailed in corporate mission statements, but mostly because they are effective at increasing consumers' involvement with and preference for the sponsoring brand or retail chain.

Unfortunately, the popularity of cause-related marketing may be eroding its effectiveness, at least within the U.S. market. In a survey of 1,066 adults polled by a commercial research firm in 2007, 36 percent said they had bought a product in the previous 12 months after learning of its maker's commitment to some social issue, but that figure was down from 43 percent in a similar survey in 2004. Only 14 percent said they paid more for a product because of its support for a cause, down from 28 percent. And just 30 percent told a family member or friend about a brand's commitment to a cause, compared to 43 percent three years earlier. Carol Cone, whose brand strategy firm conducted the survey, speculates that so many brands are now linked to worthy causes the American consumers may be suffering from "cause fatigue."

*Source:* Conrad Wilson, "Shoppers without a Cause," *Business-Week,* July 9, 2007, p. 14.

# Why People Buy Different Things: Part 1— The Marketing Implications of Psychological and Personal Influences

Even when two consumers have equal involvement with a product, they often purchase different brands for varying reasons. The information they collect, the way they process and interpret it, and their evaluation of alternative brands are all influenced by psychological and personal characteristics. Some of the important psychological, or thought, variables that affect a consumer's decision-making process include *perception, memory, needs,* and *attitudes.* The consumer's personal characteristics, such as *demographic and lifestyle variables,* influence these psychological factors.

## Perception and Memory

*Perception* is the process by which a person selects, organizes, and interprets information. When consumers collect information about a high-involvement service such as a cruise, they follow a series of steps, or a hierarchy of effects. *Exposure* to a piece of information, such as a new product, an ad, or a friend's recommendation, leads to *attention,* then to *comprehension,* and finally to *retention* in memory. Once consumers have fully perceived the information, they use it to evaluate alternative brands and to decide which to purchase.

The perception process is different for low-involvement products. Here, consumers have information in their memories without going through the sequence of attention and comprehension. Exposure may cause consumers to retain enough information so that they are familiar with a brand when they see it in a store.

Two basic factors—*selectivity* and *organization*—guide consumers' perceptual processes and help explain why different consumers perceive product information differently. *Selectivity* means that even though the environment is full of product information, consumers pick and choose only selected pieces of information and ignore the rest. For high-involvement purchases, consumers pay particular attention to information related to the needs they want to satisfy and the particular brands they are considering for purchase. This *perceptual vigilance* helps guarantee that consumers have the information needed to make a good choice. For low-involvement products, consumers tend to selectively screen out much information to avoid wasting mental effort. The average consumer is exposed to over 1,000 ads every day plus information from other sources such as catalogs, websites, and friends. Consumers must be selective in perceiving this information to cope with the clutter of messages.

Consumers also tend to avoid information that contradicts their current beliefs and attitudes. This *perceptual defense* helps them avoid the psychological discomfort of reassessing or changing attitudes, beliefs, or behaviors central to their self-images. For example, many smokers avoid antismoking messages, or play down their importance, rather than admit that smoking may be damaging to their health.

### Memory Limitations
Even though consumers are selective in perceiving product information, they remember only a small portion of it. This limitation of the human memory concerns marketers since much marketing activity deals with communicating information to potential consumers to improve their attitudes toward a given brand. What can marketers do—if anything—to improve the memorability of their messages?

There are different theories of how the human memory operates, but most agree that it works in two stages. Information from the environment is first processed by the *short-term memory,* which forgets most of it within 30 seconds or less because of inattention or displacement of new incoming information. Some information, however, is transferred to *long-term memory,* from which it can be retrieved later. Long-term memory has a nearly infinite storage capacity, but the amount of product information actually stored there is quite limited. For information to be transferred to long-term memory for later recall, it must be *actively rehearsed and internalized.* It takes from 5 to 10 seconds of rehearsal to place a chunk of information in long-term memory. This is a long time relative to the fraction of a second necessary to perceive that piece of information. Therefore, new pieces of information swamp the old one before it can be transferred unless consumers find it sufficiently relevant to warrant focusing their attention.[17]

This is why print media and interactive electronic media, such as websites, are good for communicating complex or technical information about high-involvement products. Consumers can control the pace at which such information is received and can take the time necessary to comprehend, rehearse, and remember it. Similarly, this explains why television advertising for low-involvement products should focus on a few simple pieces of information, such as brand name, symbol, or key product attributes, and be repeated frequently. Otherwise, the information will never make it into the consumer's long-term memory.

**Perceptual Organization**  Another mental factor determining how much product information consumers remember and use is the way they organize the information. People do not view and remember each piece of information they receive in isolation. Instead, they organize information through the processes of categorization and integration. *Categorization* helps consumers process known information quickly and efficiently: "I've seen this ad before so I don't have to pay much attention." It also helps people classify new information by generalizing from past experience. An ad for a new cereal with a high vitamin and mineral content, for instance, is interpreted in light of consumers' experience with other nutritional cereals. This can cause a problem if consumers' experiences have not been very favorable.

*Integration* means that consumers perceive separate pieces of related information as an organized whole. For example, the picture, headline, copy, and location of a magazine ad interact to produce a single overall reaction to the ad and the brand advertised. Similarly, consumers integrate information about various characteristics of a brand, such as its price and the retail stores that carry it, to form an overall image of the brand.

**Effects of Stimulus Characteristics on Perception**  Consumers' personal characteristics—such as their particular needs, attitudes, beliefs, and past experiences with a product category—influence the information they pay attention to, comprehend, and remember. The characteristics of the message itself and the way it is communicated also influence consumers' perceptions. The ad's color, size, and position within a magazine or a TV program influence consumers' attention to the message and the brand image the ad produces in consumers' minds. We examine these factors in Chapter 13 when we discuss advertising and promotion decisions.

# Needs and Attitudes

An *attitude* is a positive or negative feeling about an object (say, a brand) that predisposes a person to behave in a particular way toward that object. Attitudes derive from a consumer's evaluation that a given brand provides the benefits necessary to help satisfy a particular need. These evaluations are multidimensional; consumers judge each brand on a set of dimensions or attributes weighted by their relative importance.

**Fishbein Model**  Martin Fishbein pioneered a model that specified how consumers combine evaluations of a brand across multiple attributes to arrive at a single overall attitude toward that brand. His model is expressed as follows:

$$\text{Attitude}_A = \sum_{i=1}^{k} B_i I_i$$

where

$\text{Attitude}_A$ = Consumer's overall attitude toward Brand A

$B_i$ = Consumer's belief concerning the extent to which attribute $i$ is associated with Brand A

$I_i$ = The importance of attribute $i$ to the consumer when choosing a brand to buy

$k$ = The total attributes considered by the consumer when evaluating alternative brands in the product category

$i$ = Any specific product attribute

Exhibit 4.9 applies the Fishbein model to Paul MacDonald's evaluation of alternative cruises. This application is ***compensatory*** because it assumes that MacDonald's overall attitude toward a given cruise is determined by the weighted sum of the ratings for that cruise on all relevant attributes. Thus, a poor evaluation on one attribute is compensated for by a strong evaluation of another attribute. It also assumes that the cruise with the highest total score is the one MacDonald is predisposed to buy.

**Noncompensatory Attitude Models**  As suggested by Exhibit 4.9, the mental processes involved in forming an attitude are quite complex because consumers must evaluate each alternative brand on every attribute. In some purchase situations, particularly with low-involvement products, consumers may adopt a simpler approach and evaluate alternative brands on only one attribute at a time. Such an approach is ***noncompensatory*** because a poor evaluation of a brand on one attribute cannot be offset by a strong evaluation on another. For instance, one noncompensatory model, the lexicographic model, suggests that consumers evaluate brands on the most important attribute first. If one brand appears clearly superior on that dimension, the consumer selects it as the best possible choice. If no brand stands out on the most important attribute, the consumer evaluates the alternative brands on the second most important attribute, and so forth.[18]

**Marketing Implications of Attitude Models**  Although the different attitude models provide insights into the ways consumers evaluate competitive product offerings, their implications for marketers are similar. The models suggest that to design appealing product offerings and structure effective marketing programs, marketers must have information about (1) the attributes or decision criteria consumers use to evaluate a particular product category, (2) the relative importance of those attributes to different consumers, and (3) how consumers rate their brand relative to competitors' offerings on important attributes.

Multiattribute models are especially helpful in formulating marketing strategies. They do so by showing the consumer's ideal combination of product/service attributes, each of which is weighted as to its relative importance. Clustering those respondents with similar "ideals" enables the marketer to better understand not only what different sets of consumers want, but also how they perceive the various brands relative to the ideal brand.

# Exhibit 4.9

A COMPENSATORY MULTIATTRIBUTE MODEL OF ATTITUDES TOWARD ALTERNATIVE CRUISES

Our hypothetical consumer, Paul MacDonald, is interested in taking a Caribbean cruise lasting not more than seven days sometime during the months of January or February at a reasonable price. As the table indicates, he uses five attributes (choice criteria) to make a comparison between three alternative cruises. On the basis of information gathered from advertising, travel agents, promotional materials received from a number of cruiselines, and friends, he rates the three different cruises on each of the five attributes as follows:

| | | RATINGS | | |
| Service attribute | Importance weight (0–10) | A | B | C |
| --- | --- | --- | --- | --- |
| Demographics—other passengers | 10 | 8 | 8 | 8 |
| Entertainment | 10 | 8 | 10 | 9 |
| Ports of call | 8 | 8 | 9 | 9 |
| Low fares | 7 | 9 | 8 | 8 |
| Size/steadiness of ship | 6 | 9 | 8 | 8 |

Using the formula in the text, MacDonald calculates that an overall attitude score for Cruise A equals $(10 \times 8) + (10 \times 8) + (8 \times 8) + (7 \times 9) + (6 \times 9) = 341$. His overall attitude scores for the other two cruises: Cruise B = 356 and Cruise C = 346.

Consequently, MacDonald prefers and will be predisposed to buy Cruise B, the cruise toward which he has the most positive attitude. Although the demographics of other passengers was one of the most important attributes, it played no significant role in determining which cruise he would buy because there were no significant differences between the three cruises on that attribute. Instead the *determinant attribute*—that which had the biggest impact on which cruise MacDonald would prefer—was *entertainment*.

---

The firm can then decide which segments to target and how best to position its product-market entries.

## Attitude Change    The multiattribute attitude models of consumer choice suggest various ways marketers might change consumer attitudes favorably for their brands versus competing brands. These are discussed briefly below.

1. *Changing attitudes toward the product class or type to increase the total market*—thereby increasing sales for a particular brand. For example, a frozen-orange-juice seller once attempted to make its product acceptable as a refreshing drink throughout the day. This type of attitude change involves primary demand and is difficult to accomplish.

2. *Changing the importance consumers attach to one or more attributes.* For instance, a number of food manufacturers have spent large sums warning about the dangers of high cholesterol. After increasing the importance consumers attach to lowering their cholesterol, manufacturers can then promote their brands as an appropriate part of a low-cholesterol diet.

3. *Adding a salient attribute to the existing set.* For instance, Colgate-Palmolive added triclosan, an antibiotic that fights gingivitis, to its Total brand of toothpaste and promoted it heavily. Similarly, a brand might be linked to a social cause, as discussed in Exhibit 4.8.

4. *Improving consumers' ratings of the brand on one or more salient attributes via more extensive or effective advertising and promotion.* This is the most common attempt, particularly during a brand's introduction to the market or after product improvements have been made.

5. *Lowering the ratings of the salient product characteristics of competing brands.* This can be attempted via comparative advertising, which has increased in recent years. For example, one nutritional cereal regularly compares the amount of vitamins and minerals its brand provides in an average serving with those provided by specific other brands.

# Demographics, Personality, and Lifestyle

**Demographics**   Demographics influence (1) the nature of consumers' needs and wants, (2) their ability to buy products or services to satisfy those needs, (3) the perceived importance of various attributes or choice criteria used to evaluate alternative brands, and (4) consumers' attitudes toward and preferences for different products and brands. For example, older consumers spend more on medical care and travel and less on home furnishings and clothing than do younger groups; the presence of young children obviously affects the purchasing of a variety of goods and services; and better-educated people spend more on reading materials and foreign travel than do those with less education.

**Personality and Self-Concept**   A consumer's buying behavior is also influenced by his or her *personality*—the set of enduring psychological traits that lead a person to make distinctive and consistent responses to factors in his or her environment. An individual's personality is usually described in terms of traits such as sociability, self-confidence, dominance, adaptability, introversion, and the like.

Personality can be useful for explaining why different people buy different things because brands are also perceived to have personalities, and consumers are likely to choose brands whose personalities match their own. In a classic study, the following traits were commonly used to define *brand personalities* in the United States:[19]

- Sincerity (honest, wholesome, down-to-earth, cheerful)
- Excitement (imaginative, spirited, daring, up-to-date)
- Competence (reliable, successful, intelligent)
- Sophistication (upper-class, charming)
- Ruggedness (tough, outdoorsy)

Brand personalities in other countries are defined with some of these same traits, but other traits are unique to specific cultures. For instance, a "peacefulness" dimension replaces "ruggedness" in both Japan and Spain, and "competence" is overshadowed by "passionate" in Spain.[20]

Many well-known brands are perceived to be strong on one dimension, though some are seen as having multidimensional personalities. For instance, MTV is associated with excitement and Campbell soup with sincerity, while Levi's jeans are seen as rugged, youthful, and authentic. Consumers tend to choose brands with personalities that match either their own *self-concept* (the way they actually see themselves) or their *ideal self-concept* (the kind of person they would like to be), but this tendency is probably stronger for high-involvement, publicly consumed goods and services than for low-involvement items.[21]

**Lifestyles**   Two people of similar age, income, education, and even occupations do not necessarily live their lives in the same way. They may have different opinions, interests, and activities. As a result, they are likely to exhibit different patterns of behavior—including buying different products and brands and using them in different ways and for different purposes. These broad patterns of activities, interests, and opinions—and the behaviors that result—are referred to as *lifestyles.* To obtain lifestyle data, consumers are asked to indicate the extent to which they agree/disagree with a series of statements having to do with such things as price consciousness, family activities, spectator sports, traditional values, adverturesomeness, and fashion.

Lifestyle typologies or psychographic profiles have been developed by several advertising agencies and market research firms. Global Scan, developed by Backer Spielvogel & Bates ad agency, measures a variety of consumer attitudes, activities, and values among a sample of 3,500 consumers in the United States and 1,000 respondents from other countries.[22]

# Exhibit 4.10

GLOBAL SCAN'S LIFESTYLE PSYCHOGRAPHIC SEGMENTS AND THE PROPORTION OF PEOPLE IN EACH SEGMENT
ACROSS THREE COUNTRIES

- Strivers: Young people (median age 31) who live hectic, time-pressured lives. They strive hard for success. They are materialistic, seek pleasure, and demand instant gratification.

- Achievers: They have achieved some of the success that strivers aim for. They are affluent, assertive, and upward bound. They are very status conscious and buy for quality and are slightly older than strivers.

- Pressured: This group cuts across age groups and is composed mainly of women who face constant financial and family pressure. They do not enjoy life as much as they could and feel generally downtrodden.

- Adapters: These are older people who maintain time-honored values but keep an open mind. They live comfortably in a changing world.

- Traditional: They hold onto the oldest values of their countries and cultures. They resist change and prefer routines and familiar products.

*Source: Going Global: International Psychographics* (Ithaca, NY: American Demographics Books, 1991).

These measures are then matched against respondents' media viewing habits, product use, and purchase patterns. With this survey data, Global Scan has identified five lifestyle segments, summarized in Exhibit 4.10. The exhibit also shows the proportion of consumers that fall into each segment in the United States, the United Kingdom, and Japan. The size of the various segments varies across countries. For instance, Japan's more traditional and stable culture includes a larger proportion of "Traditionals" and "Adapters" than the United States.

An alternative lifestyle typology, called VALS 2, has been developed by the research firm Strategic Business Insights.[23] We will examine the lifestyle profiles identified by these various typologies, and their usefulness for defining and understanding market segments, in greater detail in Chapter 7.

# Why People Buy Different Things: Part 2— The Marketing Implications of Social Influences

Information and social pressures received from other people influence a consumer's needs, wants, evaluations, and product or brand preferences. Social influences are particularly apparent when consumers purchase high-involvement, socially visible goods or services. The social influences affecting consumers' purchase decisions include culture, subculture, social class, reference groups, and family. These five categories represent a hierarchy of social influences, ranging from broad, general effects on consumption behavior—such as those imposed by the culture we live in—to more specific influences that directly affect a consumer's choice of a particular product or brand. For a simplified view of this hierarchy of social influences, see Exhibit 4.11.

## Culture

*Culture* is the set of beliefs, attitudes, and behavior patterns (customs and folkways) shared by members of a society and transmitted from one generation to the next through socialization. Cultural values and beliefs tend to be relatively stable over time, but they can

## Exhibit 4.11

SIMPLIFIED HIERARCHY OF SOCIAL FORCES AFFECTING CONSUMER BEHAVIOR change from one generation to the next in response to changing conditions in society. For example, the baby boomers born in the United States between 1946 and 1960 have somewhat different values and behavior patterns from those of their parents. They tend to live a more health-conscious lifestyle (e.g., to eat less red meat) and to concern themselves more with personal grooming than did their parents at the same age.

And as the boomers approach retirement age, they appear even more committed to maintaining healthy, active lifestyles—and less likely to fully retire at an early age—than previous generations of senior citizens.[24]

Cultural differences across countries create both problems and opportunities for international marketers. For example, Pillsbury wanted to take advantage of the cultural evolution concerning working women in Japan. About 50 percent of married women in Japan now work outside the home. Consequently, they represent an attractive market for convenience foods, such as Green Giant frozen vegetables. The problem is that many feel guilty about using such products because they seem inconsistent with traditional cultural values. Therefore, in addition to touting the convenience of Green Giant vegetables, Pillsbury's advertising also stressed the nutrition and flavor benefits of freezing vegetables at the peak of ripeness. As a result, Green Giant's Japanese sales increased 50 percent in the first year of the ad campaign.[25]

**Subculture**   There are many groups of people in nearly every country who share common geographic, ethnic, racial, or religious backgrounds. They continue to hold some values, attitudes, and behavior patterns that are uniquely their own. Such groups are referred to as *subcultures.* For example, the average American family now has two wage earners who probably share decisions relating to vacations, car, financial instruments, and major furniture items. In contrast, Korean-Americans as a subculture in America are much more inclined to favor the male in almost all decisions, including food.[26]

## Social Class

Every society has its status groupings largely based on similarities in income, education, and occupation. Because researchers have long documented the values of the various classes (typically thought of as five—upper, upper-middle, middle, working, and lower), it is possible to infer certain behavior concerning some products and services, including class members' reactions to advertising. For example, higher-status people are more critical of advertising, react better to more individualized messages, appreciate humor and sophistication, and look down a bit on ads that stress economy. Lower-status people respond to ads that are strongly visual and show practical solutions to their everyday problems.

## Reference Groups

These include a variety of groups that affect consumer behavior through normative compliance, value-expressed influence, and informational influence. The first is most effective when there are strong normative pressures (for instance, from a college fraternity or exclusive club); when social acceptance is important (serving of certain foods to guests); and when the use of a product is conspicuous (women's fashion clothing). Value-expressive influence involves conforming to gain status within one's group.

Informational influence involves the use of certain influentials to help assess the merits of a given product/service. The opinions of such individuals often legitimize the purchase of a certain product or service. Over 40 percent of Americans seek the advice of family and friends when shopping for doctors, lawyers, and auto mechanics. Word of mouth is also important with respect to restaurants, entertainment, banking, and personal services.[27]

**The Impact of Social Media**   Social media like YouTube, Facebook, and Twitter may be increasing the informational influence of reference groups, particularly among younger consumers. A recent survey found that, while most consumers start their online information search by going to a search engine like Google (58 percent of respondents) or a manufacturer's website (24 percent), nearly half the respondents said they followed up with additional information from the social media. Thirty percent used social media to help eliminate from contention the brands their friends did not like and 28 percent said they relied on their friends for news about hot new products or brands.[28]

# The Family

The family is a reference group, but because of its importance, we discuss it separately. First, it serves as the primary socialization agent, helping members acquire the skills, knowledge, and attitudes to function as consumers in the marketplace. Consequently, it has a great and lasting influence on its younger members' attitudes toward various brands and stores. It is likely that many of the product-purchase decisions by a given generation are influenced by parents, even grandparents. Children can also socialize their parents by introducing them to new products such as food, personal care items, and the personal electronics products like 4G phones. For example, nearly half of all young people age 12 to 19 sometimes cook meals for their family.[29]

Family members tend to specialize in the purchase of certain products either because of their interest or expertise or the role structure of the family. Wives, in most western societies, have the most say in the purchases of food and household products, children's clothes and toys, and over-the-counter drugs. In a similar vein, joint decisions apply on the purchase of cars, homes, vacations, major appliances, furniture, home electronics, and long-distance telephone carriers. As education increases, more joint decision making occurs.

The influence of various family members varies substantially across countries. Generally, the more traditional the society, the more men hold the power. In the more egalitarian countries, such as the Scandinavian nations, decisions are more likely to be made jointly. As women become better educated and more influential as wage earners in developing nations, more joint decision making will happen.

**Family Life Cycle**   When people leave home and start their own households, they progress through distinct phases of a *family life cycle.* The traditional cycle in the most industrialized nations includes young singles, young marrieds without children, young marrieds with children, middle-aged marrieds with children, middle-aged marrieds without dependent children, older marrieds, and older unmarrieds.

Each phase of the life cycle brings changes in family circumstances and purchasing behavior. For example, young singles' purchases tend to concentrate on nondurable items, including food away from home, clothing, and entertainment. Young marrieds without children are typically more affluent because both spouses usually work away from home. They are a major market for such durables as automobiles, furniture, and appliances. Young marrieds with children probably have the least discretionary income, but they are the major market for single-family dwellings, infant products and clothing, and child care services. Middle-aged couples without children usually have the most discretionary income. They are a major market for many luxury goods and services, such as expensive cars and international travel. Finally, the older marrieds and unmarrieds typically have less disposable income but are nevertheless an important market for medical products and services as well as hobby and craft items.

Of course, there are exceptions to and elaborations of the traditional family life cycle, especially the growing number of single-parent families and affluent seniors. These groups are of increasing importance to marketers.[30]

# TAKE-AWAYS

1. Not all purchase decisions are equally important or psychologically involving for the consumer. People engage in a more extensive decision-making process, involving a more detailed search for information and comparison of alternatives, when buying high-involvement goods and services than when purchasing more mundane, low-involvement items.

2. Because of the differences in the decision-making process, a given marketing strategy will not be equally effective for both high- and low-involvement products. The consumer marketer's first task, then, is to determine whether the majority of potential customers in the target segment are likely to be highly involved with the purchase decision or not.

3. Because consumers are generally unwilling to spend much time or effort evaluating alternative brands in a low-involvement product category before making a purchase, marketers need to focus their promotional messages on only a few frequently repeated points and to distribute such products extensively to make them convenient for customers to buy.

4. Regardless of the consumer's level of involvement with a product category, consumers often prefer different brands because of differences in their psychological or personal characteristics, such as their perceptions, memories, attitudes, and lifestyles. Understanding how such characteristics influence consumers' decisions in a product category provides an important foundation for marketing decisions concerning the definition of market segments, the selection of target markets, and the design of marketing programs to appeal to those markets.

5. Regardless of the consumer's level of involvement with a product category, consumers often prefer different brands because of differences in their social relationships, such as their culture, social class, reference groups, and family circumstances. Understanding how such social influences impact consumers' decisions in a product category provides an important foundation for marketing decisions concerning the definition of market segments, the selection of target markets, and the design of marketing programs to appeal to those markets.

# ENDNOTES

1. Christopher Palmeri, "Carnival: Plenty of Ports in a Storm," *Business-Week*, November 15, 2004, pp. 76–78; Amy Gunderson, "Oman, Anyone? More Ships, More Ports of Call," *New York Times*, February 26, 2006, Section 5, pp. 7, 12; Nick Kaye and Hilary Howard, "Where Cruisers Are Headed," and "Too Much of a Good Thing?" *The New York Times*, February 17, 2008, p. TR8; and "Damn the Torpedoes," *The Economist*, February 11, 2010; and the Carnival Corporation 2009 Annual Report at *www.carnival.com*.

2. Henry Assael, *Consumer Behavior and Marketing Action* (Cincinnati: South-Western College Publishing, 1995), chap. 1.

3. For a detailed discussion of how consumers perceive, evaluate, and buy services, see Valarie Zeithaml, Mary Jo Bitner, and Dwayne Gremler, *Services Marketing*, 5th ed. (New York: McGraw-Hill, 2009), chaps. 3–5.

4. "You Choose," *The Economist*, December 18, 2010, pp. 123–125.

5. Keith B. Murray, "A Test of Services Marketing Theory: Consumer Information Acquisition Activities." *Journal of Marketing* 55 (January 1991), p. 13.

6. Joseph Palenchar, "MarketSource Survey Finds What Drives People to Buy," *www.twice.com*, September 13, 2010.

7. James Surowiecki, "A Buyer's Christmas," *The New Yorker*, December 24 and 31, 2007, p. 50.

8. David Kirkpatrick and Daniel Roth, "Why There's No Escaping the Blog," *Fortune*, January 10, 2005, pp. 44–50.

9. Jena McGregor, "Consumer Vigilantes," *BusinessWeek*, March 3, 2008, pp. 39–42.

10. Kirkpatrick and Roth "Why There's No Escaping The Blog." ... Also see Stephen Baker and Heather Green, "Beyond Blogs," *BusinessWeek*, June 2, 2008, pp. 45–50.

11. For a detailed review of the academic literature concerning how consumers make decisions, see J. Edward Russo and Kurt A. Carlson, "Individual Decision Making," in Bart Weitz and Robin Wensley, eds., *Handbook of Marketing* (London: Sage Publications, 2002), pp. 372–408.

**12.** Julie Schlosser, "Cashing In on the New World of Me," *Fortune*, December 13, 2004, pp. 244–50; Anthony Bianco, "The Vanishing Mass Market," *BusinessWeek*, July 12, 2004, pp. 61–72; and "The Printed World." *The Economist*, February 12, 2011, pp. 77–79.

**13.** Zeithaml, Bitner and Gremler, *Services Marketing*, chap. 13.

**14.** Ibid., chap. 7.

**15.** Aimee L. Stern, "Do The Right Thing," *BusinessWeek Online*, January 31, 2000; and Conrad Wilson, "Shoppers without a Cause," *BusinessWeek*, July 9, 2007, p. 14.

**16.** Yumiko Ono, "'Non-smearing' Lipstick Makes a Vivid Imprint for Revlon," *The Wall Street Journal*, November 16, 1995, p. B1.

**17.** For a more detailed discussion, see Joseph W. Alba, J. Wesley Hutchinson, and John G. Lynch, Jr., "Memory and Decision Making," in Harold H. Kassarjian and Thomas S. Robertson, eds., *Handbook of Consumer Theory and Research* (Englewood Cliffs, NJ: Prentice Hall, 1992), pp. 1–49.

**18.** There are several other noncompensatory models that suggest consumers follow somewhat different mental processes in arriving at their preferred brand. For a more detailed discussion of attitude models, see J. Paul Peter and Jerry Olson, *Consumer Behavior* (New York: McGraw-Hill, 2008), chap. 6.

**19.** Jennifer L. Aaker, "Dimensions of Measuring Brand Personality," *Journal of Marketing Research* 34 (August 1997), pp. 347–56.

**20.** Jennifer L. Aaker, Veronica Benet-Martinez, and Jordi Garolera, "Consumption Symbols as Carriers of Culture: A Study of Japanese and Spanish Brand Personality Constructs," *Journal of Personality and Social Psychology* 81 (March 2001), pp. 492–508.

**21.** Timothy R. Graeff, "Consumption Situations and the Effects of Brand Image on Consumers' Brand Evaluations," *Psychology and Marketing* 14 (January 1997), pp. 49–70.

**22.** American Demographics, *Going Global: International Psychographics* (Ithaca, NY: American Demographics, 1991).

**23.** For more information about the VALS survey, see *www.strategic businessinsights.com/vals*.

**24.** Louise Lee, "Love Those Boomers," *BusinessWeek*, October 24, 2005, pp. 94–102.

**25.** Jack Russell, "Working Women Give Japan Culture Shock," *Advertising Age*, January 1995, pp. 1, 24.

**26.** John Steere, "How Asian-Americans Make Purchasing Decisions," *Marketing News*, March 24, 1996, p. 9.

**27.** Chip Walker, "Word of Mouth," *American Demographics*, July 1995, p. 38.

**28.** Courtney Rubin, "Shoppers Combine Search, Social Media to Fuel Decisions," *www.inc.com*. February 25, 2011.

**29.** "The Microwave Generation," *American Demographics*, September 1995, p. 24. See also Deborah Roedder John, "Consumer Socialization of Children: A Retrospective Look at Twenty-Five Years of Research," *Journal of Consumer Research* 26 (December 1999), pp. 183–213.

**30.** "Over 60 and Overlooked," *The Economist*, August 10, 2002, pp. 51–52; and Michelle Conlin, "Unmarried America," *BusinessWeek*, October 20, 2003, pp. 106–16.

# CHAPTER FIVE

# Understanding Organizational Markets and Buying Behavior

## DHL Supply Chain: Building Long-Term Relationships with Organizational Buyers[1]

IN 2005, THE EXEL COMPANY—a global leader in supply chain management services headquartered in the United Kingdom—was acquired in a "friendly" merger by Deutsche Post World Net, the German logistics behemoth that is also the parent of DHL express freight. Exel was incorporated as a separate business unit within Deutsche Post's Logistics Division labeled DHL Supply Chain.

The business unit's primary focus is on providing warehousing and ground-based transport services to contractual customers in more than 170 countries from the company's 2,500 distribution centers around the world. In recent years, however, the DHL Supply Chain competitive strategy has concentrated on differentiating the operation by offering customers a broader range of integrated and efficient logistics services than its competitors. To that end, it has invested to build capabilities in packaging, integrated information management, e-commerce support, and recycling services. The firm's salespeople attempt to convince large potential customers in target industry segments—such as the retailing, automotive, life sciences, electronics, and technical equipment industries—that some or all of their necessary supply chain management activities could be performed more effectively or efficiently if outsourced to DHL. Account teams work closely with customers to design custom-tailored programs of integrated services, monitor the performance of those

programs, and suggest areas for improvement and expansion.

## Building Long-Term Relationships with Customers

Key aspects of the Supply Chain Division's competitive and marketing strategies, and of the development of its relationships with customers over time, are illustrated by the firm's long-running association with the Dutch printing systems manufacturer Océ. The relationship began in the 1970s when Exel transported a consignment of printing systems to a customer in the Netherlands. In the intervening years the relationship has expanded dramatically. Today, the services DHL Supply Chain performs for Océ include freight management, inventory control, technical and customer service support, and recycling.

DHL transports new printing systems from Océ's manufacturing plant to a distribution center in Veghel in the Netherlands, where systems are configured, tested, and then shipped to Océ's customers as they are sold. When a new printing system is delivered, a DHL technical driver gives on-site instruction on how to use the machine and perform simple maintenance tasks. Also, the firm's mobile technicians are available to perform equipment testing and repair on customer premises.

Finally, DHL developed a "reverse logistics" service for Océ after a customer asked the firm to take back its old printing system when a new one was delivered. The firm's technicians examine all returned systems and, with approval from Océ, undertake an appropriate course of action, from cleaning, to refurbishing, to recycling of the machine's component materials.

## Long-Term Relationships Enhance Long-Term Performance

DHL Supply Chain's success at building lucrative long-term logistics relationships with organizational customers has contributed greatly to its revenue and market share in recent years. The unit generated revenues of over €13 billion in 2010, making it by far the market share leader with over 8.4 percent of the €135 billion global market for supply chain services (the next leading competitor had only a 3 percent share).

But perhaps more important for the unit's future, the experience and competencies it has developed working with customers over the years is helping it win new clients. For instance, DHL Supply Chain recently announced the signing of a three-year contract worth over €130 million per year with Jaguar and Land Rover. Under the contract, DHL Exel will be managing Jaguar and Land Rover suppliers to ensure they are shipping the right materials and components to the right plants at the right time, as well as overseeing in-plant logistics.

# Marketing Challenges Addressed in Chapter 5

The fact that the DHL Supply Chain Division markets its logistics services to organizational customers rather than individual consumers makes it like the great majority of business firms. Worldwide, organizational markets account for more than twice the dollar value of purchases as consumer markets. About half of all manufactured goods in most countries are sold to organizational buyers. In addition, organizations such as Cargill, Nestlé, and BP buy nearly all minerals, farm and forest products, and other raw materials for further processing. Finally, organizations buy many services from accounting firms, banks, financial advisers, advertising agencies, law firms, consultants, railroads, airlines, security firms, and other suppliers.

As we'll see later, organizational customers are different in some ways from consumers, and those differences have important implications for designing effective marketing programs. But at the most basic level, marketers need to answer the same set of questions about organizational markets as about consumer markets in order to develop a solid foundation for their marketing plans. Who are the target customers and what are their needs and wants? How do those customers decide what to buy and what suppliers to buy from? Do their decision processes vary depending on their past experiences, the nature of the product being purchased, and other situational factors? If so, what are the marketing implications of those variations? This chapter provides a framework to help you address these questions.

**STRATEGIC ISSUE**

*Marketers need to answer the same set of questions about organizational markets as about consumer markets in order to develop a solid foundation for their marketing plans.*

We begin our examination of "who is the customer?" by comparing organizational markets to consumer markets and pointing out differences between the two types of customers; differences that often dictate varying marketing approaches. One of those differences is simply the number of participants in the purchase decision. While consumers are influenced by family and friends, they often decide what to buy—and make the actual purchase—on their own. That is typically not the case in organizational purchasing, especially when the product or service involved is relatively complex and expensive. For instance, a number of top managers from purchasing, manufacturing, finance, and other functions were involved in negotiating Jaguar and Land Rover's new contract with DHL Supply Chain, and managers from several levels within Océ are involved in reviewing and renegotiating the firm's service agreement each quarter. Therefore, we will discuss the different kinds of participants in organizational purchase decisions, the roles they play, and the different kinds of marketing messages and activities appropriate for each group.

Next, we examine the process that organizational customers go through in deciding what to buy and from whom. As with individual consumers, this process varies depending on the past experience the organization has in buying the particular product or service and with a given supplier. As illustrated by the association between DHL and Océ, a primary goal should be to develop long-term relationships—and ideally cooperative alliances—with customers to ensure repeat purchases and capture full lifetime value. We discuss these issues and their implications for marketing programs, as well as the impact the internet and other information technologies are having on firms' strategies for strengthening customer relationships.

Finally, organizational purchasing processes also vary depending on the kinds of goods or services being purchased. Océ's purchase of integrated logistics services costing millions of euros was more complex, required more information, and focused on different criteria than the company's more routine purchase of office supplies or copper wire. Therefore, we conclude this chapter with an examination of how organizational purchasing processes differ across various categories of goods and services and the implications of those differences for designing effective marketing programs.

# Who Is the Customer?

## A Comparison of Organizational versus Consumer Markets

Organizations—including manufacturing firms, service producers, wholesalers, retailers, nonprofit organizations such as churches and museums, and governments—all buy things. They buy many of the same goods and services as households, such as computers, office supplies, cars, airline tickets, and telephone service. Thus, what distinguishes organizational markets from consumer markets is often not the kinds of products being purchased. Instead, the crucial differences from a marketing viewpoint are (1) the motivations of the buyer: what the organization will do with the product and the benefits it seeks to obtain; (2) the demographics of the market; and (3) the nature of the purchasing process and the relationship between buyer and seller. Some of these differences are summarized in Exhibit 5.1 and discussed below.

**Purchase Motives—Derived Demand**     Individual consumers and households buy goods and services for their own personal use and consumption. Organizational buyers purchase things for one of three reasons: (1) to facilitate the production of another product or service, as when Toyota buys sheet steel, engine components, or computerized

## Exhibit 5.1

DIFFERENCES BETWEEN ORGANIZATIONAL AND CONSUMER MARKETS

### Demand characteristics

The demand for industrial goods and services is

1. Derived from the demand for consumer goods and services.
2. Relatively inelastic—price changes in the short run are not likely to affect demand drastically.
3. More erratic because small increases or decreases in consumer demand can, over time, strongly affect the demand for manufacturing plants and equipment.
4. More cyclical.

### Market demographics

Organizational buyers, when compared with buyers of consumer goods, are

1. Fewer in number.
2. Larger.
3. Geographically concentrated.

### Buyer behavior and buyer–seller relationships

Organizational markets are characterized by the following when compared with the markets for consumer goods:

1. Use of professional buying specialists following prescribed procedures.
2. Closer buyer–seller relationships.
3. Presence of multiple buying influences.
4 More apt to buy on specifications.

---

welding machines; (2) for use by the organization's employees in carrying out its operations (office supplies, computer software, advertising agency services); or (3) for resale to other customers, as when a retailer such as Target buys a truckload of towels to be distributed to its many stores and sold to individual consumers.

Given these reasons for purchasing, organizational demand for goods and services is in many cases derived from underlying consumer demand. Océ's demand for DHL's logistics services, for instance, depends on the number of printing systems purchased by its customers. Fluctuating economic conditions in an industry can change a firm's production schedule, plant and equipment utilization, and materials and parts inventories. These changes affect the firm's demand for materials, components, equipment, logistics services, and more. In other words, derived demand tends to be relatively erratic and cyclical, making accurate sales forecasting and planning more difficult.

**Market Demographics**    Another major difference between consumer and organizational markets is the number, size, and geographic dispersion of customers. Organizational markets tend to have fewer potential customers, but on average they buy much larger volumes than consumers do. In many industries, the largest organizations also tend to cluster in one or a few geographic areas, as with the concentration of major banks and financial service firms in New York, London, Frankfurt, Zurich, and Tokyo.

**Purchasing Processes and Relationships**    Because of the complexity of many of the goods and services and of the large volumes typically involved, organizational purchase decisions often involve evaluation processes focused on detailed, formally specified criteria. These processes are typically carried out by specialized purchasing managers with a great deal of input and influence from other members of the organization.

## What Do the Unique Characteristics of Organizational Markets Imply for Marketing Programs?

The fact that the demand for many organizational goods and services is derived from underlying consumer demand not only makes it harder to forecast sales, but it also limits the marketer's ability to influence demand among organizational buyers. Toyota's demand for steel is unlikely to be increased in the short term by price cuts, persuasive advertising messages, or quantity discounts and other kinds of promotions. Until consumer demand for the firm's cars and trucks expands, increasing steel purchases would simply produce bigger materials inventories, tie up more working capital, and lower profitability.

Therefore, the forward-looking company selling to organizational markets needs to keep one eye on possible changes in organizations' buying behavior for its product and another eye on trends in the underlying consumer markets. Some firms even engage in marketing actions aimed at stimulating demand in those consumer markets in hopes of increasing demand from their organizational customers. For instance, Monsanto aggressively promoted its warranty for Wear-Dated carpets made from its high-quality synthetic fibers in hopes of stimulating consumers' selective demand for such carpets. The bottom line is that even organizational marketers need a solid understanding of consumer behavior.

The complexity of many of the goods and services organizations buy, the extensive decision process involved, and the demographics of organizational markets also have marketing implications. These factors facilitate the use of **direct selling,** with its emphasis on personal communications through company salespeople and vertically integrated distribution channels. Organizational marketers also tend to be heavy users of "high-involvement" media, such as trade journals, product brochures, and websites.

Another upshot of the derived nature of demand in organizational markets, as well as of the complex products and large dollar values involved, is that interdependence between buyers and sellers tends to be greater. The economic success of the marketer depends greatly on the economic success of the organizational customer. The marketer is part of the customer's **supply chain** and is therefore relied on for services such as coordinated delivery schedules, maintenance, spare parts availability, and efficient order handling. This high level of mutual interdependence encourages the development and maintenance of long-term relationships and alliances between the parties.[2] It also demands that supplier firms be customer-oriented and have all their functional activities—including production, R&D, finance, logistics, and customer service—focused on providing superior customer value. As one authority argues, "By its very nature, [organizational] marketing requires that all parts of the business be customer-oriented and that all marketing decisions be based on a complete and accurate understanding of customer needs."[3]

**STRATEGIC ISSUE**

*High level of mutual interdependence encourages the development and maintenance of long-term relationships and alliances between the parties.*

## The Organizational Customer Is Usually a Group of Individuals

Organizations are social constructions. Organizations do not buy things. Rather, individual members, usually more than one, make purchase decisions on the organization's behalf. Similarly, organizations do not form relationships with other organizations. Relationships are built and maintained among their individual members. Consequently, to understand how organizational purchasing decisions are made, the marketer must first understand the roles performed by different individuals within the organization and their personal interests and concerns.

## Participants in the Organizational Purchasing Process   Organizational purchasing often involves people from various departments. These participants in the buying process can be grouped as users, influencers, gatekeepers, buyers, and deciders.[4]

*Users:* The people in the organization who must use or work with the product or service often have some influence on the purchase decision. For example, drill-press operators might request that the purchasing agent buy a particular brand of drills because they stay sharp longer and reduce downtime in the plant.

*Influencers:* Influencers provide information for evaluating alternative products and suppliers. They are usually technical experts from various departments within the organization. Influencers help determine which specifications and criteria to use in making the purchase decision.

*Gatekeepers:* Gatekeepers control the flow of information to other people in the purchasing process. They primarily include the organization's purchasing agents and the suppliers' salespeople. Gatekeepers influence a purchase by controlling the information that reaches other decision makers. An organization does not decide to buy a new product, for example, unless information about its existence and advantages over alternatives is brought to the decision makers' attention.

*Buyers:* The buyer is usually referred to as a **purchasing agent** or **purchasing manager.** In most organizations, buyers have the authority to contact suppliers and negotiate the purchase transaction. In some cases they exercise wide discretion in carrying out their jobs. In other cases, they are tightly constrained by specifications and contract requirements determined by technical experts and top administrators. And more recently, as we shall see, technology has enabled some firms to automate parts of the buyer's role in the form of computerized reorder and logistics management systems and web auctions.

*Deciders:* The decider is the person with the authority to make a final purchase decision. Sometimes buyers have this authority, but often lower-level purchasing managers carry out the wishes of more powerful decision makers.

## The Organizational Buying Center   For routine purchases with a small dollar value, a single buyer or purchasing manager may make the purchase decision. For most high-value organizational purchases, several people from different departments participate in the decision process. The individuals in this group, called a **buying center,** share knowledge and information relevant to the purchase of a particular product or service.

A buyer or purchasing manager is almost always a member of the buying center. The inclusion of people from other functional areas, however, depends on what is being purchased. When the purchase is a major new installation, the high dollar value of the purchase usually dictates that the firm's chief executive and its top financial officer actively participate in the final decision. For purchases of key fabricating parts for the manufacture of the final product, R&D, engineering, production, and quality-control people are likely to be added. For accessory equipment, such as new office equipment, an experienced user of the equipment (say, a secretary or office manager) might participate in the decision.

Different members of the buying center may participate—and exert different amounts of influence—at different stages in the decision process. For example, people from engineering and R&D often exert the greatest influence on the development of specifications and criteria that a new component must meet, while the purchasing manager often has more influence when it comes time to choose among alternative suppliers. The makeup of the buying center also varies with the amount of past experience the firm has in buying a particular product or service. The buying center tends to be smaller—and the relative influence of the purchasing manager greater—when reordering items the firm has purchased in the past than when buying a new product. In general, though, the typical buying center has at least five or six members and often has many more, including people from outside the firm, such as technical advisers and distribution channel members.[5]

These variations in the relative influence of different members of the buying center across types of purchase decisions and stages in the buying process are illustrated in Exhibit 5.2. The exhibit summarizes the results of a survey of 231 manufacturing firms where managers were asked to indicate the relative influence of various functional departments at different stages in the procurement of component parts. The influence of each department not only varied across stages in the buying process but also depended on whether the purchase was a new buy or a reorder.

**Marketing Implications**    Because employees of a customer's firm may be active at different stages of the purchase process and have different interests and concerns, an important part of planning a marketing program aimed at organizational customers involves determining which individuals to target, how and when each should be contacted, and what kinds of information and appeals each is likely to find most useful and persuasive. Fortunately, in many cases the roles played by various members of the buying center are sufficiently consistent across similar types of firms in an industry that a marketing manager can tailor different promotional messages and sales policies for specific members. For example, in smaller firms in the construction industry presidents and vice presidents exert significantly more influence at all stages in the decision process than do purchasing agents or construction engineers, while the situation is reversed in large firms, reflecting increasing job specialization and decentralization of

## Exhibit 5.2

THE RELATIVE INFLUENCE OF VARIOUS FUNCTIONAL DEPARTMENTS AT DIFFERENT STAGES IN TWO TYPES OF ORGANIZATIONAL PURCHASING DECISIONS

*Sources:* Reprinted from *Industrial Marketing Management,* E. Nauman, D. J. Lincoln, and R. D. McWilliams, "The Purchase of Components: Functional Areas of Influence," pp. 113–22. © 1984, with permission of Elsevier. See also Jeffrey E. Lewin and Naveen Donthu, "The Influence of Purchase Situation on Buying Center Structure and Involvement: A Select Meta-Analysis of Organizational Buying Behavior Research," *Journal of Business Research* 58 (October 2005), pp. 1381–90; and Allison Emright, "It Takes a Committee to Buy into B-To-B," *Marketing News,* February 15, 2006, pp. 12–13.

## Exhibit 5.3   COMMUNICATING VALUE TO DIFFERENT MEMBERS OF A BUYING CENTER WITH TAILORED ADVERTISEMENTS

Different members of a firm's buying center value different things when choosing suppliers and products. At Honeywell's MICRO SWITCH Division, the marketing staff responsible for fiber-optic products develops customized advertisements for the different members of customers' buying centers—design engineers, production engineers, engineering managers, and purchasing agents. Design and production engineers see value in leading-edge technologies and products that are easy to design, install, and use. Engineering management is concerned with supplier capabilities, including a proven track record and good service. Purchasing agents see value in low cost and reliable delivery.

Recognizing that different business and technical functions value different things, Bob Procsal, marketing manager for fiber-optic products, carefully chooses different messages and media to communicate to each buying center member. For instance, ads stressing the products' advanced technical features and high performance levels run in technical magazines aimed at design and production engineers, while messages emphasizing Honeywell's years of experience and position as a worldwide leader in advanced switching technology are targeted at engineering managers.

Does the added effort and expense of customized advertisements pay? Bob Procsal thinks it does. He reports that inquiries about the company's line of fiber-optic products increased 50 percent after this practice was implemented.

*Source:* Adapted from Eric N. Berkowitz, Roger A. Kerin, Steven W. Hartley, and William Rudelius, *Marketing,* 5th ed. (Burr Ridge, IL: Richard D. Irwin, 1997), pp. 190–91.

purchasing in bigger companies.[6] A manager marketing to this industry might develop account management policies directing the salesforce to seek appointments with top executives when calling on smaller firms, but to initiate contacts through the purchasing department in larger organizations. Another example involving the development of different advertising appeals and the use of different media to reach buying center members is summarized in Exhibit 5.3.

Similarly, customers' buying centers are likely to involve a wider variety of participants when they are considering the purchase of a technically complex, expensive product, such as a computer network, than when the purchase involves a simpler product or service. Consequently, firms such as IBM selling technically complex capital equipment often deploy multifunctional sales teams or utilize "multilevel" selling, with different salespeople calling on different members of the buying center to give each the kinds of information that person will find most relevant.[7]

# How Organizational Members Make Purchase Decisions

Organizational purchase decisions often involve extensive information search and evaluation processes similar to those consumers use when buying high-involvement items. As with individual consumers, however, the way specific organizational purchase decisions are made can vary with the firm's level of past experience and other aspects of the buying situation.

## Types of Buying Situations

Organizations encounter three kinds of buying tasks or situations: the straight rebuy, the modified rebuy, and new-task buying.[8]

A **straight rebuy** involves purchasing a common product or service the organization has bought many times before. Such purchases are often handled routinely by the purchasing department with little participation by other departments. Such purchases are almost automatic, with the firm continuing to purchase proven products from reliable, established vendors. In straight rebuy situations, all phases of the buying process tend to be short and routine. Even so, when large quantities are involved, the need for quality assurance, parity pricing, and on-time delivery to minimize inventory requires a competent salesforce to help the supplier maintain a continually satisfying relationship with the buyer over time. The rapid spread of computerized reordering systems, logistical alliances, and the like, have made the development and maintenance of long-term relationships between suppliers and their customers increasingly important in the purchase of familiar goods and services.[9] We shall examine the nature of such relationships, and how recent technological developments have facilitated their development, in a later section of this chapter.

A **modified rebuy** occurs when the organization's needs remain unchanged, but buying center members are not satisfied with the product or the supplier they have been using. They may desire a higher-quality product, a better price, or better service. Here buyers need information about alternative products and suppliers to compare with their current product and vendor. And as we'll see, web-based technology—such as business-to-business auctions organized by firms like FreeMarkets, Inc. (*www.FreeMarkets.com*) or by industry sites like e-Steel.com (*www.e-Steel.com*) or PlasticsNet.com (*www.PlasticsNet.com*)—is making it easier for organizational buyers to make such comparisons, at least on the price dimension. Therefore, modified rebuys present good opportunities for new suppliers to win the organization's business if they can deliver better value than the firm's current vendor.

**New-task buying** occurs when an organization faces a new and unique need or problem—one in which buying center members have little or no experience and, thus, must expend a great deal of effort to define purchasing specifications and to collect information about alternative products and vendors. Each stage of the decision process is likely to be extensive, involving many technical experts and administrators. The supplier's reputation for meeting delivery deadlines, providing adequate service, and meeting specifications is often a critical factor in selling a product or service to an organization for the first time. Because the buying center members have limited knowledge of the product or service involved, they may choose a well-known and respected supplier to reduce the risk of making a poor decision.

## The Purchase Decision-Making Process

As Exhibit 5.4 suggests, the stages in the organizational purchase decision-making process—at least for modified rebuy and new-task purchases—correspond quite closely with consumers' high-involvement purchases. However, the exhibit also suggests that some activities at each stage and their execution differ. More people are involved in organizational purchase decisions, the capability of potential suppliers is more critical, and the postpurchase evaluation process is more formalized. We examine other unique features of each stage of the organizational purchase decision process next.[10]

**Recognition of a Problem or Need**    The organizational purchasing process starts when someone in the firm recognizes a need that can be satisfied by buying some good or service. As we have seen, though, while consumers may buy things impulsively to satisfy psychological or social needs, most of an organization's needs are derived from the demand for the goods or services they produce or resell to their own customers. In other

## Exhibit 5.4

THE ORGANIZATIONAL DECISION-MAKING PROCESS FOR NEW-TASK PURCHASES

**Recognition of a problem or need**
- Derived demand
- Requirements planning
- Determining product specifications

**Search for information about products and suppliers**
- Value analysis
- Make-or-buy decisions
- Information about potential suppliers

**Evaluation and selection of suppliers**
- Vendor analysis

**Purchase decision**
- Purchasing contract
- Just-in-time purchasing arrangements

**Postpurchase evaluation and feedback**

words, most organizational purchases are motivated by the needs of the firm's production processes and its day-to-day operations.

In some cases, need recognition may be almost automatic, as when a computerized inventory system reports that an item has fallen below the reorder level or when a piece of equipment wears out. In other cases, a need arises when someone identifies a better way of carrying out day-to-day operations. Océ expanded the range of logistics services it buys from DHL over the years, for instance, as it discovered activities that the logistics expert can perform more effectively or efficiently.

Finally, changes in the organization's operations can create new needs; for instance, top management may decide to produce a new product line that requires new components or raw materials. Or there may be changes in the firm's objectives, resources, market conditions, government regulations, or competition. Needs, then, may be recognized by many people within the organization, including users, technical personnel, top management, and purchasing agents.

**Requirements Planning**   Instead of simply monitoring inventories and reordering when they run low, some firms attempt to forecast future requirements so as to plan their purchases in advance. Requirements planning governs the purchase of raw materials and fabricating components as well as supplies and major installations. One result of such planning is often the signing of long-term purchase contracts, particularly for products projected to be in short supply or to increase in price. Requirements planning can also lead to lower costs and better relations between a purchaser and its suppliers.

**Determining Product Specifications**    The need for particular goods and services is usually derived from a firm's production or operation requirements and, therefore, must meet specific technical requirements. Technical experts from the firm's R&D, engineering, and production departments are often involved early in the purchase decision. When the firm needs a unique component or piece of equipment, it might even seek help from potential suppliers in setting the appropriate specifications. For example, automobile manufacturers consult their parts suppliers before finalizing specs for a new model. Increasingly, suppliers are active participants in the design and development of new components or systems.

**Search for Information about Products and Suppliers**    Once specifications for the desired product/service are developed, purchasing (and possibly other departments) performs a **value analysis.** This systematic appraisal of an item's design, quality, and performance requirements helps to minimize procurement costs. It includes an analysis of the extent to which the product might be redesigned, standardized, or processed using less-expensive production methods. A cost analysis that attempts to determine what the product costs a supplier to produce is also part of a value analysis. Such information helps the purchasing agent better evaluate alternative bids or negotiate favorable prices with suppliers.

**Make-or-Buy Decisions**    Sometimes a firm has the option of producing some components and services internally (advertising, marketing research) or buying them from outside suppliers. Economic considerations typically dominate such decisions, although in the long run other factors may be important. For example, the Spanish retailer Zara makes many of the high-fashion items sold in its 5,000 stores around the world at its own plant in Galicia rather than outsourcing production to lower-cost Asian suppliers. Maintaining tight control over design, production, and distribution enables the firm to bring new fashions to its store shelves in less than four weeks, and to quickly make modifications in response to sales figures and customer feedback. Similarly, some high-tech firms make their own components in order to develop and protect proprietary technology and expertise.[11]

**Information about Potential Suppliers**    Because many firms evaluate a supplier's performance on a regular basis, there is often considerable information about that supplier's quality of performance on file. Where new suppliers are involved, the purchasing department typically engages in an in-depth investigation before qualifying that firm as a potential supplier. An investigation would include such information as the firm's finances, reputation for reliability, and the ability to meet quality standards; information that can be obtained from personal sources (such as salespersons, trade shows, other firms, and consultants) and nonpersonal sources including catalogs, advertising, trade literature, and websites.

**Evaluation and Selection of Suppliers**    Like individual consumers, organizational buyers evaluate alternative suppliers and their offerings by using a set of **choice criteria** reflecting the desired benefits. The criteria used and the relative importance of each attribute vary according to the goods and services being purchased and the buyer's needs. Always important are the supplier's ability to meet quality standards and delivery schedules. Price is critical for standard items such as steel desks and chairs, but for more technically complex items, such as computers, a broader range of criteria enters the evaluation process.

**Vendor Analysis**    Some purchasing departments construct quantitative ratings of potential suppliers to aid in the selection process. These ratings look very much like the multiattribute, compensatory attitude model we discussed for individual consumers. The procedure involves selecting a set of salient attributes and assigning to each a weight reflecting its relative importance. Suppliers are then rated by summing their weighted scores across all attributes.

Such ratings serve several useful purposes, including facilitating the comparison of alternative suppliers, providing a basis for discussions with suppliers about their performance, and controlling the number of qualified suppliers. The end result of a vendor analysis is typically the development of a list of approved suppliers. General Electric, for example, works only with vendors that are top-rated in an analysis of quality, technology, price, and other factors. The company finds regular vendor analysis a more efficient way to ensure the quality of the components it buys than waiting to inspect parts when they are received.[12]

This step in the buying process, along with the previous steps, seems to imply that the individuals making up the buying center respond only to economic arguments. But industrial buyers are social entities *in addition* to being interested in the economics of the situation. For example, producers of marine diesel engines for large boats understand the need to make such engines aesthetically appealing since the owners of such craft take pride in opening an engine hatch to reveal a sleek, chromed engine. In general, the more similar the suppliers and their offerings, the more likely it is that social factors will affect the buying decision.

**What If the Customer Makes Unethical Demands of Its Suppliers?**   As we saw in Chapter 2, a supplier's ethics can have a direct effect on its success in the marketplace because organizational buyers are more likely to purchase from firms they consider ethical.[13] Ethical behavior plays a crucial role in establishing the trust and cooperation necessary for the development and maintenance of long-term relationships with customers. But what if members of the buying organization engage in or demand unethical practices?

One questionable practice that some buyers engage in is **reciprocity,** which occurs when an organization favors a supplier that is also a customer or potential customer for the organization's own products or services. Although this situation is relatively common, it can cause serious problems, including undermining the morale of purchasing and sales personnel who are constrained in the way they do their jobs. Also, reciprocal buying is illegal when it substantially injures free competition among alternative suppliers.

Another unethical practice that causes headaches for many suppliers—particularly in global markets where there are great differences in cultural values and legal restrictions—is the demand for bribes as a precondition for winning a purchase. Ethical Perspective 5.1 examines this issue.

It is not always easy to know when a bribe is a bribe. For example, one common practice in high-tech industries has been for small start-ups planning an initial public offering (IPO) of common stock to give shares to executives in firms that are potential customers. While giving away such "friends and family" shares prior to an IPO is not illegal, one likely motive for the practice is the hope that the favored executives will help steer big purchase contracts to the companies in which they hold stock, thereby increasing the value of their holdings.[14]

**The Purchase**   The purchase agreement between a supplier and an organizational customer can take several forms, ranging from individual spot contracts on the open market, to long-term purchasing contracts covering a year or more, to ongoing informal relationships based on cooperation and trust rather than legal agreements. In the past, long-term purchasing contracts were popular because they enabled an organization to concentrate its purchases with one or a few suppliers, reduce transaction costs, and gain scale economies

## ETHICAL PERSPECTIVE 5.1
### *Bribery in Organizational Purchasing*

Bribery can take many forms ranging from small-value Christmas gifts to large sums of money. In the United States, gifts of high value are typically condemned. Most organizations do not want the decisions of their purchasing personnel unduly influenced by large gifts from a prospective supplier. Bribery is not officially condoned anywhere in the world, but, in the past, most countries' antibribery laws were not as restrictive or as rigorously enforced as those in the United States.

U.S. laws—particularly the Foreign Corrupt Practices Act (FCPA), which punishes firms that bribe government or company officials in foreign trade—have real teeth, including hefty fines and prison sentences. Consequently, most U.S. firms avoid paying major bribes to foreign customers and have sought other ways to influence people and win contracts. Some take foreign officials on junkets to Disney World. Others use local agents or distributors who—known to them or not—do the dirty work. And many multinationals do make small "facilitation" payments to hasten building inspections, telephone installations, customs clearances, and the like.

Despite such actions, the strict U.S. antibribery laws may have put American firms at a competitive disadvantage in many countries around the world.

One government report indicates that bribes were allegedly offered by foreign competitors on 294 international contracts worth $145 billion between 1994 and 1999, and that is probably just the tip of the iceberg.

However, commercial bribery—especially the bribing of government officials—is getting riskier. More than 30 countries have passed antibribery laws in recent years, and U.S. officials have stepped up enforcement of the Foreign Corrupt Practices Act (FCPA). The number of open FCPA investigations is at an all-time high, and penalties are up.

Fines imposed on firms are also getting bigger, both in the United States and in Europe. For instance, in 2009 U.S. courts fined construction firms KBR and Halliburton $579 million over bribes paid to obtain contracts in Nigeria, and they hit Siemens, a German conglomerate, with an $800 million fine. The German authorities subsequently fined Siemens a similar amount.

*Sources:* Robert Greenberger, "Foreigners Use Bribes to Beat U.S. Rivals, New Report Concludes," *The Wall Street Journal*, October 12, 1995, p. B1; *Addressing the Challenges of International Bribery and Fair Competition* (Washington, DC.: U.S. Department of Commerce, July 1999); Eamon Javers, "Steering Clear of Foreign Snafus," *BusinessWeek*, November 12, 2007, p. 76; "Ungreasing the Wheels," *The Economist* November 21, 2009, pp. 68–69; and Dionne Searcy, "U.K. Law on Bribes has Firms in a Sweat," *The Wall Street Journal* online (www.wsj.com) December 28, 2010.

through quantity discounts and the like. For example, an **annual requirements contract** obligated a supplier to fill all of a buyer's needs for a specific product at a consistent, usually discounted, price over a year.

One problem with long-term legal contracts, though, is that they must precisely specify all the details of a purchase agreement, including technical specifications, prices, credit terms, and so on. But in today's rapidly changing economic and technical environments, it can be difficult for the parties to foresee what their needs and market conditions will be like months or years into the future. It can be difficult to adjust the terms of a formal contract in response to unforeseen technical improvements, cost changes, or market conditions. This inflexibility of long-term contracts is a major reason their popularity has declined in favor of increased reliance on spot market contracts, or auctions, on one hand and less formal long-term relationships between customers and suppliers on the other.[15] The increased reliance on both of these approaches has been facilitated by a common factor: the growth of telecommunications technology and the internet.

### One Impact of Technology: The Growth of Auctions or E-exchanges

Over the past few years, a number of internet firms have emerged to help organizations cut their purchasing costs. The earliest entrants, such as Commerce One and Ariba, focused on improving the efficiency of organizations' search for information and evaluation of alternative products and suppliers. They developed electronic catalogs that reduced clients' transaction costs by automating the collection of product information, orders, and payments.

For firms with cash-flow problems, there are barter markets, such as Itex (*www.itex.com*), where participants offer to trade goods or services in a variety of categories. They operate similarly to other online marketplaces like eBay, but with no cash involved.

More recently, sellers' auction websites have emerged in a number of industries. These provide lively global spot markets for standard processed materials such as steel, chemicals, and plastics. For example, ChemConnect (*www.chemconnect.com*) is an exchange for buyers and sellers of bulk chemicals such as benzene. The site's user-friendly design attracted a large number of potential buyers and sellers. As a result ChemConnect is now the largest online spot market for chemical trading, with over a million barrels traded daily.[16]

The websites that may have the greatest future impact on organizational purchasing behavior, however, are those that facilitate buyers' auctions. Such auctions invite qualified competing suppliers to submit bids to win a contract where the buyer has specified all of the purchase criteria in great detail, except the price. By enabling all suppliers to see what the competition is bidding in real time, these auctions have the potential to greatly increase price competition and lower buyers' acquisition costs in some cases by as much as 30 or 40 percent.[17]

However, because buyers' auctions are feasible only when the buyer is able to specify *all* its requirements except price—including all technical and performance attributes of the good or service, delivery schedules, inventory arrangements, payment schedules, and the like—they work best for purchases where the buyer has experience to draw upon, and where those requirements are unlikely to change rapidly. One service offered by auction sites such as FreeMarkets (*www.FreeMarkets.com*) is to help clients examine their needs and clearly spell out every aspect of their request for quotes (RFQs) so potential suppliers will know exactly what they're bidding for. Thus, buyers' auctions are like "modified rebuy" situations where the buyer knows the physical requirements of the purchase but wants to see whether an alternative supplier might offer a better price.

Because auctions throw every purchase up for grabs among alternative suppliers, they work against the development of a cooperative long-term relationship with a given supplier. And they are unlikely to replace such relationships where the product or service being purchased is very technically complex or innovative, is highly customized to the buyer's unique requirements, or requires specialized equipment or other investments to produce. Auctions are also unlikely to replace long-term cooperation between a buyer and a trusted supplier where there are substantial savings to be gained from logistical alliances, as discussed in the next section. Consequently, while the proportion of global business-to-business online sales volume accounted for by auctions or e-exchanges is predicted to increase steadily for the foreseeable future, other forms of purchasing arrangements, including long-term alliances and partnerships, will continue to dominate.[18]

**Logistical Alliances**   Technology also has changed organizational purchasing over the past decade by facilitating logistical alliances involving the sharing of sales and inventory data and computerized reordering. Initially, such systems involved electronic data interchange through dedicated telephone or satellite links and were mainly limited to large firms. More recently, software for developing such systems on the web and protecting the security of proprietary data has improved substantially, thereby lowering costs and increasing their availability to smaller firms.

Consumer package goods manufacturers such as Procter & Gamble have formed **supply chain management alliances** with mass merchandisers such as Walmart and Target. Sales information from the retailer's checkout scanners is shared directly with the supplier's computers, which figure out when to replenish the stock of each item and schedule deliveries to appropriate distribution centers or even individual stores. Such paperless exchanges reduce sales and purchasing expenses, cut mistakes and billbacks, minimize inventories, decrease out-of-stocks, and improve cash flow. Recent technological enhancements—such as item-level radio frequency identification (**RFID**) tags—help such alliances deliver even more benefits to both organizational buyers and their retail customers, as illustrated by the experience of Mitsukoshi department stores described in Exhibit 5.5.

**Performance Evaluation and Feedback**  When a purchase is made and the goods delivered, the buyer's evaluation of both product and supplier begins. The buyer inspects the goods on receipt to determine whether they meet the required specifications. Later, the department using the product judges whether it performs to expectations. Similarly, the buyer evaluates the supplier's performance on promptness of delivery and postsale service.

In many organizations this process is done formally through reports submitted by the user department and other persons involved in the purchase. This information is used to evaluate proposals and select suppliers the next time a similar purchase is made.

# The Marketing Implications of Different Organizational Purchasing Situations

The extensive purchasing process we have been talking about applies primarily to new-task purchases, where an organization is buying a relatively complex product or service for the first time. Buyers in such circumstances tend to collect a lot of information about

---

**Exhibit 5.5**  JAPANESE DEPARTMENT STORE USES RADIO FREQUENCY IDENTIFICATION TAGS TO IMPROVE INVENTORY CONTROL, PURCHASING, AND CUSTOMER SERVICE

**M**itsukoshi, one of Japan's leading luxury department stores, began using radio frequency identification (RFID) tags to track individual inventory items in its ladies shoe departments in 2005. Each pair of shoes on display and every box in the stockroom (or "backyard" as the Japanese refer to it) carries a tiny radio transmitter tag with a unique ID number whose signal can be received anywhere in the department. Sales associates are equipped with PDAs capable of reading the RFID signals, and a customer kiosk housing an RFID reader is installed on the selling floor. Customers can scan through—or the salesperson can display—a full range of styles and colors, and determine whether a particular shoe is available in the right size, without the sales associate making endless trips to the stockroom. As a result, salespeople are able to service more shoppers and suggest more options. The average Mitsukoshi customer tries on 70 percent more shoes in roughly the same amount of shopping time as before the new system was installed.

Ongoing analysis of the detailed RFID data concerning every pair of shoes sold in each store provides clues to managers about what is selling quickly and where there may be size or color gaps in the assortment. Mitsukoshi's suppliers also receive automatic notification when a store's inventory of a specific stock-keeping unit (SKU) falls below a reorder threshold, thus speeding up replenishment and reducing stockouts.

In the first year, the new item-level RFID system enabled Mitsukoshi to achieve a 10 percent increase in year-over-year sales volume. About one half of that increase is attributed to improved cooperation with suppliers leading to faster replenishment and fewer stockouts, and the other half to improved customer service. The program has been so successful that it is being expanded to other fashion items, such as designer jeans.

*Sources:* Susan Reda, "Stepping Up the RFID Effort," on the stores .org website, *www.stores.org/archives/2006/3/cover.asp*, March 2006. For a more critical view of RFID Technology, see Leigh Phillips, "Future internet Privacy Worries Europe," *www.businessweek .com/globalbiz*, October 9, 2009.

alternative products and suppliers and to engage in extensive comparisons before making a final purchase decision. Such situations are relatively favorable to potential new suppliers who have never sold to the organization. Such newcomers can win the organization's business *if* they can provide superior product benefits, superior customer service, or better prices—in other words, better customer value—*and if* they can convince the customer of their superiority through an effective sales pitch, a user-friendly website, and/or other promotional efforts. (Good value means nothing if nobody knows about it.) Potential new suppliers may even be able to engage in product development efforts aimed at winning the new customer. This is why entrepreneurial start-ups tend to prosper in emerging categories where product designs are still in flux and there are few entrenched competitors with close ties to potential customers; they are more likely to get a full hearing and have a better chance to differentiate themselves from other suppliers.

One major reason for establishing long-term cooperative relationships with major customers is to become an active partner in designing—and setting the specifications for—the next generation of the customer's products. In the process, the supplier may have a major influence on the purchase criteria for major materials and components of the new product, thereby gaining the inside track on winning the purchase contract for those new-task purchases.

At the other extreme is the straight rebuy, where the customer is reordering an item it has purchased many times before. These purchases tend to be more routine and computerized. From the seller's viewpoint, being the established, or "in," supplier in such purchase situations provides a major competitive advantage because the customer spends little or no effort evaluating alternatives. Therefore, established suppliers should develop procedures to maintain and enhance their favored position with current customers. As we'll discuss in Chapter 13, for instance, many firms have developed "key account" policies and appoint cross-functional teams to service major customers to help ensure their satisfaction and retention. New technologies have made it easier for established suppliers to strengthen their ties to customers through supply chain management systems and logistical alliances.[19]

For "out" suppliers, who do not have well-established relationships with an organizational customer, however, the marketing challenge is more difficult. Such competitors must try to move the buyer away from the relatively routine reordering procedures of the straight rebuy toward the more extensive evaluation processes of a modified rebuy purchase decision. They must attempt to interest the buyer in modifying the purchase criteria by promising superior product performance, better service on one or more dimensions, or an equivalent package at a better price.[20] Historically, "out" suppliers—particularly small, unknown start-ups with few marketing resources—had a hard time surmounting this challenge. As with congressional elections, incumbents were firmly entrenched. But the emergence of web-based auctions may help level the playing field for such suppliers, at least for those efficient enough to compete largely on price.

### Developing Long-Term Buyer–Supplier Relationships
From a supplier's perspective, developing logistical alliances and computerized reorder systems can help tie major customers to the firm and increase the proportion of purchases they make from the supplier. But as DHL's evolving relationship with Océ illustrates, long-term relationships between suppliers and their organizational customers often involve much more than merely linking their computer systems and sharing inventory data. DHL frequently gets involved in improvement projects aimed at developing customized services to meet Océ's specific needs.

**STRATEGIC ISSUE**

*Long-term relationships between suppliers and their organizational customers often involve much more than merely linking their computer systems and sharing inventory data.*

**Trust between Supplier and Customer Develops Person-to-Person**   Such complex relationships not only involve a great deal of cooperation between the parties, but they also require *mutual trust*. Before making a substantial investment in training its employees to perform preinstallation testing of Océ's printing systems, DHL had to trust Océ to continue purchasing its services long enough to recoup that investment. Similarly, Océ had to trust DHL to measure up to its own high standards when servicing its customers. In other words, both parties must trust one another to avoid opportunistic behaviors that would advance their own short-term self-interest at their partner's expense.[21]

Organizations develop trust through the actions of individual members of the firm. Therefore, company salespeople, account teams, logistics managers, and customer service personnel often play crucial roles in winning customer trust and loyalty. Unfortunately, this can make buyer–supplier relationships vulnerable to personnel turnover. Suppliers can minimize such problems by (1) developing effective corporate policies and performance standards with respect to customer service, (2) instituting training programs and succession planning for customer contact personnel, and (3) fostering and rewarding a strong customer orientation within the corporate culture.[22]

**Conditions Favoring Trust and Commitment**   While mutual trust is important for the development and maintenance of long-term commitments between suppliers and their organizational customers, it is not always easy to develop. First, trust tends to build slowly. Thus, the parties must have some history of satisfying experiences with one another to provide a foundation for trust. It also helps if each party brings an established reputation for fair dealing within its industry.[23]

From the customer's perspective, a firm is more likely to trust and develop a long-term commitment to a supplier when that supplier makes dedicated, customer-specific investments, as DHL has done in developing customized services for individual customers. Such investments send a powerful signal about the vendor's credibility and commitment to the relationship since the assets are not easily deployable elsewhere.

There are many other actions a firm can take to initiate, build, and maintain long-term relationships with organizational customers. Such actions become even more important as a product-market matures, sales growth slows, and competition becomes more intense. Consequently, we will examine **customer relationship management** programs in more detail in Chapter 16 when we discuss marketing strategies for mature markets.

In markets characterized by complex and uncertain technical environments, such as where competing technologies are emerging simultaneously, as in the networking software industry, customers are less likely to develop a long-term orientation toward a single supplier. Because firms in such circumstances cannot tell which supplier's technology will eventually become the industry standard, they are more likely to keep their options open by spreading their purchases across multiple suppliers if it is economically feasible to do so.[24]

# Purchasing Processes in Government Markets

Federal, state, and local governments and their various agencies are major buyers of many goods and services. However, a government's purchasing processes tend to be different in some respects from those of a business organization. For one thing, government organizations tend to require more documentation and paperwork from their suppliers because their spending decisions are subject to public review. Thus, although most governments provide would-be suppliers with detailed guides describing their procedures and requirements, some suppliers complain about excessive bureaucracy, costly paperwork, and red tape.[25]

Another difference is that government organizations typically require suppliers to submit bids, and contracts are usually awarded to the lowest bidder who meets the minimum standards specified in the contract. In some cases, though, a government unit will make allowances for a supplier's superior product quality or customer service. They also sometimes purchase on a negotiated or "cost-plus" contract basis, particularly when the product being purchased will require a lengthy development period (a hydroelectric dam) or major and uncertain R&D investments (a new weapons system), or when there are few alternative suppliers to compete for the contract.

These differences in governmental purchasing processes make many standard marketing strategies and tools less relevant and effective than in other organizational markets. For example, since a government purchase contract usually describes the desired product specifications in great detail, and since contracts are usually awarded to the lowest bidder, a strategy of product differentiation via superior features or performance would not likely be successful, particularly if it resulted in higher costs. For the same reason, comparative advertising appeals or personal sales demonstrations have little impact. Nevertheless, many organizations—such as Rockwell, Goodyear, and 3M—have created separate government marketing departments or sales teams. Their task is to anticipate government needs and projects, participate in or influence the development of product specifications, gather competitive intelligence, carefully prepare bids, and expedite postsale activities and services.[26] The lessons learned in selling to governments may become much more relevant in private-sector markets as web-based buyers' auctions for standardized materials and components proliferate.

# Selling Different Kinds of Goods and Services to Organizations Requires Different Marketing Programs

Organizational buying processes tend to vary dramatically depending on what is being bought. Different types of goods and services require sellers to employ varying marketing strategies and actions to be successful in organizational markets. Marketers commonly classify industrial goods according to the uses made of the product by organizational purchasers. With this in mind, *six categories of industrial goods and services* can be identified: raw materials, component materials and parts, installations, accessory equipment, operating supplies, and business services. Exhibit 5.6 describes these categories and their major characteristics and marketing implications.

## Raw Materials

Raw materials are goods receiving little or no processing before they are sold, except what is necessary for handling and shipping. Purchased primarily by processors and manufacturers, they are inputs for making other products. The two types of raw materials are *natural products* (fish, lumber, iron ore, and crude petroleum) and *farm products* (fruits, vegetables, grains, beef, cotton, and wool). Processors and manufacturers purchase nearly all natural products and about 80 percent of all farm products. Retailers or consumers buy the remaining 20 percent directly without any processing.

**Implications for Marketing Decision Makers**   The supply of most natural products is limited; in recent decades, there have been some shortages. Often only a few large firms produce particular natural products, and in some countries those producers have

## Exhibit 5.6

CATEGORIES, CHARACTERISTICS, AND MARKETING IMPLICATIONS OF GOODS AND SERVICES BOUGHT BY ORGANIZATIONS

| Category | Description | Characteristics and marketing implications |
|---|---|---|
| Raw material | Relatively unprocessed goods that become a portion of a final product (farm products, lumber, etc.) | Limited supply, few producers; distribution is a key function, price is a critical competitive variable |
| Component parts and materials | Processed goods that become a portion of a final product (engines, microchips, etc.) | High-volume purchases, long-term contracts; fierce competition among suppliers, requires good service and nurturing of relationships with buyers; Web auctions also important for standard components |
| Installations | Major capital goods used to produce final product, but not part of the final product (plant installations, production machinery, etc.) | Long-lasting; involved in production of many units of the final product over several years; involve large dollar outlays; capital budgeting committee involved in purchase decision; sold directly from manufacturer; personal selling and system design services are crucial |
| Accessory equipment | Finished goods that facilitate production of a final product (trucks, hand tools, etc.) | Enduring but less so than installations; more standardized, more frequently purchased, and less costly than capital equipment; less complex buying; intermediaries may be involved |
| Operating supplies | Finished goods that facilitate repair, maintenance, and ongoing operations (office supplies, repair parts, etc.) | Analogous to consumer convenience goods, frequently purchased and consumed in a short time; standardized; broad market; heavy use of channel intermediaries; web-based wholesalers and catalog sites becoming important |
| Business services | Provide special expertise to facilitate ongoing operations (law firms, advertising agencies, etc.) | Long-term relationships with customers; supplier's qualifications, experience, and reputation critical to success; purchase decision often made by top executives |

been nationalized. These supply conditions give producers the power to limit supplies and administer prices, as with the Organization of Petroleum Exporting Countries (OPEC). Such supply conditions encourage processors and manufacturers to seek ways to ensure adequate supplies for the future by negotiating long-term purchase contracts (often at premium prices) or by purchasing the raw materials sources. For example, many large steel manufacturers own iron ore mining and processing operations.

When the supply—and therefore the price—of a critical raw material is volatile and unpredictable, long-term purchase agreements may not be viable. Consequently, a buyer may have to adjust its own marketing strategy to cushion the impact of rapidly changing commodity costs. A good example of such an adjustment is provided by the Swiss food giant Nestlé, as discussed in Exhibit 5.7.

Natural materials are generally bulky and low in unit value; therefore, producers try to minimize their handling and transportation costs. Distribution channels for natural materials tend to have few middlemen; most materials are marketed directly to processors and manufacturers.

The marketing problems associated with natural products are quite different from those of agricultural products, which are produced by many relatively small farms located far from consumer markets. Also, many of these products are produced seasonally. Thus, the distribution channels for most agricultural materials involve middlemen who buy products from

**Exhibit 5.7   VOLATILE COMMODITY COSTS FORCE NESTLÉ TO MAKE STRATEGIC ADJUSTMENTS**

As the world's largest food and beverage company, Nestlé spends more than $30 billion a year on raw materials; mostly agricultural products. The company buys 10 percent of the world's coffee crop, 12 million metric tons of milk, and more than 300,000 tons of cocoa.

Because of increased global demand for food and a variety of factors limiting world supply—such as drought, violent storms, and political turmoil—the price of almost all the major commodities the company purchases more than doubled in the four years from 2006 to 2010. The firm expects raw material costs to increase $3 billion in 2011, the biggest increase ever.

Nestlé tried to moderate commodity prices by working with farmers and producer cooperatives around the world to improve production practices and increase crop yields. But a recent report from the International Monetary Fund suggests it may take years before agricultural output increases enough to make a significant dent in worldwide food prices.

Consequently, Nestlé crafted a competitive strategy that assumes commodity prices will remain volatile—but generally follow an upward trend—for the foreseeable future. The first part of that strategy is to offset increases in commodity costs which the firm cannot control with reduction in operating costs in areas where the firm does have some control. For example, the firm redesigned the bottles for its Poland Spring water and reduced the amount of plastic used by 35 percent.

Second, Nestlé aims for a steady stream of gradual price increases for most of its products, regardless of whether their ingredients costs rise or fall in the short term. This reduces price volatility at the retail level and helps avoid shocking consumers with occasional large price increases.

Finally, the firm's strategy emphasizes the development of unique, high-quality products that can command a premium price. Ingredient costs account for a smaller percentage of the revenue generated by such products. For example, by packaging its highest-quality coffee in single-serve capsules for its Nespresso coffee machines, Nestlé can command about 10 times the price per cup that competitors get for unground beans. And the company has built Nespresso into a $3 billion business that is growing over 20 percent a year.

*Source:* Tom Mulier, "Nestlé's Recipe for Juggling Volatile Commodity Costs," *Bloomberg Businessweek*, March 21, 2011, pp. 29–30.

a large number of farmers, collect them in a central location (such as a grain elevator), and store them for shipment throughout the year to processors and exporters. Since there is little difference among the products grown by different farmers, branding is relatively unimportant. There is usually little promotional activity, except for cooperative advertising campaigns funded by trade groups to stimulate primary demand for a product. An example is a promotional campaign to persuade health-conscious adults to drink more milk.

## Component Materials and Parts

As with raw materials, component materials and parts are purchased by manufacturers as inputs for making other products. *Component materials* differ, though, in that they have been processed to some degree before they are sold (for instance, flour bought by a baker). *Component parts* are manufactured items assembled as part of another product without further changes in form (electric motors for washing machines, batteries for new cars).

### Implications for Marketing Decision Makers
Manufacturers buy most component materials and parts in large quantities; therefore, they are usually sold direct, without the use of middlemen. However, wholesale distributors sell to smaller manufacturers in some lines of trade.

To avoid disrupting production runs, sellers must ensure a steady, reliable supply of materials and parts, especially when a just-in-time (JIT) management system is being used by the buyer. This system's objective is to eliminate inventories at the customer's manufacturing site, which requires the timely delivery of 100 percent quality (zero-defect) products. This relieves the customer of any incoming inspection. A vendor's failure on quality or delivery can close a customer's operation so the resulting penalties are severe.

A JIT system is costly to set up and cannot be effectively implemented without a continuing and close working relationship between buyer and seller. This may explain why a growing proportion of the purchases of component materials and parts, particularly in situations where the components are standardized and the buyer is able to specify all requirements in detail, are being made through electronic buyer auctions such as FreeMarkets, Inc.[27] (*www.FreeMarkets.com*). Competitive bidding by suppliers can provide some of the cost saving benefits of JIT systems without the time and effort necessary to build close cooperation.

## Installations

Installations are the buildings and major capital equipment that manufacturers and service producers use to carry out their operations. They are expensive and long-lived; examples are factory buildings constructed for a manufacturer, office buildings built for government agencies, computers used by the Internal Revenue Service, presses used by an automobile manufacturer, and airplanes purchased by Ryanair.

**Implications for Marketing Decision Makers**　The marketing of installations presents a real challenge because there are few potential customers at any one time, and the average sale is very large. Many installations are custom-made to fit a particular customer's needs; therefore, sellers must provide some engineering and design services before making a sale. Often a long period of negotiation precedes the final transaction. Firms selling installations must usually provide many postsale services, such as installing the equipment, training the customer's personnel in its use, providing maintenance and repair services, and sometimes financing.

Because of the small number of buyers, the large dollar volume of each sale, and the custom engineering involved, distribution is usually direct from producer to customer. Sometimes wholesale distributors provide replacement parts and repair services for equipment already in operation. For similar reasons, promotional emphasis is usually on personal selling versus advertising. High-caliber, well-trained salespeople are critically important in the marketing of installations.

## Accessory Equipment

As with installations, **accessory equipment** includes industrial machines and tools that manufacturers, services producers, and governments use to carry out their operations. The difference is that although installations determine the scale of operations of the firms that buy and use them, accessory equipment has no such impact since it consists of tools and machines with relatively short lives and small price tags. They consist of such goods as personal computers, desks, file cabinets, and hand tools.

**Implications for Marketing Decision Makers**　Because this product category includes a wide range of specific items, it is hard to generalize about the most common or appropriate marketing strategies for accessory equipment. In some cases, as with Hyster forklifts and Xerox office equipment, the producers sell accessory equipment directly. Their presale and postsale service requirements are substantial, but the dollar value of the average sale is high enough to justify direct distribution. When there are many different types of potential customers scattered around the country, the average order size is small, and the product does not require much technical service, producers use wholesale distributors (for instance, Makita power tools). Web-based catalog sites, such as Commerce One (*www.CommerceOne.com*), are also becoming increasingly important in this category.

Personal selling, either by the producer's or a distributor's salesforce, remains the most important promotional method for accessory equipment, but because most products in this category are standardized and not technically complex, advertising, brand name promotions, and company websites are also important.

## Operating Supplies

**Operating supplies** do not become a part of the buyer's product or service, nor are they used directly in producing it. Instead, these supplies facilitate the buying organization's day-to-day operations. They are usually low-priced items purchased frequently with a minimum of decision-making effort. Examples include heating fuel, floor wax, typing paper, order forms, paper clips, and pencils.

### Implications for Marketing Decision Makers   These supplies are purchased in small quantities by many different organizations, so wholesale middlemen, including those with extensive websites such as Office Depot, are typically used to distribute them. Price is usually the critical decision variable, and there tends to be little brand loyalty.

## Business Services

Many business services producers, or facilitating agencies, have special areas of expertise used and paid for by other organizations. These include security and guard services, janitorial services, equipment repair services, public warehouses, transportation agencies, consulting and marketing research services, advertising agencies, and legal and accounting services.

### Implications for Marketing Decision Makers   Services are intangible and are purchased before they can be evaluated by the buyer. Thus, the supplier's qualifications, past performance, and reputation become critical determinants of the success of the marketing effort. Price is less important in selling business services because a lawyer or consultant with an outstanding reputation can often charge much more for a given service than one who is less well known. Also, price often serves as an indicator of quality, especially when there are no other quality cues.[28]

Because services are often tailored to the specific needs of a given customer, personal selling and negotiation are important elements in most services producers' marketing programs. This selling is often done by high-level executives in the service producer's organization. The negotiation process can be lengthy; for instance, an ad agency team spends months developing proposals and making presentations to a prospective client before finding out whether it has landed the new account. This selling task is often worth the effort, though, for once a relationship is established between a service supplier and a customer, it tends to be maintained over a long time, as in the case of DHL and Océ. Many companies employ the same law firm, advertising agency, or logistics services firm for years or even decades.

# TAKE-AWAYS

1. While organizational customers are different in some ways from consumers, marketers need to answer a similar set of questions to develop a solid foundation for their marketing plans. Who are our target customers? What are their needs, wants, and preferences? How do those customers decide what to buy and what suppliers to buy from?

2. Organizations buy things for one of three reasons: (1) to facilitate the production of another product or service, (2) for use by the organization's employees in carrying out its operations, or (3) for resale to other customers.

3. Organizations are social constructions. Therefore, "organizations" do not buy things. Rather, individual employees—usually more than one from different departments and organizational levels—make purchase decisions on the organization's behalf. Understanding the personal motivations of these individuals, and their

influence on different stages of the purchasing process, is essential for marketing success.

4. The internet is simultaneously encouraging two opposing trends in organizational purchasing: (1) the growing use of short-term spot market contracts via web-based auctions and (2) the strengthening of long-term buyer–supplier relationships via the sharing of sales and inventory data and the development of supply chain alliances.

5. The mutual interdependence of organizational buyers and their suppliers makes long-term cooperative relationships crucial for customer retention and marketing success. For firms that sell a significant portion of their output to a few large customers, the stakes are very high. Building trust and commitment at multiple levels in both firms—on an individual-to-individual basis—can be a key factor in establishing and maintaining long-term customer relationships that are profitable to both parties.

# ENDNOTES

1. This opening case example is based on material found in "A Moving Story," *The Economist,* December 7, 2002, pp. 65–66; Deutsche Post's 2010 Annual Report, and other material found on the Deutsche Post World Net website, *www.dpwn.de.*

2. For example, see F. Robert Dwyer, Paul H. Schurr, and Sejo Oh, "Developing Buyer–Seller Relationships," *Journal of Marketing* 51 (April 1987), pp. 11–27; Shankar Ganesan, "Determinants of Long-Term Orientation in Buyer–Seller Relationships," *Journal of Marketing* 58 (April 1994), pp. 1–19; and Das Narayandas and Kasturi Rangan, "Building and Sustaining Buyer–Seller Relationships in Mature Industrial Markets," *Journal of Marketing* 68 (July 2004), pp. 63–77.

3. Frederick E. Webster, Jr., *Industrial Marketing Strategy* (New York: John Wiley & Sons, 1991), p. 14. Also see Bob Donath, "To Perform Marketing, Think Purchasing," *Marketing News,* July 17, 2000, p. 12.

4. Thomas V. Bonoma, "Major Sales: Who Really Does the Buying?" *Harvard Business Review,* May–June 1982, pp. 111–19. Also see Susan Lynn, "Identifying Buying Influences for a Professional Service: Implications for Marketing Efforts," *Industrial Marketing Management,* May 1987, pp. 119–30.

5. For a comprehensive review of buying-center research, see Morry Ghingold and David T. Wilson, "Buying Center Structure: An Extended Framework for Research," in *A Strategic Approach to Business Marketing,* Robert Spekman and David T. Wilson, eds. (Chicago: American Marketing Association, 1985), pp. 18–93. See also Robert D. McWilliams, Earl Naumann, and Stan Scott, "Determining Buying Center Size," *Industrial Marketing Management* 21 (February 1992), pp. 43–50; Richard G. Jennings and Richard E. Plank, "When the Purchasing Agent Is a Committee: Implications for Industrial Marketing," *Industrial Marketing Management* 24 (November 1995), pp. 411–19; Jeffery E. Lewin and Naveen Donthu, "The Influence of Purchase Situation on Buying Center Structure and Involvement: A Select Meta-Analysis of Organizational Buying Behavior Research," *Journal of Business Research* 58 (October 2005), pp. 1381–90; and Allison Enright, "It Takes a Committee to Buy into B-to-B," *Marketing News,* February 15, 2006, pp. 12–13.

6. Joseph A. Bellizzi, "Organizational Size and Buying Influences," *Industrial Marketing Management* 10 (1981), pp. 17–21.

7. For a more detailed discussion of these and other account management policies aimed at reaching the various members of a customer's buying center, see Mark W. Johnson and Greg W. Marshall, *Churchill/Ford/Walker's Sales Force Management,* 7th ed. (New York: McGraw-Hill/Irwin, 2003), chaps. 3 and 4.

8. Patrick J. Robinson, Charles W. Faris, and Yoram Wind, *Industrial Buying and Creative Marketing* (Boston: Allyn and Bacon, 1967). See also Erin Anderson, Wujin Chu, and Barton Weitz, "Industrial Buying: An Empirical Exploration of the Buyclass Framework," *Journal of Marketing* 51 (July 1987), pp. 71–86.

9. Wolfgang Ulaga and Andreas Eggert, "Value-Based Differentiation in Business Relationships: Gaining and Sustaining Key Supplier Status," *Journal of Marketing* 70 (January 2006), pp. 119–36.

10. For a more detailed discussion of the organizational purchase decision-making process, see Wesley J. Johnson and Jeffrey E. Lewin, "Organizational Buying Behavior: Toward an Integrative Framework," *Journal of Business Research* 35 (1996), pp. 1–15.

11. For examples, see Pete Engardio, "The Future of Outsourcing," *BusinessWeek,* January 30, 2006, pp. 50–58; and "Global Stretch—When Will Zara Hit Its Limits?" *The Economist,* March 12, 2011, p. 76.

12. Robin Y. Bergstrom, "Hanging a Vision on Quality," *Production,* July 1993, pp. 56–61. See also Wolfgang Ulaga and Andreas Eggert, "Value-Based Differentiation in Business Relationships."

13. I. Frederick Trawick, John E. Swan, Gail W. McGee, and David R. Rink, "Influence of Buyer Ethics and Salesperson Behavior on Intention to Choose a Supplier," *Journal of the Academy of Marketing Science* 19 (Winter 1991), pp. 17–23.

14. Linda Himelstein and Ben Elgin, "Tech's Kickback Culture," *BusinessWeek,* February 10, 2003, pp. 74–77.

**15.** Jan B. Heide, "Interorganizational Governance in Marketing Channels," *Journal of Marketing* 58 (January 1994), pp. 71–85; and Ganesan, "Determinants of Long-Term Orientation in Buyer–Seller Relationships."

**16.** Julia Angwin, "Top Online Chemical Exchange Is Unlikely Success Story," *The Wall Street Journal*, January 8, 2004, p. B1.

**17.** Shawn Tully, "Going, Going, Gone! The B2B Tool That Really Is Changing the World," *Fortune,* March 20, 2000, pp. 132–45.

**18.** Olga Kharif, "B2B, Take 2," *BusinessWeek*, November 25, 2003, pp. 24–25; and George S. Day, Adam J. Fein, and Gregg Ruppersberger, "Shakeouts in Digital Markets: Lessons from B2B Exchanges," *California Management Review* 45 (Winter 2003), pp. 131–51.

**19.** Ulaga and Eggert, "Value-Based Differentiation in Business Relationships."

**20.** Jan B. Heide and Allan M. Weiss, "Vendor Consideration and Switching Behavior for Buyers in High-Technology Markets," *Journal of Marketing* 59 (July 1995), pp. 30–43.

**21.** Robert M. Morgan and Shelby D. Hunt, "The Commitment-Trust Theory of Relationship Marketing," *Journal of Marketing* 58 (July 1994), pp. 20–38; and Kenneth H. Wathne and Jan B. Heide, "Opportunism in Interfirm Relationships: Forms, Outcomes, and Solutions," *Journal of Marketing* 64 (October 2000), pp. 36–51.

**22.** Jan B. Heide and Kenneth H. Wathne, "Friends, Businesspeople, and Relationship Roles: A Conceptual Framework and Research Agenda," *Journal of Marketing* 70 (July 2006), pp. 90–103; and Fred Selnes and James Sallis, "Promoting Relationship Learning," *Journal of Marketing* 67 (July 2003), pp. 80–95.

**23.** Ganesan, "Determinants of Long-Term Orientation in Buyer–Seller Relationships." See also Robert W. Palmatier, Rajiv P. Dant, Dhruv Grewal, and Kenneth R. Evans, "Factors Influencing the Effectiveness of Relationship Marketing: A Meta-Analysis," *Journal of Marketing* 70 (October 2006), pp. 136–53.

**24.** Matthew Swibel and Janet Novack, "The Scariest Customer," *Forbes,* November 10, 2003, pp. 96–97; see also Jan B. Heide and George John, "Alliances in Industrial Purchasing: The Determinants of Joint Action in Buyer–Supplier Relationships," *Journal of Marketing Research,* February 27, 1990, pp. 24–36.

**25.** Valarie Zeithaml, Mary Jo Bitner, and Dwayne Gremler, *Services Marketing,* 5th ed. (New York: McGraw-Hill, 2009), chap. 5.

**26.** Don Hill, "Who Says Uncle Sam's a Tough Sell?" *Sales and Marketing Management,* July 1988, pp. 56–60.

**27.** Tully, "Going, Going, Gone!"

**28.** Zeithaml, Bitner, and Gremler, *Services Marketing.*

# CHAPTER SIX

# Measuring Market Opportunities: Forecasting and Market Knowledge

## Intel's Secret Weapon[1]

GENEVIEVE BELL HAS A RADICAL IDEA. Bell, the only female among Intel's roster of top technical talent dubbed Intel Fellows, and Director of Intel's User Experience Group, thinks the world would be a better place if we can better understand how people would like to use technology, rather than tossing technology that people don't really want into the market at an alarming pace. Bell was given her own lab at Intel in 2010, an event that may change Intel, or even the future of technology itself.

"Imagine," says Bell, "If we were willing to take on board the ways in which PCs don't work and applied that to other technologies such as our refrigerators or televisions. If your fridge said, "I'm terribly sorry, you cannot have that cold milk until I've rebooted myself and downloaded new drivers!" or your TV said, "You cannot watch the end of the cricket match because I am defragging my hard drive," we would all go insane."

### Bell's Charter at Intel

In Bell's view, her charter at Intel is straightforward, "To provide insights and inspire innovation." Her team of social scientists, interaction designers and human factors engineers is charged with setting research directions, leading new product strategy and definition, and driving consumer-centric product innovation and thinking across the company. All this is everyday work for this wiry-haired woman who as a very small girl used to kill things—frogs and the like—growing up in an aboriginal community in Australia's outback.

Why is there a role like Bell's at Intel today? "I joined Intel in 1998," she recalls, "There was a collective sense in Intel's senior management that they didn't know what was going to happen when PCs became mass market. They knew they had market research, they knew they had the skills to size markets and how to survey people, and a little bit of usability work was going on even then, but I think the sense of what was missing was this notion about what was motivating people, what did they care about and was there an opportunity if you understood the things to drive new uses of technology."

"For many years thereafter, a part of every presentation I gave, every class I taught, every meeting I attended was explaining what an anthropologist was, what ethnography was, what was user centered design and why it was going to be a useful tool at Intel." In her 13 years at Intel, Bell has fundamentally changed how the company envisions, plans, and develops its product platforms.

## How Do Anthropology and Ethnography Work?

Bell and her team spend their time hanging out wherever they can find users of technology—people on holiday, people in their workplace, people at home with their families in every corner of the planet. "At Intel, we try to start with people first—we ask questions about who they are and what they care about, we also ask questions about technology: What do you love about it, how does it frustrate you, what do you hate about it, what can't you live without?"

One of the key tools in the modern anthropologist's toolkit is the digital camera. Says Bell, "We can now put digital cameras in the hands of our research participants. There is nothing like the film a five-year-old takes of its own home—you realize that electrical outlets are everywhere and furniture is really badly designed." Seeing the world as it really is and though other people's eyes is what anthropologists do that traditional market researchers often miss.

## What is Bell Learning about Generation X?

One of the questions Bell and her team are sometimes asked is whether today's Generation X—who seem to be digitally connected all the time—are somehow different from their parents' generation. "I don't think it's as easy as we sometimes think," says Bell. "We fall into the trap of assuming that what you are and what you do at 16 is what you will do for the rest of your life. I don't know why we believe that because we were all 16 once, and we mostly don't behave now as we did then."

In a study of early adopters of social networking technology, Bell spoke to a young woman who had just had a baby and was no longer blogging as much.

"Have you ever tried to breast-feed a baby and use a laptop?" the woman asked. "It's just not going to happen. It is much easier to go back to watching television. It doesn't demand so much when I have this other thing I'm trying to do!"

## Can Bell's Work Make a Difference?

Bell, who brings to her craft a doctorate in anthropology from Stanford University, has become one of the world's leading thinkers on the mash-up of humanity and technology. She has worked tirelessly to get Intel chip designers to not simply build ever-faster chips and market them everywhere. The internet, in many parts of the world, means text on a cell phone, so Intel's speedy but pricey Celeron chips are not very relevant in some markets. Intel's cheaper and less power-hungry Atom chips are a better way to go. "Genevieve and her team make us engineers think differently," says Stephen Pawlowski, who leads Intel's chip architecture research team. "We intend to use Bell's expertise heavily as we focus on emerging growth markets."

Perhaps if Bell has her way, one day we'll all be using PCs that actually start when we ask them to start, and stop when we are done. Or if she fails in her quest, Apple will continue its inroads into the PC, smartphone, and other consumer electronics markets with its legendary skills at doing what Bell hopes Intel can do. And the rest of us will continue to be subservient to the products we buy, rather than masters of them.

As Bell puts it, "Anthropology continues to be a really important way to bring voices into the technology realm that really need to be there. Ruth Benedict, an early anthropologist, had a great line—"The role of the anthropologist is to make the world safe for people." Let's hope people like Benedict and Bell prevail!

# Marketing Challenges Addressed in Chapter 6

Entrepreneurs and managers in established firms like Intel need to develop knowledge about their market and industry and synthesize that knowledge into tangible plans that their organizations can act on. These plans can take many forms. For entrepreneurs a business plan may be needed to raise the necessary capital to start the venture. For new product managers in established firms, marketing plans must be developed to win support and resources to permit the product's launch. In organizations of all kinds, annual budgets are prepared to guide decision making for the coming year. These decisions determine staffing, investments in productive capacity, levels of operating expense, and so on. In almost every case, these planning and budgeting activities begin with a sales forecast. Once a sales figure is agreed to, the various activities and investments needed to support the planned sales level are budgeted.

In Chapter 6, we deal with some key issues that enable managers and entrepreneurs to bring life to their dreams. First, we address the challenges in estimating **market potential** and **forecasting** sales, for both new and existing products or businesses. We provide a menu of evidence-based forecasting methods, each of which is useful in some situations, but not others, and we discuss their limitations. We also examine the process by which innovative new products diffuse into the market over time, a source of insight into the particularly difficult task of forecasting sales of innovative new products.

> **STRATEGIC ISSUE**
>
> *We provide a menu of evidence-based forecasting methods, each of which is useful in some situations, but not others.*

Finally, we briefly address the informational needs of the forecasting task—as well as the tasks addressed in the earlier chapters of this book that enable managers and entrepreneurs to understand their market and competitive contexts—to provide guidance on to how to gather, collect, and report data relevant to marketing decision making (i.e., **marketing research**).

The portion of the chapter that deals with marketing research has two objectives. First, we want to enable every reader to be an informed and critical user of marketing since most marketing decision makers rely, in part, on such research to guide key corporate-level and business-level decisions, as was discussed in Chapter 2. Second, we want to provide readers with at least a rudimentary level of competence in designing and carrying out marketing research studies of various kinds, so that they can, even on minimal budgets, obtain useful market and competitive insights to inform their decision making. Depending on hunches—instead of carefully though-out research inquiries, even modest ones done quickly—can be risky.

> **STRATEGIC ISSUE**
>
> *We want to enable every reader to be an informed and critical user of marketing research.*

# Every Forecast Is Wrong!

We know of no manager who has ever seen a forecast that came in *exactly* on the money. Most forecasts turn out too high, some too low. Forecasting is an inherently difficult task because no one has a perfect crystal ball. The future is inherently uncertain, especially in today's rapidly changing markets. Consumer wants and needs shift, buffeted by the winds of ever-changing macro trends. Competitors come and go. New technologies from Intel and others sweep away old ones. Some forecasts are based on extensive and expensive research, others on small-scale inquiries, and still others on uninformed hunches. As we have seen, however, forecasting plays a central role in all kinds of planning and budgeting in all kinds of businesses and other organizations. Given the stakes and the risks entailed in being *very* wrong with a forecast, some effort to prepare an **evidence-based forecast,** instead of a wild guess, is almost always called for, even if time and money are scarce. So forecast we must. But how?

# A Forecaster's Tool Kit: A Tool for Every Forecasting Setting

Before choosing a method to prepare a forecast, one first must know what is to be estimated or forecasted. First, there's the size of the potential market, that is, the likely demand from all actual and potential buyers of a product or product class. An estimate of **market potential** often serves as a starting point for preparing a sales forecast, which we explore in more detail later in this chapter.

Such estimates are particularly crucial for aspiring entrepreneurs, where levels of risk and uncertainty are especially high. Such was the case for two business school graduates, who set out to build a pay telephone business, African Communications Group (ACG), in Tanzania in the early 1990s, before the wave of cell telephone development washed across sub-Saharan Africa. Monique Maddy and Come Laguë knew that, to obtain the financing they would need and to obtain the necessary licenses, they would have to prepare a credible business plan. They also knew that among the most critical elements of any business plan was the sales forecast. Not only would the sales numbers serve as a starting point from which most of the other numbers in the plan would be developed, but they would serve as a key litmus test for prospective investors.

If the sales forecast was well supported and credible, Maddy and Laguë believed the rest of the pieces would fall into place. The secondary data they gathered convinced them that the market and industry were sufficiently attractive. But coming up with hard numbers for market potential and sales revenue was another story altogether.

For starters, they knew that prospective investors would want to know how large the potential market for telephone services would be in the coming years, measured perhaps in several ways: in numbers of telephone users, in numbers and/or minutes of calls, and in dollars or Tanzanian shillings. This market was composed of those consumers who were likely to have both the willingness and ability to buy and would use a phone card or one of ACG's other services at one of ACG's pay phones. There was also the size of the currently **penetrated market,** those who were actually using pay phones in Tanzania at the time of the forecast. Investors would also want to know these figures—the size of the potential and penetrated markets for the market segments Maddy and Laguë intend to serve, their **target market.** They would also need a **sales forecast,** in which they predicted sales revenues for ACG for five years or so. How might Maddy and Laguë do these things?

Established organizations employ two broad approaches for preparing a sales forecast: top-down and bottom-up. Under the top-down approach, a central person or persons take the responsibility for forecasting and prepare an overall forecast, perhaps using aggregate economic data, current sales trends, or other methods we describe shortly. Under the bottom-up approach, common in decentralized firms, each part of the firm prepares its own sales forecast, and the parts are aggregated to create the forecast for the firm as a whole. For an example of how managers at Gap Inc. retailing divisions combine both methods to forecast next-year sales, see Exhibit 6.1.

The bottom-up logic also applied to Maddy and Laguë's task. They could break their anticipated demand into pieces and sum the components to create the summary forecast. These pieces could be market segments, such as small retailers, mobile businesspeople,

## Exhibit 6.1    FORECASTING NEXT YEAR'S SALES AT GAP

At international retailer Gap Inc., forecasting sales for the next year for each of its key brands—Gap, Banana Republic, and Old Navy—is an important process that drives a host of decisions, including how much merchandise to plan to buy for the coming year. Both top-down and bottom-up approaches are used.

At Old Navy, for example, each merchandiser generates a forecast of what level of sales his or her category—women's knit tops, men's jeans, and so on—can achieve for the next year. Group merchandise managers then provide their input and sum these numbers to create a total forecast from a merchandising perspective. A second bottom-up forecast is generated by the store operations organization, summing stores and groups of stores. Simultaneously, a top-down figure is prepared at headquarters in California, using macroeconomic

data, corporate growth objectives, and other factors. The three forecasts are then compared, differences debated, and a final figure on which to base merchandise procurement and expense budgets is determined. Though the effort to prepare such a forecast is considerable, the broad involvement in the process helps to ensure both knowledgeable input to the forecast as well as subsequent commitment to "make the numbers." Most important, Old Navy finds that the different processes together with the ensuing discussion lead to substantially better forecasts.

*Source:* Marshal L. Fisher, Ananth Raman, and Anna Sheen McClelland, "Rocket Science Retailing Is Almost Here: Are You Ready?" *Harvard Business Review,* July–August 2000. For more on Gap, see *www.gap.com.*

consumers, and so on, or product lines, such as revenue from phone cards or individual pay phones, voice-mail fees, pager fees, and the like.

Using the bottom-up approach presented numerous advantages. First, this approach would force them to think clearly about the drivers of demand for each market segment or product line and thus better understand the real potential of their business and its parts. Second, they would be forced to make explicit assumptions about the drivers of demand in each category, assumptions they could debate—and support with evidence gathered from their research—with prospective investors and which they could later verify as the business unfolds. Third, such an approach facilitated "what if" planning. Various combinations of market segments and/or product lines could be combined to build a business plan that looked viable.

What forecasting methods, or tools, could Maddy and Laguë choose from? There are six major evidence-based methods for estimating market potential and forecasting sales: statistical methods, observation, surveys, analogy, judgment, and market tests. A seventh method, not evidenced-based—the SWAG method (Silly Wild-@*# Guess)—is not condoned here, though there is little else to support some forecasts!

## Statistical and Other Quantitative Methods

**Statistical methods** use past history and various statistical techniques, such as multiple regression or time series analysis, to forecast the future based on an extrapolation of the past.[2] This method is typically not useful for ACG or other entrepreneurs or new product managers charged with forecasting sales for a new product or new business, since there is no history in their venture on which to base a statistical forecast.

 In established firms, for established products, statistical methods are extremely useful. When Michelin, the tire manufacturer, wants to forecast demand for the replacement automobile tire market in Asia for the next year, it can build a statistical model using such factors as the number and age of vehicles currently on the road in Asia, predictions of GDP for the region, the last few years' demand, and other relevant factors to forecast market potential as well as Michelin's own replacement tire sales for the coming year. Such a procedure is likely to result in a more accurate forecast than other methods, especially because Michelin has years of experience with which to calibrate its statistical model.

As with all forecasting methods, statistical methods have important limitations. Most important of these is that statistical methods generally assume that the future will look very much like the past. Sometimes this is not the case. US WEST (now CenturyLink), the regional Bell telephone company serving the Rocky Mountain and Northwest regions of the United States, ran into trouble when its statistical models used to predict needs for telephone capacity failed to allow for rapidly increasing use of the internet, faxes, and second lines for teenagers in American homes. Suddenly, the average number of lines per home skyrocketed, and there was not enough physical plant—cable in the ground, switches, and so on—to accommodate the growing demand. Consumers had to wait, sometimes for months, to get additional lines, and they were not happy about it!

Similarly, if product or market characteristics change, statistical models used without adequate judgment may not keep pace. When tire manufacturers produce automobile tires that last 80,000 miles instead of 30,000 to 50,000 miles, the annual demand for replacement tires is reduced. If automobile manufacturers were to change the number of wheels on the typical car from four, the old statistical models would also be in trouble. For example, many large-capacity pickup trucks sold in the United States feature six wheels.

Other quantitative methods, especially useful for new products, have also been developed. These include methods to mathematically model the diffusion of innovation process for consumer durables[3] (discussed later in this chapter) and conjoint analysis,[4] a method to forecast the impact on consumer demand of different combinations of attributes that might be included in a new product.

## Observation

Another method for preparing an evidence-based forecast is to directly observe or gather existing data about what real consumers do in the product-market of interest. Maddy and Laguë conducted a study of pay phone use in Tanzania to find out how many minutes per day the typical pay phone was used. Their study showed that an average of 150 three-minute calls were made per day at the 60 working pay phones then provided by other companies in Dar es Salaam. Revenue for most pay phones fell into the US $100 to $150 range.[5]

Like statistical methods, **observation-based forecasting** is attractive because it is based on what people actually *do*. If behavioral or usage data can be found from existing secondary sources—in company files, at the library, or on the internet—data collection is both faster and cheaper than if a new study like the one Maddy and Laguë conducted must be designed and carried out. For new-to-the-world products, however, observation is typically not possible, and secondary data are not available, since the product often does not yet exist, except in concept form. Had there been no pay phones in Tanzania or a similar country, observation would not have been possible. Market tests and concept tests, which we discuss later in this section, are two ways to get real purchase data about new-to-the-world products.

## Surveys or Focus Groups

Another common way to forecast sales or estimate market potential is to conduct surveys or focus groups. These methods can be done with various kinds of respondents. Consumers, after being shown a statement of the product concept (a **concept test**) or a prototype or sample of the product, can be asked how likely they are to buy, creating a **survey of buyers' intentions.** Buyers can also be asked about their current buying behavior: what they currently buy, how often, or how much they use. Salespeople can be asked how much they are likely to sell, completing a **survey of salesforce opinion.** Experts of various kinds—members of the distribution channel, suppliers, consultants, trade association executives, and so on—can also be surveyed.

As part of their research in Dar es Salaam, Maddy and Laguë surveyed pay phone customers to find out more about them. A whopping 65 percent were using a pay phone because they lacked access to another working phone—good news for the ACG concept! Sixty-three percent were business customers, 20 percent were students or teachers, and 17 percent were other nonbusiness customers. Business customers spent an average of US$10 per week for 14 pay phone calls, and nonbusiness customers spent US$6 per week for 12 calls.[6] By combining these data with demographic data on the Tanzanian population, Maddy and Laguë now had what they needed to prepare an evidence-based, bottom-up forecast of market potential, market segment by market segment.

Surveys and focus groups possess important limitations, however. For one, what people *say* is not always what people *do*. Consumer surveys of buyer intention are always heavily discounted to allow for this fact. For one common approach to doing so, see Exhibit 6.2.

Second, the persons who are surveyed may not be knowledgeable, but if asked for their opinion, they will probably provide it! Third, what people imagine about a product concept in a survey may not be what is actually delivered once the product is launched. If consumers are asked if they will buy an "old world pasta sauce with homemade flavor," they

**STRATEGIC ISSUE**

*Surveys and focus groups possess important limitations, however. For one, what people say is not always what people do.*

## Exhibit 6.2

A SURVEY OF BUYERS' INTENTIONS: WHAT PEOPLE SAY IS NOT WHAT THEY DO

When Nestlé's refrigerated foods division in the United States was considering whether to acquire Lambert's Pasta and Cheese, a fresh pasta company, it wanted to forecast the likely first-year sales volume if the acquisition were completed. To do so, Nestlé used a concept test in which consumers were asked, among other things, how likely they were to try the fresh pasta product. The results were as shown in the first two columns in the following table.

| Purchase Intent | % Response | Rule of Thumb Reduction for Forecasting Purposes | Percentage of Market Deemed Likely to Actually Buy |
|---|---|---|---|
| Definitely would buy | 27% | Multiply by .8 | 27% × .8 = 21.6% |
| Probably would buy | 43% | Multiply by .3 | 43% × .3 = 12.9% |
| Might or might not buy | 22% | Count as zero | |
| Probably or definitely would not buy | 8% | Count as zero | |
| Totals | 100% | | 21.6% + 12.9% = 34.5% |

Even though 70% of consumers surveyed indicated they were likely to buy, Nestlé's experience indicated that these "top two box" percentages should be cut sharply: "definitely" responses were reduced by 20%, while "probably" responses were reduced by 70%; and "maybe" responses were considered as "no." These adjustments, shown in columns three and four, reduced the 70% figure by more than half, to 34.5%. Most consumer product manufacturers who employ concept tests use similar rules of thumb when interpreting purchase intent data for forecasting purposes because they have learned that what people *say* they will buy exceeds what they will *actually* buy. Similar logic is useful in a variety of forecasting situations.

*Source:* Marie Bell and V. Kasturi Rangan, "A Survey of Buyers' Intentions: What People Say Is Not What They Do" from *Nestlé Refrigerated Foods: Contadina Pasta and Pizza,* case no. 9-595-035. Boston: Harvard Business School, 1995. Copyright © 1995 by the President and Fellows of Harvard College. Reprinted by permission. For more on Nestlé, see *www.nestle.com.*

will surely provide a response. Whether they will actually *like* the taste and texture of the sauce that the lab develops is another story!

In general, statistical and observational methods, where adequate data or settings are available in which to apply them, are superior to survey methods of forecasting because such methods are based, at least in part, on what people have *actually done* or bought (e.g., the number of old cars actually on the road or the length of pay phone calls in Tanzania), while survey methods (Are you likely to buy replacement tires this year? How often are you likely to use a pay phone?) are based on what people *say,* a less reliable indicator of their future behavior.

## Analogy

An approach often used for new product forecasting where neither statistical methods nor observations are possible is to forecast the sales or market potential for a new product or product class by **analogy.** Under this method, the product is compared with similar historical data that *are* available. When Danone, the leading marketer of yogurt in Europe, plans to introduce a new flavor, its managers look at the sales history of earlier introductions to forecast the sales for the newest flavor. This method is also used for new-to-the-world high-technology products, for which product prototypes are often either not available or extremely expensive to produce. Rather than conduct surveys to ask consumers about their likelihood to buy a product they can hardly imagine (What would someone have said in 1978 about his or her likelihood to buy a personal computer?), forecasters consider related product introductions with which the new product may be compared.

Indeed, Apple, in developing its now wildly successful music business, had a number of available analogs with which to shed light on the likely demand for paid downloading of music from iTunes and for the demand for a user-friendly portable device—the iPod—on which to play them. First, Napster, the free peer-to-peer music-sharing site, was all the rage with consumers (though not with the music publishing industry, which eventually convinced the courts that Napster was illegal). Second, the Sony Walkman had sold more than 300 million units, proving there was vibrant demand for a portable music player. The use of analogs like these, as well as antilogs—previous examples one explicitly decides *not* to copy—is a crucial approach for many entrepreneurs as they mold their initial ideas into more refined versions that will actually work.[7]

As always, there are limitations. First, the new product and its pricing are never exactly like that to which the analogy is drawn. Downloaded music from Napster was free, but Apple planned to ask consumers to pay for their tunes. What price should Apple charge, and would customers with free downloads available be willing to pay anything at all? Second, market and competitive conditions may vary from when the analogous product was launched. Such conditions must be taken into account.

## Judgment

While we hesitate to call this a forecasting method of its own, since capable and informed judgment is required for *all* methods, sometimes forecasts are made *solely* on the basis of experienced **judgment,** or intuition. Some decision-makers are intuitive in their decision processes and cannot always articulate the basis for their judgments. Said a footwear buyer at Nine West Group, an international manufacturer and retailer of shoes and fashion accessories, "Trend forecasting is a visceral thing that cannot be trained. I rely on my sense of color and texture, but at times I cannot explain why I feel a certain way.... I just know."[8] Those with sufficient forecasting experience in a market they know well may be quite accurate in their intuitive forecasts. Unfortunately, it is often difficult for them to defend their forecasts against those prepared by evidence-based methods when the two differ. Nonetheless, the importance of experienced judgment in forecasting, whether it is used solely and intuitively or in concert with evidence-based methods, cannot be discounted.

## Market Tests

**Market tests** of various kinds are the last of our six commonly used forecasting methods. Used largely for new consumer products, market tests such as **experimental test markets** may be done under controlled experimental conditions in research laboratories or in live **test markets** with real advertising and promotion and distribution in stores.

Use of live test markets has declined over the past few decades for two reasons. First, they are expensive to conduct because significant quantities of the new product must be produced and marketing activities of various kinds must be paid for. More importantly, in today's data-intensive environment, especially for consumer products sold through supermarkets and mass merchants, competitors can buy the data collected through scanners at the checkout and learn the results of the test market without bearing the expense. More diabolically, competitors can engage in marketing tactics to mislead the company conducting the test by increasing sampling programs, offering deep discounts or buy-one-get-one-free promotions, or otherwise distorting normal purchasing patterns in the category. Experimental test markets, on the other hand, are still commonly used.

The coming of the internet has made possible a new kind of market test: an offer directly to consumers on the web. Offers to chat rooms, interest groups, or e-mail lists of current customers are among the common approaches. Use of such techniques has increased due to companies' ability to carry out such tests quickly and at low cost. We explore these and other internet marketing strategies in greater detail in Chapter 14.

## Psychological Biases in Forecasting

To a varying degree, the effectiveness of all of the forecasting methods we've just reviewed is often undermined by excessive optimism on the forecaster's part, especially in new product or new venture settings. Forecasters often fall prey to what Dan Lovallo and Daniel Kahneman call the planning fallacy, a tendency to make decisions based on delusional optimism rather than on a rational weighting of possible gains and losses and the probabilities thereof.[9] A solution they espouse, based on the systematic use of multiple analogs, is discussed in Exhibit 6.3.

## Mathematics Entailed in Forecasting

Regardless of the method used, the ultimate purpose of the forecasting exercise is to end up with numbers that reflect what the forecaster believes is the most likely outcome, or sometimes a range of outcomes under different assumptions, in terms of future market potential or for the sales of a product or product line. The combination of judgment and other methods often leads to the use of either of two mathematical approaches to determine the ultimate numbers: the chain ratio calculation or the use of indices. See Exhibit 6.4 and Exhibit 6.5 for examples applying these mathematical calculations

## Exhibit 6.3 MANAGING THE VIEW THROUGH YOUR ROSE-COLORED GLASSES

Even in new product and new venture settings, virtually nothing is completely new. Many similar products or ventures have undoubtedly preceded yours. Even in the theatre, there are only 36 literary plots: Leonard Bernstein's *West Side Story* is Shakespeare's *Romeo and Juliet,* set in New York's Harlem in the 1950s. Dan Lovallo and Daniel Kahneman argue that the overoptimistic, rosy view can be mitigated by systematically assembling a class of similar projects, laying out the distribution of actual outcomes of those projects from best to worst, and then positioning the current project in that distribution. The resulting forecast will be far more accurate. This "outside view," as they call it, is much more likely to yield realistic estimates because it bypasses the cognitive and organizational biases that tend to hype the more typical "inside view" that's based on the project itself.

*Sources:* John Mullins and Randy Komisar, *Getting to Plan B: Breaking Through to a Better Business Model,* Boston: Harvard Business Press, 2009; and Dan Lovallo and Daniel Kahneman, "Delusions of Success," *Harvard Business Review,* July 2003.

to arrive at sales forecasts. Both mathematical approaches begin with an estimate of market potential (the number of households in the target market in Exhibit 6.4; the national market potential for a product category in Exhibit 6.5). The market potential is then multiplied by various fractional factors that, taken together, predict the portion of the overall market potential that one firm or product can expect to obtain. In Exhibit 6.4, which shows the more detailed of the two approaches, the factors reflect the appeal of the product to consumers, as measured by marketing research data and the company's planned marketing program.

## Exhibit 6.4

CHAIN RATIO FORECAST: TRIAL OF FRESH PASTA

Once Nestlé's research on fresh pasta had been completed (see Exhibit 6.2), it used the chain ratio method to calculate the total number of households who would try their fresh pasta. The chain ratio calculation went like this

| Research Results for: | Data from Research | Chain Ratio Calculation | Result |
|---|---|---|---|
| Number of households in target market | 77.4 million | | |
| Concept purchase intent: adjusted figure from Exhibit 6.2 | 34.5% will try the product | 77.4 million × 34.5% | 26.7 million households will try *if aware* |
| Awareness adjustment: based on planned advertising level | 48% will be aware of the product | 26.7 million × 48% | 12.8 million households will try *if they find product at their store* |
| Distribution adjustment: based on likely extent of distribution in supermarkets, given the introductory trade promotion plan | The product will obtain distribution reaching 70% of U.S. households | 12.8 million × 70% | 9.0 million will try the product |

Similar chain ratio logic is useful in a variety of forecasting settings.

*Source:* Marie Bell and V. Kasturi Rangan, "Chain Reaction Forecast: Trial of Fresh Pasta, from *Nestlé Refrigerated Foods: Contadina Pasta, and Pizza,* case no. 9-595-035 (Boston: Harvard Business School Publishing, 1995). Copyright © 1995 by the President and Fellows of Harvard College. Reprinted by permission. For more on Nestlé, see *www.nestle.com.*

## Exhibit 6.5    ESTIMATING MARKET POTENTIAL USING INDICES

In many countries there are published indices of buying behavior, including the "Annual Survey of Buying Power" published by *Sales and Marketing Management* in the United States. The Buying Power Index (BPI) is a weighted sum of a geographical area's percentage of national buying power for the area, based on census income data (weight = .5), plus the percentage of national retail sales for the area (weight = .3), plus the percentage of national population located in the area (weight = .2). If this calculation comes to 3.50 for a given state or region, one might expect 3.5% of sales in a given category (toys, power tools, or whatever) to come from that geographical area.

**Category development indices** (CDIs) are similar indices that report the ratio of consumption in a certain *category* (for instance, restaurant sales) to population in a defined geographical area. Trade associations or trade magazines relevant to the *category* typically publish such indices. Ratios greater than 1.0 for a particular geographic area (perhaps metropolitan Chicago) indicate that the area does more business than average (compared to the country as a whole) in that category. **Brand development indices** (BDIs) compare sales for a given *brand* (for example, Pizza Hut restaurants) to population. Companies that use BDI indices typically calculate them for their own use. The ratio of the BDI to the CDI for a given area is an indicator of how well a brand is doing, compared to its category overall, in that area. These various indices are useful for estimating market potential in defined geographic areas. They are, however, crude numbers, in that they do not consider differences in consumer behavior from region to region. The CDI or BDI for snowmobiles in Minnesota (with its freezing winters) is far higher than in balmy Texas, for example. Attempting to rectify this imbalance by increasing the snowmobile advertising budget in Texas would be difficult!

# Rate of Diffusion of Innovations: Another Perspective on Forecasting

**STRATEGIC ISSUE**

*Diffusion theory is useful to managers in predicting the likely adoption rate for new and innovative goods or services.*

Before entrepreneurs or established marketers invest in the development and introduction of an innovation, they want to know how rapidly the innovation is likely to be adopted by the target market. The faster the adoption rate, the faster will be the rate at which the innovative new product's sales ramp up. **Diffusion of innovation** theory seeks to explain the adoption of an innovative product or service over time among a group of potential buyers. Lack of awareness and limited distribution typically limit early adoption. As positive word about the product spreads, the product is adopted by additional consumers. Diffusion theory is useful to managers in predicting the likely adoption rate for new and innovative goods or services.

## The Adoption Process and Rate of Adoption

The **adoption process** involves the attitudinal changes experienced by individuals from the time they first hear about a new product, service, or idea until they adopt it. Not all individuals respond alike; some tend to adopt early, some late, and some never. If plotted on a cumulative basis, the percentage of people adopting a new product over time resembles a S curve. Although the curve tends to have the same shape regardless of the product involved, the length of time required differs among products—often substantially.

The time dimension is a function of the rate at which people in the target group (those ultimately adopting) move through the five stages in the adoption process. Generally, the speed of the adoption process depends heavily on the following factors: (1) the risk (cost of product failure or dissatisfaction), (2) the relative advantage over other products, (3) the relative simplicity of the new product, (4) its compatibility with previously adopted ideas, and behavior, (5) the extent to which its trial can be accomplished on a small-scale basis, and (6) the ease with which the central idea of the new product can be communicated.[10] Some new products move quickly through the adoption process (a new breakfast cereal), while others take years. Risk minimization via guarantees and reliable and prompt service can be helpful as can the ability to demonstrate the product's uniqueness in meeting the customer's needs. Source credibility is also important.

The rate at which an innovative new product category passes through the adoption process is also a function of the actions taken by the product's marketers. Thus, the diffusion process may be faster when there is strong competition among competitors, when they have favorable reputations, and when they allocate substantial sums to R&D (to improve performance) and marketing (to build awareness). Early cellular telephones scored high on most of the key adoption factors.

## Adopter Categories

Early adopters differ from later adopters. If we use time of adoption as a basis for classifying individuals, five major groups can be distinguished: innovators, early adopters, early majority, late majority, and laggards. See Exhibit 6.6 for an illustration and Exhibit 6.7 for the approximate size and characteristics of each group.[11] Because each category comprises individuals who have similar characteristics and because individuals differ substantially across categories, these adopter groups can be considered market segments. Thus, one would use a different set of strategies to market a new product to the early adopter group than to market it to the late majority group. For a discussion of the challenges in transitioning marketing efforts from group to group, see Exhibit 6.8.

## Implications of Diffusion of Innovation Theory for Forecasting Sales of New Products and New Firms

Optimistic entrepreneurs or new product managers sometimes wax euphoric about the prospects for the innovations they plan to bring to market. They naively forecast that their innovations will capture 10 or 20 percent of the market in its first year. How likely is it that a truly innovative new product, even a compellingly attractive one, will win all of the innovators plus most of the early adopters in its first year

## Exhibit 6.6

DIFFUSION OF INNOVATION CURVE

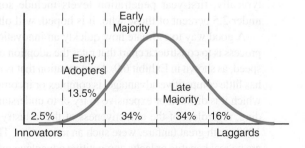

# Exhibit 6.7

SIZE AND CHARACTERISTICS OF INDIVIDUAL ADOPTER GROUP

- **Innovators** represent the first 2.5 percent of all individuals who ultimately adopt a new product. They are more venturesome than later adopters, more likely to be receptive to new ideas, and tend to have high incomes, which reduces the risk of a loss arising from an early adoption.

- **Early adopters** represent the next 13 to 14 percent who adopt. They tend to be more a part of the local scene, are often opinion leaders, serve as vital links to members of the early majority group (because of their social proximity), and participate more in community organizations than do later adopters.

- The **early majority** includes 34 percent of those who adopt. These individuals display less leadership than early adopters, tend to be active in community affairs (thereby gaining respect from their peers), do not like to take unnecessary risks, and want to be sure that a new product will prove successful before they adopt it.

- The **late majority** represents another 34 percent. Frequently, these individuals adopt a new product because they are forced to do so for either economic or social reasons. They participate in community activities less than the previous groups and only rarely assume a leadership role.

- **Laggards** comprise the last 16 percent of adopters. Of all the adopters, they are the most "local." They tend to participate less in community matters than members of the other groups and stubbornly resist change. In some cases, their adoption of a product is so late it has already been replaced by another new product.

---

# Exhibit 6.8   CROSSING THE CHASM: A DIFFICULT TRANSITION IN THE DIFFUSION PROCESS

In Geoffrey Moore's classic book on the marketing of high-technology products, Moore explores the challenges of crossing the "chasm," as he calls it, in the diffusion process between the early adopters and the early majority. For many high-tech products, innovators and early adopters have quite different needs from early majority customers. They are often willing to adopt a revolutionary new product that is not yet very user-friendly or whose product features have not yet been fully developed. Their own technical skill enables them to adapt such a product to their needs and resolve some of the uncertainties inherent in the product's perhaps still-unclear potential. Their self-perception as an innovator gives them comfort in trying new products before others do. Early majority buyers, on the other hand, typically require easier-to-use products, whose benefits are clearly defined, and for which there is proof that the product will perform. Taking a product from the first group of buyers to the second is a difficult challenge, one that is compounded by the fact that buyers in the innovator and early adopter groups are not likely to associate or talk with buyers in the early majority group.

*Source:* Geoffrey A. Moore, *Crossing the Chasm* (New York: HarperCollins, 1991).

---

on the market? History suggests that such penetration levels are rare at the outset. More typically, first-year penetration levels include some but not all of the innovators, well under 2.5 percent of those who, it is hoped, will ultimately adopt!

A good way to estimate how quickly an innovation is likely to move through the diffusion process is to construct a chart that rates the adoption on the six key factors influencing adoption speed, as shown in Exhibit 6.9. An innovation that is risky for the prospective user to try or buy, has little competitive advantage, is complex or incompatible with current user behavior, and for which it is difficult or expensive to try or to understand its benefits is likely to face tough sledding, regardless of the attractiveness of the industry. Personal robots, introduced in the early 1980s with great fanfare, were such an innovation. Thus, introducing a new product that delivers no real benefits or lacks competitive advantage into *any* industry, regardless of its high-tech profile, is likely to be an unpleasant experience!

## Exhibit 6.9

COMPARISON OF RATE OF ADOPTION OF CELLULAR PHONES AND EARLY PERSONAL COMPUTERS FOR HOME USE

| Adoption Factor | Cell Phones | | Home Computers | |
|---|---|---|---|---|
| Risk | +/– | Moderate risk: Cell phones were given away to attract early adopters who agreed to one year's usage. | – | An expensive investment wasted, if it turned out not to be useful. |
| Relative advantage | + | Enabled people to make and receive phone calls from anywhere—in the car or at the beach! | – | It was not clear, in the early days of personal computing, what the advantages of a PC were in the home. |
| Relative simplicity | + | Early cell phones were easy to use. | – | Early PCs were inordinately complex to use. |
| Compatibility with current behavior | + | Just like making or receiving a phone call at home or office. | – | Lots of learning required to use. |
| Ease of small-scale trial | +/– | Easy to demonstrate, but contracts required. | +/– | One could visit a store for hands-on trial but couldn't understand the "bits, bytes, and RAM." |
| Ease of communication of benefits | – | "Make or receive calls anywhere" is easy to understand. | – | Benefits were not clear, thus not communicable. |

Key:
+Favorable for rapid adoption
–Unfavorable for rapid adoption

# Cautions and Caveats in Forecasting

## Keys to Good Forecasting

A key goal of good forecasting is to identify the full range of possibilities about the future, not some illusory set of certainties that are, in fact, not certain at all.[12]  There are two important keys to improve the credibility and accuracy of a set of forecasts of sales and market potential. The first of these is to make explicit the **assumptions** on which the forecast is based. This way, if there is debate or doubt about the forecast, the *assumptions* can be debated, and data to support the assumptions can be obtained. The resulting conversation is far more useful than stating mere opinions about whether the forecast is too high or too low. For ACG, the combination of observational and survey forecasting methods enabled Maddy and Laguë to articulate the assumptions on which their revenue forecasts were based and to support those assumptions with data. Their evidence-based forecast was instrumental in their obtaining US$3.5 million in start-up capital to get their venture off the ground.[13]

> ## STRATEGIC ISSUE
>
> *There are two important keys to improve the credibility and accuracy of forecasts of sales and market potential.*

The second key to effective forecasting is to use multiple methods. When forecasts obtained by different methods converge near a common figure, greater confidence can be placed in that figure. The procedure used at Gap Inc. to forecast next year's sales (see Exhibit 6.1) is an example of such an approach. Where forecasts obtained by multiple methods diverge, the assumptions inherent in each can be examined to determine which set of assumptions can best be trusted. Ultimately, however, any forecast is almost certainly wrong. Contingency plans should be developed to cope with the reality that ultimately unfolds.

# Common Sources of Error in Forecasting

Several sources of potential error in forecasts should be recognized. First, forecasters are subject to anchoring bias, where forecasts are perhaps inappropriately "anchored" in recent historical figures, even though market conditions have markedly changed, for better or worse.[14]

Second, capacity constraints are sometimes misinterpreted as forecasts. Someone planning to open a car wash that can process one car every seven minutes would probably be amiss in assuming sufficient demand to actually run at that rate all the time. A restaurant chain that is able to turn its tables 2.5 times each night, on average, must still do local market research to ascertain how much volume a new restaurant will really generate. Putting similar 80-table restaurants in two trade areas with different population makeup and density, with different levels of competition, will result in different sales levels.

Another source of error in forecasting is incentive pay. Bonus plans can cause managers to artificially inflate or deflate forecasts, whether intentionally or otherwise. "Sandbagging"—setting the forecast or target at an easily achievable figure in order to earn bonuses when that figure is beaten—is common.

Finally, unstated but implicit assumptions can overstate a well-intentioned forecast. While 34.5 percent of those surveyed (after adjustments, as shown in Exhibit 6.2) may indicate their willingness to buy a new grocery product, such as fresh pasta, for such a forecast to pan out requires that consumers actually are *made aware* of the new product when it is introduced and that the product *can actually be found* on supermarket shelves. Assumptions of **awareness** and **distribution coverage** at levels less than 100 percent, depending on the nature of the planned marketing program for the product, should be applied to such a forecast, using the chain ratio method (see Exhibit 6.4).

In today's fast-changing world that is becoming harder and harder to predict, these common sources of error in forecasting are only the beginning of the challenge that forecasters must address. In their new book, *Future Ready: How to Master Business Forecasting*, Steve Morlidge and Steve Player argue that, in many companies, today's forecasting culture—based on a command-and-control mind set, an annual budget-driver schedule, and a predict and comply approach—has simply gone wrong (See Exhibit 6.10).[15]

# Why Data? Why Marketing Research?

In the first portion of this chapter, we provided several approaches to forecasting, each of which requires that data be collected. Similarly, the first five chapters of this book provided frameworks for gaining a better understanding of market and competitive conditions and of what buyers in a given market want and need—what we call **market knowledge.**[16] Obtaining market knowledge also requires data, and so far we've provided little discussion of exactly how one might best find the necessary data. Without relevant and timely data, market knowledge is generally incomplete and often ill-informed, based perhaps on hunches or intuition that may or may not be correct. For an example of how Starbucks uses qualitative marketing research to systematically tap into its customers' ideas and suggestions, see Exhibit 6.11.

Without adequate market knowledge, marketing decisions are likely to be misguided. Products for which there is little demand may be introduced, only to subsequently fail. New markets may be entered, despite market or industry conditions that make success unlikely. Attractive product-markets may be overlooked. Products may be marketed to the wrong target market, when consumers in another market segment would like the product better. Pricing may be too high, reducing sales, or too low, leaving money on the table. Advertising and promotion monies may be poorly spent. Second-best distribution

## Exhibit 6.10

MASTERING FORECASTING

Let's face it. It is nigh on impossible to predict the future. The world is too complex and too dynamic to do so with any confidence. So what is a forecaster to do? Morlidge and Player offer six pragmatic suggestions about what to do and how to do it, as shown in the table below.

| Issue | What to Stop Doing | What to Start Doing |
|---|---|---|
| Purpose | Stop using the budget process and accounting structure to drive your forecasts | Start recognizing the distinction between targets (what you hope will happen) and forecasts (what you think will happen) and the gap between them |
| Time | Stop producing forecasts on the accounting department's timetable | Start producing rolling forecasts, and update them based on the rate of change of the variables that drive your decisions |
| Models | Stop relying on a single approach | Start using different types of models and approaches in combination |
| Measurement | Stop measuring the quality of your forecasts informally | Start routinely measuring forecast error to find biases, rather than focusing on accuracy |
| Risk | Stop forecasting single-point outcomes | Start assessing alternative potential outcomes |
| Process | Stop treating forecasting as an optional exercise | Start building forecasting into the fabric of your managerial processes |

*Source:* Steve Morlidge and Steve Player, *Future Ready: How to Master Business Forecasting* (Chichester, West Sussex, UK: John Wiley and Sons, Ltd, 2010). For more on Steve Morlidge, see *http://www.satoripartners.co.uk/About_Me.html.*

## Exhibit 6.11    STARBUCKS LISTENS, "SPLASH STICKS" ARE THE RESULT

In January 2008, Starbucks founder Howard Schultz returned to his former CEO role, in an effort to reinvigorate the company following a string of disappointing performance figures. One of the first things Schultz did was to launch an online listening post, MyStarbucksIdea.com, in order, as Schultz put it, to instill what he calls "a seeing culture" into the company. It quickly became clear that Starbucks customers weren't reticent. More than 10,000 of them wanted something to plug the hole in the lid on their take-out coffee that would prevent spilling. The result? Starbucks' reusable "splash stick" does just that.

The Starbucks system and others like it, such as Dell's IdeaStorm.com, are powered by new "Ideas" software from Salesforce.com. "It's like a live focus group that never closes," says Marc Benioff, Salesforce's chairman and CEO. The Starbucks website is backed by 48 specially trained "idea partners" who host the online discussions that ensue. They also act as advocates for customers' ideas so they get a fair hearing inside the company. Chris Bruzzo, Starbucks' chief technology officer, says the purpose of MyStarbucksIdea.com was to "open up a dialogue with customers and build up this muscle inside our company." MyStarbucksIdea.com is but one manifestation of how online tools are reshaping the practice of marketing research and leading to a better understanding of what customers want.

*Source:* Jeff Jarvis, "The Buzz from Starbucks Customers," *BusinessWeek* European Edition, April 28, 2008. For more on Starbucks, see *www.starbucks.com.*

channels may be chosen. These outcomes are all too common. Most often, they result from ill-formed or underinformed marketing decisions. Thoughtfully designed, competently executed marketing research can mitigate the chances of such unpleasant outcomes.

Thus, in the remainder of this chapter, we address the challenge of obtaining market knowledge, including the development of systems to track pertinent market information inside and outside the firm, as well as the design and implementation of more targeted studies intended to collect information about a particular marketing problem. We begin by discussing the principal kinds of **market knowledge systems** used in companies large and small, and we show how such systems can improve the timeliness and quality of marketing decisions.

## Customer Relationship Management: Charting a Path toward Competitive Advantage

Marketing is rapidly becoming a game where information, rather than raw marketing muscle, wins the race for competitive advantage. There are four commonly used market knowledge systems on which companies rely to keep pace with daily developments: internal records regarding marketing performance (in terms of sales and the effectiveness and efficiency of marketing programs), marketing databases, competitive intelligence systems, and systems to organize client contact. Taken together, these systems lie at the heart of the systematic practice of **customer relationship management** (CRM). Effective use of CRM is likely to result in happier, higher-volume, more loyal customers. Few of these systems that made modern CRM possible existed in their current form until developments in data processing and telecommunications made them cost-effective.

> **STRATEGIC ISSUE**
>
> *Marketing is rapidly becoming a game where information, rather than raw marketing muscle, wins the race for competitive advantage.*

## Internal Records Systems

Every Monday morning, each retail director at the headquarters of Nine West Retail Stores, a leading operator of shoe specialty stores, receives the "Godzilla Report," a tabulation of detailed sales and inventory information about the fastest-selling items in Nine West stores from the prior week.[17] By style and color, each director learns which items in his or her stores are selling fast and need to be reordered. A similar report provides information about all other styles currently in Nine West's stores, so that slow sellers can be marked down or transferred to stores where those styles are in higher demand. Additional reports aggregate sales information by style and color; by merchandise category (e.g., dress or casual); by store, area, or region; and for various time periods. The information provided by these reports constitutes the backbone of Nine West's decision-making about which shoes to offer in which of its stores. Imagine how much more difficult the retail director's job would be without today's point-of-sale systems to collect and report such data! Imagine the potential advantage Nine West has over shoe retailers who lack such information.

Every marketer, not just retailers, needs information about "what's hot, what's not." Unfortunately, accounting systems generally do not collect such data. Typically, such systems just track dollars of revenue, with no information about *which* goods or services were sold. Thus, marketers need **internal records systems** to track what is selling, how fast, in which locations, to which customers, and so on. Providing input on the design of such systems so that the right data are provided to the right people at the right time is a critical marketing responsibility in any company. But what constitutes critical marketing information varies from company to company and industry to industry.

> **STRATEGIC ISSUE**
>
> *Every marketer, not just retailers, needs information about "what's hot, what's not." Unfortunately, accounting systems generally do not collect such data.*

Nine West retail directors need to know which styles and colors are selling, in which stores, at what rate. Wal-Mart believes its key suppliers need to know its store-by-store item and category sales data, so it provides password-protected online access to such data to some suppliers. Telemarketers need to know which callers are producing sales, at what times of day, and for which products. Marketers of kitchen gadgets through infomercials on late-night television need to know which ads on which stations in which cities are performing, in order to place media spending where it will be most productive. Companies selling their wares to industrial markets through outside salesforces need to know not only which products are selling to which customers, but also which salespeople are selling how much, at what margins and expense rates, and to whom. The salesforce, too, needs information about status of current orders, customer purchasing history, and so on.

For those charged with developing or updating internal record systems in their companies, we provide, in Exhibit 6.12, a series of questions to help marketing decision makers specify what internally generated sales data are needed, when, for whom, in what sequence, and at what level of aggregation.

## Marketing Databases Make CRM Possible

In the technology boom of the late 1990s, several companies launched extensive and expensive projects to help them better manage customer relationships through enhanced use of customer data. Although many large-scale CRM projects have failed to show an adequate return on investment, CRM has proved to be very successful in managing marketing campaigns and in serving customers more effectively and more efficiently. For a discussion of how one charity has benefited from such tools, see Exhibit 6.13.

The purpose of CRM is to develop a unified and cohesive view of the customer from every touch point within the company, whether by telephone, over the web, by mail, or in person, and, in so doing, to increase profitability and shareholder value. CRM, when implemented successfully, is a cross-functional process that requires coordination and broad-based strategic thinking. The goal of most CRM efforts is to profitably win a

## Exhibit 6.12

DESIGNING AN INTERNAL RECORDS SYSTEM FOR MARKETING DECISION MAKERS

| Questions to Ask | Implications for a Chain Footwear Retailer | Implications for an Infomercial Marketer of Kitchen Gadgets |
| --- | --- | --- |
| *What information* is key to providing our customers with what they want? | Need to *know* which shoes sell, in which stores and markets, at what rate | Need to *know* which gadgets sell, in what markets, at what rate |
| *What regular marketing decisions* are critical to our profitability? | Decide which shoes and shoe categories to buy more of, which to buy less of or get rid of, in which stores and markets to sell them | *Decide* on which specific TV stations, programs, and times of day to place infomercials for which gadgets |
| *What data* are critical to managing profitability? | Inventory turnover and gross margin | Contribution margin (gross margin less media cost) per gadget sold |
| *Who* needs to know? | Buyers and managers of merchandise categories | Media buyers, product managers |
| *When* do they need to know for competitive advantage? | For hottest sellers, need to know before competitors, to beat them to reorder market. For dogs, need to know weekly, to mark them down. | Need to know daily, for prior night's ads, to reallocate media dollars |
| In what *sequence* and at what *level of aggregation* should data be reported? | Sequence of report: hot sellers first, in order of inventory turnover. Aggregation: by style and color for buyers, by category for merchandise managers | Sequence of report: hot stations and programs first, in order of contribution margin per gadget sold. Aggregation: By stations/programs for media buyers, by gadget for product managers |

## Exhibit 6.13    CUSTOMER RELATIONSHIP MANAGEMENT (CRM) PROJECTS— A CAMPAIGN MANAGEMENT SUCCESS STORY

Campaign management software allows marketers to design and execute marketing programs that allow them greater control and accountability and that produce better results than in the past. The veterinary charity PDSA in the United Kingdom uses software to manage its database of 3.5 million supporters, its 11 million transactions, and 22 million lines of previous mailing history. Because it is a charity, PDSA realizes that not every supporter wishes to be permanently included in its database, and the system allows for this to be factored in. PDSA uses the database to effectively target customers for its mail shot campaigns and pulls in between €10 million and €12 million in contributions per year.

The European bank ING has used a Dutch software company to implement a CRM system that allows it to identify its customers who never respond to mailshots, thereby reducing their mailings by 30 percent, or 46 million. Other vendors help companies pinpoint customers who are most likely to defect to competitors, thereby reducing customer churn.

*Sources:* "Ringing the Changes," *Precision Marketing,* September 20, 2002; and Michael Dempsey, "FT Report—FT-IT—Getting Back to Basics in Battle to Win Customers," *Financial Times,* November 6, 2002. For more on PDSA, see *www.pdsa.org.uk.*

growing share of key customers' business while finding lower-cost but effective ways of serving less valuable customers. A key element in such efforts is the use of marketing databases, often in conjunction with call centers where many customer contacts occur.

Databases created for CRM purposes typically capture information about most or all of the following for each customer.[18]

- Transactions: Complete transaction detail, including dates, items purchased, and prices paid.
- Instances of customer contact: Whether sales calls, call center inquiries, service requests, or whatever, a CRM system should capture the detail of each and every customer contact with the company.
- Customer demographics: Relevant descriptive data to facilitate market segmentation and target marketing are crucial.
- Customer responses: A CRM system should capture linkages between marketing activities and customer action. Did the customer respond to an e-mail? A direct mail shot? A face-to-face sales call?

Many companies have become quite sophisticated about using marketing databases. Catalog marketers such as Lands' End and L. L. Bean, based in the United States, know who are their best customers and what categories they tend to buy. Online marketers such as Amazon use "cookies," electronic signatures placed at a customer's personal computer, so they not only keep track of what each customer has bought, but also recognize the customer when he or she logs on to their site. Airlines track members of their frequent flyer programs and target some with special promotions. Supermarket chain Tesco in the United Kingdom uses its loyalty cards to track and analyze customer buying patterns and to offer customers coupons and incentives tailored to their buying behavior. Tesco uses its analysis in deciding product placement on shelves, managing coupon campaigns, and tailoring product portfolios to individual stores.[19]

**STRATEGIC ISSUE**

*Designing marketing databases that take effective advantage of customer data that companies are in a position to collect requires that several major issues be considered.*

Designing marketing databases that take effective advantage of customer data that companies are in a position to collect requires that several major issues be considered: the cost of collecting the data, the economic benefits of using the data, the ability of the company to keep the data current in today's mobile society, and the rapid advances in technology that permit the data to be used to maximum advantage.

Collecting information, then storing and maintaining it, always costs money. If a company wants to know more about the demographics and lifestyles of its best customers, in addition to their purchasing histories, it must obtain demographic and lifestyle data about them. Doing so is more difficult than it sounds; many people are unwilling to spend much time filling out forms that ask nosy questions about education, income, whether they play tennis, and what kind of car they drive. The cost of collecting such information must be weighed against its value. What will be done with the information once it is in hand? Marketers planning to build their own databases need also to consider several increasingly important ethical issues, as discussed in Ethical Perspective 6.1.

## ETHICAL PERSPECTIVE 6.1
### Ethical Issues in Database Marketing, internet Marketing, and Marketing Research

New technologies relating to the gathering and use of information about consumers and their behavior, interests, and intentions raise a host of legal and ethical questions. These new technologies have the potential to harm individuals when such information "is used without their knowledge and/or consent, leading them to be *excluded from* or *included in* activities in such a way that they are harmed economically, psychologically, or physically." Examples include the improper disclosure of a person's credit rating, denying medical insurance to an individual based on confidential information, and a person's being placed on target lists for direct mail and telemarketing. The depth of privacy concerns varies from country to country, a critical issue for internet marketers, given their global reach.

Ethical issues in marketing research stem, in large part, from the interaction between the researcher and respondents, clients, and the general public. For instance, respondents should not be pressured to participate, should have the right to remain anonymous, and should not be deceived by fake sponsorship.

Client issues involve the confidentiality of the research findings and the obligation to strive to provide unbiased and honest results regardless of client expectations. The public is very much involved when they are exposed to a sales solicitation disguised as a marketing research study or issuing from data obtained from "volunteer surveys" using write-ins or call-ins.

In discussing the reliability of, and ethical issues involved with, marketing research studies, a *Wall Street Journal* article noted that many studies "are little more than vehicles for pitching a product or opinion." An examination of hundreds of recent studies indicated that the business of research has become pervaded by bias and distortion. More studies are being sponsored by companies or groups with a financial interest in the results. This too often leads to a bias in the way questions are asked.

Because of shortages in time and money, sample sizes are being reduced to the point that, when groups are further broken into subgroups, the margin of error becomes unacceptable—assuming a probability sample was used. In addition to sample size, the way the sampling universe is defined can bias the results. Thus, in a Chrysler study showing that people preferred Chrysler's cars to Toyota's, a sample of only 100 respondents was used in each of two tests, and none owned a foreign car. Thus, the respondents may well have been biased in favor of U.S. cars.

In addition to the preceding problems, subjective sampling procedures are often used, data analysis may be flawed, or only the best conclusions are reported. Frequently researchers are hired whose views on the subject area being researched are known to be similar to those of the client. In an attempt to regulate the marketing research industry, several codes of conduct and ethics have been developed. For the United States these include published codes by the American Marketing Association, the American Association for Public Opinion Research, the Marketing Research Association, and the Council of American Survey Research Organizations. In the United Kingdom, the Market Research Society has developed an ethical Code of Conduct that all members are required to adhere to. Similar organizations have developed localized guidelines in other countries. For one such listing of organizations in other countries, see the British Market Research Association website at *www.bmra.org.uk*.

*Sources:* Paul N. Bloom, Robert Adler, and George R. Milne, "Identifying the Legal and Ethical Risks and Costs of Using New Information Technologies to Support Marketing Programs," in *The Marketing Information Revolution*, Robert C. Blattberg, Rashi Glazer, and John D. C. Little, eds. (Boston: Harvard Business School Press, 1994), p. 294; Cynthia Crossen, "Studies Galore Support Products and Positions, But Are They Reliable?" *The Wall Street Journal*, November 14, 1991, pp. A1 and A8; and Thomas E. Weber, "Europe and U.S. Reach Truce on Net Privacy, but What Comes Next?" *The Wall Street Journal*, June 19, 2000, p. B1.

Building or accessing marketing databases is but a small part of any effective CRM effort, however. Implementing such an effort requires four key steps:[20]

- Gaining broad-based organizational support for creating and adopting a CRM strategy.
- Forming a cross-functional CRM team with membership from all functions that have customer contact.
- Conducting a needs analysis that identifies both customer and business needs.
- Developing a CRM strategy to guide implementation.

One of the things that some CRM efforts make possible is segmenting markets according to the lifetime value of customers, rather than by more traditional means. **Customer lifetime value** (CLV) refers to the margins that a customer generates over a lifetime less the cost of serving the customer. Calculating CLV is not a trivial task; it requires both historical purchasing data and forecasting of future customer purchases which, as we've seen, is always somewhat tenuous. Nevertheless, research conducted by Deloitte Consulting found that companies that use CLV metrics are 60 percent more profitable than firms that do not.[21]

The rapid rise in so-called two-sided markets—in which one set of customers who pay little or nothing (Google search users, for example) are essential to attract a completely different and more lucrative set of customers (advertisers who buy ads that arise in response to Google searches)—has led to an even more vexing challenge than the calculation of customer lifetime value in a conventional sense. This challenge is to figure out the value of both kinds of customers: those who search (and are not asked to pay), in Google's case, and those who pay, the advertisers.

Marketing academicians and marketers themselves are beginning to address this and similar kinds of problems, using sophisticated models that help marketers decide on which set of customers to spend marketing dollars, when, and in what pattern over time.[22] Well-educated marketing graduates with an affinity for web analytics are well placed to make meaningful contributions to their employers or to start new kinds of businesses themselves to address complex issues like these.

## Why CRM Efforts Fail

Unfortunately, there have been many instances of CRM installations that were unsuccessful, sometimes dramatically so. All of us have experienced infuriating occasions where wading through endless levels of telephone prompts and poorly trained or soulless customer service representatives has damaged or destroyed, rather than enhanced, the customer relationship the company sought to build. Research by Bain & Co. suggests that there are four major pitfalls to watch out for:[23]

- Implementing CRM without first developing a strategy.
- Putting CRM in place without changing organizational structure and/or processes.
- Assuming that more CRM is better.
- Failure to prioritize which customer relationships are most worth investing in.

## Client Contact Systems

One good starting point for developing CRM capabilities in companies having limited resources is to put in place salesforce automation software. Such software helps companies disseminate real-time product information to salespeople to enable them to be more productive and more able to satisfy customer needs. Such software also allows companies to effectively capture customer intelligence from salespeople, keep track of it for use on later sales calls, and even transfer it to other salespeople in the event of a salesperson leaving the company. Several low-cost software applications that run on PCs are available. ACT and Goldmine are two of the best-known programs in this arena, and Salesforce.com (see *www.salesforce.com* for a free trial) offers a web-based product. These programs keep track of clients' names, addresses, phone and fax numbers, and so on—along with all kinds of personal tidbits, such as their spouse's and children's names and the kind of wine the client likes to drink—and they also provide an organized way to make notes about each contact with the customer.

CRM is a topic about which whole chapters—even entire books—have been written, so we've just scratched the surface with our treatment here. There are a couple of good websites for those interested in learning more about CRM. One is *www.crmdaily.com*, which provides daily updates on the latest happenings in the CRM field. Another is *www.1to1 .com*, the website of the Peppers and Rogers group, a leading consultancy in this arena.

## Competitive Intelligence Systems[24]

In today's fast-paced business climate, keeping up with competitors and the changing macroenvironment is no easy task. Competitive intelligence (CI) is a systematic and ethical approach for gathering and analyzing information about competitors' activities and related business trends. It is based on the idea that more than 80 percent of all information is public knowledge. The most important sources of CI information include companies' annual and other financial reports, speeches by company executives, government documents, online databases, trade organizations, as well as the popular and business press. The challenge is to find the relevant knowledge, analyze it, and share it with the decision-makers in the organization, so they can use it. The critical questions that managers setting up a CI system should ask are:

- How rapidly does the competitive climate in our industry change? How important is it that we keep abreast of such changes?
- What are the objectives for CI in our company?
- Who are the best internal clients for CI? To whom should the CI effort report?
- What budget should be allocated to CI? Will it be staffed full- or part-time?

In companies that operate in industries with dynamic competitive contexts, the use of full-time CI staff is growing.

## Marketing Research: A Foundation for Marketing Decision Making

We now turn briefly to the **marketing research** task: the design, collection, analysis, and reporting of research intended to gather data pertinent to a *particular* marketing challenge or situation. The word *particular* is very important. Marketing research is intended to address carefully defined marketing problems or opportunities. Research carried out without carefully thought-out objectives usually means time and money down the tubes! Some marketing problems commonly addressed through marketing research include tracking customer satisfaction from unit to unit or year to year (**tracking studies**); testing consumer responses to elements of marketing programs, such as prices or proposed advertising campaigns; and assessing the likelihood that consumers will buy proposed new products.

**STRATEGIC ISSUE**

*Research carried out without carefully thought-out objectives usually means time and money down the tubes!*

## Exhibit 6.14

STEPS IN THE MARKETING RESEARCH PROCESS: WHAT CAN GO WRONG?

| Steps | What Frequently Goes Wrong? |
| --- | --- |
| 1. Identify managerial problem and establish research objectives. | Management identifies no clear objective, no decision to be made based on the proposed research. |
| 2. Determine data sources (primary or secondary) and types of data and research approaches (qualitative or quantitative) required. | Primary data are collected when cheaper and faster secondary data will do. Quantitative data are collected without first collecting qualitative data. |
| 3. Design research: type of study, data collection approach, sample, etc. | These are technical issues best managed by skilled practitioners. Doing these steps poorly can generate misleading or incorrect results. |
| 4. Collect data. | Collector bias: hearing what you want to hear. |
| 5. Analyze data. | Tabulation errors or incorrect use or interpretation of statistical procedures may mislead the user. |
| 6. Report results to the decision maker. | Some users do not really want objective information—they want to prove what they already believe to be true. |

We begin by presenting a model of the marketing research process that sets forth the many decisions that must be made to conduct effective and actionable marketing research. The steps in the marketing research process are shown in Exhibit 6.14. As this exhibit shows, the marketing research process is fraught with numerous opportunities for error. That's why it's so important that all who play influential roles in setting strategy for their firms or who use marketing research results for decision making be well-informed and critical users of the information that results from market research studies. To this end, we now address each of the steps in the marketing research process, from a decision-making point of view.

## Step 1: Identify the Managerial Problem and Establish Research Objectives

As for any other form of human endeavor, if you don't have clear objectives, any road will get you there! The same is true for conducting marketing research. A good place to start is to ask what the managerial problem or question is that a proposed program of research might address. Maddy and Laguë's initial inquiries about starting a telecommunications business in Tanzania had numerous managerial questions to be answered. How attractive is the telephone market in Tanzania? What segments are most attractive? How large is the market, and how fast is it likely to grow? Is the industry attractive? Who are the key competitors and what competitive advantages might they have and not have if we enter? What telecommunications wants and needs are not well satisfied currently, for which groups of consumers? How likely are consumers to use the system we propose to put in place? How much might they be willing to pay? What incentives would retailers or others need to sell our phone cards or to place our pay phones on their premises? Taking each of these managerial questions, one at a time, and applying appropriate analytical frameworks to each of them—such as macro trend analysis and Porter's five forces (Chapter 3), and so on— provides clear guidance for the kind of information the researcher needs. The result is a set of **research objectives** (e.g., determine market size and growth rate, assess supplier power in this industry, and so on) that will drive the research.

# Step 2: Determine the Data Sources and Types of Data Required

This step is critical in determining the cost-effectiveness and timeliness of the research effort. The researcher must answer two key questions at this stage: Should I gather data from primary or secondary sources? Whichever type of data sources are called for, do I need qualitative or quantitative research to satisfy my research objectives, or both?

**Primary or Secondary Sources?**    **Primary data** are data collected from individual research subjects using observation, a survey, interviews, or whatever. The data are then gathered and interpreted for the particular research objective at hand. **Secondary data** already exist—on the internet, in government documents, in the business press, in company files, or wherever. Someone has already done the primary data collection and placed the data where others can access it, whether easily or with difficulty, whether free or at some cost.

Which is better—primary or secondary data? *If* (and it's an important *if*) a research objective can be met using secondary data, that's usually the best course to follow. Why?

**STRATEGIC ISSUE**

*Which is better—primary or secondary data?*

First, it's usually quicker to find the data somewhere than to collect information from scratch. Imagine having to collect demographic data about Tanzania without the Tanzanian census! Second, it's usually less costly to simply find existing secondary data than to collect the information as primary data all over again. Third, secondary data are typically based on what people actually *do,* or how they actually *behave.* Surveys, a common form of primary data, are based on what people *say.* The two are not the same, as we saw earlier in the forecasting portion of this chapter.

For Maddy and Laguë, secondary data, if available, should answer several of their research questions, such as those on market and industry attractiveness, *if* Tanzania's government has made gathering and reporting such data a priority. Often, the availability and quality of a country's secondary data, from government as well as other sources, correlates closely with its degree of economic development. Refer to Exhibit 3.14 in Chapter 3 for a list of some commonly used websites for market and industry analysis. Similar sources are available for most developed countries. To explore consumers' willingness to use the innovative system of pay phones and calling cards that Maddy and Laguë proposed to develop, primary data were necessary. It is unlikely that a study to evaluate the attractiveness of such a system to consumers had already been conducted.

**Qualitative or Quantitative Data and Research Approaches?**    Where secondary data are to be collected, the researcher needs to decide whether qualitative data, such as that concerning sociocultural trends in Tanzania, or quantitative data, such as the number of households in a particular income group in Dar es Salaam, are required. Most secondary research studies require both qualitative and quantitative data.

If primary data are necessary, a decision must be made about whether to collect that data using qualitative or quantitative research approaches. **Qualitative research** usually involves small samples of subjects and produces information that is not easily quantifiable. Qualitative data may yield deeper insights into consumer behavior than are available from quantitative research. For this reason, qualitative research is often conducted first and used to guide subsequent quantitative research. An important drawback of qualitative research, however, is that its generally small samples may not fairly represent the larger population. Most experienced marketing researchers would say, "*Never generalize* from qualitative research. Always follow up with a quantitative study to test the hunches developed in the qualitative study." Such

**STRATEGIC ISSUE**

*Never generalize from qualitative research.*

statements presume, however, that adequate research resources are available to conduct additional studies. Often, and particularly in entrepreneurial settings, such is not the case, and decision makers are forced to rely, albeit tenuously, on small-scale qualitative studies.

**Quantitative research** collects data that are amenable to statistical analysis, usually from large enough samples so that inferences may be drawn with some confidence to the population from which the subjects in the sample are drawn. The principal benefit of quantitative research lies in its measurement of a population's attitudes toward or likely response to products or marketing programs. Because of their larger sample sizes and quantitative metrics, greater confidence can be placed in quantitative studies, when conducted properly, using appropriate sampling procedures and statistical techniques. We address these issues in more detail in subsequent sections of this chapter.

### Qualitative Research Techniques

There are seemingly as many qualitative research techniques as there are stars in the sky.[25] The most common ones, however, are focus groups and interviews of various kinds.[26] A focus group typically consists of 8 to 12 consumers from the marketer's target market brought together at a research facility to discuss a particular marketing problem, such as attitudes toward a proposed new product and various possible features.

A skilled moderator conducts the focus group, records the conversation on audio- and/or videotape, and writes a report of the findings. Typically, two or more groups are conducted for a single research project. Focus groups have significant limitations: They are subject to data distortion caused by a dominant person in the group, their results are difficult to interpret, and they are neither representative of nor generalizable to a larger population, due to their small sample size and convenience samples. They are one way, however, to begin a research inquiry or to gather at least some information when research budgets are tight.[27] In-depth interviews are another, perhaps better, approach.

A set of qualitative research methods whose use is growing fast among marketing professionals is the use of ethnographic and anthropological approaches, like those Genevieve Bell and her team employ at Intel, as we saw at the outset of this chapter. Such approaches have been used by many other high-tech companies to better understand consumers' real needs. Among the results of such efforts was Nokia's insight about the need for very simple and inexpensive but dust-proof cell phones in India. More than 200 million of Nokia's low-price Model 1100 handset were sold between 2003 and 2007, contributing to the rapid growth of cell phone penetration in India and other emerging markets that took hold at about that time.[28] Alas, not all companies, whether tech-driven or otherwise, actually seek and are willing to invest in an in-depth understanding of what consumers really need.

### Quantitative Research Techniques

In most quantitative research, questionnaires are used that enable the researcher to measure the subjects' responses on quantitative scales. These scales enable the researcher to compare product attributes, the responses of demographically different consumers, and other differences in order to better understand what consumers prefer, how satisfied they are with one product compared to others, and so on. Where statistically significant differences are found, managers can be relatively certain at some known level of confidence that the differences uncovered in the research reflect those actually found in the whole population. Examples of several kinds of quantitative scales commonly used in such research are shown in Exhibit 6.15.

Novice researchers, or those whose budgets are limited, can sometimes obtain useful market knowledge from small-scale research that begins with some qualitative research, perhaps several interviews, and concludes with a quantitative study using measures such as those shown in Exhibit 6.15. Gaining experience with such research, even in a class

## Exhibit 6.15

SOME COMMONLY USED TYPES OF SCALES FOR QUANTITATIVE MARKET RESEARCH

| Type of scale | Description | Example |
|---|---|---|
| Semantic Differential Scale | A scale connecting two bipolar words or phrases | How satisfied are you with your provider of cable TV? Not at all satisfied 1 2 3 4 5 6 7 Extremely satisfied |
| Likert Scale | A statement with which the respondent shows the amount of agreement/disagreement | I am extremely satisfied with my provider of cable TV. Strongly agree 1 2 3 4 5 6 7 Strongly disagree |
| Quality Rating Scale | Rates some attribute on a scale from "excellent" to "poor" | My cable TV service, overall, is:<br>Poor   Fair   Good   Very Good   Excellent |
| Importance Scale, using semantic differential attribute format | Rates the importance of some. attribute | How important are the following criteria to your satisfaction with your cable TV provider? |

<table>
<tr><td></td><td>Not at all<br>important</td><td>Extremely<br>important</td></tr>
<tr><td>Answers the phone quickly</td><td colspan="2">1 2 3 4 5 6 7</td></tr>
<tr><td>Prompt repair service</td><td colspan="2">1 2 3 4 5 6 7</td></tr>
<tr><td>Cleans up after installation</td><td colspan="2">1 2 3 4 5 6 7</td></tr>
<tr><td>Service never goes dark</td><td colspan="2">1 2 3 4 5 6 7</td></tr>
</table>

| Intention-to-Buy Scale | Measures how likely the respondent is to buy at some price | How likely are you to sign up for the new InterGalactic Channel for an extra $9.95 per month? |
|---|---|---|

| | |
|---|---|
| Definitely | _____ |
| Probably | _____ |
| Might or might not | _____ |
| Probably not | _____ |
| Definitely not | _____ |

project setting, provides future managers with some appreciation for the conduct of marketing research and the limitations to its interpretation.

## Step 3: Design the Research

Designing secondary research is a simple matter of finding sources of informations sufficient to satisfy the research objectives and ensuring that the sources are credible.

For primary qualitative research, such as focus groups or interviews, detailed guides are prepared for conducting the research to specify what questions are to be asked. For primary quantitative research, research design is the most technical and most difficult step in conducting the research. The key decisions to be made in primary research design are to determine the data collection method and prepare the research instrument, determine how to contact the participants in the research, and design the sampling plan.

### Determine the Data Collection Method and Prepare the Research Instrument
The most common methods of collecting primary data are observation, survey, and experiment. Observation is just that: observing subjects using pay phones in Tanzania, in Maddy and Laguë's case. Typically, a form is prepared on which the observer

records what is being observed, perhaps minutes of use and gender of the user, among other things. Many companies favor the use of observation to better understand not only consumers, but also salespeople and distribution channel members.

Surveys involve writing a questionnaire, which, will include questions and either scaled answers (such as those shown in Exhibit 6.15) or spaces for open-ended answers. Demographic information about the respondent is also usually requested to aid in market segmentation and market targeting decisions, which we address in Chapters 7 and 8. Constructing survey questions and formats for the answers is more difficult than one might expect and is beyond the scope of this book, but several sources cited in this chapter, as well as Exhibit 6.15, can help bring the reader up to speed on these tasks.[29]

Experiments are studies in which the researcher manipulates one or more variables, such as price or product features, either within the context of a survey or in a laboratory or field setting, in order to measure the effect of the manipulated variable on the consumer's response. One common use of experiments is to examine the consumer's likelihood to buy a new product at different price points. Different respondents are given different prices for the product, and the researcher tests differences in consumers' likelihood to buy as the price changes. This procedure entails less bias than asking consumers what they would be willing to pay for a product, the typical answer to which is "as little as possible!"

**Determine the Contact Method**    Once a data collection method is chosen, the researcher must decide how to contact those who will participate in the research. Common choices include face-to-face (perhaps in a shopping mall or a public place), mail, telephone, fax, e-mail, and the internet. Exhibit 6.16 shows some of the trade-offs among these methods. A significant problem with survey research is that those who choose *not* to participate when asked ("We're eating dinner now, and please don't call back!") may differ from those who *do* participate. This nonresponse bias may distort the results of the research. Response rate can also be a problem, since many who are asked to participate will not do so. Response rates for mail surveys generally run about 10 to 15 percent. The other types are better or worse, as shown in Exhibit 6.16. Thus, for a mail survey, 6 to 10 times the number of surveys the researcher hopes to receive must be mailed.

Increasingly, marketing research of all kinds, especially surveys, is moving from more costly face-to-face or telephone contact methods to online approaches. Proponents argue that there are benefits in doing so. First, it's fast, easy, and in some cases free, thanks to numerous websites like *www.zoomerang.com* that offer easy-to-use online survey tools. Second, respondents can choose when to take the survey, so they may provide more thoughtful, more complete answers. And researchers can ask more sensitive questions because the process is less intrusive.[30]

## Exhibit 6.16

Pros and Cons of Different Contact Methods for Survey Research

| Method | Response rate | Cost | Timelines | Nonresponse bias |
|---|---|---|---|---|
| **Face-to-Face** | High | High | Slow | Low |
| **Mail** | Low | Low | Slow | High |
| **Telephone** | Moderate | Moderate | Fast | Moderate |
| **Fax** | Moderate | Low | Fast | High |
| **E-mail** | Low | Low | Fast | High |
| **Internet** | Low | Low | Fast | High |

Significantly, some of the world's largest users of marketing research, including Procter & Gamble, are turning more and more to online methods. P&G's global consumer and market knowledge officer Joan Lewis expects surveys to decline sharply in importance by 2020. The rise in social media is the reason why. "The more people see two-way engagement and being able to interact with people all over the world, I think the less they want to be involved in structured research," she said. "If I have something to say to that company now, there are lots of ways to say it. We are all brought into the research industry with the almost dogmatic belief that representation is everything," Ms. Lewis said, noting that she doesn't discount the importance of having samples representative of a population for some research. "But we need to get away from the notion that being representative of something is the only way to learn."[31]

But critics have significant concerns, the main one being that it's difficult to ensure that the huge pools of online respondents are representative of the wider population. The fact that respondents are not selected randomly violates a core tenet of probability-based sampling and interpretation of the results, notes Stanford professor Jon A. Krosnick, who has studied polling for eight years. Gary Langer, Director of Polling at ABC News, says the pools of volunteer participants—lured by gifts or cash—who take some polls are simply poll-taking clubs. ABC refuses to run the results of nonrandom polling.[32]

### Design the Sampling Plan

Selecting a sample of participants for observational, survey, or experimental research requires that three questions be answered:

1. Who is the population (or universe) from which the sample of **respondents** will be drawn?
2. What sample size is required to provide an acceptable level of confidence?
3. By what method, probability sampling (also called random sampling) or nonprobability sampling (such as convenience sampling), will the sample be selected?

We'll discuss each of these issues briefly.[33] First, the population from which the sample is to be drawn must be clearly specified. Typically, it consists of the target market, defined in demographic or behavioral terms (e.g., users of pay telephones in Tanzania), although excluding current nonusers might not be a good idea for Maddy and Laguë if they hope to expand the market.

Second, the sample must be large enough to provide confidence that statistical data, such as mean responses to survey questions, are *truly* within some narrow-enough range, sometimes called the **margin of error.** In general, the larger the sample size, the smaller the margin of error. If Maddy and Laguë observed only three pay phones in their research, they could not be very confident that the average daily minutes of use at those phones was representative of use for 60 pay phones in Tanzania. A larger sample would give them more confidence. Exhibit 6.17 provides rough approximations of the margin of sampling error associated with different sample sizes.

Third, the idea behind **probability,** or **random, sampling** is that every person in the population has an equal chance of being selected. If **nonprobability samples,** such as **convenience samples,** are used, the sample may be biased. If Maddy and Laguë observe consumers using pay phones in the international departure lounge at the airport in Dar es Salaam, this sample would not reflect usage by the general Tanzanian population. Convenience samples are used quite often for marketing research because true random samples are more difficult and costly to reach. The nonresponse problem makes almost all samples potentially biased in the same way. An astute user should always ask about the sample selection method. If the method is not random, the user should inquire about how the sample was selected to look for any source of bias that might distort the research results.

### STRATEGIC ISSUE

*An astute user should always ask about the sample selection method. If the method is not random, the user should inquire about how the sample was selected.*

## Exhibit 6.17

MARGIN OF ERROR ASSOCIATED WITH DIFFERENT SAMPLE SIZES

Assume a poll of eligible voters is taken to determine which candidate is in the lead. Suppose the results are that Jones has 45% of the voters in her corner. Smith has 41%, and 14% are undecided. Can we conclude that Jones leads Smith? It depends, in part, on the sample size of the poll.

| Sample size | Approximate margin of error for 95% confidence level | Implications for the Jones and Smith race (in which Jones appears to be leading) |
| --- | --- | --- |
| 100 | 10 percentage points | Jones has 45% plus or minus 10%, or 35% to 55%. |
| | | Smith has 41% plus or minus 10%, or 31% to 51%. |
| | | Smith could be leading by as much as 51% to 35%. |
| 500 | 4–5 percentage points | Jones has 45% plus or minus 4.5%, or 40.5% to 49.5%. |
| | | Smith has 41% plus or minus 4.5%, or 36.5% to 45.5%. |
| | | Smith could be leading by as much as 45.5% to 40.5%. |
| 1,000 | 3 percentage points | Jones has 45% plus or minus 3%, or 42% to 48%. |
| | | Smith has 41% plus or minus 3%, or 38% to 44%. |
| | | Smith could be leading by as much as 44% to 42%. |

What will the headlines say? Probably that Jones leads Smith, 45 percent to 41 percent, if the sample size is 1,000, typical In national or statewide political polls. Is this a fair conclusion?

## Step 4: Collect the Data

By now, the hardest parts of the research process are complete, though the most time-consuming parts have just begun. The data collection contributes more to overall error than any other step in the process. In some cases, especially where entrepreneurs or marketers conduct marketing research themselves instead of contracting with a third party for data collection, collector bias can be a problem. The person collecting the data might, in his or her enthusiasm for the product, bias the respondents so they tell the researcher what they think he or she wants to hear. Errors in face-to-face or telephone surveys include those that derive from nonresponse by some respondents; selection errors by the interviewer (i.e., selecting respondents who are not members of the specified population); the way the interviewer asks the questions; the interviewer's interpretation and recording of answers; and even interviewer cheating. In surveys conducted by fax, e-mail, or over the internet, an additional problem is that the researcher does not know who actually replied to the survey. The data collection effort can be substantial. To complete 100 surveys in the United Kingdom with randomly selected homes using random digit dialing, several hundred phone numbers will likely be required and 1,000 dialings!

## Step 5: Analyze the Data

When the data have been collected, the completed data forms must be processed to yield the information the project was designed to collect. The forms are checked to see that instructions were followed, that the data are complete, and that the data are logical and consistent within each respondent's form. Typically, the data are then entered into computer files; percentages and averages are computed; and comparisons are made between different classes, categories, and groups of respondents. Often, sophisticated statistical analyses are required.

## Step 6: Report the Results to the Decision Maker

This is where the rubber meets the road. If the research study began with clearly defined objectives, reporting the results simply returns to those objectives and reports what was found. Where research is carried out without clear objectives, reporting can be difficult, as no clear conclusions may be available. Lots of marketing research money is wasted in some companies because of poorly specified research objectives.

## What Users of Marketing Research Should Ask

The research process described in the preceding section makes clear where many of the potential stumbling blocks are in designing and conducting marketing research. The informed and critical user of marketing research should ask the following questions, ideally before implementing the research or if necessary subsequent to its completion, to ensure that the research is unbiased and the results are trustworthy.

1. What are the objectives of the research? Will the data to be collected meet those objectives?
2. Are the data sources appropriate? Is cheaper, faster secondary data used where possible? Is qualitative research planned to ensure that quantitative research, if any, is on target?
3. Are the planned qualitative and/or quantitative research approaches suited to the objectives of the research? Qualitative research is generally better for deep insights into consumer behavior, while quantitative research is better for measurement of a population's attitudes and likely responses to products or marketing programs.
4. Is the research designed well? Will questionnaire scales permit the measurement necessary to meet the research objectives? Are the questions on a survey or in an interview or focus group unbiased? ("Isn't this a great new product? Do you like it?") Do the contact method and sampling plan entail any known bias? Is the sample size large enough to meet the research objectives?
5. Are the planned analyses appropriate? They should be specified *before* the research is conducted.

## Rudimentary Competence: Are We There Yet?

One objective we set at the outset of this chapter was to provide the reader with at least a rudimentary level of competence in designing and carrying out marketing research studies. Entire courses dealing with marketing research are offered in nearly every business school marketing curriculum and half a chapter does little justice to the detail and technical expertise involved in this important craft. Nonetheless, by reading this chapter and a few of the cited reference sources on particular research techniques, the reader should be able to conduct at least some useful research for a class project or even a low-budget entrepreneurial venture. Such research, despite its limitations, will give the reader an experiential base useful in assessing research done by others, and it will surely yield greater insights into the marketing problem than will hunches alone. Given the importance of marketing research in marketing and strategic decision making today, we encourage every business student from every business discipline to try his or her hand at it.

In the remaining chapters in this book, we shall return from time to time to the marketing research topic and show how marketing research informs not only market and competitive analysis and customer understanding, but also the design and implementation of marketing programs.

In recent years, a wide variety of software applications have been developed to aid marketers in conducting marketing research and applying it and other data to specific marketing problems. Various trade magazines publish annual directories that list providers of these tools and other services that facilitate marketing research.[34] In subsequent chapters, we'll point out specific applications for which such applications are commonly used.

# TAKE-AWAYS

1. Every forecast and estimate of market potential is wrong! *Evidence-based* forecasts and estimates, prepared using the tools provided in this chapter, are far more credible—and generally more accurate—than hunches or wild guesses. A menu of evidence-based forecasting approaches is provided in this chapter.

2. Forecasts have powerful influence on what companies do, through budgets and other planning procedures. Thus, forecasting merits significant management attention and commitment.

3. Superior market knowledge is not only an important source of competitive advantage, but it also results in happier, higher volume of, and more loyal customers. Thus, the systematic development of market knowledge is a critically important activity in any organization.

4. Much can go wrong in marketing research and often does. Becoming an informed and critical user of marketing research is an essential skill for anyone who seeks to contribute to strategic decision making. Tools for obtaining this skill are presented in this chapter.

# ENDNOTES

**1.** This material is drawn from Stephen Prentice, "Intel's Genevieve Bell: An Anthropologist at the Cutting Edge of Technology and Society: A Gartner Fellows Interview," April 23, 2010; Rob Enderle, "Intel's Secret Weapon", *TG Daily, http://www.tgdaily.com/hardware-opinion/50438-genevieve-bell-intel*; *http://www.gartner.com/displaydoument?id1358720*; Mike Magee, "Intel's Genevieve Bell Drank Water out of Frogs", TechEye, *http://www .techeye.net/chips/*; Michael V. Copeland, "Intel's Cultural Anthropologist," *Fortune* European Edition, September 27, 2010, pp. 16–17; Intel, "Mobile Etiquette Mishaps Are Running Rampant", *Hoteliers,* March 17, 2011, *http:// www.4hoteliers.com/4hots_nshw.php?mwi8403*; and the Intel website at *http://www.intel.com/pressroom/kist/bios/gbell.htm.*

**2.** Kenneth D. Lawrence, Ronald K. Klimberg, and Sheila M. Lawrence, *Fundamentals of Forecasting Using Excel* (New York: Industrial Press, 2009).

**3.** See Frank M. Bass, "A New Product Growth Model for Consumer Durables," *Management Science,* January 1969, pp. 215–27; and Trichy V. Krishnan, Frank M. Bass, and V. Kumar, "Impact of a Late Entrant on the Diffusion of a New Product/Service," *Journal of Marketing Research,* May 2000, pp. 269–78.

**4.** For more on conjoint analysis, see Vithala Rao, *Applied Conjoint Analysis* (New York: Springer Publishing, 2009).

**5.** Anita M. McGahan, *African Communications Group (Condensed)* (Boston: Harvard Business School Publishing, 1999).

**6.** McGahan, *African Communications Group (Condensed).*

**7.** For more on analogs and antilogs and their use in developing evidence-based forecasts and business models, see John Mullins and Randy Komisar, *Getting to Plan B: Breaking Through to a Better Business Model* (Boston: Harvard Business Press, 2009).

**8.** Colin Welch and Ananth Raman, *Merchandising at Nine West Retail Stores* (Boston: Harvard Business School Publishing, 1998).

**9.** Dan Lovallo and Daniel Kahneman, "Delusions of Success," *Harvard Business Review,* July 2003.

**10.** Everett M. Rogers, *Diffusion of Innovations* (New York: Free Press, 1983).

**11.** Rogers, *Diffusion of Innovations.*

**12.** Paul Saffo, "Six Rules for Effective Forecasting," *Harvard Business Review,* July–August 2007.

**13.** Dale O. Coxe, *African Communications Group* (Boston: Harvard Business School Publishing, 1996).

**14.** Amos Tversky and Daniel Kahneman, "Judgment under Uncertainty," *Science* 185 (1974), pp. 1124–31.

**15.** Steve Morlidge and Steve Player, *Future Ready: How to Master Business Forecasting* (Chichester, West Sussex, UK: John Wiley and Sons, Ltd, 2010).

**16.** Li and Calantone define market knowledge as "organized and structured information about the market." See Tiger Li and Roger J. Calantone, "The Impact of Market Knowledge Competence on New Product Advantage: Conceptualization and Empirical Examination," *Journal of Marketing,* October 1998, pp. 13–29.

**17.** Welch and Raman, *Merchandising at Nine West Retail Stores.*

**18.** Russell S. Winer, "A Framework for Customer Relationship Management," *California Management Review* 43 (*Summer 2001*), pp. 89–105.

**19.** "Marketing—Clubbing Together," *Retail Week,* November 8, 2002.

**20.** For more on this topic, see V. Kumar and Werner J. Reinartz, *Customer Relationship Management* (Hoboken, NJ: John Wiley & Sons, 2006).

21. Sudhir Kale, "CRM Failure and the Seven Deadly Sins," *Marketing Management* 13 (April 2004), pp. 42–46.

22. For one such approach, see Sunil Gupta and Carl F. Mela, "What Is a Free Customer Worth?" *Harvard Business Review,* November 2008, pp. 102–109.

23. Darrell K. Rigby, Frederick F. Reichfeld, and Phil Schafter, "Avoid the Four Perils of CRM," *Harvard Business Review,* February 2002, pp. 101–9.

24. Information in this section comes from the Society of Competitive Intelligence Professionals website at *www.scip.org.*

25. For additional qualitative research techniques. See Abbic Griffin, "Obtaining Customer Needs for Product Development", in M.D. Rosenau, ed. *The PDMA Handbook of New Product Development* (New York: John Wiley and Sons, 1996): and Gerald Zaltman, "Rethinking Marketing Research: Putting the People Back to", *Journal of Marketing Research,* November 1997, pp. 424–37.

26. The definitive guide to conducting in-depth long interviews is Grant McCracken. *The Long Interview* (Newbury Park, CA: Sage Publications, 1988). For an adaptation of McCracken's approach to new product and new venture settings, where discovering the "unknown unknowns" is a primary research objective. See John W. Mullins, "Discovering

Unknown Unknown's." *MIT Sloan Management Review,* Summer 2007, pp. 17–21.

27. The survey research methods section of the American Statistical Association offers useful guides to conducting focus groups and surveys. Downloadable PDF files may be found at *www.whatisasurvey.info.*

28. Darren Murph, "Nokia's 1100 Handset Over 200 Million Served," engadget mobile, *http://mobile.engadget.com/2007/05/07/nokias-1100-handset-over-200-million-served/*, May 7, 2007.

29. For more on questionnaire design, see any marketing research text, such as Joseph F. Hair, Jr., Robert P. Bush and David J. Oninau. *Marketing Research* (Burr Ridge, JL: Irwin/McGraw-Hill, 2008.)

30. Bun Helm, "Online Potts: How Good Are They?" *Business Week* European Edition, June 16, 2008. pp. 86–87.

31. Jack Neff, "Will Social Media Replace Surveys as a Research Tool?". *Advertising Age* March 21, 2011. *http://adage.com/article/news/p-g-surveys-fade-consumers-reach-brands-social-media/149509/.*

32. Helm, "Online Polls: How Good Are They?"

33. For more on sampling, see Hair, Bush, and Oninau, *Marketing Research.*

34. For example, see "Directory of E-marketing Services." *Marketing News.* September 29, 2003, pp. 12–20.

# CHAPTER SEVEN

# Targeting Attractive Market Segments

## The Developing World's Emerging Middle Class[1]

FOR MANY YEARS, IN THE eyes of Western marketers, there were only two market segments in the developing world—the very rich (of which there were not very many, but they had plenty of money to spend)—and everyone else, all very poor. With the 2004 publication of C. K. Prahalad's landmark book, *The Fortune at the Bottom of the Pyramid,* eyes were opened to the aggregate purchasing power of the world's poorest citizens, often defined as those earning less than $2 per day. Prahalad called attention to what a few companies had already figured out, that if you packed shampoo in single-portion sachets, poor consumers could and would buy it, even though the large economy size bottle sold in the west was completely irrelevant.

Today, a new reality is emerging all over the developing world. Rapid economic development has spawned a large and growing middle class, a middle class with discretionary spending power and a plethora of unmet needs that local and foreign marketers are just starting to serve. But targeting the developing world's new middle class isn't as simple as following the old division between rich and poor, for this new group is a heterogeneous one, whose composition varies from country to country.

### The New Middle Class: Who and How Large?

There are two common approaches to defining this new middle class, which sits just above the poor in Prahalad's pyramid: in absolute terms without regard to local conditions or in relative terms, wherein what's "middle" is defined more locally. Central to the middle class notion is a reasonable amount of income that is discretionary—perhaps one-third, according to Diana Farrell of the National Economic Council in the United States—which goes to goods and services other than food and shelter. Most of the time, this means holding a steady job with salary and some benefits or running a small business whose employees go beyond the immediate family.

If one defines middle class as those having incomes greater than Brazil's average income and less than Italy's—roughly between $12 and $50 per person per day—the middle class population in emerging markets was about 250 million in 2000 and 400 million in 2005. But such an approach omits very large numbers of people in India and China who are clearly middle class but don't earn $12 per day. Martin Ravallion of the World Bank uses a range of $2 to $13 at 2005 purchasing-power parity prices, above the accepted poverty line in the developing world but below the American one. By his definition, India's middle class population rose from 147 million to 264 million from 1990 to 2005 and China's from 174 million to 806 million. The middle class in emerging markets globally nearly doubled over that period, from 1.4 billion to 2.6 billion. It now accounts for more than half of the developing world's population, up from one-third in 1990.

Shasi Thanoor, an Indian commentator, argues that the middle class is a category that is "more sociological than logical." It is, of course, an income category, but it's also a set of attitudes, even a mindset. And new kinds of spending patterns, too. These households spend proportionately less on food and housing, so they have money to spend on private education, health care, motorcycles, modern kitchens, air conditioners, and more. McKinsey believes that India's middle class will reach 580 million people by 2025. For marketers, this phenomenon holds powerful implications in market segmentation terms.

## Targeting India's New Middle Class

Consider Dinaz Vervatwala, owner of a growing chain of fitness studios in India's fast-growing high-tech hot spot, Hyderabad. Vervatwala pioneered the aerobics industry in Hyderabad in 1993, opening her first fitness studio to serve upscale women in the posh Banjara Hills neighborhood. Hyderabad has grown rapidly in recent years, and her business has grown with it. The growth of high-tech industries in Hyderabad—from software to business process outsourcing and more—has created a new market of fitness customers having a blend of Indian and Western attitudes and aspirations.

As we write, there are four Dinaz's Fitness Studios in Hyderabad (*www.dinazs.com*), employing more than 50 people in total, each the product of a range of important marketing decisions. What socioeconomic level should Vervatwala target? What level of service do customers want, and what price will they pay for it? Where should new stores be located? Should she continue to target women, or should she expand her sights to include men (so far, not the case)? Each of these decisions required Vervatwala to think clearly about not just the growing market that was readily apparent, but about the market segments within it that she wanted to target, where to find them and how best to serve them.

## Targeting: One Ingredient in Marketing Success

As Dinaz Vervatwala foresaw, Hyderabad's rapid growth has created a growing middle class of customers she was eager and willing to serve. But it's not just fitness studios that are growing in India. By 2007, India had more cell phone users than America. China had twice as many. In banking, ICICI, a large Indian bank, added 4 million new customers in 2008, most of them previously unbanked and living in India's second and third tier cities, where much of the growth in India's middle class is taking place. But bricks and mortar weren't a part of the effort. ICICI's mobile phone banking innovations and vigorous cost-cutting reduced its transaction costs to levels far below those of its competitors.

Market segmentation decisions are not confined to small entrepreneurial companies like Dinaz's, of course. In March 2011, Vikram Pandit, CEO of CitiBank, announced that CitiBank, attracted by the explosion in trade and capital flows within and into emerging market countries like Brazil, China, and India, planned to become the world's "largest emerging markets financial services company." CitiBank already earns more than half its profits from developing countries.

Some observers argue that Asia, in particular, has reached a tipping point. The Chinese already buy more cars and more cell phones than Americans and will soon surpass them in computers, too, not to mention numerous other categories where the same thing is happening. Targeting attractive market segments in these rapidly growing markets and developing marketing strategies that are tailored to serve the chosen segments is what good marketers, whether entrepreneurs like Dinaz Vervatwala or bankers like those at ICICI and CitiBank, do.

# Marketing Challenges Addressed in Chapter 7

Targeting the most attractive market segments is an issue that arises for marketers everywhere, not just in emerging economies. Different groups of customers—different market segments—have different wants and needs, both tangible and intangible. Fitness *aficionadas* may measure their progress by stepping on the scale, but the real benefits that Dinaz Vervatwala offers—overall appearance, energy, and attitude—are more difficult to quantify. In virtually any market, if different segments can be clearly identified, specific goods or services with specific marketing programs can be developed to meet the physical needs of the customer (pounds lost or kept at bay, muscles finely toned, endurance enhanced) as well as the emotional needs that consumers attach to their favorite pursuits (looking good in the clubs or at work).

In Chapter 7, we draw on the foundation of market knowledge and customer understanding established in the first six chapters to introduce what are probably the most important and fundamental tools in the marketer's tool kit: **market segmentation** and **target marketing.** Together with differentiation and brand positioning, which we address in Chapter 8, these tools provide the platform on which most effective marketing programs are built. Learning to apply these tools effectively, however, requires addressing several important questions. Why do market segmentation and target marketing make sense? Why not sell the same fitness services—or bank accounts, automobiles, or whatever—to everyone? How can potentially attractive market segments be identified and defined? Finally, how can these segments be prioritized so that the most attractive ones are pursued? Answering these questions should enable an entrepreneur, a venture capital investor in Silicon Valley or Hyderabad, or a marketing manager in a multinational firm to decide which market segments should be targeted and provide insight into which investments should be made.

# Do Market Segmentation and Target Marketing Make Sense in Today's Global Economy?

Market segmentation is the process by which a market is divided into distinct subsets of customers with similar needs and characteristics that lead them to respond in similar ways to a particular product offering and marketing program. Target marketing requires evaluating the relative attractiveness of various segments in terms of market potential, growth rate, competitive intensity, and other factors and the firm's mission and capabilities to deliver what each segment wants, in order to choose which segments it will serve. Brand positioning entails designing product offerings and marketing programs that can establish an enduring competitive advantage in the target market by creating a unique brand image, or position, in the customer's mind. Dinaz Vervatwala founded her fitness studio in part because she saw a market segment—women in Banjara Hills—whose needs were not being fully met. She chose to target this segment because fitness training was growing in popularity and because she had particular knowledge and expertise she could bring to the party. She positioned her fitness studios as the ones that were focused on womenly without any ogling males anywhere nearby.

These three decision processes—market segmentation, target marketing, and positioning—are closely linked and have strong interdependence. All must be well considered and implemented if the firm is to be successful in managing a given product-market relationship. No matter how large the firm, however, its resources are usually limited compared with the number of alternative market segments available for pursuit. Thus, a firm must make choices. Even in the unusual case where a firm can afford to serve all market segments, it must determine the most appropriate allocation and deployment of its marketing effort *across* segments. In East Africa, for example, to reach rural villages. Coca-Cola relies on more than 13,000 small distributors—many of whom use pushcarts and hand trucks—to reach local mom and pop retailers.[2] By tailoring its promotion and distribution methods by market and market segment, Coke's sales in Africa surpassed $550 million in 2009.[3] But are all these analyses and conscious choices about which segments to serve and how best to serve these really necessary?

## Most Markets Are Heterogeneous

Because markets are rarely homogeneous in benefits wanted, purchase rates, and price and promotion elasticities, their response rates to products and marketing programs differ. Variation among market segments in product preferences, size and growth in demand, media habits, and competitive structures further affect the differences and response rates. Thus, markets are complex entities that can be defined (segmented) in a variety of ways. As New York–based trend tracker Tom Vierhile notes, "what consumers really appear to hunger for are products that fit their unique needs, wants, and desires. They want products that talk just to them. . . . and appeal just to them on an emotional level."[4] The critical issue is to find an appropriate segmentation scheme that will facilitate target marketing, positioning, and the formulation of successful marketing strategies and programs.

## Today's Market Realities Often Make Segmentation Imperative

Market segmentation has become increasingly important in the development of marketing strategies for several reasons. First, population growth in many developed countries has slowed, and more product-markets are maturing. This sparks more intense competition in existing markets as firms seek growth via gains in market share and encourages companies to find new markets they've not served previously. Often, as they search for faster-growing markets, their attention turns to the developing world, where the enormous diversity in demographic profiles and market conditions makes careful market segmentation and targeting essential. Nokia, for example, has targeted the fast-growing Indian market, where a majority of the population lives in rural areas. In doing so, it's had to adapt the design of its cell phones, adding dust-proof keypads and eliminating other features to make its phones affordable to India's low-income masses. When Nokia's researchers discovered that many cell phones in India were used by more than one person, Nokia developed handsets with multiple address books.[5] By developing products uniquely suited to the Indian market and various segments therein, Nokia has become the market leader.[6]

Second, such social and economic forces as expanding disposable incomes, higher educational levels, and more awareness of the world have produced customers with more varied and sophisticated needs, tastes, and lifestyles than ever before. This has led to an outpouring of goods and services that compete with one another for the opportunity of satisfying some group of consumers.

Third, there is an increasingly important trend toward microsegmentation in which extremely small market segments are targeted. For a discussion of how one company built itself into a multimillion-dollar business while serving a very small niche (see Exhibit 7.1). This trend has been accelerated in some industries by new technology such as computer-aided

## Exhibit 7.1   CAN UNDER ARMOUR BECOME ANOTHER NIKE?

Kevin Plank did not set out to create a cult around athletic underwear—he simply wanted a comfortable T-shirt to wear under his football pads that would wick moisture away from his skin and protect him from heat exhaustion during practice. After hunting through all the sporting goods shops, Kevin realized that there was not a single product on the market that met his needs. He set out to create one. In March 1996, just before graduation, Kevin had some T-shirts sewn up in Lycra and found that he had solved a common problem for all of his teammates.

Under Armour, the company that was soon born in his grandmother's basement, made its first sale of 200 shirts for $12 apiece to the football team at Georgia Tech. Kevin ended his company's first year with sales of $17,000. Under Armour was marketed by word-of-mouth from happy, satisfied customers and grew with sales to athletic teams in colleges. The company got its big break due to a product placement in the Oliver Stone football movie *Any Given Sunday*. Buzz from the movie and a first-time ad in

*ESPN Magazine* during the movie premiere boosted Under Armour sales to $1.35 million in 1999. Under Armour's sales in 2001 drove triple-digit growth in its category and led industry peers at *Sporting Goods Business* to recognize the company as "Apparel Supplier of the Year." Under Armour's sales soared to U.S. $55 million in 2002, more than $400 million in 2006, and more than $850 million in 2009.

The underserved niche market segment that Kevin Plank discovered and his success have not gone unnoticed. Ironically, recent entrants to this segment are Nike and Reebok. Will Under Armour be able to withstand the competitive heat? Kevin Plank's reaction? "I'll never let them see me sweat."

*Sources:* Company website: *http://www.underarmour.com*; Elaine Shannon, "Tight Skivvies; They're What Everyone's Wearing This Season. Here's Why," *Time*, January 13, 2003, p. A1; and Stanley Holmes, "Under Armour May Be Overstretched," *Business-Week European Edition*, April 30, 2007, p. 65; Matt Townsend, "Under Armour's Daring Half-Court Shot," *Bloomberg Businessweek*, European Edition, November 1–7, 2010, pp. 24–25.

design, which has enabled firms to mass-customize many products as diverse as T-shirts and coffee mugs, even designer jeans and cars. Mass customization websites such as CaféPress and Zazzle in the United States and Spreadshirt in Europe now make it possible for consumers to order T-shirts and other custom-designed products in quantities of one or one thousand, with almost instant delivery. No longer must everyone at the company picnic wear exactly the same T-shirt, since companies like these let everyone choose their own style, size, and color, and even the slogan.[7]

Finally, many marketing organizations have made it easier to implement sharply focused marketing programs by more sharply targeting their own services. For example, many new media have sprung up to appeal to narrow interest groups. In the United Kingdom, these include special interest magazines, such as *Wanderlust* and *Autocar;* radio stations with formats targeted to different demographic groups, such as classical music, rock, country, and jazz, not to mention chat shows of various kinds; and cable TV channels, such as Sky Sport and the Discovery Channel. Also, more broad-based magazines, such as *Time, The Economist,* and *Hello,* offer advertisers the opportunity to target specific groups of people within their subscription base. An advertiser can target specific regions, cities, or postal codes, or even selected income groups.

## How Are Market Segments Best Defined?

There are three important steps in the market segmentation process:

- **Identify a homogeneous segment that differs from other segments.** The process should identify one or more relatively homogeneous groups of prospective buyers with regard to their wants and needs and/or their likely responses to differences in the elements of the marketing mix—the 4 Ps (product, price, promotion, and place). For Dinaz Vervatwala, women were targeted even though most other fitness clubs in India targeted men and women.

- **Specify criteria that define the segment.** The segmentation criteria should measure or describe the segments clearly enough so that members can be readily identified and accessed, in order for the marketer to know whether a given prospective customer is or is not in the target market and in order to reach the prospective customer with advertising or other marketing communication messages. Like most retailers, Vervatwala targets well-defined trading areas in placing new studios.
- **Determine segment size and potential.** Finally, the segmentation process should determine the size and market potential of each segment for use in prioritizing which segments to pursue, a topic we address in more detail later in this chapter. In most developed countries, detailed demographic data showing what kind of people live where is readily available.

Given these objectives, what kinds of segmentation criteria, or descriptors, are most useful? Segmentation decisions are best made in one of three ways: based on *who* the customers are, based on *where* they are, or based on *how they behave* relevant to the market in question. The three approaches apply in both consumer and organizational markets. We examine each of these approaches as follows.

## Who They Are: Segmenting Demographically

While firm demographics (age of firm, size of firm, industry, etc.) are useful in segmenting organizational markets, we usually think of demographics in terms of attributes of individual consumers, as shown in Exhibit 7.2. Some examples of demographic attributes used to segment consumer markets are as follows:

- *Age.* Since mobile phone penetration has reached almost saturation levels in Europe and the United Kingdom, mobile service providers are focusing attention on the 55–65 and 65-plus segment to improve usage and penetration. Their high disposable incomes and their ability to devote time to new habits are seen as a lucrative market opportunity.[8] At the other end of the demographic scale, Red Bull has built a following among youth worldwide (see Exhibit 7.3).

## Exhibit 7.2

SOME OF THE MORE COMMONLY USED DEMOGRAPHIC ATTRIBUTES*

| Demographic Descriptors | Examples of Categories |
| --- | --- |
| Age | Under 2, 2–5, 6–11, 12–17, 18–24, 25–34, 35–49, 50–64, 65 and over |
| Sex | Male, female |
| Household life cycle | Young, single; newly married, no children; youngest child under 6; youngest child 6 or over; older couples with dependent children; older couples without dependent children; older couples retired; older, single |
| Income | Under $15,000, $15,000–24,999; $25,000–74,999; etc. |
| Occupation | Professional, manager, clerical, sales, supervisor, blue collar, homemaker, student, unemployed |
| Education | Some high school, graduated high school, some college, graduated college |
| Events | Birthdays, graduations, anniversaries, national holidays, sporting events |
| Race and ethnic origin | Anglo-Saxon, African-American, Italian, Jewish, Scandinavian, Hispanic, Asian |

*Others include marital status, home ownership, and presence and age of children.

## Exhibit 7.3   RED BULL'S TARGETED APPROACH WINS ACROSS THE GLOBE

Austria-based Red Bull is a company with one product that accounts for nearly all of its revenue; an energy drink containing the amino acid taurine. While working for Unilever, Dietrich Mateschitz traveled often to Asia, where he tried syrups that Asian businessmen drank to revitalize. His experience there led him to spot a market opportunity, and after modifying the drink to appeal to Western palates, he launched Red Bull in 1986. Its signature, a slim, silver-colored, 8.3-ounce can, has been an enormous hit with its target youth segment across the globe. By 2005, its global revenue had passed the $1.8 billion mark.

From Stanford University on California's West Coast to the beaches of Australia and Thailand, Red Bull has managed to maintain its hip, cool image, with virtually no mass-market advertising. It has instead opted for a grass-roots campaign. "In terms of attracting new customers and enhancing consumer loyalty, Red Bull has a more effective branding campaign than Coke or Pepsi," said Nancy F. Koehn, professor of business administration at Harvard Business School and author of *Brand New: How Entrepreneurs Earned Consumers' Trust from Wedgwood to Dell*. Red Bull used Collegiate Brand Managers to promote the drink via free samples handed out at student parties. The company also organized extreme sports events, for example, cliff diving in Hawaii or skateboarding in San Francisco, reinforcing the brand's extreme, on-the-edge image.

*Sources:* Jill Bruss, "Alternatively Speaking: Alternative Beverages Keep the Industry Abuzz with New Products (Category Focus)," *Beverage Industry* 1, November 2002; Nancy F. Koehn, *Brand New: How Entrepreneurs Earned Consumers' Trust from Wedgwood to Dell* (Boston: Harvard Business School Press, 2001); and Kerry A. Dolan, "The Soda with Buzz," *Forbes,* March 28, 2005.

---

- *Sex.* In Australia, Toyota launched an online information service aimed at women, recognizing that women make up 50 percent of Toyota's sales and directly influence 8 out of 10 vehicle purchases.[9] As many marketers are discovering, however, thinking about all men or all women as a single market segment is usually naive. Understanding segments within the male population, for example, can bring out insights previously missed.[10]

- Among women, sharply targeted segmentation schemes can often deliver attractive results. A plethora of juice-based dietary cleansing brands targeting the urban get-thin-quick segment has emerged in recent years. New York's Organic Avenue and BluePrint Cleanse, Los Angeles-based Cooler Cleanse and iZo Cleanze arc among them. We get "a *lot* of mommies," reports BluePrint co-founder Erica Huss Jones. But Dr. Michael D. Gershon of Columbia University's Department of Anatomy and Cell Biology is less than enthralled. There's "nothing but danger associated with" cleansing, he says. "It is a practice to be condemned.[11]

- *Income.* Higher-income households purchase a disproportionate number of cellular phones, expensive cars, and theater tickets. In 2000, Nokia started a wholly owned subsidiary, Vertu, to create an ultra-exclusive mobile telephone and services built around the phone, targeting the same customers who buy luxury watches and custom-made cars.[12]

- *Occupation.* The sales of certain kinds of products (e.g., work shoes, automobiles, uniforms, and trade magazines) are tied closely to occupational type. The increase in the number of working women has created needs for specialized goods and services including financial services, business wardrobes, convenience foods, automobiles, and special-interest magazines.

- *Education.* There is a strong positive correlation between the level of education and the purchase of travel, books, magazines, insurance, theater tickets, and photographic equipment.

- *Race and ethnic origin.* More and more companies are targeting these segments via specialized marketing programs. In the United States, car companies have found ways to cater to the needs of the multicultural segment, which is estimated to comprise 32 percent of the U.S. population in 2010. A distinctive trend that had already emerged by 2002 was Asian-Americans' affinity for upscale cars—they accounted for 15 percent of BMW and 9 percent of Mercedes Benz sales.[13]

Demographic descriptors are also important in the segmentation of industrial markets, which are segmented in two stages. The first, *macrosegmentation,* divides the market according to the characteristics of the buying organization using such attributes as age of firm, firm size, and industry affiliation (SIC code in the United States). The international counterpart of SIC is the trade-category code.

The second stage, *microsegmentation,* groups customers by the characteristics of the individuals who influence the purchasing decision—for instance, age, sex, and position within the organization. International markets are segmented in a similar hierarchical fashion, starting with countries, followed by groups of individuals or buying organizations.

## Where They Are: Segmenting Geographically

Different locations or regions vary in their sales potential, growth rates, customer needs, cultures, climates, service needs, and competitive structures, as well as purchase rates for a variety of goods. For example, more pickup trucks are sold in the Southwest United States, more vans in the Northeast, and more diesel-fueled cars in Europe. More and more advertisers are taking advantage of geographic media buys. Uni-Marts, Inc., a convenience store operator of over 400 stores, focuses on small towns and rural areas, thereby avoiding big competitors. In the first 25 years of its history, it never recorded a loss.[14]

Nestlé, in order to reach the 800,000 Brazilians who live in the Amazon River basin, chartered a boat stocked with more than 300 of its brands, including Nescafé instant coffee, Maggi soups and seasonings, and Leche Ideal, Nestlé's fortified powdered milk. Says Nestlé Brazil CEO Ivan Zurita, "We're going to pick up the customer where he is."[15]

Geographic segmentation is used in both consumer and organizational markets and is particularly important in retailing and many services businesses, where customers are unwilling to travel very far to obtain the goods or services they require. Thus, one way to segment retail markets is by distance or driving time from a particular location. The area included within such a geographically defined region is called a **trade area.**

## Geodemographic Segmentation

Marketers targeting emerging markets in the developing world must pay particular attention to market segmentation within the geographic regions they target. Virtually every developing country contains a small segment of extremely wealthy people, a rapidly growing but perhaps relatively small middle class, and large numbers of people who are poor by Western standards. The first two of these demographic groups are most often found in the cities, while many poor live either in rural areas or in urban slums. Treating the people of any developing country as a single market segment is not likely to bring success.

In emerging and developed markets alike, many segmentation schemes involve *both* demographic and geographic factors. Thus, retailers usually want to know something about the people who live within, perhaps, a two-mile or five-mile radius of their proposed new store. Neiman Marcus, the upscale department store, might target one demographic group within a given trade area, and Wal-Mart, a discounter, might target another. Claritas (*www.claritas.com*) and other sources offer low-cost reports based on census data that show the demographic profile of the population residing within any given radius of a particular street corner or shopping center location in the United States. These reports are useful in assessing the size and market potential of a market segment defined by a particular trade area. Geodemographics also attempts to predict consumer behavior by making demographic, psychographic, and consumer information available at the block and zip code or postal code levels. Claritas's PRIZM service classifies all U.S. households into

66 demographically and behaviorally distinct clusters, each of which, in turn, is assigned to one of 14 social groups and 11 life stage groups.[16] Claritas offers similar datasets for other countries as well.

# How They Behave: Behavioral Segmentation

There is no limit to the number of insightful ways successful marketers have segmented markets in behavioral terms. Kevin Plank of Under Armour initially targeted college and university athletic teams. Mountain bike makers Specialized and Gary Fisher target bicyclists who wish to ride on single-track trails or back-country terrain. Europe's easy Jet airline originally targeted leisure travelers. Gatorade's original target market consisted of athletes who needed to replenish water and salts lost through perspiration. This simple segmentation scheme created a whole new category of "sports beverages," which grew to include entries from Coke (Powerade) and Pepsi (All Sport), though Gatorade still dominates the category. This onetime niche market has grown into a multibillion-dollar market in the United States alone.[17]

These examples all demonstrate the power of highly specific behavioral descriptors in defining sharply focused market segments, based not on *who* the target consumers are or *where* they live, but based on what they *do*. In virtually every consumer and organizational market there are segments like these just waiting to be identified and targeted by insightful marketers. Behavioral attributes can take many forms, including those based on consumer needs; on product usage patterns; on more general behavioral patterns, including lifestyle, which often cuts across demographic categories or varies within them; and, in organizational markets, on the structure of firms' purchasing activities and the types of buying situations they encounter. We examine some of these forms next.

**Consumer Needs**   Customer needs are expressed in **benefits sought** from a particular product or service. Different individual customers have different needs and thus attach different degrees of importance to the benefits offered by different products. In the end, the product that provides the best bundle of benefits—given the customer's particular needs—is most likely to be purchased. For an example of how targeting a distinct set of consumer needs has taken a late entrant to the top of the car rental industry, see Exhibit 7.4.

Since purchasing is a problem-solving process, consumers evaluate product or brand alternative on the basis of desired characteristics and how valuable each characteristic is to the consumer—**choice criteria.** Marketers can define segments according to these different choice criteria in terms of the presence or absence of certain characteristics and the importance attached to each. Firms typically single out a limited number of benefit segments to target. Thus, for example, different automobile manufacturers have emphasized different benefits over the years, such as Volvo's safety versus Jaguar's styling, quickness, and status.

In organizational markets, customers consider relevant benefits that include product performance in different use situations. For example, supercomputers are bought because they meet the high-speed computational requirements of a small group of customers such as governments, universities, and research labs. Other considerations in the purchase of industrial products/services include on-time delivery, credit terms, economy, spare parts availability, and training.

**Product Usage and Purchase Influence**   In addition to highly specific behavioral attributes such as those just discussed, there are more general product-related attributes as well. They include product usage, loyalty, purchase predisposition, and purchase influence, all of which can be used to segment both consumer and industrial markets.

## Exhibit 7.4    ENTERPRISE RENT-A-CAR: TARGETING PAYS OFF

In 1963, Jack Taylor added car rentals to his small auto-mobile leasing business. Taylor's strategy was to serve a completely different target market than the majors, Hertz and Avis, and provide replacement cars for people involved in accidents or breakdowns and those who were grounded while their cars were being serviced. Serving this market required a completely different sort of service—delivering the car to the customer, for example—than the majors provided. "This stuff is a lot more complicated than handing out keys at the airport," says Andy Taylor, Jack's son and now chairman and CEO. The business grew steadily, if unexceptionally, until the 1990s, when the younger Taylor stepped on the gas and cruised past Hertz and Avis to take the number one spot in the U.S. market, with a fleet of 500,000 vehicles and more than $6 billion in revenue for the still privately held company. Europe followed and the initial entry has already begun, into the U.K., Ireland, and Germany.

While Enterprise now serves target segments beyond the car-replacement market, its clear focus on a narrowly defined segment that the majors had ignored provided the beachhead and an impregnable foundation on which the company was able to grow. Equally important, the strong customer service culture and decentralized decision-making that were crucial to the initial strategy have become the lynchpin of the company's wider success. Enterprise measures each of its branches each month in terms of both profitability and customer service (two questions are asked of each customer: Are you satisfied with our service? Would you come back?), and no one gets promoted from branches that have below-average customer service scores, no matter how strong their financial performance. Enterprise has found that customers who answer "completely satisfied" on question one are three times more likely to come back.

Clear targeting. Exceptional customer service. It's a combination that's kept Enterprise rolling for nearly 50 years.

*Source:* Simon London, "Driving Home the Service Ethic," *Financial Times,* June 3, 2003.

**Product usage** is important because in many markets a small proportion of potential customers makes a high percentage of all purchases. In organizational markets, the customers are better known, and heavy users (often called *key accounts*) are easier to identify.

For Coca-Cola, differences in products usage rates provide clues to where its growth prospects are most attractive. North Americans bought $2.6 billion worth of Coke in 1989, and just $2.9 billion in 2009. So Coke is looking elsewhere for growth, like Kenya, for example, where annual per capita consumption is just 39 servings, compared to 665 servings in Mexico, whose people guzzle more Coke than anywhere else. Coke providers refrigerated coolers to the mom and pop *dukas* where Kenyans shop, and even prescribes exactly how they should be stocked: half-liter bottles of Coke at the top, Fanta in the middle, and large bottles at the bottom.[18]

Market segmentation based on sources of **purchase influence** for the product category is relevant for both consumer and organizational markets. Many products used by various family members are purchased by the wife, but joint husband–wife decisions are becoming more common. Children's products, prescription drugs, and gifts are clearly influenced by a variety of family members. In organizational markets, several individuals or units with varying degrees of influence participate in buying decisions.

**Lifestyle**    Segmentation by lifestyle, or psychographics, segments markets on the basis of consumers' activities, interests, and opinions—in other words, what they do or believe, rather than who they are in a demographic sense. From such information it is possible to infer what types of products and services appeal to a particular group, as well as how best to communicate with individuals in the group. Even among demographic groups that might at first glance seem homogeneous, behavioral segmentation based on lifestyle is identifying new target markets for savvy marketers (see Exhibit 7.5).

## Exhibit 7.5   MARKETING TO BABY BOOMERS: RETHINKING THE RULES

By 2006, more than half the baby boomers in the United States—those born between 1946 and 1964—had turned 50 or older. With combined spending power of more than $1 trillion per annum among the 50- to 60-year-olds alone, this growing market simply cannot be ignored. What marketers are discovering, though, is that these aging customers aren't all the same. Demographic segmentation just won't do. Behavior is the key. Consumers aged 50+ buy a quarter of all Vespa motor scooters in the United States. Better still for Vespa, with their empty-nester spending power, they tend to buy the top-of-the-line models. But that doesn't mean all boomers are fantasizing about their younger days. Indeed, wrinkles and gray hair are in among many boomers,

along with healthier diets and lifestyles to help them age gracefully.

But are these consumers counting their days until they can retire to the shuffleboard court or bingo parlor? Hardly. As a result, Del Webb, the retirement-community division of Pulte Homes Inc., is changing the way it markets its properties, with more emphasis on the varied and active lifestyles that many of tomorrow's retirees will lead. "We have to keep up with residents," says David G. Schreiner, vice president for active-adult business development at Del Webb. "The War Generation was far more predictable and consistent, but this generation gives you a bunch of paradoxes."

*Source:* Louise Lee, "Love Those Boomers," *BusinessWeek,* October 24, 2005.

Stanford Research Institute (SRI) has created a U.S. segmentation service (called VALS 2), which builds on the concept of self-orientation and resources for the individual. *Self-orientation* is based on how consumers pursue and acquire products and services that provide satisfaction and shape their identities. In doing so, they are motivated by the orientations of principle, status, and action. Principle-oriented consumers are motivated by abstract and idealized criteria, while status-oriented consumers shop for products that demonstrate the consumer's success. Action-oriented consumers are guided by the need for social or physical activity, variety, and risk-taking. *Resources* include all of the psychological, physical, demographic, and material means consumers have to draw on. They include education, income, self-confidence, health, eagerness to buy, intelligence, and energy level—on a continuum from minimal to abundant.

Based on these two dimensions, VALS 2 defines eight segments that exhibit distinctive behavior and decision-making—actualizers, fulfillers, achievers, experiencers, believers, strivers, makers, and strugglers. Claritas and similar commercial organizations identify each of the respondents as to their VALS type, thereby permitting a cross-classification of VALS type with the product usage and personal information collected by such companies. Thus, users can determine what each VALS segment bought, what their media habits are, and similar data. The VALS system has been further developed in Europe and Asia. Those interested in the VALS segmentation scheme can complete a short survey on the VALS website (log onto *www.sric-bi.com/VALS/presurvey/shtml*) and discover the VALS segment to which they belong.

**STRATEGIC ISSUE**

*Those interested in the VALS segmentation scheme can complete a short survey on the VALS website and discover the VALS segment to which they belong.*

**Organizational Behavioral Attributes** Purchasing structure and buying situation segmentation attributes are unique to organizational markets. **Purchasing structure** is the degree to which the purchasing activity is centralized. In such a structure the buyer is likely to consider all transactions with a given supplier on a company-wide or global basis, to emphasize cost savings, and to minimize risk. In a decentralized situation, the buyer is apt to be more sensitive to the user's need, to emphasize product quality and fast delivery, and to be less cost-conscious. Some marketers segment their markets accordingly and target customers whose purchasing structure is similar (companies who buy centrally from one location to meet their global needs, for example).

The **buying situation** attribute includes three distinct types of situations: straight rebuy, a recurring situation handled on a routine basis; modified rebuy, which occurs when some an element, such as price or delivery schedules, has changed in a client–supplier relationship; and a new buying situation, which may require the gathering of considerable information and an evaluation of alternative suppliers. Business-to-business marketers seeking new customers often find the buying situation to be a useful way to decide which new customers to target.

## Innovative Segmentation: A Key to Marketing Breakthroughs

At the beginning of this section, we identified three steps in the market segmentation process:

- Identify a homogeneous segment that differs from others.
- Specify criteria that define the segment.
- Determine segment size and potential.

Skilled marketers, such as the creators of Under Armour athletic wear, Red Bull energy drinks, and Enterprise Rent-a-Car, know that following this process to an insightful and innovative market segmentation scheme is often the key to marketing breakthroughs. Often, combinations of different attributes are used to more precisely target an attractive segment: perhaps some behavioral dimension together with a carefully defined demographic profile within some geographic region. Generally, it is useful to know the demographic profile of the target market to be pursued, even if the driving force behind the segmentation scheme is geographical and/or behavioral in nature, because understanding the demographic profile of a target market enables the marketer to better choose targeted advertising media or other marketing communication vehicles.

As several examples in this section have shown, at the foundation of many a marketing breakthrough one often finds an insightful segmentation scheme that is sharply focused in a *behavioral* way. Marketers with superior market knowledge are probably more likely to generate the insights necessary to define market segments in these innovative and meaningful ways. Sometimes these insights are counterintuitive, even surprising (see Exhibit 7.6).

**STRATEGIC ISSUE**

*At the foundation of many a marketing breakthrough one often finds an insightful segmentation scheme that is sharply focused in a behavioral way.*

## Choosing Attractive Market Segments: A Five-Step Process

Most firms, not even Coca-Cola, no longer aim a single product and marketing program at the mass market. Instead, they break that market into homogeneous segments on the basis of meaningful differences in buyer behavior or in the benefits sought by different groups of customers. Then they tailor products and marketing programs to the particular desires and idiosyncrasies of each segment. *But not all segments represent equally attractive opportunities for the firm.* To prioritize target segments by their potential, marketers must evaluate their future attractiveness and their firm's strengths and capabilities relative to the segments' needs and competitive situations.

Within an established firm, rather than allowing each business unit or product manager to develop an approach to evaluate the potential of alternative market segments, it is

**STRATEGIC ISSUE**

*Most firms no longer aim a single product and marketing program at the mass market.*

## Exhibit 7.6   ILLITERATE CONSUMERS: A SEGMENT WORTH TARGETING?

Some 21–23 percent of United States consumers simply do not have the basic language and numeracy skills that are necessary to effectively navigate today's typical retail shopping environment. In many developing countries, the proportion of consumers who are functionally illiterate is even higher. But these groups have surprising purchasing power, controlling $380 billion in spending in the United States alone in 2003. Because these consumers do not assimilate information in the same way literate consumers do, however, various kinds of marketing efforts—from price promotions, to retail signage, to the packaging of "new and improved" products, most of which are words- and numbers-based—are wasted on, or even misleading

to, this consumer population. Such tactics may even cause these consumers to switch away from the brands being promoted. Some marketers are addressing this opportunity, however, and have found ways to better meet these consumers' needs. Employee training to help reduce customers' possible losses of self-esteem (what happens if they don't have enough money at checkout), the use of pictorial information alongside word information, and other measures can make these consumers both loyal and profitable.

*Source:* Madhubalan Viswanathan, José Antonio Rosa, and James Edwin Harris, "Decision Making and Coping of Functionally Illiterate Consumers and Some Implications for Marketing Management," *Journal of Marketing* 69 (January 2005), pp. 15–31.

often better to apply a common analytical framework across segments. With this approach, managers can compare the future potential of different segments using the same set of criteria and then prioritize them in order to decide which segments to target and how resources and marketing efforts should be allocated. One useful analytical framework managers or entrepreneurs can use for this purpose is the **market-attractiveness/competitive-position matrix.** As we saw in Chapter 2, managers use such models at the corporate level to allocate resources across businesses, or at the business-unit level to assign resources across product-markets. We are concerned with the second application here.

Exhibit 7.7 outlines the steps involved in developing a market-attractiveness/competitive-position matrix for analyzing current and potential target markets. Underlying such a matrix is the notion that managers can judge the attractiveness of a market (its profit potential) by examining market, competitive, and environmental factors that may influence profitability. Similarly, they can estimate the strength of the firm's competitive position by looking at the firm's capabilities or shortcomings *relative* to the needs of the market and the competencies of likely competitors. By combining the results of these analyses with other considerations, including risk, the mission of the firm, and ethical issues (see Ethical Perspective 7.1), conclusions about which markets and market segments should be pursued can be reached.

The first steps in developing a market-attractiveness/competitive-position matrix, are to identify the most relevant variables for evaluating alternative market segments and the firm's competitive position regarding them and to weight each variable in importance. Note, too, that Exhibit 7.7 suggests conducting a forecast of future changes in market attractiveness or competitive position in addition to, but separately from, an assessment of the current situation. This reflects the fact that a decision to target a particular segment is a strategic choice that the firm will have to live with for some time.

## Step 1: Select Market-Attractiveness and Competitive-Position Factors

An evaluation of the attractiveness of a particular market or market segment and of the strength of the firm's current or potential competitive position in it builds naturally on the kind of opportunity analysis developed in Chapter 3. Managers can assess both dimensions

# Exhibit 7.7

STEPS IN CONSTRUCTING A MARKET-ATTRACTIVENESS/COMPETITIVE-POSITION MATRIX FOR EVALUATING POTENTIAL TARGET MARKETS

1. Choose criteria to measure market attractiveness and competitive position.

2. Weight market attractiveness and competitive position factors to reflect their relative importance.

3. Assess the current position of each potential target market on each factor.

4. Project the future position of each market based on expected environmental, customer, and competitive trends.

5. Evaluate implications of possible future changes for business strategies and resources requirements.

 ETHICAL PERSPECTIVE 7.1
### Eat Chocolate, Get Fit?

In 2003, Cadbury's, the British confectionery company, launched a "Sports for Schools" promotion, emulating an earlier and very successful promotion that Tesco, the leading grocer in the United Kingdom, had run called "Computers for Schools." Cadbury's offered to buy fitness equipment for schools in exchange for tokens obtained through consumer purchases of Cadbury's confectionery.

Following howls of protest in the media, in which the program was characterized as a perverse incentive for children to eat more of a product widely considered to be associated with child obesity, a growing problem in the United Kingdom and elsewhere, Cadbury's withdrew the program.

As the U.K.'s Food Commission calculated, "Cadbury's wants children to eat 2 million kilograms of fat (more than 4 million pounds)—to get fit." According to the Food Commission's calculations, a netball that sold for £5 in sporting goods stores would require consumer tokens from £38 worth of Cadbury products.

These £38 worth of products would, in turn, involve consuming more than 20,000 calories and over 1,000 grams of fat. In targeting children and families with this promotion, Cadbury's overlooked or misunderstood consumers' rising concerns over child obesity.

Empirical research by Craig Smith and Elizabeth Cooper-Martin indicates that ethical concerns such as those that arose here are particularly likely to arise over targeting strategies where the target market is perceived as vulnerable and where the products concerned are, in any sense, perceived to be harmful. Thus, it's not necessarily the products themselves that lead to ethical concerns, but targeting and market segmentation decisions to which insufficient ethical consideration is given. As Smith and Cooper-Martin note, "Marketing managers should be alert to public disquiet over the ethics of certain targeting strategies," especially when consumer vulnerability and product harm enter the equation.

*Sources:* N. Craig Smith, "Out of Leftfield: Societal Issues as Causes of Failure of New Marketing Initiatives," *Business Strategy Review*, Summer 2007; and N. Craig Smith and Elizabeth Cooper-Martin, "Ethics and Target Marketing: The Role of Product Harm and Consumer Vulnerability," *Journal of Marketing* 61 (July 1997), pp. 1–20.

on the basis of information obtained from analyses of the environment, industry and competitive situation, market potential estimates, and customer needs. To make these assessments, they need to establish criteria, such as those shown in Exhibit 7.8, against which prospective markets or market segments can be evaluated. Both market and competitive perspectives are necessary.

**Market-Attractiveness Factors**   As we saw in Chapter 3, assessing the attractiveness of markets or market segments involves determining the market's size and growth rate and assessing various trends—demographic, sociocultural, economic, political/legal, technological, and natural—that influence demand in that market. An even more critical factor in determining whether to *enter* a new market or market segment, however, is the degree to which *unmet customer needs,* or needs that are currently not being well served, can be identified. In the absence of unmet or underserved needs, it is likely to be difficult to win customer loyalty, regardless of how large the market or how fast it is growing. "Me-too" products often face difficult going in today's highly competitive markets.

**Competitive-Position Factors**   As we showed in Chapter 3, understanding the attractiveness of the industry in which one competes is also important. Entering a segment in a way that would place the firm in an unattractive industry or increase its exposure therein may not be wise. Of more immediate and salient concern, however, is the degree to which the firm's proposed product entry into the new market or segment will be sufficiently *differentiated* from competitors, given the critical success factors and product life-cycle conditions already prevalent in the category. Similarly, decision-makers need to

## Exhibit 7.8

FACTORS UNDERLYING MARKET ATTRACTIVENESS AND COMPETITIVE POSITION

**Market-Attractiveness Factors**

Customer needs and behavior
- Are there unmet or underserved needs we can satisfy?

Market or market segment size and growth rate
- Market potential in units, revenue, number of prospective customers
- Growth rate in units, revenue, number of prospective customers
- Might the target segment constitute a platform for later expansion into related segments in the market as a whole?

Macro trends: Are they favorable, on balance?
- Demographic
- Sociocultural
- Economic
- Political/legal
- Technological
- Natural

**Competitive-Position Factors**

Opportunity for competitive advantage
- Can we differentiate?
- Can we perform against critical success factors?
- Stage of competing products in product life cycle: Is the timing right?

Firm and competitor capabilities and resources
- Management strength and depth
- Financial and functional resources: marketing, distribution, manufacturing, R&D, etc.
- Brand image
- Relative market share

Attractiveness of industry in which we would compete
- Threat of new entrants
- Threat of substitutes
- Buyer power
- Supplier power
- Competitive rivalry
- Industry capacity

know whether their firm has or will be able to acquire the resources it will take—human, financial, and otherwise—to effectively compete in the new segment. Simply put, most new goods or services need to be either better from a consumer point of view or cheaper than those they hope to replace. Entering a new market or market segment without a source of sustainable competitive advantage is often a trap.

## Step 2: Weight Each Factor

Next, a numerical weight is assigned to each factor to indicate its relative importance in the overall assessment. Weights that Under Armour's Kevin Plank might have assigned to the major factors in Exhibit 7.8 are shown in Exhibit 7.9. Some users would rate each bullet point in Exhibit 7.8 independently, assigning a weight to each one.

The task of weighting the factors—as well as determining them in the first place— gets more complicated as companies reach out to new and different markets, like the growing middle class in the developing world. Both the scores and the weights placed on different factors may differ in emerging versus developed markets, for example, and the factors and their weights may differ across markets where a category is relatively mature versus nascent. Macro trends are generally more favourable for Coca-Cola in emerging markets with rapidly growing middle classes, for example, than in North America or western Europe, where both population growth and Coke consumption are relatively flat.

## Step 3: Rate Segments on Each Factor, Plot Results on Matrices

This step requires that evidence—typically both qualitative and quantitative data—be collected to objectively assess each of the criteria identified in Step 1. For Under Armour the assessment of the various factors might have looked as shown in Exhibit 7.9. While more detailed evidence than we discuss here should have been, and no doubt was, gathered, Plank might have reached the following conclusions:

## Exhibit 7.9

ASSESSING THE ATHLETIC UNDERWEAR MARKET SEGMENT AT UNDER ARMOUR'S INCEPTION

|  | Weight | Rating (0–10 Scale) | Total |
|---|---|---|---|
| **Market-attractiveness factors** | | | |
| Customer needs and behavior: unmet needs? | .5 | 9 | 4.5 |
| Segment size and growth rate | .2 | 7 | 1.4 |
| Macro trends | .3 | 9 | 2.7 |
| **Total: Market attractiveness** | **1.0** | | **8.6** |
| **Competitive-position factors** | | | |
| Opportunity for competitive advantage | .4 | 6 | 2.4 |
| Capabilities and resources | .2 | 5 | 1.0 |
| Industry attractiveness | .4 | 5 | 2.0 |
| **Total: Competitive position** | **1.0** | | **5.4** |

## Market-Attractiveness Factors

- Unmet needs for wicking underwear for athletic teams have been identified and are well understood. Score: 9.
- The athletic team segment is small, but easily identified and reached and might lead to other segments in the future. Score: 7.
- Macro trends are largely favorable: Sports are "in," number of people in athletically active demographic groups is growing, and niche brands for other athletic pursuits (e.g., Patagonia for outdoor people) have been successful. Score: 9.

## Competitive-Position Factors

- Opportunity for competitive advantage is modest: Proposed garments will be differentiated, but are easily imitated; Under Armour, as a new firm, has no track record. Score: 6.
- Resources are extremely limited, though the founder knows the athletic community. Score: 5.
- Five forces are mixed: Entry barriers are very low (unfavorable), buyer power and supplier power are low (favorable), there is little threat of substitutes (favorable), and rivalry among existing firms is modest. Score: 5.

Mere armchair judgments about each criterion are not very credible and run the risk of taking the manager or entrepreneur into a market segment that may turn out not to be viable. It is especially important to undertake a detailed analysis of key competitors, especially with regard to their objectives, strategy, resources, and marketing programs. Similarly, compelling evidence that a proposed entry into a new segment will satisfy some previously unmet needs, and do so in a way that can bring about sustainable competitive advantage, is called for. Both qualitative and quantitative marketing research results are typically used for this purpose. Once these assessments have been made, the weighted results can be plotted on a **market-attractiveness/competitive-position matrix** like the one shown in Exhibit 7.10.

> **STRATEGIC ISSUE**
>
> *Compelling evidence that a proposed entry into a new segment will satisfy some previously unmet needs, and do so in a way that can bring about sustainable competitive advantage, is called for.*

## Exhibit 7.10

MARKET-ATTRACTIVENESS/COMPETITIVE-POSITION MATRIX, FOR UNDER ARMOUR AT INCEPTION

● = Market attractiveness and competitive position with Under Armour at inception

## Step 4: Project Future Position for Each Segment

Forecasting a market's future is more difficult than assessing its current state. Managers or entrepreneurs should first determine how the market's attractiveness is likely to change over the next three to five years. The starting point for this assessment is to consider possible shifts in customer needs and behavior, the entry or exit of competitors, and changes in their strategies. Managers must also address several broader issues, such as possible changes in product or process technology, shifts in the economic climate, the impact of social or political trends, and shifts in the bargaining power or vertical integration of customers.

For example, **Eons.com,** the fast-growing social networking site for U. S. baby boomers, is banking on expectations that today's baby boomers will remain active as they pass the age of 50. Jeff Taylor, Eons's founder (who was founder and CEO of the job site **Monster.com**), says people in previous generations may have "dried up like a raisin" as they got older, but not today's baby boomers. "They're pumping up life, having fun on the flip side of 50," he says. Many 50-plus consumers have been using cell phones, the internet, and other high-tech gadgets for two or three decades, so Taylor figures that his target market will be internet-savvy. Some will be looking for love, too. The erotic poems and racy photos posted in the site's "Fun, Flirting, and Sex After 50" section suggest that Eons's users haven't turned into raisins just yet![19]

Once they have determined any changes likely to occur in market attractiveness, managers must next determine how the business's competitive position in the market is likely to change, assuming that it responds effectively to projected environmental changes but the firm does not undertake any initiatives requiring a change in basic strategy. The expected changes in both market attractiveness and competitive position can then be plotted on the matrix in the form of a vector to reflect the direction and magnitude of the expected changes. Anticipating such changes may be especially important in today's internet age and in today's increasingly integrated and competitive global economy.

## Step 5: Choose Segments to Target, Allocate Resources

Managers should consider a market segment to be a desirable target only if it is strongly positive on at least one of the two dimensions of market attractiveness and potential competitive position

and at least moderately positive on the other. In Exhibit 7.10, this includes markets positioned in any of the three cells in the upper right-hand corner of the matrix. However, a business may decide to enter a market that currently falls into one of the middle cells under these conditions: (1) managers believe that the market's attractiveness or their competitive strength is likely to improve over the next few years; (2) they see such markets as stepping-stones to entering larger, more attractive markets in the future; or (3) shared costs or synergies are present, thereby benefiting another entry.

Under Armour used its growth in the apparel category and its retailer relationships to expand to the range of its apparel and, more recently, to enter the market for athletic footwear. However, both its 2008 entry into the cross-trainers category and its 2009 entry into running flopped. Undeterred, Under Armour launched its Micro G basketball shoe in October 2009, taking on Nike and its firmly entrenched 95 percent share in the basketball category. Will Under Armour be able to successfully migrate from its original niche underwear segment into footwear? Nike does not seem worried. Says Nike spokesman Derek Kent, "We thrive on competition of any kind. We expect to further expand our leadership position."[20]

## Exhibit 7.11

IMPLICATIONS OF ALTERNATIVE POSITIONS WITHIN THE MARKET-ATTRACTIVENESS/COMPETITIVE-POSITION MATRIX FOR TARGET MARKET SELECTION, STRATEGIC OBJECTIVES, AND RESOURCE ALLOCATION

|  |  | **Competitive Position** | | |
|  |  | Weak | Moderate | Strong |
| **Market Attractiveness** | **High** | Build selectively:<br>• Specialize around limited strengths<br>• Seek ways to overcome weaknesses<br>• Withdraw if indications of sustainable growth are lacking | DESIRABLE POTENTIAL TARGET<br>Invest to build:<br>• Challenge for leadership<br>• Build selectively on strengths<br>• Reinforce vulnerable areas | DESIRABLE POTENTIAL TARGET<br>Protect position:<br>• Invest to grow at maximum digestible rate<br>• Concentrate on maintaining strength |
|  | **Moderate** | Limited expansion or harvest:<br>• Look for ways to expand without high risk; otherwise, minimize investment and focus operations | Manage for earnings:<br>• Protect existing strengths<br>• Invest to improve position only in areas where risk is low | DESIRABLE POTENTIAL TARGET<br>Build selectively:<br>• Emphasize profitability by increasing productivity<br>• Build up ability to counter competition |
|  | **Low** | Divest:<br>• Sell when possible to maximize cash value<br>• Meantime, cut fixed costs and avoid further investment | Manage for earnings:<br>• Protect position<br>• Minimize investment | Protect and refocus:<br>• Defend strengths<br>• Seek ways to increase current earnings without speeding market's decline |

*Sources:* Adapted from George S. Day, *Analysis for Strategic Market Decisions* (St. Paul: West, 1986), p. 204; and S. J. Robinson, R. E. Hitchens, and D. P. Wade, "The Directional Policy Matrix: Tool for Strategic Planning," *Long Range Planning* 11 (1978), pp. 8–15.

The market-attractiveness/competitive-position matrix offers general guidance for strategic objectives and allocation of resources for segments currently targeted and suggests which new segments to enter. Thus, it can also be useful, especially under changing market conditions, for assessing markets or market segments from which to withdraw or to which allocations of resources, financial and otherwise, might be reduced. Exhibit 7.11 summarizes one observer's generic guidelines for strategic objectives and resource allocations for markets in each of the matrix cells.

# Different Targeting Strategies Suit Different Opportunities

Most successful entrepreneurial ventures target narrowly defined market segments at the outset, as did Dinaz Vervatwala and Kevin Plank, for two reasons. One, doing so puts the nascent firm in position to achieve early success in a market segment that it understands particularly well. Second, such a strategy conserves precious resources, both financial and otherwise. But segmenting the market into narrow niches and then choosing one niche to target is not always the best strategy, particularly for established firms having substantial resources. Three common targeting strategies are **niche-market, mass-market,** and **growth-market** strategies.

## Niche-Market Strategy

This strategy involves serving one or more segments that, while not the largest, consist of a sufficient number of customers seeking somewhat-specialized benefits from a good or service.

Nestlé did just this in launching its exclusive—and pricey, at 10 times the price per cup compared to buying unground beans at the supermarket—Nespresso brand of coffee, packed in single-serve capsules for high-end consumers who would like to enjoy an espresso or cappuccino at home. Nespresso has become a $3 billion business, growing at more than 20 percent annually.[21] Such a strategy is designed to avoid direct competition with larger firms that are pursuing the bigger segments. Infact, overall coffee consumption is down in some countries, even though sales of specialty coffees in coffee bars such as Starbucks or Coffee Republic have boomed in recent years, though four-dollar lattes have become less fashionable in the currently distressed global economy. For an example of an American bank pursuing a niche market strategy in a services business, see Exhibit 7.12.

## Mass-Market Strategy

A business can pursue a mass-market strategy in two ways. First, it can ignore any segment differences and design a single product-and-marketing program that will appeal to the largest number of consumers. The primary object of this strategy is to capture sufficient volume to gain economies of scale and a cost advantage. This strategy requires substantial resources, including production capacity, and good mass-marketing capabilities. Consequently, it is favored by larger companies or business units or by those whose parent corporation provides substantial support. For example, when Honda first entered

---

### Exhibit 7.12    PNC Bank Targets Generation Y

When it comes to banking, the members of Generation Y—those aged 18–34, by PNC Financial Services' definition, including many of the readers of this book—have different needs from their parents' generation. The most important of these differences, banking-wise, is that they tend to be clueless about how to manage their money. Some, in this debit card day and age, don't even know how to balance a checkbook because they rarely write checks. As Michael Ley, the PNC executive who led a project to target these customers says, "This group understands how to research online, but they said, 'We need help helping ourselves.'"

PNC decided that Gen Y was worth targeting, so they developed a new online product called the "Virtual Wallet." Virtual Wallet consists of three accounts: "Spend," "Reserve," and "Growth," all linked together with a user-friendly interface. What sets Virtual Wallet apart from other banks' products is features such as getting account balances by text message. Colleen Rohlf, a 24-year-old

teacher from Pittsburgh, doesn't have to worry any more about exactly how much money is in her account and doesn't have to worry about going online to find out. "I always know how much money I have," she says.

PNC likes this target market because it tends to hold higher balances than others and because Virtual Wallet customers rarely call customer service or show up in a branch office, keeping handling costs down. By late 2008, PNC had signed up more than 20,000 Virtual Wallet customers, of which 70 percent fell into the Gen Y demographic. With an average of 130 new customers signing on daily, PNC expected to break even in about two years, a year less than a conventional brick-and-mortar branch would take. As Gen Y grows up, PNC plans to add additional user-friendly tools for loans, investments, and other financial services.

*Source:* Burt Helm, "User-Friendly Finance for Generation Y," *BusinessWeek*, European Edition, December 8, 2008, p. 66.

the American and European motorcycle markets, it targeted the high-volume segment consisting of buyers of low-displacement, low-priced cycles. Honda subsequently used the sales volume and scale economies it achieved in that mass-market segment to help it expand into smaller, more-specialized segments of the market.

A second approach to the mass market is to design separate products and marketing programs for the differing segments. This is often called **differentiated marketing.** For example, Marriott and Europe's Accor do this with their various hotel chains. Although such a strategy can generate more sales than an undifferentiated strategy, it also increases costs in product design, manufacturing, inventory, and marketing, especially promotion.

## Growth-Market Strategy

Most companies would probably prefer to make life simple and sell more or less identical products wherever they go. In fact, some do. Boeing, whose largest markets for passenger jets are now in India and China, sells more or less the same planes there that they sell elsewhere. Automakers like Ford and Toyota design cars on global platforms. An Apple iPod is an iPod wherever you go. But for most companies, segmenting global markets presents similar, if not more daunting, challenges compared to segmenting their home markets.[22]

Businesses pursuing a growth-market strategy often target one or more fast-growth segments, even though these segments may not currently be very large. It is a strategy often favored by smaller companies to avoid direct confrontations with larger firms while building volume and share. Most venture capital firms invest only in firms pursuing growth-market strategies because doing so is the only way they can earn the 30 percent to 60 percent annual rates of return on investment that they seek for portfolio companies.

VC-backed Zynga, the multiplayer online gaming company whose games are played by more than 120 million users, hitched its wagon to fast-growing Facebook, whose user base has grown at a torrid pace. Founded in 2007, privately held Zynga's revenues were thought to have surpassed $450 million in 2010. "Only a few companies are so privileged to get the rocket-ship growth that Zynga has," crows Reid Hoffman, co-founder of LinkedIn and a Zynga director and investor.[23]

A growth-market strategy usually requires strong R&D and marketing capabilities to identify and develop products appealing to newly emerging user segments, plus the resources to finance rapid growth. The problem, however, is that fast growth, if sustained, attracts large competitors. The acquisition of Playfish by longtime gaming leader Electronic Arts in November 2010 may give Zynga a run for its money.[24] The goal of the early entrant is to have developed an enduring competitive position via its products, service, distribution, costs, and its brand by the time competitors enter. In the online world, however, such positions can be fleeting.

## Global Market Segmentation

One traditional approach to global market segmentation in the developed world was to view a country as a single segment comprising all consumers. As we have seen earlier in this chapter, this approach is seriously flawed because it relies on country variables rather than consumer behavior, assumes homogeneity *within* the country segment, and ignores the possibility of the existence of homogeneous groups of consumers *across* country segments.

More and more companies are approaching global market segmentation by attempting to identify consumers with similar needs and wants reflected in their behavior in the marketplace in a range of countries. This intercountry segmentation enables a company to develop reasonably standardized programs requiring little change across local markets, thereby resulting in scale economies. Star TV's launch of a Pan-Asian satellite television service broadcasting throughout Asia in English and Chinese is an example of such a strategy. By 2011, Star reached more than 400 million viewers in 53 Asian countries.[25]

There are many reasons—beyond mere ambitions to grow—why companies expand internationally. Some companies go international to defend their home position against global competitors who are constantly looking for vulnerability. For example, Caterpillar, through a joint venture with Mitsubishi Heavy Industries, has for more than 30 years made a substantial investment in Japan to deny its Japanese competitor, Komatsu, strength at home, thereby taking away its profit sanctuary. Had Cat not been successful in doing so, Komatsu would have been able to compete more aggressively with Cat, not only in the United States, but also in other major world markets.

Another reason a firm may go overseas and target a specific country is to service customers who are also engaging in global expansion. In recent years Japanese automobile companies that have created U.S. and other overseas manufacturing facilities have encouraged their parts suppliers to do the same. Firms also enter overseas markets to earn foreign exchange and, in some cases, are subsidized by their governments to do so. Others, like Coca-Cola, ramp up their international growth when opportunities for growth in their home markets falter.

Whatever the motivation, though, the challenges entailed in crossing borders are always tricky. Companies that "go global" need to decide when to standardize their offerings, and when to tailor them to local needs in what remains a highly diverse global marketplace. Says Singapore-based brand strategist Martin Roll, "Contrary to many predictions, the flattening of the world has not flattened unique cultural ant national characteristics, or the idiosyncratic preferences of customers."[26] The need for marketers to hone their skills at segmenting markets and targeting those they see as the most attractive appears not to be going away any time soon.

# TAKE-AWAYS

1. Marketers and entrepreneurs who find new and insightful ways to segment mature markets often uncover opportunities for uncontested market entry and rapid growth.

2. Sharply focused target marketing enables marketers to differentiate from mass-market leaders by giving consumers in a narrowly defined market segment what they want.

3. Focused market entry strategies conserve resources and facilitate early success.

4. The five-step procedure provided in this chapter identifies segments having the highest potential.

5. The market-attractiveness/competitive-position matrix is a useful analytical framework for deciding which markets or market segments to enter and from which to withdraw.

# ENDNOTES

**1.** Information to prepare this section was taken from John Parker, "Burgeoning Bourgeoisie" special report, *The Economist,* February 24, 2009, pp. 3–6; "Who's in the Middle?" "Burgeoning Bourgeoisie" special report, *The Economist,* February 24, 2009, p. 4; and the Dinaz's Fitness Studios website at *www.dinazs.com.* David Pilling, Kathrin Hille, and Amy Kazmin, "Stroll to a New Status." *Financial Times,* January 5, 2011, p. 11; Donal Griffin, "Pandit Stakes Citi's Future on Emerging Markets," *Bloomberg Business week* European Edition, March 21–27, 2011, pp. 49–50;

**2.** Duane D. Stanford, "Coke's Last Round," *Bloomberg Businessweek,* November 1–7, 2010, pp. 54–61.

**3.** Marc Gunther, "The World's New Economic Landscape," *Fortune* European Edition, July 26, 2010, pp. 81–82.

**4.** Shelley Emling, "Buyers Want It to Be All About Me," *International Herald Tribune,* January 21–22, 2006, p. 16.

**5.** Gunther, "The World's New Economic Landscape."

**6.** Jack Ewing, "First Mover in Mobile," *BusinessWeek,* European Edition, May 14, 2007, p. 60.

**7.** To see the vast array of customized products that such websites offer, see w*ww.cafepress.com, www.zazzle.com, or www.spreadshirt.com.*

**8.** "NMA WIRELESS—Silver Texters," *New Media Age,* November 28, 2002, p. 35.

**9.** "Service for Women," *North West News,* October 10, 2001, p. 20.

**10.** Nanette Byrnes, "Secrets of the Male Shopper," *BusinessWeek,* European Edition, September 4, 2006, pp. 45–51.

**11.** Gillian Reagan, "Nothing Tastes as Good as Skinny Feels," *Bloomberg Businessweek* European Edition, February 21–27, 2011.

**12.** Mark Levine, "The $19,450 Phone," *The New York Times,* December 1, 2002, p. 66.

**13.** Jean Halliday, "Sector Survey: Pinning Down the Numbers: Automakers Attempt to Quantify Their Share of the Market," *Advertising Age,* December 2, 2002, p. 50.

**14.** Mora Somassundarm, "Uni-Marts Inc.'s Small Town Strategy for Convenience Stores Is Paying Off," *The Wall Street Journal,* November 20, 1995, p. B5A; Tom Dochat, "Uni-Marts Ponders Options," *Harrisburg Patriot,* November 5, 2002, p. D02.

**15.** Gunther, "The World's New Economic Landscape."

**16.** See *www.claritas.com.*

**17.** Michael Arndt, "Quaker Oats Is Thirsty for Even More Gatorade Hits," *www.businessweek.com/bwdaily/dnflash/feb2000/nf202c.htm,* February 2, 2000.

**18.** Stanford, "Coke's Last Round."

**19.** Laura Petrecca, "Tech Giants Target Older Users—and Their Cash," *USA Today,* November 30, 2007, p. 5A.

**20.** Matt Townsend, "Under Armour's Daring Half-Court Shot," *Bloomberg Businessweek* European Edition, November 1–7, 2010, pp. 24–25.

**21.** Tom Mulier, "Nestlé's Recipe for Juggling Volatile Commodity Costs," *Bloomberg Businessweek* European Edition, March 21–27, 2011.

**22.** Gunther, "The World's New Economic Landscape."

**23.** Douglas MacMillan, "Zynga and Facebook, It's Complicated," *Bloomberg Businessweek* European Edition, April 26–May 2, 2010, pp. 47–48.

**24.** Ibid.

**25.** STAR TV website at *www.startv.com/corporate/about/index.htm.*

**26.** Gunther, "The World's New Economic Landsape" p. 82.

# CHAPTER EIGHT

# Differentiation and Brand Positioning

## Fast Food Turns Healthy[1]

THERE ARE MANY REASONS WHY CON-SUMERS around the world have made the fast-food industry one of the world's fastest growing over the past four decades, but healthy eating isn't one of them. At least not until Subway, the ubiquitous U.S.-based sandwich chain, decided in the late 1990s that its downscale image had to go. Subway had grown from a single store in 1965 to a nationwide chain of stores whose sales volume had long since surpassed $1 billion. But it was known more for its belly-busting foot-long sandwiches and its gaudy yellow décor than for anything else. Subway needed a makeover—a new positioning in the marketplace—something that would distinguish Subway from its fat- and sugar-purveying competitors.

### The Jared Diet

Fortuitously for Subway, at about the same time as the company decided to remake its image by adding some healthier sandwiches, a rotund college student at Indiana University who happened to live next door to the local Subway outlet decided that getting winded by dragging his 425-pound body across campus wasn't much fun. Jared Fogle, a regular customer of the Subway store, saw the new healthier sandwiches—less than seven grams of fat, the signs proclaimed—and decided it was time to go on a diet. For lunch, it would be a six-inch turkey, no mayo, no oil, and hold the

cheese, please. For dinner, a footlong veggie sub, a bag of baked potato chips, and a diet beverage.

The other element in his weight-loss strategy was walking. No more riding the campus bus. No more elevators. "Walking was the key," said Fogle. "I walked an average of 1.5 miles a day, five days a week. It may not sound like a lot, but it sure was better than what I was doing." A year later, he was down to 180 pounds on his 6-foot-2-inch frame. An editor at the student newspaper wrote about Jared's feat, the national media picked up the story, and before long Fogle was Subway's spokesman—"Jared, the Subway Guy."

### Repositioning Fuels Subway's Growth

To reflect the new positioning, the stores' interiors were updated. The dated graphics depicting the New York City subway system were dumped, and images of fresh tomatoes and other vegetables took their place. New heart-healthy sandwiches and, later, Atkins-friendly wraps—bowing to the growing popularity of the carbohydrate-controlled Atkins diet—were introduced. Jared went on a national tour, appearing in more than two dozen heart walks a year, as well as on talk shows everywhere.

Subway's new image as a place where you could get healthy fast food and all the hoopla that Jared generated paid the chain and its franchisees a twofold dividend. It helped stores grow their sales, as concerns over obesity became a compelling public health issue at the dawn of the new millennium. It enticed more people to sign up as franchisees and open new Subway stores in the United States and abroad. The results?

In 2001, Subway surpassed McDonald's as the most ubiquitous fast-food operator in the United States, with 13,247 stores at year-end, opening 904 stores in 2001 to McDonald's 295.

## Value: A Second Dimension to Subway's Positioning

In 2004, Stuart Frankel, owner of two small Subway sandwich shops in Florida, struggled with the fact that sales were always soft on weekends. He decided to offer every foot-long sandwich for $5—weekends only—a savings of about a dollar. Sales soared, and overall profits rose, too, despite higher food costs.

In 2007, as the financial crisis took hold, with devastating effect in much of Florida, Steve Sager, Subway's development agent for 225 Florida stores, decided to copy Frankel's idea in a troubled Fort Lauderdale store. Sales doubled on the first day, and

the store nearly ran out of bread and meat. Eventually, the idea caught the attention of Jeff Moody, Subway's marketing chief, who saw the $5 footlong as the basis for a value-oriented message that wouldn't conflict with Subway's existing "Eat Fresh" image and might help Subway compete with McDonald's dollar menu and drive traffic into Subway's stores. In March 2008 Moody, in the same week that venerable investment banker Bear Stearns collapsed, took the promotion into national distribution with a catchy new jingle. Within weeks, 3,600 videos of people performing Subway's hokey jingle appeared on YouTube, and Fogel was serenaded with the song by college students at the NCAA Final Four basketball tournament.

As its reputation for healthy and value-priced fast food grew, Subway's appeal to both franchisees and consumers grew as well. It won plaudits from *Entrepreneur* magazine (the Number One Franchise Opportunity for 2009) and from the Zagat Survey, which rated Subway as the top overall provider of "Healthy Options" in its 2009 fast-food survey. Though McDonalds still held the lead in total sales, by 2009 Subway had passed both Burger King and Wendy's in market share. Now the world's largest submarine sandwich chain, Subway by late-2011 had more than 35,000 stores in 97 countries.

## Marketing Challenges Addressed in Chapter 8

As the Subway example illustrates, the success of a brand offered to a given target market depends on how well it is positioned within that market segment—that is, how well it performs *relative to* competitive offerings and to the needs of the target audience. **Brand positioning** (or repositioning, in the case of Subway) refers to both the place a brand occupies in customers' minds relative to their needs and competing brands and to the marketer's decision-making intended to create such a position. Positioning comprises both competitive *and* customer considerations.

Brand positioning is basically concerned with differentiation. Ries and Trout, who popularized the concept of positioning, view it as a creative undertaking whereby an existing brand in an overcrowded marketplace of similar brands can be given a distinctive position in the minds of targeted prospects. While their concept was concerned with an existing brand, it is equally applicable for new brands.[2] While typically thought of in relation to the marketing of consumer goods, it has equal value for industrial goods and for services, which require essentially the same procedure as consumer goods. Because services are characterized by their intangibility, perishability, consumer participation in their delivery, and the simultaneous nature of their production and consumption, they are generally more difficult for marketers to position successfully, notwithstanding Subway's success.

In Chapter 8, we take the final step in preparing the foundation on which effective marketing programs are based. Drawing on decisions made about target markets, as discussed in Chapter 7, we address the critical question: "How should a business position its product offering—whether goods or services—so customers in the target market perceive the offering as providing the benefits they seek, thereby giving the product an advantage over current and potential future competitors?"

As we shall see, the brand positioning decision is a strategic one, with implications not only for how the firm's goods or services should be designed, but also for developing the

other elements of the marketing mix. Pricing decisions, promotion decisions, and decisions about how products are to be distributed all follow from and contribute to the effectiveness of the positioning of the product in its competitive space. Thus, the material in this chapter provides a foundation for virtually all of the strategic decision-making that follows in the balance of this book.

# Differentiation: One Key to Customer Preference and Competitive Advantage

Why do customers prefer one product, whether a good or a service, over another? In today's highly competitive markets, consumers have numerous options. They can choose from dozens of best-selling novels to take along on an upcoming vacation. They can buy the novel they choose from an online merchant such as Amazon.com, from large chain booksellers such as Barnes and Noble or their online counterparts, from book clubs, from a local bookstore, or in some cases from their nearby supermarket or mass merchant. They can even borrow the book at their local library and not buy it at all! Whether it's goods such as books or services such as libraries, consumers make choices such as these nearly every day. In most cases, consumers or organizational customers choose what they buy for one of two reasons: what they choose is *better,* in some sense, or *cheaper.* In either case, the good or service they choose is, in some way, almost always *different* from others they could have chosen.

Differentiation is a powerful theme in developing business strategies, as well as in marketing. As Michael Porter points out, "A company can outperform its rivals only if it can establish a difference that it can preserve. It must deliver greater value to customers or create comparable value at a lower cost, or both."[3] Most of the time, differentiation is why

people buy. They buy the latest John Grisham novel because they know it will be a page-turner, different from the last Grisham they read, and hard to put down. They buy it from Amazon.com because they know Amazon will have it in stock and its one-click ordering system takes only a minute. Or they buy it from the megastore because it's fun to browse there or from their local bookseller because they feel good about supporting their local merchants. They buy it at the supermarket because it's convenient. All these book-selling strategies are different, and they appeal to different consumers (i.e., different market segments) at different points in time, for different book-buying purposes. If these strategies did not vary, consumers would have no reason to use some of them, and they would buy their books where they were cheapest or most convenient, though even in such a case, the cheaper pricing or greater convenience would still constitute differences.

## Differentiation among Competing Brands

As we saw in Chapter 7, customers in one market segment have wants and needs that differ in some way from those of customers in other segments. Brand positioning allows the marketer to take advantage of and be responsive to such differences and position particular goods and services to better meet the needs of consumers in one or more of these segments. These differences are often physical. Subway's Atkins-friendly wraps and some of its sandwiches really do contain much less fat than a fast-food hamburger. But differences can also be perceptual, as when athletic footwear and apparel, for example, benefit from endorsements by Roger Federer, Kobe Bryant, or other famous athletes. Creating *both* physical and perceptual differences, using all the elements of the marketing mix—product, pricing, promotion, and distribution decisions—is what effective brand positioning seeks to accomplish.

## Physical Positioning

One way to assess the current position of a brand relative to competitors is on the basis of how various brands compare on some set of objective physical characteristics. In many cases, a physical positioning analysis can provide useful information to a marketing manager, particularly in the early stages of identifying and designing new product offerings. Sometimes, physical differences provide the basis for entirely new product lines, even new companies, as the example of Geox shoes in Exhibit 8.1 demonstrates.

### Exhibit 8.1    YOUR FEET WANT TO BREATHE

Nearly 20 years ago, Mario Moretti Polegato was out hiking under the hot summer sun of his native Italy. In an effort to relieve the discomfort of his sweaty feet, Polegato poked holes in the soles of his hiking shoes. "Why doesn't anyone make shoes that can breathe?" he wondered. After trying unsuccessfully to sell his idea of breathable shoes to Nike and Adidas, he decided to strike out on his own. Polegato founded Geox in 1995, starting with children's shoes and later adding adult styles. Customers responded. In 2007, his Milan-listed company sold 21 million pairs of shoes, some $1.2 billion worth, everything from rhinestone-studded but breathable sandals fit for a night on the town to earthy moccasins to a new line of athletic footwear. Thousands of tiny holes in the sole of every Geox shoe lets air in but keeps water out.

In Polegato's view, most athletic shoe makers focus on performance and competitive advantage. The Geox mind-set—it's all about comfort—is different. He says, "Feet have to breathe."

*Source:* Jennifer L. Schlenker, "Geox Takes On the Goliaths of Sport," *BusinessWeek*, European Edition, April 14, 2008, p. 58. For more on Geox see *www.geox.com*.

Despite being based primarily on technical rather than on market data, physical comparisons can be an essential step in undertaking a positioning analysis, which sets the foundation for brand positioning decisions. This is especially true with the competitive offerings of many industrial goods and services, which buyers typically evaluate largely on the basis of such characteristics. In addition, it contributes to a better marketing/R&D interface by determining key physical product characteristics; helps define the structure of competition by revealing the degree to which the various brands compete with one another; and may indicate the presence of meaningful product gaps (the lack of products having certain desired physical characteristics), which, in turn, may reveal opportunities for a new product entry, such as Polegato's breathable shoes.

## Limitations of Physical Positioning

A simple comparison of only the physical dimensions of alternative offerings usually does *not* provide a complete picture of relative positions because, as we noted earlier, positioning ultimately occurs in customers' minds. Even though a brand's physical characteristics, package, name, price, and ancillary services can be designed to achieve a particular position in the market, customers may attach less importance to some of these characteristics than, or perceive them differently from, what the firm expects. Also, customers' attitudes toward a product are often based on social or psychological attributes not amenable to objective comparison, such as perceptions of the product's aesthetic appeal, sportiness, or status image (for example, in the United States, French wine from Bordeaux has traditionally been thought of as expensive or as an accompaniment to French food). Consequently, **perceptual positioning analysis**—whether aimed at discovering opportunities for new product entries or evaluating and adjusting the position of a current offering—is critically important.

> **STRATEGIC ISSUE**
>
> A simple comparison of only the physical dimensions of alternative offerings usually does not provide a complete picture of relative positions.

## Perceptual Positioning

Consumers often know very little about the essential physical attributes of many of the brands they buy, especially household products. The same is true for many services. Even if they did, they might not understand the physical attributes well enough to use them as a basis for choosing between competitive offerings. (For the major differences between physical and perceptual product positioning analyses, see Exhibit 8.2.) Many consumers do not want to be bothered about a product's physical characteristics because they are not buying these physical properties but rather the benefits they provide. While the physical properties of a product certainly influence the benefits provided, a consumer can typically evaluate a product better on the basis of what it *does* than what it *is*. Thus, for example, a headache remedy may be judged on how quickly it brings relief, a toothpaste on the freshness of breath provided, a beer on its taste, and a vehicle on how comfortably it rides.

The evaluation of many goods and services is subjective because it is influenced by factors other than physical properties, including the way products are presented, our past experiences with them, and the opinions of others. Thus, physically similar products may be perceived as being different because of different histories, names, and advertising campaigns. For example, Sri Lankan tea producer Dilmah positions its teas in the same way wine has been positioned for years (see Exhibit 8.3).

## Exhibit 8.2

COMPARISON OF PHYSICAL AND PERCEPTUAL POSITIONING ANALYSES

| Physical Positioning | Perceptual Positioning |
|---|---|
| • Technical orientation | • Consumer orientation |
| • Physical characteristics | • Perceptual attributes |
| • Objective measures | • Perceptual measures |
| • Data readily available | • Need for marketing research |
| • Physical brand properties | • Perceptual brand positions and positioning intensities |
| • Large number of dimensions | • Limited number of dimensions |
| • Represents impact of product specs | • Represents impact of product specs and communication |
| • Direct R&D implications | • R&D implications need to be interpreted |

## Exhibit 8.3  NOT YOUR ORDINARY CUP OF TEA

"What's grown on that field," says the Dilmah Group's Dilhan Fernando, "will differ drastically from what's grown over here." Fernando and his brother Malik think it's high time for a revolution in the way tea is blended and marketed.

Their Ceylon teas, as they call them, harking back to Sri Lanka's colonial heritage, are positioned like fine wine, with elegant packaging extolling the subtly distinctive flavors of teas grown on a single hillside.

In the declining and still relatively fragmented global tea industry, which has lost $70 billion in sales to coffee in recent years, Dilmah has risen out of nowhere. Founded in the midst of Sri Lanka's civil war in 1988, it now ranks as the third-largest stand-alone tea brand, behind Unilever's Lipton and Associated British Foods' Twinings and about even with Tetley, owned by India's Tata Group.

The multinational players scoff at Dilmah's success. "The wine analogy is fairly ridiculous," says John Cornish, Twinings' international marketing director. But William Gorman, executive chair of Britain's Tea Council, says, "Dilmah is a very interesting company. This is an industry that has been incredibly slow to innovate, and Dilmah has shown it how."

With Starbucks having acquired Tazo Tea in 1999 and other boutique brands also making headway, Dilmah's positioning strategy may be just the ticket to turning tea's sales trend around. With a growing number of chic Dilmah T-bars now open in countries where the majors have limited clout—65 bars and rising, in places such as Poland, Kazakstan, and the United Arab Emirates—the Fernando brothers are making sure they don't leave distribution and brand awareness to chance.

*Source:* Eric Ellis, "Vintage Ceylon," *Fortune*, International Edition, June 25, 2007, pp. 22–24. For more on Dilmah, see *www.dilmahtea .com.*

# Levers Marketers Can Use to Establish Brand Positioning

Customers or prospective customers perceive some physical as well as other differences between goods or services within a product category, of course. Marketing decision-makers seeking to win a particular position in customers' minds will seek to endow their brand with various kinds of attributes, which may be categorized as follows:

- *Simple physically based attributes.* These are directly related to a single physical dimension such as quality, power, or size. While there may be a direct correspondence between a physical dimension and a perceptual attribute, an analysis of consumers' perception of products on these attributes may unveil phenomena of interest to a marketing strategy. For instance, two cars with an estimated gasoline mileage of 23.2 and 25.8 miles per gallon may be perceived as having similar gasoline consumption.

- *Complex physically based attributes.* Because of the presence of a large number of physical characteristics, consumers may use composite attributes to evaluate competitive offerings. The development of such summary indicators is usually subjective because of the relative importance attached to different cues. Examples of composite attributes are the speed of a computer system, roominess of a car, and a product or service being user-friendly.
- *Essentially abstract attributes.* Although these perceptual attributes are influenced by physical characteristics, they are not related to them in any direct way. Examples include the sexiness of a perfume, quality of a French wine, and prestige of a car. All of these attributes are highly subjective and difficult to relate to physical characteristics other than by experience.
- *Price.* A brand's price may imply other attributes, such as high or low quality.

The importance of perceptual attributes with their subjective component varies across consumers and product classes. Thus, it can be argued that consumers familiar with a given product class are apt to rely more on physical characteristics and less on perceptual attributes than consumers who are less familiar with that product class. It can also be argued that while perceptual positioning is essential for many consumer goods, such is not necessarily the case for many industrial goods.

Even though there is considerable truth in these statements, perceptual attributes must be considered in positioning most products. One reason is the growing similarity of the physical characteristics of more and more brands. This increases the importance of other, largely subjective dimensions. Consider, for example, whether Nike's Zoom Kobe VI basketball shoes would have sold as well without basketball star Kobe Bryant endorsement and his presence in their ads.

**STRATEGIC ISSUE**

*Perceptual attributes must be considered in positioning most brands.*

## Preparing the Foundation for Marketing Strategies: The Brand Positioning Process

Positioning a new brand in customers' minds or repositioning a current brand involves a series of steps, as outlined in Exhibit 8.4. These steps are applicable to goods and services, in domestic or international markets, and to new and existing brands. Thus, when we say "brand" in the rest of this chapter and those that follow, we include both existing goods and services and planned new products—goods or services—that do not yet exist. We do not suggest that the determinant product attributes and the perceptions of consumers of various competitive offerings will remain constant across countries or other market segments; in fact they are likely to vary with most products. After managers have selected a relevant set of competing offerings serving a target market (Step 1), they must identify a set of critical or determinant product attributes important to customers in that target market (Step 2).

Step 3 involves collecting information from a sample of customers about their perceptions of the various offerings, and in Step 4 researchers analyze this information to determine the brand's current position in customers' minds and the intensity thereof (does it occupy a dominant position), as well as those of competitors.

Managers then ascertain the customers' most preferred combinations of determinant attributes, which requires the collection of further data (Step 5). This allows an examination of the fit between the preferences of a given target segment of customers and the current positions of competitive offerings (Step 6). Finally, in Step 7, managers write a concise

## Exhibit 8.4

STEPS IN THE POSITIONING PROCESS FOR GOODS AND SERVICES

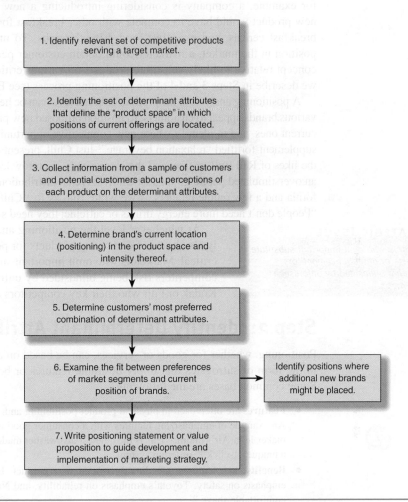

1. Identify relevant set of competitive products serving a target market.

2. Identify the set of determinant attributes that define the "product space" in which positions of current offerings are located.

3. Collect information from a sample of customers and potential customers about perceptions of each product on the determinant attributes.

4. Determine brand's current location (positioning) in the product space and intensity thereof.

5. Determine customers' most preferred combination of determinant attributes.

6. Examine the fit between preferences of market segments and current position of brands.

Identify positions where additional new brands might be placed.

7. Write positioning statement or value proposition to guide development and implementation of marketing strategy.

statement that communicates the positioning decision they have reached. A discussion of these steps in the positioning process takes up most of the remainder of this chapter.

## Step 1: Identify a Relevant Set of Competitive Products

Positioning analyses are useful at many levels: company, business unit, product category, and specific product line or brand. At the company or business unit level, such analyses are useful to determine how an entire company or business unit is positioned relative to its competitors. Even countries can be thought of as having brand positions in the marketplace. Unfortunately for Chinese manufacturers, a string of toy recalls for safety reasons, incidents of poisonous pet foods, and other scares mean that the words "Made in China" do not ring with confidence in consumers' ears. Positioning that says "cheap" in the mind of the consumer is not what quality and globally oriented Chinese companies such as personal computer manufacturer Lenovo and brewer Tsingtao want to hear.[4]

At the product category level, the analysis examines customers' perceptions about types of products they might consider as substitutes to satisfy the same basic need. Suppose, for example, a company is considering introducing a new instant breakfast drink. The new product would have to compete with other breakfast foods, such as bacon and eggs, breakfast cereals, and even fast-food drive-throughs. To understand the new product's position in the market, a marketer could obtain customer perceptions of the new product concept relative to likely substitute products on various critical determinant attributes, as we describe in Steps 3 and 4 of the positioning process (see Exhibit 8.4).

A positioning analysis at the product or brand level can be helpful to better understand how various brands appeal to customers, to position proposed new products or brands or reposition current ones, and to identify where new competitive opportunities might be found. The new supplement-fortified "relaxation beverage," Just Chill, presents itself as a clear alternative to the likes of Red Bull, coffee, and the increasingly overcrowded energy drink category. Will an overstimulated public go for Just Chill? Its retail distribution is confined to Southern California and a few online retailers as we write. But, as Just Chill creator Max Baumann says, "People don't need more energy drinks or caffeine; they need something to chill them out."[5]

At whichever level the positioning analysis is to be done, the analyst's choice of competing products (or product categories or firms) is critical. Marketers who omit important substitute products or potential competitors risk being blindsided by unforeseen competition. Just ask Kodak or Fuji who their key competitors are today!

## Step 2: Identify Determinant Attributes

Positioning, whether for goods or services, can be based on a variety of attributes—some in the form of surrogates that imply desirable features or benefits as a positioning base. Some common bases are the following.[6]

- **Features** are often used in physical product positioning and, hence, with industrial products. An example of emphasizing features with a consumer good is U.S. high-end home appliance maker Jenn-Air's claim; "This is the quietest dishwasher made in America." Amazon.com has a unique "1-click®" ordering system.

- **Benefits,** like features, are directly related to a product. Examples here include Volvo's emphasis on safety, Toyota's emphasis on reliability, and Norelco's promising a "close and comfortable shave."

- **Parentage** includes who makes it ("At Fidelity, you're not just buying a fund, a stock, or a bond—you're buying a better way to manage it") and prior products ("Buying a car is like getting married. It's a good idea to know the family first—followed by a picture of the ancestors of the Mercedes-Benz S class model").

- **Manufacturing process** is often the subject of a firm's positioning efforts. An example is Jaeger-LeCoultre's statement about its watches; "We know it's perfect, but we take another 1,000 hours just to be sure."

- **Ingredients** as a positioning concept is illustrated by some clothing manufacturers' saying their shirts are made only of organic cotton.

- **Endorsements** are of two types—those by experts ("Discover why over 5,000 American doctors and medical professionals prescribe this Swedish mattress"—Tempur-Pedic) and those via emulation as with Kobe Bryant wearing Nike shoes.

- **Comparison** with a competitor's product is common ("Tests prove Pedigree is more nutritious than IAMS, costs less than IAMS, and tastes great, too"—Pedigree Mealtime pet food).

- **Proenvironment** positioning seeks to portray a company as a good citizen ("Because we recycle over 100 million plastic bottles a year, landfills can be filled with other things, like land, for instance"—Phillips Petroleum, part of Conoco Phillips).

● **Price/quality** is used in cases such as Walmart successfully positioning itself as the lowest-price seller of household products.

Theoretically, consumers can use many attributes to evaluate competing brands, but the number actually influencing a consumer's choice is typically small, partly because consumers can consider only attributes of which they are aware. The more variables used in positioning a given brand, the greater the chance of confusion and even disbelief on the part of the consumer. The positioning effort must be kept as simple as possible and complexity should generally be avoided at all costs. Subway's positioning is based on only two elements, healthy and good value. Even marketers of bottled water are seeking to differentiate and better position their products (see Exhibit 8.5).

In using one or more attributes as the basis of a brand's positioning effort, it is important to recognize that the importance attached to these attributes often varies. For example, while the brands of soap or shampoo provided by a hotel may be an attribute that some consumers use in evaluating hotels, most are unlikely to attach much importance to this when deciding which hotel chain to patronize. Bedding, however, is another story, as specialty linens maker Anichini has found. Its exquisite bedding helps luxury boutique hotels and resorts like the Bacara Resort in Santa Barbara, California, stand out from the sameness of the ubiquitous—and in some people's minds, boring—chain hotels.[7] Even an important attribute may not greatly influence a consumer's preference if all the alternative brands are perceived to be about equal on that dimension. Deposit safety is an important attribute in banking, but most consumers perceived all banks to be about equally safe, at least until the recent financial crisis. Consequently, deposit safety has not been a **determinant attribute:** It does not play a major role in helping customers to differentiate among the alternatives and to determine which bank they prefer.

Marketers should rely primarily on determinant attributes, whether benefits or features, in defining the product space in a positioning analysis. The question is: "How can a marketer find out which product dimensions are determinant attributes?" Doing so typically requires conducting some kind of marketing research. This brings us to Step 3.

## Exhibit 8.5   CAN YOU POSITION BOTTLED WATER?

The growth category called bottled water has suddenly come to a screeching halt. Growth in the United States in 2008 slowed to 2 percent, down from near-double-digit rates earlier. Environmental concerns are the driver, at least in part. The energy costs and pollution that the bottled products generate are far higher compared to plain old tap water, which arrives in your home or workplace much more efficiently. The slump was expected to turn into a full-fledged downturn in 2009, as budget-squeezed customers turn to the tap.

Big players such as Coca-Cola, PepsiCo, and Nestle are jostling for position to reverse the decline. "But it's all just water," you might say. Not so fast. They are scrambling to offer products that put something in the bottle other than just plain water. Coke's Dasani has introduced a flavored version called Dasani Essence. Pepsi's SoBe Lifewater added stevia, a new all-natural sweetener. Other companies are focused on refillable bottles, a bit better environmentally, at least at the margin. Meanwhile water filter manufacturers, such as Clorox's Brita and Procter & Gamble's PUR, are enjoying healthy sales increases.

Who will prosper in this shakeout? It's too soon to tell, but positioning one bottled water as fundamentally different from another is a stern test of these companies' marketing prowess or, as some observers lament, an indicator of consumer marketing run amok.

*Source:* Christopher Palmeri and Nanette Byrnes, "Coke and Pepsi Try Reinventing Water," *BusinessWeek,* European Edition, March 2, 2009, p. 58.

# Step 3: Collect Data about Customers' Perceptions for Brands in the Competitive Set

Having identified a set of competing brands, the marketer needs to know what attributes are determinant for the target market and the product category under consideration. He or she also needs to know how different brands in the competitive set are viewed on these attributes. Typically, this market knowledge is developed by first conducting qualitative research, perhaps interviews or focus groups, to learn which attributes are determinant. Then quantitative research follows, perhaps a survey of consumers about their perceptions, to gather data on how competing brands score on these attributes. Later in this chapter, we discuss several statistical and analytical tools that are useful at this step of the positioning process.

# Step 4: Analyze the Current Positions of Brands in the Competitive Set

Whether the positioning process is directed at a new brand not yet introduced or repositioning one that already exists, it is important to develop a clear understanding of the positioning of the existing brands in the competitive set (see Step 1). There are two useful tools for doing so. One is the **positioning grid,** also called a **perceptual map.** The other is the **value curve.** The positioning grid provides a visual representation of the positions of various products or brands in the competitive set in terms of (typically) two determinant attributes. Where more than two attributes are to be considered in a positioning analysis, multidimensional grids, or multiple grids, are produced. Alternatively, a value curve, which comprises more than just two dimensions, can be generated (see following).

But not all brands exist in the awareness of most consumers. A brand that is not known by a consumer cannot, by definition, occupy a position in that consumer's mind. Often the awareness set for a given product class is three or fewer brands. Thus, many if not most brands have little or no position in the minds of many consumers. Consider coffee bars, which, in recent years, have become ubiquitous in cities worldwide. In London, three major chains dominate—Starbucks, Coffee Republic, and Caffé Nero—each with its own ambience and image with consumers. There are also several smaller chains and numerous independents, most of which are largely unknown—thus with no clear positioning—to most Londoners.

With consumers having so many coffee bars to choose from already—often several shops within a few hundred feet of each other on any busy street—for a new coffee bar entrant to be successful, it must adopt a clear positioning in consumers' minds to give consumers a reason to switch. Determining the attributes on which the brand's positioning will be based is a key outcome of the positioning process and a driver of the marketing communication strategy, as well as the marketing strategy overall, that will ultimately be developed. Without clear guidance about the intended position of the brand, advertising agencies, salesforces, and others charged with building the awareness and recognition of the product in the marketplace will be ill-equipped to do this important job.

**Building a Positioning Grid**   An example of what can be done with data gathered in Step 3 is found in Exhibit 8.6, which shows the results obtained from a classical study that portrays how a sample of consumers positioned a number of women's clothing retailers in the Washington, D.C., area. Respondents rated the various stores on the two determinant attributes of value and fashionability. Some stores, such as Nordstrom and Kmart, occupy relatively distant positions from one another, indicating that consumers see them as very different. Other stores occupy positions comparable to one another (Neiman Marcus, Saks) and thus are considered relatively alike, meaning the intensity of competition between these stores is likely to be considerably greater than for those that occupy widely divergent positions.

The store positioning shown in Exhibit 8.6 also provides useful information about possible opportunities for the launching of a new store or the repositioning of an existing one. Positioning for a new store could be done by examining the positioning map for empty spaces (competitive gaps) where no existing store is currently located. There is such a gap in the upper-right quadrant of the "value/fashionability" map in Exhibit 8.6. This gap may represent an opportunity for developing a new entry or repositioning an old one that is perceived to offer greater fashionability than Nordstrom at a lower price. Of course, such gaps may exist simply because a particular position is either (1) impossible for any brand to attain because of technical constraints or (2) undesirable since there are few prospective customers for a brand with that set of attributes. It is important that positioning grids be built on a foundation of well-designed marketing research, rather than naive hunches. Several software tools have been developed for designing positioning studies and analysing the results, some of which we identify in Exhibit 8.7.

**Building a Value Curve**    Given that crafting strategies involves making choices—choices about what *not* to do, as well as what to do—another useful tool for positioning

## Exhibit 8.6

PERCEPTUAL MAP OF WOMEN'S CLOTHING RETAILERS IN WASHINGTON, D.C.

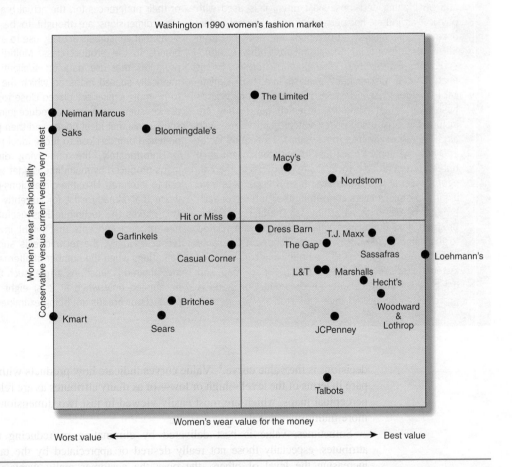

*Source:* Adapted from Douglas Tigert and Stephen Arnold, "Nordstrom: How Good Are They?" *Babson College Retailing Research Reports,* September 1990, as shown in Micheal Levy and Barton A. Weitz, *Retailing Management* (Burr Ridge, IL: Richard D. Irwin. 1992), p. 205.

## Exhibit 8.7    SOFTWARE TOOLS FOR POSITIONING DECISION MAKING

Software tools useful for making positioning decisions include applications that identify important determinant attributes, as well as statistical applications that can plot positioning grids from market research data.

*Conjoint analysis:* As we mention in Step 5 of the positioning process, it is important to learn which key attributes are important to consumers. Conjoint analysis is one tool for doing so. Conjoint analysis determines which combination of a limited number of attributes consumers most prefer. The technique is helpful for identifying appealing new product designs and important points that might be included in a product's advertising. Although it can provide some insights about consumer preferences, it cannot provide information about how consumers perceive the positioning of existing products in relation to product dimensions. Conjoint analysis is one way to narrow down a set of product attributes to those most important to consider in product design and positioning decisions. Most often, it is used with physical attributes, not perceptual ones. Several widely used conjoint analysis applications are available from Sawtooth Software, Inc. (*www.sawtoothsoftware.com*).

*Factor analysis and discriminant analysis:* Factor analysis and discriminant analysis are two statistical techniques useful in constructing positioning grids based on actual marketing research data. They are included in most broad-based statistical packages, such as SPSS MR (*www.spss.com/spssmr*). To employ factor analysis, the analyst must first identify the salient attributes consumers use to evaluate products in the category under study. The analyst then collects data from a sample of consumers concerning their ratings of each product or brand on all attributes. The factor analysis program next determines which attributes are related to the same underlying construct ("load" on the same factor). The analyst uses those underlying constructs or factors as the dimensions for a product space map, and the program indicates where each product or brand is perceived to be located on each factor.

Discriminant analysis requires the same input data as factor analysis. The discriminant analysis program then determines consumers' perceptual dimensions on the basis of which attributes best differentiate, or discriminate, among brands. Once again, those underlying dimensions can be used to construct a product space map, but they are usually not so easily interpretable as the factors identified through factor analysis. Also, as with factor analysis, the underlying dimensions may be more a function of the attributes used to collect consumer ratings than of the product characteristics that consumers actually consider to be most important.

*Multidimensional scaling:* Unlike the other techniques in which the underlying dimensions identified depend on the attributes supplied by the researcher when collecting data, multidimensional scaling produces dimensions based on consumer judgments about the similarity of, or their preferences for, the actual brands. These underlying dimensions are thought to be the basic dimensions that consumers actually use to evaluate alternative brands in the product class. Multidimensional scaling programs that use data on similarities construct geometrically spaced maps on which the brands perceived to be most similar are placed close together. Those that use consumer preferences produce joint space maps that show consumer ideal points and then position the most-preferred brands close to those ideal points.

Unfortunately, the underlying dimensions of the maps produced by multidimensional scaling can be difficult to interpret. Also, the dimensions identified are only those that already exist for currently available brands. This makes the technique less useful for investigating new product concepts that might involve new characteristics. Finally, the technique is subject to statistical limitations when the number of alternative brands being investigated is small. As a rule, such techniques should be applied only when at least eight or more different products or brands are being examined.

---

decisions is the value curve.[8] Value curves indicate how products within a category compare in terms of the level—high or low—of as many attributes as are relevant. Thus, unlike perceptual maps, which are most easily viewed in just two dimensions, value curves are more multidimensional.

Sometimes, value is best delivered by eliminating or reducing the level of some attributes, especially those not really desired or appreciated by the target customer, and increasing the level of others, the ones the customer really wants. Let's imagine that in addition to the data shown on the perceptual map in Exhibit 8.6, we have data about

## Exhibit 8.8

VALUE CURVES FOR NEIMAN MARCUS, JC PENNEY, AND SEARS

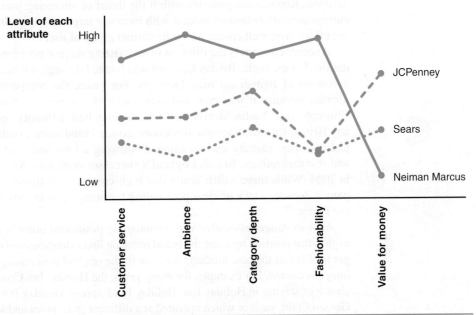

several other variables for three stores: Neiman Marcus, Sears, and JC Penney: We could build value curves for the three retailers by plotting these hypothetical data as shown in Exhibit 8.8.

The value curves show that, among other things, Sears and JC Penney choose to compete by reducing their level of customer service, ambience, category depth, and fashionability, presumably in order to deliver increased value for money. Neiman Marcus offers higher levels of customer service, ambience, category depth, and fashionability, presumably because the target customer it seeks to serve is willing to pay for these attributes.

**Marketing Opportunities to Gain a Distinct Position**   In situations where one or a limited number of brands dominate a product class (or type) in the minds of consumers, the main opportunity for competitors generally lies in obtaining a profitable position within a market segment *not* dominated by a leading brand. Competing head-on against the leaders on the basis of attributes appropriated by larger competitors is not likely to be effective.

A better option is to concentrate on an attribute prized by members of a given market segment. Toyota, with its traditional baby-boomer customer base getting older, launched its Scion brand in 2004, targeted at American youth. Instead of transitional mass marketing, the Scion team used edgy internet-based marketing, including making virtual Scions available for virtual purchase on Second Life, a website that was then growing in popularity with the younger set.[9] Scion's hip, youthful image has helped the new brand score with its Generation Y target market.

**Constraints Imposed by an Intense Position**   Although marketers should generally seek a distinctive and intense position for their brands, attaining such a position imposes constraints on future strategies. If shifts in the market environment cause customers to reduce the importance they attach to a current determinant attribute, marketers may have difficulty repositioning a brand with an intensely perceived position on that attribute. Repositioning carries with it the threat of alienating part or all of the product's current users regardless of success with its newly targeted group. Success in its repositioning efforts may well ensure losing its current group of users.

Another concern is the dilution of an existing intense position as a result of consolidation. For example, British Leyland was formed through a series of mergers involving a number of British car manufacturers. For years, the company did not have a clear identity because it was new and manufactured a variety of brands, including Rover, Triumph, and Austin-Morris. Most Europeans had difficulty spontaneously recalling any British car manufacturer since once-strong brand names such as Austin and Morris had lost their identity and meaning. Following a long series of divestitures, buyouts, and reorganizations, British Leyland's successor company, MG Rover, went bankrupt in 2005. While there's little doubt that high-cost manufacturing contributed to the company's demise, a lack of clear positioning for many of its brands was surely a contributing factor.[10]

Another danger associated with an intensely positioned brand is the temptation to overexploit that position by using the brand name on line extensions and new products. The danger here is that the new products may not fit the original positioning and the brand's strong image is diluted. For example, for many years, the Holiday Inn Group offered travelers the choice of staying in Holiday Inn, Holiday Inn Express, Holiday Inn Select, or Holiday Inn Garden Court, each of which operated at a different price point and service offering. Such a diverse offering bearing a single brand can be very confusing to consumers.

**Limitations of Product Positioning Analysis**    The analysis depicted in Exhibit 8.6 is often referred to as *product positioning* because it indicates how alternative products or brands are positioned relative to one another in customers' minds. The problem with this analysis is that it does not tell the marketer which positions are most appealing to customers.[11]   Thus, there is no way to determine if there is a market for a new brand or store that might locate in an "open" position or whether the customers in other market segments prefer brands or stores with different attributes and positions. To solve such problems, it is necessary to measure customers' preferences and locate them in the product space along with their perceptions of the positions of existing brands. This is called a **market positioning analysis.** We deal with this issue in Step 5.

# Step 5: Determine Customers' Most Preferred Combination of Attributes

There are several ways analysts can measure customer preferences and include them in a positioning analysis. For instance, survey respondents can be asked to think of the ideal brand within a category—a hypothetical brand possessing the perfect combination of attributes (from the customer's viewpoint). Respondents could then rate their ideal product and existing products on a number of attributes. An alternative approach is to ask respondents not only to judge the degree of similarity among pairs of existing brands, but also to indicate their degree of preference for each. In either case, the analyst, using the appropriate statistical techniques, can locate the respondents' ideal points relative to the positions of the various existing brands on the product space map.

Another method of assessing customers' preferences and trade-offs among them is a statistical technique called *conjoint analysis*.[12]   Customers are surveyed and asked their preferences among various real or hypothetical product configurations, each with attributes that are systematically varied. By analyzing the resulting data, the marketer can learn which of several attributes are more important than the others. These results can then be used in positioning analyses such as those described here.

Whichever approach is used, the results will look something like Exhibit 8.9, which shows a hypothetical cluster of ideal points for one segment of women's clothing consumers. As a group, this segment would seem to prefer Nordstrom over any other women's clothing retailer on the map.

There are, however, several reasons not all customers in this segment are likely to prefer Nordstrom. First, the ideal points of some customers are actually closer to Macy's than Nordstrom. Second, customers whose ideal point is equidistant between the two stores may be relatively indifferent in their choice of which store to patronize. Finally, customers sometimes may patronize stores somewhat further away from their ideal—particularly when buying low-involvement, nondurable goods or services—to

## Exhibit 8.9

PERCEPTUAL MAP OF WOMEN'S CLOTHING RETAILERS IN WASHINGTON, D.C.,
SHOWING THE IDEAL POINTS OF A SEGMENT OF CONSUMERS

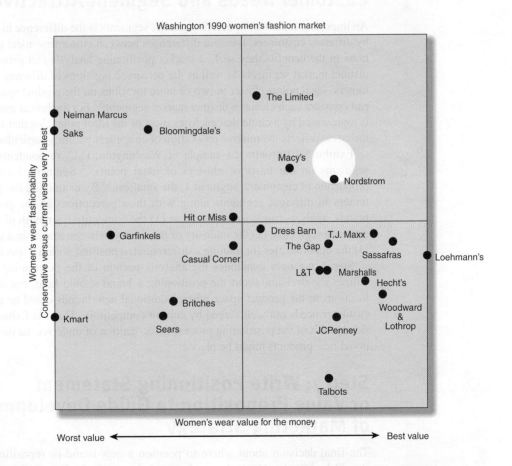

*Source:* Adapted from Douglas Tigert and Stephen Arnold, "Nordstrom: How Good Are They?" *Babson College Retailing Research Reports,* September 1990.

assess the qualities of new stores, to reassess older stores from time to time, or just for the sake of variety.

Using price as one dimension of a positioning grid, or as a key dimension on which a brand is positioned, is typically not very useful unless price is a key driver of the market-ing strategy. This is the case for two reasons. First, price is easily imi-table by competitors. Unless the firm has a clear cost advantage over its competitors, by virtue of its processes or other sources of efficiency, using low price as a basis for positioning can be a fast road to a price war that no one (except consumers) will win.

Second, claims that one's brand—whether a good or a service—is low-priced are some-times not very credible because so many marketers make such claims. It is often better to position around more enduring differentiators and let price speak more subtly for itself. Walmart, an exception, has been able to sustain its low-price positioning in the United States because its costs and its prices on many items, compared to its chief competitors, actually are lower.

## Step 6: Consider Fit of Possible Positions with Customer Needs and Segment Attractiveness

An important criterion for defining market segments is the difference in the benefits sought by different customers. Because differences between customers' ideal points reflect varia-tions in the benefits they seek, a market positioning analysis can simultaneously identify distinct market segments as well as the perceived positions of different brands. When cus-tomers' ideal points cluster in two or more locations on the product space map, the analyst can consider each cluster a distinct market segment.[13] For analytical purposes, each cluster is represented by a circle that encloses most of the ideal points for that segment; the size of the circle reflects the relative proportion of customers within a particular segment.

Exhibit 8.10 groups the sample of Washington, D.C. respondents into five distinct segments on the basis of clusters of ideal points.[14] Segment 5 contains the largest proportion of customers; segment 1, the smallest.[15] By examining the preferences of cus-tomers in different segments along with their perceptions of the positions of existing brands, analysts can learn much about (1) the competitive strength of different brands in different segments, (2) the intensity of the rivalry between brands in a given segment, and (3) the opportunities for gaining a differentiated position within a specific target segment.

Step 6 not only concludes the analysis portion of the positioning process and crys-tallizes the decision about the positioning a brand should hold, but it also can uncover locations in the product space where additional new brands could be positioned to serve customer needs not well served by current competitors. Thus, as Exhibit 8.4 suggested, a side benefit of the positioning process is recognition of underserved positions where addi-tional new products might be placed.

## Step 7: Write Positioning Statement or Value Proposition to Guide Development of Marketing Strategy

The final decision about where to position a new brand or reposition an existing one should be based on both the market targeting analysis discussed in Chapter 7 and the results of a brand positioning analysis. The position chosen should match the prefer-ences of a particular market segment and should take into account the current positions of competing brands.

## Exhibit 8.10

PERCEPTUAL MAP OF WOMEN'S CLOTHING RETAILERS IN WASHINGTON, D.C.,
SHOWING FIVE SEGMENTS BASED ON IDEAL POINTS

Washington 1990 women's fashion market

*Source:* Adapted from Douglas Tigert and Stephen Arnold, "Nordstrom: How Good Are They?" *Babson College Retailing Research Reports,* September 1990.

It should also reflect the current and *future* attractiveness of the target market (its size, expected growth, and environmental constraints) and the relative strengths and weaknesses of competitors. Such information, together with an analysis of the costs required to acquire and maintain these positions, allows an assessment of the economic implications of different market positioning strategies.

Most successful products are positioned based on one or, at most, two determinant attributes, whether physical or perceptual. Using more attributes simply confuses customers.

**STRATEGIC ISSUE**

*Most successful products are positioned based on one or, at most, two determinant attributes.*

Domino's Pizza in the United States, in its early days, focused its positioning solely on its fast delivery, since that was the principal dimension on which it established its competitive advantage. While there are many things Domino's could have said about the pizza itself, it chose to focus its positioning on its key point of differentiation: fast delivery. Later, when fast delivery became common in the pizza industry, Domino's added a heat retention device to its delivery containers and added a second positioning attribute: hot. Papa John's, a later entrant in the pizza business, positions its offering around a single attribute, the quality of its pizza, with its promotional phrase "Better ingredients. Better pizza."

Where there are no real product differences, as in so-called **me-too products,** or no differential benefits to the user, not only is success hard to achieve, but also ethical issues may arise. For an example of ethical issues involving positioning in the pharmaceutical industry, see Ethical Perspective 8.1.

Once the desired positioning for the product has been determined, it's a good idea to write it down so those charged with developing and implementing the marketing strategy have a clear understanding of what is intended for the product and where it will fit in its competitive set. Two approaches are commonly used for doing so. In the classical approach, a **positioning statement** is written. A more recent approach, one adopted by a growing number of firms, involves writing a **value proposition** for the product.

### Writing a Positioning Statement or a Value Proposition    A positioning statement is a succinct statement that identifies the target market for which the product is intended and the product category in which it competes and states the unique benefit the product offers. An example of a positioning statement that reflects Volvo's marketing strategy in the United States is shown in Exhibit 8.11.

A value proposition is similarly explicit about what the product does for the customer (and sometimes, what it does not do) and typically also includes information about pricing relative to competitors. Both positioning statements and value propositions should generally reflect a **unique selling proposition (USP)** that the product embodies. In this sense, they reflect the basis on which the marketer intends to win sustainable competitive advantage by differentiating the product from others in its competitive space.

The notion of the USP has been oversold, however, since in many product categories, especially mature ones, customers are more interested in the degree to which particular products meet their already well-established needs rather than the degree to which they differ from others. Newness and differentiation are not always what the customer wants! We address this issue later in this chapter.

A value proposition is another way to clearly and succinctly state a product's positioning. In its shortest form, a value proposition typically looks like this:

- Target market
- Benefits offered (and not offered)
- Price range (relative to competitors)

Exhibit 8.11 also provides a value proposition for Volvo. More fully developed value propositions sometimes identify the best competing alternatives available to the customer

---

 **ETHICAL PERSPECTIVE 8.1**
*Positioning in the Pharmaceutical Industry—An Ethical Quagmire*

Under constant and ever-increasing pressure to perform, the pharmaceutical industry is frequently cited for practices that are ethically questionable. An article in the British journal *The Lancet* provided an assessment of advertisements in Spanish medical journals in 1997 for antihypertensive (drugs used to treat high blood pressure) and lipid-lowering (i.e., cholesterol-lowering) drugs. The advertisements studied in a six-month period (264 different ads for antihypertensives and 23 different ads for lipid-lowering drugs)

made a total of 125 referenced claims. After excluding the 23 claims that did not have published data, the researchers found that in 44 percent of the cases, the published data did not support the statements made in the ads. This study is a note of caution for doctors who prescribe medicines based on the evidence of reported research on drugs.

Is such marketing really in the best long-term interests of the shareholders?

*Source:* Pilar Villanueva, Salvador Peiró, Julián Librero, and Inmaculada Pereiró, "Accuracy of Pharmaceutical Advertisements in Medical Journals," *The Lancet,* January 4, 2003.

## Exhibit 8.11

POSITIONING STATEMENT AND VALUE PROPOSITION FOR VOLVO AUTOMOBILES IN THE UNITED STATES

| Positioning Statement | Value Proposition |
|---|---|
| For upscale American families, Volvo is the automobile that offers the utmost in safety. | • Target market: Upscale American families<br>• Benefits offered: Safety<br>• Price range: 20% premium over similar cars |

and specify the benefits, in measurable terms, that the customer can expect to receive by using the proposed product. Detailed value propositions such as these are particularly helpful in positioning industrial goods and services, where quantifiable customer benefits are often essential to make the sale.

### STRATEGIC ISSUE

> It is important that the positioning statement or value proposition states benefits that the user of the product will obtain, rather than features or attributes of the product itself.

It is important that the positioning statement or value proposition states **benefits** that the user of the product will obtain, rather than **features** or attributes of the product itself or vague or ambiguous platitudes about high quality or excellent service. By *benefits,* we mean the resulting measurable end-use consequences that the user will experience through the use of the product, in comparison to others.

The marketer generally writes positioning statements and value propositions for use internally and by others, such as advertising agencies engaged to develop the marketing strategy. They are short and succinct and are typically *not* written in catchy consumer language, though catchy **slogans** and **tag lines** for communication with customers often follow. They are most commonly written for a product line or a brand, as is the case in our Volvo example, but sometimes for a single product or for a business as a whole. For products, they play several important roles. They provide direction for R&D and product development about what kind of attributes should be built into the product (side-door airbags, for example, in Volvo's case). They provide direction for those who create advertising campaigns about what the focus of those campaigns should be (for example, Volvo's ads almost always focus on safety, even though Volvo could say other things about its cars). The value proposition also provides direction for pricing decisions.

Thus, in a very real sense, the positioning statement or value proposition constitutes the foundation upon which the marketing strategy is built. More broadly, when used at the business level, as they sometimes are, these statements articulate the strategic direction toward which the company's activities in all arenas should be directed. Promising a certain sort of positioning, or value, to the target market is one thing. Delivering it is another. Clear and concise positioning statements and value propositions can play important roles in effectively executing the intended strategy.

## The Outcome of Effective Positioning: Building Brand Equity

Brand equity is the term marketers use to refer to the value created by establishing customer preference for one's brand. It reflects how consumers feel, think, and act toward the brand, and it has implications for the prices and profits the brand can achieve in the marketplace and for the market capitalization of the company owning the brand.[16] When companies create differences between their brands and other brands, differences that consumers view as meaningful, brand equity is the result. Effective positioning decisions that lead to effective marketing programs are critical to this process.

Consider Procter & Gamble, arguably one of the world's most successful marketers over the past century. Its market capitalization of $180 million in 2011 is due in large part to the brand equity it has built for its portfolio of brands in the more than 140 countries in which it does business. As P&G's global marketing officer James Stengel notes about consumers, "They want to trust something. People really do care what's behind the brand, what's behind the business. They care about the values of a brand and the values of a company. We can never be complacent about that. Businesses and brands that are breaking records are those that inspire trust and affection and loyalty by being authentic, by not being arrogant, and by being empathetic to those they serve."[17]

In India, for example, P&G sells shampoo one sachet at a time, rather than in the giant economy-size bottles found in American showers, reflecting Indian consumers' limited purchasing power. In North America, P&G has turned its trusted detergent brand, Tide, into a growth machine by adding innovative new cleaning products such as the Tide Stain Stick that people can carry with them.[18]

## Managing Brand Equity

While brand positioning decisions are crucial in large companies such as P&G and to the development of new brands, whether goods or services, in entrepreneurial start-ups, there are two ongoing issues that are essential if whatever brand value that's been built is to be maintained and grown: brand reinforcement and brand revitalization.

Some companies have maintained strong brands for many decades—for example, P&G's Tide, Crest, and Pampers, Wrigley's gum, Coca-Cola, Disney, and numerous others. Other brands with substantial brand equity are more recent phenomena—including Nike, Dell Apple, and Google, all of which made *BusinessWeek's* 2011 list of the 100 best global brands.[19] All of these companies, young and old, nurture and protect their brands, ensuring that the products that bear their brands stand for something consistent and that marketing messages reinforce the brand strategy and personality.

Sometimes, however, market conditions or marketing mistakes make it necessary to revitalize a brand that has lost its lustre. The emergence of new competitors or changes in consumer tastes and preferences can affect a brand's fortunes, sometimes for the worse. For an example of how one automobile brand is working to remake its stuffy and outdated image, see Exhibit 8.12.

Additionally, rebranding can sometimes help marketers achieve a more unified approach in their marketing efforts. Federated Stores, a collection of U.S. department stores operating under a variety of hundred-year-old brands of their long-departed founders—from Wanamakers in Philadelphia to Marshall Field in Chicago—was unable to build a coherent nationwide marketing strategy. "Since we weren't a national brand, I couldn't even advertise during the Macy's Thanksgiving Day Parade," says Federated CEO Terry Lundgren.[20] Federated was printing 16 different shopping bags, running 16 different catalogs, and buying merchandise locally in 16 different regions across the United States.

Despite a lot of push-back from local managers, Lundgren thought there was an opportunity to take advantage of the Macy's parade and put the Macy's brand on most of the Federated stores. Converting more than 600 stores from their former nameplates and creating a centralized hut localized strategy took nearly five years, but has delivered impressive results. Same-store sales were up 4.6 percent and Macy's nearly doubled its operating profit in 2010 over 2009. Says Lundgren of the rebranding decision, "If we hadn't made that decision a few years ago, the external environment would have forced it on us. It was the right choice.[21]

As we have seen in this chapter, brand positioning is much more than a one-time exercise. It's an ongoing, never-ending process, one in which the best marketers keep abreast of market and competitive changes in order to maintain and grow the brand equity they have built. Positioning decisions, important as they are, only set the foundation for the development and implementation of effective marketing programs, however. It is those marketing programs whose job is to deliver on the brand promise. Developing and implementing marketing programs and strategies is the focus of much of the remainder of this book. Before turning to those issues, we wrap up our work on positioning by identifying some of the growing array of software tools to aid in the positioning process, and we address a few caveats to which attention should be given along the way.

## Some Caveats in Positioning Decision Making

We noted earlier in this chapter that it's generally desirable to identify a unique selling proposition that clarifies how the product is differentiated from others. A book by Patrick Barwise and Seán Meehan argues, however, that contrary to conventional wisdom, buyers only rarely look for uniqueness. They argue that the degree to which a brand can grow to dominate its category is a reflection of how many users in the category believe it delivers the main category benefits.[22] They say the infinitesimal differentiators that some marketers worry so much about make little real difference. Thus, they argue that marketing strategists should focus their efforts on delivering the benefits that matter most to the target customer—even if other competitors do so as well—and not worry so much about inventing trivial differences that don't really matter.

A second caveat is the question of whether, if one is to differentiate, the focus should be on features—tangible attributes of the good or service itself, such as Volvo's side-door airbags and other safety features—or the benefits the features deliver—safety, in Volvo's case. At the end of the day, customers buy what they buy, whether goods or services, in order to obtain certain benefits. They could care less about features for their own sake. Thus, it's the benefits that matter.

But words are cheap, for marketers as well as for politicians' election-year promises. To be credible in telling the benefits story, marketers must back up their words with features that actually deliver the benefits that are promised. The challenge for marketing strategists is to keep benefits as the focus of the value proposition and at the top of everyone's mind—copywriters, salespeople, everyone who sells in one way or another—but find a way to credibly support and effectively communicate the benefits that are claimed. Doing so is far more difficult than it sounds, which is why so many ads and so many salespeople talk about features instead of benefits.

# TAKE-AWAYS

1. Clear and distinctive positioning that differentiates a brand from others with which it competes is usually essential for developing a winning marketing strategy.

2. The positioning process outlined in this chapter helps decision makers choose a position that maximizes their chance of establishing sustainable competitive advantage.

3. Distinctive and intense positioning is best accomplished when based on one or at most two attributes. More are likely to be confusing to customers.

4. Writing clear and succinct positioning statements or value propositions can play an important role in ensuring effective development and execution of a marketing strategy. This chapter provides templates for writing these materials.

5. Effective brand positioning decisions establish the foundation upon which successful marketing strategies and programs are built, thereby setting the stage for the creation of brand equity.

**Self-diagnostic questions to test your ability to apply the analytical tools and concepts in this chapter to marketing decision making may be found at this book's website at www.mhhe.com/ mullins8e.**

# ENDNOTES

1. The Subway case example is drawn from Jessica Pasley, "Jared of Subway Fame Touts Healthy Lifestyle at Heart Walk Kickoff," *The Reporter,* Vanderbilt Medical Center, October 3, 2003; CNN.com, "Jared the Subway Guy, Superstar," November 17, 2003, *www.cnn.com/2003/SHOWBIZ/ TV/11/17/subway/guy.ap/*; Matthew Boyle, "The Accidental Hero," *BusinessWeek* European Edition, November 16, 2009, pp. 58–61; and the Subway Restaurants website at *www.subway.com.*

2. Al Ries and Jack Trout, *Positioning: The Battle for Your Mind* (New York: Warner Books, 1982).

3. Michael Porter, "What Is Strategy?" *Harvard Business Review,* November–December 1996, p. 62.

4. Dexter Roberts, "China's Brands: Damaged Goods," *BusinessWeek,* European Edition, September 24, 2007, p. 47.

5. Adam Baer, "The Big Chill," *Hemispheres,* April 2011, pp. 50–52.

6. Adapted from C. Merle Crawford and C. Anthony Di Benedetto, *New Products Management* (Burr Ridge, IL: McGraw-Hill/Irwin, 2008).

7. See the company's website at *www.anichini.com.*

8. For more on strategy making as choices, see Constantinos C. Markides, *All the Right Moves: A Guide to Crafting Breakthrough Strategy* (Cambridge, MA: Harvard Business School Press, 2000). For more on value curves, see W. Chan Kim and Renée Mauborgne, "Value Innovation: The Strategic Logic of High Growth," *Harvard Business Review* (January–February, 1997), pp. 103–12.

9. Roland Jones, "Can Toyota's Scion Keep Its Edge?" *www.msnbc.msn .com/id/17688646/*, March 21, 2007.

10. Lindsay Brooke, "Mini: The Real Story," *Automotive Industries,* April 2002. For more on BL's history, see also "British Leyland Motor Corporation," *http://en.wikipedia.org/wiki/British_Leyland.*

11. Existing brands' attractiveness can be inferred from current sales volumes and market shares. The position occupied by the share leader is obviously more appealing to a greater number of customers than are the positions occupied by lesser brands.

12. For more on conjoint analysis, see Vithala Rao, *Applied Conjoint Analysis* (New York: Springer Publishing, 2009).

13. When using preference data to define market segments, however, the analyst should also collect information about customers' demographic characteristics, lifestyle, product usage, and other potential segmentation variables. This enables the analyst to develop a more complete picture of the differences among benefit segments. Such information can be useful for developing advertising appeals, selecting media, focusing personal selling efforts, and designing many of the other elements of a marketing program that can be effective in appealing to a particular segment.

14. The size of the individual circles in Exhibit 8.10 is fictitious and designed for illustrative purposes only.

15. The map in Exhibit 8.10 shows five distinct preference segments but only one set of perceived product positions. The implication is that consumers in this sample were similar in the way they perceived existing brands but different in the product attributes they preferred. This is the most common situation; customers tend to vary more in the benefits they seek than in how they perceive available products or brands. Sometimes, however, various segments may perceive the positions of existing brands quite differently. They may even use different determinant attributes in assessing these positions. Under such circumstances, a marketer should construct a separate market-positioning map for each segment.

16. Kevin Lane Keller, *Strategic Brand Management,* 3rd ed. (Upper Saddle River, NJ: Prentice Hall, 2008).

17. Geoff Colvin, "Selling P&G," *Fortune,* International Edition, September 17, 2007, p. 82.

18. Ibid., pp. 81–87.

19. "100 Best Global Brands," *Bloomberg BusinessWeek,* November 29, 2011.

20. Terry Lundgren, "Hard Choices," *Bloomberg Businessweek,* November 29–December 5, 2010, p.104.

21. Macy's Inc 2010 Annual Report at *http://www.macysinc.com/Investors/ vote/2010_ar.pdf.*

22. Patrick Barwise and Seán Meehan, *Simply Better: Winning and Keeping Customers by Delivering What Matters Most* (Cambridge, MA: Harvard Business School Press, 2004).

# SECTION THREE

# DEVELOPING STRATEGIC MARKETING PROGRAMS

# CHAPTER NINE

# Business Strategies: A Foundation for Marketing Program Decisions

## Business Strategies and Marketing Programs at 3M[1]

THE MINNESOTA MINING AND MANU-FACTURING Company, better known as 3M, began manufacturing sandpaper a century ago. Today it is the leader in dozens of technical areas from fluorochemistry to fiber optics. The firm makes more than 60,000 different products, which generated $26.7 billion in global sales in 2010. The company produced $5.9 billion in operating profits.

As you might expect of a firm with so many products, 3M is organized into a large number of strategic business units (SBUs). The company contains 38 such SBUs or product divisions organized into six market sectors:

- The Industrial and Transportation Sector makes a variety of tapes, abrasives, adhesives, filters, and specialty chemicals for industrial applications ranging from electronics to aerospace to automobile manufacturing.
- The Health Care Sector markets a variety of medical, surgical, pharmaceutical, and dental products and services.
- The Consumer and Office Sector offers products for homes and offices, such as Post-it brand repositionable notes and Scotch brand tapes.

- The Electro and Communications Sector supplies connecting, splicing, and protective products for electronics and telecommunications markets.
- The Display and Graphics Sector is a world leader in the sale of films and reflective materials for electronic displays, touch screens, commercial graphics, and traffic control.
- The Safety, Security and Protection Services Sector makes a wide variety of products ranging from respirators for worker safety to cleaning supplies to fire-protection products.

While 3M has acquired many smaller firms over the years, its growth strategy has focused primarily on internal new product development, emphasizing both improved products for existing customers and new products for new markets. One formal objective assigned to every business unit is to obtain at least 30 percent of annual sales from products introduced within the past four years. The company supports its growth strategy with an R&D budget of more than $1.45 billion, almost 5.5 percent of total revenues.

The company also pursues growth through the aggressive development of foreign markets for its many products. A seventh organizational sector is responsible for coordinating the firm's marketing efforts across countries. In 2010, 3M attained $17.4 billion in sales—68 percent of its total revenue—from outside the United States.

Differences in customer needs and life-cycle stages across industries, however, lead 3M's various business units to pursue their growth objectives in different ways. The Industrial Tape Division within the Industrial and Transportation Sector, for example, operates in an industry where both the product technologies and the customer segments are relatively mature and stable. Growth in this group results from extending the scope of adhesive technology (for instance, attaching weather-stripping to auto doors), product improvements and line extensions targeted at existing customers, and expansion into global markets.

In contrast, the firm's Drug Delivery Systems Division within the Health Care Sector develops new medical applications for emerging technologies developed in 3M's many R&D labs. It sells a variety of technologies for the delivery of medications that are inhaled or absorbed through the skin. Most of the unit's growth comes from developing new products, often through alliances with other pharmaceutical firms, aimed at new markets.

The competitive strategies of 3M's various business units also differ. For instance, the industrial tape unit is primarily concerned with maintaining its commanding market share in existing markets while preserving or even improving its profitability. Its competitive strategy is to differentiate itself from competitors on the basis of product quality and excellent customer service.

But the drug delivery systems unit's strategy is to avoid head-to-head competitive battles by being the technological leader and introducing a stream of unique new products. To be successful, though, the unit must devote substantial resources to R&D and to the stimulation of primary demand. Thus, its main objective is volume growth; and it must sometimes sacrifice short-run profitability to fund the product development and marketing efforts needed to accomplish that goal.

These differences in competitive strategy, in turn, influence the strategic marketing programs within the various business units. For instance, the firm spends

little on advertising or sales promotion for its mature industrial tape products. However, it does maintain a large, well-trained technical salesforce that provides valuable problem-solving assistance and other services to customers and informed feedback to the firm's R&D personnel about potential new applications and product improvements.

In contrast, the pioneering nature of the drug delivery unit's technologies calls for more extensive promotion to attract potential alliance partners, develop awareness among prescribing physicians, and stimulate primary demand. Consequently, the unit devotes a relatively large portion of its revenues to advertising in technical journals aimed at the pharmaceutical industry, physicians, and other medical professionals. It also supports a well-trained salesforce, but those salespeople spend much of their time demonstrating new technologies and building relationships with drug manufacturers who are prospective customers and partners.

While different business and marketing strategies make sense for business units facing different market and competitive conditions, they pose a dilemma for top management. Can a variety of competitive strategies and marketing programs be consistent with, and effective under, a single corporate strategy or company policy? George Buckley had to address this issue when he took over as 3M's CEO in 2005. His predecessor had instituted a "six sigma" program throughout the firm. Six sigma is a quality control approach for systematically analyzing a problem (e.g., high shipping costs) and then using data to solve each component of the problem. It seeks to use rigorous statistical analysis to remove variability from a process, thereby reducing defects, improving quality, and lowering costs.

Six sigma's objectives and methods make good sense for mature businesses like 3M's Industrial Tape unit where the product line is well-established and improving quality and lowering costs are important means of maintaining profitability. But what about a business whose competitive strategy focuses on innovation and new product development, like the Drug Delivery Systems unit? As one management guru points out, "The more you hardwire a company for total quality management (e.g., six sigma), the more it is going to hurt breakthrough innovation. The mindset that is needed, the capabilities that are needed, the metrics that are needed . . . for discontinuous innovation are fundamentally different."

Consequently, CEO Buckley has made adjustments in the firm's corporate strategy to accommodate some of the differences in objectives and competitive strategies across the firm's business units. For instance, while he has continued to emphasize six sigma goals and projects in 3M's mature businesses, he has loosened the reins a bit by de-emphasizing the six sigma approach in the firm's research labs and some of its pioneering business units.

## Marketing Challenges Addressed in Chapter 9

The situation at 3M again illustrates that large firms with multiple businesses usually have a hierarchy of strategies extending from the corporate level down to the individual product-market entry. As we saw in Chapter 2, corporate strategy addresses such issues as the firm's mission and scope and the directions it will pursue for future growth. Thus, 3M's corporate growth strategy focuses primarily on developing new products and new applications for emerging technologies.

The major strategic question addressed at the business-unit level is, How should we compete in this business? For instance, 3M's industrial tape unit attempts to maintain its commanding market share and high profitability by differentiating itself on the basis of high product quality and good customer service. The drug delivery unit, on the other hand, seeks high growth via aggressive new product and market development.

Finally, the strategic marketing program for each product-market entry within a business unit attempts to allocate marketing resources and activities in a manner appropriate for accomplishing the business unit's objectives. Thus, most of the strategic marketing programs within 3M's drug delivery unit involve relatively large expenditures for marketing research and introductory advertising and promotion campaigns aimed at achieving sales growth.

One key reason for 3M's continuing success is that all three levels of strategy within the company have usually been characterized by good internal and external consistency, or **strategic fit.** The company's managers have done a good job of monitoring and adapting their strategies to the market opportunities, technological advances, and competitive threats in the company's external environment. The firm's marketing and sales managers play critical roles both in developing market-oriented strategies for individual products and in influencing and helping to formulate corporate and business-level strategies that are responsive to environmental conditions. At the same time, those strategies are usually internally compatible. Each strategy fits with those at other levels as well as with the unique competitive strengths and competencies of the relevant business unit and the company as a whole. As 3M's new CEO discovered, however, maintaining good strategic fit in a firm with many diverse business units may require some adjustments to one or more levels of strategy.

Recent empirical evidence shows that when there is a good fit between a business's competitive strategy and the strategic marketing programs of its various product or service offerings, the business will achieve better results in terms of sales growth, market share, and profitability than when the two levels of strategy are inconsistent with one another.[2]

Therefore, this chapter focuses on what marketing decision makers can and should do to help ensure that the strategic marketing plans they develop are appropriate in light of the available resources and competitive thrust of the business that is their organizational home.

First, we examine the question of how a business might choose to compete. What generic competitive strategies might a business pursue,

### STRATEGIC ISSUE

*When there is a good fit between a business's competitive strategy and the strategic marketing programs of its various product or service offerings, the business will achieve better results.*

and in what environmental circumstances is each strategy most appropriate? We'll also explore whether the same kinds of competitive strategies are relevant for small, single-business organizations and entrepreneurial start-ups as for large multi-SBU firms such as 3M and whether technological shifts, such as the growth of e-commerce, are likely to give birth to new competitive strategies or make some old ones obsolete.

Next, we examine the interrelationships between different business competitive strategies and elements of the strategic marketing programs for the various products within the business. How does—or should—a particular competitive strategy influence or constrain marketing programs for the business's product offerings? And what happens if the market positioning or specific marketing actions that would be most effective for appealing to a product's target customers do not fit very well with the competitive strategy of the larger business unit? For example, as some of the products made by the drug delivery unit at 3M—such as the inhalers they make for delivering asthma medications—become well-established and mature, they may require marketing actions (e.g., more competitive pricing) that are not consistent with the aggressive product development strategy of the business unit. What should 3M and the marketing manager responsible for inhalers do under such circumstances?

## How Do Businesses Compete?

As mentioned, the essential strategic question at the SBU level is, How are we going to compete in this business? Thus, business strategies are primarily concerned with allocating resources across functional activities and product-markets to give the unit a sustainable advantage over its competitors. Of course, the unit's core competencies and resources, together with the customer and competitive characteristics of its industry, determine the viability of any particular competitive strategy.[3] The 3M drug delivery unit's strategy of gaining revenue growth via technological leadership and aggressive new product and market development, for instance, will continue to work only if the firm's R&D, engineering, and marketing competencies and resources continue to outweigh those of its competitors. Consequently, most SBUs pursue a single competitive strategy—one that best fits their market environments and competitive strengths—across all or most of the product-markets in which they compete. The question is, What alternative strategies are available to a business unit? What are the basic, or generic, competitive strategies most SBUs choose to pursue?

## Generic Business-Level Competitive Strategies

Researchers have identified general categories of business-level competitive strategies based on overall patterns of purpose, practice, and performance in different businesses. As we saw in Chapter 8, Michael Porter distinguishes three strategies—or competitive positions—that businesses pursue to gain and maintain competitive advantages in their various product-markets: (1) *overall cost leadership;* (2) *differentiation*—building customer perceptions of superior product quality, design, or service; and (3) *focus,* in which the business avoids direct confrontation with its major competitors by concentrating on narrowly defined market niches. Porter describes firms that lack a distinctive strategy as being "stuck in the middle" and predicts that they will perform poorly.[4]

Robert Miles and Charles Snow identified another set of business strategies based on a business's intended rate of product-market development (new product development, penetration of new markets).[5] They classify business units into four strategic types: *prospectors, defenders, analyzers,* and *reactors.* Exhibit 9.1 describes each of these business

# Exhibit 9.1

DEFINITIONS OF MILES AND SNOW'S FOUR BUSINESS STRATEGIES

### Prospector

- Operates within a broad product-market domain that undergoes periodic redefinition.
- Values being a "first mover" in new product and market areas, even if not all of these efforts prove to be highly profitable.
- Responds rapidly to early signals concerning areas of opportunity, and these responses often lead to new rounds of competitive actions.
- Competes primarily by stimulating and meeting new market opportunities, but may not maintain strength over time in all markets it enters.

### Defender

- Attempts to locate and maintain a secure position in relatively stable product or service areas.
- Offers relatively limited range of products or services compared with competitors.
- Tries to protect its domain by offering lower prices, higher quality, or better service than competitors.
- Usually not at the forefront of technological/new product development in its industry; tends to ignore industry changes not directly related to its area of operation.

### Analyzer

- An intermediate type; makes fewer and slower product-market changes than prospectors, but is less committed to stability and efficiency than defenders.
- Attempts to maintain a stable, limited line of products or services, but carefully follows a selected set of promising new developments in its industry.
- Seldom a first mover, but often a second or third entrant in product-markets related to its existing market base—often with a lower-cost or higher-quality product or service offering.

### Reactor

- Lacks any well-defined competitive strategy.
- Does not have as consistent a product-market orientation as its competitors.
- Not as willing to assume the risks of new product or market development as its competitors.
- Not as aggressive in marketing established products as some competitors.
- Responds primarily when it is forced to by environmental pressures.

---

*Source:* Robert E. Miles and Charles C. Snow, *Organizational Strategy, Structure, and Process* (Palo Alto, CA: Stanford University Press, 1978). Copyright © 2003 by the Board of Trustees of the Leland Stanford Jr. University.

strategies briefly. As you can see, businesses pursuing a *prospector strategy* focus on growth through the development of new products and markets. 3M's drug delivery business unit illustrates this. *Defender businesses* concentrate on maintaining their positions in established product-markets while paying less attention to new product development, as is the case with 3M's industrial tape business unit. The *analyzer strategy* falls in between these two. An analyzer business attempts to maintain a strong position in its core product-market(s) but also seeks to expand into new—usually closely related—product-markets. Finally, *reactors* are businesses with no clearly defined strategy.

Even though both the Porter and Miles and Snow typologies have received popular acceptance and research support, neither is complete by itself. For example, a *defender business unit* could pursue a variety of competitive approaches to protect its market position, such as offering the lowest cost or differentiating itself on quality or service.

Thus, we have combined the two typologies in Exhibit 9.2 to provide a more comprehensive overview of business strategies. Exhibit 9.2 classifies business strategies on two primary dimensions: the unit's desired rate of product-market development (expansion) and the unit's intended method of competing in its established product-markets.

Each of our strategic categories could be further subdivided according to whether a business applies the strategy across a broadly defined product-market domain or concentrates on a narrowly defined segment where it hopes to avoid direct confrontation with major competitors (the *focus* strategy of Porter). Although this distinction is useful, it is more germane to a discussion of the business's target market strategy (as discussed in Chapter 7) than to its competitive strategy. Most businesses compete in a reasonably consistent way across all of their product-markets, whether their domain is broad or narrow.

Exhibit 9.2 describes only six business strategies, rather than the eight that one might expect. We view reactor and prospector business units as two homogeneous categories.

Evidence suggests that a substantial portion of businesses fall into the reactor category. One study, for instance, found that 50 out of 232 businesses examined could be classified as reactors.[6] By definition, however, such businesses do not have well-defined or consistent approaches either to new product development or to ways of competing in existing product-markets. In other words, reactors have no clear competitive strategy. Therefore, we will largely ignore them during the rest of this discussion.

Prospectors are also shown as a single strategic category in Exhibit 9.2 because the desire for rapid new product or market development is the overriding aspect of their strategy. There is little need for a prospector business to consider how it will compete in the new product-markets it develops because it will face little or no competition—at least not until those markets become established and other firms begin to enter.

## Exhibit 9.2

COMBINED TYPOLOGY OF BUSINESS-LEVEL COMPETITIVE STRATEGIES

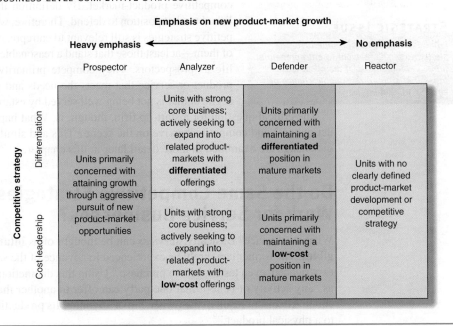

# Do the Same Competitive Strategies Work for Single-Business Firms and Start-ups?

Even small firms with a single business and only a few related product offerings or start-ups with a single product must decide how they will compete. And just like an SBU in a major corporation such as 3M, their competitive strategies should be tailored to their unique resources and competencies and aimed at securing a sustainable advantage over existing or potential competitors. Therefore, the same set of generic competitive strategies are just as appropriate for small firms as for business units within larger ones. For example, Pinkberry frozen yogurt shops have captured a significant portion of the upscale ice cream/gelato/frozen yogurt market in the United States with a differentiated defender strategy. They have successfully differentiated their stores by (1) hiring and training friendly, enthusiastic store personnel, (2) offering more flavors and many more unique toppings than competitors, and (3) generating promotional buzz via celebrity endorsements. Their strategy enabled them to expand to 120 shops in only five years, even though the U. S. frozen dessert market is mature.

Impressively, too, Pinkberry has been able to generate substantial global sales by adapting their flavors and toppings to local cultures and tastes. For instance, they offer green tea flavored yogurt in Asian shops, date and pistachio toppings in Kuwait, and Nutrella spread in Russia. By adjusting their differentiated defender strategy from country to country the firm has been able to generate more than a quarter of its income from outside the United States, and that portion is expected to grow in the future.[7]

However, there is one important difference between single-business and multi-SBU organizations. In smaller single-business firms the distinction between business-level competitive strategy and marketing strategy tends to blur and the two strategies blend into one. Pinkberry's competitive strategy, for instance, is essentially the same as the market positioning of its stores: shops that offer high-quality frozen yogurt with tons of unique flavors and toppings and fast, friendly customer service.

Another difference applies to entrepreneurial start-ups. Most start-ups do not have the resources to succeed by competing as a "me-too" competitor in a well-established and highly competitive product-market. By definition they do not have an established market position to defend. Therefore, while the taxonomy of competitive strategies is still relevant to entrepreneurial firms, in reality most of them—at least those that stand a reasonable chance of success—begin life as prospectors. They compete primarily by developing a unique product or service that meets the needs and preferences of a customer segment that is not being well served by established competitors.

The critical question for a start-up firm, though, is, What happens when the new product matures and competitors arrive on the scene? This and similar issues related to strategic change are examined in more detail later in this chapter.

# Do the Same Competitive Strategies Work for Service Businesses?

What is a service? Basically, *services* can be thought of as **intangibles** and *goods* as **tangibles.** The former can rarely be experienced in advance of the sale, while the latter can be experienced, even tested, before purchase.[8] Using this distinction, a **service** can be defined as "any activity or benefit that one party can offer to another that is essentially intangible and that does not result in the ownership of anything. Its production may or may not be tied to a physical product."[9]

We typically associate services with nonmanufacturing businesses, even though service is often an indispensable part of a goods producer's offering. Services such as applications engineering, system design, delivery, installation, training, and maintenance can be crucial for building long-term relationships between manufacturers and their customers, particularly in consumer durable and industrial products businesses. Thus, almost all businesses are engaged in service to some extent.

Many organizations are concerned with producing and marketing a service as their primary offering rather than as an adjunct to a physical product. These organizations include public-sector and not-for-profit service organizations, such as churches, hospitals, universities, and arts organizations. The crucial question is this: To be successful, must service organizations employ different competitive strategies than goods manufacturers?

The framework we used to classify business-level competitive strategies in Exhibit 9.2 is equally valid for service businesses. Some service firms, such as Super 8 or Days Inn in the lodging industry, attempt to minimize costs and compete largely with low prices. Other firms, like Marriott, differentiate their offerings on the basis of high service quality or unique benefits. Similarly, some service businesses adopt prospector strategies and aggressively pursue the development of new offerings or markets. For instance, American Express's Travel Related Services Division has developed a variety of new services tailored to specific segments of the firm's credit-card holders. Other service businesses focus narrowly on defending established positions in current markets. Still others can best be described as analyzers pursuing both established and new markets. For instance, Emirates, an airline whose competitive strategy is discussed in Exhibit 9.3, might best be described as a low-cost analyzer.

## Exhibit 9.3   EMIRATES AIRLINE—COMPETING FOR BUSINESS TRAVELERS WHILE BUILDING NEW MARKETS

Habib Fekih was traveling the Mideast as a salesman for European planemaker Airbus in 1985, the year Dubai's ruling family started a small airline called Emirates to shuttle Pakistani workers between Karachi and Dubai aboard two leased planes. "Nobody believed Emirates could be a successful airline," recalls Fekih, who now heads Airbus' Mideast subsidiary. "It was the joke of the day."

Emirates is a joke no longer. It has grown into the world's tenth-largest airline, earning $964 million in profits in 2010 on sales of nearly $12 billion.

One important factor underlying Emirates' success is simply the geographic location of Dubai. It provides a convenient hub that has enabled Emirates to offer more convenient routes for business travelers shuttling between Europe or the United States and Asia. And the rapid growth of many Asian economies in recent years has, in turn, generated increased demand and new customers for Emirates' flights.

Of course, many other airlines fly between Asia and the West, so Emirates has attempted to strengthen and defend its share of that market by offering good service with very low fares. Aggressive expansion via the purchase of new planes from Boeing and Airbus has made the company's fleet of 142 all wide-body jets the youngest and most efficient of any airline. And when its recent order of 90 Airbus A380 super-jumbo jets is delivered, it will be even more efficient. The A380's operating costs are 12 percent lower than the newest 747, and it carries about 500 passengers. Therefore, Emirates's cost per passenger mile are lower than any other intercontinental airline, and will be even lower in coming years. This allows the company to charge lower fares while still maintaining good service, expanding its routes to "secondary" airports like Manchester in the UK and Kolkata in India, and still make money; In other words, to implement a very successful low-cost analyzer strategy.

*Sources:* Steve Rothwell and Andrea Rothman, "Emirates Wins with Big Planes and Low Costs," *Bloomberg Businessweek,* July 5, 2010, pp. 18–19; "Rulers of the New Silk Road," *The Economist,* July 5, 2010, pp. 75–77; and the Emirates Group's 2009–2010 Annual Report on the firm's website, *www.ekgroup.com.*

A study of the banking industry provides empirical evidence that service businesses actually do pursue the same types of competitive strategies as goods producers. The 329 bank CEOs who responded to the survey had little trouble categorizing their institution's competitive strategies into one of Miles and Snow's four types. Fifty-four of the executives reported that their banks were prospectors, 87 identified their firms as analyzers, 157 as defenders, and 31 as reactors.[10]

## Do the Same Competitive Strategies Work for Global Competitors?

In terms of the strategies described in Exhibit 9.2, businesses that compete in multiple global markets almost always pursue one of the two types of analyzer strategy. They must continue to strengthen and defend their competitive position in their home country—and perhaps in other countries where they are well-established—while simultaneously pursuing expansion and growth in new international markets.

When examined on a country-by-country basis, however, the same business unit might be viewed as pursuing different competitive strategies in different countries. For instance, while 3M's industrial tape group competes like a differentiated defender in the United States, Canada, and some European countries where it has established large market shares, it competes more like a prospector when attempting to open and develop new markets in emerging economies such as China and Mexico.

This suggests that a single SBU may need to engage in different functional activities (including different strategic marketing programs)—and perhaps even adopt different organizational structures to implement those activities—across the various countries in which it competes. For example, Huawei Technologies Co., located in Shenzhen, China, was able to compete very effectively in its home market as a low-cost analyzer. The company earned $2.4 billion in revenues in 2001 selling internet switches and routers patterned after the equipment manufactured by Cisco Systems and Alcatel, but at prices as much as 40 percent lower. However, only 10 percent of those revenues came from outside China. In order to compete more effectively in the developed markets of Europe and North America, Huawei had to expand its product line and develop new equipment with more innovative features and greater functionality. In other words, it had to compete more like a prospector in those markets. Consequently, the firm greatly increased its R&D spending and product development efforts. It also developed marketing programs geared to generating brand awareness and trial among potential customers. For the time being, Huawei relies heavily on alliances with established distributors and value-added resellers to develop and implement marketing programs in developed markets. For instance, the Vierling Group serves as Huawei's distributor in Germany, and the firm has also signed a distribution deal with IBM. As a result of these strategic adjustments, Huawei's contract sales topped $28.5 billion in 2010, and nearly two-thirds of those sales came from outside China.[11]

## Will the Internet Change Everything?

Some analysts argue that the internet will change the way firms compete. The internet makes it easier for buyers and sellers to compare prices, reduces the number of middlemen necessary between manufacturers and end users, cuts transaction costs, improves the functioning of the price mechanism, and thereby increases competition.[12] One possible outcome of all these changes is that it will be harder for firms to differentiate themselves on any basis other than low price. All the business-level competitive strategies focused on differentiation will become less viable, while firms pursuing low-cost strategies will be more successful.

While we agree that the internet has increased both efficiency and competitiveness in many product-markets, we doubt that competition will focus exclusively on price. For one thing, innovation is likely to continue—and probably accelerate—in the future. Unique new products and services will continue to emerge and provide a way for the innovator to gain a competitive advantage, at least in the short term. Thus, firms with the resources and competencies necessary to produce a continuing stream of new product or service offerings that appeal to one or more customer segments—that is, to effectively implement a prospector strategy—should be successful regardless of whether they are the lowest-cost producers in their industries. Amazon, the largest e-tailer as of early 2011, is generally not the lowest priced.

In addition, the internet is primarily a communications channel. While it facilitates the dissemination of information, including price information, the goods and services themselves will continue to offer different features and benefits. As customers gather more information from the internet and become better informed, they are less likely to be swayed by superficial distinctions between brands. But if a firm offers unique benefits that a segment of customers perceive as *meaningful,* it should still be able to differentiate its offering and command a premium price, at least until its competitors offer something similar.

Finally, the internet will make it easier for firms—both manufacturers and retailers—to customize their offerings and personalize their relationships with their customers. Such personalization should differentiate the firm from its competitors in the customer's eyes and improve customer loyalty and retention. For instance, in Chapter 5 we discussed the role of the internet in developing logistical alliances among organizational buyers and their suppliers. Consumer goods and services firms, internet portals, and social networking sites are also using the internet's interactive capabilities to acquire and communicate information and build customer relationships. For example, about 40 percent of shoppers who buy clothing at Lands' End—both men and women—choose a customized garment tailored to their personal dimensions over the standard-sized equivalent, even though each customized garment costs more and takes longer to arrive. And customers who customize are more loyal to the company. Reorder rates for custom-clothing buyers are 35 percent higher than for buyers of Land's End's standard items.[13]

**STRATEGIC ISSUE**

*The internet will make it easier for firms to customize their offerings and personalize their relationships with their customers.*

## How Do Competitive Strategies Differ from One Another?

In Chapter 2 we said that all strategies consist of five components or underlying dimensions: scope (or breadth of strategic domain), goals and objectives, resource deployments, a basis for achieving a sustainable competitive advantage, and synergy. But the generic strategies summarized in Exhibit 9.2 are defined largely by their differences on only one dimension: the nature of the competitive advantage sought. Each strategy also involves some important differences on the other four dimensions—differences that are outlined in Exhibit 9.4 and discussed below. Those differences provide insights concerning the conditions under which each strategy is most appropriate and about the relative importance of different marketing actions in implementing them effectively.

## Differences in Scope

Both the breadth and stability of a business's domain are likely to vary with different strategies. This, in turn, can affect the variables the corporation uses to define its various businesses. At one extreme, defender businesses, whether low-cost or differentiated, tend

## Exhibit 9.4

HOW BUSINESS STRATEGIES DIFFER IN SCOPE, OBJECTIVES, RESOURCE DEPLOYMENTS, AND SYNERGY

| Dimensions | Low-cost defender | Differentiated defender | Prospector | Analyzer |
|---|---|---|---|---|
| • *Scope* | Mature/stable/well-defined domain; mature technology and customer segments | Mature/stable/well-defined domain; mature technology and customer segments | Broad/dynamic domains; technology and customer segments not well-established | Mixture of defender and prospector strategies |
| • *Goals and objectives* | | | | |
| Adaptability (new product success) | Very little | Little | Extensive | Mixture of defender and prospector strategies |
| Effectiveness (increase in market share) | Low | Low | High | Mixture of defender and prospector strategies |
| Efficiency (ROI) | High | High | Low | Mixture of defender and prospector strategies |
| • *Resource deployment* | Generate excess cash (cash cows) | Generate excess cash (cash cows) | Need cash for product development (question marks or stars) | Need cash for product development but less so than do prospectors |
| • *Synergy* | Need to seek operating synergies to achieve efficiencies | Need to seek operating synergies to achieve efficiencies | Danger in sharing operating facilities and programs—better to share technology/marketing skills | Danger in sharing operating facilities and programs—better to share technology/marketing skills |

to operate in relatively well-defined, narrow, and stable domains where both the product technology and the customer segments are mature.

At the other extreme, prospector businesses usually operate in broad and rapidly changing domains where neither the technology nor customer segments are well established. The scope of such businesses often undergoes periodic redefinition. Thus, prospector businesses are typically organized around either a core technology that might lead to the development of products aimed at a broad range of customer segments or a basic customer need that might be met with products based on different technologies. The latter is the approach taken by 3M's drug delivery systems business. Its mission is to satisfy the health needs of a broad range of patients with new products developed from technologies drawn from other business units within the firm.

Analyzer businesses, whether low-cost or differentiated, fall somewhere in between the two extremes. They usually have a well-established core business to defend, and often their domain is primarily focused on that business. However, businesses pursuing this intermediate strategy are often in industries that are still growing or experiencing technological changes. Consequently, they must pay attention to the emergence of new customer segments and/or new product types. As a result, managers must review and adjust the domain of such businesses from time to time.

# Differences in Goals and Objectives

Another important difference across generic business-level strategies with particular relevance for the design and implementation of appropriate marketing programs is that different strategies often focus on different objectives. SBU and product-market objectives might be specified on a variety of criteria, but to keep things simple, we focus on only three performance dimensions of major importance to both business-unit and marketing managers:

1. *Effectiveness.* The success of a business's products and programs relative to those of its competitors in the market. Effectiveness is commonly measured by such items as *sales growth* relative to competitors or *changes in market share.*

2. *Efficiency.* The outcomes of a business's programs relative to the resources used in implementing them. Common measures of efficiency are *profitability* as a percent of sales and *return on investment.*

3. *Adaptability.* The business's success in responding over time to changing conditions and opportunities in the environment. Adaptability can be measured in a variety of ways, but the most common ones are the *number of successful new products* introduced relative to competitors or the *percentage of sales accounted for by products introduced within the last five years.*

However, it is very difficult for any SBU, regardless of its competitive strategy, to simultaneously achieve outstanding performance on even this limited number of dimensions, because they involve substantial trade-offs. Good performance on one dimension often means sacrificing performance on another.[14] For example, developing successful new products or attaining share growth often involves large marketing budgets, substantial up-front investment, high operating costs, and a shaving of profit margins—all of which reduce ROI. This suggests that managers should choose a competitive strategy with a view toward maximizing performance on one or two dimensions, while expecting to sacrifice some level of performance on the others, at least in the short term. Over the longer term, of course, the chosen strategy should promise discounted cash flows that exceed the business's cost of capital and thereby increase shareholder value.

As Exhibit 9.4 indicates, prospector businesses are expected to outperform defenders on both new product development and market-share growth. On the other hand, both defender strategies should lead to better returns on investment. Differentiated defenders likely produce higher returns than low-cost defenders, assuming that the greater expenses involved in maintaining their differentiated positions can be more than offset by the higher margins gained by avoiding the intense price competition low-cost competitors often face. Once again, both low-cost and differentiated analyzer strategies are likely to fall between the two extremes.[15]

# Differences in Resource Deployments

Businesses following different strategies also tend to allocate their financial resources differently across product-markets, functional departments, and activities within each functional area. Prospector—and to a lesser degree, analyzer—businesses devote a relatively large proportion of resources to the development of new product-markets. Because such product-markets usually require more cash to develop than they produce short term, businesses pursuing these strategies often need infusions of financial resources from other parts of the corporation. In portfolio terms, they are "question marks" or "stars."

Defenders, on the other hand, focus the bulk of their resources on preserving existing positions in established product-markets. These product-markets are usually profitable; therefore, defender businesses typically generate excess cash to support product and market development efforts in other business units within the firm. They are the "cash cows."

Resource allocations among functional departments and activities within the SBU also vary across businesses pursuing different strategies. For instance, marketing budgets tend to be the largest as a percentage of an SBU's revenues when the business is pursuing a prospector strategy; they tend to be the smallest as a percentage of sales under a low-cost defender strategy. We discuss this in more detail later.

## Differences in Sources of Synergy

Because different strategies emphasize different methods of competition and different functional activities, a given source of synergy may be more appropriate for some strategies than for others.

At one extreme, the sharing of operating facilities and programs may be an inappropriate approach to gaining synergy for businesses following a prospector strategy. And to a lesser extent, this may also be true for both types of analyzer strategies. Such sharing can reduce an SBU's ability to adapt quickly to changing market demands or competitive threats. Commitments to internally negotiated price structures and materials, as well as the use of joint resources, facilities, and programs, increase interdependence among SBUs and limit their flexibility. It is more appropriate for such businesses to seek synergy through the sharing of a technology, engineering skills, or market knowledge—expertise that can help improve the success rate of their product development efforts. Thus, 3M's drug delivery systems business attempts to find medical applications for new technologies developed in many of the firm's other business units.

At the other extreme, however, low-cost defenders should seek operating synergies that will make them more efficient. Synergies that enable such businesses to increase economies of scale and experience curve effects are particularly desirable. They help reduce unit costs and strengthen the strategy's basis of competitive advantage. The primary means of gaining such operating synergies is through the sharing of resources, facilities, and functional activities across product-market entries within the business unit or across related business units.[16] Emerson Electric, for instance, formed an "operating group" of several otherwise autonomous business units that make different types of electrical motors and tools. By sharing production facilities, marketing activities, and a common salesforce, the group was able to reduce the costs of both per-unit production and marketing.

# Deciding When a Strategy Is Appropriate: The Fit between Business Strategies and the Environment

Because different strategies pursue different objectives in different domains with different competitive approaches, they do not all work equally well under the same environmental circumstances. The question is, Which environmental situations are most amenable to the successful pursuit of each type of strategy? Exhibit 9.5 outlines some major market, technological, and competitive conditions—plus a business units' strengths relative to its competitors—that are most favorable for the successful implementation of each generic business strategy. We next discuss the reasons each strategy fits best with a particular set of environmental conditions.

## Appropriate Conditions for a Prospector Strategy

A prospector strategy is particularly well suited to unstable, rapidly changing environments resulting from new technology, shifting customer needs, or both. In either case, such industries tend to be at an early stage in their life cycles and offer many opportunities for

## Exhibit 9.5

ENVIRONMENTAL FACTORS FAVORABLE TO DIFFERENT BUSINESS STRATEGIES

| External factors | Prospector | Analyzer | Differentiated defender | Low-cost defender |
|---|---|---|---|---|
| Industry and market | Industry in introductory or early growth stage of life cycle, many potential customer segments as yet unidentified and/or undeveloped. | Industry in late growth or early maturity stage of life cycle, one or more product offerings currently targeted at major customer segments, but some potential segments may still be undeveloped. | Industry in maturity or decline stage of life cycle; current offerings targeted at all major segments; sales primarily due to repeat purchases/replacement demand. | Industry in maturity or decline stage of life cycle; current offerings targeted at all major segments; sales primarily due to repeat purchase/ replacement demand. |
| Technology | Newly emerging technology; many applications as yet undeveloped. | Basic technology well developed but still evolving; product modifications and improvements—as well as emergence of new competing technologies—still likely. | Basic technology fully developed and stable; few major modifications or improvements likely. | Basic technology fully developed and stable; few major modifications or improvements likely. |
| Competition | Few established competitors; industry structure still emerging; single competitor holds commanding share of major market segments. | Large number of competitors, but future shakeout likely; industry structure still evolving; one or more competitors hold large shares in major segments but continuing growth may allow rapid changes in relative shares. | Small to moderate number of well-established competitors; industry structure stable, though acquisitions and consolidation possible; maturity of markets means relative shares of competitors tend to be reasonably stable over time. | Small to moderate number of well-established competitors; industry structure stable, though acquisitions and consolidation possible; maturity of markets means relative shares of competitors tend to be reasonably stable over time. |
| Business's relative strengths | SBU (or parent) has strong R&D, product engineering, and marketing research and marketing capabilities. | SBU (or parent) has good R&D, product engineering, and marketing research capabilities, but not as strong as some competitors'; has either low-cost position or strong sales, marketing, distribution, or service capabilities in one or more segments. | SBU has no outstanding strengths in R&D or product engineering; costs are higher than at least some competitors'; SBU's outstanding strengths are in process engineering and quality control and/or in marketing, sales, distribution, or customer services. | SBU (or parent) has superior sources of supply and/or process engineering and production capabilities that enable it to be low-cost producer; R&D, product engineering, marketing, sales, or service capabilities may not be as strong as some competitors'. |

new product-market entries. Industry structure is often unstable because few competitors are present and their relative market shares can shift rapidly as new products are introduced and new markets develop.

Because they emphasize the development of new products and/or new markets, the most successful prospectors are usually strong in, and devote substantial resources to, two broad areas of competence: first, R&D, product engineering, design, and other functional areas that identify new technology and convert it into innovative products; second, marketing research, marketing and sales—functions necessary for the identification and development of new market opportunities.

In some cases, however, even though a prospector business has strong product development and marketing skills, it may lack the resources to maintain its early lead as product-markets grow and attract new competitors. For example, Minnetonka was the pioneer in several health and beauty-aid product categories with brands like Softsoap liquid soap and Check-Up plaque-fighting toothpaste. However, because competitors like Procter & Gamble and Colgate-Palmolive introduced competing brands with advertising and promotion budgets much larger than Minnetonka could match, the firm was eventually forced to change its strategy and concentrate on manufacturing products under licenses from larger firms.

## Appropriate Conditions for an Analyzer Strategy

The analyzer strategy is a hybrid. On the one hand, analyzers are concerned with defending—via low costs or differentiation in quality or service—a strong share position in one or more established product-markets. At the same time, the business must pay attention to new product development to avoid being leapfrogged by competitors with more technologically advanced products or being left behind in newly developing application segments within the market. This dual focus makes the analyzer strategy appropriate for well-developed industries that are still experiencing some growth and change as a consequence of evolving customer needs and desires or continuing technological improvements.

Automobile manufacturing is an example of such an industry. Competitors are relatively few and well-established, the market is relatively mature except in emerging economics like China, but technology continues to advance. And recent changes in the industry's environment—such as rising fuel prices and concerns over the impact of auto emissions on global warming—have underscored the need for more efficient and ecologically friendly technologies. Thus, auto manufacturers around the world, including Toyota, Honda, General Motors, and many others, are investing billions in a variety of different technologies to develop a new generation of cars, as described in Exhibit 9.6.

The actions of Toyota and Honda illustrate one problem with an analyzer strategy. Few businesses have the resources and competencies needed to successfully defend an established core business while generating revolutionary new products at the same time. Success on both dimensions requires strengths across virtually every functional area, and few businesses (or their parent companies) have such universal strengths. Also, defending a successful core business can produce a corporate culture and policies that are difficult to change and that may resist the kind of innovative thinking and risk taking needed to develop radical new products. Therefore, analyzers are often not as innovative in new product development as prospectors. And they may not be as profitable in defending their core businesses as defenders.

## Appropriate Conditions for a Defender Strategy

A defender strategy makes sense only when a business has something worth defending. It is most appropriate for units with a profitable share of one or more major segments in a relatively mature, stable industry. Consistent with the "constant improvement" principles

## Exhibit 9.6   ANALYZER STRATEGIES IN THE AUTO INDUSTRY

Given that Toyota was already selling 300,000 of its Prius gas–electric hybrid cars annually by 2008, it was in the strongest position to respond to the double whammy of rising gas prices and growing concerns over the impact of exhaust emissions on global warming that caught the auto industry off guard that year. The firm's strategy, at least for the short term, was to rapidly expand its hybrid offerings and invest in R&D to further improve their efficiency. New hybrid models—including one in the firm's luxury Lexus line—were introduced in 2009 along with a lighter, more fuel-efficient version of the Prius.

Longer term, the company is eyeing plug-in electric cars. To that end, Toyota has created a special battery research division, complete with more than 100 engineers and technicians. As a first step, Toyota plans to introduce a plug-in version of the Prius hybrid in 2012.

Honda also plans to beef up its hybrid offerings in the short term, but it also offers new clean-diesel engines, which are purportedly 25 percent more fuel efficient than gas engines, in its larger cars—including those that carry the luxury Acura brand.

For the longer term, Honda is focusing on fuel cell vehicles which run on liquid hydrogen and emit only water. In 2008 the firm began production on a fuel cell model called the FCX Clarity which can go 280 miles on a tank of hydrogen and boast better fuel efficiency than comparable gas or hybrid cars. While Honda will lease just 200 Claritys in Japan and the United States through the early 2010s, it hopes to have the technology ready for the mass market within 10 years. But since every Clarity currently costs an estimated $1 million to produce, cost reductions via economies of scale and experience will be critical for the car's future.

Many other auto companies are placing their bets on electric motors. Electric cars come in two varieties. Pure electric cars, like the Nissan Leaf and the Mitsubishi i-MiEV (introduced in 2010) can be driven for 100 miles or so before they need to be plugged in and recharged. Range-extenders, like the General Motors' Volt (introduced as the Ampera in Europe in 2010), can be recharged either by plugging into an outlet or by a small onboard gas engine.

And all of the current competitors are nervously looking over their shoulders in anticipation of electric vehicles from China. The Chinese government is supporting electric car technology more than any other country. Beijing has already pledged over $17 billion for R&D, the installation of charging stations, customer subsidies, and the like.

Katsuaki Watanabe, Toyota's president, declared, "Without focusing on measures to address global warming and energy issues, there can be no future for our auto business." The interesting question is which of the many new technologies being pursued will prove the most effective and appealing means of addressing those issues.

*Sources:* Ian Rowley, "Japan's New Green Car Push," *www.businessweek.com*, July 2, 2008; "A Sparky New Motor," *The Economist*, October 9, 2010, pp. 89–90; and Brian Dumaine, "China Charges into Electric Cars," *Fortune*. November 1, 2010, pp. 138–48.

of total quality management, most successful defenders initiate process improvements, product improvements, or line extensions to help protect and strengthen their established positions. But they devote relatively few resources to basic R&D or the development of innovative new products. Thus, a defender strategy works best in industries where the basic technology is not very complex or where it is well-developed and unlikely to change dramatically over the short term. For instance, Pillsbury's prepared-dough products SBU—now part of the General Mills Company—has pursued a differentiated defender strategy for years. The unit generates substantial profits from well-established refrigerated dough products like Pillsbury Crescent rolls and Grands biscuits. But while it has introduced a number of line extensions over the years, most have been reconfigurations of the same basic dough-in-a-can technology, such as Soft Breadsticks.

**Differentiated Defenders**   To effectively defend its position by differentiation, a business must be strong in those functional areas critical for maintaining its particular competitive advantages over time. If a business's differentiation is based on superior product quality, those key functional areas include production, process engineering, quality control, and perhaps product engineering to develop product improvements. The effort to develop and maintain a quality differentiation can be worthwhile, though, because evidence suggests that superior product quality has a strong impact on a business's return on investment—an important performance objective for defenders.[17]

Regardless of the basis for differentiation, marketing is also important for the effective implementation of a differentiated defender strategy. Marketing activities that track changing customer needs and competitive actions and communicate the product offering's unique advantages through promotional and sales efforts to maintain customer awareness and loyalty are particularly important.

**Low-Cost Defenders**   Successful implementation of a low-cost defender strategy requires the business to be more efficient than its competitors. Thus, the business must establish the groundwork for such a strategy early in the growth stage of the industry. Achieving and maintaining the lowest per-unit cost usually means that the business has to seek large volume from the beginning—through some combination of low prices and promotional efforts—to gain economies of scale and experience. At the same time, such businesses must also invest in more plant capacity in anticipation of future growth and in state-of-the-art equipment to minimize production costs. This combination of low margins and heavy investment can be prohibitive unless the parent corporation can commit substantial resources to the business or unless extensive sharing of facilities, technologies, and programs with other business units is possible.

In recent years, some firms—particularly those in more developed economies—have tried to reduce their costs by outsourcing production and a few other corporate functions, such as customer call centers and human resources departments. However, outsourcing can lead to problems, like reduced quality control and more complicated logistics, that may raise the firm's costs in other areas. And because the efficiencies gained through outsourcing can be easily duplicated by competitors, it is not an effective way to build a *sustainable* low-cost advantage.[18]

The low-cost defender's need for efficiency typically forces the standardization of product offerings and marketing programs across customer segments to achieve scale effects. Thus, such a strategy is usually not so effective in fragmented markets desiring customized offerings as it is in commodity industries such as basic chemicals, steel, or flour, or in industries producing low-technology components such as electric motors or valves.

While low-cost defenders emphasize efficiency and low price as the primary focus of their competitive strategy, it is important to keep in mind that businesses pursuing other strategies should also operate as efficiently as possible given the functional activities necessary to implement those strategies. Some of the most effective businesses are those that work *simultaneously* to lower costs and improve quality and service.[19] And operating efficiency is likely to become even more critical as the internet makes it easier for customers to compare prices across alternative suppliers or to obtain low-price bids via "buyers' auction" sites, such as *www.MetalSite.com,* as discussed in Chapter 5.

# How Different Business Strategies Influence Marketing Decisions

Business units typically incorporate a number of distinct product-markets. A given entry's marketing manager monitors and evaluates the product's environmental situation and develops a marketing program suited to it. However, the manager's freedom to design such a program may be constrained by the business unit's competitive strategy. This is because different strategies focus on different objectives and seek to gain and maintain a competitive advantage in different ways. As a result, different functions within the SBU— and different activities within a given functional area, such as marketing—are critical for the success of different strategies.

There are, therefore, different key success factors inherent in the various generic business strategies. This constrains the individual marketing manager's freedom of action in two basic ways. First, because varying functions within the business unit are more important under different strategies, they receive different proportions of the SBU's total resources. Thus, the SBU's strategy influences *the amount of resources committed to marketing* and ultimately the budget available to an individual marketing manager within the business unit. Second, the SBU's choice of strategy influences both the kind of *market and competitive situation* that individual product-market entries are likely to face and the *objectives* they are asked to attain. Both constraints have implications for the design of marketing programs for individual products within an SBU.

### STRATEGIC ISSUE

*The SBU's strategy influences the amount of resources committed to marketing and ultimately the budget available.*

It is risky to draw broad generalizations about how specific marketing policies and program elements might fit within different business strategies. While a business strategy is a general statement about how an SBU chooses to compete in an industry, that unit may comprise a number of product-market entries facing different competitive situations in various markets. Thus, there is likely to be a good deal of variation in marketing programs, and in the freedom individual marketing managers have in designing them, across products within a given SBU. Still, a business's strategy does set a general direction for the types of target markets it will pursue and how the unit will compete in those markets. And it does have some influence on marketing policies that cut across product-markets. Exhibit 9.7 outlines differences in marketing policies and program elements that occur across businesses pursuing different strategies, and those differences are discussed below.

## Product Policies

One set of marketing policies defines the nature of the products the business will concentrate on offering to its target markets. These policies concern the *breadth or diversity of product lines,* their *level of technical sophistication,* and the target *level of product quality* relative to competitors.

Because prospector businesses rely heavily on the continuing development of unique new products and the penetration of new markets as their primary competitive strategy, policies encouraging broader and more technically advanced product lines than those of competitors should be positively related to performance on the critical dimension of share growth. The diverse and technically advanced product offerings of 3M's drug delivery systems SBU are a good example of this.

Whether a prospector's products should be of higher quality than competitors' products is open to question. Quality is hard to define; it can mean different things to different customers. Even so, it is an important determinant of business profitability. Thus, Hambrick suggests that in product-markets where up-to-the-minute styling or technical features are key attributes in customers' definitions of quality, high-quality products may play a positive role in determining the success of a prospector strategy. In markets where the critical determinants of quality are reliability or brand familiarity, the maintenance of relatively high product quality is likely to be more strongly related to the successful performance of defender businesses, particularly differentiated defenders.[20]

# Exhibit 9.7

DIFFERENCES IN MARKETING POLICIES AND PROGRAM COMPONENTS ACROSS BUSINESSES
PURSUING DIFFERENT STRATEGIES

| | STRATEGY | | |
| --- | --- | --- | --- |
| Marketing policies and program components | Prospector | Differentiated defender | Low-cost defender |
| *Product policies* | | | |
| • Product-line breadth relative to competitors | + | + | − |
| • Technical sophistication of products relative to competitors | + | + | − |
| • Product quality relative to competitors | ? | + | − |
| • Service quality relative to competitors | ? | + | − |
| *Price policies* | | | |
| • Price levels relative to competitors | + | + | − |
| *Distribution policies* | | | |
| • Degree of forward vertical integration relative to competitors | − | + | ? |
| • Trade promotion expenses as percent of sales relative to competitors | + | − | − |
| *Promotion policies* | | | |
| • Advertising expenses as percent of sales relative to competitors | + | ? | − |
| • Sales promotions expenses as percent of sales relative to competitors | + | ? | − |
| • Salesforce expenses as percent of sales relative to competitors | ? | + | − |

Key:  Plus sign (+) = greater than the average competitor.

Minus sign (−) = smaller than the average competitor.

Question mark (?) = uncertain relationship between strategy and marketing policy or program component.

Differentiated defenders compete by offering more or better choices to customers than do their competitors. For example, 3M's commercial graphics business, a major supplier of sign material for truck fleets, has strengthened its competitive position in that market by developing products appropriate for custom-designed signs. Until recently, the use of film for individual signs was not economical. But the use of computer-controlled knives and a new Scotch-brand marking film produce signs of higher quality and at lower cost than those that are hand-painted. This kind of success in developing relatively broad and technically sophisticated product lines should be positively related to the long-term ROI performance of most differentiated defender businesses.

However, broad and sophisticated product lines are less consistent with the efficiency requirements of the low-cost defender strategy. For one thing, maintaining technical sophistication in a business's products requires continuing investments in product and process R&D. For another, broad, complex lines can lead to short production runs and larger inventories. Some of the efficiency problems associated with broader, more-customized product lines may disappear, however, with continuing improvements in computer-assisted design and manufacturing, process reengineering, three-dimensional printing, and the like.[21]

Instead of, or in addition to, competing on the basis of product characteristics, businesses can distinguish themselves relative to competitors on the *quality of service* they offer. Such service might take many forms, including engineering and design services, alterations, installation, training of customer personnel, or maintenance and repair services. A policy of high service quality is particularly appropriate for differentiated defenders because it offers a way to maintain a competitive advantage in well-established markets.[22]

The appropriateness of an extensive service policy for low-cost defenders, though, is more questionable if higher operating and administrative costs offset customer satisfaction benefits. Those higher costs may detract from the business's ability to maintain the low prices critical to its strategy, as well as lowering ROI—at least in the short term. Further, a study of 71 SBUs pursuing a range of competitive strategies suggests that investments aimed at improving service efficiency and thereby reducing costs generally do not have as positive an impact on a unit's financial performance as service improvements aimed at increasing revenues via improved customer satisfaction and loyalty.[23]

## Pricing Policies

Success in offering low prices relative to those of competitors should be positively related to the performance of low-cost defender businesses—for low price is the primary competitive weapon of such a strategy. However, such a policy is inconsistent with both differentiated defender and prospector strategies. The higher costs involved in differentiating a business's products on either a quality or service basis require higher prices to maintain profitability. Differentiation also provides customers with additional value for which higher prices can be charged. Similarly, the costs and benefits of new product and market development by prospector businesses require and justify relatively high prices. Thus, differentiated defenders and prospectors seldom adhere to a policy of low competitive prices.

## Distribution Policies

Some observers argue that prospector businesses should show a greater degree of *forward vertical integration* than defender businesses.[24] The rationale for this view is that the prospector's focus on new product and market development requires superior market intelligence and frequent reeducation and motivation of distribution channel members. This can best be accomplished through tight control of company-owned channels. However, these arguments seem inconsistent with the prospector's need for flexibility in constructing new channels to distribute new products and reach new markets.

Attempting to maintain tight control over the behavior of channel members is a more appropriate policy for defenders who are trying to maintain strong positions in established markets. This is particularly true for defenders who rely on good customer service to differentiate themselves from competitors. Thus, it seems more likely that a relatively high degree of forward vertical integration is found among defender businesses, particularly differentiated defenders, while prospectors rely more heavily on independent channel members—such as manufacturer's representatives or wholesale distributors—to distribute their products.[25]

Because prospectors focus on new products where success is uncertain and sales volumes are small in the short run, they are likely to devote a larger percentage of sales to *trade promotions* than are defender businesses. Prospectors rely on trade promotion tools such as quantity discounts, liberal credit terms, and other incentives to induce cooperation and support from their independent channel members.

## Promotion Policies

Extensive marketing communications also play an important role in the successful implementation of both prospector and differentiated defender strategies. The form of that communication, however, may differ under the two strategies. Because prospectors must constantly work to generate awareness, stimulate trial, and build primary demand for new and unfamiliar products, high advertising and sales promotion expenditures are likely to bear a positive relationship to the new product and share-growth success of such businesses. The drug delivery SBU at 3M, for instance, devotes substantial resources to advertising in professional journals and distributing samples of new products, as well as to maintaining an extensive salesforce.

Differentiated defenders, on the other hand, are primarily concerned with maintaining the loyalty of established customers by adapting to their needs and providing good service. These tasks can best be accomplished—particularly in industrial goods and services industries—by an extensive, well-trained, well-supported, salesforce.[26] Therefore, differentiated defenders are likely to have higher salesforce expenditures than are competitors.

Finally, low-cost defenders appeal to their customers primarily on price. Thus, high expenditures on advertising, sales promotion, or the salesforce would detract from their basic strategy and may have a negative impact on their ROI. Consequently, such businesses are likely to make relatively low expenditures as a percentage of sales on those promotional activities.

# What If the Best Marketing Program for a Product Does Not Fit the Business's Competitive Strategy?

What should a marketing manager do if the market environment facing a particular product or service demands marketing actions that are not consistent with the overall competitive strategy of the business to which it belongs? What if, for example, the product's target market is rapidly becoming more mature and competitive, but it is housed in a prospector business unit that does not have the cost structure or the personnel to allow the aggressive pricing or excellent customer service that may be needed for the product to compete successfully? Or what if newly emerging technology demands that a mature product category undergo an innovative redesign even though the defender SBU does not have extensive R&D and product development capabilities?

If a business unit is focused on a single product category or technological domain—as is the case with 3M's industrial tape unit—the ideal solution might be for the whole SBU to change its strategy in response to shifting industry circumstances. As the product category matures, for instance, the SBU might switch from a prospector to an analyzer strategy, and ultimately to one of the defender strategies.

The problem is that—as we shall see in Chapter 17—effective implementation of different business strategies requires not only different functional competencies and resources but also different organizational structures, decision-making and coordination processes, reward systems, and even personnel. Because such internal structures and processes are hard to change quickly, it can be very difficult for an entire SBU to make a successful transition from one basic strategy to another.[27] For example, many of Emerson Electric's SBUs historically were successful low-cost defenders, but accelerating technological change in their industries caused the corporation to try to convert them to low-cost analyzers who would focus more attention on new product and market development. Initially, however, this attempted shift in strategy resulted in some culture shock, conflict, and mixed performance outcomes within those units.

In view of the implementation problems involved, some firms do not try to make major changes in the basic competitive strategies of their existing business units. Instead, they might form new prospector SBUs to pursue emerging technologies and industries rather than expecting established units to handle extensive new product development efforts.

Similarly, as individual product-market entries gain successful positions in growing markets, some firms move them from the prospector unit that developed them into an existing analyzer or defender unit, or even into a newly formed SBU, better suited to reaping profits from them as their markets mature. For example, a number of innovative products developed at 3M, such as Post-it repositionable notes, have enjoyed sufficient success that new business units were formed to concentrate on defending them as their markets matured. Many successful entrepreneurial start-ups eventually reorganize into two or more business units, one to continue prospecting new products and markets and another to defend the firm's initial product offering as its market matures.

Finally, some firms that are technological leaders in their industries may divest or license individual product-market entries as they mature rather than defend them in the face of increasing competition and eroding margins. This approach is relatively common at firms such as 3M and DuPont.

Because the marketing manager responsible for a given product-market entry is usually most closely tuned-in to changes in the market environment, he or she bears the responsibility for pointing out any mismatches between what is best for the product and the capabilities of the organizational unit to which it belongs. The marketer should develop a marketing strategy that makes the most sense in light of a detailed analysis of the available customer and competitive information and present a strong case for the resources necessary to implement the plan. If those resources are not available within the business unit, or if the marketing strategy is inconsistent with the SBU's objectives or competitive strategy, top management faces a choice of moving the product to a more benign unit of the firm or rejecting the recommended strategy. If the strategy is rejected, the marketer will likely have to make compromises to the strategy to make it fit better with the competitive thrust of the SBU, even though an attractive opportunity may be lost. But if the marketer has great confidence in the recommended strategy, he or she might opt to quit the firm and pursue the opportunity elsewhere, as was the case with Jim Watkins as discussed in Exhibit 9.8.

## Exhibit 9.8   JIM WATKINS TAKES A HIKE

When he was a product manager at the Pillsbury Company in the early 1970s, James D. Watkins became convinced that microwave technology represented a major opportunity for the packaged food industry. Consequently, he developed a marketing plan that proposed the pioneering development and aggressive introduction of a line of microwavable food products, starting with microwave popcorn. However, the business unit he worked for—and the entire Pillsbury Company at that time—was focused on defending strong positions in established markets, largely through incremental line extensions and product improvements. In other words, it was pursuing more of an analyzer strategy. As a result, top management rejected Watkins's proposal as being too risky and requiring resources and capabilities that were in short supply.

Watkins subsequently quit Pillsbury, founded a new firm called Golden Valley Microwave, attracted venture capital, hired some food scientists to do the necessary R&D, and began to market ActII microwave popcorn through large mass merchandisers such as Walmart. As Watkins had predicted in his original marketing plan, the availability of microwavable foods spurred a rapid increase in consumer demand for microwave ovens, which in turn increased demand for more microwavable foods. His new company grew rapidly, and a few years later he sold it to ConAgra for many millions of dollars.

But don't be too critical of Pillsbury. Like a good analyzer, the company avoided playing the risky role of the pioneer, but it eventually responded to the growing potential of microwave technology and successfully launched its own line of microwavable foods, including popcorn.

# TAKE-AWAYS

1. Research suggests that a business is likely to achieve superior revenue growth, market share, and profitability when there is a good fit between its competitive strategy and the strategic marketing programs of its various product or service offerings.

2. Business-level competitive strategies can be usefully categorized into (1) prospector strategies focused on growth via the development of new products and markets; (2) defender strategies primarily concerned with defending strong positions in established markets through either low prices or offering customers superior value in terms of product quality or service; and (3) analyzer strategies, which are hybrids of the other two strategies.

3. The generic competitive strategies described in the previous point apply equally well to services and physical products, single-product start-ups and multidivisional corporations, and global and domestic operations, and they are unlikely to change dramatically due to the rise of e-commerce.

4. Because the various business-level strategies focus on different objectives and seek to gain a competitive advantage in different ways, marketing may play a different role under each of the strategies, and varying marketing actions may be called for.

5. The marketing decision maker's job is to develop a sound, evidence-based marketing strategy for his or her offering and to make a persuasive case for its support. If that strategy does not fit the objectives or available resources and competencies of the business unit in which the product is housed, top management may choose to move the product to a more amenable unit or require adjustments to the strategy.

**Self-diagnostic questions to test your ability to apply the analytical tools and concepts in this chapter to marketing decision making may be found at this book's website at www.mhhe.com/mullins8e.**

# ENDNOTES

1. Material for this example was obtained from The *3M Company 2010 Annual Report* and other information found on the company's website, *www.3m.com;* Jerry Useem, "Scotch Tape Plus Innovation Equals?", *Fortune,* August 12, 2002, pp. 127–32; Brian Hindo, "At 3M, A Struggle between Efficiency and Creativity," *BusinessWeek—Indepth,* June 2007, pp. in8–in14; and Will Daley, "3M Moves Most Capital Spending Outside U. S. for First Time," *Bloomberg Businessweek Online* (*www.Businessweek.com*), April 26, 2011.

2. Stanley F. Slater and Eric M. Olson, "Marketing's Contribution to the Implementation of Business Strategy: An Empirical Analysis," *Strategic Management Journal* 22 (November 2001), pp. 1055–67; Eric M. Olson, Stanley F. Slater, and G. Tomas Hult, "The Performance Implications of Fit among Business Strategy, Marketing Organization Structure, and Strategic Behavior," *Journal of Marketing* 69 (July 2005), pp. 49–65; and Stanley F. Slater, Eric M. Olson, and G. Thomas M. Hult, "Worried about Strategy Implementation? Don't Overlook Marketing's Role," *Business Horizons* 53 (2010), pp. 469–79.

3. C. K. Prahalad and Gary Hamel, "The Core Competence of the Corporation," *Harvard Business Review* 68 (May–June 1990), pp. 79–91.

4. Michael E. Porter, *Competitive Strategy* (New York: Free Press, 1980). Also see Michael E. Porter, *Competitive Advantage: Creating and Sustaining Superior Performance* (New York: Free Press, 1985).

5. Robert E. Miles and Charles C. Snow, *Organizational Strategy, Structure, and Process* (New York: McGraw-Hill, 1978). For another taxonomy of business-level competitive strategies that incorporates elements of both the Porter and Miles and Snow frameworks, see Michael Treacy and Fred Wiersema, *The Discipline of Market Leaders* (Reading, MA: Addison-Wesley, 1995).

6. Charles C. Snow and Lawrence G. Hrebiniak, "Strategy, Distinctive Competence, and Organizational Performance," *Administrative Science Quarterly* 25 (1980), pp. 317–35.

7. Leslie Patton, "Pinkberry Looks Abroad to Keep Its Cool," *Bloomberg Businessweek.* May 2, 2011, pp. 18–20.

8. Theodore Levitt, *The Marketing Imagination* (New York: Free Press, 1986), pp. 94–95.

9. Philip Kotler and Gary Armstrong, *Principles of Marketing* (Englewood Cliffs, NJ: Prentice Hall, 1989), p. 575.

10. Daryl O. McKee, P. Rajan Varadarajan, and William M. Pride, "Strategic Adaptability and Firm Performance: A Market-Contingent Perspective," *Journal of Marketing,* July 1989, pp. 21–35.

11. Bruce Einhorn and Ben Elgin, "The Well-Heeled Upstart on Cisco's Tail," *BusinessWeek,* October 28, 2002, p. 91; and Bruce Einhorn, "The World's Most Influential Companies—Huawei," *BusinessWeek.* December 22. 2008, p. 5l; and Huawei Technologies Co. 2010 Annual Report on the company's website at *www.huawei.com.*

12. For examples, see Rajiv Lal and Miklos Savary, "When and How Is the Internet Likely to Decrease Price?" *Marketing Science* 18 (Fall 1999), pp. 485–503; Paul Markillie, "A Perfect Market: A Survey of E-Commerce," *The Economist,* May 15, 2004, pp. 13–20; and Florian Zettlemeyer, Fiona Scott Morton, and Jorge Silva-Risso, "How the Internet Lowers Prices: Evidence from Matched Survey and Automobile Transaction Data," *Journal of Marketing Research* 43 (May 2006), pp. 168–81.

13. Larry Chiagouris and Brant Wansley, "Branding on the Internet," *Marketing Management* 9 (Summer 2000), pp. 35–38; Faith Keenan, Stanley Holmes, Jay Greene, and Roger O. Crockett, "A Mass Market of One," *BusinessWeek,* December 2, 2002, pp. 68–72; Julie Schlosser, "Cashing in on the New World of Me," *Fortune,* December 13, 2004, pp. 244–50; and Nanette Byrnes, "More Clicks at the Bricks," *BusinessWeek,* December 17, 2007, pp. 50–52.

14. Gordon Donaldson, *Managing Corporate Wealth* (New York: Praeger, 1984). Also see Spencer E. Ante, "Giving the Boss the Big Picture," *BusinessWeek,* February 13, 2006, pp. 48–50.

**15.** Donald C. Hambrick, "Some Tests of the Effectiveness and Functional Attributes of Miles and Snow's Strategic Types," *Academy of Management Journal* 26 (1983), pp. 5–26; and McKee, Varadarajan, and Pride, "Strategic Adaptability and Firm Performance."

**16.** Robert W. Ruekert and Orville C. Walker, Jr., "The Sharing of Marketing Resources across Strategic Business Units: The Effects of Strategy on Performance," in *Review of Marketing* 1990 (Chicago: American Marketing Association, 1990).

**17.** Robert D. Buzzell and Bradley T. Gale, *The PIMS Principles: Linking Strategy to Performance* (New York: Free Press, 1987), chap. 6.

**18.** Peter Engardio, "The Future of Outsourcing," *BusinessWeek,* January 30, 2006 pp. 50–64; and Peter Engardio, "Can the U. S. Bring Jobs Back from China?" *BusinessWeek*, June 30, 2008, pp. 39–43.

**19.** For example, see Ronald Henkoff, "Cost Cutting: How to Do It Right," *Fortune,* April 9, 1990, pp. 40–49.

**20.** Hambrick, "Some Tests of Effectiveness."

**21.** Keenan, et al., "A Mass Market of One"; and Anthony Bianco, "The Vanishing Mass Market," *BusinessWeek,* July 12, 2004, pp. 61–72; and "The Printed World," *The Economist,* February 12, 2011, pp. 77–79.

**22.** Wolfgang Ulaga and Andreas Eggert, "Value-Based Differentiation in Business Relationships: Gaining and Sustaining Key Supplier Status," *Journal of Marketing* 70 (January 2006), pp. 119–36.

**23.** Roland T. Rust, Christine Moorman, and Peter R. Dickson, "Getting Return on Quality: Revenue Expansion, Cost Reduction, or Both?" *Journal of Marketing* 66 (October 2002), pp. 7–24.

**24.** Miles and Snow, *Organizational Strategy, Structure, and Process;* and Hambrick, "Some Tests of Effectiveness."

**25.** Although Hambrick argues for the reverse relationship, data from his study of 850 SBUs actually support our contention that defenders have more vertically integrated channels than do prospectors. See Hambrick, "Some Tests of Effectiveness."

**26.** Jaclyn Fierman, "The Death and Rebirth of the Salesman," *Fortune,* July 25, 1994, pp. 80–91; and Ulaga and Eggert, "Value-Based Differentiation in Business Relationships."

**27.** Connie J. G. Gersick, "Revolutionary Change Theories: A Multilevel Exploration of the Punctuated Equilibrium Paradigm," *Academy of Management Review* 16 (1991), pp. 10–36; and Michael L. Tushman, William H. Newman, and Elaine Romanelli, "Convergence and Upheaval: Managing the Unsteady Pace of Organizational Evolution," *California Management Review* 29 (1986), pp. 29–44.

# CHAPTER TEN

# Product Decisions

## Product Decisions in a Services Business[1]

*g* **A**LMOST NO ONE LIKES BANKS. From surly tellers to long lines, from "bankers' hours" to fees for just about everything, consumers are fed up. But Prudential, the big British insurer, was convinced things didn't have to be this way. Way back in October 1998, Prudential launched Egg, which has gone on to become one of Europe's largest online financial services providers.

*i* Egg, unlike many in the banking industry, believes superlative customer service is the key to growth. But can such service be delivered online? "The aim of all Egg's communication is to make the customer feel like an individual," says Patrick Muir, Egg's director of marketing. "We want to make money easier to understand and easier to manage."

Offering great customer service is easy to say, but is much harder to deliver consistently. Egg has succeeded by making a series of decisions about the product it offers—various services, in its case, rather than goods—and then managing its execution and service delivery very well through the use of technology. Banking with Egg is a far cry from conventional banking or most other applications of customer relationship management technology, for that matter, which often infuriate rather than please customers.

What were the product decisions that helped Egg succeed? First, Egg offers its customers a variety of channels of communication. There's the internet, of course, but Egg doesn't stop there. Egg TV offers interactive access from the comfort of one's living room. Further, Egg's 1,200 call center associates are available round the clock to help customers who want to speak to a real person. "You actually have a conversation with someone, rather than sticking with a rigid script," says Muir. What Egg also does differently is to offer a wide variety of financial services. Checking accounts, savings, credit cards with cashback discounts financed out of retailers' commission to Egg, mortgages, even insurance. Egg's wide range of financial services offers one-stop shopping to Egg customers. And each Egg customer can access a personal balance sheet that displays all his or her assets and liabilities on one screen. Even accounts with other online providers can be included.

Egg's multichannel strategy provides customers with more access points and enables them to access their money where, when, and as they wish. At home? Use Egg TV. At the office? Use the internet. On holiday at a beach resort? Find an internet café, and access your account. Egg says it's committed to mobile banking, too, as wireless technology deployment permits.

Egg's technology gives it a comprehensive customer-by-customer view that enables Egg to come up with suitable products and service to offer, based on each customer's own profile. "We want to put great offers in front of our customers that we believe are right for them rather than pushing unwanted products through hard-hitting sales campaigns," says Muir.

Egg's early results spoke for themselves. In 1999, it won 22 percent of net new deposits in the U.K. banking system. Within 18 months of launch, Egg had attracted more than one million customers. By 2002, brand awareness had reached 88 percent and its customers numbered over 2.1 million.

Egg's success in the United Kingdom led management to believe it could replicate the Egg model elsewhere. But its foray across the English Channel was not à la mode. French consumers didn't respond in the same way Brits had, and by 2004, Prudential was forced to shut down the French operation, posting an overall loss for the year of £107 million. But it was not just the French business that fared poorly. Prudential sold Egg's investments business to Fidelity at a small loss and put its investment wrap business, Funds Direct, up for sale.

Chastened by these setbacks, management refocused on its basic UK business, returned the company to profitability, and—with Egg's stock price in the tank—bought the company back from its public shareholders, taking it private. In May 2007, having returned the business to health, Prudential then sold Egg to CitiGroup for £546 million, or just over $1 billion.

Despite the somewhat rocky road it has traveled, Egg's service-centric focus has served it well. Whether that focus is sufficient to fuel future growth in the hotly competitive online finance industry, where just about every brick-and-mortar bank is also now online, remains to be seen. But CitiGroup's billion-dollar bet suggests that it believes Egg still has room to run.

# Marketing Challenges Addressed in Chapter 10

As the story of Egg illustrates, decisions about product attributes—whether for goods or services—can make a huge difference in attracting customers. In this chapter, we examine the first of the four Ps—the many kinds of **product decisions** that marketers must make to provide the value that customers want. As we shall see, such decisions include those about attributes to include in the product (such as Egg's decision to offer account access via interactive TV), how to package the product (the level of access that Egg offers its customers), as well as decisions about branding, services related to the product, warranties, and so on. These decisions grow out of the need to differentiate one's products from those of competitors, as we discussed in Chapter 8, the brand positioning chapter. As we observed in Chapter 8, going to market with an undifferentiated product can be hazardous.

Thus, Chapter 10 addresses several critical questions that marketers face in differentiating their offerings from those of their competitors. How should our product offering, whether a good or a service, be designed to give it a chance to win competitive advantage? What product decisions must we make to deliver the benefits and value promised in our positioning statement or value proposition? Finally, given the importance of new products in the long-term success of most firms, how can new product development be managed, from a process perspective, to ensure a timely flow of new products that enjoy favorable reception by customers? Answering these questions thoughtfully, using evidence-based and up-to-date market knowledge as a foundation, often gives the firm its best chance to offer goods and services that consumers want—as opposed to products its engineers can develop ("It's the latest technology!"), its merchants are excited about ("I have a hunch purple will be hot this year!"), or its CEO loves.

In the first portion of the chapter, we address the *content* of product decision making: decisions about product quality and features, packaging, brand names, related services, and so on. These decisions, which we refer to as **whole product** or **augmented product**

## Exhibit 10.1

THE AUGMENTED PRODUCT CONCEPT

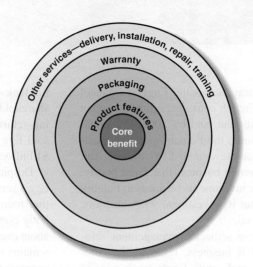

decisions (see Exhibit 10.1), are applicable to both new and existing products, and they comprise the heart of any marketer's product decision making. Then we address the *process* of **new product development.** An abundance of recent evidence indicates that *how* the new product development process is managed—whether for **new-to-the-world products** born in high-tech research labs or simple **product modifications** or **line extensions**—can have important implications for time to market and, ultimately, for product success or failure. Finally, to close the chapter, we examine product decisions over the product life cycle, from product introduction to a product's maturity and possible decline.

## Product Design Decisions for Competitive Advantage

A **product** can be defined as anything that satisfies a want or need through use, consumption, or acquisition. Thus, products include objects (TVs, radios, cars), services (medical, educational), places (New York, Moscow), people (Barack Obama and other politicians everywhere), activities (entering a contest or visiting a weight-loss clinic), and ideas (have you hugged your kids today?).

Conceptually, products should be thought of as problem solvers since they are purchased because of the core benefits they provide—not because of the product per se.[2] Jain Irrigation Systems, a marketer of drip-irrigation technology in India, found that it needed to sell more than just its gear. Guidance on choosing appropriate crops for a farmer's fields, given the local soil conditions and terrain, as well as after-market service, like replacing any parts where maintenance had been improper or the local rats had gnawed through them, were essential.[3]

**STRATEGIC ISSUE**

*Most customers are far more interested in benefits than they are in features.*

What is important is how the *consumer* perceives the product as satisfying a need, *not* how the *seller* sees the product. The seller must turn the wanted benefits into a tangible product with **features,** as well as other elements, of the augmented product, or attributes that will provide the intended satisfaction better than competitive products. But benefits and features are not the same. **Features** are the tangible or intangible attributes given the product by its designers. **Benefits** are the solutions to customer problems or needs delivered by the product. Thus, what Jain Irrigation really sells is not tubes and connectors. It sells reduced water usage—in a country where water is an increasingly scarce resource—and higher crop yields. Ultimately, most customers are far more interested in *benefits* than they are in *features,* though marketers sometimes forget this fact in designing ads or other marketing communications messages.

## Goods and Services: Are the Product Decisions the Same?

What is a service? As we discussed in Chapter 9, services can be thought of as *intangibles* versus goods as *tangibles.* Thus, services can rarely be experienced in advance of the sale, while tangible goods can be directly experienced, even tested, before purchase.

As we have seen with Egg, the principles entailed in product decision making apply to services as well as goods. Thus, when we say **product** in this book we mean both **goods** and **services.** As shown in Exhibit 10.2, different kinds of goods and services often call for different marketing strategies, but the decision-making content and processes for both goods and services are similar.

## Product Quality and Features Decisions

A well-developed positioning statement or value proposition plays an important role in designing products, whether goods or services. It tells the product's designers what benefits are to be delivered, so designers can imbue the product with the necessary features or other attributes, such as those we've seen at Egg, to deliver those benefits. Positioning makes clear how the product—an account with Egg—is to be differentiated from other products in its category.

As we have seen in the brand positioning chapter, products—whether goods or services—can be differentiated by both physical and perceptual means. One important dimension on which goods or services are physically differentiated is on the basis of quality—seeking to be better, in some sense, in the customers' eyes than competing products (see Exhibit 10.3). Differentiating on quality can occur on any of the eight dimensions of quality for goods—attributes

## Exhibit 10.2

MARKETING STRATEGY IMPLICATIONS OF CONSUMER GOODS CLASSIFICATION

|  | Examples | Strategy elements typically stressed |
| --- | --- | --- |
| Convenience goods and services | Dentifrice, soap, razor blades, magazines, many packaged food products, haircuts | Maximum distribution (product availability), consumer advertising (awareness and brand recognition), merchandising (in-store displays) |
| Shopping goods and services | Color TVs, cars, major appliances, homes, car repair, family doctors | Available in limited number of stores, personal selling important, limited to extensive advertising, seller often offers financing, warranties, and postpurchase service |
| Specialty goods and services | Musical instruments, stereo equipment, some brands of men's clothing, college consultants | Limited distribution, high price, strong advertising to promote brand uniqueness and to inform where available locally |
| Unsought goods and services | Certain medical services, personal liability insurance, encyclopedias | Strong promotion, including personal selling |

## Exhibit 10.3   SOFT FOOTBALL HELMETS FOR TOUGH ATHLETES

Industrial designer Bert Straus has worked on everything from sports equipment to streetcars. He and his small Pennsylvania company, Protective Sports Equipment, Inc., want to make head injuries to football players a thing of the past. His multilayered Gladiator helmet—foam on the outside and inside, sandwiching a harder middle layer—is designed to distribute the energy of impact. Straus is hoping to win approval for his Gladiator helmet from a national standards group.

Mark Kelso, a hard-hitting safety for the Buffalo Bills and now an investor in Straus's company,

switched to an earlier Straus model, the ProCap, after suffering concussions. Former NFL player Steve Wallace, who also wore the ProCap, is convinced that Straus' multilayered helmets are better than the current two-layer models. "I never had another concussion when I wore it." If the Gladiator wins approval, a large market of college and youth teams—not to mention the National Football League—awaits.

Source: James Strengold, "Innovator: Bert Straus," *Bloomberg Businessweek*, December 13–19, 2010, p. 44.

like reliability, durability, and performance[4]—or the five dimensions of service quality: empathy, assurance, responsiveness, reliability, and tangibles.[5]

So how should decisions about product features be made? Typically, consumers' choice criteria are limited to relatively few attributes or quality dimensions for a given product category. Thus, most products use only a few dimensions of quality as the basis on which they compete. Attempting to differentiate on too many features can be confusing to consumers and can lead to "feature fatigue."[6]

**STRATEGIC ISSUE**

*How should decisions about product features be made?*

Feature fatigue was blamed for making 2010 a flat year in television, leaving retailers like Best Buy stacked to the rafters with unsold flat-screen TVs.[7] Decisions about which dimensions of quality should be designed into a product are driven by earlier choices about the product's target market and positioning. When the product and product category, its users, and its uses are well understood, the marketing research techniques discussed in Chapter 6 can be employed to determine consumer needs and assess consumer preferences for products having various features. Some analytical techniques (and software packages for running them) commonly employed in determining the best set of features for a product are discussed in Exhibit 10.4.

In some situations, especially when the task is to design a breakthrough product that differs significantly from prior products, traditional marketing research is less likely to elicit the information needed to design a new product. For such situations, new techniques

## Exhibit 10.4

### MARKETING DECISION SUPPORT TOOLS FOR NEW PRODUCT DECISION MAKING

| Tool or technique | Software packages | What they do |
|---|---|---|
| Brand development software | NamePro® from the Namestormers, www.namestormers.com | Helps create distinctive, memorable brands for goods or services |
| Quality function deployment | QFD/CAPTURE; see www.qfdcapture.com | Measures links between known customer needs, engineering characteristics, and product design features to assess product preferences |
| Conjoint analysis | Several programs from Sawtooth Software, see www.sawtoothsoftware.com | Assesses consumers' preferred trade-offs among different product attributes |

## Exhibit 10.5   BIKES AS BIKES USED TO BE

In the summer of 2007, 55-year-old grandmother Alice Wilkes bought a brand new Trek bicycle, her first in more than 40 years. But it wasn't a mountain bike or a sleek road racer, and she didn't buy tight cycling clothes to go with it. "I like to feel free, with the wind flying up my sleeves," she says.

What Wilkes bought was an outgrowth of some ethnographic research that product design firm IDEO carried out for Shimano, the Microsoft of the cycling industry. Shimano components—from gears to brakes to derailleurs—are found on the majority of bikes these days, and sales of bicycles have been down in recent years. When the bike industry is down, so, too, is Shimano. So Shimano's senior manager for product development and marketing, David Lawrence, asked IDEO to find out why people weren't riding as much any more, and come up with some solutions that might energize the industry. IDEO sent its designers and researchers into the homes of baby boomers who no longer ride. They discovered that the lack of riding wasn't because people were getting lazy or out of shape. Many were simply intimidated by the increasing technical complexity and the hard-core nature of something that once had been just plain fun, rather than the serious sport that cycling had become. Perhaps what was needed were "just plain bikes." As Lawrence put it, cycling "had gone from fun to being a sport, and no one had noticed."

The result was coasting bikes, like the Trek model that Wilkes tools around on, that look and work much like the bikes of yesteryear. Pedaling backward even puts on the brakes. And Shimano's new automatic shifting technology means that Wilkes never has to shift gears. Her bike does it for her. Easy and fun, just as cycling used to be. And a big comfortable seat, too! Lance Armstrong, eat your heart out!

*Source:* Jay Greene, "Return of the Easy Rider," *BusinessWeek* European Edition, September 17, 2007, pp. 78–81.

have been developed to go beyond what consumers can easily articulate and uncover needs they may not have yet identified (see Exhibit 10.5). The use of techniques such as ethnography and empathic design is one way to respond to critics who charge that excessively customer-led decision processes can blind companies to the needs of customers it does not currently serve.[8] Companies that adopt a true **market orientation** use techniques such as these to obtain a broader view of their markets than their current customers can provide.

## Branding Decisions

As we saw in Chapter 8, **branding** identifies and helps differentiate the goods or services of one seller from those of another. It consists of a name, sign, symbol, or some combination thereof. Branding is important to consumers because it simplifies shopping, facilitates the processing of information concerned with purchase options, provides confidence that the consumer has made the right decision, helps to ensure quality, and often satisfies certain status needs.

Through its branding efforts, a company improves its brand equity position, which consists of four major asset categories—brand name awareness, brand loyalty, perceived quality, and brand association. Thus, given the value-enhancing power of branding, it is not surprising that more and more attention is being given to managing brands, especially in terms of developing a winning brand identity. The latter will be discussed in Chapter 13, in which we focus in greater detail on advertising.

**STRATEGIC ISSUE**

*The decision issue here is what brand to give to a new product.*

The decision issue we address here is what brand to give to a new product. This decision may involve developing a new brand, as Toyota did when it introduced its upscale Lexus automobiles into the United States, or using one of the firm's existing brands, as Toyota did with the introduction of its Toyota Prius model.

**Branding Strategies**   A company has a number of branding-strategy options, one of which is whether to brand each individual product or to use a family brand name. **Individual branding** requires the company to provide each product or product line with a distinctive name. This type of branding is practiced by such firms as Procter & Gamble (Tide and Ariel detergent, Crest toothpaste), Diageo (Smirnoff vodka, Guiness stout, Baileys Irish Cream, Jose Cuervo tequila), and Accor hotels (Mercure, Novotel, Motel 6). Individual branding reduces a company's risk in that a new product failure is not readily associated with the firm's other products. Further, it enables a firm to compete via multiple entries within the same product class.

When developing a new brand, whether in a new or existing company, one key decision is whether to have the brand clearly indicate what the product is or stands for (*Burger* King, *Pizza* Hut, *Healthy* Choice cookies) or to develop a brand whose meaning must be built (Amazon, Nestlé, McDonald's). The former approach may make it easier and less costly to build market awareness and gain customer trial at the outset, but it can limit the flexibility to adapt to changing market conditions (witness Kentucky Fried Chicken's name change to KFC when *fried* became a negative attribute due to trends toward healthier eating). The former approach, however, is viewed by some as generic and boring and may make it harder to build an image for and differentiate one's brand. Positioning guru Al Ries argues that the latter approach, whereby a brand is based on its own distinctive name (eBay, Google), is probably better than the generic approach (Auction.com, Diapers .com) in today's rapidly changing and highly competitive marketplace.[9]

**Family branding** uses the same brand name to cover a group of products or product lines. There are several variations of family branding including its use primarily with related items (Campbell's soups and Dyson vacuum cleaners), its use with all company items regardless of whether they are use-related (General Electric is an example), and the use of a family name combined with individual product names (Kellogg's Raisin Bran cereal).

The major arguments for using family branding are reduced costs and transfer of customer satisfaction from one product to another bearing the same name. This approach also makes it easier to launch product modifications such as new package sizes and types, or new products, as when Nike extended its footwear brand to cover athletic clothing. Family branding can also increase the impact of shelf facings in stores and make feasible the promotion of a product line comprising many low-volume items.

**Brand extension** involves the use of a family brand name established in one product class as a vehicle to enter another product class. A majority of the new products introduced to supermarkets and drugstores fall in this category.

The rationale for an extension is that the contribution of the brand name to the extension will be positive. The critical question here is the extent to which the brand name can provide a point of differentiation, including a quality association. Examples here include Arm and Hammer Carpet Deodorizer, Duracell Durabeam flashlights, and the use of the HP (Hewlett-Packard) name on thousands of items. By providing such an association, brand extensions can facilitate the acceptance of a new product by providing it with instantaneous familiarity. Bad brand extensions occur when the name adds little or no benefit to the extension and may cause confusion and, at worst, stimulate negative attribute association.

**Cobranding**   Cobranding uses multiple brand names with a single product or service offering, such as Häagen-Dazs's Baileys Irish Cream ice cream.[10] Cobranding is just getting started worldwide but is expected to grow.

**Global Branding**   Building a global brand is often difficult for a variety of reasons: the meaning of the brand name evoking negative associations in some countries, the presence of strong local brands, and the heavy investments required. Still, if successful, the scale effects can dramatically enhance sales and profits. Ketchup-maker Heinz has built a small sauce brand that it acquired in 1998, ABC, into the world's second largest-selling soy sauce, after Japan's Kikkoman. ABC, whose home market is Indonesia, is seeking further growth at home by taking an exotic new product to Indonesian consumers: ketchup.[11]

### Corporate Identity and Family Branding as a Source of Synergy

Corporate identity—together with a strong corporate brand that embodies that identity—can help a firm stand out from its competitors and give it a sustainable advantage in the market. *Corporate identity* flows from the communications, impressions, and personality projected by an organization. It is shaped by the firm's mission and values, its functional competencies, the quality and design of its goods and services, its marketing communications, the actions of its personnel, the image generated by various corporate activities, and other factors.

In order to project a positive, strong, and consistent identity, firms as diverse as Caterpillar, Walt Disney, and The Body Shop have established formal policies, criteria, and guidelines to help ensure that all the messages and sensory images they communicate reflect their unique values, personality, and competencies. One rationale for such corporate identity programs is that they can generate synergies that enhance the effectiveness and efficiency of the firm's marketing efforts for its individual product offerings. By focusing on a common core of corporate values and competencies, every impression generated by each product's design, packaging, advertising, and promotional materials can help reinforce and strengthen the impact of all the other impressions the firm communicates to its customers, employees, shareholders, and other audiences, and thereby generate a bigger bang for its limited marketing bucks. For example, by consistently focusing on values and competencies associated with providing wholesome family entertainment, Disney has created an identity that helps stimulate customer demand across a wide range of product offerings—from movies to TV programs to licensed merchandise to theme parks and cruise ships.

### Retailer and Distributor Brands

In recent years, private label **store brands** have gained considerable ground versus national brands. Such labels represent over $50 billion at retail in the United States and a 20 percent share of all items purchased in supermarkets, drug chains, and mass merchandisers. Private labels have won even greater success in Europe, taking a 45 percent share of retail products sold locally.[12]

The explanation for the increasing importance of store brands is that over the last two decades, the national and global brands regularly increased their prices along with massive distributions of coupons, thereby training consumers to shop on price. They also undertook large numbers of line extensions and, in general, focused less on brand equity. Such fast-growing discounters as Walmart and France's Carrefour have moved aggressively to take advantage of the price vulnerability of many national brands. Strong retailer brands have also become very important in the soft goods trade. Ralph Lauren and a number of European retailers such as Burberry and Laura Ashley have opened their own U.S. stores.

But there are some countertrends to the above. A number of consumer goods companies have been acquired over the past several years at substantial multiples of their book value because of the value of their brand names (for instance, the acquisition of Richardson/Vicks by Procter & Gamble and various liquor brands by Diageo). The reasoning behind such acquisitions is the high cost of creating a well-known brand and the low success rate of new products. Thus, buying popular brands can be a shortcut to growth.

# Packaging Decisions

A product's package serves several functions—protecting, facilitating use of, and promoting the product, as well as providing information about the product and its use. The protection function is critical in both transport and storage. Protecting an item under a variety of temperatures and moisture conditions and against being crushed or dropped during handling is no small undertaking.

Because of increasing competition among brands within stores, packages have become an extension of the product and a way of identifying and differentiating products that can lead to increased loyalty and growth in sales. Packaging often facilitates use of the product, as in aerosol cans and disposable and unbreakable bottles. Packaging can also increase consumer safety, as proved by child-proof tops on drugs and tamper-resistant packages.

Packaging can give a product strong promotional support at the point of purchase. Many more potential customers may see the package than see advertising—and at more opportune times. More and more sellers are attempting to develop a common package design for their products, thereby creating a greater impact on the consumer. Allowing for the needs of varied groups of consumers is a real challenge, however (see Exhibit 10.6).

Increasingly firms are recognizing the need to use environmentally sensitive packages. Given the growing concern about the disposal of solid waste, more recyclable and biodegradable materials are being used.

Because consumers purchase a high percentage of supermarket items on impulse, packaging is especially important for such items. Packaging also can play an important role in the marketing of services. The blue suits and white shirts worn by high-priced strategy consultants are an example. The distinctive store décor of the various beauty salon chains is another.

# Services Decisions and Warranties

The service component of a product can include a variety of activities; the following are among the more common:

- Delivery reliability.
- Warranty.
- Repair and maintenance (including response time, spare parts availability, and effectiveness).
- Efficient handling of complaints and returns.
- Credit availability.

## Exhibit 10.6   *Universal Design Meets Growing Acceptance*

Universal design is the concept of designing products and their packages in such a manner that the product or package can easily be used by people other than average healthy adults—the handicapped, the aging, and so on. The universal design movement has spawned numerous efforts to rethink how ordinary products and packages are designed (round doorknobs, for example, are difficult for arthritic hands to open; lever handsets are much easier). An entire conference at the School of Packaging at Michigan State University was held in 2006 with an interdisciplinary focus on such issues as the biomechanics of aging, cognition and aging, and their impact on packaging and the packaging industry.

*Source:* Faraday Packaging Partnership, Events, at *www .faraday-packaging.com.*

- Prompt inquiries handling.
- Buyer personnel training.
- Prompt claim settlement.
- Fast price quotations.
- Fast order processing.

Companies that excel at providing service find it a substantial competitive advantage. In most markets, it is a significant part of a firm's quality rating. In many, it is more important than the product itself. Service is not just a competitive weapon; it also strongly affects the overall level of profitability since it typically costs more to get a new customer than to keep an old one. The more service-sensitive the market (the importance of service versus physical attributes), the greater the opportunity for profits. To be effective, a firm's service program generally must contain performance standards and be monitored regularly.

Warranties can play important roles in reducing the customer's risk of purchase and enhancing quality perceptions, thereby enhancing sales. Catalog retailer Lands' End's slogan "Guaranteed, period" is such an example. Similarly, Dell's offer of extended three-year on-site warranties for computers it sells on its website helps reduce any concerns customers may have about buying Dell products sight unseen.

Warranties are only part of the story in assuring customer satisfaction, however. Sometimes, products fail to perform as planned, and customers have unsatisfactory experiences with them that take the company beyond the terms of its warranties. The operating profit of Bridgestone Corp, the makers of Firestone tires, fell by 27 percent in 2001 following a poorly managed product recall that resulted from nearly 300 reports of Firestone tire failure on Ford's hot-selling Explorer SUV. Putting the consumer first, even when it is costly to do so, at least in the short term, can be difficult for some companies to do. But as one former Firestone executive remarked, "They just don't have a clue how to handle this."[13]

## Managing Product Lines for Customer Appeal and Profit Performance

Whether a **product line** is too short or too long depends on the extent to which the market can be segmented and how the company wants to position itself. Much also depends on what stage the product-market evolution is in. A short product line is desirable during the early stages, given the difficulties of managing a long line. It is also generally more profitable given the economies of scale and that it simplifies the inventories of both the company and its channel members. In the longer term, however, a short line can come under fire as competitors segment the market and develop more specialized products to meet the needs of these segments. Thus, to survive and prosper, short lines must be uniquely positioned against competitors—and the firm must be able to maintain the line's differential advantage.

Longer product lines generally come about through a series of **line extensions,** in which additional products are developed to serve more narrowly targeted, or even different, market segments. But too few companies subject their product lines to a regular audit to determine which products, if any, should be dropped.[14] Too often a firm rationalizes the continuation of certain products on the basis that they are at least covering direct costs, perhaps even making a contribution to fixed costs. Such reasoning overlooks the opportunity costs of not getting rid of them, including the disproportionate amount of management time spent on weak products. Substantial profit increases can often result from the elimination of weak items. Japan's Shiseido Co., its largest cosmetics group, moved to profitability by streamlining product lines and improving inventory control.[15]

The criteria for identifying weak products focus largely on the trend of the product's contribution to profit. Each such item should then be evaluated on such considerations as future sales of the item's product type or class, its future market share assuming no changes in the product or its marketing, future market share assuming certain product and marketing changes, anticipated changes in the marketing of competitive products (including the price), the effect of dropping the product on the company's channels of distribution, the cost of dropping the item (layoffs and inventory clearances), and the effect of dropping the product on the sales and profits of the firm's other items because of joint costs or other factors.

## Product Systems

Among the most strategically important product line decisions in today's hotly competitive markets are those related to the development of **product systems,** whereby different product work together to create barriers to competition. Gillette sells razors and blades, selling razors at low prices to generate high-margin recurring revenue on the razor blades. Hewlett-Packard sells printers and ink cartridges. Inkjet cartridges are so lucrative for HP that they could practically give away the printers for free (see Exhibit 10.7).

Apple, in its transformation from a marginally profitable maker of personal computers into a consumer electronics powerhouse, has used product systems like the iPod MP3 player and the iTunes music store to support its attractive profit margins on hardware—the iPod—by selling the software—the iTunes—at break-even pricing, effectively and ingeniously turning Gillette's razor and razor blade model upside down. And by building common elements of usability into its iPod, iPhone, and iPad, Apple should help publishers like *Time* and *Sports Illustrated* take advantage of today's latest digital technology.[16]

---

### Exhibit 10.7    CHAMPAGNE FOR YOUR PRINTER

Hewlett-Packard, Epson, and the other makers of inkjet printers know a cash cow when they see one. At the equivalent of more than $2,000 per liter, ink for your printer is far pricier than a bottle of Dom Perignon! Printer consumables—principally those little black cartridges that we cannot live without—account for half of HP's printer and imaging division's sales and most of its profits. It's no wonder that HP stuffs postage-paid envelopes into its packages so its customers will recycle their cartridges into raw materials for other plastic products, rather than refill them at one of the growing number of cartridge consumables stores. The printer companies' profits are spawning a new industry to serve those who would refill cartridges, rather than recycling or disposing of them. "Inkjet refilling is a very lucrative market," says Bill McKinney, CEO of InkTec Zone, a growing company that markets inkjet-filling machines to retailers wanting to cash in on these profits. Fortunately for the printer makers, though, some 86% of consumers still buy new brand-name cartridges, thereby making low prices on printers possible. Will the cartridge cash cow disappear? If so, printer prices are bound to rise.

*Sources:* Drew Cullen, "Bring on the Empty Cartridges," *The Register*, November 12, 2003, at *www.theregister.co.uk/2003/11/12/bring_on_the_empty_cartridges/*; and ClickPress, "Liquid Gold Rush: Turning Inkjet Cartridges into Gold," at *www.clickpress.com/releases/detailed/7143005cp.shtml.*

# New Product Development Process Decisions

As the Egg example that opened this chapter illustrates, a firm's growth and profitability is significantly influenced by how well it succeeds in making product decisions, improving present products, and adding new ones to serve new markets or market segments. But developing new products is a costly and risky undertaking, as companies around the world have learned. This section examines a process by which a firm can better exploit the opportunities for new products and minimize the inherent risks.[17] Before detailing this process, we need to discuss the role of new products in long-term profitability, new product success rates, and the major reason why new products fail.

## The Importance of New Products to Long-Term Profitability

An abundance of research has established that new products constitute the lifeblood of long-term firm success and provide a central mechanism for firms' adaptation to rapidly changing markets and the opportunities they offer. Radical innovations, defined as those based on new technology and that offer substantial increases in customer benefits, may be particularly important but tend to come from a minority of companies.[18]

There are a number of ways to classify new products. One of the simplest ways is to divide new products into four major classes: new to the world, new to the firm, product-line extensions, and product improvements. Only a small percentage of products are new to the world. The vast majority are either **product-line extensions** or **product improvements.** The rationale for this focus on line extensions is—Why spend a lot of time and money to introduce a new product when most fail and it's much less expensive and faster to introduce an extension or an improvement? But is this the best way to go?

## New Product Success and Failure

Introducing new products is a notoriously risky business, as most new products—more than half, by many estimates—fail. They don't usually fail for technical reasons, either. They fail because not enough people want to buy them.[19] Thus, a crucial factor in successful new product development is to ensure that an adequate understanding of customer needs, preferences, and requirements is developed. Doing so is not as easy as it sounds, however.

As we saw in Chapter 6, there is a wide array of marketing research tools that, at least in theory, should enable marketers to gain the customer understanding they require. In practice, though, it is not always easy for customers to articulate what they want, particularly with new-to-the-world products or product ideas that they can scarcely imagine. For this reason, some companies, such as Bang & Olufsen, the high-end

**STRATEGIC ISSUE**

*In practice, it is not always easy for customers to articulate what they want.*

Danish electronics maker, don't bother doing marketing research on new product ideas (see Exhibit 10.8). Most companies, however, work diligently to understand how large the market is for new products, how fast that market is growing (using approaches and frameworks such as those discussed in Chapter 3), and to understand what customers really want and will pay for. For some—like Google, 3M, and Intel—these efforts along with these companies' willingness to develop technology that may not pay off any time soon, have led to consistent new product success over many years and well-deserved reputations for their product innovation prowess.[20]

## Exhibit 10.8   At Bang & Olufsen, Designers Rule the Roost

CEO Torben Ballegaard Sorensen, of Bang & Olufsen, says it's often the case that consumers don't really know what they want. Thus, B&O doesn't engage in extensive marketing research or follow an exhaustive new product development process. Instead, B&O's ideas and the sometimes revolutionary products that flow from them arise not as the result of market analysis, "but rather a deep understanding of how our consumers live," he says. And who has that understanding at B&O? A half dozen or so highly creative designers, not B&O managers.

Depending on the instincts of quirky designers is not for everyone, however. And counting on the ability of managers to manage such individuals raises additional complications. But B&O wants its designers, none of whom are even employees, to call the shots, even when that means telling the engineers that a standard 2-inch screen with a black plastic frame simply won't do for its new high-end cell phone. An elegant, frameless 2.1-inch screen is what designer Torsten Valeur had in mind. Samsung, the supplier, simply had to cancel its $2 million order and get what Valeur wanted in the first place.

But, thanks to Valeur's snazzy design, B&O's Serene cell phone sells nicely at its $1,275 price point. More generally, its designers' ability to intuit what B&O's luxury customers want and will pay for means its BeoLab 5 stereo speakers, cranking out a thumping 2,500 watts per speaker, fetch $19,700 a pair. Its 50-inch BeoVision 9 plasma TV swivels to adjust itself to where you are sitting, a nice feature, for those who already have everything else money can buy. It's a mere $19,900. Just think, for under $50,000, you can outfit the family with designer cell phones, a great sound system, and the TV, too!

*Source:* Jay Greene, "Where Designers Rule," *BusinessWeek* European Edition, November 5, 2007, pp. 46–51.

# Organizing for New Product Development

At the outset of the development process, the firm must decide whether to keep its development activities in-house or go outside via subcontracting or some form of joint venture. The rationale for the latter is that large, integrated bureaucratic companies find it difficult during times of rapid technological changes to compete against smaller, more-focused companies that are highly flexible and can motivate their employees using stock incentives and bonuses. As a result, companies like Procter & Gamble, British Telecom, and IBM are building innovation networks with other companies to open up their innovation processes.

Other companies are using another prime source to spur innovation—the customer.[21] A new trend toward **cocreation** is bringing customers or prospective customers directly into the product development process. The idea underlying cocreation is that rather than inventing new goods or services on their own, companies engage their customers in the process. Facebook, for example, benefits from the more than 20,000 software applications that have been developed by Facebook users. Under the cocreation mantra, companies don't bother to imagine, create, or deliver many of the new products. Instead, they provide a platform on which customers can do so. Cocreation defies the conventional organizational logic of having to own and protect one's new goods and services, and calls for new skills and mind-sets to make it possible.[22]

Another new customer-driven approach is **collective customer commitment.**[23] Under this approach, companies systematically solicit new product ideas from customers and ask for purchase commitments *before* going into production. While this idea is not a new one— indeed, business-to-business marketers, real estate developers, and others have long done so—it helps avoid expensive failures by ensuring demand before large production investments are made. This approach is now being extended into consumer markets, aided by the highly efficient customer engagement possibilities that the internet brings (see Exhibit 10.9).

## Exhibit 10.9    THREADLESS TURNS ONLINE MARKETING RESEARCH INTO REVENUE

Each and every week, customers evaluate more than 400 new submissions for T-shirt designs on the website of Chicago-based Threadless .com. In 2000, Threadless founders Jake Nickeli and Jacob DeHart figured the best way to build their business was to let customers not only design their T-shirts, but evaluate which were the best designs. The Threadless community includes ordinary consumers and hobbyists, as well as hot-shot graphic designers, whose evaluations determine which styles Threadless produces and which it does not. Customers don't just say which designs they like, however. They indicate their willingness to buy.

Threadless examines the data, considers any possible legal issues and how the new styles fit into the overall Threadless product line, and produces a few or as many as a dozen new designs each week, putting the name of the winning designs' creators on the labels and giving each of them a $2,000 reward plus a $500 gift certificate. To date, Threadless has paid out more than $1 million to its creators. It's a way to get winning design solutions at minimal cost, and a great way to build an engaged customer community as well.

*Source:* Susumu Ogawa and Frank T. Piller, "Reducing the Risks of New Product Development," *MIT Sloan Management Review,* Winter 2006, pp. 65–71.

For many companies, though, product innovation still happens largely internally, where customer insight is developed concurrently with product and process engineering to speed new products to market. Empirical research indicates that the way product development is best organized depends, in part, on the nature of the product under development. For line extensions and product improvements, where the degree of innovation is minor, relatively bureaucratic procedures appear to be better at getting products to market quickly. For more radical innovations, cross-functional teams are more efficient, both for **time-to-market** and cost considerations.[24]

A reduction in time to market can have a strong, positive effect on the product's profitability, especially in fast-cycle industries in which product life cycles are short. Improved profitability results from extending the product's sales life, creating opportunities to charge a premium price, providing for development and manufacturing cost advantages, and reducing the risks of a marketing shift since the development process started.

## Key Decisions in the New Product Development Process

Given the importance of new products—whether goods or services—in long-term firm success, much attention has been paid to the generation and assessment of new product ideas and to improving the process of getting new products to market.[25] One result of this attention has been the development of so-called **stage-gate systems** for managing new product development from **idea generation** to **product launch**.[26] A diagram of the stage-gate system is shown in Exhibit 10.10.

In a stage-gate system, an idea for a new product must pass through a series of gates at each of which its merit is examined before it is allowed to continue its journey toward market introduction. Between each gate, various analyses and development activities are conducted. The point is to "kill" ideas that lack strategic or market potential early in the process, before significant resources are spent on these ideas, as well as to pave the way for high-potential ideas so that they not only get to

**STRATEGIC ISSUE**

*The point is to "kill" ideas that lack strategic or market potential early in the process, before significant resources are spent on these ideas, as well as to pave the way for high-potential ideas.*

## Exhibit 10.10

STAGE-GATE NEW PRODUCT DEVELOPMENT SYSTEM

*Source:* Paul O'Connor, "Implementing a Stage-Gate Process: A Multi-Company Perspective," *Journal of Product Innovation Management* 11 (1994), p. 185. Blackwell Publishers.

market quickly but also have the "right" attributes to enhance their likelihood of market success. Simple new products, such as line extensions or product improvements, sometimes skip stages in the process, going directly from idea status to Stage 2, 3, or 4, for example. More innovative products whose market acceptance is unclear or whose product performance is uncertain typically must pass muster at each gate. Similarly, stages in the process are sometimes conducted concurrently, and backward loops in the process are common when the results of the analysis at a given stage do not support passing the product to the next stage.

**Managing the Stage-Gate Process**    Though the stage-gate process may appear lengthy and tedious, a principal goal of using such processes is to improve the speed with which a firm brings new products to market. This is accomplished in three principal ways. First, clear milestones are set at each gate to encourage new product teams to move quickly through the necessary activities to get through the next gate. Second, resource commitments are made along the way to ensure that inadequate resources, whether human or financial, do not delay promising products. Third, concurrent engineering is employed, whereby both market analyses and technical progress proceed concurrently. Previously, it was common for R&D to develop a product and "throw it over the wall" to marketing, who were asked to sell it. Marketing would then throw it back, asking for changes to make the product more acceptable to customers, and so on, through several iterations. By the time the tossing ended, a competitor's product may have won the race to market. Thus, here, as with most other business processes, implementation is critical. In some fast-moving markets, firms seek **first-mover advantage,** whereby theirs is the first entrant in a new product category. There is much talk, especially in high technology and internet marketing circles, about the importance of first-mover advantage. As is discussed in Exhibit 10.11, however, bringing the *right* product to market and updating it to keep it ahead of competing products are far more important in the long run than being first to market, especially with a product that does not offer what customers really want or need.

## Exhibit 10.11  BEST BEATS FIRST

There is much talk in business school classrooms and in the pages of business plans about first mover advantage. Indeed, many aspiring entrepreneurs are so enamored with being first to market that they seem to feel that little else matters.

But how important is first-mover advantage? A candid look at business history in the 20th century indicates that being *best* in market is far more important than being *first* to market, notwithstanding the benefits that being first can bring to early leaders in any category. A 1999 review by Lambert and Slater of recent studies of first-mover advantage, as well as an abundance of anecdotal evidence [see Markides and Geroski (2004) and Collins (2000)], makes it clear that first movers are often successfully leapfrogged by later competitors, who benefit from the ability to observe and improve upon the market offerings of the early entrants. Where is VisiCalc, the first personal computer spreadsheet today? Where is Osborne, the first portable personal computer? Why are Palm Pilots now ubiquitous, while Apple's earlier Newton failed? Thus, while faster time to market can provide a competitive edge, entrants who fail to introduce the right product or improve on their early offerings risk being overtaken by followers whose offerings are more attractive. As Collins observes, being best is typically far better than being first.

*Sources: Constantinos C. Markides and Paul A. Geroski, Fast Second: How Smart Companies Bypass Radical Innovation to Enter and Dominate New Markets, Jossey-Bass: 2004; Jim Collins, "Best Beats First," Inc., August 2000, pp. 48–51; Denis Lambert and Stanley F. Slater, "First, Fast, and On Time: The Path to Success. Or Is It?" Journal of Product Innovation Management, 1999, pp. 427–38.*

**Deciding Who Staffs the Gates, and How Many Gates**   In most companies or business units using stage-gate systems, a cross-disciplinary team is appointed to staff the gates. As new product ideas pass through the process, this team considers market, technical, and manufacturing or service deliverability criteria in deciding which ideas should pass through to the next stage. At minimum, marketing, R&D, and production perspectives are necessary, as is the presence of someone having the clout to commit resources needed for further development. One study showed that selecting gatekeepers who score high on measures of creativity, such as the MBTI® Creativity Index, enhances both the speed and productivity of the new product development process.[27]

The number of gates employed in the process varies in different firms, as some steps shown in Exhibit 10.10 can be combined or broken into additional steps.

**Gate 1: Idea Generation and Initial Screening Decisions**   To have an effective new product strategy, a firm needs to establish objectives for its new product effort. In what customer markets does it wish to grow? What capabilities does it have? What product lines should be expanded? In a large multidivisional firm, which divisions should get greater R&D and new product funds? These decisions, which were addressed from a strategic perspective in Chapter 9, provide guidance for idea generation. Typically, a substantial number of new product ideas must be generated to get one successful product. Ideas for new products can come from customers, as we have seen earlier in this chapter; from the company's own staff, R&D people, the salesforce, product managers, marketing researchers; from members of its distribution channels; even from competitors. Whatever the source, at Gate 1 an initial screening is made to determine the idea's **strategic fit.** Does the idea align with the company's mission, does it take advantage of or strengthen its competencies, and are the resources needed to develop and market the product available? If the answer to any of these questions is no, the idea will likely be rejected. Some ethical considerations in making these decisions are discussed in Ethical Perspective 10.1.

## ETHICAL PERSPECTIVE 10.1
### Issues in Idea Generation and Screening

Business is often criticized for excessive production of me-too products, which leads to waste in the economic system. This is a difficult criticism to refute except to note that under certain conditions the development of a me-too product is justified, such as when it can be produced at a lower price or made available to more people. Some consumers argue that business produces too many wasteful products. But what is such a product? Also, most companies don't create the desire for wasteful products; it already exists.

There is also reverse criticism that business fails to produce products that are needed, such as products for people with unusual physical attributes (too tall, too short). In the medical field the development of new drugs is inhibited by risk (vaccines for children) and the uneconomic size of the market. In the latter case, the U.S. government provides federal funds for the development and marketing of so-called *orphan drugs* having only a very limited application.

It seems clear that sellers need to design safety into their products, but to what extent? Often consumers are not willing to pay the price of the added safety, as was initially the case with flame-resistant children's pajamas and auto seat belts. Both were finally mandated by the federal government. How a product is positioned and communicated affects how a product is used and, thus, can relate to safety (car acceleration and braking power). And what should a

company do when one of its products is designed for an innocent use but contributes to violence, like a high-powered toy water gun that can shoot a variety of liquids, some not so pleasant to the person on the receiving end?

In recent years societies around the world have become increasingly concerned about the impact of products and their packaging on the environment. There are several ways in which both new and old products can harm the environment—through the use of destructive raw materials (asbestos and lead), the use of a manufacturing process that pollutes (use of chemicals in the production of paper), the use of the final product (automobiles and air pollution), and the disposal of the used product (tires, motor oil, beverage containers).

Firms vary in their response to the ecological problem. Some largely ignore the problem, while others go so far as to disinvest in businesses that may harm the environment. Since being ethically right is not always the most profitable position, firms face the question of how best to trade off the environmental benefits versus profits. Small businesses (some of which account for considerable pollution) in particular are often hard pressed to take even a reasonable environmental point of view because of their lack of funds and technological know-how.

*Source:* Philip R. Cateora, *International Marketing*, 7th ed. (Burr Ridge, IL: Richard D. Irwin, 1990), pp. 149–54.

**Gate 2: Secondary Screening Decisions**    In Stage 1, prior to reaching Gate 2, managers are typically asked to undertake preliminary assessments of the idea's technical and market feasibility. First, can the product be developed and delivered? For a high-technology product, will the technology pan out? Second, how large is the market, and what is the estimated market potential for the proposed product? Will customers like it? This screening is typically based largely or entirely on secondary data and on the market and technical know-how resident in the company. The tools presented in Chapter 6 for estimating market potential are useful at this stage. A "classic" qualitative scoring model used by some companies at Gate 2 is shown in Exhibit 10.12.

## STRATEGIC ISSUE

*To invest new product development resources wisely, it is necessary to "kill" weak ideas at Gate 2, because significant resources in marketing research and in product development are likely to be incurred for products that pass this gate.*

To invest new product development resources wisely, it is necessary to "kill" weak ideas at Gate 2, because significant resources in marketing research and in product development are likely to be incurred for products that pass this gate. Thus, a weak screening process can waste resources on obvious losers or misfits and can lead to a creeping commitment to the wrong projects. An overly rigid process, on the other hand, can lead to lost opportunities.

# Exhibit 10.12

NEW PRODUCT SCORING MODEL

| (1) | | (2) Very Good (10) | | (3) Good (8) | | (4) Average (6) | | (5) Poor (4) | | (6) Very Poor (2) | | (8) | (9) |
|---|---|---|---|---|---|---|---|---|---|---|---|---|---|
| Subfactor | Subfactor weight | EP | EV | EP | EV | EP | EV | EP | EV | EP | EV | Total EV | Subfactor evaluation |
| Product superiority | 1.0 | 0.1 | 1.0 | 0.2 | 1.6 | 0.5 | 3.0 | 0.2 | 0.8 | — | | 6.4 | 6.4 |
| Unique features for users | 1.0 | 0.1 | 1.0 | 0.2 | 1.6 | 0.4 | 2.4 | 0.2 | 0.8 | 0.1 | 0.2 | 6.0 | 6.0 |
| Reduce customers' costs | 3.0 | 0.3 | 3.0 | 0.4 | 3.2 | 0.2 | 1.2 | 0.1 | 0.4 | — | | 7.8 | 23.4 |
| Higher quality than competitors | 1.0 | 0.1 | 1.0 | 0.2 | 1.6 | 0.5 | 3.0 | 0.2 | 0.8 | — | | 6.4 | 6.4 |
| Does unique task for user | 2.0 | 0.5 | 5.0 | 0.4 | 3.2 | 0.1 | 0.6 | — | — | — | | 8.8 | 17.6 |
| Priced lower than competing products | 2.0 | — | | 0.2 | 1.6 | 0.5 | 3.0 | 0.3 | 1.2 | — | | 5.8 | 11.6 |
| | 10.0 | | | | | | | | | | Total value of factor | | 71.4 |

Note: EP = estimated probability as judged by management. EV = expected value, computed by multiplying the rating's numerical value by the estimated probability.

**Gate 3: Decisions on the Business Case**   If an idea successfully passes the tests at Gate 2, a more detailed investigation, the subject of Stage 2, is made into the market potential for the proposed product. Such an investigation includes a comprehensive customer, market, and competitive analysis using the tools and analytical frameworks provided in Chapters 3 through 6. Primary research is customarily done at this stage. Thus, some resources are now invested in research, and development of product prototypes is sometimes done to support these research efforts. For many technology-based products, development before this point has likely been limited to basic research, and actual development of a truly functional product has awaited confirmation of the business case. Decisions at Gate 3, while based on similar criteria as those at Gate 2, are based on greater depth of information and are the last chance to stop before proceeding with full-scale development of the product and of the marketing plan for introducing it.

**Gate 4: Postdevelopment Review Decisions**   During Stage 3, the technological development of the actual product design proceeds, and a marketing plan, including a total product/service offering (as we noted earlier in this chapter), is developed. A critical decision here is to settle on the product's design and its particular features.

An analysis of more than 200 new products revealed that product design was the most important single factor in their success for a number of reasons.[28] First, it can influence costs by its choice of materials and shapes, which strongly influence the manufacturing processes. Second, it can call favorable attention to the product in a crowded marketplace, as was the case with Swatch watches, which used a number of unusual forms to call attention to its line of watches. Third, it creates impressions concerning other product attributes. For example, the Apple iPhone had a simple compact form designed to emphasize that it was user-friendly. And fourth, product design enhances our lives by the satisfaction we derive from seeing and using beautiful artistic products.[29]

In addition to product design and specific product features, pricing and channels are determined at this stage, along with brand name, packaging, and a planned marketing communications program. Additional marketing research may be needed to complete this process. These technological and marketing activities proceed in tandem, with considerable communication along the way, so that the "over the wall" problem is avoided. There are two possible causes why a product would fail to pass Gate 4, as many do. The first is that stumbling blocks are encountered with the technology or product design or with the projected costs of the final version of the product, thereby calling into question whether the product will actually work as planned or whether it will provide target customers with good value for the money. The second is the discovery, during marketing planning, that market or competitive conditions that now prevail raise questions about the marketability of the product. The entry of an unforeseen competitor, for example, is often the cause for abandoning or delaying a previously attractive product idea at Gate 4. Thus, gatekeepers at Gate 4 must take a careful look at whether the product is likely to perform, whether the marketing plan is likely to lead to market acceptance for the product, and whether the degree of acceptance is sufficient to merit further development. Making a "no-go" decision at this point is often difficult, however, given the considerable momentum the product already enjoys within the company. Failing to do so, however, in the face of cautionary market or product evidence, is one reason that many new products fail.

### Gate 5: Precommercialization Business Analysis Decisions

Gate 5 is the last hurdle before the product is rolled out. To clear Gate 5, the product must often pass muster in a **test market,** in companies with budgets large enough to afford this step. Two major kinds of test markets are commonly used by large consumer products firms to prepare for Gate 5: field and laboratory test markets. Smaller firms, whose budgets may not allow for formal market tests, may simply begin marketing the product, assessing early results as they go. With the advent of the internet, some firms now turn the stage-gate process upside down and simply begin selling on the internet or in limited channels as a form of market learning quite different from traditional marketing research. We address a disciplined set of approaches for doing so later in this chapter.

In a **field test market,** the marketing plan for the product is typically implemented in a small geographical area to ensure that it will deliver the expected results. This test seeks to obtain an estimate of the sales that will be achieved once the product is rolled out into the broader market, given the planned marketing strategy and marketing budget.

In the past, the big food-, household-, and personal care–products companies typically used a sample composed of a few small cities as the test market—and did so for between 12 and 18 months. The cost of such research was often several million dollars. Increasingly such companies want faster and less-expensive ways of testing their products, and not only for cost reasons. More importantly, and unfortunately, field test markets give competitors the opportunity to evaluate the results, even to the point of introducing their own new products. In a classic case, General Mills was sufficiently impressed by a Procter & Gamble test market to quickly introduce its own version of the test product under the Betty Crocker brand name, which quickly became the best seller.[30] These concerns have led to increasing use of **laboratory test markets.**

In laboratory test markets, which are used most commonly for packaged consumer products, the procedure measures the process by which a consumer adopts a new product, consisting of three major steps: **awareness, trial,** and **repeat buying.**

In the lab procedure, respondents representative of the target audience see commercials about the new product imbedded in a TV program. Then they are given the option of buying such a product in a simulated store also stocked with competing brands. If they choose the test product, then researchers make follow-up interviews to determine the extent of satisfaction (including preference over their regular brand) and repurchase intentions. These tests have the advantage of relatively low costs ($60,000–$80,000) *and* confidentiality. Their biggest disadvantage is the small range of products that can be accommodated and that they provide little or no information about the difficulty of obtaining and maintaining distribution.

Marketing managers working toward Gate 5, or in entrepreneurial companies much earlier in the process, are faced with decisions about whether and how to use scarce resources for market testing, in order to reduce the risk of a possibly unsuccessful market launch. Decisions about whether to conduct a market test, and whether to do so in the field or in a laboratory, must consider the likelihood of competitive interference with a field test, competitors' ability to benefit themselves from such a test, and the company's willingness and ability to spend money on test marketing.

## Stage 5: Commercialization Decisions

At this point, the horse is "out of the barn," but key strategic decisions remain about how to roll out the product in hopes of winning competitive advantage. **Commercialization** requires considerable coordination between the various functional areas. Large sums may be required even if the new product is a brand extension. Because marketing is responsible for making the new product available, developing awareness of its unique properties, inducing trial, and fostering repeat purchases, its role is critical.

There are a number of different commercialization strategies. One is to forgo market testing and move directly to a rollout region by region or nationally from the outset. Such a strategy is used when there is little risk, as is usually the case with brand extensions and when copying a competitor's product that has experienced successful test marketing. For industrial products, the use of the internet and e-mail to contact large accounts facilitates and accelerates the introduction.

Another commercialization strategy involves using a different kind of test market—one that is not necessarily representative of the target audience. Some companies use a rollout test versus a more elaborate market test, provided the results from the market simulation studies are strongly positive. Thus, they launch their product in, say, 10 percent of the country and rely on fast sales results data to check how well the product is doing. As global consumer goods markets become more similar, more companies are testing in a few countries, then following with a global rollout. For example, after Colgate successfully launched a new shampoo in the Philippines, Australia, Mexico, and Hong Kong, it was rolled out in Europe, Asia, Latin America, and Africa.[31]

Choices among the above strategies are based on the trade-offs between risk, the need to cash-flow the introduction, and the speed with which competitors are likely to react, among other factors. We'll examine alternative marketing strategies for the commercialization of new products, and the market conditions where each makes most sense, in greater detail in Chapter 15.

# Limitations of Stage Gate Thinking and Processes

Stage-gate thinking is useful in companies of all ages and sizes. Even in new startups or in small or young companies whose resources—both human and financial—are limited, the simultaneous creativity and discipline entailed in stage-gate thinking can serve as a foundation for entrepreneurial initiative while balancing these factors with some measure of discipline. Such balance can help mitigate the risk of costly new product failures that could lead a precarious young company to bankruptcy.

On the other hand, critics of the overly restrictive role of planning—in both large and nascent companies alike—argue that most of the time, the best-laid plans do not typically predict how success is won (see Exhibit 10.13). More often, what eventually works is a product different than that which was initially proposed, sold to different consumers than originally intended, and used for something that its inventor had not even imagined. Who could possibly have imagined all the different ways in which personal computers, cell phones, the internet, and other technological innovations have changed people's behavior, even their lives?

Thus in their new book *Getting to Plan B,* John Mullins and Randy Komisar argue that a more open-minded, experimental, and data-driven approach to innovation—one fundamentally different from the more linear, traditional approaches like the stage-gate processes—is needed to maximize innovators' chances for success.[32]

## Exhibit 10.13    CAN BIG COMPANIES REALLY INNOVATE?

A growing chorus of entrepreneurially-inclined voices argues persuasively that for new products—or new companies—based on ideas where there is considerable uncertainty, the inherent assumption that the new product development process and its outcomes can be planned is dead wrong. Computer scientist Bill Joy, a co-founder of Sun Microsystems and now a venture capital investor, puts it even more bluntly. "Big companies almost never innovate." Joy argues that the main problem in most big companies is that they simply fail to undertake small, quirky, controversial projects that might fail, but also have the potential to grow.

Many entrepreneurs, on the other hand, are putting to use a new set of approaches to the innovation challenge based not on planning (After all, who can really plan how a genuine innovation will pan out?), but on rapid and low-cost experimentation. "Fail early and fail inexpensively" is their mantra. Sometimes dubbed the Lean Startup approach, it relies on a minimum viable product or prototype that's far less developed than what the innovator probably envisions, validated learning (from customers' actual feedback and purchases—or not), and rigorous measurement using actionable metrics. As the validated learning arrives from the marketplace through a series of build-measure-learn cycles, the idea is to change course—or "pivot" in the new entrepreneurial vernacular—and quickly adapt to what the market is saying.

By rigorously examining the untested assumptions—or "leaps of faith"—in entrepreneurs' initial plans, this process often mercifully kills the initial concept and results in better products that customers actually want to buy. Planning it is not. But disciplined it is. And effective, too.

*Source:* Bill Joy, "Large Problem: How Big Companies Can Innovate," *Fortune,* November 15, 2004, p. 214; John Mullins and Randy Komisar, *Getting to Plan B: Breaking Through to a Better Business Model,* Harvard Business Press: 2009; and Eric Reis, *The Lean Startup: How Today's Entrepreneurs Use Continuous Innovation to Create Radically Successful Businesses,* Crown Business: 2011.

# Product Decisions over the Product Life Cycle

While product decisions are perhaps most visible and dramatic at the time new products are introduced, what happens after the launch—sometimes many years thereafter—has substantial influence on a product's profitability over its lifetime. The **product life cycle** offers important insights into how decision making—for the product itself and for other elements of the marketing mix—is likely to evolve.

The product life cycle is concerned with the sales history of a product or product class. The concept holds that a product's sales change over time in a predictable way and that products go through a series of five distinct stages: introduction, growth, shakeout, maturity, and decline (see Exhibit 10.14). Each of these stages provides distinct opportunities and threats, thereby affecting the firm's strategy as well as its marketing programs. Despite the fact that many new products do not follow such a prescribed route because of premature failure, the concept is valuable in helping management look into the future and better anticipate what changes will need to be made in marketing programs.

At the beginning (the **introductory stage**), a new product's purchase is limited because members of the target market are insufficiently aware of its existence; also, the product often lacks easy availability. As more people learn about the product and it becomes more readily available, sales increase at a progressively faster rate (the **growth stage**). Growth slows as the number of buyers nears the maximum and repeat sales become increasingly more important than trial sales. As the number of both buyers and their purchases stabilizes, growth becomes largely a function of population growth in the target market. At the end of the growth period—just before maturity—the **shakeout** or **competitive turbulence stage** occurs. This is characterized by a decreasing growth rate that results in strong

# EXHIBIT 10.14

GENERALIZED PRODUCT LIFE CYCLE

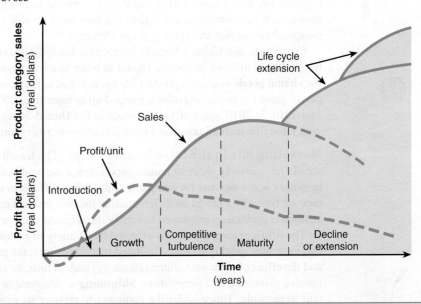

*Source:* From George S. Day, *Analysis for Strategic Marketing Decisions,* © 1986 South-Western, a part of Carnegie Learning, Inc. Reproduced by permission. *www.cengage.com/permissions.*

price competition, forcing some products or firms to exit or sell out. The **mature stage** is reached when the net adoption rate holds steady—that is, when adopters approximate dropouts. When the latter begin to exceed new first-time users, the sales rate declines and the product is said to have reached its final or **decline stage.**

Many products do not go through the product life cycle curve shown in Exhibit 10.14 because a high percentage are aborted after an unsatisfactory introductory period. Other products seemingly never die (Scotch whiskey, TVs, automobiles). The shape of the life cycle curve varies considerably between and within industries but is typically described as "S"-shaped.

**Fads,** such as some trendy online ventures, sometimes enter suddenly, experience strong and quick enthusiasm, peak early, and enter the decline stage shortly thereafter. Thus, even when successful, their life cycle is unusually short and is typically depicted in the form of an inverted V.

## Market and Competitive Implications of Product Life Cycle Stages

The various stages of the product life cycle present different opportunities and threats to the firm. By understanding the characteristics of the major stages, a firm can do a better job of setting forth its objectives and formulating its strategies as well as developing its action plans, as briefly summarized in Exhibit 10.15.

**Introductory Stage**    There is a vast difference between pioneering a product class and a product type. The former is more difficult, time-consuming, expensive, and risky, as, for example, when the telephone was introduced versus the introduction of the cellular phone. The introductory period, in particular, is apt to be long, even for relatively simple product classes such as packaged food products. Because product type and subtype entries usually emerge during the late-growth and maturity stages of the product class, they have shorter introductory and growth periods. Once the product is launched, the firm's goal should be to move it through the introductory stage as quickly as possible. Research, engineering, and manufacturing capacity are critical to ensure the availability of quality products. Where service is important, the firm must be able to provide it promptly (as in postpurchase service and spare parts availability).

Companies like China's Shanda Interactive, Europe's Playfish, and California's Zynga have taken in millions in venture capital in order to move through the introductory stage of the **virtual goods** industry's product life cycle as fast as they can. Zynga, maker of the multiplayer game Farmville and others, ramped up to more than 240 million users per month by mid-2010. In 2010, sales of virtual goods in the United States alone—like a plum tree for your Farmville orchard priced at a mere 25 cents—were expected to double to $1.6 billion.[33]

**Marketing Mix in the Introductory Stage**    The length of the *product line* typically should be relatively short to reduce production costs and hold down inventories, though inventory is not an issue for companies like Zynga. Efforts to establish competitive advantage are typically focused on differentiating the new product or product line from solutions customers previously employed to satisfy the targeted want or need.

The firm's *pricing* is strongly affected by a variety of factors: the product's value to the end user; how quickly it can be imitated by competitors; the presence of close substitutes; and the effect of price on volume (elasticity) and, in turn, on costs. Basic strategic choices involve skimming and penetration. **Skimming** is designed to obtain as much margin per unit as possible. This enables the company to recover its new product investments more quickly. Such a strategy is particularly appropriate in niche markets and where consumers are relatively insensitive to price, as was the case in the sale of cellular phones to business

# Exhibit 10.15

EXPECTED CHARACTERISTICS AND RESPONSES BY MAJOR LIFE CYCLE STAGES

| STAGES IN PRODUCT LIFE CYCLE | | | | | |
|---|---|---|---|---|---|
| **Stage characteristics** | **Introduction** | **Growth** | **Shakeout** | **Mature** | **Decline** |
| Market growth rate (constant dollars) | Moderate | High | Leveling off | Insignificant | Negative |
| Technical change in product design | High | Moderate | Limited | Limited | Limited |
| Segments | Few | Few to many | Few to many | Few to many | Few |
| Competitors | Few | Many | Decreasing | Limited | Few |
| Profitability | Negative | High | Low | High for market-share leaders | Low |
| **Firm's normative responses** | | | | | |
| Strategic marketing objectives | Stimulate primary demand | Build share | Build share | Hold share | Harvest |
| Product | Quality | Continue quality improvements | Rationalize | Concentrate on features | No change |
| Product line | Narrow | Broad | Rationalize | Hold length of line | Reduce length of line |
| Price | Skimming or penetration | Reduce | Reduce | Hold or reduce selectively | Reduce |
| Channels | Selective | Intensive | Intensive | Intensive | Selective |
| Communications | High | High | High | High to declining | Reduce |

executives early in the product life cycle. **Penetration pricing** enables the firm to strive for quick market development and makes sense when there is a steep experience curve, which lowers costs; a large market; and strong potential competition.

The importance of *distribution* and channel intermediaries varies substantially from consumer to industrial goods. The latter are often sold direct, but with few exceptions consumer goods use one or more channel intermediaries. Product availability is particularly important with consumer goods because of the large amounts spent on promotion to make consumers aware of the product and to induce usage. Distribution is easier if the company uses the same channels for its other products and has a successful track record with new product introductions.

During the introductory period, *promotion* expenditures involving advertising and the salesforce are typically a high percentage of sales, especially for a mass-market, small-value product. Many dot-coms spent themselves to failure for promotional purposes. For industrial goods, personal selling costs are apt to be much higher than advertising costs.

The communications task at the outset is to build awareness of the new product's uniqueness, which is typically an expensive undertaking. Further, the promotional expenditures (such as in-store displays, premiums, coupons, samples, and off-list pricing) required to obtain product availability and trial can be substantial. For industrial products, the time required to develop awareness of the product's uniqueness is often extensive due to the number of people in the buying center and the complexity of the buying systems.

Not all consumer packaged goods companies, however, especially cash-strapped entre-preneurial ventures, accept the conventional wisdom about the high cost of building aware-ness and obtaining retail distribution. Companies like Nantucket Nectars in the United States and Innocent Drinks in the United Kingdom used quirky public relations efforts and a patient buildup of distribution in relatively small-scale distribution channels to build brand awareness before seeking distribution in supermarkets and other mass-market out-lets. By doing so, they were able—over time—to create sufficient customer demand that the big chains had little choice but to carry their products.

Other young companies use a deep understanding of key channel partners to win wide-spread distribution much earlier and less expensively than would otherwise be likely. Method, an innovative marketer of household cleaning products, used superior package design developed by high-profile designers, upscale positioning and pricing, and effective public relations to convince Target, the U.S. discount chain, that Method's products could help Target differentiate its offering from that of Walmart. Method went from start-up to $100 million in retail sales in six short years using this strategy.[34]

### Growth Stage

This stage starts with a sharp increase in sales. Important product improvements continue in the growth stage, but at a slower rate. Increased brand differen-tiation occurs primarily in product features. The product line expands to attract new seg-ments, offering an array of prices and different product features.

Zipcar, a pioneer in the fast-growing car-sharing industry, has put its pedal to the metal in an effort to stay ahead of car-rental players like Hertz, which has awakened to the poten-tial of Zipcar's model. Zipcar customers no longer need to own cars, saving an average of $600 per month, according to Zipcar's research. Instead, they grab a nearby Zipcar when they need one, paying by the hour, and saving the planet as well, since people drive only when they really need to. To maintain its lead, Zipcar has entered partnerships with employers (8,500 of them, including Gap, Nike and Lockheed Martin) and city govern-ments with large fleets (Washington, D.C. expected to save $1 million by switching to Zipcar in 2009), and it has acquired similar competitors to reach scale more quickly.[35]

During the latter part of the growth stage, the firm—especially the dominant one—makes every effort to extend growth by adding new segments, lowering costs, improv-ing product quality, adding new features, and trying to increase product usage among present users.

**Marketing Mix Changes** While the *product line* generally expands to attract new market segments, the quest for competitive advantage shifts to differentiation from other entrants in the product class. *Prices* tend to decline during the growth period and price dif-ferences between brands decrease. The extent of the decline depends on cost-volume rela-tionships, industry concentration, and the volatility of raw material costs. If growth is so strong that it outpaces supply, there is little or no pressure on price; indeed, it may enable sellers to charge premium prices.

During this period sellers of both industrial and consumer goods strive to build a chan-nel or a direct-sales system that provides maximum product availability and service at the lowest cost. If this can be accomplished, rivals are placed at a disadvantage, even to the extent of being excluded from some markets. This is particularly the case with some con-sumer goods for which the number of intermediaries in any one market is limited. A brand must attain some degree of distribution success in advance of the mature stage, because channel members then tend to disinvest in less-successful brands.

*Promotion costs* (advertising and personal selling) become more concerned with building demand for a company's brand (selective demand) than demand for the product class or type (primary demand). Firms strive to build favorable attitudes toward their brand on the basis of its unique features. Communications are also used to cultivate new segments. Even though promotion costs remain high, they typically decline as a percentage of sales.

### Shakeout Stage

The advent of this period is signaled by a drop in the overall growth rate and is typically marked by substantial price cuts. As weaker competitors exit the market, the stronger firms gain share. Thus, major changes in the industry's competitive structure occur. In France, mobile telephone users are eagerly anticipating the entry of Free, an upstart company which, having revolutionized France's internet industry has set its sights on the mobile telecom giants (see Exhibit 10.16).

During shakeout the firm must *rationalize* its product line by eliminating weaker items, emphasize creative promotional pricing, and strengthen its channel relationships. To a considerable extent, what happens during the shakeout is predetermined by how well each brand has been positioned in relation to its targeted segments, its distribution system, and its relative costs per unit.

### Marketing Mix Changes

In addition to entering into more direct *price* competition, firms make every effort to maintain and enhance their *distribution* system. Channel intermediaries use this downturn in industry sales to reduce the number of products carried and, hence, their inventories. Weaker competitors often have to offer their intermediaries substantial inducements to continue stocking all or even part of their line. *Promotion costs may increase*, particularly for low-share firms, as companies attempt to maintain their distribution by offering customers buying incentives.

### Mature Stage

When sales plateau, the product enters the mature stage, which typically lasts for some time. Most products now on the market are in the mature stage. Stability in terms of demand, technology, and competition characterizes maturity. Strong market leaders, because of lower per-unit costs and the lack of any need to expand their facilities, should enjoy strong profits and high positive cash flows. But there is always the possibility of changes in the marketplace, the product, the channels of distribution, the production

---

## Exhibit 10.16   A Maverick Entrepreneur Takes on the French Telecom Giants

As a teenager, Xavier Niel started a business that provided weather forecasts, stock quotes, matchmaking services and more on Minitel, a French precursor of what we know as the internet today. After a detour into the sex shop business, Niel returned to his digital roots, setting up Free in 1999. Free introduced Europe's first triple-play offer of broadband, free nationwide phone calls, and 100 TV channels for a mere €29.99 per month, when market leader Wanadoo was charging €15 for broadband alone.

Fast forward to 2009. Free's parent company, Iliad, where Niel is deputy chairman and director of strategy, won France's fourth mobile license for the bargain price of €240 million in an auction in which there were no other bidders, after convincing the government to return the auction at a reduced opening price. But is it wise for Iliad to take on France's well-entrenched incumbents head-on? "This is the instincts of Xavier Niel against the rest of the world," says Francois Godard, an analyst at Enders Analysis. "I think he has a sixth sense—like Steve Jobs, he has a flair, an understanding that at the right moment there is an opportunity. He sees mobile as expensive in France, and he's right."

Is a telecom shakeout looming when Free launches its 3G network in 2012? Whatever happens, French mobile users are likely to be the winners.

*Source:* Ross Tieman, "Wired for Success," *Financial Times Boldness in Business*, March 17, 2011, pp. 40–43.

processes, and the nature and scope of competition. The longer the mature stage lasts, the greater the possibility of change. If the firm does not respond successfully to a change but its competitors do, then a change in industry structure may occur.

Carpigiani, a privately held Italian firm that has long dominated the market for small-batch machines that manufacture and dispense ice cream from posh gelato to creamy soft-serve, has deftly navigated changes in its mature market to win nearly a 50 percent global share, according to its managing director Gino Cocchi. Carpigiani machines at chains as varied as McDonald's, Pizza Hut, and the fast-growing Cold Stone Creamery specialty stores have kept millions of consumers not only licking their lips on warm summer days, but have made ice cream a year-round proposition. Carpigiani's strict adherence to quality and hygiene ensure that its ice cream and gelato is not only delicious, but safe to eat.[36]

**Marketing Mix Changes**  Because of technical maturity, the various brands in the marketplace become more similar; therefore, any significant breakthroughs by R&D or engineering that help to differentiate the product or redirect its cost can have a substantial payout. One option is to add value to the product that benefits the customer by improving the ease of use (voice-activated dialing with cellular phones), by incorporating labor-saving features, or by selling systems rather than single products (adding extended service contracts). Increasingly, *service* becomes a way of differentiating the offering. *Promotion* expenditures and *prices* tend to remain stable during the mature stage. But the nature of the former is apt to change; media advertising for consumer goods declines and in-store promotions, including price deals, increase. The price premium attainable by the high-quality producer tends to erode. The effect of experience on costs and prices becomes smaller and smaller. Competition may force prices down, especially when the leading competitors hold similar shares. For consumer goods, *distribution* and in-store displays (shelf facings) become increasingly important, as does effective cost management.

**Decline Stage**  Eventually most products enter the decline stage, which may be gradual (canned vegetables/hot cereals) or extremely fast (some prescription drugs). The sales pattern may be one of decline and then petrification as a small residual segment still clings to the use of the product (tooth powder versus toothpaste). Products enter this stage primarily because of superior substitutes (internet search over encyclopedias) or a shift in consumer tastes, values, and beliefs.

As sales decline, costs increase, and radical efforts are needed to reduce costs and the asset base. Even so, if exit barriers are low, many firms vacate the market, which increases the sales of remaining firms, thereby delaying their exit. Stronger firms may even prosper for a time. If the curve is a steep decline followed by a plateau, then some firms can adjust. If the firm is strong in some segments vacated by its competitors, then it may experience a sufficient increase in market share to compensate for loss of sales elsewhere.

**Marketing Mix Changes**  Marketing expenditures, especially those associated with *promotion,* usually decrease as a percentage of sales in the decline stage. *Prices* tend to remain stable if the rate of decline is slow, there are some enduring profitable segments and low exit barriers, customers are weak and fragmented, and there are few single-product competitors. Conversely, aggressive pricing is apt to occur when decline is fast and erratic, there are no strong unique segments, there are high exit barriers, a number of large single-product competitors are present, and customers have strong bargaining power. For consumer goods, marketing activity centers on *distribution*—persuading intermediaries to continue to stock the item even though they may not promote it. For industrial products the problem may center around maintaining the interest of the salesforce in selling the item.

# Strategic Implications of the Product Life Cycle

The product life cycle model is a framework that signals the occurrence of opportunities and threats in the marketplace and the industry, thereby helping the business better anticipate change in the product's strategic market objective, its strategy, and its marketing program. As Exhibit 10.17 indicates, there is a strong relationship between the market and industry characteristics of each stage, the entry's market share objectives, and the level of investment, which, in turn, strongly affect cash flow and profit.

**Introductory and Growth Stages**  Because the introduction of a new product often requires large investments, most firms sustain a rather sizable short-term loss. As the product moves into the growth stage, sales increase rapidly; hence, substantial investments continue. Profitability is depressed because facilities have to be built in advance to ensure supply. The firm with the largest share during this period should have the lowest per-unit costs due to scale and learning effects. If it chooses to decrease its real price proportionate to the decline in its costs, it dries up the investment incentives of would-be entrants and lower-share competitors. The innovating firm's share is likely to erode substantially during the growth stage. Nevertheless, it must still make large investments, for even though it is losing share, its sales are increasing. New entrants and low-share sellers are at a substantial disadvantage here. They must not only invest to accommodate market growth, but also to gain market share.

**Mature and Declining Stages**  As the product enters the mature stage, the larger-share sellers should be able to reap the benefits of their earlier investments. Given that the price is sufficient to keep the higher-cost sellers in business, that growth investments are no longer needed, and that most competitors may no longer be striving to gain share, the leader's profitability and positive cash flow can be substantial. But the leader needs to continue making investments to improve its product and to make its manufacturing, marketing, and physical logistics more efficient.

## Exhibit 10.17

RELATIONSHIP OF STRATEGIC MARKET POSITION OBJECTIVE, INVESTMENT LEVELS, PROFITS, AND CASH FLOW TO INDIVIDUAL STAGES IN THE PRODUCT LIFE CYCLE

### STAGES IN THE PRODUCT LIFE CYCLE

| Stage | Strategic market objective | Investments | Profits | Cash flow |
|---|---|---|---|---|
| Introduction | For both innovators and followers, accelerate overall market growth and product acceptance through awareness, trial, and product availability | Moderate to high for R&D, capacity, working capital, and marketing (sales and advertising) | Highly negative | Highly negative |
| Growth | Increase competitive position | High to very high | High | Negative |
| Shakeout | Improve/solidify competitive position | Moderate | Low to moderate | Low to moderate |
| Mature | Maintain position | Low | High | Moderate |

# Limitations of the Product Life Cycle Framework

The product life cycle model's major weakness lies in its normative approach to prescribing strategies based on assumptions about the features or characteristics of each stage. It fails to take into account that the product life cycle is, in reality, driven by market forces expressing the evolution of consumer preferences (the market), technology (the product), and competition (the supply side). Thus, whether for goods or services, there are no simple cookbook answers for what a brand's marketing strategy should look like at a given stage in its product life cycle. Careful and creative planning, combined with effective implementation, is what most often leads to winning marketing strategies and long-term success.

# TAKE-AWAYS

1. Decisions about product design—including product features, brand names, related services, and warranties, for both goods and services—are among the most critical elements in differentiating one's brand from others to achieve competitive advantage. Factors to consider in making product decisions are provided in this chapter.

2. While speed to market is important in today's fast-paced business climate, bringing the *right* products to market and keeping them current are far more important than seeking first-mover advantage for a product that customers don't want.

3. Decisions about the depth and breadth of product lines must be carefully considered in market segmentation terms. Product lines that are too long or too short can place the company at a competitive disadvantage.

4. Customer-driven innovation approaches like cocreation and collective customer commitment can reduce the likelihood of new product failure and create high levels of customer engagement.

5. *How* the new product development process is managed, from a process perspective, is as important as *what* product decisions are made. The stage-gate system can help companies strike a balance between entrepreneurial creativity and business discipline in their new product efforts.

6. Though new products constitute the lifeblood of long-term success for most firms, most new products fail! Thus, product decisions, in both content and process terms, are critical to the successful implementation of business strategies.

7. Regardless of the nature of the playing field, developing and regularly updating winning marketing strategies are important, too! In developing strategies to build and sustain competitive advantage, marketing decision makers are more likely to win the competitive war by adjusting their strategies as the markets and industries in which they compete evolve through the stages of the product life cycle. Specific tools and frameworks for managing this task are provided in the balance of this book.

**Self-diagnostic questions to test your ability to apply the analytical tools and concepts in this chapter to marketing decision making may be found at this book's website at www.mhhe.com/mullins8e.**

# ENDNOTES

1. Based on "What's Egg?" *ABA Banking Journal,* September 2002, p. 60; and "On Whose Face?" *Economist,* May 20, 2000, p. 31; and company reports on www.egg.com.

2. See Stephen L. Vargo and Robert F. Lusch, "Evolving to a New Dominant Logic for Marketing," *Journal of Marketing* 68 (January 2004), pp. 1–17, for a discussion of the ongoing shift in thinking from marketing as the exchange of goods to marketing as focused on service provision.

3. Amy Kazmin, "Farming for the Future," *Financial Times Boldness in Business,* March 17, 2011, pp. 30–35.

4. David A. Garvin, *Managing Quality: The Strategic and Competitive Edge,* Free Press, 1988.

5. Valarie A. Zeithaml, A. Parasuraman, and Leonard L. Berry, *Delivering Quality Service: Balancing Customer Perceptions and Expectations,* Free Press, 1990. World Trade Organization News, "World Trade Slows Sharply in 2001 amid the Uncertain International Situation," October 19, 2001, *http://www.wto.org/English/news_e/pres01)e/pr249_e.htm.*

6. Debora Viana Thompson, Rebecca W. Hamilton, and Roland Rust, "Feature Fatigue: When Product Capabilities Become Too Much of a Good Thing," *Journal of Marketing Research* 42 (November 2005), pp. 431–42.

7. John Helyar, "How Marketing Missteps Stalled TV Sales," *Bloomberg Businessweek* European Edition, January 24–30, 2011.

8. For more on such research approaches, see Leonard and Rayport, "Spark Innovation through Empathic Design." For an approach to discovering needs that customers are unlikely to easily articulate, see John W. Mullins, "Discovering Unk-Unks," *MIT Sloan Management Review,* Summer 2007, pp. 17–21.

9. See Al Ries and Laura Ries, *The 11 Immutable Laws of Internet Branding* (New York: HarperBusiness, 2000).

10. Lance Leuthesser, Chiranjier Kohli, and Rajneesh Suri, "2 + 2 = 5? A Framework for Using Co-Branding to Leverage a Brand," *Journal of Brand Management* 2 (September 2003), pp. 35–47.

11. Matthew Boyle, "The Ketchup King Prospers," *BusinessWeek* European Edition, September 8, 2008, p. 28.

12. Private Label Manufacturers Association, *http://www.plma.com;* and John Stanley, "Brands versus Private Labels," *http://retailindustry.about .com/library/UC/02/UC_stanley2.htm.*

13. Irene M. Kunil and Dean Foust, "They Just Don't Have a Clue How to Handle This," *BusinessWeek,* September 18, 2000, p. 43.

14. Nirmalya Kumar, "Kill a Brand, Keep a Customer," *Harvard Business Review,* December 2003, pp. 86–95.

15. Irene M. Kunii, "Japan's Quick Studies in Survival," *BusinessWeek Online,* November 18, 2002.

16. "Steve Jobs and the Tablet of Hope," *The Economist,* January 30, 2010, p. 79; "A Smashing Success," *The Economist,* September 18, 2010, p. 82.

17. See "Producer Power," *The Economist,* March 4, 1995, p. 70, for a discussion of two classics that throw light on the problem of product development. Both books conclude that "far from being a matter of luck and prayer, the ability to produce outstanding products can be planned and managed just like any other bit of corporate life," The two books—now classics—are *Product Development Challenge,* ed. Kim Clark and Steven Wheelwright, and *Product Juggernauts,* by Jean-Phillipe Dischamps and P. Ranganath Nayak.

18. See Alina B. Sorescu, Rajesh K. Chandy, and Jaideep Prabhu, "Sources and Financial Consequences of Radical Innovation: Insights from Pharmaceuticals," *Journal of Marketing* 67, October 2003, pp. 82–102; and Richard Leifer, Christopher M. McDermott, Gina Colarelli O'Connor, Robert W. Verizer, Jr., Lois S. Peters, and Mark Rice, *Radical Innovation: How Mature Companies Can Outsmart Upstarts* (Boston: Harvard Business School Press, 2000).

19. Susumu Ogawa and Frank T. Piller, "Reducing the Risks of New Product Development," *MIT Sloan Management Review,* Winter 2006, pp. 65–71.

20. Marc Gunther, "3M's Innovation Revival," *Fortune* European Edition, September 27, 2010; John Markoff, "Google at Wheel, with No Hands," *International Herald Tribune,* October 11, 2010, p. 1.

21. For a review of various approaches to customer-driven innovation, see Eric von Hippel, *Democratizing Innovation* (Cambridge, MA: MIT Press, 2005).

22. Geoff Colvin, "Here It Is. Now You Design It!" *Fortune* European Edition, May 26, 2008, p. 16.

23. Ogawa and Piller, "Reducing the Risks of New Product Development."

24. Eric M. Olson, Orville C. Walker, Jr., and Robert W. Rueckert, "Organizing for Effective New Product Development: The Moderating Role of Product Innovativeness," *Journal of Marketing,* January 1995, p. 48.

25. See Shona L. Brown and Kathleen M. Eisenhardt, "Product Development: Past Research, Present Findings, and Future Directions," *Academy of Management Review* 7/e, no. 2 (1995), pp. 343–78.

26. The stage-gate system is described in R. G. Cooper, "Stage-Gate System: A New Tool for Managing New Products," *Business Horizons,* May–June 1990, pp. 44–54. A useful guide for implementing such systems is Paul O'Connor, "Implementing a Stage-Gate Process: A Multi-Company Perspective," *Journal of Product Innovation Management* 11 (1994), pp. 183–200.

27. See Greg Stevens, James Burley, and Richard Devine, "Creativity + Business Discipline = Higher Profits Faster from New Product Development," *Journal of Product Innovation Management* 16 (1999), pp. 455–68.

28. Robert G. Cooper and Elko Kleinschmidt, "New Products: What Separates the Winners from the Losers," *Journal of Product Innovation Management,* September 1987, p. 169.

29. Peter H. Bloch, "Seeking the Ideal Form: Product Design and Consumer Response," *Journal of Marketing,* July 1995, pp. 16–18.

30. Christopher Poer, "Will It Sell in Podunk? Hard to Say," *BusinessWeek,* August 10, 1992, p. 46.

31. Ibid.

32. John Mullins and Randy Komisar, *Getting to Plan B: Breaking Through to a Better Business Model* (Boston: Harvard Business Press, 2009).

33. Ari Levy and Joseph Galante, "Who Wants to Buy a Digital Elephant?" *Bloomberg Businessweek* European Edition, March 8, 2010, pp. 64–65.

34. Laura Hemrika and Nicola Blue, "Method U.K. (A)" (London Business School, 2008).

35. Paul Keegan, "The Best New Idea in Business," *Fortune* European Edition, September 14, 2009, pp. 58–64.

36. ". . . and a Sweet Success," *The Economist,* August 18, 2007, pp. 55–56.

# CHAPTER ELEVEN

# Pricing Decisions

## Ryanair: Low Prices, High Profits— but Increasing Costs[1]

WHEN THE RYAN FAMILY LAUNCHED Ryanair as Europe's first low-fare, no-frills airline in 1985, travelers wondered how the firm would ever make money offering €99 fares from Dublin to London when the cheapest flights available on British Airways or Aer Lingus cost more than twice as much. But the Irish company has grown into one of Europe's largest and most profitable airlines with 7,000 employees and flying nearly one thousand different routes to 155 airports in 26 countries. Over the first decade of the 21st century, at a time when the global airline industry collectively lost nearly $50 billion, Ryanair earned healthy profits in 9 out of the 10 years; most recently making a net profit of €319 million on revenues of €2.9 billion in 2010.

From the beginning, the firm's executives have pursued a very straightforward corporate strategy. It focused exclusively on providing low-cost air transportation for consumers within the European Union, and it sought a competitive advantage by offering the lowest fares of any airline operating in Europe.

Of course, a low-price competitive strategy can be profitable only when the firm's costs are also low. Therefore, all of Ryanair's functional activities and operating policies are designed with efficiency in mind. For instance, the firm owns rather than leases its airplanes, and nearly all 232 of those planes are Boeing 737s, thereby allowing standardization of maintenance activities and parts inventories. The company also concentrates its flights

to and from underutilized regional airports such as Stansted outside of London and Charleroi south of Brussels. Such airports offer the company more favorable terms with respect to taxes, facilities fees, and ground-handling charges than more popular and congested airports closer to major cities. The lack of congestion helps reduce turnaround times and thereby lowers costs by increasing utilization rates for planes and flight crews. It also helps Ryanair achieve the best on-time record of any European airline, 89 percent.

The firm's operating efficiencies have helped it successfully implement its low-price competitive strategy and hold its average fare below €35; substantially lower than even easyJet's, its strongest low-price competitor. Unfortunately, many of Ryanair's cost savings come at the expense of customer comfort and convenience. Not only do customers have to find their way to and from small airports far from the big cities, they have to carry and stow their own bags and do without meals, drinks, and other in-flight services. And there is not much room for them to stretch out and relax during their flights since Ryanair carries 15 percent more seats per aircraft than traditional airlines. It is even difficult for customers to buy their tickets because the company pays no fees to computer reservation systems and no commissions to travel agents. Indeed, the company has instituted so many customer unfriendly policies in its relentless pursuit of efficiency—such as surcharges for such things as using its wheelchairs—that several newspapers, including *The Guardian,* have created reader competitions dedicated to describing Ryanair horror stories.

Advertising and promotion, however, are among the few areas where Ryanair has not tried to cut costs below its competitors. With the exception of the sales commissions mentioned above, the company's marketing costs are about the same per passenger–kilometer as those of more traditional airlines. Even the most frugal flyers would not seek out Ryanair's cheap fares without being aware—and being frequently reminded—that they exist. And the firm must also maintain an extensive website and call center to facilitate the direct sale of tickets.

While Ryanair's low-cost/low-price strategy has been very successful so far, there may be some turbulence in the company's future. For the past decade, the firm has relied on rapid growth, attained largely by adding new routes and more planes, to bring in new customers. But given that the company has adopted a more modest growth objective of 5 to 10 percent per year through 2015, the question is whether it can continue to generate enough repeat business from past customers to maintain its revenue stream and profitability. While there is clearly a sizable segment of customers who are willing to sacrifice comfort and convenience for low fares, how large is that segment across the various countries that Ryanair serves, and how much comfort and convenience are those consumers willing to give up? While Ryanair's cost structure should enable it to make money at lower fares than the major airlines can match, some consumers may see those low fares as a poor value since they have to schlep their own bags and land at remote airports. And the number of such convenience-oriented consumers may increase as the European economies get stronger.

On the other hand, the double whammy of high fuel prices and slow economic growth have forced the full-service airlines to cut expensive customer services, but without being able to match Ryanair's low costs and cheap fares. In order to survive, those carriers are cutting flights to smaller cities, charging extra for baggage and snacks, and reducing the seats available for frequent flyers. With competition like that, maybe Ryanair's low-cost, no-frills flights aren't such a lousy value after all.

# Marketing Challenges Addressed in Chapter 11

Pricing is an area where managers "feel the most pressure to perform and the least certain that they are doing a good job. The pressure is intensified because, for the most part, managers believe that they don't have much control over price. It is dictated by [the firm's costs and by forces in] the market."[2] And those forces have increased in recent years. The maturing of many basic industries, slower growth, improved productivity, the growing power of retailers and their private labels, the increased aggressiveness of low-cost global competitors such as Ryanair, and the growing ability of customers to compare suppliers' prices on the internet have made many markets more price competitive.

The perception that price decisions are dictated by factors beyond the marketer's control, however, is a dangerous one. As we shall see later in this chapter, many firms base their pricing decisions largely on what is necessary to recover their costs or match competitors. For instance, a company may try to determine the costs of making a product or delivering a service and then add a standard markup to achieve a target return on investment. Such an approach can be justified given that firms cannot price their products or services below cost, at least not for long.

The danger is that prices set solely on the basis of cost or competitive considerations may not reflect **customer value:** the customer's perception of what the product or service is really worth. The price may be higher than the customer is willing to pay, resulting in a loss of potential sales and market share. Alternatively, the price may be much lower than customers think the product is worth, resulting in low margins and the sacrifice of potential profits. While pricing a product below its perceived value may delight customers and stimulate short-term demand, it may also depress the earnings the firm needs to compensate its employees, fund capital investments, and pay for the product development and other marketing activities necessary for long-term growth. Even small mistakes in this direction can have major implications for the firm. For example, for a company with 8 percent profit margins, a 1 percent improvement in price realization would boost the firm's margin dollars by 12.5 percent.[3]

The critical question addressed in this chapter is, How can a marketer determine a price that captures a fair share of the value customers receive from a product or service without violating the constraints imposed by its strategic objectives, cost structure, and competitive environment? To answer that question, the first part of this chapter describes a price-setting process that begins by considering a variety of strategic, market demand, cost, and competitive factors. It then discusses methods that different firms use to set a price level, with emphasis on methods geared to reflecting the product's value as perceived by customers in the target market.

Determining an appropriate price level for a product or service is complicated, and most firms do not charge the same list price to every customer all the time. Instead, they develop a **price structure** that establishes guidelines for adapting the price to variations in costs and demand across different markets. Consequently, the last half of this chapter examines some price adjustments marketers often make to accommodate differences across (1) geographic territories, (2) national boundaries, (3) levels of the distribution channel, (4) types of distribution channels, especially the internet, (5) items within the product line, and (6) customer segments.

## A Process for Making Pricing Decisions

A manager's freedom to select a price for a given good or service is constrained by several factors. First, the firm's costs determine the floor of the range of feasible prices—at least longer term. At the other extreme, the price sensitivity of demand for the product determines the ceiling of the range of acceptable prices. Beyond some price level, most potential customers seek less costly substitutes, such as private labels, or do without the good or service.

Where should managers set a product's price within the range of feasible prices? There are a number of ways to calculate a price,[4] but whichever one is used should consider situational factors. Such factors include (1) the business strategy and the other components of the marketing mix with which it must be compatible, (2) the extent to which the product is perceived to differ from competitive offerings in quality or level of customer service, (3) competitors' costs and prices, and (4) the availability and prices of possible substitutes.

Given the variety of factors to consider when setting a price, the following paragraphs describe, and Exhibit 11.1 diagrams, a step-by-step procedure for managers to follow. This process is particularly appropriate for first-time pricing decisions, as when a firm introduces a new product or enters a bid for nonroutine contract work. It includes several steps involving detailed analyses of demand, costs, and the competition. First, however,

## Exhibit 11.1

PRICE-SETTING DECISION PROCESS

**Influences and constraints:**
- SBU and marketing strategies
- Target market characteristics
- Product characteristics
- Competitor characteristics
- Company strengths and weaknesses
- Environmental influences
  Economic trends
  Legal restrictions

- Set strategic pricing objective
- Estimate demand, price elasticity of demand, and perceived value
- Determine costs and their relationship to volume
- Examine competitors' prices and costs
- Select a method for calculating price
- Set a price level
- Adapt price structure to meet variations in demand and cost across geographic territories, market segments, sales channels (e.g., the internet), etc.

managers must establish a pricing objective consistent with the firm's business and marketing strategies.

# Strategic Pricing Objectives

The strategic pricing objective should reflect what the firm hopes to accomplish with the product in its target market. When the business strategy, the target market, and the positioning strategy for the product are all clearly defined, then formulating objectives and policies for the marketing program elements, including price, can be relatively simple. For instance, Ryanair's business strategy of being the lowest-cost competitor in Europe makes the most appropriate pricing objectives and policies rather obvious.

We examine marketing objectives for different market and competitive situations, and their implications for the marketing mix components, in more detail in Chapters 15 and 16. But to clarify the role of price in different marketing programs, we discuss some strategic pricing objectives next and summarize them in Exhibit 11.2. The exhibit also suggests the conditions under which each objective is appropriate and the implications for choosing a price level within the range of feasible prices.

## Exhibit 11.2

STRATEGIC PRICING OBJECTIVES

| Objective | Conditions where most appropriate | Implications for relative price level |
|---|---|---|
| Maximize sales growth and penetration | Product-market is in introductory or growth stage of life cycle; firm is early entrant; target customers are sensitive to price; firm has low-cost position and is pursuing a low-cost business strategy; firm can gain experience-curve effects with increasing volume; low price may preempt potential competitors. | Set relatively low price—slightly above costs; penetration pricing policy aimed at winning new customers, expanding realized demand, and capturing as large a market share as possible. |
| Maintain quality or service differentiation | Product-market is in growth or maturity stage of life cycle; firm's offering is perceived to have a quality or service advantage over competitive offerings; firm does extensive advertising to maintain the product's quality image; firm has high costs; firm is pursuing differentiated defender strategy; target customers are relatively insensitive to price. | Set price high relative to competitors to cover high production, distribution, and advertising costs; price high to reinforce prestige image. |
| Maximize current profit | | |
| • Skimming | Product-market is in introductory or early growth stage of life cycle; firm is the first entrant; firm is pursuing a prospector strategy; firm has limited capacity; advanced technology or other barriers prevent immediate entry by competitors. | Set price very high to appeal to only the most price-insensitive customer segment; as market matures and competitors enter, firm can (a) reduce price to attract new segments, or (b) withdraw from the product-market. |
| • Harvesting | Product-market is in late maturity or decline stage of life cycle; firm is pursuing differentiated defender strategy; there is no basis (e.g., product improvements, increased promotion) to sustain product demand or competitive position into the future; product is cash cow funding growth in other product-markets. | Set price to maintain margins and maximize profit or return on investment even though some customers may switch to competitive brands or substitutes. |
| Survival | Firm's product has a weak competitive position, but major shortcomings are correctable; firm needs to buy time and maintain cash flow to make necessary adjustments; product-market is still in growth or maturity stage of life cycle. | Reduce price, perhaps even below total cost, as long as price covers variable costs and makes a contribution to overhead. |
| Social objectives | Firm is a not-for-profit organization; costs are subsidized in part by tax revenues or contributions; one or more segments need the good or service but are unwilling or unable to pay full costs. | Set low price, perhaps below total cost for some segments, to stimulate or subsidize demand. |

**Maximize Sales Growth**    When a firm is an early entrant into a new product-market with the potential for substantial growth, its objective may be to maximize its product's rate of sales growth (in units). This suggests it should set a relatively low price to attract as many new customers as quickly as possible and to capture a large share of the total market before it becomes crowded with competitors. This low-priced strategy is called **penetration pricing.** It is appropriate when, in addition to a large market,

1. Target customers are relatively sensitive to price.
2. The firm's costs are low compared to competitors' and the SBU is pursuing a low-cost strategy.

3. Production and distribution costs per unit are likely to fall substantially with increasing volume.

4. Low prices may discourage potential competitors from entering the market.

However, there is major risk in using low prices to achieve maximum sales growth in the short term as a base for future profits. If market, competitive, or technological conditions change, those future profits may never be realized.

### Maintain Quality or Service Differentiation

When a firm has a strong competitive position based on superior product quality or customer service, its primary pricing objective is to generate sufficient revenue to maintain that advantage. Such a firm usually asks a premium price for its product for two reasons: First, it needs additional revenue to cover the R&D, production, distribution, and advertising costs it takes to maintain both the reality and the perception of superior quality or service. Second, customers are usually willing to pay more for a superior offering; high quality decreases the elasticity of demand.[5]

A premium price policy is most appropriate for businesses pursuing differentiated defender strategies, as is the case with Europe's traditional, full-service airlines like British Airways and Air France. However, there are limits to the price premium customers are willing to pay for superior quality and performance. Those limits may change with shifting economic and competitive conditions. Thus, a premium price strategy is most appropriate when target customers attach relatively greater importance to quality or service attributes than to price, such as business travelers who are willing to pay more for flights convenient to major cities.

### Maximize Current Profit: Skimming

When firms pioneer the development of a new product-market, sometimes their pricing objective is to maximize short-run profits. They adopt a **skimming price policy,** setting the price very high and appealing to only the least price-sensitive segment of potential customers. This can also be accomplished over time, as in "periodic discounting," when the seller prices high at the beginning of each period and low at the end. Examples include off-season travel fares, peak-load pricing by utilities, and markdowns of fashion goods.[6] Skimming is particularly appropriate for businesses pursuing prospector strategies involving investments in the development and commercialization of a stream of new products. Such businesses may not have the production capacity to fill a large initial demand for any one new product. They must try to recoup their development costs quickly so they can fund the next generation of new product ideas. Skimming works best when the new product involves proprietary technology, when the higher price reinforces the image of a superior product, or when other barriers discourage competitors from quickly entering the market and undercutting the pioneer's price. Skimming is most relevant to a small market because a large market is more apt to attract competitors.

### Maximize Current Profit: Harvesting

At the other end of the life cycle, some product-markets decline rapidly as customer preferences change or new technologies and substitute products are introduced. Often it is too late to divest the product and earn a reasonable return, so firms facing this situation adopt a **harvesting** strategy to maximize short-term profits before demand for the product disappears. This typically involves cutting marketing, production, and operating costs of the product, while setting a relatively high price to maintain margins and maximize profits.[7] The opportunity to accomplish this ideal state depends largely upon exit barriers. If large barriers are present, then competitors will exert a downward pressure on prices. If few barriers are present, marginal competitors will exit and falling supplies may drive prices up.

The risk of maximizing short-run profits for a declining product is that demand can decline even faster as price-sensitive customers switch to competing brands or substitute products. Therefore, this is an appropriate strategy only where there is no way—such as by making product improvements or increasing promotion—to sustain market demand and the item's competitive position very far into the future.

**Survival**    Sometimes businesses with an established product in a market expected to grow or experience stable demand well into the future run into trouble because of strategic mistakes, such as failing to adapt to customers' changing desires or to competitive threats, or building excess capacity. If such mistakes are correctable, the firm may adopt a pricing objective of simply keeping the product alive while strategic adjustments are made. Because short-term profits are less important than survival for such products, this situation usually demands a low price to attract enough demand to keep the plant operating and maintain cash flow. So long as the price covers variable costs and at least contributes to fixed costs, the firm may be able to buy time to correct its competitive weaknesses.

**Social Objectives**    Some organizations may forgo possible profits—at least among some price-sensitive customer segments—by offering a low price to those customers to achieve some broader social purpose. This is most common among not-for-profit organizations such as performing arts organizations and public hospitals, especially if subsidized by government agencies, foundations, or private contributions and not relying on sales as their sole source of revenue. In reality, they are simply shifting the price "reduction" burden to organizations or individual contributors who are willing to subsidize one or more price-sensitive segments to achieve some social purpose. For example, performing arts organizations often offer substantial discounts to students. This is not just a strategy for building loyal future audiences. It also provides intellectual benefits to a customer group that would otherwise be unable to afford them.

## Estimating Demand and Perceived Value

Demand sets the ceiling on the range of feasible prices for a product. Even before that ceiling is reached, however, the total number of customers willing to buy during a given period varies according to the price charged. The familiar **demand curve** depicts this variation in the quantity demanded at different prices.

In most cases there is an inverse relation between a product's price and the quantity demanded: the higher the price, the less people want to buy. Thus, the typical demand curve has a negative, or downward, slope. However, prestigious products (such as expensive wines and liquors) and those whose quality is difficult to objectively judge sometimes have positively sloping demand curves. Some customers use price as an indicator of the prestige or quality of such products, and they are induced to buy more as the price increases.[8]

**Factors Affecting Customers' Price Sensitivity**    The demand curve sums the reactions of many potential buyers to the alternative prices that might be charged for a product. The curve's degree of slope reflects the fact that different buyers have different sensitivities to the product's price.

Thomas Nagle identified specific factors influencing variations in sensitivity to price across customers and products. Exhibit 11.3 summarizes these factors. Each factor reflects three basic phenomena that determine customers' willingness and ability to pay for a good or service. First, buyers' willingness to pay a given price for a product is influenced by their perceptions and preferences: their needs, desires, awareness of, and attitude toward, the item in question.

## Exhibit 11.3

FACTORS AFFECTING CUSTOMERS' SENSITIVITY TO PRICE

**Buyer's perceptions and preferences**

| | |
|---|---|
| Unique-value effect | Customers are less price-sensitive when they perceive the product or service provides unique benefits; there are no acceptable substitutes. |
| Price-quality effect | Customers are less price-sensitive when they perceive the product or service offers high quality, prestige, or exclusiveness. |

**Buyer's awareness of and attitude toward alternatives**

| | |
|---|---|
| Substitute-awareness effect | Customers are less price-sensitive when they are relatively unaware of competing brands or substitute products or services. |
| Difficult-comparison effect | Customers are less price-sensitive when it is difficult to objectively compare the quality or performance of alternative brands or substitutes. |
| Sunk-investment effect | Customers are less price-sensitive when the purchase is necessary to gain full benefit from assets previously bought. |

**Buyer's ability to pay**

| | |
|---|---|
| Total-expenditure effect | Customers are less price-sensitive when their expenditure for the product or service is a relatively low proportion of their total income. |
| End-benefit effect | Customers—particularly organizational buyers purchasing raw materials or component parts—are less price-sensitive when the expenditure is a relatively small proportion of the total cost of the end product. |
| Shared-cost effect | Customers are less price-sensitive when part of the cost of the product or service is borne by another party (e.g., when part of the cost of medical services is covered by health insurance, or when a salesperson's travel costs are covered by an expense account). |
| Inventory effect | Customers are less price-sensitive in the short run when they cannot store large quantities of the product as a hedge against future price increases. |

*Source:* Thomas T. Nagle, *The Strategy and Tactics of Pricing: A Guide to Profitable Decision Making.* © 1987. Reproduced by permission of Pearson Education, Inc., Upper Saddle River, NJ.

Second, the price, availability, and attractiveness of alternative brands and substitute products affect buyers' willingness to buy the product. So do the prices of complementary items that customers must buy to gain full value from the product. For example, the rising price of gasoline has dampened consumer demand for large, fuel-inefficient sport utility vehicles.

Finally, the size of their incomes relative to the price influences customers' ability to pay for a product or service. Taken together, these factors determine the **perceived value** a potential customer will associate with a given product-market entry, and thus the price he or she is willing to pay. Later in this chapter, we discuss how perceived value might be estimated for a given customer segment and used as a basis for setting a price level.

**Price Elasticity of Demand**   The larger the proportion of price-sensitive customers in a product's market, the more sensitive overall demand is to a change in the product's price. This degree of responsiveness of demand to a price change is referred to as the **price elasticity of demand.** The following formula calculates the price elasticity of demand for a product or service:

$$\text{Price elasticity of demand}(E) = \frac{\text{Percentage change in quantity demanded}}{\text{Percent change in price}}$$

If, for instance, a seller raised the price of a product by 2 percent and demand subsequently fell by 6 percent, the price elasticity of demand for that product would be –3 (with the minus sign reflecting the inverse relationship between price and demand), indicating substantial **elasticity.** Conversely, if a 2 percent increase produced only a 1 percent decline in the quantity demanded, then price elasticity is –½ indicating that demand is **inelastic.** If a 2 percent price increase leads to a 2 percent decline in quantity, price elasticity is **unitary.** In such a case the seller's total revenue stays the same because the smaller quantity sold is offset by the higher price.

There are major problems in using price elasticity—as discussed above—to help set price in any precise way. These difficulties include the failure to consider the response of competitors to the company's change in price; that demand may be inelastic for a given price change, but elastic for a larger amount; that elasticity is measured in terms of sales revenues not profit margins (one reason being it doesn't take into account scale effects); that a lowering of price may affect the sales of other items in the company's product line (for example, cannibalization); and that it ignores any societal benefits accorded the company for benefiting low-income segments via a price reduction.

**Methods for Estimating Demand**    Many firms, particularly larger ones, attempt to estimate the demand curves for their products through marketing research. This is easier said than done, though, for two reasons: First, laboratory or test-market experiments can provide insights into the price–demand relationship for a product, but do not reflect the likely reactions of competitors to different prices or changes in price over time. Underestimating the aggressiveness and impact of such reactions can lead to debilitating price wars, particularly in mature industries suffering from excess production capacity.[9] A second problem researchers encounter when trying to empirically estimate demand curves is that *effects of nonprice factors,* such as changes in economic conditions or in other components of the marketing mix, must be controlled or measured. Thus, if a firm conducted a test market in which it increased advertising expenditures at the same time it lowered prices, researchers could not tell how much increased volume was a result of the sensitivity of demand to price and how much was a result of the heavier advertising.

Keeping these two problems in mind, there are a number of ways for marketers to estimate a product's demand curve.[10] One approach is to survey a sample of consumers, or bring them into a laboratory setting, and ask them how much of the product they would buy at different possible prices. The artificiality of this approach, however, and the fact that respondents are not required to "put their money where their mouth is" leads to questions about the validity of the findings. More realistic approaches include estimating the price–quantity relationship via the regression analysis of historical sales using consumer panel data, in-store experiments where a product's price is systematically varied, or multiple test markets. However, the expense of the latter limits their use.

Recently, software providers like SAP and Profit Logic Inc. have developed programs that sift through massive databases available on a corporate intranet with information about past orders, promotions, product revenues, inventory levels in warehouses and stores, and the like. Historically, this wealth of information was usually divided among different departments, or even different firms in the distribution channel, but the new programs are bringing it all together via the internet. The programs' sophisticated algorithms then crunch historical sales, pricing, and inventory data to estimate the response of different customer segments to different price levels or price promotions. While such programs are expensive and can be difficult to implement initially, many analysts expect them to greatly improve the future accuracy of firms' demand estimates and pricing decisions.[11]

# Estimating Costs

Demand and perceived value set the ceiling on the range of feasible prices a firm might charge for a product, but costs determine the floor. A firm's costs take two forms: fixed and variable. **Fixed costs** (or **overhead**) are constant in the short term, regardless of production volume or sales revenue. They include rent, interest, heat, executive salaries, and functional departments—such as purchasing and R&D—needed to support the products made by the firm. Because total fixed costs remain constant in the short term regardless of volume, the **fixed cost per unit** of a product declines as a firm produces and sells more of the product in a given period.

**Variable costs** vary in magnitude directly with the level of production, but they remain constant *per unit* regardless of how many units are produced. They involve such things as the costs of materials, packaging, and labor needed to produce each unit of the product.

**Total costs** equal the sum of fixed and variable costs for a given level of production. The product's price must cover this total cost figure—divided by the number of units produced—if it is to be economically viable in the long run.

**Marketing mix** costs, which may include both fixed and variable costs as well as other costs such as retailers or distributors' markups that don't even appear on the company's books, must also be considered in determining the level at which a product's price will be set. For example, it is common for a greater portion of the consumer's dollar to be spent on **distribution channel markups** than for a product's actual manufacturing cost. Similarly, in some product categories—diet aids and colognes, among others—the cost to promote the product, establish its brand name, and acquire customers can be higher—sometimes far higher—than manufacturing costs. For new products in categories such as these, marketers are faced with a clear choice between setting a high price together with a substantial promotional budget to communicate the product's benefits and attract customers, or a low penetration price along with little promotional support. Either strategy can be viable, depending on market and competitive conditions. Setting a high price with too little promotional support, however, is likely to lead to sales problems. Similarly, setting a low price alongside an aggressive promotional program can lead to profit and cash flow problems, as many dot-com retailers learned the hard way. Thus, price setting for a product cannot occur in isolation. It requires considering the costs of the planned overall marketing mix for the product, including product, promotion, and distribution decisions.

**Measuring Costs**    The firm's cost accounting system provides managers with information about the fixed and variable costs associated with each of the company's products. Even though it is a relatively simple matter to measure each product's variable costs, fixed costs present a problem. The analyst has the option of using full costing (which involves allocating indirect costs) or direct costing (often referred to as the contribution margin approach because it takes into account only variable costs). These topics are covered in depth in Chapter 18 and will not be discussed here.

Examining the impact on a product's contribution is a useful way to evaluate the economic viability of marketing program components directly linked to a specific product. However, it does not provide enough detailed information for a manager to judge whether a given price is adequate to cover the total costs incurred by that product. Consequently, many firms are beginning to revise their cost accounting systems to provide more accurate product-cost information to managers. They often develop multiple systems for financial reporting, cost control, and product-cost measurement purposes. **Activity-based costing systems**—which allocate costs across individual products by directly observing the level of various functional activities such as shipping, receiving, supervising, and selling that are devoted to each item in the line—often generate very different estimates of the total costs associated with a given product than does the firm's standard cost control system. But such activity-based cost estimates are often more useful for making strategic marketing decisions, such as setting prices, because they reduce some of the distortions inherent in the allocation of indirect costs within standard cost accounting systems while avoiding the imprecision of the contribution margin approach.[12]

**Cost and Volume Relationships**    A product's average cost per unit—and the price necessary to cover that cost—varies with the quantity produced. Managers should take two different volume–cost relationships into account when making pricing decisions. The first relationship involves **economies of scale.** In the short run, scale economies result from more complete use of available capacity. In the long run, companies can gain further economies by constructing larger and more efficient facilities. The average cost per unit is high if few units are produced, but it falls as production approaches the plant's capacity because fixed costs are spread over more units. This is why excess capacity is anathema to the profitability and competitive cost position of a product, particularly in mature, commodity-like product categories where margins tend to be low. If, however, a company tries to produce more than capacity, average costs per unit would rise. The overworked machinery would break down more often, workers would get in each other's way, and other inefficiencies would occur.

The second volume–cost relationship involves the **experience curve**—the fall in production and marketing costs per unit as a firm gains accumulated experience. Regardless of a firm's plant size, its average costs per unit decline as it gains experience. Its production workers discover efficient shortcuts, procurement costs fall, and the accumulated impact of past advertising and marketing efforts may enable the firm to succeed with smaller per-unit marketing expenditures.

# Analyzing Competitors' Costs and Prices

To achieve a desired strategic competitive position for a product or service in its target market, the manager must take competitors' costs and prices into account. To successfully implement a low-cost strategy, for instance, the manager must be sure that the product's costs are truly lower than any competitor's and that those lower costs are reflected in the product's relative price. Thus, the manager needs to learn and track the price, cost, and relative quality of each competitor's offer. For example, the continued success of Ryanair's low-price strategy obviously depends on the firm's ability to hold its total costs and prices well below those of other airlines—especially other no-frills carriers like easyJet—while offering a reasonably comparable choice of destinations, flight times, and customer services.

Competitors' costs are harder to measure than their prices. Reverse engineering can be used to take apart competing products and estimate the cost of their components, packing, and production processes. Because the costs associated with services are often largely fixed, such as the costs of labor, physical facilities, and the like, a manager can estimate competitors' relative cost positions in a service industry by comparing their numbers of employees or the number and size of outlets and then looking at efficiency ratios like sales per employee or sales per square foot. And there is usually a relationship between costs and market share—the higher the relative share, the lower the relative cost is likely to be based on scale and learning effects.

# Methods Managers Use to Determine an Appropriate Price Level

Given the complexity of the concerns involved in setting a price—and the frequent incompleteness of information about demand and costs—managers often rely on rules of thumb to set list prices. Although these practical pricing methods are unlikely to produce an optimal—or profit-maximizing—price, they are all based on a set of relevant considerations. These various pricing methods fall into three categories: cost-oriented pricing, competition-oriented pricing, and demand, or customer-oriented, pricing.

## Cost-Oriented Methods

Perhaps the simplest and most commonly used pricing method is to add a standard markup to the cost of the product. This kind of **cost-plus,** or **markup, pricing** does not explicitly consider the price sensitivity of demand or the pricing practices of competitors. But it is convenient and easy to apply—important considerations when a firm faces hundreds or thousands of pricing decisions each year, as in the case of retail stores and wholesaling institutions. It is also widely used among firms that must submit competitive bids for a variety of projects, as is the case with construction firms.

The typical procedure for determining price under the markup approach is to first calculate the cost per unit by adding variable cost to fixed costs divided by an expected level of unit sales:

$$\text{Unit cost} = \text{Variable cost} + \frac{\text{Fixed cost}}{\text{Expected unit sales}}$$

To find the price, add a desired markup on retail to the unit cost (or divide unit cost by 1 minus the desired percent markup):

$$\text{Markup price} = \frac{\text{Unit cost}}{\left(1 - \text{Desired percent markup on retail}\right)}$$

Suppose, for instance, that a small-appliance manufacturer produces a line of electric coffeemakers and expects to sell 50,000 in the coming period. Fixed costs of $500,000 are associated with producing the coffeemakers, and variable costs are $10 per unit. The unit cost for each coffeemaker would be

$$\text{Unit cost} = \$10 + \frac{\$500,000}{50,000} = \$10 + \$10 = \$20$$

Suppose further that the manufacturer wants to earn a markup (or margin on selling price) of 30 percent. The markup price would be

$$\text{Markup price} = \frac{\$20}{\left(1 - .30\right)} = \frac{\$20}{.7} = \$28.57$$

This approach largely ignores the price sensitivity of demand. It assumes a level of sales *before* the price is set. Furthermore, if the manager's assumption about likely sales volume is wrong, the desired markup is not achieved. A shortfall in units sold would mean that fixed costs would be spread over fewer units and the realized markup would be smaller than desired.

In the distributive trades, retailers and wholesalers often add standard markups to what they paid for the item to attain a margin sufficient to cover overhead and provide a profit. These standard markups do not explicitly consider variations in demand. However, they have evolved in a way that reflects general variations in price sensitivity across products. In supermarkets, for instance, markups on selling price range from as low as 10 percent on baby foods to more than 50 percent on some toiletries and greeting cards.[13] The products with the lowest markups tend to be frequently purchased, commodity-like items for which many consumers make price comparisons.

**Rate-of-return,** or **target return, pricing** is similar in principle to, but somewhat more sophisticated in practice than, markup pricing. This cost-oriented approach brings one more cost element into the pricing decision—the cost of capital tied up in producing and distributing the product. The objective is to set a price yielding a target rate of return on investment. This pricing approach is common at automobile companies that price their cars to achieve a target of 15 to 20 percent return on investment.

Operationally, this pricing approach demands that managers (1) estimate the unit sales volume of the product, (2) figure unit costs (variable costs plus overhead attributable to the product), (3) estimate the amount of capital involved in producing and selling the product, and (4) select a target rate of return on investment. They can then determine the price as follows:

$$\text{Target return price} = \text{Unit cost} + \frac{\text{Desired percent return} \times \text{Capital invested in product}}{\text{Unit sales}}$$

For example, suppose our small-appliance manufacturer has invested $1 million in facilities and equipment to produce and distribute its coffeemakers and wants to make a 20 percent return on that investment. The target return price for each coffeemaker would be

$$\text{Target return price} = \$20 + \frac{.20 \times \$1,000,000}{50,000 \text{ units}} = \$20 + \frac{\$200,000}{50,000} = \$24$$

When managers make these estimates accurately, the target return method results in a more rational pricing decision than the simpler markup method. As typically practiced, however, this method does not explicitly consider the interaction between alternative prices and demand.

What happens if the price is set on the basis of an overly optimistic sales estimate? As with markup pricing, the realized return falls below the target level because fixed costs have to be covered by a smaller unit volume. The impact of such variations in volume can be examined by preparing a **break-even analysis.** Suppose our appliance manufacturer decided to price its coffeemakers at $26. With variable costs of $10 per unit and fixed costs of $500,000, the break-even chart in Exhibit 11.4 indicates that the product's **break-even volume** is 31,250 units—the volume necessary to just cover total costs. To calculate this result, use the following formula:

$$\text{Break-even volume} = \frac{\text{Fixed cost}}{\text{Price} - \text{Variable cost}} = \frac{\$500,000}{\$26 - \$10} = 31,250 \text{ units}$$

If we also consider the $1 million of capital invested in the product and the manufacturer's target return of 20 percent (or $200,000), the chart shows that the firm must sell 43,750 to achieve the desired return. Break-even analysis can also calculate break-even and target return volumes at different price levels. Exhibit 11.5 indicates how these volumes vary for our product example over a range of prices. Break-even analysis, however, suffers from the same limitations as other cost-oriented pricing methods. It does not explicitly consider

## Exhibit 11.4

BREAK-EVEN CHART SHOWING BREAK-EVEN AND TARGET RETURN VOLUME

## Exhibit 11.5

BREAK-EVEN AND TARGET RETURN VOLUMES FOR ALTERNATIVE SELLING PRICES

| Selling price | Fixed costs ($000) | Per unit average variable cost | Target return ($000) | Break-even volume (units) | Target return volume (units) |
|---|---|---|---|---|---|
| $18 | $500 | $10 | $200 | 62,500 | 87,500 |
| 20 | 500 | 10 | 200 | 50,000 | 70,000 |
| 24 | 500 | 10 | 200 | 35,714 | 50,000 |
| 26 | 500 | 10 | 200 | 31,250 | 43,750 |
| 28 | 500 | 10 | 200 | 27,778 | 38,889 |
| 30 | 500 | 10 | 200 | 25,000 | 35,000 |

the price sensitivity of demand or the likely reactions of competitors. Therefore, managers must rely on their own judgment to decide how likely it is that the product's actual volume will reach or exceed the break-even level associated with each alternative price.

# Competition-Oriented Methods

Some companies key their pricing decisions to what competitors are charging for similar offerings and pay relatively less attention to their own costs or demand schedules. This is not to say that their prices and competitors' prices are always the same; some firms may add a premium or discount their price below the industry average. Such competition-oriented pricing is also found in mature industries where little product differentiation and a few strong competitors make it difficult for one firm to change its price without precipitating a competitive reaction. Under such circumstances, a common industry price structure reflects the collective wisdom about finding the price that will yield a fair return and minimize the chances that a price war will jeopardize the profits of all industry firms.

Firms that pursue competition-oriented pricing approaches do not ignore cost or return-on-investment considerations. Instead, they try to control costs to make adequate returns at prices consistent with those of competitors. But if this cannot be done (for instance, because the firm is less efficient), the target rate of return may be the factor that is changed.

In some cases, firms adopt a **going-rate,** or **competitive parity,** pricing approach, where they try to maintain prices equal to those of one or more major competitors. This has been common in oligopolistic industries with little product differentiation and a few large competitors, as in steel, paper, and fertilizer. Price virtually ceases to be a controllable element of the marketing mix under such circumstances. No firm can increase its price without some assurance that others will follow, because most customers would switch to lower-priced competitors. Similarly, a firm would be reluctant to price below the competition lest other companies also cut their prices and reduce profits for all concerned. Consequently, prices are usually quite stable in such industries until a **price leader** decides an increase in industry prices is necessary to meet increased costs and maintain returns.

The ability of a firm to be a price leader whose pricing decisions are emulated by other companies is not determined solely by its size or market share. The leader also tends to be one of the most efficient firms in the industry; that is, it is one of the last to feel the need for a price increase. Often leaders are also perceived to have good marketing expertise and have had past success in making price increases stick. Even so, there is no guarantee that a given price leader can maintain its position. "Follower" firms are particularly likely to cut prices below the leader during periods of overcapacity and to increase prices faster than the leader during periods of high inflation.

In industries where product quality, service, or availability vary across brands, a firm may still base its pricing on what its competitors are charging, but try to hold its prices either below or above the competition. Such **discount** or **premium price policies** usually reflect differences in positioning strategies. Ryanair's low-price strategy is a good example of a discount price policy. Once again, however, such a policy is sustainable only if the firm can maintain a total cost advantage over its competitors.

**Sealed bidding** is common in some businesses, especially in dealing with governments. In such situations buyers request a formal bid with no later opportunity for change. In public procurement the bids are opened publicly, enabling bidders to learn what competitors bid. Such is not typically the case with private bidding.

One approach used to set a bid price is an **expected value** model based on the following formula:

$$E(X) = P(X)Z(X)$$

where $X$ = bid price, $Z(X)$ = the profit at the bid price, $P(X)$ = the probability of an award at the bid price, and $E(X)$ = the expected profit of a bid. The price the company bids is the one yielding the highest expected profit. But such models suffer because of the subjectivity of the probability estimates and objectives other than profit to take into account, such as the possibility of follow-on work, capacity availability, and need to keep the workforce intact.[14]

### Internet Auction Sites Make Accurate Cost Estimates More Critical

The internet might make old-fashioned sealed bidding procedures obsolete. Instead of asking for a single submission of sealed bids from alternative suppliers, government agencies are likely to turn to internet auctions where suppliers can adjust their bids in response to those of competitors.

Recall that in Chapter 5 we discussed the rapid growth of auction websites, particularly in business-to-business markets.[15] Some business-to-business sites focus on **seller's auctions.** These sites are usually specialized by industry and facilitate global spot markets for relatively standardized materials, component parts, used equipment, and the like. On *www.MetalSite.com,* for example, a steelmaker such as LTV can offer a block of sheet or rolled steel whenever its plants have excess capacity and inventories grow too large. Potential buyers then enter bids for the steel over two or three days, and the highest bid wins. Similarly, *www.acunet.com* runs a popular wholesale auction for used cars.

More recently, **buyer's auction (or reverse auction)** sites have emerged in a number of industries where qualified suppliers are invited to compete for a contract where the buyer has specified all the technical requirements and purchase criteria in detail, except the price. Because the buyer must be able to specify all its requirements before suppliers can submit firm bids, such auctions are likely to work best for purchases where the buyer has past experience to draw on and where those requirements are unlikely to change rapidly, as, for example, when BMW buys seats or bumpers for one of its current car models.

Most analysts believe that, in markets where they are appropriate, both kinds of internet auctions will work to increase price competition. Whether that turns out to be the case or not, one thing is clear: To be profitable selling goods or services at auction a firm must work to hold its costs down relative to its competitors, and it must have an accurate understanding of what those costs are.

When selling excess inventory on a seller's auction site, for instance, the firm may be willing to accept a bid that is below its full cost as long as that bid covers variable costs and makes a contribution to fixed costs. This is particularly true if the product or service would otherwise go unsold and contribute nothing to cover fixed costs, as is the case with empty seats on an airline flight or empty hotel rooms on weekends. Nevertheless, the selling firm must know what its fixed and variable costs are with some certainty before it can decide whether a bid will provide enough revenue to cover variable cost and therefore be worth accepting.

The critical question facing managers bidding for contracts on a buyer's auction site is, How low should we go? Winning too many contracts by bidding prices that are too low to cover costs and provide a reasonable return on invested capital is a good recipe for failure in the long run. Conversely, buyers who use such auctions need to recognize the possible negative effects they can have on their relations with suppliers. If the savings a firm realizes from a reverse auction means decreased margins for an incumbent supplier, that supplier may feel the firm is opportunistically forcing it to make price concessions. Such feelings are probably not conducive to maintaining cooperative long-term relationships with valued suppliers.[16]

# Customer-Oriented Methods

### Pricing to Capture the Value Perceived by the Customer   Perhaps the key concept in setting a price is the notion of *perceived value.* Whether the product offering is an industrial product or service that delivers primarily economic and functional benefits or a consumer item whose benefits are more psychological, potential customers usually have some idea of what constitutes a good or bad price. They develop such perceptions by comparing the prices being charged by a firm and its competitors to the benefits or value they think they can derive from purchasing the product or service. The essential purpose of the price level set by the marketing manager, then, should be to enable the firm to capture the value of the product as perceived in the mind of the customer.

## Exhibit 11.6

METHODS FOR ESTIMATING PERCEIVED CUSTOMER VALUE

1. Industrial engineering methods:
   - Internal engineering assessment: Physical laboratory tests within the firm.
   - Field value-in-use assessments: Customer field trials or interviews determining economic benefits to using the product.
   - Indirect survey questions: Customer estimates of the effects of product changes on firm operations used to infer the value of product attributes.

2. Overall estimates of customer value:
   - Focus group value assessment: Willingness-to-pay questions in a small group setting.
   - Direct survey questions: Willingness-to-pay questions in a survey format.

3. Decomposition approaches:
   - Conjoint analysis: A method for estimating customer trade-offs of product attributes.
   - Benchmarks: Customer indication of willingness to pay for incremental (or fewer) attributes that can be compared to an example from the product category.

4. Compositional approach:
   - Direct customer questions about the value of product attributes.

5. Importance ratings:
   - Customer rank ordering or rating of the importance of product attributes as well as comparisons between competitors.

*Source:* James C. Anderson, Dipak C. Jain, and Pradeep K. Chintagunta, "Customer Value Assessment in Business Markets: A State-of-Practice Study," *Journal of Business-to-Business Marketing* 1 (1993), pp. 3–29.

While a firm's costs establish a minimum floor for long-term profitability, customers generally do not care what those costs are. The only thing important to them is the value they are likely to receive for the price they pay. Thus, one danger of cost-oriented (or even competition-oriented) pricing methods is that they can produce prices that are lower than perceived value, causing the firm to "leave money on the table." Such approaches might also result in prices that exceed many customers' perceptions of value, resulting in lost sales and competitive vulnerability.

Of course, the perceived value of a given product offering can vary from customer to customer. When setting a price level within a strategic marketing program, however, the manager should try to determine an "average" perceived value for the customers in a particular target market segment. Such a determination typically requires research. Exhibit 11.6 summarizes a variety of methods for calculating customer value, ranging from reverse-engineering methods aimed at estimating the economic benefits generated by the product's performance to more common survey research approaches for measuring customers' perceptions.

### Estimating Customer Value by Assessing Value-in-Use

One of the most useful ways to estimate customer value, particularly for industrial products and consumer durables, is by assessing the product's **value-in-use.** The value-in-use assessment process begins with the selection of a reference product, usually the product the customer is currently using or a major competitor's product. The manager then calculates the incremental benefits to the customer—in monetary terms—of using his or her product instead of the reference product. These benefits may be the result of improved performance and additional features, or improved efficiency and reduced costs over the life cycle of the product. In either case, the additional monetary value of the manager's product added to the price of the reference product [(1) + (2) in Exhibit 11.7] equals the **economic value** of the manager's product to the customer: the maximum amount the customer should be willing to pay, assuming that she is fully informed about the product and the offerings of competitors.

For example, suppose New Holland introduces a new farm tractor to compete with a particular John Deere model. The John Deere is priced at $25,000. However, field use trials indicate that the New Holland tractor will use on average $2,000 less fuel over its 15-year productive life, and it has a more user-friendly hitch system that will save 100 hours of the farmer's time, worth (if we assume the farmer's time is valued at $20 an hour) another $2,000. Finally, the New Holland comes with a superior air-conditioned cab and a Bose stereo system, which a survey of farmers suggests is worth another $1,000 to potential buyers. Thus, if we add the additional cost savings and benefits provided by the New Holland model to the price of the reference product, we get $25,000 + $2,000 + $2,000 + $1,000 = $30,000. This is the total economic value-in-use to the average farmer of the New Holland tractor.

Therefore, $30,000 is the maximum amount a farmer should be willing to pay for the new tractor, *assuming* that he or she has all the relevant information. But while providing such "complete" information should obviously be the goal of New Holland's salesforce and promotional materials, it is unlikely such a state of complete information will usually exist. Therefore, the manager must anticipate some discounting on the customer's part due to lack of knowledge about the product's benefits, competitive offerings, the perceived risk of buying something new, and so on. Therefore, as indicated in Exhibit 11.7, the customer's actual *perceived* value of the New Holland tractor (3) is likely to be somewhat less than the tractor's actual economic value-in-use.

The difference between the value perceived by the customer and the manufacturer's marginal cost defines the range of possible prices. Suppose, for instance, that a farmer perceives the New Holland tractor to be worth $3,000 more than the John Deere, or $28,000, and that New Holland's marginal cost of producing another tractor (including the dealer's margin, etc.) is $20,000. New Holland's managers could set the price anywhere between those two figures. From New Holland's perspective, it might seem desirable to set the price as close to the customer's perceived value as possible. The customer should be willing to pay such a price since the farmer would receive benefits equal to the cost. By capturing all of the incremental value the company has created, New Holland would fatten its profit margin and return on investment. However, there are sound strategic reasons for setting a price that shares at least some of the economic value with the customer [as indicated by (4) in Exhibit 11.7]. If New Holland's price is exactly equal to the perceived incremental

**STRATEGIC ISSUE**

*The difference between the value perceived by the customer and the manufacturer's marginal cost defines the range of possible prices.*

## Exhibit 11.7

THE "VALUE-IN-USE" APPROACH TO DETERMINING A CUSTOMER'S PERCEPTION OF VALUE

value of the tractor in the customer's mind, then he or she will be indifferent between the two tractors; either tractor will leave the farmer equally well off after he pays for it. Therefore, passing some of the incremental value along to the customer in the form of a lower price provides an inducement to purchase the New Holland instead of the competing brand. Such inducements give the salesforce a strong argument to persuade potential purchasers. They also can be particularly important in achieving some strategic pricing objectives, such as when the firm is pursuing a penetration strategy to maximize sales growth.

**Perceived Value Can Change but Prices Are Sticky**    The perceived value of a product—and therefore the demand for that product at a given price—often varies with changes in economic and social conditions. For instance, more expensive national brands of consumer goods tend to lose market share to cheaper private labels during economic recessions. Ideally, a company and the firms in its distribution channel should adjust a product's price from time to time to reflect changes in its perceived value.

But frequent price changes can be difficult and costly to implement, especially for retailers who carry thousands of stock-keeping units (SKUs) in inventory. Consequently, retail prices tend to be "sticky," particularly for consumer convenience goods. Retailers tend to perpetuate past prices even though they could generate higher margins by adjusting them to reflect changing demand conditions. Recent research suggests that retail prices are particularly sticky in product categories with a high proliferation of SKUs, and for brands with low market shares or low price elasticities.[17]

**Other Perceptual Pricing Issues**    Often, a number of psychological factors can influence customers' perceptions of the relationship between a product's price and its value. Thus, many firms use such practices as customary pricing, price lining, psychological pricing, and promotional pricing. All of these are particularly popular in consumer nondurable product categories.[18]

In some product categories consumers expect a single **customary price** for the product. Candy bars, for example, sold for many years at a customary price of 10 cents. When increasing costs put pressure on manufacturers' margins, they elected to reduce the size of the bar rather than upset customers' expectations by raising the price.

**Price lining** is another common customer-oriented pricing practice, especially among retailers. It involves selling all products in a category at one of several predetermined "price points" or levels. Each price line represents a different level of quality. For example, different brands of men's shirts in the same store might be priced at $29.95, $34.95, and $39.95. This practice helps customers make quality comparisons, assuming the price differences can be easily associated with differences in quality, including the number and type of features offered. It also simplifies pricing decisions for the retailer and guides the retail buyer in deciding which brands to stock.

In **psychological pricing** the firm takes advantage of the fact that many consumers use price as an indication of quality. For example, Heublein successfully repositioned its Popov brand of vodka by substantially raising its price. The 8 percent price increase reduced the brand's market share by 1 percent but produced a 30 percent increase in profit.[19] Some perfumes are priced high to elevate their status as a gift.

Another common psychological pricing practice is called *odd pricing*. For instance, a product or service might be priced at $29.95 instead of $30.00, 19 cents instead of 20 cents, or $39,950 instead of $40,000. Odd prices convey the psychological impression of a lower price.[20] A final demand-oriented pricing practice is the use of **promotional pricing** to transmit a message about the product in conjunction with, or sometimes in lieu of, advertising or other forms of promotional activity. The most common form

**ETHICAL PERSPECTIVE 11.1**
*When Is a "Sale" a Sale?*

Because many customers in most product and service categories are price sensitive and are motivated to find the best value for their money, promotional pricing is both common and effective, particularly among retailers. Unfortunately, some firms engage in practices that attempt to deceive the customer. For instance, deception can occur when a retailer prices an item at an unusually high level for a short period and then discounts it for the remainder of the selling period and promotes it as being on sale. Since very little of the item is sold at the artificially high "regular" price, the "sale" price is in reality the regular price.

Bait-and-switch is another practice that is not only unethical but illegal as well. It involves a retailer advertising an unusually low price on one or more popular brands to attract customers. Once in the store, customers are told the sale items have been sold out or are otherwise dissuaded from buying the advertised items. Instead, the salesperson attempts to sell the customer a higher-priced/higher-margin substitute.

of promotional pricing is the familiar sale: the offer of a reduced price on the product for a limited time. Unfortunately, some firms are overly aggressive in their promotional pricing tactics, which can give rise to ethical concerns, as discussed in Ethical Perspective 11.1.

# Deciding on a Price Structure: Adapting Prices to Market Variations

Even though determining a product's price level is a complicated process, most firms do not stop with the selection of a single list price. Instead, the final step in the pricing process is usually to develop a **price structure** that adapts the price to variations in cost and demand across geographic territories, national boundaries, types of customers, and items within the product line.

## Geographic Adjustments

Within a domestic market, firms with only one or a few plants must adjust prices for the variations in transportation costs of selling to customers in different parts of the country. One approach is called **FOB origin pricing:** The manufacturer places the goods "free on board" a transportation carrier. At this point the title and responsibility passes to the customer, who pays the freight from the factory to the destination. Advocates argue that this is the fairest way to allocate freight charges: Each customer picks up its own costs. The disadvantage, though, is that the manufacturer may be at a cost disadvantage when trying to sell to customers in distant markets.

The opposite alternative is **freight absorption pricing.** Here the seller picks up all or part of the freight charges. New competitors trying to penetrate new markets and smaller competitors in maturing industries trying to increase their share sometimes use this approach. Their rationale is that if they can obtain more business, their average unit costs will fall enough to compensate for the high freight costs.

Most firms use a compromise approach to deal with variations in transportation costs. One method is **uniform delivered pricing,** where a standard freight charge—equal to the average freight cost across all customers—is assessed every customer, regardless of location. This lowers the overall cost to distant customers, but raises costs for customers near the company's plant. Nevertheless, the approach is popular because it is easy to administer and enables the firm to maintain a single nationally advertised price. **Zone pricing** is another compromise approach that falls between FOB and uniform delivered pricing. Here the company divides the country into two or more pricing zones. It charges all customers within the same zone the same delivered price, but a higher price is set for distant zones than for those closer to the plant.

## Global Adjustments

Geographic adjustments become even more complicated when the geographic areas involve different countries. In addition to reflecting transportation costs, prices in different countries may also have to be adjusted for different exchange rates, variations in competition, market demand, or strategic objectives (volume growth versus profit generation), and different governmental tax policies or legal regulations.

In some cases, firms attempt to minimize such adjustments by adopting a highly standardized global pricing policy similar to an FOB origin policy in the domestic market. They charge the same price around the world and require each customer to absorb all freight and import duties. Such a policy has the obvious virtue of simplicity, but it fails to respond to variations in local demand or competitive conditions.

Other firms charge a transfer price to their various national branches or subsidiaries but then give local managers in each country wide latitude to charge their customers whatever price they think most appropriate. Although sensitive to variations in local conditions, such a policy may lead to arbitrage involving the transshipment of goods across countries when price differences exceed the freight-and-duty costs separating the markets. There is also the question of control and whether the strategic objectives of local managers are always consistent with the higher business and corporate objectives.

For all the above reasons, most firms follow an intermediate approach to global pricing.[21] Corporate management establishes an acceptable range of prices. Local country managers are then given the flexibility to select the price within that range that is best suited to local demand and competitive conditions, though their decisions are often subject to strategic review and approval by top management. Thus, a firm might allow local managers to set a high price in countries where the product has a strong competitive position and high perceived value, but demand more competitive prices in other nations. For instance, Zara—the Spanish purveyor of fashion goods—charges prices as much as 60 percent higher in China than in European countries. This reflects the fact that rapid economic growth has increased discretionary income for Chinese consumers, that those consumers tend to see high prices as indicators of high fashion and quality, and that there is a relative lack of competition among fashion retailers in China. The question, of course, is how long the company can maintain such large price differentials as it expands its online catalog and as more Chinese consumers travel to other countries.[22]

**Countertrade**    An additional pricing problem often arises when selling to customers in developing economies, which may lack sufficient hard currency to pay for their purchases. Such customers may offer items other than money as payment. While many companies dislike such deals, it is often in their best economic interest to facilitate them via a set of activities known as *countertrade*. For example, given the sharp devaluation of the Argentine peso and the resulting decline in new auto sales a few years ago, Toyota began bartering pickup trucks in Argentina for a trade-in and 44 tons of soybeans.[23] Countertrade can take a variety of forms, several of which are discussed in Exhibit 11.8.

## Exhibit 11.8

GLOBAL COUNTERTRADE

Countertrade, which occurs in international transactions where the potential customer lacks sufficient hard currency to pay for a purchase, can take a variety of forms. These include:

- *Barter.* Barter involves the direct exchange of goods with no money and no third party involved. For instance, a German firm might agree to build a steel plant in Mexico in exchange for a given amount of Mexican oil.

- *Compensation deals.* Here the seller agrees to take some percentage of the payment in cash and the rest in goods, as when Boeing sells airplanes to Brazil for 70 percent cash and an agreed-upon number of tons of coffee.

- *Buyback arrangements.* Under such arrangements a seller offers a plant, equipment, or technical expertise to a customer and agrees to accept as partial payment products manufactured with the equipment or training supplied. For example, a U.S. chemical company built a plant for an Indian company in return for some cash and a volume of chemicals to be made in the plant.

- *Offsets.* The seller is compensated in cash but agrees to spend a substantial amount of that cash with the customer or its government over a stated time period. For instance, Pepsi sells its cola syrup to Russia for rubles and agrees to buy Russian vodka at a given rate for sale in the United States.

*Source:* Adapted from Stephen S. Cohen and John Zysman, "Countertrade, Offsets, Barter, and Buybacks," *California Management Review,* Winter 1986, pp. 41–56. Copyright © 1986, by The Regents of the University of California. Reprinted from the *California Management Review,* Vol. 28, No. 2. By permission of The Regents.

## Discounts and Allowances

Firms relying on independent wholesalers and retailers to distribute their products must adjust their list prices to motivate and reward these firms to perform needed marketing activities.[24] We discuss programs for gaining reseller support in more detail in the next chapter, but briefly describe price discounts and allowances—basic tools used in creating such programs—in the next sections.

**Trade Discounts**     To induce wholesalers and/or retailers to carry a product and perform their usual marketing activities in its support, manufacturers offer **trade (or functional) discounts** from the suggested retail list price. Such discounts vary, depending on the intermediary's wholesale or retail level in the channel and the specific activities they are expected to perform. A manufacturer who distributes stereo speakers through a channel of independent wholesale distributors and retailers, for instance, might have a suggested retail price of $100 for each speaker and a trade discount schedule of 50/15. The 50 represents the percent discount from list price offered to retailers who carry the product. The 15 is the discount offered to the wholesaler. Thus, a retailer would pay $50 for each speaker ($100 − [.5 × $100]). The wholesaler would pay the manufacturer $42.50 ($50 − [.15 × $50]).

**Quantity Discounts**     To encourage channel members, or even ultimate customers, to purchase more of the product, a manufacturer might offer a price reduction for ordering in large quantities. The **quantity discount** often increases as order size increases. For example, a firm might offer no additional discount on orders of 50 units or less, a 2 percent discount off list on orders of 51 to 100 units, 4 percent off on orders of 101 to 500 units, and 5 percent off on orders of more than 500 units. To avoid charges of illegal price discrimination against smaller purchasers, the size of such discounts should be justified by the cost savings that manufacturers gain by filling larger orders. These savings include reductions in per-unit selling, order processing, transportation, and inventory carrying costs. In addition to cost savings, quantity discounts help move more inventory closer to the ultimate customer, thereby encouraging more impulse purchases and reducing the probability of stockouts occurring among wholesalers or retailers in the distribution system.

**Cash Discounts**    A **cash discount** is a price reduction to encourage customers to pay their bills promptly. A common example of such a discount is "2/10, net 30." This means that payment in full is due within 30 days, but the buyer can deduct 2 percent from the price if payment is made within 10 days. Such discounts help reduce the capital the seller has tied up in accounts receivable and lower collection costs and bad debts.

**Allowances**    Allowances are similar to discounts in that they are inducements to encourage channel members or final customers to engage in specific behaviors in support of the product. One common example in consumer durable goods categories—particularly automobiles—is the **trade-in allowance.** This is essentially a price reduction granted to customers for turning in an old item when buying a new one. Such allowances help customers recoup the value from their used products and thereby encourage more frequent replacement purchases. **Promotional allowances** such as cooperative advertising programs reward distributors or retailers for advertising the product at the local level. Other promotional allowances may induce retailers to devote more shelf space, personal selling effort, or point-of-purchase promotional material to the product. Payment of such allowances is often contingent upon the retailer's meeting a specific sales volume goal, but they can amount to substantial sums. For instance, Safeway Inc., a large supermarket chain, reported supplier promotion payments amounted to $2.1 billion in 2002.[25]

**Price-Off Promotions**    This is one of the simplest kinds of sales promotion since all that's involved is a temporary reduction in the product's price. A similar popular promotion increases the amount of product provided while holding the price constant—like Pepsi's offer of 15 cans of soda for the normal price of a 12-pack. Price-off promotions may be the most effective way to boost sales temporarily; however, they suffer from several disadvantages. Often they only transfer future sales to the present as loyal customers stock up. Another problem is that competitors can easily copy them. Also, they may lead consumers to the notion that the product should be bought only below the suggested retail price if promotional deals are offered frequently.

**Coupons, Rebates, and Refunds**    The proportion of consumer promotion dollars devoted to **cents-off coupons** declined somewhat during the 1990s. As redemption rates fell to about 2 percent and processing costs increased, many consumer goods manufacturers attempted to cut their couponing budgets and emphasize "value pricing" or "everyday low price" policies instead. Such actions were also motivated by other drawbacks of heavy reliance on coupons, including the potential for fraud—ranging from counterfeiting to misredemption by retailers—and the fact that it is difficult to gain a competitive advantage using such a ubiquitous tactic.

Nevertheless, couponing remains the dominant form of price-oriented promotion in the United States. Approximately 300 billion coupons are distributed each year, and a recent survey found that 100 percent of manufacturers who sell consumer goods through supermarkets still devote at least some of their promotion dollars to coupons.[26]

What accounts for the continuing popularity of coupons? Coupons can be an effective way to target discounts to specific customer segments, particularly as information technology makes it possible for firms to collect more detailed information about customers. For instance, by combining a computer database of purchase histories with a direct mail program, a marketer can direct coupons to the most price-sensitive households while maintaining higher regular prices for less price-oriented buyers.[27] Coupons are also useful for accomplishing specific strategic marketing objectives, such as motivating first-time buyers to try a product or encouraging the purchase of larger package sizes.

**"Deal-a-day" website coupons** are particularly effective for attracting first-time customers because they reassure potential buyers that their peers also find the deal attractive, and they guarantee the seller that a substantial number of customers will be attracted or they won't have to pay for the promotion. For example, Groupon—the most successful such site—posts one deal each day in each of the various cities where it operates. If enough subscribers sign up for the deal, they receive a coupon by e-mail the next, and Groupon gets a finder's fee. Michelle Johnson of the Vitality Unlimited Spa near St. Louis reports attracting 600 new customers by offering a $68 massage for $30, and nearly 70 percent of those Groupon visitors have since booked a second massage at full price.[28]

**Rebates** reduce the price of the product through a money refund offer. Such offers typically require the consumer to mail some proof of purchase to the manufacturer to receive the refund. In recent years rebates have been used extensively by producers of durable goods, including automobiles, major appliances, and cameras, because they can move excess inventories quickly.

**Premiums** are attempts to attract buyers by offering a product or service free or at a substantially reduced price to encourage the purchase of another product. Premiums can be included in a package, sent by mail, or via another product (a free soft drink with the purchase of a pizza). Premiums can even be to some extent self-liquidating—as when the consumer sends in a package and 50 cents for a premium.

## Differential Pricing

**Differential pricing** (also known as discriminatory pricing) occurs when a firm sells a product or service at two or more prices not determined by proportional differences in cost. This is usually done to adjust to differences in the price sensitivities or preferences of various customer segments. Prices may even vary on a customer-to-customer basis in organizational markets or consumer durable categories where the final price is determined through negotiation. For example, automobile retailers were once noted for such pricing practices, but the wide availability on the internet of manufacturers' invoice prices has made aggressive haggling over price a much less common event when shopping for a new car.[29]

Some common differential pricing adjustments targeted at particular customer segments include:

- *Time pricing.* Prices might be adjusted seasonally, across days of the week, or across hours of the day to capitalize on predictable fluctuations in demand over time. Movie theaters, for instance, often charge higher prices for evening shows than for early matinees, and hotels charge less for weekend occupancy.

- *Location pricing.* The same product or service might be priced differently at various retail locations to capitalize on local demand or the intensity of competition. Even within a single theater, seats in some locations are typically more expensive because many theater-goers are willing to pay more to sit near the stage.

- *Customer segment pricing.* Perhaps the most common differential pricing practice is to charge different prices to customer segments that vary in their willingness or ability to buy. Many arts organizations, for example, offer lower prices to senior citizens whose fixed incomes might otherwise prohibit their attendance.

**Conditions Allowing Differential Pricing**   It is not always possible or wise to set different prices for essentially the same product. For such a differential pricing policy to work, first there must be identifiable customer segments with different price sensitivities. Second, the customer segments must either be physically separated from one another or the firm must institute control procedures to ensure that the segment paying the lower price cannot resell the product to customers paying the higher price. Obviously, too, the cost to the manufacturer of segmenting and monitoring the market should not exceed the extra revenue generated by the discriminatory pricing. And the firm should be confident that resentment among customers asked to pay the higher price or competitive conditions in the market will not leave it vulnerable to competitive attacks in the high-price segments. Consumer resentment is particularly likely if they are aware that different people pay different prices for what they perceive to be essentially the same product or service. Thus, the perceived unfairness of differential pricing can be offset by customizing the product or service, differentiating the offerings sold via different distribution channels, or communicating a social or economic rationale to justify the price differences (e.g., elderly customers get a lower price because they have limited incomes).[30]

### The Internet Facilitates Differential Pricing
As we have mentioned before, many analysts argue that the internet will make product categories more price competitive. It is also making it easier to identify—and charge different prices to—customer segments with different price sensitivities. For example, there are software programs that let a web-based seller examine the click-streams of visitors to its site. If the individual examines a number of alternatives without making a purchase, he or she might be identified as a high-involvement, price-sensitive shopper and therefore be offered lower prices.[31]

The internet also enables firms, especially service firms, to do more differential pricing by allowing them to change prices quickly at different times of the day or week (i.e., time pricing) or in response to unused capacity, as when airlines make last-minute special fares available on their websites.

### Legal Considerations[32]
Price discrimination is not the legal issue in the United States today that it was in the past. It is important to note, however, that the Robinson-Patman Act outlaws price discrimination among buyers of goods of "like grade and quality" where the effect may be to "injure, destroy, or prevent competition." Because individual consumers buy goods and services for their own use and are not competing with one another, the law usually does not prevent discriminatory pricing of consumer goods at the retail level because there is no injury to competition. To legally offer different prices for the same product to retailers, distributors, or industrial buyers, the manufacturer must be sure that the buyers involved are not in direct competition, or that the difference in prices offered is justified by differences in the cost of doing business with the different buyers. This cost defense, for example, is the rationale for offering the quantity discounts mentioned in the preceding section. Because transportation and order processing costs are usually lower for large orders, firms can legally pass those cost savings on to the buyer as a discount or lower price.

In addition to price discrimination, the Sherman Act prohibits both horizontal and vertical price fixing. In the case of the former, competitors agree to maintain a given price. The latter involves an agreement between manufacturers and retailers to sell products at a certain price. The Miller Tyding Act (1937) was passed to permit such vertical price fixing, but in 1976, Congress passed the Consumer Goods Pricing Act, which made such pricing once more illegal. Predatory pricing is also illegal under the Sherman Act because it involves selling below cost to drive one or more competitors out of the market.

In addition to legal concerns, differential price adjustments can raise some ethical issues as well. One such issue concerns the inherent "fairness" of charging higher prices to some customers simply because they are not very price sensitive or reside in a different geographic area or market segment, as discussed in Ethical Perspective 11.2.

## ETHICAL PERSPECTIVE 11.2
### Ethical Concerns over Differential Prices

While the issue of the equity or fairness of charging different prices to different customers is primarily a concern of the law, evaluating the fairness of the price charged to a particular customer can also involve ethical considerations. For instance, just because a customer attaches a high value to a given product or service and is therefore willing to pay a high price does not necessarily mean it is always ethical—or in the firm's best long-term interest—to charge such a price. Consider the case of AZT, a drug treatment for symptoms of AIDS. When the drug was first introduced by Wellcome PLC, a yearlong treatment cost $10,000. The company argued that the high price was necessary to compensate for the heavy investment involved in developing such a drug for a relatively small market. In addition, potential customers attached a high value to any drug that offered promise for ameliorating AIDS symptoms. However, public reaction to AZT's high price was so negative that the company eventually reduced it substantially, but only after some damage had probably been done to the firm's image and reputation.

Similarly, in a somewhat less "high involvement" product category, shoppers complained to Amazon when they realized the company was testing different prices for the same items in different markets. Amazon abandoned the test in just five days and went back to uniform pricing.

For a discussion of other ethical issues, see Gwendolyn K. Ortmeyer, "Ethical Issues in Pricing," in N. Craig Smith and John A. Quelch, eds., *Ethics in Marketing* (Burr Ridge, IL: Richard D. Irwin, 1993); and Faith Keenan, "The Price Is Really Right," *BusinessWeek*, March 31, 2003, pp. 62–67.

# Product-Line Pricing Adjustments

Pricing decisions become even more complicated when a firm produces a line of several models or styles that potential customers perceive as bearing some relationship to one another. In such cases, firms need to adjust the prices of various models to reflect customers' perceptions of their relative value. In theory, producers should determine the prices for all the products in the line simultaneously, taking into account not only the price elasticity of demand for each model, but also the cross-elasticities among them. A **cross-elasticity** is the percentage change in sales of one product induced by a 1 percent change in the price of another product that is assumed to be a close substitute.

Because of the difficulties in estimating such cross-elasticities, however, firms seldom use this approach. About the best that managers can do is to price each item separately and then adjust those prices to reflect the likelihood that customers will trade up or down and will perceive the prices of the related items to be fair and reasonable. Since some products require the use of other products (razors and razor blades or printers and ink cartridges), the seller may price one product lower to stimulate the sale of the other.

Many companies offer optional features with their basic product. Automobile companies offer such extras as bigger engines, special tires, sun roofs, higher-quality sound systems, and leather interiors—all for an extra cost. Luxury cars include most such features as standard equipment and many retailer's use them as a way of bargaining with consumers. Such practices make it difficult to price these options in any realistic way. A somewhat similar situation exists when firms sell a basic service for a fixed amount and then charge an additional amount based on the extent of usage (telephone companies and their long-distance charges).

Sellers often **bundle** the various items in their product line and sell the bundle at a price less than the total of the items if priced separately (McDonald's meals for children, season subscriptions to concerts, option packages offered by car companies). Since some customers may not want the bundle, provision must be made to allow purchase of individual items.

# TAKE-AWAYS

1. Pricing decisions involve an inherent conflict between (1) the need to win customers by allowing them to retain a portion of the value inherent in a product or service and (2) the need to maintain profit margins sufficient to compensate employees, fund growth, and satisfy the firm's various stakeholders.

2. The price of a good or service must be high enough to cover per unit costs—at least in the long term—but cannot exceed its value as perceived by the customer. Therefore, the region between unit cost and perceived value represents the range of feasible prices.

3. The decision about what price to select from within the range of feasible prices should be based on a careful analysis of competitors' costs and prices, the product's strategic objectives, and consistency with other components of the marketing plan.

4. Perhaps the key concept in setting a price is the notion of perceived value. An essential purpose of the price set by a marketing manager should be to enable the firm to capture a fair share of the value of the product as perceived by the intended customer.

5. The final step in deciding what price to charge for a product or service involves the development of a price structure that adapts the price to variations in cost and demand across geographic territories, national boundaries, customer segments, and items within the product line.

**Self-diagnostic questions to test your ability to apply the analytical tools and concepts in this chapter to marketing decision making may be found at this book's website at www.mhhe.com/mullins8e.**

# ENDNOTES

1. This case example is based on material found in "Lining Up for Profits," *The Economist,* November 12, 2005, pp. 71–73; Mark Scott, "Ryanair Faces Future Trouble," *www.businessweek.com/globalbiz/europeinsight,* June 6, 2008; Suzanne Kapner, "Flying the Unfriendly Skies," *Fortune,* July 7, 2008, p. 30; Felix Gillette, "The Duke of Discomfort," *Bloomberg Businessweek,* September 6, 2010, pp. 58–61; and Ryanair's 2010 annual report available at *www.ryanair.com.*

2. Robert J. Dolan, "How Do You Know When the Price Is Right?" *Harvard Business Review,* September–October 1995, p. 174.

3. Dolan, "How Do You Know When the Price Is Right?"

4. For a detailed review of pricing methods and research, see Chezy Ofir and Russell S. Winer, "Pricing: Economic and Behavioral Models," in Bart Weitz and Robin Wensley, eds., *Handbook of Marketing* (London: Sage Publications, 2002).

5. Y. K. Shetty, "Product Quality and Competitive Strategy," *Business Horizons,* May–June 1987, pp. 46–52; David A. Garvin, *Managing Quality* (New York: Free Press, 1988), pp. 70–74; and Jan-Benedict E. M. Steenkamp, Harald J. Van Heerde, and Inge Geyskens, "What Makes Consumers Willing to Pay a Price Premium for National Brands over Private Labels?" *Journal of Marketing Research* 47 (December 2010), pp. 1011–24.

6. Gerard J. Tellis, "Beyond the Many Faces of Price: An Integration of Pricing Strategies," *Journal of Marketing,* October 1986, p. 146.

7. Kathryn Rudie Harrigan and Michael E. Porter, "End-Game Strategies for Declining Industries," *Harvard Business Review,* July–August 1983, pp. 111–20. To truly maximize current profit, of course, the product's price should be set exactly at the point where the marginal revenue gained from the last item sold equals the marginal cost of producing and selling that item. In reality, though, most firms do not have adequate knowledge of their demand and cost functions to determine the profit-maximizing price with such precision.

8. Wilfred Amaldoss and Sanjay Jain, "Pricing of Conspicuous Goods: A Competitive Analysis of Social Effects," *Journal of Marketing Research* 42 (February 2005), pp. 30–42.

9. Akshay R. Rao, Mark E. Bergen, and Scott Davis, "How to Fight a Price War," *Harvard Business Review,* March–April 2000, pp. 107–16; and Thomas T. Nagel, "Managing Price Competition," *Marketing Management* 2 (Spring 1993), pp. 36–45.

10. For a more detailed discussion of how to estimate demand and its elasticity, see Paul W. Farris, Neil T. Bendle, Phillip E. Pfeifer, and David J. Reibstein, *Marketing Metrics,* 2nd ed. (Upper Saddle River, NJ: Pearson Education, Inc., 2010), chap. 7.

11. Faith Keenan, "The Price Is Really Right," *BusinessWeek,* March 31, 2003, pp. 62–67.

12. Robin Cooper and Robert S. Kaplan, "Measure Costs Right: Make the Right Decisions," *Harvard Business Review,* September–October 1988, pp. 96–103.

13. "Supermarket 1998 Sales Manual," *Progressive Grocer,* July 1998.

14. H. Michael Hayes, Per V. Jenster, and Nels Erik Aaby, *Business Marketing* (Burr Ridge, IL: Richard D. Irwin, 1996), p. 306.

15. Steven Kaplan and Mohanbir Sawhney, "E-Hubs: The New B2B Marketplaces," *Harvard Business Review,* May–June 2000, pp. 97–103; Paul Markillie, "A Perfect Market: A Survey of E-Commerce," *The Economist,* March 15, 2004, pp. 3–20; and Timothy J. Mullaney, "E-Biz Strikes Again," *BusinessWeek,* May 10, 2004, pp. 80–90.

16. Sandy D. Jap, "The Impact of Online Reverse Auction Design on Buyer–Supplier Relationships," *Journal of Marketing* 71 (January 2007), pp. 146–59.

17. Shuba Srinivasan, Koen Pauwels, and Vincent Nijs, "Demand-Based Pricing versus Past-Price Dependence: A Cost-Benefit Analysis," *Journal of Marketing* 72 (March 2008), pp. 15–27.

18. Erin Anderson and Duncan Simester, "Mind Your Pricing Cues," *Harvard Business Review* (September 2003), pp. 96–103.

19. Jeffery H. Birnbaum, "Pricing of Products Is Still an Art, Often Having Little Link to Costs," *The Wall Street Journal,* November 25, 1981, p. 25.

**20.** Mark Stiving and Russell S. Winer, "An Empirical Analysis of Price Endings with Scanner Data," *Journal of Consumer Research* (June 1997), pp. 57–68.

**21.** Warren J. Keegan, *Global Marketing Management,* 7th ed. (Englewood Cliffs, NJ: Prentice Hall, 2001), chap. 13.

**22.** "Global Stretch," *The Economist,* March 12, 2011, p. 76.

**23.** Leslie Moore, "For Wary Argentines, the Crops Are Cash," *New York Times,* December 1, 2002, BU6.

**24.** Michael V. Marn and Robert L. Rosiello, "Managing Price, Gaining Profit," *Harvard Business Review,* September–October 1992, pp. 84–94.

**25.** David Henry, "Accounting Games in the Grocer's Aisle," *Business-Week,* April 14, 2003, p. 64.

**26.** Cox Direct, *19th Annual Survey of Promtional Practices* (Largo, FL: Cox Direct, 1997).

**27.** "Targeting Couponing Slows Redemption Slide," *Marketing News,* February 12, 1996, p. 11; and Faith Keenan, "The Price Is Really Right."

**28.** Jessi Hemple, "Social Media Meets Retailing," *Fortune,* March 22, 2010, p. 30.

**29.** Paul Markillie, 'Motoring Online,' a section within "A Survey of Consumer Power," *The Economist,* April 2, 2005, pp. 11–12.

**30.** Lan Xia, Kent B. Monroe, and Jennifer L. Cox, "The Price Is Unfair! A Conceptual Framework of Price Fairness Perceptions," *Journal of Marketing* 68 (October 2004), pp. 1–15.

**31.** Scott Woolley, "I Got It Cheaper Than You," *Forbes,* November 2, 1998, pp. 82–84.

**32.** For a more detailed discussion of the legal aspects of pricing, see Thomas T. Nagle and Reed K. Holden, *The Strategy and Tactics of Pricing* (Englewood Cliffs, NJ: Pearson/Prentice Hall, 2006), chap. 14.

# CHAPTER TWELVE

# Distribution Channel Decisions

## Selling Soft Drinks in Africa—Coke Builds a Distribution System[1]

THE U.S. COLA MARKET has long been mature and has suffered declining revenue over the past five years. That has motivated companies like Coca-Cola and PepsiCo to diversify their product lines by adding bottled water, fruit juices and the like, and to seek future growth in undeveloped markets—such as many of the countries in Africa. Coke has been in Africa since 1929, is currently selling in every African country, and is the continent's largest employer with 65,000 employees and 160 plants. But the firm is gearing up for what it predicts will be a major and sustained increase in future sales volume. In 2000 about 59 million African households earned $5,000 or more, which is the point where families begin to spend half their income on nonfood items. Forecasts suggest that number could grow to 106 million households by 2014. Important too, Coke's management believes that, in spite of recent turmoil in the Muslim countries of North Africa and in Ivory Coast and Zimbabwe, African governments will become more stable, democratic, and focused on economic development. Consequently, the company plans to invest $12 billion on the continent over the next 10 years, more than twice as much as in the previous decade.

Of course, the diverse populations, low discretionary incomes, and underdeveloped transportation and distribution systems found in many African nations call for some very different marketing actions than Coke has pursued in the United States and Europe. For example, most soft drinks in Africa are sold in returnable glass bottles which Coke refills as many as 70 times before they are recycled. Returnable bottles help hold costs and prices down so the company can reach more of what it calls "economically diverse" customers. Consumers, in effect, pay only for the liquid in the bottle. And that liquid may also be somewhat different. While the company focuses heavily on its signature soft-drink brands like Coca-Cola and Sprite, it is also building new juice bottling plants to capture a growing middle-class demand for mango, orange, and other tropical fruit juices.

As any soft drink executive will tell you, though, the key to marketing success is to get the product "cold and close" to the customer. And that is the major challenge Coke faces in countries with very few vending machines or supermarkets, thousand of very small retail shops, and marginal transportation infrastructure. To meet this challenge, Coke has helped develop about 4,000 manual distribution centers in a number of African countries. Rosinje Distributors in Nairobi Kenya, for instance, stores cases of soft drinks from the nearby bottling plant in three shipping containers, which serve as a warehouse. Ten salespeople then use two-wheeled dollies to deliver Coke, Fanta, Mango juice, and Stony Ginger Beer to about 345 small shops and beverage kiosks in the neighborhood. With no room for inventory, many shopkeepers order as little as a case a day. And given the lousy roads and congestion, its easier to deliver to them by hand. Coke and its bottlers teach these minidistributors how to run their operations as efficiently as possible, and help provide the shopkeepers they serve with coolers, signage, point-of-sale materials, and the like. As a result, manual distributors like Rosinje have become important players in the African market, moving as much as 25,000 cases per month. They currently employ 12,000 Africans and generate $500 million in annual revenue. It's not surprising, then, that Coke plans to develop 1,200 more in the near future.

## Marketing Challenges Addressed in Chapter 12

The importance of good distribution decisions in designing a marketing plan is simple: Customers won't buy your good or service unless it is readily available when and where they want to buy it. An effective distribution channel makes the right quantities of the right product available in the right place at the right time to satisfy the target customer. An efficient distribution channel also reduces the costs of marketing and acquiring the product.

As Coca-Cola's experience in Africa makes apparent, however, the manager really faces two separate but closely related sets of decisions concerning distribution channels. First come **channel design** decisions concerned with developing a channel structure that links the firm's marketing strategy with the needs of its target market. These decisions focus on questions such as how many levels of middlemen should be included in the distibution system and what types of institutions, and how many of each, should be included at each level. Unfortunately, as Coca-Cola discovered in Kenya, sufficient numbers of appropriate middlemen may not exist in developing markets. In that case, channel design may involve facilitating the development of new institutions through financial assistance, extensive training programs, promotional materials, and the like.

Once a product's distribution channel has been designed, a second set of decisions concerns how that channel should be managed. **Channel management** decisions involve the development of policies and procedures to gain and maintain the cooperation of—and often to form mutually beneficial long-term relationships with—the various institutions within the channel. Such decisions focus on selecting and recruiting individual channel members, motivating them to perform specific marketing functions on behalf of the supplier's product or service, coordinating their efforts, assessing their performance, and resolving conflicts that arise.

This chapter examines both the channel design and channel management decisions a marketer faces.[2] We begin by discussing the economic rationale for having multiple institutions involved in distributing a given product or service. Why are channels involving networks of many independent firms often more efficient and effective than distributing things directly from the producer to the consumer?

Next, we discuss the various marketing objectives a distribution channel might be designed to accomplish. We then examine some alternative channel designs for both consumer and organizational goods and services, including the various types of institutions and the numbers of those institutions that might be included in a distribution channel given different objectives and strategic circumstances.

Finally, we examine the major issues involved in managing an existing channel, starting with various legal mechanisms, such as vertical integration and franchising, that some firms employ to control channel activities. However, because most channel systems consist of networks of legally independent firms, we devote most of our attention to examining the incentives that can be used to motivate those firms to act in concert with the manufacturer's marketing program. We conclude with a discussion of channel conflicts and the strategies firms employ to resolve them.

## Why Do Multifirm Marketing Channels Exist?

As noted in our first chapter, someone must perform a number of marketing functions or activities before a producer and a customer can exchange goods or services—transportation and storage; communication of information via advertising, personal selling, and sales promotion; feedback (marketing research); financing; and such services as installation and repair. Sometimes the customer performs most of the marketing activities in an exchange, as when a family takes a drive through the country to buy vegetables at a farmer's roadside stand. In other cases, a producer may distribute goods or services directly to end users, for example, through mail-order catalogs or the internet. Most goods are, however, distributed through systems consisting of a variety of middlemen such as retailers, wholesalers, and agents. Thus, a **marketing channel** is

> the set of interdependent organizations involved in the process of making a product or service available for consumption or use by consumers or industrial users.[3]

Many services are distributed through marketing channels, too. Due to their intangible nature, services often do not require the physical distribution activities, such as transportation and storage, that are necessary for goods. Nevertheless, many marketing activities are still necessary to facilitate exchanges with service customers, such as communicating information, customizing the service to a particular customer's needs, personal selling, and financing. Many of these activities are performed by independent middlemen; sometimes by franchised retailers such as McDonald's fast-food outlets, and in other cases by agent middlemen like insurance agents, travel agents, or stockbrokers.

The rationale for marketing channels lies in the trade-off between costs and benefits. Performing marketing activities costs money, which is reflected in the final selling price of the product or service. Such costs vary widely across products and customers, but are often substantial—on average about 50 percent of the retail price of most consumer package goods with about half that being the retailer's margin. The rest consists of the marketing expenses of the manufacturer and wholesale middlemen. Although the marketing costs for many industrial goods such as sheet steel or basic chemicals tend to be considerably lower since they are sold in large quantities to a smaller number of regular customers, they still account for 10 to 15 percent of the final selling price.

Would consumers be better off buying directly from the manufacturer and bypassing channel intermediaries? Usually not. It's a classic marketing truth that although middlemen can be eliminated, someone must still perform the marketing functions. Middlemen often perform the needed functions at a lower cost than either the customer or the manufacturer could by themselves. This is particularly true when a product must be distributed

## Exhibit 12.1

Ways by Which Using Middlemen Improves Market Efficiency

- *Functional efficiency:* Middlemen can often perform one or more marketing activities more efficiently than manufacturers or their customers because of their specialization and greater economies of scale. For example, they can spread costs across different manufacturers and thus perform the selling function at a lower cost.

- *Scale efficiency:* By purchasing goods in large quantities, storing them, and then breaking them down into the smaller quantities their customers prefer, middlemen enable manufacturers and their customers to operate more efficiently. Rather than having to make small production runs to fill the orders of individual customers, manufacturers can achieve the economies of large-scale production. And their customers can buy smaller quantities without having their capital tied up in large inventories.

- *Transactional efficiency:* Through their various activities, wholesalers and retailers make it possible for customers to acquire wide assortments of products from a single source with one transaction. This reduces the time and effort that businesses and consumers expend in finding and purchasing the goods they need.

to large numbers of geographically dispersed customers. See Exhibit 12.1 for a discussion of the various ways marketing efficiency can be improved using middlemen.

However, not all middlemen perform a full range of marketing functions, nor are they equally efficient or effective. Therefore, the first step in designing a distribution channel for a given product is to determine what objectives the channel must accomplish and their relative importance.

## Designing Distribution Channels: What Are the Objectives to Be Accomplished?

Managers can design distribution channels to accomplish one or more of the following objectives: (1) increase the availability of the good or service to potential customers, (2) satisfy customer requirements by providing high levels of service, (3) ensure promotional effort, (4) obtain timely and detailed market information, (5) increase cost–effectiveness, and (6) maintain flexibility. As summarized in Exhibit 12.2, the achievement of each of these objectives can be measured and thus can be used to evaluate the performance of a particular channel. However, there are trade-offs among these various objectives, and they are not all equally relevant for all types of products or market circumstances. Consequently, we briefly discuss in the following sections each of these objectives and the conditions where each might be given greater emphasis.

## Product Availability

The most important objective for any distribution channel is to make the product conveniently available for customers who want to buy it. For consumer goods, two aspects of availability must be considered. The first is to attain the desired level of coverage in terms of appropriate retail outlets. Because retailers differ in their sales volume, manufacturers need to weight the relative importance of each retailer on the basis of its percent of sales within the product category in question. The resulting figure is referred to as the percent of **all commodity volume (ACV).** For example, a packaged food item may be carried by only 40 percent of an area's food stores. But it may have 70 percent ACV because it is handled primarily by supermarkets accounting for a large proportion of the total sales of such products. The second important aspect of availability for consumer products is the item's positioning within the store. One way to measure performance here is the percentage

# Exhibit 12.2

DISTRIBUTION CHANNEL OBJECTIVES AND MEASUREMENT CRITERIA

| Performance objective | Possible measures | Applicable products and channel level |
|---|---|---|
| **Product availability:** | | |
| • Coverage of relevant retailers. | • Percent of all commodity volume (ACV). | • Consumer products (particularly convenience goods) at retail level. |
| • In-store positioning. | • Percent of shelf-facings or display space gained by product, weighted by importance of store. | • Consumer products at retail level. |
| • Coverage of geographic markets. | • Frequency of sales calls by customer type; average delivery time. | • Industrial products; consumer goods at wholesale level. |
| **Meeting customer service requirements:** | | |
| • Installation, training, repair, reliability, order cycle time, etc. | • Number of service technicians receiving technical training; monitoring of customer complaints; customer satisfaction level. | • Industrial products, particularly those involving high technology; consumer durables at retail level; consumer and commercial services. |
| **Promotional effort:** | | |
| • Effective point-of-purchase (P-O-P) promotion. | • Percent of stores using special displays and P-O-P materials, weighted by importance of store. | • Consumer products at retail level. |
| • Effective personal selling support. | • Percent of salespeople's time devoted to product; number of salespeople receiving training on product's characteristics and applications. | • Industrial products: consumer durables at all channel levels; consumer convenience goods at wholesale level. |
| **Market information:** | | |
| • Monitoring sales trends, inventory levels, competitors' actions. | • Quality and timeliness of information obtained. | • All levels of distribution. |
| **Cost-effectiveness:** | | |
| • Cost of channel functions relative to sales volume. | • Middlemen margins and marketing costs as percent of sales. | • All levels of distribution. |
| **Flexibility:** | | |
| • Ability to switch to new channels or types of middlemen as conditions change. | • Amount of specialized assets or dedicated investments devoted to current channel.<br><br>• Number of long-term legal commitments to current channel members. | • All levels of distribution; product or service categories experiencing rapid market development or technological change. |

of available shelf or display space devoted to the brand, weighted by the importance of the store.

For industrial products—and for assessing channel performance at the wholesale level for consumer products—the relevant issue of availability is whether the industrial customer or retailer has the opportunity to place an order and obtain the product when it is needed. This is a question of the adequacy of market coverage. Firms can assess coverage by measuring how often customers in a territory are called on by company or distributor salespeople *and* by the time required to fill and deliver an order (i.e., order cycle time). Cycle time measures are particularly relevant when dealers are able to purchase their requirements directly from a firm's website, or when they are linked to a manufacturer via an electronic reorder system.

Product availability is an important objective for all distribution channels. The appropriate *degree* of availability varies with the characteristics of the product and the target customers, particularly the product's importance to those customers and the amount of time and effort they will expend to obtain it. For example, consumer convenience goods, such as packaged foods and health products, demand immediate availability since most customers are unwilling to devote much effort to obtaining a particular brand. As Coca-Cola understands, soft-drink sales go up when the product is "cold and close" to the ultimate consumer. At the other extreme, immediate availability is less critical for unique and important products such as consumer specialty goods or major industrial equipment and installations.

Market and competitive factors also influence a firm's *ability to* achieve a desired level of availability for its product. When demand is limited or when the brand holds a small relative share of the total market, wholesalers or retailers willing to carry it may be difficult to find. The firm may have to offer extra incentives and inducements to achieve an adequate level of product availability. On the other hand, a brand's strong competitive position makes it easier to attain extensive retail coverage and shelf space. Also, as we'll discuss in more detail later, firms can enhance at least some aspects of availability through effective use of the internet.

# Meeting Customers' Service Requirements

A second channel objective, which is closely related to availability but broader in scope, is to achieve and maintain some target level of satisfaction in meeting the service requirements of target customers. This tends to be a particularly crucial objective for analyzer and defender businesses attempting to differentiate themselves from competitors on one or more service dimensions. Some service requirements that might be targeted for consumers, industrial end users, or other members of the distribution channel (e.g., the firm's "intermediate customers" such as distributors or retailers) include:

1. **Order cycle time,** which refers to how long it takes the manufacturer to receive, process, and deliver an order.
2. **Dependability,** which relates to the consistency/reliability of delivery. This is probably the most important element of distribution service, especially for those using just-in-time delivery systems.
3. **Communication** between buyer and seller, which enables both parties to resolve problems at an early stage.
4. **Convenience,** meaning that the system is sufficiently flexible to accommodate the special needs of different customers.
5. **Postsale services,** which help the customer attain full benefits over the life of the product. Such service might include installation, user training, help lines to resolve technical glitches, repair, and spare parts availability. Such services can be particularly important in the distribution of consumer durable goods and technically complex industrial products, such as computer systems, major software applications, manufacturing machinery, and the like.

Monitoring customer complaints, and the ongoing measurement of customer (or channel member) satisfaction, retention, and loyalty levels are all appropriate measures of whether the firm is meeting its customer service targets. As we saw in Chapter 4, monitoring customer complaints can also provide useful guidance for improving a firm's product and service quality levels in the future. For example, Dell Computer monitors blogs criticizing the firm's products or service and attempts to correct the problems discussed. The company also started Idea-Storm where customers offered more than 8,500 suggestions for improvement in the first year, voted on those suggestions 600,000 times, and left 64,000 comments. More than a dozen of those ideas have been implemented so far.[4]

## Promotional Effort

Another common channel objective is to obtain strong promotional support from channel members for the firm's product, including the use of local media, in-store displays, and cooperation in special promotion events. Gaining broad retailer support for in-store promotions is particularly important for low-involvement, convenience goods.[5] Both the amount and quality of personal selling effort that channel members devote to particular products can be critical. Strong selling support is particularly important when (1) firms are marketing technically complex and expensive consumer durables or industrial goods, (2) the market is highly competitive, or (3) a differentiated defender is trying to sustain a competitive advantage based on superior product quality or customer service.

## Market Information

Because of their proximity to the marketplace, middlemen are often relied on for fast and accurate feedback of information about such things as sales trends, inventory levels, and competitors' actions. A high level of channel feedback is particularly important for firms in highly competitive industries characterized by rapid changes in product technology or customer preferences, such as the computer and fashion industries. Feedback is crucial for firms pursuing prospector business strategies since they depend on the early identification of new product and market development opportunities for their success.

## Cost-Effectiveness

Channels must be designed to minimize the costs necessary to attain the firm's channel objectives. The cost-effectiveness of the distribution channel is of particular concern to businesses pursuing low-cost analyzer or defender strategies. However, there is often a trade-off between channel costs, particularly those associated with physical distribution activities such as transportation and inventory storage, and achieving high levels of performance on many of the other objectives we have examined, such as product availability and meeting customer service requirements. We will examine these trade-offs in more detail when we examine the pros and cons of alternative channel designs.

## Flexibility

Well-entrenched channels where the members have long-standing commitments or substantial mutual investments can be hard to change in response to shifting market or competitive conditions. Consequently, some firms, particularly those pursuing prospector strategies in new or rapidly growing or technically turbulent product categories, consider channel flexibility an important goal. A flexible channel is one where it is relatively easy to switch channel structures or add new types of middlemen without generating costly economic or legal conflicts with existing channel members.

# Designing Distribution Channels: What Kinds of Institutions Might Be Included?

There are four broad categories of institutions that a manager might decide to include in the distribution channel: merchant wholesalers, agent middlemen, retailers, and facilitating agencies. Each of these categories is defined in Exhibit 12.3 and discussed below.

## Merchant Wholesalers

Some types of merchant wholesalers engage in a full range of wholesaling functions while others specialize in only limited services. But both buy goods from various suppliers (that is, they take title) and then resell those goods to their commercial customers, either industrial buyers or other resellers such as a retailer. They are compensated by the margin between the price they pay and the price they receive for the goods they carry. Approximately 400,000 merchant wholesalers are operating in the United States, including sales branches maintained by manufacturing firms.[6]

## Agent Middlemen

The primary role of agent middlemen is to represent other organizations in the sale or purchase of goods or services. Agents do not take title to, or physical possession of, the goods they deal in. Instead, they specialize in either the buying or selling function. There are about 45,000 agent middlemen in the United States, of which manufacturer's agents and sales agents are the two major types used by producers.[7]

### Manufacturer's Agents or Manufacturer's Reps
These usually work for several manufacturers, carry noncompetitive, complementary merchandise in an exclusive territory, and concentrate only on the selling function. They are important where a manufacturer's sales are not sufficient to support a company salesperson in a particular territory. Manufacturer's reps are common in the industrial equipment, automotive supply, footwear, and toy industries.

## Exhibit 12.3

### INSTITUTIONS FOUND IN MARKETING CHANNELS

| Institution | Definition |
|---|---|
| Merchant wholesalers | Take title to the goods they handle; sell primarily to other resellers (e.g., retailers), industrial and commercial customers rather than to individual consumers. |
| Agent middlemen | Include manufacturer's representatives and brokers. Also sell to other resellers, industrial or commercial customers, but do not take title to the goods. Usually specialize in the selling function and represent client manufacturers on a commission basis. |
| Retailers | Sell goods and services directly to ultimate consumers for their personal, nonbusiness use. Usually take title to goods they handle; are compensated by the margin between the price they pay for those goods and the price they receive from their customers. |
| Facilitating agencies | Include advertising agencies, marketing research firms, collection agencies, trucking firms, and railroads; specialize in one or more marketing functions, work on a fee-for-service basis to help clients perform those functions more effectively and efficiently. |

*Note:* Terms such as *distributor* and *jobber* refer to wholesalers, especially those handling industrial goods. The term *dealer* may refer to either a wholesaler or retailer.

**Sales Agents**    In contrast, **sales agents** usually represent only one manufacturer and are responsible for the full range of marketing activities needed by that producer. Because they have a wider range of responsibilities, their commissions are much larger than those of manufacturer's reps. Sales agents are used primarily by small firms or start-ups that have limited marketing capabilities. They are particularly common in the electronics, apparel, and home furnishing industries.

**Brokers**    These are independent firms whose purpose is to bring buyers and sellers together for an exchange. Unlike agents, brokers usually have no continuing relationship with a particular buyer or seller. The producers of seasonal products such as fruits and vegetables and the real estate industry use brokers extensively.

**E-Hubs[8]**    These emerging forms of business-to-business internet sites serve the same major function as brokers; they help bring potential buyers and sellers together for an exchange. Also like a broker, the e-hub is usually compensated by commissions from one or both parties.

Some hubs focus on broad product categories of frequently purchased goods and services that are not industry specific, such as office supplies, airline tickets, or janitorial supplies, and add value by giving buyers in a range of industries access to a "virtual catalog" of offerings from an array of suppliers. While the hub is not directly responsible for performing any of the physical distribution functions, such as transportation or storage, it may maintain relationships with third-party facilitating agencies such as UPS to help ensure that buyers get what they pay for in a timely manner. Examples of this kind of hub include W.W. Grainger and *www.BizBuyer.com.*

Other hubs are more industry-specific, bringing buyers and sellers together within a single product category. They create value by enabling one-stop shopping by purchasers. For example, *www.PlasticsNet.com* allows plastics processors to issue a single purchase order for hundreds of plastics products sourced from a diverse set of suppliers. Because the products they offer tend to be specialized, industry-specific hubs often work with established merchant wholesalers (distributors) in their industry to ensure product availability and reliable delivery. Other examples include SciQuest in the life sciences industry and Chemdex in specialty chemicals.

## Retailers

Retailers sell goods and services directly to final consumers for their personal, nonbusiness use. Because retailers usually take title to the goods they carry, their compensation is the margin between what they pay for the merchandise and the prices they charge their customers. Retailing is a major industry in the United States, with over 1.6 million retail establishments.

Retail stores can be categorized in many different ways, such as by the type of merchandise carried (supermarkets, drugstores), breadth of product assortments (specialty or department stores), pricing policies (discount or specialty stores), or nature of the business's premises (e-tailers, mail-order retailers, vending-machine operators, traditional stores). One useful classification scheme groups stores according to their method of operation—low margin/high turnover versus high margin/low turnover.

The former compete primarily on a price basis. To keep volume high while minimizing inventory investments, **low-margin/high-turnover** stores usually concentrate on fast-moving items—such as food, health and beauty aids, basic clothing items, and housewares—and carry a relatively limited selection in each product category. Examples of such retailers include mass-merchandise discounters, wholesale clubs, most supermarket and drug chains, and some specialty chains in such areas as women's clothing, shoes, hardware, office supplies, and building supplies (e.g., Home Depot and Lowe's).

To profit, low-margin/high-turnover retailers must minimize their costs. Their focus on standardized, prepackaged merchandise helps lower personnel costs by reducing or eliminating in-store sales assistance. It also enables them to centralize many purchasing and store operating decisions, thus reducing the number of administrative personnel needed. Many such operations—particularly the mass merchandisers—also minimize their capital investment by operating out of freestanding, no-frills facilities near major traffic arteries; locations where land costs, rents, and taxes are low. Many specialty store chains, however, operate out of sizable malls.

At the other extreme, **high-margin/low-turnover** retailers differentiate themselves with unique assortments, quality merchandise, good customer service, and a prestigious store image. They focus on shopping or specialty goods, usually carrying a narrow range of product categories but offering deep assortments of styles and sizes within each category. They also emphasize prestigious national brands or exclusive goods unavailable elsewhere. Tiffany's, for example, carries many one-of-a-kind crystal and jewelry items. This category includes most department stores and upscale specialty stores.

## Nonstore Retailing

These institutions fit the definition of a retailer, but we discuss them separately because they don't have a fixed bricks-and-mortar physical location and most do not enable customers to personally inspect the merchandise or take immediate possession. This category includes direct selling (e.g., door-to-door sales and telemarketing), mail-order catalogs, TV shopping, vending machines, and websites.

There are several varieties of retail websites, including web start-ups like Amazon and iTunes.com that exist solely on the web and do not have any physical stores, websites developed by large catalog retailers (Lands' End, L.L. Bean) to leverage their direct-delivery operations, and websites developed by established bricks-and-mortar retailers like Target and Tesco to leverage their brand names and customer service skills.

Historically, an established brand name and customer base typically enabled the catalog and bricks-and-mortar retailers to attract customers to their websites at lower cost than the web start-ups. However, survey results suggest that retail websites in general have not done a great job of satisfying customers, particularly on basic customer service dimensions, although the bricks-and-mortar sites have been more successful at keeping those buyers coming back for repeat purchases than the start-ups.[9]

Many of the start-ups began life as "virtual" businesses that outsourced many of the physical distribution functions such as inventory storage and delivery. But because of the critical importance of good customer service for developing a satisfied and loyal customer base, some of those start-ups have begun developing their own physical distribution and fulfillment competencies to gain tighter control over those activities. For instance, Amazon has invested hundreds of millions of dollars in warehouses and inventory to help ensure fast, reliable delivery. As a result, repeat customers now account for the vast majority of Amazon's orders.[10]

Similarly, bricks-and-mortar stores have sought more creative uses for their websites and other communication channels as their customers have changed the way they shop. A summary of survey results detailing some of these changes in shopping behavior is presented in Exhibit 12.4. The bottom line is that many customers who make their purchases within a store rely on the retailer's website—as well as those of manufacturers and competing retailers and bloggers—to compare features, brands, and prices before they make a purchase.

## Exhibit 12.4

HOW IN-STORE PURCHASERS USE THE INTERNET

**Percent of in-store shoppers . . . who:**

| | |
|---|---|
| 69 | Research products online before going to a store to make a purchase. |
| 62 | Have looked at least once at an online peer review before making a purchase. |
| 61 | Want to be able to scan bar codes and access information on other stores' prices. |
| 39 | Compared a product's features and price across retail outlets before buying. |
| 9 | Used a cell phone to text-message a friend or relation about a product while shopping. |

*Source:* Data reported in Nanette Byrnes, "More Clicks at the Bricks," *BusinessWeek,* December 17, 2007, p. 51.

To help in-store salespeople remain relevant as their customers use the internet to become increasingly savvy, some retailers have revamped their job descriptions, training programs, and incentives. At Best Buy, for instance, 30 percent of store staff have been redeployed from specific departments to roam the entire store. Their job is to understand all the electronic gadgets in the store, how they work together, and how a customer can get the best performance from a product when she or he gets it home. To get those salespeople up to speed, the company has them meet with manufacturers' reps, attend frequent training programs, and—when customers are scarce—play with the products.[11]

### Auction Sites Facilitate Retail Start-ups

Auction sites like eBay and China's TaoBao not only provide a convenient way for consumers to sell possessions they want to get rid of, they also enable entrepreneurs to start new retail businesses with minimal capital and red tape. In the United States, 724,000 professional sellers relied on eBay as either their primary or secondary source of sales revenue in 2010. And eBay-based start-ups have become popular in Europe where government regulations and scarce venture capital have historically posed problems for small retailers. Starting an eBay business is relatively easy for anyone with broadband and inventory and shipping software, which is readily available for a few thousand dollars. And European logistics companies such as Deutsche Post offer services tailored to small e-commerce operations. Consequently, more than 60,000 entrepreneurs in both Germany and Britain, 15,000 in France, and 10,000 in Italy earn at least 25 percent of their income as eBay merchants. As a result, the diversity of products available to consumers and their price competitiveness are increasing rapidly.[12]

## Channel Design Alternatives

Deciding which channel members to include when designing a distribution system depends in part on whether the good or service is to be sold to individual consumers or organizational customers. Therefore, we begin our examination of alternative channel designs by enumerating the options available for distributing consumer versus industrial goods. But the choice also depends, as we'll see in subsequent sections, on the firm's competitive strategy and resources and therefore on the relative importance of the various channel objectives we discussed earlier.

# Alternative Consumer Goods Channels

Five channel designs are commonly used to distribute consumer goods and services, as shown in Exhibit 12.5. Channel A involves direct distribution from the producer to the consumer. This is becoming a more popular channel, particularly for products targeted at two-wage-earner households where time is of the essence. As noted earlier, a number of technologies can be employed to achieve direct distribution, including direct mail catalogs, telephone or door-to-door selling, interactive cable TV, and manufacturers' websites. Channel B in Exhibit 12.5 involves producers that sell directly to retailers, who in turn sell to consumers. Such channels are typically used when the retailers are large enough to perform their own wholesaling functions or to form efficient logistical alliances with the manufacturer, as is the case for chains like Walmart, Sears, and Marks & Spencer. This kind of channel is also appropriate for distributing specialty goods such as designer fashions, expensive watches, or even greeting cards through selected retail outlets like Hallmark Card shops. Of course, the retailers involved in such channels may be traditional bricks-and-mortar operations, internet start-ups, or some combination of the two.

Channel C uses both a wholesaler and a retailer and is most common for low-cost, frequently purchased items extensively distributed through a large number of retailers. Because many of the retailers in such channels are small, the manufacturer's cost of dealing with them directly would be prohibitive. Thus, before it could distribute soft drinks through the many small retail shops and beverage kiosks in Kenya, Coca-Cola had to first sponsor and train enough wholesale distributors to service them efficiently. This channel system is common for such products as packaged food items, liquor, and health and beauty aids. Channel D, where an agent sells to wholesalers who in turn sell to retailers, is used when the manufacturer is too small, or its product line too narrow, to justify a company salesforce. In some cases, particularly where a small producer sells to retail chains that are large enough to take care of their own wholesaling functions, an agent may be employed to sell directly to the retailers, as shown in Channel E.

# Exhibit 12.5

MARKETING CHANNELS FOR CONSUMER GOODS AND SERVICES

## Exhibit 12.6

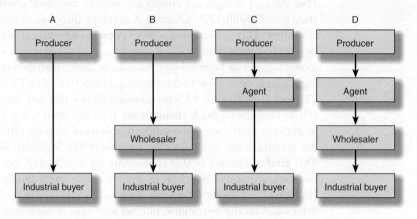

## Alternative Industrial Goods Channels

Exhibit 12.6 illustrates four alternative channel designs for distributing industrial goods. Direct distribution (Channel A) is much more common for industrial goods and services than it is in the consumer sphere. It is particularly popular when buyers are large and well-known, the product or service is technically complex and of high unit value, and the selling function requires technical expertise or extended negotiation. For example, large computer systems, commercial aircraft, and consulting services are sold through direct distribution.

Many industrial goods manufacturers distribute through wholesalers (industrial distributors), as in Channel B. While a manufacturer loses some control over such activities as the negotiation of sales contracts, installation, and maintenance by using distributors, wholesalers can improve distribution efficiency by lowering costs for such functions as selling, storage, and transportation. This is particularly likely when the product is standardized, there are many potential buyers with similar requirements, the average order value is relatively small, and the item is easy to handle and store.

The two other industrial goods channels involve the use of agents or brokers, either to sell directly to customers, as in Channel C, or to wholesalers, as in Channel D. Manufacturers too small to support a company salesforce most frequently use agents. For example, Stake Fastener Company, a small producer of industrial fasteners, uses agents to call on its customers rather than employing a company salesforce. Larger firms also employ agents, particularly to call on smaller customers or to cover low-potential geographic areas.

## Which Alternative Is Best? It Depends on the Firm's Objectives and Resources

As we pointed out earlier, there are trade-offs among the various objectives a company might try to accomplish with its distribution channel; it's generally impossible to design a channel that performs well on all of them. In addition, each of the alternative designs outlined above are better suited for attaining some objectives than others. Therefore, the decision about which alternative to adopt depends on which distribution objectives are considered most important, which is influenced by the business's competitive strategy and the other components of the marketing program, including characteristics of the product itself.

The following sections briefly examine the alternative channel designs most appropriate for the various objectives outlined earlier. For any given objective, channel design decisions may be further influenced by the availability of human and financial resources within the firm and by factors in the environment, such as technological developments.

## Availability and the Satisfaction of Customer Service Requirements

**Consumer Goods and Services**    For consumer goods and services, achieving a desired level of product availability is largely a matter of gaining the cooperation of appropriate numbers and types of retail outlets. A manufacturer can pursue three basic **strategies of retail coverage**—intensive, exclusive, or selective distribution (see Exhibit 12.7). The best strategy for a given product depends on the nature of the product, the target market pursued, and the competitive situation.

**Intensive Distribution**    Such a strategy uses the maximum possible number of retailers and is most appropriate for low-involvement, frequently purchased convenience goods such as candy, soft drinks, deodorants, and razor blades. This strategy maximizes product availability, which generates greater product recognition and more impulse buying. However, firms that adopt intensive distribution often experience implementation and cost problems. Individual retailers may be more reluctant to carry the product or to cooperate fully with the manufacturer's marketing program than if they were given an exclusive right to carry the product in their territory. Also, gaining cooperation from a large proportion of available retailers is a problem when total demand for the product is relatively small or when the brand is not the share leader in its product category.

**Exclusive Distribution**    This strategy relies on only one retailer or dealer in a given geographic territory. It is most appropriate when the product is a high-involvement specialty or shopping good. Exclusive distribution is also useful when a firm wants to

## Exhibit 12.7

COMPARISON OF INTENSIVE, EXCLUSIVE, AND SELECTIVE RETAIL COVERAGE STRATEGIES

| | Retail coverage | Major strength | Major weakness | Products most appropriate for |
|---|---|---|---|---|
| Intensive | Maximum | Maximizes product availability | Lack of retailer support | Low-involvement consumer convenience goods |
| Exclusive | Single | Matches retailer clientele with target market; facilitates close cooperation with retailer | Risk of relying on single retailer | High-involvement specialty or shopping goods |
| Selective | Limited | Provides adequate coverage but not at expense of manufacturer–retailer cooperation | Difficult to implement given interstore competition, especially where discounts may occur | Infrequently purchased shopping goods |

differentiate its product on the basis of high quality, prestige, or excellent customer service. The main advantages of exclusive distribution are that the manufacturer can choose retailers whose clientele match its target market, and that there will be close cooperation in implementing the producer's merchandising and customer service programs. Examples of products that are exclusively distributed include Ethan Allen furniture and Rolls-Royce automobiles. The major disadvantage of exclusive distribution is the risk involved in relying on a single retailer in a given territory.

**Selective Distribution**    This is a compromise between the other two extremes since it uses more than one but fewer than all available retailers in a geographic area. It is an appropriate strategy for shopping goods. Most brands of automobiles are distributed this way.

### Implications for Channel Design

In general terms, the greater the strategic importance of availability and the more intensive the desired level of retail coverage, the more likely wholesalers and/or agents are to be used. Intensive distribution requires large numbers of retail outlets, many of which are small, independently owned operations. The personal selling, order processing, inventory storage, and delivery costs involved in servicing such a large network of retailers would be prohibitive for most manufacturers. Therefore, channel designs such as B and C in Exhibit 12.5 are most common for large, deep-pocketed firms seeking intensive distribution, while channel designs D and E are used by smaller firms needing intensive distribution. Firms with exclusive or selective distribution goals are likely to employ channel design B in order to interface directly with their retailers.

### Industrial Goods and Services

In organizational markets, availability and customer service objectives tend to go together because it is order cycle time (the time it takes for customers to place orders and have the goods delivered to their plants or offices) and delivery dependability that tend to be most important for keeping customers satisfied. Historically, firms that wanted to provide fast and reliable delivery had to design channels with a relatively large number of "distribution points"—either wholesale distributors or company-owned warehouses and sales branches. Many distribution points were necessary to ensure adequate inventories would be available to avoid out-of-stock conditions and that those inventories would be close enough to the customer to allow quick delivery. Consequently, firms that tried to differentiate themselves on the basis of excellent customer service tended to rely on channels with substantial numbers of wholesale distributors, such as Channel B in Exhibit 12.6 (for companies that could afford a field salesforce) or Channel D (for those that could not). The reason, once again, had to do with the trade-offs between good customer service and physical distribution costs. Unless the producer was pursuing only a few very large customers or had sufficient sales volume and resources to make substantial investments in warehouses and field salespeople, the selling, storage, and transportation functions necessary to provide quick and reliable service could usually be performed more efficiently by independent distributors. As we'll see later, however, this historical trade-off between customer service levels and physical distribution costs is changing as the result of improved communication technologies and the logistical alliances they have made possible.

### The Impact of the Internet on Availability and Customer Service

Some analysts argue that the internet will lead to the "death of distance"; the geographic locations of sellers and their customers will no longer be relevant when they engage in transactions in cyberspace.[13] Consequently, they argue that the internet will facilitate the availability of all sorts of goods and services—both consumer and industrial. Keep in mind, though, that there are two aspects of availability from the customer's point of view. The first has to do with product search: identifying available alternatives, collecting information about them, and placing an order. The second concerns product **acquisition** or order cycle time: how long it takes to gain physical possession of the product at the location where it is to be used or consumed.

Websites, whether sponsored by the manufacturer or by wholesalers, retailers, or e-tailers who are members of the distribution channel, have clearly enhanced the search aspect of availability. Potential customers can learn about available brands, compare features and prices, and make purchases any time of the day or week without ever getting up from their computer. And in many product categories, "aggregator" sites, or e-hubs, bring together many buyers and sellers under one virtual roof, enabling potential customers to compare alternatives and decide on a final purchase all at one site.

On the other hand, the internet is not much help with the acquisition or physical distribution aspects of availability, at least not in most product categories. While it can help coordinate inventories and delivery schedules among channel members, it can't help move the physical product from the producer to the customer's home or plant, unless the product, like music or books, can be delivered in digital form. In fact, many e-tailers, such as RedEnvelope, outsource inventory storage and delivery activities to an established wholesaler or order fulfillment specialists. Therefore, channels incorporating traditional bricks-and-mortar wholesalers and retailers with the ability to provide quick delivery likely have a competitive advantage on the acquisition/order cycle time dimension,[14] particularly for consumer convenience and impulse items, fashion goods and big-ticket durables that need to be tried out or tried on before purchase, and industrial components where quick and reliable delivery are critical.

**STRATEGIC ISSUE**

*The internet is not much help with the acquisition or physical distribution aspects of availability, at least not in most product categories.*

# Promotional Effort, Market Information, and Postsale Service Objectives

One of the most vexing questions facing a manager who must rely on independent agents, wholesalers, and/or retailers is how to get them to do what he or she thinks is best for the product. This is particularly important when it comes to achieving high levels of promotional effort within the channel, collecting timely market information, and servicing customers after the sale. Achieving these objectives requires substantial effort and expense on the part of the middleman, but many of the benefits accrue to the manufacturer or service producer.

As we'll see, firms can attempt to control the activities related to these objectives by writing detailed legal contracts, such as franchise agreements, or to motivate voluntary effort from their channel members by providing appropriate incentives, such as cooperative advertising allowances or liberal service cost reimbursements. In many cases, though, firms can gain better control of such activities by using more direct, vertically integrated distribution channels, such as Channel A in Exhibits 12.5 and 12.6. It's easier to control a company salesforce and company-owned warehouses, retail outlets, or websites than it is to monitor the behaviors of many independent middlemen[15] and find acceptable replacements for those who perform poorly.[16]

The replacement problem is particularly difficult when an intermediary must invest in specialized (or **transaction-specific**) assets, such as extensive product training or specialized capital equipment, in order to sell the manufacturer's good or service effectively. It's more difficult to find—or to develop—replacement channel members when such specialized assets are required. Thus, the theory of **transaction cost analysis** (TCA) argues that when substantial transaction-specific assets are involved, the costs of using and administering independent channel members are likely to be higher than the costs of managing a company salesforce and/or distribution centers. This is because TCA assumes independent channel members will pursue their own self-interest—even at the expense of the manufacturer they represent—when they think they can get away with it. For instance, they might provide only cursory postsale service or expend too little effort calling on smaller accounts because they are unlikely to earn big commissions from such activities. Because independent intermediaries are more likely to get away with such behavior when it is difficult for the manufacturer to monitor or replace them, the transaction cost of using independent agents or wholesalers under such circumstances is likely to be high.[17]

Recently, though, both managers and researchers have questioned TCA's assumption that independent intermediaries will always put their own short-term interests ahead of those of the manufacturer when they can avoid getting caught and replaced. Many argue that when both manufacturer and intermediary believe their relationship can be mutually beneficial for years into the future, norms of trust and cooperation can develop.[18] Such beliefs and norms are essential for the development of effective long-term relationships and alliances among channel partners.

## Cost-Effectiveness

As pointed out earlier, firms often face a trade-off between high product availability and short order cycle times on one hand and higher distribution costs on the other. To service the large number of retailers necessary to provide intensive distribution of consumer products typically requires many salespeople, widely dispersed warehouses, and large inventories. Similarly, guaranteeing fast and reliable delivery to organizational customers, especially smaller ones, demands a relatively large number of wholesale distribution points. Therefore, the manager's task is to design a marketing channel that minimizes physical distribution costs subject to the constraint of achieving some target level of product availability and customer service.

**Make-or-Buy Decisions**    One issue that has a bearing on distribution costs is the choice among different types of institutions at each channel level. Would the firm be better off financially performing the functions necessary to achieve the desired level of customer service itself in a vertically integrated system or could independent intermediaries perform them more efficiently? In other words, for a given service level, are more direct, vertically integrated channel designs—such as Channels A and B in Exhibit 12.5 or Channel A in Exhibit 12.6—more cost-effective than channels incorporating independent wholesalers and/or agent middlemen?

To answer this question, the manager needs to compare the relative costs of performing the necessary selling, storage, order processing, and transportation functions across the various alternative institutions for different levels of sales volume. For instance, at each sales level the margins that would have to be paid to wholesale distributors could be compared to the costs the firm would incur if it took over the sales and distributive functions necessary to support that level of volume. Similarly, the costs of maintaining a company salesforce can be compared to the commissions earned at various volume levels by external agents, such as manufacturer's reps.

The results of this analysis typically vary by the amount of sales projected. For physical distribution activities to be handled efficiently in-house, the firm's products must generate sufficient sales volume to achieve economies of scale. At lower volume levels, independent wholesale distributors are usually less costly because they can spread their fixed costs across the many different suppliers they represent, and the aggregated sales of all those suppliers' products enable greater scale economies.

Similarly, the fixed costs of using external agents are lower than those of using a company salesforce because there is usually less administrative overhead and agents do not receive a salary or reimbursement for selling expenses. But costs of using agents tend to rise faster as sales volume increases because agents usually receive larger commissions than company salespeople. Thus, agents are typically more cost-efficient at lower levels of sales but less so as volumes increase. This helps explain why agents tend to be used by smaller firms or by larger firms in their smaller territories where sales are too low to justify a company salesforce.

## Supply Chain Management—The Impact of New Technologies and Alliances

Recent developments may be changing the historical trade-offs between distribution costs and customer service levels. New data collection, communication, materials handling, and transportation technologies are enabling firms to reengineer their distribution processes in ways that increase customer service levels while *simultaneously* reducing costs. These new processes are commonly referred to as **supply chain management** (although consumer package goods firms that distribute through supermarkets have labeled them **efficient consumer response [ECR]** programs).

Much of the resulting improvement in customer service on dimensions such as order cycle time and dependability has been due to the electronic interchange of sales and inventory data—and the development of computerized ordering systems—between manufacturers and their channel partners. As we saw in Chapter 5, sales information from a retailer's checkout scanners can be sent directly to either a wholesaler's or a manufacturer's computer, which figures out when to replenish each product and schedules deliveries to appropriate warehouses or stores. It is even possible to track each individual package via Radio Frequency Identification (RFID) tags and wireless technology as it moves through a distribution channel.[19] And, as we saw in the relationship between DHL and Océ, logistics service firms or transportation agencies such as trucking or airfreight companies may also be included in these supply chain alliances to facilitate timely order processing and delivery.

Logistical alliances based on electronic data interchange are often able to reduce the total amount of inventory needed via improved coordination of the stocks kept at various levels in the distribution channel, quicker order processing, and speedier delivery. Thus, the number of wholesale distribution points required to provide a given level of customer service is often reduced. These reductions cut inventory carrying costs (the costs of capital tied up in inventory), storage costs, and damage to the stock. In most cases such reductions in inventory costs are more than sufficient to offset the costs of the computers and telecommunications equipment and the more costly modes of fast transportation usually involved in logistical alliances. For example, one study suggests that widespread adoption of such systems could reduce the average length of time it takes dry grocery products, such as cake mixes, soups, and pasta sauces, to reach the ultimate consumer from more than 100 days down to only 60 days. It is estimated that this would save consumers about 11 percent of their current grocery bills.[20]

Another potential benefit of improved logistical cooperation in the food industry is the reduction of "shrink"—the amount of perishable food that is thrown away because of spoilage. It is estimated that about $20 billion worth of food is dumped by retailers each year in the United States alone. By improving the speed of order delivery, the monitoring and forecasting of consumer demand, and thereby reducing inventories and the size of in-store displays, Stop & Shop—a grocery chain owned by Holland's Ahold—was able to cut shrink by a third in 2007, saving over $50 million, eliminating 36,000 tons of rotten food, and improving customer satisfaction with the freshness and quality of the chain's produce.[21]

## Flexibility

Different channel designs involve different levels of commitment and loss of flexibility by manufacturers. Generally, vertically integrated systems are difficult to alter quickly, particularly when a firm has made substantial investments in physical (buildings) and human resources (salespersons). Channels involving independent middlemen are often more flexible, especially if the firm does not have to sign long-term contracts to gain their support. Manufacturers facing uncertain and rapidly changing market or competitive environments often rely on independent reps or wholesalers to preserve the adaptability of their distribution channels. Conversely, firms operating in relatively mature and stable markets, and defenders whose efficiency or good service is more critical than flexibility, might attach greater importance to the increased control inherent in vertical integration.[22] However, making major changes in channel design can lead to substantial conflict and resistance even when that channel is made up of independent middlemen, especially if channel members have had a long and profitable relationship with the supplier. Note, for instance, the very negative reaction of many independent electronics retailers when Apple began opening its company-owned stores.[23]

## Multichannel Distribution

Companies are increasingly using multiple channels. Some use **dual (two-channel) distribution** systems—as, for example, when a manufacturer of industrial goods uses wholesalers to sell small accounts and its own salesforce to handle large accounts. An increase in the number of target segments typically forces many companies to use more than two channels. For example, a manufacturer of brake fluid distributes its product (*a*) directly to General Motors, Ford, and BMW for use in new cars; (*b*) through major oil companies that wholesale the fluid to their retail stations for use in servicing cars; and (*c*) through auto parts wholesalers to retail auto parts stores to reach do-it-yourself customers.

Multichannel systems can create conflict and control problems. Conflicts can arise if different channel members try to pursue the same customer segment, and multiple channels are harder for the manufacturer to coordinate and control than a simpler system. Nevertheless, such systems often provide more complete market coverage with greater efficiency, which can provide a competitive advantage.

A variation of multichannel systems is the **hybrid system.**[24] While multichannel systems employ separate channels to reach different target segments (e.g., service stations versus do-it-yourselfers), the members of a hybrid system perform complementary functions for the same customer segment. As Exhibit 12.8 indicates, for example, a supplier might rely on its own website and salespeople to contact customers and generate sales, employ an independent wholesaler or fulfillment organization to deliver the goods, and then use a company help line and independent service centers to provide service after the sale. Some analysts expect such hybrid systems to become the most common channel design in the future, largely because the internet is making it easier to effectively coordinate a large number of functional specialists. Also, by outsourcing or offshoring some of those specialized functions, firms can often provide a given level of customer service more efficiently.[25]

## Exhibit 12.8

EXAMPLE OF A HYBRID MARKETING CHANNEL

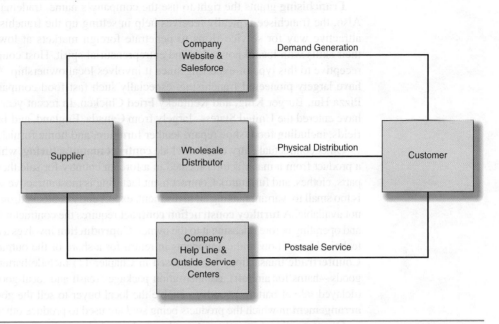

## Channel Design for Global Markets

When designing marketing channels to reach customers in more than one country, the manager faces a couple of additional issues. First, when entering a new national market for the first time, he or she must decide on an entry strategy. Subsequently, a decision must be made whether to rely on middlemen in the firm's home country that specialize in selling to foreign markets or to deal directly with foreign middlemen who operate in those markets.

## Market Entry Strategies

There are three major ways of entering a foreign country—via export; by transferring technology and the skills needed to produce and market the goods to an organization in a foreign country through a contractual agreement; and through direct investment.

**Exporting** is the simplest way to enter a foreign market because it involves the least commitment and risk. It can be direct or indirect. The latter relies on the expertise of domestic international middlemen: **export merchants,** who buy the product and sell it overseas for their own account; **export agents,** who sell on a commission basis; and **cooperative organizations,** which export for several producers, especially those selling farm products. Direct exporting uses foreign-based distributors/agents or operating units (branches or subsidiaries) set up in the foreign country.

**Contractual entry modes** are nonequity arrangements that involve the transfer of technology and/or skills to an entity in a foreign country. In **licensing,** a firm offers the right to use its intangible assets (technology, know-how, patents, company name, trademarks) in exchange for royalties or some other form of payment. Licensing is less flexible and provides less control than exporting. Further, if the contract is terminated, the licensor may have developed a competitor. It is appropriate, however, when the market is unstable or difficult to penetrate.

**Franchising** grants the right to use the company's name, trademarks, and technology. Also, the franchisee typically receives help in setting up the franchise. It is an especially attractive way for service firms to penetrate foreign markets at low cost and to couple their skills with local knowledge and entrepreneurial spirit. Host countries are reasonably receptive to this type of exporting since it involves local ownership. American companies have largely pioneered franchising, especially such fast-food companies as McDonald's, Pizza Hut, Burger King, and Kentucky Fried Chicken. In recent years foreign franchisers have entered the United States—largely from Canada, England, and Japan—in a variety of fields, including food, shoe repair, leather furniture, and home furnishings.

Other contractual entry modes include **contract manufacturing,** which involves sourcing a product from a manufacturer located in a foreign country for sale there or elsewhere (auto parts, clothes, and furniture). Contract manufacturing is most attractive when the local market is too small to warrant making an investment, export entry is blocked, and a quality licensee is not available. A **turnkey construction contract** requires the contractor to have the project up and operating before releasing it to the owner. **Coproduction** involves a company's providing technical know-how and components in return for a share of the output, which it must sell. **Countertrade** transactions (as discussed in Chapter 11) include barter (direct exchange of goods—hams for aircraft), compensation packages (cash and local goods), counterpurchase (delayed sale of bartered goods to enable the local buyer to sell the goods), and a **buyback arrangement** in which the products being sold are used to produce other goods.

**Overseas direct investment** can be implemented in two ways—through joint ventures or sole ownership. **Joint ventures** involve a joint ownership arrangement (such as between a U.S. firm and one in the host country) to produce and/or market goods in a foreign country. Today, joint ventures are common because they avoid quotas and import taxes and satisfy government demands to produce locally. They also have the advantage of sharing investment costs and gaining local marketing expertise. For example, Sir Richard Branson's Virgin Books Ltd. recently partnered with a group of Indian entrepreneurs, who were running a comics distribution business, to form a new venture called Virgin Comics LLC. The joint venture plans to build India into a multibillion-dollar comic book market by combining Virgin's capital and production expertise with the Indians' distribution system to appeal to the country's 500 million teenagers with mythic tales and possibly animated movies and TV shows. There may also be substantial opportunities to export some of the firm's offerings to the West via Virgin's established retail channels.[26]

A **sole ownership** investment entry strategy involves setting up a production facility in a foreign country. Direct investment usually allows the parent organization to retain total control of the overseas operation and avoids the problems of shared management and loss of flexibility. This strategy is particularly appropriate when the politics of the situation require a dedicated local facility.

High risks are associated with direct investment. Nevertheless, direct investments everywhere are accelerating because companies have concluded that capturing and retaining customers demands constant innovation and a rapid, flexible response to the dynamics of the environment.

# Channel Alternatives[27]

Two major types of international channel alternatives are available to a domestic producer. The first involves the use of domestic middlemen who provide marketing services from a domestic base and the second is the use of foreign middlemen.

**Domestic Middlemen**   While convenient to use, these may suffer from a lack of knowledge about a specific foreign market and their inability to provide the kind of local representation offered by foreign-based middlemen. The more common **merchant middlemen** (those taking title) include the **export merchant,** who takes physical possession of the goods (mostly manufactured), has a broad line, and sells in his own right; the **export jobber,** who handles mostly bulky and raw materials (but does not take physical control of them); and **trading companies,** which sell manufactured goods to developing countries and buy back raw materials and unprocessed goods.

**Agent middlemen** include **brokers; buying offices** (primarily concerned with searching for and purchasing merchandise upon request); **selling groups** (an arrangement by which various producers cooperate to sell their goods overseas); the **export management company,** which operates in the name of its principal; and the **manufacturer's export agent (MEA),** which specializes in only a few countries and has a short-term relationship with its clients.

**Foreign Middlemen**   In contrast to dealing with domestic middlemen, a manufacturer may decide to deal directly with **foreign middlemen.** This shortens the channel, thereby bringing the manufacturer closer to the market. A major problem is that foreign middlemen are some distance away and therefore more difficult to control than domestic ones. Since many foreign middlemen, especially merchant middlemen, are prone to act independently of their suppliers, it is difficult to use them when market cultivation is needed.

Wholesalers around the world, while performing similar functions, vary tremendously in size, margins, and service quality. A broad generalization is that the less developed a country, the smaller the wholesaler and the more fragmented the wholesale channels. In recent years, however, the emergence of wholesaler-sponsored voluntary chains has tended to consolidate distribution power in the hands of a smaller number of wholesalers. Also, there is a worldwide trend of vertical integration from the wholesale or retail level to the manufacturer. And the growth of national wholesalers in many countries has made it easier for manufacturers to distribute their product(s) nationwide.

**Retail Structures in Foreign Countries**   These vary tremendously across countries because of differences in the cultural, economic, and political environments; for example, a generalization is that the size of retail stores increases as gross national product per capita increases. Both European and Japanese retailing are following a path similar to that pioneered by the United States with respect to store size, self-service, discounting, automation (use of electronic checkout counters), expansion of national chains, and direct marketing. And as we saw with Coca-Cola's activities in Africa, the effectiveness and efficiency of both retailers and wholesale distributors are being improved in some cases with the help of training programs, promotional materials, and inventory planning advice from large multinational manufacturers. Another good example of this sort of proactive approach to improving the retail distribution of a firm's products in foreign lands is provided by Procter & Gamble's program to increase its revenues in rural China, as discussed in Exhibit 12.9.

It is also becoming increasingly possible to promote and sell goods and services directly over the internet almost anywhere. The online population was estimated to be 2.09 billion in the year 2011, with 272 million in North America, 476 million in Europe, 943 million in the Asia-Pacific region, 216 million in South America, 48 million in Africa, and 68 million in the Middle East.[28] As we have seen, however, while the internet enables firms to contact customers and generate orders, they must still rely on foreign middlemen to carry out the necessary physical distribution functions.

## Exhibit 12.9   PROCTER & GAMBLE AND THE CHINESE GOVERNMENT WORK TO IMPROVE RURAL RETAILERS

Since Procter & Gamble, the consumer package goods giant, first introduced Head & Shoulders, Pampers, and many other brands to mainland China in 1988, it has enjoyed steady growth. The firm racked up $2.5 billion in revenues in fiscal 2006, and its wholly owned China business unit employs 6,300 people, many of whom work in the firm's extensive sales and wholesale distribution network.

While much of P&G's past growth came from large retailers in China's biggest cities, company managers expect that future growth will come from the rural countryside where there are more than 700 million potential first-time buyers for many of P&G's products. Since family incomes in the countryside average less than one-third of those in the cities, however, P&G has been developing new brand extensions and packaging to lower costs and prices, and to appeal to rural cultural preferences.

Since retail stores in rural China tend to be small, numerous, and unsophisticated, the firm has also had to expand its distribution network to reach them. The firm relies on a group of wholesale subdistributors and their vans to deliver a variety of P&G products as well as sales aids like posters, display racks, and the like to hundreds of small shops. And the firm signed an agreement with China's Commerce Ministry in 2007 whereby P&G promises to help renovate existing retail outlets, design and build new ones, and train local shopkeepers in some 10,000 small villages in the art of retailing. The government supports the program as a means of reducing the flow of counterfeit goods and spurring economic development in the countryside, while P&G hopes that improving the effectiveness and efficiency of China's rural retailers will lower its distribution costs and gain increased local promotion of its many brands.

*Sources:* Dexter Roberts, "Scrambling to Bring Crest to the Masses," *BusinessWeek,* June 25, 2007, pp. 72–73; and Jennifer Reingald, "Can P&G Make Money in Places Where People Earn $2 a Day?" *Fortune,* January 17, 2011, pp. 86–91.

## Channel Design for Services

Producers of services also face the problem of making their outputs available to targeted customer segments. In some cases, this results in forward vertical integration involving decisions about branch outlets—as in bank services that are accessible through branch banks (some of which may be located in supermarkets) and automatic tellers. Another example is a hospital that establishes outpatient clinics to serve the specific health needs of various community segments, such as high-stress or drug- or alcohol-dependent groups.

Ordinarily, the marketing of services does not require the same kind of distribution networks as does the marketing of tangible goods. Marketing channels for services tend to be short—direct from the creator or performer of the service to the end user—hence the emphasis on franchising (discussed later in this chapter).

Some services require the use of longer channels, however. Health care services use a variety of channel systems other than the traditional fee system employed by many doctors and hospitals in selling directly to the consumer. Health maintenance organizations (HMOs) sometimes use a vertically integrated system, where consumers pay a monthly charge to an organization (such as Baptist Medical Systems-HMO, Inc.) that coordinates the services of all the health care needs of its constituents. Hotels rely increasingly on indirect channels for their bookings. Intermediaries include travel agents who may deal directly with a hotel or contact another intermediary holding blocks of rooms, sales representatives who represent a number of noncompeting hotels or resorts, airlines that provide tour packages that include hotels, and automated reservation services that maintain a computerized inventory of available rooms travel agents can tap into for a fee, e-hubs that enable business buyers to reserve rooms online, and "name-your-own-price" sites such as *www.priceline.com* where hotels can dispose of excess capacity if potential buyers offer an acceptable price.[29]

# Channel Management Decisions

Designing the perfect channel to accomplish the firm's objectives is one thing; getting the middlemen to carry the product and perform the desired functions is another. In recent years manufacturers—and in some cases large wholesalers and retailers—have developed **vertical marketing systems** (VMSs) to improve coordination among channel members, thereby improving their performance. Greater coordination and cooperation in VMSs have led to greater marketing effectiveness and distribution economies by virtue of their size, bargaining power, and the elimination of duplicated functions. As a result, VMSs have become the dominant form of channel arrangement, particularly in the distribution of consumer goods and services.

This section discusses the various types of VMSs and how firms can develop and maintain such systems. Next, we examine the sources of power and the inducements and incentives that channel members use to gain the support of other system members. Finally, we identify possible sources of conflict in VMSs and some resolution mechanisms that firms use to preserve cooperation within their channels.

## Vertical Marketing Systems

Firms attempt to develop and manage integrated distribution systems in one of four ways: (1) a corporate VMS, which involves a vertically integrated system; (2) a contractual VMS, which formulates agreements spelling out a coordinated set of rights and obligations for members of the system; (3) an administered VMS, in which one firm uses its economic position or expertise to provide inducements for cooperation from other members; or (4) a relational VMS, where cooperation between two or more channel partners is based on norms of mutual trust and the expectation that cooperation will increase the total system's success and thereby make all members better off in the long term. Each of these four types is shown in Exhibit 12.10 and discussed next.

**Corporate VMSs**   In these systems firms achieve coordination and control through corporate ownership. In most cases, this is the result of forward integration by a manufacturer of the functions at the wholesale—and perhaps even the retail—levels. For example, many industrial firms have their own salesforces, warehouses, or branch sales offices. **Backward integration** occurs when a retailer or wholesaler assumes ownership of institutions that normally precede them in their distribution channels. Such integration is common among large supermarket chains.

The primary advantage of these systems is the tight control they provide over personal selling, promotion, distribution, and customer service activities. Such control is particularly important when the product is technically complex; when specialized knowledge or facilities are needed to sell, distribute, and/or service the product; and when few capable independent middlemen are available. Corporate VMSs are not without their disadvantages, which include the large capital investment required and less flexibility than conventional systems.

**Contractual VMSs**   In such systems independent firms at different levels of production and distribution coordinate their programs through contracts that spell out the rights

# Exhibit 12.10

VERTICAL MARKETING SYSTEMS

and duties of each party. The intent is to obtain greater economies and market impact than they could achieve alone. Contractual VMSs have had the greatest growth of any channel system in recent years. There are many kinds of contractual systems, but the three basic types are **wholesaler-sponsored voluntary chains, retailer cooperatives,** and **franchise systems**.

*Wholesaler-sponsored voluntary chains* are formed by getting independent retailers to sign contracts in which they agree to standardize their selling practices and to purchase a certain portion of their inventories from the wholesaler. The Independent Grocers Alliance (IGA), Western Auto, and Ben Franklin are among the best-known wholesaler-sponsored voluntaries.

*Retailer cooperatives* are groups of independent retailers who form their own co-operative chain organizations. Typically, they agree to concentrate their purchases by forming their own wholesale operations. In many cases they also engage in joint advertising, promotion, and merchandising programs. Profits are passed back to the member retailers in proportion to their purchases. Such cooperatives are particularly common in the grocery field, where Associated Grocers and Certified Grocers are examples.

In *franchise systems*[30] a channel member can coordinate two successive stages in the distribution channel by offering franchise contracts that give others the right to participate in the business provided they accept the agreement terms and pay a fee. Such contracts usually specify a variety of operational details—including which members of the system will perform specific functions and how—as well as mechanisms to evaluate members' performance and to terminate members who fail to perform adequately.

Franchising has great versatility. Such systems operate in almost every business area and cover a wide variety of goods and services. There are four major types of franchise systems.

1. **Manufacturer–retailer franchise systems** account for the largest number of franchisees and the largest volume of sales and are common in the automotive (Chrysler and Ford) and petroleum industries (Exxon, Shell, and BP).

2. **Manufacturer–wholesaler franchise systems** are exemplified by the soft-drink industry; Coca-Cola and Pepsi sell syrup concentrate to franchised wholesale bottlers that then carbonate, bottle, sell, and distribute soft drinks to retailers in their territories. In recent years, however, Coca-Cola has acquired several of its larger and previously independent bottlers to gain control over its distribution channel and has formed new bottlers via joint ventures in developing markets like Kenya.

3. **Wholesaler–retailer franchise systems** are similar to wholesaler-sponsored voluntary chains, but the retail franchisees agree to conduct and coordinate their operations according to detailed standards specified by the franchise agreement. Examples include Rexall drugstores and SuperValu supermarkets.

4. **Service sponsor–retailer franchise systems** are the most familiar to consumers. Examples include McDonald's, Burger King, and Kentucky Fried Chicken in fast foods; Holiday Inn and Ibis Hotels in lodging; Hertz and Avis in car rentals; Midas and Precision Tune in auto repair; and Manpower in employment services.

The popularity of franchise systems from a customer's point of view derives from their ability to deliver consistent quality at a convenient location and a reasonable price. From the franchiser's perspective, such systems provide a legal basis for exercising some control over franchisees without the large capital investments required by a vertically integrated system. On the other side, franchisees can gain access to the franchiser's operational expertise, brand recognition, and loyal customers in exchange for providing local capital and management oversight.

**Administered VMSs**   Firms using this system coordinate the necessary activities at successive stages of distribution through the informal guidance and influence of one of the parties (rather than through ownership or contractual agreements). The administrator is typically the manufacturer, but in some cases the role is performed by a large retailer or wholesaler, such as Tesco or Walmart. Usually, the administration of such systems develops a detailed merchandising program in which the manufacturer spells out shelf-space arrangements, a promotional calendar, pricing policies, and guidelines for other activities to be followed by its wholesalers and retailers.

To encourage the other members of the distribution channel to go along with its merchandising program, the channel administrator typically relies on its superior economic or expert power (as described in a later section) to provide incentives for cooperation. Therefore, administered VMSs are typically designed and managed by the most powerful member. As a result, however, the performance outcomes that are rewarded may be more reflective of the powerful member's objectives than of the interests of the system as a whole. And there is often a tendency for the administrator to use its power to "share the pain" when economic conditions are tough but to "hog the gain" during the good times.

**Relational VMSs**   Relational VMSs also rely on economic rewards—and often contractual agreements, as well—to specify what is expected of each channel member and to provide incentives for cooperation. However, in relational systems what is expected of each partner may change by mutual agreement as market or competitive conditions change, and the economic incentives depend more on the long-term market success of the entire system than on the power and largess of the strongest member.

As we have seen, such relational systems or alliances are often more effective and efficient than more traditional systems. This is largely because of the extensive and rapid sharing of information, cost savings resulting from better coordination of activities and less duplication of efforts, and the cooperative search for innovative ways for the system to gain a competitive advantage over other systems.

However, the open sharing of internal operating data and innovative ideas for improving efficiency and sales performance requires substantial mutual trust and long-term commitments from each partner. As we discussed in Chapter 5, trust tends to build slowly. Thus, the partners in a relational system must typically have some history of satisfying experiences with one another to provide a foundation for trust and a history of mutually rewarding performance outcomes to motivate continued commitment for the long haul.[31]

## Sources of Channel Power

As mentioned, the channel leader in an administered VMS typically coordinates the actions of other members by exercising power over them. Channel member A has power over channel member B to the extent that A can get B to do something that B would not do if left alone.

The power of any firm within a distribution channel is inversely proportional to how dependent the other channel members are on that firm. Thus, the extent of Firm A's power over Firm B is determined by A's ability to deliver rewards desired by B, and by B's ability to attain those rewards outside of a relationship with A (that is, by the alternatives open to B). Thus, sources (or bases) of power within channel relationships include the following:

- **Economic power** exists when channel members perceive that a firm can mediate economic rewards for them if they follow its directives.
- **Coercive power** is based on a perception that one channel member will punish another for failure to cooperate. It is the inverse of economic power, since such punishments usually take the form of a reduction in or withholding of economic rewards. For example, a manufacturer might threaten to withdraw a retailer's exclusive territorial rights if the retailer's performance does not meet expectations.
- **Expert power** stems from a perception that one channel member has special knowledge or expertise that can benefit other members of the system. Because of the reputations of firms like Unilever and Procter & Gamble as savvy marketers, middlemen are often willing to abide by their merchandising suggestions.
- **Referent power** is based on the belief that the benefits generated are likely to continue. A channel member that has earned substantial profits from a manufacturer over the years may be willing to accede to its suggestions or requests, without demanding any additional rewards.
- **Legitimate power** flows from the belief that one channel member has the right to make certain decisions or demands and to expect compliance from other members. Legitimate power is usually the result of ownership or contractual agreements, but in some instances it is based on moral authority or common beliefs about what is right and proper. For example, most middlemen would agree that a food manufacturer has the right to print expiration dates on its packages and to expect middlemen to remove outdated packages from the shelves as a means of protecting the product's quality and the consumer's health.

Of course, economic rewards and expertise are exchanged among partners in relational VMSs as well, but such exchanges tend to be relatively symmetrical—both parties benefit—rather than being dominated by one powerful member. Therefore, when one party in a relational VMS accedes to the requests or suggestions of a partner, that response often reflects the partner's referent power, a belief that the relationship will continue to be mutually beneficial in the future.[32]

## Channel Control Strategies

Two strategies used by manufacturers to improve their perceived economic power and to gain better cooperation from channel members are a pull and a push strategy.

**Pull Strategy**   When pursuing this strategy, a manufacturer focuses primarily on building selective demand and brand loyalty among potential customers through media advertising, consumer promotions, extended warranties and customer service, product improvements, line extensions, and other actions aimed at winning customer preference. Thus, by building strong consumer demand, the manufacturer increases its ability to promote economic rewards in the form of large sales volumes to its channel members in return for their cooperation. A share leader or most prestigious brand in its category has substantial power to influence other channel members, particularly if the product is in the growth stage of its life cycle.

But what if the manufacturer is introducing a new product with no past sales history? In such situations, the manufacturer must convince prospective channel members that its marketing program can quickly build strong customer demand and loyalty for the new brand. Such efforts at persuasion are most likely to be successful when the manufacturer has substantial resources to devote to the new product's marketing program, is perceived to have a great deal of marketing expertise, and has an extensive track record of past new product successes. Thus, pull strategies are commonly employed by large consumer goods marketers such as Procter & Gamble, Unilever, Frito-Lay, and Diageo PLC. Such companies have the deep pockets necessary to implement pull strategies, and their products typically have sufficiently broad appeal to make an aggressive consumer promotion and advertising program worthwhile.

**Push Strategy**   Smaller firms with limited resources, those without established reputations as savvy marketers, and those attempting to gain better channel support for existing products with relatively small shares and volumes often have difficulty achieving cooperation solely on the promise of future sales and profits. In such situations firms usually adopt a **push strategy** in which much of the product's marketing budget is devoted to direct inducements to gain the cooperation of wholesalers and/or retailers. Typically, a manufacturer offers channel members a number of rewards, each aimed at motivating them to perform a specific function or activity on the product's behalf. The rationale is that by motivating more wholesalers or retailers to carry and aggressively sell the product, more customers are exposed and persuaded to buy it.

Most small and medium-sized marketers of consumer goods employ push strategies because they lack the necessary resources for, or sell products whose relatively narrow appeal cannot justify, the expense involved in a pull strategy. The growing number of energy bars—Clif bars, Luna bars, Balance bars, and others—are examples of products marketed largely through push strategies, even though some limited consumer promotion does appear for these products.

## Trade Promotions—Incentives for Motivating Channel Members

Manufacturers typically use a combination of incentives to gain reseller support and push their products through the channel. Most of these incentives constitute **sales promotion** activities. As we shall see in the next chapter, sales promotions are incentives designed to stimulate the purchase or sale of a product in the short term. There are two categories of sales promotion activities: (1) **consumer promotions,** such as coupons, rebates, and contests, aimed at stimulating consumer purchases; and (2) **trade promotions,** which encourage resellers to engage in activities that will support and increase local sales of the product. In the next chapter we will discuss how both types of sales promotion can

**STRATEGIC ISSUE**

*Manufacturers typically use a combination of incentives to gain reseller support and push their products through the channel.*

be combined with other communications tools such as advertising, personal selling, and publicity to create integrated marketing communications programs. In this section, we focus on the variety of trade promotion incentives and their role in motivating reseller support.

Different trade promotion incentives motivate resellers to engage in different functions or activities on the manufacturer's behalf. By combining various rewards, manufacturers can tailor trade incentives to the specific marketing and distribution needs of a product and its target customers. Exhibit 12.11 lists a variety of reseller incentives along with the functional activities that each is appropriate for motivating.

**Incentives to Increase Reseller Purchases and Inventories**   For new products, the most critical objective is simply to get wholesalers or retailers to stock the new item. Manufacturers unable to build much pull for their products by stimulating selective demand often have to offer more direct inducements to build distribution. They can offer higher margins than are typical for the category, introductory discounts for a limited time, or even agree to give selected resellers exclusive rights to the product in their local territory (although exclusive territories are not appropriate for convenience goods requiring extensive distribution). In many cases, the manufacturer must also pay a onetime fee, called a **slotting allowance,** to induce retailers to stock the product on their shelves. The growing popularity of slotting allowances, however, raises ethical concerns, as discussed in Ethical Perspective 12.1.

Once a product has achieved adequate distribution, the manufacturer's purpose changes to one of maintaining adequate inventories of the product as close to the end customer as possible to minimize out-of-stock conditions. This usually involves offering some form of **quantity discount** tied to the volume of a reseller's purchases. Similar incentives include **buy-back allowances,** where the producer offers a discount on a future second order based on the size of the initial order, and **free goods,** where the manufacturer rewards volume purchases with additional merchandise at no cost. Of course, the manufacturer may also try to form logistical alliances or relationships involving electronic data interchange and computerized reordering with their larger resellers. As we have seen, such alliances help ensure that adequate stocks are available while reducing the volume of inventory (and the associated costs) that resellers must carry.

## Exhibit 12.11

INCENTIVES FOR MOTIVATING CHANNEL MEMBER PERFORMANCE

| Functional performance dimensions | Examples of channel incentives |
|---|---|
| Increased purchases/carry larger inventories | Larger margins, exclusive territories, buy-in promotions, quantity discounts, seasonal discounts, buy-back allowances, free goods, shelf-stocking programs, slotting allowances |
| Increased personal selling effort | Sales training programs, instructional materials, incentive programs for channel members' salespeople |
| Increased local promotional effort | |
| • Local advertising | Cooperative advertising; advertising allowances; print, radio, or spot TV ads for use by local retailers |
| • Increased display space | Promotion allowances tied to shelf space |
| • In-store promotions | Display racks and signs, in-store demonstrations, in-store sampling |
| • Price promotions | Off-invoice allowances |
| Improved customer service | Service training programs, instructional materials, high margins on replacement parts, liberal labor cost allowances for warranty service |

### ETHICAL PERSPECTIVE 12.1
#### Do Slotting Allowances Stack the Deck against Small Firms?

The heavy reliance on trade promotions, which account for about two-thirds of the marketing budgets of U.S. consumer package goods firms, to gain channel member support can make it difficult for small firms to introduce new products. This is especially true for slotting allowances because the size of the allowance demanded by retailers tends to be larger for new products which have a relatively low probability of generating big sales volumes and profits. Since small firms and entrepreneurial start-ups tend to have limited promotional resources and unknown brands, they often have to pay bigger allowances to gain retailer acceptance than larger, well-established firms. While this practice makes good economic sense from the perspective of a retailer who must allocate scarce shelf space among a large number of new

products, it may have a negative effect on new business formation, competition, and the availability of product innovations in the larger economy.

However, a recent study of more than 1,000 new products suggests that slotting allowances do a reasonably good job of helping retailers allocate shelf space efficiently and balancing the risk of new product failure between manufacturers and retailers. The researchers conclude that the positive effects of these benefits on channel efficiency probably outweigh the negative effects that slotting allowances may have on competition by making market access more difficult for smaller manufacturers.

*Sources:* Frank V. Cespedes, "Ethical Issues in Distribution," in N. Craig Smith and John A. Quelch, eds., *Ethics in Marketing* (Burr Ridge, IL: Richard D. Irwin, 1993), chap. 12; David Henry, "Accounting Games in the Grocer's Aisle," *BusinessWeek*, April 14, 2003, p. 64; and K. Sudhir and Vithala R. Rao, "Do Slotting Allowances Enhance Efficiency or Hinder Competition?" MSI Report #05–122 (Cambridge, MA: Marketing Science Institute, 2005).

**Incentives to Increase Personal Selling Effort**   To motivate and assist resellers in upgrading the knowledge and professionalism of their salespeople, manufacturers can provide instruction manuals, training seminars, or detailed training programs held at the manufacturer's headquarters. Some firms also attempt to increase the amount of effort their resellers' salespeople devote to their products by offering incentives directly to those sales personnel. Such programs usually take the form of sales contests. The rewards may be monetary—sometimes called **push money** or **spiffs**—or in the form of merchandise or travel. However, manufacturers should obtain approval from each reseller before initiating such programs.

**Incentives to Increase Local Promotional Effort**   Middlemen can play an important role in advertising and promoting a manufacturer's product in their local areas, particularly for consumer goods. Thus, to stimulate more local advertising, many manufacturers offer **cooperative advertising programs** that pay a percentage of a reseller's expenses for local advertising up to some limit based on that reseller's sales of the product. Firms may also offer retailers **promotional allowances** tied to the amount of shelf or display space they devote to a product. To further encourage in-store promotions, many manufacturers offer free racks, signs, and other materials for use in point-of-purchase (P-O-P) displays.

Producers may also encourage periodic or seasonal price promotions featuring their product by providing **off-invoice discounts** for limited periods. The intention of such discounts is to encourage the reseller to pass along the savings to customers in the form of a special promotional price or sale event. One problem with such discounts, though, is that resellers may simply pocket the money as a means of increasing their own margins.

**Incentives to Improve Customer Service**   For consumer durables and industrial products, manufacturers often rely on distributors or retailers to provide product-related services, such as installation and repair, to the final customer. One way for firms to strengthen the quality of such service is to provide detailed instructional materials or company-sponsored training programs for their dealers' service technicians. Many firms, such as Caterpillar, are now making detailed repair guidelines and technical assistance available to dealers over the internet.[33] Manufacturers also offer high margins on replacement parts or liberal labor cost reimbursements to reward resellers for performing warranty service.

### The Changing Role of Incentives in Relational Distribution Systems

In channel systems where the manufacturer has forged successful long-term relationships with major resellers, the primary incentive for continued cooperation among the parties is focused on the improved sales volumes and reduced operating costs such cooperation can generate. Consequently, some of the specific trade promotion incentives discussed above are less important and less frequently used in such systems. As mentioned, for instance, logistical alliances and computerized reordering systems can reduce the amount of inventory that resellers must carry to avoid out-of-stock problems (though many manufacturers continue to offer quantity discounts to resellers based on their total sales volume during the year to encourage aggressive sales effort on behalf of their products). Similarly, some firms have reduced or eliminated off-invoice price promotions in favor of "everyday low prices" aimed at improving resellers' average margins. The purpose is to smooth out manufacturing schedules and inventories by discouraging resellers from stocking up during promotion periods. Some manufacturers continue to offer periodic price promotions, but they pay discounts to their resellers only on goods that were actually sold to consumers at a promotional price.[34]

# Channel Conflicts and Resolution Strategies

Regardless of how well a manufacturer administers its channel system, some amount of **channel conflict** is inevitable. Some conflict is essential if members are to adapt to change. Conflict should result in more effective and efficient channel performance, *provided* it does not become destructive. Disagreements among channel members can occur for several reasons, including incompatible goals, unclear rights and responsibilities, and misperceptions and poor communication.

Because channel conflict is inevitable, the challenge is not to eliminate it but to manage it better. Firms can pursue several approaches aimed at recognizing and resolving potential conflicts early before they cause a breakdown of cooperation in the system. These include involving channel members in policy decisions (use of dealer advisory boards), increasing interaction among personnel at all levels (a manufacturer's salespersons making sales calls with each of its distributors), focusing on common goals, and the use of mediation and arbitration.

A manufacturer might also proactively adjust policy to defuse the source of conflict or increase the incentives and rewards available to channel members to lessen the economic consequences of contentious issues. For example, Hallmark created a separate line of greetings cards for sale through mass merchandisers to reduce the amount of direct competition with its traditional retail card shops, and it created a website that helped those retailers attain discounts from other, noncompeting suppliers and thereby improve their profits.

There are legal constraints on how much and what kinds of power can be used to resolve conflicts or control channel members' actions. This is most apt to be the case when the firm uses an exclusive or selective distribution strategy and/or attempts to dictate how the channel intermediary will perform in marketing the product. In recent

## Exhibit 12.12

SUMMARY OF NONPRICE LEGAL CONSTRAINTS IN THE UNITED STATES

1. *Exclusive dealing.* The requirement that a channel member sell or lease only the seller's products is illegal if the requirement substantially lessens competition.

2. *Tying contracts.* This requires a buyer to take products other than the one wanted and, with some exceptions, is illegal per se. **Reciprocity,** wherein a buyer refuses to do business with a supplier unless that firm buys its products, is similar to tying contracts and is illegal when coercion is involved and substantial commerce is affected.

3. *Territorial restrictions.* This involves the granting of a geographical monopoly to a buyer for a given product. The decision here rests on the effect of intrabrand restrictions on interbrand competition. **Resale restrictions** on the type of customer the buyer can sell to are handled on much the same basis.

4. *Refusal to deal.* The right of a seller to select its customers—or to stop selling to one—is legal as long as it does not substantially lessen competition or foster a restraint of trade.

5. *Promotional allowances and services.* These must be offered to all resellers on proportionally equal terms and must be used for the purposes intended (e.g., advertising allowances must be used to pay for advertising).

6. *Incentives for resellers' employees.* Such incentives (e.g., push money) are generally acceptable, provided they do not injure competition substantially.

years, the U.S. courts have begun to use more of a rule-of-reason approach to potential offenses rather than finding specific practices inherently illegal. Even so, vertical relationships are covered by the major antitrust acts—Sherman, Clayton, and FTC. See Exhibit 12.12 for a brief discussion of the major nonprice legal constraints imposed by the federal government.

# TAKE-AWAYS

1. The importance of good distribution decisions in designing a marketing plan is simple: Customers won't buy your good or service unless it is conveniently available when and where they want to buy it.

2. Distribution channel decisions have a major economic impact because distribution costs, many of which do not even appear in the firm's income statement, often exceed the costs of producing a good or service.

3. Channel design involves decisions about the appropriate types and numbers of middlemen to include in the distribution channel in order to link the marketing strategy for the good or service to the needs of the target customers.

4. Distribution channels can be designed to accomplish a number of objectives, including maximizing the product's availability, satisfying customer service requirements, encouraging promotional effort, obtaining timely market information, minimizing distribution costs, and maintaining flexibility. However, each design alternative is better for achieving some objectives than others, and there are trade-offs across objectives; increasing

availability and customer service, for example, tends to increase distribution costs. Therefore, good channel design decisions require compromise and careful judgment.

5. A manufacturer or service provider can attempt to gain the support and direct the efforts of its channel partners through vertical integration, by legal contracts (e.g., franchise agreements), by providing economic incentives, and/or by developing mutually beneficial relationships based on trust and the expectation of future benefits. Given the large investments required for vertical integration and the difficulty of writing enforceable contracts when market conditions are changing rapidly, the development of effective incentives and long-term relationships with channel members is increasingly vital to the market success of most firms.

**Self-diagnostic questions to test your ability to apply the analytical tools and concepts in this chapter to marketing decision making may be found at this book's website at www.mhhe.com/mullins8e.**

# ENDNOTES

**1.** This opening case example is based on material found in Duane D. Stanford, "Coke's Last Round," *Bloomberg Businessweek*, November 1, 2010, pp. 54–61.

**2.** For a summary of academic research on distribution channel design and management, see Erin Anderson and Anne T. Coughlan, "Channel Management: Structure, Governance, and Relationship Management," in Bart Weitz and Robin Wensley, eds., *Handbook of Marketing* (London: Sage Publications, 2001), pp. 223–47; and Gary L. Frazier, "Organizing and Managing Channels of Distribution," *Journal of the Academy of Marketing Sciences* 27 (Spring 1999), pp. 226–40.

**3.** Louis W. Stern and Adel I. El-Ansary, *Marketing Channels*, 3rd ed. (Englewood Cliffs, NJ: Prentice Hall, 1992), p. 1.

**4.** Jeff Jarvis, "Love the Customers Who Hate You," *BusinessWeek*, March 3, 2008, p. 58.

**5.** Paul Markillie, 'Warfare in the Aisles,' a section within "A Survey of Consumer Power," *The Economist*, April 2, 2005, pp. 6–8.

**6.** You can check the U.S. Census Bureau's most current wholesale and retail trade statistics at its website: *www.census.gov/econ*.

**7.** Ibid.

**8.** The following discussion is based largely on material found in Steven Kaplan and Mohanbir Sawhney, "E-Hubs: The New B2B Marketplaces," *Harvard Business Review*, May–June 2000, pp. 97–103. See also Stewart Scharf, "Grainger: Tooled Up for Growth," *BusinessWeek Online*, April 25, 2006.

**9.** Timothy J. Mullaney and Robert D. Hof, "E-Tailing Finally Hits Its Stride," *BusinessWeek*, December 26, 2004, pp. 36–37. Also see, Edward J. Fox, Alan L. Montgomery, and Leonard M. Lodish, "Consumer Shopping and Spending across Retail Formats," *The Journal of Business* 77 (April 2004), pp. S25–S60.

**10.** Heather Green, "How Hard Should Amazon Swing?" *BusinessWeek*, January 14, 2002, p. 38; Robert Hof, "Amazon's Costly Bells and Whistles," *BusinessWeek Online*, February 3, 2006; and Peter Burrows, "Bezos: How Frugality Drives Innovation," *BusinessWeek*, April 28, 2008, pp. 64–66.

**11.** Nanette Byrnes, "More Clicks at the Bricks," *BusinessWeek*, December 17, 2007, pp. 50–52; and Alan Wolf, "Best Buy Beefing Up Web, Downsizing Stores," *www.twice.com*, March 24, 2011.

**12.** Robert D. Hof, "Ebay's Rhine Gold," *BusinessWeek*, April 3, 2006, pp. 44–45; and "Pass the Parcel," *The Economist*, February 11, 2006, p. 61; and "eBayBusiness Guide," *www.startups.co.uk*, January 2011.

**13.** Leyland Pitt, Pierre Berthon, and Jean-Paul Berthon, "Changing Channels: The Impact of the Internet on Distribution Strategy," *Business Horizons*, March–April 1999, pp. 19–28.

**14.** Ranjay Gulati and Jason Garino, "Get the Right Mix of Bricks and Clicks," *Harvard Business Review*, May–June, 2000, pp. 107–14.

**15.** Bernard J. Jaworski, "Toward a Theory of Marketing Control: Environmental Context, Control Types, and Consequences," *Journal of Marketing*, July 1988, pp. 23–39.

**16.** Allen M. Weiss and Erin Anderson, "Converting from Independent to Employee Salesforces: The Role of Perceived Switching Costs," *Journal of Marketing Research*, February 1992, pp. 101–15.

**17.** Transaction cost analysis was first developed in Oliver E. Williamson, *Markets and Hierarchies: Analysis and Antitrust Implications* (New York: Free Press, 1975). For empirical evidence that largely supports TCA's predictions about the conditions under which firms will employ independent agents versus company salespeople, see Erin Anderson, "The Salesperson as Outside Agent or Employee: A Transaction Cost Analysis," *Marketing Science* 4 (1985), pp. 234–54; Erin Anderson and Barton Weitz, "Make or Buy Decisions: Vertical Integration and Marketing Productivity," *Sloan Management Review*, Spring 1986, pp. 1–19; and Jan B. Heide and George John, "The

Role of Dependence Balancing in Safeguarding Transaction-Specific Assets in Conventional Channels," *Journal of Marketing*, January 1988, pp. 20–35.

**18.** For example, see James C. Anderson and James A. Narus, "A Model of Distributor Firm and Manufacturer Firm Working Partnerships," *Journal of Marketing*, January 1990, pp. 42–58; Jan B. Heide and George John, "Do Norms Matter in Marketing Relationships?" *Journal of Marketing*, 1992; Erin Anderson and Barton Weitz, "The Use of Pledges to Build and Sustain Commitment in Distribution Channels," *Journal of Marketing Research*, February 1992, pp. 18–34; Daniel Corsten and Nirmalya Kumar, "Do Suppliers Benefit from Collaborative Relationships with Large Retailers? An Empirical Investigation of Efficient Consumer Response Adoption," *Journal of Marketing* 69 (July 2005) pp. 80–94; and Jan B. Heide, Kenneth H. Wathne, and Aksel I. Rokkan, "Interfirm Monitoring, Social Contracts, and Relationship Outcomes," *Journal of Marketing Research* XLIV (August 2007), pp. 425–33.

**19.** Gerry Khermouch and Heather Green, "Bar Codes Better Watch Their Backs," *BusinessWeek*, July 14, 2003, p. 42.

**20.** James Walsh, "Shortening the Supply Chain," *Minneapolis Star Tribune*, July 24, 1995, p. 1D. See also Ronald Henkoff, "Delivering the Goods," *Fortune*, November 28, 1994, pp. 64–78; and Joseph B. Fuller, James O'Conor, and Richard Rawlinson, "Tailored Logistics: The Next Advantage," *Harvard Business Review*, May–June 1993, pp. 87–98.

**21.** "Shrink Rapped," *The Economist*, May 17, 2008, p. 80.

**22.** Robert W. Ruekert, Orville C. Walker, Jr., and Kenneth J. Roering, "The Organization of Marketing Activities: A Contingency Theory of Structure and Performance," *Journal of Marketing*, Winter 1985, pp. 13–25; and Melissa Campanelli, "Agents of Change," *Sales and Marketing Management*, February 1995, pp. 71–75.

**23.** Nick Wingfield, "How Apple's Store Strategy Beat the Odds," *The Wall Street Journal*, May 17, 2006, p. 1.

**24.** Rowland T. Moriarity and Ursula Moran, "Managing Hybrid Marketing Systems," *Harvard Business Review*, November–December 1990, p. 146.

**25.** Pete Engardio, "The Future of Outsourcing," *BusinessWeek*, January 30, 2006, pp. 50–64.

**26.** Steve Hamm, "Speed Demons," *BusinessWeek*, March 27, 2006, pp. 68–74.

**27.** This section has benefited from Philip R. Cateora, *International Marketing*, 7th ed. (Burr Ridge, IL: Richard D. Irwin, 1990), chap. 4.

**28.** "Internet Usage Statistics—The Big Picture," Internet World Stats website, *www.internetworldstats.com*, March 31, 2011.

**29.** See Ann Coughlan, Erin Anderson, Louis W. Stern and Adel El-Ansary, *Marketing Channels*, 7th ed. (Upper Saddle River, NJ: Prentice Hall, 2006), chap. 13, for a discussion of the channels used by other service providers.

**30.** Ibid.

**31.** F. Robert Dwyer, Paul H. Schurr, and Sejo Oh, "Developing Buyer–Seller Relationships," *Journal of Marketing* 51 (April 1987), pp. 11–27; Robert M. Morgan and Shelby D. Hunt, "The Commitment-Trust Theory of Relationship Marketing," *Journal of Marketing* 58 (July 1994), pp. 20–38; and Shankar Ganesan, "Determinants of Long-Term Orientation in Buyer–Seller Relationships," *Journal of Marketing* 58 (April 1994), pp. 1–19.

**32.** Morgan and Hunt, "Commitment-Trust Theory." See also Donald V. Fites, "Make Your Dealers Your Partners," *Harvard Business Review*, March–April 1996, pp. 84–95.

**33.** Fites, "Make Your Dealers Your Partners."

**34.** For examples, see Zachary Schiller, Greg Burns, and Karen Lowry Miller, "Make It Simple," *BusinessWeek*, September 9, 1996, pp. 96–104; and David Henry, "Accounting Games in the Grocer's Aisle," *BusinessWeek*, April 14, 2003, p. 64.

# CHAPTER THIRTEEN

# Integrated Promotion Decisions

## Nano Goes Nowhere[1]

*g* IN 2005, CHAIRMAN RATAN TATA of India's Tata Group announced with great fanfare that Tata would introduce a new budget-priced automobile that would get Indian families of four or five off their motorcycles and scooters—not the safest of ways for a family to travel together—and into the new Nano. The Nano, priced at an unheard-of price point of 100,000 rupees—about $2,000, half the price of a Maruti Suzuki Alto, a low-priced leader in India—would revolutionize the way Indian families get around.

Fast forward to November 2010, nearly two years after the Nano's launch, when only 589 Nanos were shipped to dealers, marking the bottom of a steady slide in Nano sales from 9,000 units in July of that year. What had gone wrong?

For starters, there were political pressures that forced Tata to abandon its planned plant in West Bengal and move production temporarily while a planned plant for the Nano was built in Gujarat. These delays caused supply problems that limited Tata's ability to fill the advance orders that it had already taken. Then there were quality and safety issues. In mid-2010, there were fires in several Nanos, not exactly reinforcing the safety benefits that moving families off motorcycles and into automobiles was supposed to deliver. Finally, due to the hype and Tata's overwhelming number of advance bookings—200,000 cars were prebooked, of which 100,000 were planned to be delivered by the end of 2010—there was a general perception that there was

no point in trying to buy a Nano. You couldn't get one any time soon.

## Marketing Missteps

But was the problem one of supply, or was it lack of demand? Gautam Sen, editor of India's *Auto India*, says the real issue was "A total marketing failure. (Tata) thought the car would sell itself because it was the Nano and (because of) the kind of coverage it received around the world. They just took their eyes off the ball."

Observers say that Tata simply didn't get its marketing act together. The Nano targeted rural and other Indian consumers of modest means—first-time auto buyers whose current transportation was a two-wheeler—but early promotional efforts featured a special Nano website, the use of social networking on Facebook and Orkut, blogs, and online advertising. Given India's very modest online penetration at the time of the launch, this was clearly a mismatch, as most low-income consumers simply weren't online.

Worse, the positioning of the car was entirely wrong, according to Professor Sudipt Roy of the Indian School of Business. In India, "A car is an aspirational product. You can't say, 'Here is a car that's cheap, so buy it.' The car has to connect with the right segment emotionally. They have to win the battle of the mind."

## Tata Responds

To address its quality and safety issues, Tata added features—a heftier engine, power steering and windows, even an airbag—but the price rose correspondingly, to about $4,000 for high-end models and $2,700 for the base model. This sort of pricing put it nearly on par with the larger and more comfortable Alto or even a used Toyota, thereby putting it into a highly competitive market segment and creating a disconnect with the target market the Nano was intended to reach.

Tata also introduced a variety of financing incentives, though it's not clear that its target consumers, many of whom could not easily document their income in India's informal economy, could comply with lenders' credit requirements.

As Tata fought to regain the Nano's footing, General Motors, which had been planning a new model to compete with the Nano, announced in June 2011 that it was shelving its plans, as the project was deemed not to be viable.

Can Tata recover from its early missteps and make the Nano live up to its hype? Sales in 2011 began to recover from the Nano's November 2010 low point, reaching a cumulative 16,527 units through May, more than double Nano's prior-year figures, but still far below Tata's lofty original goals. Kevin Freiberg, coauthor of *Nanovation,* a book that touts the Nano as a vehicle for helping the developing world "think big," says, "We don't know. But we do know this: Tata Motors is a great company with a deep culture of commitment to the needs of the customer. We can't wait to see how they handle this situation."

## Marketing Challenges Addressed in Chapter 13

Assessing markets, analyzing industries, and uncovering customers' unsatisfied wants and needs often leads to the development of new goods or services with huge potential—at least in the eyes of the marketing managers or entrepreneurs who introduce them. So far, we've seen how these activities, together with decisions about final product configuration, pricing, and distribution—three of the four Ps—bring companies to the brink of marketing success. With these important building blocks in place, a critical marketing task remains—to let a waiting world know of the new product and invite it to purchase. The entrepreneur with a new product is not alone; countless marketing managers face similar decisions every day, not only for new products of which customers are unaware, but also for established products trying to win in today's highly competitive markets.

In Chapter 13, we address the considerable challenges entailed in the last of the four Ps—**promotion**—and we provide tools and analytical frameworks for addressing several age-old marketing questions. To whom should marketing messages be directed, inside the company and outside, to consumers and other stakeholders? How can the marketing manager most effectively and efficiently inform the target market about the product? How can the manager persuade them to try or buy? What messages should be delivered? How much should the firm spend to deliver them? In what media, or with what promotional tools? Finally, how might the manager assess whether the promotional strategy has been both effective and efficient? These are not easy questions to answer.

**STRATEGIC ISSUE**

*How can the marketing manager most effectively and efficiently inform the target market about the product?*

We begin by introducing the promotion mix, the collection of promotional elements from which marketers can choose. We then explore the communication process and the barriers that make it difficult to get promotional messages across to their intended audiences. Finally, we provide tools for marketing managers or entrepreneurs to use in answering the questions just raised, in order to prepare evidence-based marketing plans that stand a good chance of meeting their marketing objectives.

# The Promotion Mix: A Communication Tool Kit

In deciding how to best promote their products, marketing managers must decide which promotional tools to use and with whom they wish to communicate. These decisions, as we shall see, must consider the objectives the marketer has in mind, as well as the merits of and costs entailed in using different tools in the **promotion mix.** In making these decisions, the marketer is developing a promotional, or an **integrated marketing communication (IMC), plan.** Arens defines the IMC planning process as one of "building and reinforcing mutually profitable relationships with employees, customers, other stakeholders, and the general public by developing and coordinating a strategic communications program that enables them to make constructive contact with the company brand through a variety of media."[2]

The process by which the IMC plan is developed follows essentially the steps in the marketing management process that have served as the basis for the structure of this book.

Of particular importance are the steps involving segmentation, targeting, and positioning, which ideally would provide information on the choice criteria of the target audience. Setting marketing objectives and strategy for a product-market is also critical since it sets the stage for the development of the strategic marketing program, which establishes the role of the various elements in the marketing mix.

The traditional tools from which a marketer can choose in developing an IMC plan, comprising the **promotion mix,** are **advertising, personal selling, sales promotion, and public relations,** though there are other promotional tools, such as sponsorships and staged events, that do not fall neatly into any of these categories. For example, in the hope of getting hot new actors and actresses to plug their products, some marketers use companies like Backstage Creations to place their products in so-called swag suites at the Sundance Film Festival and others, where the likes of Paris Hilton have been known to walk away with as many as two dozen bags of freebies ranging from Puma sneakers to Samsung handheld computers. RevitaLash, a small cosmetics company, spent $50,000 on swag suites in 2010 and believes its ensuing press coverage was worth $2.4 million if paid for as advertising.[3] Definitions of the traditional tools or promotional elements follow, and are elaborated in Exhibit 13.1.

- **Advertising**—Any paid form of *nonpersonal* (i.e., through some medium, such as search advertising, radio, print, direct mail, or e-mail) presentation and promotion of ideas, goods, or services by an identified sponsor.
- **Personal selling**—A process of helping and persuading one or more prospects to purchase a good or service or to act on any idea through the use of an *oral* presentation (person-to-person communication).
- **Sales promotion**—Incentives designed to stimulate the purchase or sale of a product, usually in the short term.
- **Public relations**—Nonpaid, nonpersonal stimulation of demand for a product, service, or business unit by planting significant news about it or a favorable presentation of it in the media.

## Exhibit 13.1

EXAMPLES OF PROMOTIONAL ACTIVITIES

- **Advertising:** Print ads (newspaper and magazine), radio, television, billboard, direct mail, brochures and catalogs, signs, in-store displays, posters, motion pictures, web pages, banner ads, and e-mails.

- **Personal selling:** Sales presentations, sales meetings, sales training and incentive programs for intermediary salespeople, and telemarketing (either inbound or outbound).

- **Sales promotion:** Coupons, sweepstakes, contests, product samples, rebates, tie-ins, self-liquidating premiums, trade shows, trade-ins, and exhibitions.

- **Public relations:** Newspaper and magazine articles/reports, TV and radio presentations, charitable contributions, speeches, issue advertising, and seminars.

Firms spend substantial sums on their advertising and other promotional activities. Advertising expenditures in all media, including the internet, were estimated to be $544 billion worldwide in 2010.[4] And the total does not include personal selling, sales promotion, and public relations on which billions more are spent.

## Developing an Integrated Marketing Communications Plan

There are many factors to consider in developing an effective promotional, or marketing communications, program, whether for goods or services. These include the objectives the marketer has in mind, the characteristics and decision processes of the target market(s) the communication is intended to reach, and the available budget. In addition, the brand's positioning, its competitors' promotional strategies, the distribution channels through which it will be sold, the product's stage in the product life cycle, and the merits of the various elements of the promotion mix must be considered. Thus, promotional decision making is no simple task! Simply having a creative idea for an advertising campaign is not sufficient.

Each of the four main elements of the promotion mix—advertising, personal selling, sales promotion, and public relations—has its own unique strengths and weaknesses, though these vary for specific tools and media within each of the four elements. The marketer's challenge is to develop a budget that will accomplish the promotional objectives and distribute that budget across the elements of the promotion mix in the most effective and efficient manner. To do so, skilled marketers follow a five-step process like that outlined in Exhibit 13.2.

## Step 1: Define the Audience(s) to Be Targeted

In the market segmentation chapter, we identified three broad ways to segment both consumer and organizational markets: on the basis of who the customers are, where they are, and how they behave. Segmentation decisions are especially important to the marketing communications effort because they identify who the target market is, so those planning the communications effort can identify the best ways to reach the target customers.

## Exhibit 13.2

DECISION SEQUENCE FOR DEVELOPING THE PROMOTION MIX

Define the audience(s) to be targeted
(1)

Set the promotional objectives
(2)

Set the promotion budget
(3)

Design the promotion mix
(4)

Evaluate the results
(5)

Sometimes promotional messages in an integrated marketing communications program must target multiple audiences, such as for medical products. For example, Rogaine, the drug for male pattern baldness, was promoted to doctors, to encourage them to prescribe it, as well as to consumers, to encourage them to ask their doctors about the product.

Making promotional decisions without a clear idea as to who the target market is can often lead to misdirection or waste of scarce marketing funds, as was the case for Tata's launch of the Nano. An even more dramatic example of poor targeting is OurBeginning.com, a marketer of wedding invitations that advertised on the Super Bowl in 2005.[5] Women ages 18 to 30 comprise the most attractive target market for wedding invitations, since women's families still plan most weddings and most weddings are still among couples in these age brackets. Was the Super Bowl an effective and efficient way to reach this target market? It may have been effective, since many young women do watch the Super Bowl, though they may be less glued to the screen at a Super Bowl party than are their male counterparts. But it was not efficient. Only a small portion of the total Super Bowl viewing audience fell into OurBeginning. com's target market, but OurBeginnings had to pay Super Bowl prices for the *entire* viewing audience. Thus, OurBeginning.com's cost to reach its *target* customers was very high.

## Step 2: Set the Promotional Objectives

Having clearly identified the target audience for the marketing communication being planned, the marketer's next job is to decide exactly what the communication is supposed to accomplish, in measurable terms. Growth in sales and market share are often used as promotional objectives, but marketers should note that sales increases are a function of the entire marketing program, not just the promotion mix. Advertising a poorly designed or overpriced product or one that has little distribution is not likely to be successful. Appropriate promotional objectives, like other business objectives, should follow the SMART acronym: specific, measurable, attainable, relevant (to the firms' mission and overall market and competitive context), and time-bound. Thus, good promotional objectives should include four key elements:

- A statement defining the target audience.
- A statement of how some specific aspect(s) of the audience's perceptions, attitudes, or behavior should change.
- A statement of how quickly such a change is expected to occur.
- And a statement of the degree of change required.

# Step 3: Set the Promotion Budget

There are a number of ways to prepare the promotion budget, most of which work from the top down (managers first determine the total amount to be budgeted and then allocate various amounts to the different mix components). The budget-setting methods most commonly used are discussed briefly below.

The **percentage-of-sales** method is the most common. The procedure consists of setting this year's budget as a percentage of this year's anticipated sales. Under this approach, sales determine the promotional activity versus planning to achieve some desired sales objective. Even though illogical, this method has some advantages. It is simple to calculate and is risk-averse because spending is linked to sales.

The **competitive-parity** method sets the relative level of promotional spending equal to the brand's market share, or larger if an attempt is being made to increase share. Thus, if the brand's market share is 20 percent, then its budget would be its 20 percent of the total amount spent by the industry on promoting brands in that category. This method of budgeting tends to create stability in market shares among competitors and has the advantage of considering competition. Share of market budgeting is often used in connection with new products where one rule of thumb is to spend one and a half times the share objective at the end of the first or second year.

Because the **objective-and-task** method avoids most of the flaws inherent in the top-down budgeting approaches, it is the best one—though the most difficult—to use. It essentially involves three steps—first, define promotional objectives as specifically as possible; second, determine the strategies and specific tasks necessary to meet those objectives; and third, estimate the costs of performing those tasks and budget accordingly.

The objective-and-task method has the advantage of forcing firms to set specific promotional objectives through careful analysis of the specific situation. It is most effective when the results obtained from a particular promotion activity can be measured (for instance, the awareness generated among members of the target audience or the number of persons who would be exposed to the product via sampling).

Using the promotional budget strategically can deliver significant results. During the economic downturn following the 2007–2008 financial crisis, General Mills decided that a downturn was a good time to steal market share from its rivals. "In an environment where you have consumers going to the grocery stores more often and thinking about more meals at home, we think that is a great environment for brand building," says CEO Ken Powell. General Mills boosted promotional budgets when total U.S. ad spending was falling, thereby growing top-line sales at 9 to 10 percent in categories that were growing at only 5 percent.[6]

# Step 4: Design the Promotion Mix

Designing the promotion mix is itself a three-step process.

- First, marketers decide which promotion components to use: advertising, personal selling, sales promotion, public relations, or other less traditional activities.
- Second, they choose the specific activities within each component. In advertising, this involves considering such media as TV, radio, newspapers, magazines, the internet, or billboards. A consumer sales promotion could consist of coupons, free samples, or premiums, for example.
- Third, within each activity they must decide which specific vehicle to employ; for example, in advertising, this might require selecting a TV or radio program, while in sales promotion they must decide about the coupon specifics—its value, size and color, message format, and how it will be delivered.

These decisions are complex because the elements of the promotion mix are not independent; for example, a consumer sales promotion (perhaps a coupon or sweepstakes) often

requires advertising to inform the target audience about the promotion. Making specific decisions about promotion mix elements requires examining the target audience, objectives, and budget, already established in Steps 1 though 3 (see Exhibit 13.2), as well as the company's overall strategic objectives and resources, the product's stage in the product life cycle, and various market characteristics and the other elements—the kind of brand being promoted; its price and distribution—in the marketing mix. It also usually involves making a choice between advertising and personal selling as the principal driver of the promotion strategy (see Exhibit 13.3).

In practice, either advertising or personal selling generally plays a dominant role in the promotion mix, with sales promotion and/or publicity playing supporting roles. In entrepreneurial settings where budgets are tight, public relations, events, or other lower-cost methods, such as RevitaLash's use of swag suites, sometimes take the lead. When advertising

## Exhibit 13.3

STRATEGIC CIRCUMSTANCES AND THE RELATIVE IMPORTANCE OF ADVERTISING AND PERSONAL SELLING AS PROMOTIONAL TOOLS

| Advertising relatively important | | Personal Selling relatively important |
|---|---|---|
| Large | Number and dispersion of customers | Small |
| Low | Buyers' information needs | High |
| Small | Size and importance of purchase | Large |
| Little | Postpurchase service required | Much |
| Low | Product complexity | High |
| Pull | Distribution strategy | Push |
| Preset | Pricing policy | Negotiated |
| Many | Resources available for promotion | Few |

*Source:* Adapted from David W. Cravens, and Nigel Piercy *Strategic Marketing* (Burr Ridge, IL: McGraw-Hill/Irwin, 2009), p. 380. Reprinted with permission from The McGraw-Hill Companies.

dominates, the idea is to communicate with the consumer and encourage him or her to pull the product through the distribution channel, by demanding that the channel stock the product. As we saw in the previous chapter, this strategy is called a **pull strategy.** Major consumer goods marketers typically use pull strategies. When personal selling dominates, the marketer attempts to convince channel members to stock the product, so consumers will find it at their local store—a **push strategy.** Smaller consumer goods marketers who lack the budgets to pursue pull strategies typically use push strategies. Many little-advertised products found in supermarkets and mass merchants found their way to the shelf through effective push strategies.

Different elements in the promotion mix may be called on to meet different objectives. For example, advertising may be asked to develop awareness and brand recognition; the internet may be used to build a contact list or generate sales leads; personal selling may be used to complete the sale. Even when the strategic conditions and communications tasks faced by a firm favor the allocation of substantial promotional resources to the salesforce, the specific marketing objectives that salespeople are asked to pursue vary widely across firms facing different market and competitive situations. A company's sales personnel might be asked to focus on one or more of the following objectives:

- Winning acceptance of new products by existing customers.
- Developing new customers for existing products.
- Maintaining the loyalty of current customers by providing good service.
- Facilitating future sales by providing technical services to potential customers.
- Facilitating future sales by communicating product information to potential customers or influencers.
- Gathering market information.

An important part of designing the promotion mix is creating the messages to be communicated to the target audience(s). Preparing a successful message is difficult, if only because of the countless ways in which it can be constructed. Yet the payoffs from good messages are substantial. For example, simple changes in the wording of a print ad have been known to generate a substantial increase in sales for retail stores, mail-order houses, and direct mail sellers.

Getting the message just right is part of what Groupon, the fast-growing daily discount marketer, provides to its clients. Groupon user Dana Thayer of Chelsea Piers, a sports and entertainment complex in New York City, likes Groupon's off-beat style and the ability it gives her to target potential new or existing customers with tailored offers. "It's not the same old stuff," she says. Groupon sold 2,800 coupons for her 90-minute basic golf classes during March 2010, when the club wasn't very busy. And Thayer can track just how well her offers meet their objectives. "We give them a bounce-back—a card with a special offer and then we track the redemption."[7]

In concept, then, our discussion of this step highlights the remaining issues the marketer must consider in preparing a promotional plan. At the risk of being overly general, Exhibit 13.4 provides guidance in assessing some relative merits of the various elements of the promotion mix. But we have not yet provided enough specifics that the marketer charged with preparing a marketing or integrated marketing communications plan for a new or existing product can determine the specific budgets and activities necessary to meet a sales forecast. We address these important details in the balance of this chapter. First, however, comes Step 5, which assesses the results of the promotion plan, once it has been implemented.

## Exhibit 13.4

COMPARING THE MERITS OF THE PROMOTION MIX ELEMENTS

| Promotion mix element | Amount of information communicated | Credibility | Control over the message | Cost to reach one customer | Strategic suitability |
|---|---|---|---|---|---|
| Advertising | Varies: little information in a radio or TV ad, to lots on a website | Low | Good | Low | Well-suited to a **pull strategy.** |
| Personal Selling | Lots of information | Depends on the credibility of the company and the personality and sales skills of the salesperson | Poor, but training helps | Very high in developed countries, can be low in emerging markets | Well-suited to a **push strategy.** |
| Sales Promotion | Virtually no information | Not applicable | Good | Low and self-liquidating: generally pays for itself as the product is purchased | Consumer promotion supports a **pull strategy.** Trade promotion supports a **push strategy.** |
| Public Relations | Lots of information | High | Poor | Very low or nil | Supports both **pull** and **push** strategies. |

# Step 5: Evaluate the Results

This step involves finding out whether the objectives of the promotional activity have been met—sometimes via marketing research. For example, in advertising a new consumer product, after the promotional campaign had run for a designated period the company could conduct a telephone survey to determine whether the objective of generating a certain level of awareness among members of the target audience had been achieved. Further, the survey could determine what percent had tried the brand and of these how many had bought it two or more times. In this way management could obtain information about the relationship of trial to awareness. Research can also provide important insights into whether the firm attained its distribution objectives.

As we'll see later in this chapter, one of the reasons that online marketing is taking a growing share of advertisers' spending is that the results of many online promotional activities are easily measured. The growing use of online search advertising and other forms of online advertising, including behavioral targeting, which tracks a web user's behavior and offers targeted ads based on that behavior, is said by some to offer a solution to the oldest problem in advertising: "Half the money I spend on advertising is wasted; trouble is, I don't know which half." Behavioral targeting, which already makes up about 20 percent of online display advertising by value, is particularly useful among advertisers selling high-ticket items for which a period of online search is likely to precede a buying decision.[8]

# The Nitty-Gritty of Promotional Decision Making

Faced with meeting a sales forecast, how should a marketer determine the specifics of his or her promotional program? How big an ad budget is needed? In which media should it be spent? What role should personal selling play? How might the internet be used to best advantage? Are coupons or trade promotions called for? What about samples to encourage trial? Should we seek publicity through a public relations effort? We address these practical questions in this portion of the chapter.

**STRATEGIC ISSUE**

*How should a marketer determine the specifics of his or her promotional program?*

## Making Advertising Decisions

Advertising is a complex decision arena and the changing macroenvironment has made it even more so. Major social and economic changes in Western countries include a redefined family unit (fewer members, more single parents and two wage earners), which leads to less pressure to conform to traditional family values, more lifestyle options, and an increase in basic household needs. An exploding media scene, including a dramatic increase in the number of media options, not the least of which is the internet, exacerbates the challenge.

Advertising decision making is concerned with setting objectives and budgets, choosing which media types and vehicles to use with what frequency, deciding what the message should be and how to present it, and analyzing the effectiveness of the advertising program. We address these issues next.

**Setting Advertising Objectives**    Promotional objectives are important in developing an integrated promotion plan. They derive from the firm's marketing objectives and strategy and are concerned with communicating certain information about the company and its product(s) to target audiences. They help in the development of a promotion plan, which, in turn, facilitates decision making by a large number of diverse individuals both inside and outside the company. Promotional objectives serve as the basis for evaluating the advertising program once it is completed.

Advertising objectives must somehow relate to attitudes or behavior. Results can sometimes best be assessed by measuring the *process* by which the desired objectives are met. Hence the use of hierarchy-of-effect models that move prospective buyers through a series of steps—awareness, comprehension, conviction, action—to the ultimate goal of purchasing the product. Knowing the various steps in such models helps the marketer better set its advertising objectives. Thus, if most prospects are aware of the product *and* its advantages but not convinced of its uniqueness, one advertising objective would be to create conviction by demonstrating product superiority.

Another advantage of using the communication hierarchy as the basis for setting advertising objectives is that it is possible to measure the proportion of potential customers who are at each stage in the hierarchy. This means that advertising objectives can be set forth in numerical terms for a stated time period and pertaining to a defined audience group.

**STRATEGIC ISSUE**

*In setting advertising objectives, a clear understanding of precisely what the advertising is expected to accomplish, often measured in terms of attitude change, provides an ad agency or others who make the media choices and develop the ads with the direction they need to do their jobs.*

Thus, in setting advertising objectives, a clear understanding of precisely what the advertising is expected to accomplish, often measured in terms of attitude change, provides an ad agency or others who make the media choices and develop the ads with the direction they need to do their jobs. In large-company settings, where advertising enjoys multimillion-dollar budgets, marketing research is typically used to assess whether the advertising is doing its intended job, as we discuss later in this section. Setting SMART advertising objectives makes such an assessment possible.

## Setting Advertising Budgets and Making Media Choices

Whether an advertising program consists of radio or television ads, ads on the internet, print ads in magazines or newspapers, direct mail, or other media choices, setting budgets and choosing media come down to making decisions about the extent to which a message is delivered to its target audience, or **reach,** and the **frequency** with which it does so. Thus, advertisers must choose some combination of *reach* and *frequency* to attain their advertising objectives. Reach is defined as the total number of individuals or households exposed to at least one ad during a given period—typically four weeks. The term can be used in connection with a single media vehicle (a specific TV show) or a media schedule comprising a number of different vehicles. Reach is typically expressed as a percent of the target audience; for example, if the target audience was 100,000 persons and the media schedule reached 70,000, then the reach would be 70 percent. Ordinarily, costs rise at an increasing rate as higher levels of reach are sought.

There are several problems in using reach and frequency to make media decisions. The first is defining the target audience and correlating it with the audiences reached by the various media vehicles. We discuss these problems later in this section. A second problem is defining exposure—is it an opportunity to be exposed to a given message or is it an actual reading of a print ad, actual watching of a TV commercial, or actual listening to an ad on radio? It is difficult to measure exposure no matter how it is defined. Third, not all who are exposed are of equal value to the advertiser; some may not even be prospects, as we saw in the example of the Super Bowl ad for OurBeginning.com earlier in thus chapter. Fourth, how should successive exposures be weighted? Is a second exposure worth more than a third? How much? And how much time should elapse between exposures?

Reach and frequency measures are used to prepare the advertising schedule, which, in turn, determines total advertising expenditures. In estimating the cost of a given schedule, media planners simplify their task by using gross rating points (GRPs), which are calculated by multiplying reach by average frequency. Assuming a reach of 70 percent and a desired average frequency of four, the number of GRPs would then be 280. By multiplying this by an estimated cost per GRP, the cost for a proposed media schedule can be estimated. A step-by-step procedure for setting an advertising budget for a new energy beverage brand is shown in Exhibit 13.5. This example also illustrates the use of the objective-and-task method to set an advertising budget.

Exhibit 13.5 shows that various assumptions must be made about desired levels of reach and frequency in order to prepare a media budget. On what are these assumptions based? In practice, marketers rely on their prior experience to determine how much reach and frequency are necessary to deliver a certain level of results. Thus, in preparing promotional plans, marketers must draw on either their own experience, that of others within their company, or that of experts, such as ad agency personnel, to determine how large a budget, or media buy, is necessary to meet a particular objective.

The costs of advertising in various media may be found from a variety of sources. Typically, an advertising medium provides to prospective advertisers upon request a **rate card,** which specifies the nature and size of the audience it reaches and the costs of advertising in that medium. Costs are expressed in **cost per thousand** impressions (an impression is one person being exposed to the ad one time), or **CPM,** making comparisons across different kinds of media possible. Various industry sources compile such information and make

**STRATEGIC ISSUE**

*Various assumptions must be made about desired levels of reach and frequency in order to prepare a media budget. On what are these assumptions based?*

## Exhibit 13.5

SETTING AN ADVERTISING BUDGET FOR A NEW ENERGY BEVERAGE BRAND—A HYPOTHETICAL EXAMPLE

1.  Establish a market-share goal. By the end of the first year, achieve a 15 percent share of the estimated 40 million-case energy beverage market, which is expected to grow by 10 million cases per year for the next several years. This target of 6 million cases is to be obtained by attracting first-time energy beverage buyers and getting existing users to switch to the new brand. Assume some 10 million energy beverage drinkers and the net addition of 2.5 million new drinkers each year. The number of individual consumers needed to attain a 15 percent share is estimated to be about 2 million.

2(a).  Determine the percent of the target audience that needs to be made aware of the new brand in order to induce a trial and repeat usage rate (three or more bottles) that will attract 2 million consumers. The agency estimates that 40 percent of those who try a bottle of the new brand will become long-term users. This means 5 million persons must try the product. The agency further assumes that 75 percent of those who become aware of the product will try it. This translates into a need to make 6.67 million—or some 53 percent of the 12.5 million total present and prospective buyers—aware of the brand.

2(b).  Determine the number of impressions needed to obtain an awareness level of 53 percent followed by trial and repeat buying. The agency estimates that 35 impressions on average will be needed for each of 12.5 million individuals in the target audience to bring this about. Thus, the total number of impressions needed is $35 \times 12.5$ million = 437.5 million.

2(c).  Determine the number of gross rating points (GRPs) needed.* Based on needed reach and frequency (35), assume 3,500 GRPs are needed.

3.  Determine the cost of the needed 3,500 GRPs. The agency estimates an average cost per GRP of $4,000—hence, the advertising media budget would be $14 million. To this amount, the costs of ad production and marketing research have to be added.

*GRPs are computed by multiplying the *reach* by the average *frequency*. *Reach* means the different individuals (or households) exposed to an advertising schedule per time period. Reach measures the unduplicated audience exposed to a media schedule and is typically expressed as a percent of the target audience. *Frequency* is a measure of the number of times on average a person or household receives an advertising measure. Thus, it is a measure of repetition.

## Exhibit 13.6

COMPREHENSIVE SOURCES OF MEDIA AUDIENCE AND RATE INFORMATION

| Source | website address | Description |
|---|---|---|
| Standard Rate and Data Service (SRDS) | www.srds.com | Provides rates and audience information for U.S. television, radio, newspaper, magazine (both consumer and business), and direct mail media |
| BPA International | www.bpai.com | Provides circulation and traffic information for newspaper, magazine (both consumer and business), trade show, website, industry database, and wireless communication media in 25 countries |
| DMPlaza | www.dmplaza.com | Provides web information relating to the direct marketing industry, including suppliers and call center services and products |
| A. C. Nielsen | www.nielsenmedia.com | Provides, on a fee basis, North American ratings and traffic data for television, cable television, and websites based on proprietary samples who report their viewing and web traffic behavior |

it available to prospective advertisers for their use in planning promotional programs. Exhibit 13.6 provides several such sources and their internet addresses. Most business libraries have copies of these or similar publications.

**Traditional Media Types**   Of the four major types of mass media, network and cable TV has the largest share globally, followed by newspaper advertising.[9] New media, including the internet, are threatening television's historical dominance of mass-market advertising (see Exhibit 13.7), though in fast-growing emerging markets like China and Brazil, TV still dominates.[10] Each media type offers unique advantages to the advertiser, but each also has limitations.

**Television** is best at communicating images and symbols because it can demonstrate product usage and consumer reactions. It is a particularly good medium to help sell a mass market product and is seen as particularly useful for reaching the emerging middle class in the developing world. It has enormous reach—for example, in the United States almost all households have a TV set, though viewing hours have been declining; even in China 93% regularly watch TV.[11]

In spite of the apparently inexorable decline in TV viewing in Western markets, media analyst Jon Fine writes, "Waiting for ad dollars to shift decisively away from TV is like being a weatherman during a 30-year drought. You know the heavy rains have to come down at some point. It's just taking awfully long for those showers to arrive.[12] Adman and Saatchi & Saatchi CEO Kevin Roberts puts it more forcefully: "TV will be the absolute dominant screen in the world. Just look at China, look at Russia, look at India, look at Brazil, look at Indonesia and look at the way TVs are absolutely going crazy. Even in the U.S., people still spend two and a half hours a day in front of a television screen."[13] The debate about the future of TV advertising as we know it has ad agencies, marketers of all kinds, and numerous observers on the edge of their couches. It's an important question about which only time will give us an answer.

**Radio** is seen as less involving than television, but offers economy and the opportunity to target specific audiences—particular ethnicities, teenagers, senior citizens. Radio advertising—while inexpensive compared with TV and newspapers—suffers in that it reaches people mostly when they are doing something else such as working, driving, or walking. It is often used to reinforce TV advertising.

**Print media** can be more involving than broadcast media. Readers select what advertising they want to read and take as much time as they wish to read it. Thus, print is effective in communicating detailed information about a product. This is particularly important for most industrial products and high-involvement consumer goods.

There are many types of magazines based on the nature of their content and the scope of their geographical coverage—local, regional, and national. And they can be categorized on the nature of their audience ranging from general or mass appeal (*The Economist, Newsweek*), to highly specific such as those dedicated to sports (football, golf, tennis), hobbies (gardening, stamp collecting, antiques), ethnic groups (Hispanic), age groups

---

## Exhibit 13.7    UNILEVER'S AXE SWITCHES FROM TV TO THE INTERNET

As Western consumers spend more and more time on the internet, advertisers are following suit. "Ultimately it comes down to where the customer is," says Kevin George, Unilever's general manager for deodorants. Axe, Unilever's growing line of personal care products for young men, has moved the majority of its ad budget to the internet, a switch from 2002 when it launched the brand with a television-based campaign. Axe spends its online budget where young men are found, on sites such as Facebook and Heavy.com. One of its efforts featured an online game that was centered on techniques for picking up women, a theme that would have been difficult to deliver in traditional 30-second TV spots. "We all recognize our consumers are online and we all continue to share the sense that the effectiveness of a traditional 30-second television ad is continuing to erode," says Noreen Simmons, who directs Unilever's U.S. strategic media planning. Globally, internet advertising rose to 12 percent of total ad spending in 2010, up from just 7 percent in 2006, compared with TV's 38 percent in both years.

*Sources:* Kevin J. Delaney, "Once-Wary Industry Giants Embrace Internet Advertising," *The Wall Street Journal,* April 17, 2006, p. 1; *Marketing News 2010 Marketing Factbook,* p. 24. For more on Axe, see www.theaxeeffect.com.

(teens, seniors), gender (working women), and financial matters (investment opportunities). In recent years more-focused magazines in terms of market segments have gained circulation versus the larger, more-generalized ones. Newspapers' circulation has been falling, and newspapers' revenues from classified advertising have been decimated by Craigslist and others. Unless they can find ways to sharply increase revenue from putting their content online—a tenuous assumption, as many readers expect their online content to be free—their long-term viability is in question.

**Out-of-home, exhibition, and supplementary media** cover a wide variety of media types. These three categories are discussed briefly below.

- **Out-of-home.** Billboards are the most prominent media and come in a variety of shapes and sizes as well as location opportunities. These include spectacular electronic signs that feature moving messages and color graphics. Other outdoor media include transit shelters, terminals, and airports; transit vehicles—both inside and out—such as taxis, buses, and streetcars; sports stadiums (many carry the name and logo of a prominent advertiser); parking meters, public phones, and shopping malls.
- **Exhibition.** This category is dominated by in-store display materials, which include signs, banners, video displays on shopping carts, and electronic ads on in-store screens. Trade shows and exhibits are a favorite with many business-to-business marketers. In Brazil, Elemedia's ubiquitous TV screens pump out ads in elevators in hotels, office buildings, and elsewhere.
- **Supplementary.** Directories and yellow pages (both print and online) are the major media in this category.

**Direct marketing using advertising media** has been covered in part in Chapter 12 (distribution decisions). For consumer products, this approach typically involves direct mail (including catalogs and internet marketing), infomercials on late-night or cable TV, radio, and print ads with a toll-free phone number. Despite its high cost (per exposure) and despite typical response rates in the 1–2 percent range, direct mail's selectivity has enabled some companies to reap substantial profits.

Fitness guru Tony Horton of Beachbody has persuaded 3 million people to pay $140 for his company's 12-DVD fitness regimen since 2005, by promising three months of rigor and pain, in contrast to the usual weight-loss and fitness promises of spectacular results with little or no effort. Horton's next move is to expand his product line to less-intense regimens for the elderly and teens, protein supplements, and other fitness-related products.[14]

**New Media**    Among the greatest challenges facing advertisers today is how to take best advantage of the opportunities presented by the new media made possible by advances in computing and communications technology. We address these challenges in considerable detail in Chapter 14, in which we examine an array of available strategic options in the internet age. Here, we focus on the internet and other new media as communication vehicles, where new developments are causing advertisers to rethink how they spend their advertising budgets. Selected ethical issues are addressed in Ethical Perspective 13.1.

In late 1998—eons ago in internet time—J. William Gurley, a venture capitalist and columnist writing in *Fortune* magazine, predicted that internet technologies would revolutionize advertising, largely because the performance of internet ads is measurable. "On the internet an advertiser can not only measure the number of people who see his ad but can also track the number of people who 'click through' an ad to get more information from the advertiser's own web page. Armed with such data, an advertiser doesn't have to settle for spots that don't deliver customers. Unlike a print or television ad buyer—and like a direct marketer—he can pay only for messages that reach the most receptive audience."[15]

**STRATEGIC ISSUE**

*"On the internet...an advertiser doesn't have to settle for spots that don't deliver customers. Unlike a print or television ad buyer—and like a direct marketer—he can pay only for messages that reach the most receptive audience."*

## ETHICAL PERSPECTIVE 13.1
### Ethical Issues in New Media Marketing

In the early days of the web, a principal consumer concern was whether it was safe to transmit one's credit card number to buy something from a web-based merchant. Such concerns have largely gone by the wayside, as electronic shopping has proven no more risky than the bricks-and-mortar variety. Bigger concerns today have to do with privacy and unauthorized use of customer information, as played out in unwanted e-mails or unwanted monitoring of web shopping behavior. Many websites, including those of internet retailers such as Amazon.com, place so-called "cookies" on their customers' computers, to track their shopping preferences and enable enhanced customer services, like Amazon.com's One-Click® ordering. When a repeat customer logs on to Amazon.com, the site knows who she is, offers recommendations of books she may like, and permits her to purchase books with a single click. These consumer benefits, however, come at the cost of Amazon's being able to track her behavior and learn things about her that she may not wish to have the company know. If Amazon sells this information to others, such concerns are heightened. Further, Amazon is able to send her e-mails announcing promotions, such as when it adds new merchandise categories to its offering.

While consumers typically have the ability to opt in or out of such e-mail lists, knowing how to do so is not always obvious or easy. Similar concerns will arise as the use of mobile telephones for advertising grows. How many of us will want to receive unsolicited messages about bargain lunches on our cell phones? Ultimately, legislation is likely to govern how consumer information may be gathered and used by web-based and other new media marketers, though different countries are likely to pass different laws. Given the global reach of the web, does this mean that web-based marketers will have to comply with whomever passes the most restrictive laws? These and other ethical issues are far from resolved, and new technological developments will likely raise issues not contemplated today.

Gurley's prediction has been a right on target, as internet shopping and advertising have exploded. Aided by recent software innovations, advertisers measure not only how many customers "click through" an ad, but they can also determine which customers bought online, how much they bought, and what the margins were on each sale. More traditionally, advertisers can also use the internet for brand building for both web-based and traditional businesses, as we saw in Exhibit 13.7.

Company websites, now as *de rigueur* for companies as having e-mail and business cards, provide a cost-effective way to provide detailed product information about one's entire product line, as well as information of interest to investors and, unfortunately, to competitors. Websites are also good ways to build one-on-one relationships with customers, by giving them an easy place to go for information, day or night, and by offering opportunities to receive e-mail messages that might be of interest.

**Banner ads** and other forms of internet ads, including buttons, text links, pop-up windows, and other new versions that are invented regularly, can be placed on web portals or other websites. Ads can consist of text, graphics, audio, or video, and some are even interactive. In many cases, advertisers can choose how they wish to pay for such ads. They can pay for placements for a certain time period, like a billboard on a highway. They can pay on a cost-per-thousand-impressions (CPM) basis, as they do for traditional print and broadcast media. They can pay for "click-throughs" or they can pay a fee only when the customer buys, thus bearing out Gurley's 1998 prediction.

Unfortunately for internet businesses that rely on advertising-driven business models, click-through rates for many kinds of internet advertising, especially those that are not very well targeted, have plummeted as their novelty has worn off, to an average, for banner ads, of a mere 0.2 percent in 2006.[16] Targeted audiences are increasingly essential.

**Search keywords** have become a proverbial pot of gold for Google, and have grown to account for some 40 percent of online advertising.[17] Type "Tuscany vacation" into

Google and along with Google's free listings on the left side of the Google page come paid ads on the right side of the page for cheap flights to Italy, villa rentals, even cooking schools. Such ads are the holy grail of internet advertising, and the main reason for Google's lofty market capitalization. Because they are highly targeted—you would be unlikely to type "Tuscany vacation" unless you were actually considering such a trip—they're worth much more to the advertiser than most other kinds of internet ads, and are priced accordingly.

**Portal deals,** whereby marketers pay web portals for prime or exclusive positions on the portals' websites, can establish competitive advantage for marketers by enhancing the likelihood that theirs will be the site in their product category or industry that customers find first on the web. These deals are particularly popular with web-based marketers, including travel, auction, and other services.

**Social networks,** to which we devote considerable attention in Chapter 14, have emerged as yet another new medium for advertisers to consider. A variety of new entrants are building on these platforms—Facebook, Twitter, and others—to provide additional advertising possibilities, including advertising on mobile phones. By mid-2010, location-based advertising services Foursquare, Loopt, and Booyah had each signed up about 3 million users; Foursquare hit 8 million users in early 2011. Visit a Starbucks, check in with Foursquare using your smartphone, and you might get a dollar off your frappuccino.[18] Twitter, derided by some as having no viable business model, provides a cost-effective way for small companies to stay in touch with their customers in ways that larger brands are less likely to do (see Exhibit 13.8).

**E-mail** is also a rapidly growing advertising medium, one particularly well suited to building one-on-one relationships with customers. The best thing about e-mail as a medium, from an advertiser's view, is that it is virtually cost-free. Many airlines now send weekly e-mail updates on bargain weekend airfares to consumers who sign up for such services. On Tuesday or Wednesday, consumers are offered low-priced deals on flights the airlines need to fill. Those in a position to take short, spur-of-the-moment vacations appreciate the opportunities such services provide, and the airlines like having a way to fill seats, which would otherwise fly empty, without having to discount their fares to the general public. As Seth Godin in his book *Permission Marketing* points out, however, the considerable benefits attainable through e-mail marketing come only when the customer

## Exhibit 13.8    SNARKY TWEETS HELP "DAVIDS" TAKE ON GOLIATH

Someecards, a three-year-old digital newcomer to the greeting-card industry, relies on its 1.7 million followers on Twitter—versus greeting-card giant Hallmark's 2,017 followers—to carve out and retain its growing niche. Someecards' Duncan Mitchell points out that the 140-character-limited medium is a good match for his product, whose greetings sometimes run even shorter. "We believe in short-form communication," he says. "Our cards match our tweets in size. It's not a lot of extra effort to write short, snarky one-liners," and tweet.

Observer Robert Klara says that, when it comes to Twitter, the big brands are "Often left in the dust by the Indie brands with a fraction of their market share." Why? "Tweets don't just have to be brief, but cool and snarky as well," says Klara, traits that do not come very comfortably to the online marketing staff in a buttoned down publicly traded company like Hallmark.

Take OddFit, a quirky custom T-shirt company in Rhode Island. Its CEO, Javier Alonzo, recently tweeted a link to an online tutorial for breast enhancement using Photoshop. "Here's how they do it, girls," tweeted Alonzo. Imagine that from the likes of Hanes or Fruit of the Loom!

*Source:* Robert Klara, "For Smaller, Independent Brands, How Tweet It is," *Brandweek*, February 7, 2010. For more on someecards, see *www.someecards.com*. For more on Oddfit, see *www.oddfit.com*.

*gives his or her permission* to be sent marketing messages. Were this not the case, the system would be inundated with unwanted messages to the point that it would come to a screeching halt![19] The growth of unwelcome e-mails, or spam, is a customer problem that software makers are working hard to address.

**Blogging** is another fast-growing internet application. Given the ease with which anyone can now post material on the web, companies large and small are developing blogs with which they can, sometimes anonymously, promote their products or ideas or even disparage competition. There are even sites (for example, *www.betterbusinessblogging.com*) to help businesses develop their blogs!

**Podcasting,** a technology that provides a way for consumers to receive audio via the internet, is another growing web-based application. Advertisers and other providers such as CNN, the Cable News Network, provide short audio feeds that can be downloaded and listened to on a PC or on a portable MP3 player.

While the new media seem, on the surface, to be radically different from their more traditional counterparts—radio, television, and print—the logic entailed in planning their roles in promotional programs is no different than for other media. Considerations of reach, frequency, and cost—measured in cost per thousand impressions (or "hits" or "click-throughs" on the web)—provide a means of comparing their value to one another and to traditional media. **Cost per acquisition,** another measure, is useful for web advertising that results directly in actual customer purchases, a model familiar in the direct-marketing industry. To the extent that new media performance can be measured (How many extra customers does a restaurant get for weekday lunches as a result of its Groupon promotion, and at what cost per customer?), marketers will be encouraged to use them to their full economic potential.

The rapid growth of these and other new media has led to a variety of ethical issues marketers must address, including the implications of location-based services discussed in Ethical Perspective 13.2.

**International Media**　　Global advertising has been aided by the rise of globally oriented television media like CNN, MTV, and ESPN, all of which originate primarily in the United States, and a variety of other media like STAR-TV and Al Jazeera, which originate in Asia and the Middle East, respectively. The ability of media like these to deliver to

---

**ETHICAL PERSPECTIVE 13.2**
*Do You Really Want Burglars to Know Where You Are?*

The creators of PleaseRobMe.com, a simple website that publishes a live feed of location-based posts that appear on Twitter, points out that the tweeters are somewhere other than at home. The site's creators want to highlight the fact that tweeters on the likes of Foursquare and other location-based services give away information that burglars would love to have.

But the founders of location-based services and the venture capitalists backing them will have to deal with growing concerns that collecting information about people's movements may have unintended consequences.

The Centre for Democracy and Technology, a privacy advocate, argues that the privacy policies of companies that are collecting and using location-based data are "uneven at best and inadequate at worst."

Some companies are better, of course, and some worse. Loopt includes software that monitors its service for suspicious patterns of behavior, it says. But politicians are getting into the act, holding a congressional hearing in Washington to examine the implications of such services and their rapid growth. If web-savvy burglars want to take advantage of all this data, it would appear that they'd better do so soon.

Source: "Follow Me," *The Economist,* March 6, 2010, p. 81. For more on Foursquare and Loopt, see *www.foursquare.com* and *www.loopt.com.*

advertisers an international audience that spans national boundaries offers new possibilities to advertisers seeking to reach wide global audiences.

### Developing the Creative Strategy

Creative strategy derives from the product's targeting and positioning decisions coupled with what the advertising must accomplish. From this information the major selling idea for communicating the key benefits must be developed. This, in turn, generates a strategy statement—often referred to as a copy platform or creative brief (see Exhibit 13.9 for the contents of such a document). Deciding on the major selling idea or theme is the essence of the creative strategy process since it dictates the nature and scope of the various messages that collectively make up an advertising campaign, and it delivers on the positioning decisions already made as we saw in Chapter 8.

Designing creative and effective marketing communications—regardless of media, whether traditional or new—is a task that requires creativity and special expertise. Copywriters, art directors, and others who ply this trade effectively are worth their weight in gold, for there are many ineffective ads in every medium.

Domino's Pizza, faced with a deteriorating image for the quality of its pizza, decided in 2010 to confront the issue head-on. "We spent tens of millions of dollars repeating the negative," in a series of courageous documentary-style TV ads created by CP+B, an agency known for unconventional work, "with consumers saying our pizza tastes like cardboard," says CEO Patrick Doyle. "(But) we are in a dramatically different place with our customers than we were prior to doing it." A social media platform was created alongside, where customers could share their views, for better or worse. The impact was substantial. Domino's sales were up 12.9 percent in 2010, compared to Papa John's 5.5 percent and Pizza Hut's 2 percent.[20]

It is far beyond the scope of this book to explore how effective messages are best created. The issues involved in managing the creative effort, however, include decisions about the **unique selling proposition** to be delivered (based on the desired positioning of the product), the **source** of the message (Should a company spokesperson or a celebrity be used?), the nature of the **appeal** embodied in the message (Should it be primarily rational, emotional, or both? Should it compare one's own product with those of competitors? Should it use fear, humor, or music?). Effective creative strategies almost always contain at least some **emotional appeal,** and not only deliver the desired message, but also manage to attract the **attention** and **interest** of the target audience despite an extremely cluttered advertising environment. Some ads even include a **call to action,** in which the customer

## Exhibit 13.9

COPY PLATFORM CONTENTS

- Basic issue or problem advertising must address
- Advertising and communications objectives
- Target audience
- Major selling idea—or key benefits to be communicated
- Creative strategy statement (campaign theme, appeal, and execution technique)
- Supportive information

*Source:* George E. Belch and Michael A. Belch, *Introduction to Advertising and Promotion* (Burr Ridge, IL: McGraw-Hill/Irwin, 2012), p. 278.

is asked to do something (like call a toll-free telephone number, clip a coupon, or click through to a website).

In today's highly competitive markets where many competing products are at parity, and in our increasingly cluttered advertising environment, Saatchi & Saatchi's Kevin Roberts argues that making an emotional connection with consumers is what effective advertising must accomplish. "It took (Michael) Jordan to move Nike from being irreplaceable to becoming irresistible," he says. "This is because Jordan gave it aspiration, he gave it emotional connectivity. If you wear Nikes you can be like Mike."[21]

Several ethical issues are involved in developing advertising messages, including issues of morals, good taste, community values, and truth (or deception) in advertising. These issues are discussed in Ethical Perspective 13.3.

**Measuring Advertising Results**    Management must know to what extent the message was received, understood, and believed by the target audience, as well as what effect it had on the behavior of the receiver (trial, repeat buying). Message (copy) testing typically is concerned with alternative ways to present a message to the target audience. The discussion here is divided into two parts—tests made *before* the message is released on a full-run basis and tests done *after* the copy is run in the prescribed media.

---

## ETHICAL PERSPECTIVE 13.3
### *Ethical Issues in Advertising*

To many, the ethical question is more than whether advertising is deceptive. Rather, the moral issue is seen as whether advertisers have the right to encourage the purchase of a product that might be harmful to certain individuals—for instance, the sale of tobacco and liquor products in general and, especially, to young people and certain minority groups. Seagram's decided to end the liquor industry's long practice of not doing television advertising. While all three major networks continue to refuse liquor ads, some of their affiliates still may accept them.

One of the most controversial areas is advertising to children, especially on TV. Critics argue that the advertising of toys creates unreasonable expectations, that children are encouraged to eat harmful foods (sugared cereals), and that the long-term effects of TV may negatively affect children's values, beliefs, and behavior (especially with respect to violence). Sweden and Canada prohibit any advertising aimed at children; France and Japan limit the use of cartoon characters in advertising to children; and the major U.S. networks have strict guidelines for children's ads.

In the United States, where the Federal Trade Commission (FTC) has taken a generally less aggressive stance, the FTC and a variety of industry groups have tried to regulate and control deception in advertising. For a given ad to be ruled illegal, it must

have the potential to deceive a significant number of consumers as to the facts relating to a purchasing decision. However, deception is difficult to detect in many cases because of the subtle ways in which it can work. Enforcement is hindered by the fact that advertisers can legally employ *puffery*, which uses subjective claims (the "best" or "greatest") to promote the product. Many believe that since the role of advertising is to provide information relevant to the purchasing decision, puffery should be prohibited.

Deception can also occur via the use of mockups, which involve the alteration of a product or situation to get a realistic photograph of it (using mashed potatoes to represent ice cream, which melts under the photographer's lights). While the FTC has ruled that mockups are legal as long as they do not misrepresent the product's characteristics, some critics of advertising argue that many are misleading.

Endorsements and testimonials for products and services have increased in recent years. But do the individuals involved *really* use the products, or are they "hired guns"? Even though the FTC has rules governing their use, many such ads have the potential to deceive.

Partial disclosure concerning a product's attributes is yet another way consumers can be misled. An example is when an ad talks about low cholesterol but fails to mention the amount of fat or sugar the product contains.

**Before Tests**   No copy pretest can simulate exactly the conditions of exposure and the long-run effects of repetition on a particular audience group. There are, however, a number of ways to pretest message effectiveness, including the following:

- **Recall tests** of proposed print ads are inserted into a simulated magazine and respondents are told to read whatever interests them. After doing so, they are asked to "play back" ads they remember. They are also asked questions about ad credibility and product usage. Using the results, researchers can determine the extent to which the message got through and to what extent it achieved the communicator's objective(s). Unfortunately, recall scores too often reflect a brand's popularity rather than message content.

- **Sales tests** as administered by commercial research firms such as BehaviorScan measure the effects of TV commercials through the use of consumer panels located in a number of small cities. Purchases are recorded electronically by scanners at supermarket checkout counters by panel members using special ID cards. BehaviorScan can insert test TV commercials into TV programs at the individual panel household level. They select household samples on the basis of their purchase behavior history. Thus, the consumer panel becomes a single source of both purchase and viewing behavior, thereby enhancing its value. Because alternative ad treatments can be shown to different balanced samples at the same time, it is possible to measure the sales effect of one copy treatment against another based on actual purchase data.

**After Tests**   Measuring the effects of an advertising message after it has run is difficult because the results are confounded by the effects of the media used, the frequency with which the audience received the message, and other factors, including competitive activity and even the weather! *After* tests tend to measure the effectiveness of the total advertising effort. Here we look at only those *after* tests used primarily to measure message effects. Thus, for example, BMW's advertising agency reported that consumer research showed that consumers were getting the right message—namely, that a BMW is not only dynamic, but comfortable and affordable as well.

Advertisers design *after* tests in a number of ways, and they all rely on the respondent's memory, which raises the problem of how soon after running the ad the measurement should be taken. Also, testing that relies on a single measure at one moment in time does not reflect the learning that occurs with repeated exposure.

- **Recognition tests** are the most popular postexposure testing method for print media. Advertisers design these tests to measure the extent to which advertising copy is noted and read. Field workers interview people who say they have read a given issue of a magazine. Each respondent goes through the issue pointing out what was seen and read. When the respondent reports seeing an ad, the interviewer asks which parts were read. The interviewer starts each interview at a random point within the issue, so that the ratings are not affected by respondent fatigue.

- **Recall tests** are another common way to measure the effectiveness of an advertising message, especially a TV commercial, after it has been run. Respondents are typically aided in their recall. Interviewers show them a list of the advertisers and brands presented and ask which ones they have seen recently. Interviewers proceed to obtain playbacks of these ads from the respondents.

The industry has long raised questions of whether recall and recognition tests provide adequate measures of memory. Other postexposure ways of measuring the effectiveness of the message include sales tests similar to those used to test new products, inquiries (possible when coupons are used or a toll-free telephone number is made available for placing orders), and measurements of attitudinal change. The latter typically involve *before–after* measurements of the degree to which a given brand possesses certain salient features.

Where the objectives of an advertising effort involve increases in customer traffic, sales, market share, or other tangibly measurable outcomes, such measures should be taken to assess advertising effectiveness. Such measures—including cost per acquisition (to win a new customer) and cost per order (in absolute or percent-of-sales terms)—are commonly used in direct marketing and in many internet marketing contexts. Caution should be exercised, however, as other market and competitive factors—the product itself, its pricing or distribution, the weather, or competitive activities—may also have influenced the outcomes being measured. Some fast-food companies have been known to blame their ad agencies for failing to overtake McDonald's in sales per store. Many factors, from the cleanliness of the bathrooms to the toys included in kids' meals, are involved in determining consumers' fast-food decisions. The advertising is only part of the story. But blaming the ad agency is not uncommon!

## Making Personal Selling Decisions

Advertising is one of the two principal elements in the promotion mix, as we saw in Exhibit 13.3. We now turn to the second key element, personal selling. In companies like Amway, for example, personal selling lies at the heart of the promotional strategy. Since getting started in China, now its largest market, Amway, thanks largely to its 160,000 direct-selling agents there, has built a $3 billion Chinese business, constituting more than 35 percent of its worldwide sales.[22]

As the top half of Exhibit 13.10 indicates, planning a sales program involves four sets of decisions. First, the salesforce must be **organized** to facilitate the most efficient allocation of effort. Second, **account management policies** should be developed as guidelines for the way different types of customers are approached, persuaded, and serviced. Third, **deployment** decisions must be made to define territories and assign salespeople to those territories. Fourth, performance expectations—**quotas**—should be developed for each sales rep based on forecasted demand in that territory. When these four aspects of a sales program are well planned and clearly communicated, they help the sales staff understand the job requirements and the role they are expected to play in implementing the firm's strategy. That improved understanding, in turn, should help the sales staff achieve desired levels of performance.

Space does not permit us to deal in any depth in this book with these four sets of decisions. For readers interested in additional detail, there are numerous books on salesforce management that treat these topics extensively.[23] But we do want to address several key strategic issues that marketing managers must consider in planning a marketing program or preparing a marketing plan; the sales cycle, organizing the sales effort in global markets; managing customer service, an activity that new technology has the potential to influence dramatically (for better or worse); recruiting, compensating, and training salespeople; and evaluating and controlling salesforce performance.

**The Sales Cycle**   The sales cycle refers to the duration—expressed both in calendar time and number of sales visits—that it will take to meet with the various decision makers and convince them to try the product, perhaps on a limited basis at first, and then to adopt it more fully. As we saw in Chapter 5, in many business-to-business selling situations, numerous individuals in a typical client organization have influence over the purchase decision. Each of them will need to be contacted, often more than once. In some companies, annual budgeting cycles mean the purchasing window is open only at certain times of the year. Planning the sales program and determining how many—and what kind of—salespeople it will take

## Exhibit 13.10

IMPLEMENTING THE STRATEGIC SALES PROGRAM

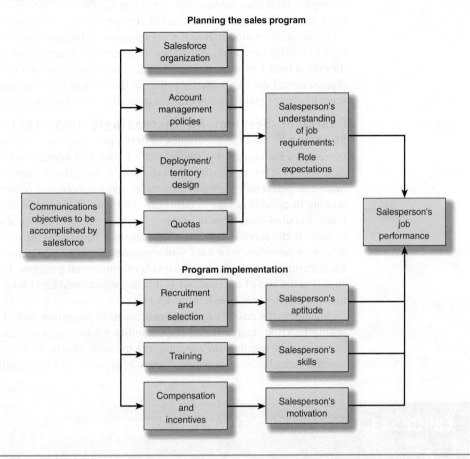

**Planning the sales program**

Salesforce organization

Account management policies

Deployment/ territory design

Quotas

Communications objectives to be accomplished by salesforce

Salesperson's understanding of job requirements: Role expectations

Salesperson's job performance

**Program implementation**

Recruitment and selection

Training

Compensation and incentives

Salesperson's aptitude

Salesperson's skills

Salesperson's motivation

to get the job done require a clear understanding of the length of the sales cycle, the number of sales calls it is likely to take to complete a sale, and the nature of the sales task at hand.

### Organizing the Sales Effort in Global Markets

As firms expand their marketing and sales efforts into other countries, they face a critical decision concerning how to organize their selling efforts across national boundaries.

While globalization obviously adds complexity to a firm's organizational design, the basic questions to be answered are the same as those faced in domestic markets. First,

should the firm rely on independent agents to represent its interests in a foreign market or hire its own company salespeople? If the firm decides to establish its own subsidiary or sales office with a dedicated company salesforce in a foreign country, a second question arises concerning the appropriate structure for that salesforce. Should it be organized geographically, by product line, by type of customer, or some other way? It is beyond the scope of this book to address these questions.[24]

Industry factors are also related to the use of agents versus company salespeople. Firms selling complex, high-tech products such as computers and pharmaceuticals are significantly more likely to rely solely on their own salespeople than firms in other industrial or consumer goods industries. The higher levels of product knowledge and postsale service required to sell such high-tech products make it relatively more desirable for firms to employ their own salespeople. By doing so, they can maintain better control over the marketing and sales efforts devoted to their products and reduce their transaction costs.

While globalization makes the organization of the salesforce more complicated, firms tend to resolve organizational issues in international markets in largely the same way as they do in their native countries. The situational and strategic factors that influence firms' organizational decisions appear to be similar in both types of markets, and those factors seem to affect organizational choices in similar ways both at home and abroad.

### Customer Service: An Increasingly Important Personal Selling Function[25]

As the economies in developed countries have become more dominated by services businesses, the importance of customer service has grown. Even in today's manufacturing businesses, intense competition, sometimes from lower-cost producers, has made competent and responsive customer service a point of differentiation for companies seeking to provide complete customer solutions. Thus, just as marketing managers must make decisions about how to best manage their salesforce, they also must decide how best to provide the service that customers demand. How many times have you called a cable television provider, your bank—or even the telephone company itself!—only to have to wade through seemingly endless levels of voice-mail prompts. Finally, you're placed on "hold" at the end of the process! Is this any way to win loyal long-term customers? There must be a better way (see Exhibit 13.11).

Managing the customer service process is an important part of managing the personal selling function. Increasingly, responsibility for customer service and "outside" sales is being brought together on company organization charts, so the two functions can work together seamlessly to serve customers effectively and efficiently, before and after the

---

### Exhibit 13.11    Is the Best Service No Service at All?

Amid all the hand-wringing about how to improve customer service in companies where customer service is a long-forgotten phrase, a book by Bill Price and David Jaffe argues that the best service, in fact, is no service at all! How can this be? People usually seek "service," they argue, when something has gone wrong. Getting things right in the first place is the real solution, for customers won't then need any "customer service." An example makes the point. By obsessing over a metric it calls contacts per order (CPO) and by working out exactly why customers contact Amazon and eliminating the need for this to happen, Amazon.com has reduced its CPO by 90 percent over the last five years.

There are four broad causes that drive customer service requests, the authors argue in their book, *The Best Service Is No Service*: quality issues ("It doesn't work," about 15 percent of customer service requests), poor processes or customer communication ("How do I ... ?" about 25 percent), basic information requests ("Where can I get ... ?" about 40 percent), and customers wanting to buy (20 percent). If the 80 percent of queries that comprise the first three categories can be reduced—through better quality, better processes, and better communication—then more attention can be paid to the last category, where additional revenue is to be found.

Among the authors' recommendations is this one: to charge those responsible for generating customer service requests, even outside suppliers, for the full cost of the customer contacts they cause. "This final step brings most of the dividends—when owners get hit in the pocket, they may pay more attention to customer service issues."

It sounds easy, doesn't it? Fix the quality, fix the processes, fix the communication, all from the customer's perspective, of course. But it's all really hard to do, which is probably why so many companies still have such dreadful customer service.

*Source:* Bill Price and David Jaffe, *The Best Service Is No Service* (Jossey Bass, 2008).

sale. Managing customer service involves thinking carefully about the firm's objectives for serving customers before the sale and adding additional objectives for aftersale service, along with people and strategies for meeting these objectives. It is no longer sufficient to simply put some people at telephones and ask them to try to help the customers as best they can. Sophisticated systems now make it possible to identify customers as they call, so customer service representatives have their account information at their fingertips, and provide detailed product knowledge to answer the customers' questions, all electronically.

Modern technology allows companies to place **call centers** in different time zones, following the sun, and calls made to a single number are automatically routed to the active call center. Technology also allows call centers to be located in places like India, which offer a lower cost basis and access to a large pool of highly skilled workers.[26] Where local knowledge is part of what customers see as good service, however, far-away call centers can be more a problem than a solution.

The growing ubiquity of social networks like Facebook is leading some companies to use social networks as a source of customer service. Figuring that customers can sometimes better help one another than their own staff people can, Intuit, the maker of accounting software like QuickBooks, routes some of its die-hard users to a site where they can exchange information with one another. Customers get quicker answers, and Intuit saves money on tech support.[27]

The growing use of smartphones, combined with cloud computing, is helping road warriors like Michael Roh of Genentech provide answers he doesn't have at his fingertips. He can deal with complex medical inquiries on the spot, as well as collaborate with colleagues. As Roh puts it, "I can do things more real-time."[28]

Companies concerned about improving their personal selling, sales management, and customer service can turn to the latest computer technologies for help. **Salesforce automation** and other decision support tools are identified in Exhibit 13.12.

Taken together, technology-based customer-focused applications such as those mentioned here, together with the growing use of database marketing, as we saw in Chapter 6, have led to growing interest in customer relationship management, or CRM, among practitioners and academics alike. A recent issue of the *Journal of Marketing* dealt

## Exhibit 13.12

### DECISION SUPPORT SOFTWARE FOR PERSONAL SELLING AND SALESFORCE MANAGEMENT

| Tool | Software package | Functions |
| --- | --- | --- |
| Salesforce Automation Software | Salesforce.com | Manages a database of customer contact information |
| Contact Management Software | ACT, from Interact Commerce Corporation, at *www.act.com* Goldmine, available (along with other sales management software) from *www.sales-tools.com* | Keeps track of client lists—including addresses, phone numbers, and other idiosyncratic client information, such as birthdays—and organizes records of prior client contact and other customer-relevant information |
| Sales Compensation Design Software | Salescom, from *www.salesforcecompensation.com* | Helps design base salary and/or incentive plans for any incentive-eligible position |
| Customer Relationship Management Software | Entice!, from *www.multiactive.com* | Integrates sales, marketing, and customer service, with e-commerce and wireless telephony, for online and offline marketing applications. |

extensively with these issues. A book like *Return on Customer* provides marketing managers with practical guidance on how they can increase the value of their customer base to increase shareholder value.[29]

All these innovations have just scratched the surface in making inside and outside sales and customer service people more efficient and effective. If one is not careful, however, some of these tools can enhance efficiency at the expense of effectiveness. Horror stories about endless waits for customer service reps in call centers or layer upon layer of keys to punch to obtain the desired automated information are not the best path to customer satisfaction. Astute marketing managers carefully assess such trade-offs. As these technologies develop, one thing is certain: Regardless of the size of one's company, selling with just a telephone, a company car, a frequent flyer card, and a pair of well-worn shoes is a thing of the past.

### Recruiting, Training, and Compensating Salespeople: The Keys to Salesforce Performance

There is no guarantee that even a very well-designed and clearly communicated sales plan will be carried out effectively. Good implementation requires that the members of the salesforce have both the ability and the desire to meet management's expectations. Thus, as the bottom portion of Exhibit 13.10 indicates, implementing the sales program requires three more sets of management actions: First, management must **recruit and select** appropriate kinds of salespeople with the aptitude for effectively carrying out the activities involved in the job. Second, management may need to provide appropriate kinds and amounts of **training** to ensure that the salespeople have the knowledge and skills needed to do their jobs. Finally, management must design an attractive package of **compensation and other incentive rewards** to motivate the salesforce to expend the effort necessary to achieve good performance. For a more detailed discussion of these key elements in sales program implementation see a text on salesforce management.[30]

### Evaluating and Controlling Salesforce Performance

Managers collect and evaluate information about their salespeople's performance and compare these data to the plan's objectives and forecasts to determine how well the salesforce is doing. The purpose is much like that of navigating a ship at sea. By determining where the ship is relative to its destination, the captain can see how well the ship is doing and make necessary corrections when it is off course.

Companies use three main approaches in monitoring the salesforce to evaluate and control sales performance.

1. **Sales analysis.** Managers monitor sales and/or gross margin for each salesperson. In addition, they break down figures by geographic territory, by each product in the line, and by different types of customers. They compare results to the forecasts and quotas in the firm's sales plan to determine which salespeople are doing well and where adjustments may be needed.

2. **Cost analysis.** They can also monitor the costs of various selling activities such as travel and entertainment expenses. Managers often examine these across individual salespeople, districts, customers, and product types. However, this does present some difficult technical challenges about how certain costs, such as administrative costs and overhead, should be allocated. When put together with the results of a sales analysis, this procedure allows managers to evaluate the profitability of different territories, products, and customer types.

3. **Behavioral analysis.** When sales volume or profitability in a territory falls below expectations, managers may be uncertain as to the cause. Perhaps the salesperson in that territory is not working hard enough or is allocating effort to the wrong activities. Or the disappointing results could be due to factors beyond the salesperson's control, such as poor economic conditions or heavy competition in the territory. To gain a better understanding of the cause—and provide a better basis for taking corrective action—many managers believe it is necessary to

monitor and evaluate the actual behavior of the salesperson as well as the outcomes of that behavior. They obtain much information for this kind of behavioral analysis from activity reports and call reports submitted by the salespeople. In addition, some firms use self-rating scales, field observations, and supervisor ratings to compile the needed information.

Many of these methods apply equally well to the evaluation of entire marketing programs, not just the salesforce; we examine this topic in more detail in Chapter 18.

At this point, we have discussed the two principal elements in the promotion mix, advertising and personal selling. The two remaining elements, sales promotion and public relations, often play a secondary or supporting role to one or both of the first two elements. In some cases, however, especially in early-stage companies with limited marketing budgets, their roles can be more substantial.

## Making Sales Promotion Decisions

The American Marketing Association defines **sales promotion** as "those marketing activities, other than personal selling, advertising, and publicity, that stimulate consumer purchasing and dealer effectiveness." Sales promotions typically offer an incentive to consumers and resellers to stimulate short-term demand for a product. As we saw in Chapter 12, sales promotion can be of two kinds: consumer promotion (targeted at consumers, often as part of a pull strategy) and trade promotion (targeted at channel members, often as part of a push strategy). Surprisingly, perhaps, more money is spent on sales promotion than on advertising in the United States and Europe. For example, Reebok launched a pan-European promotion for its new A6 shoe, using SMS offers, supported by advertising on websites like mp3.com and Yahoo, running hip-hop and dance music ads.[31] More generally, expenditures for consumer promotions have lagged (especially for coupons) in recent years and are smaller than trade promotions.

Marketers use a variety of sales promotion techniques, the primary ones being price-off promotions, premiums, sampling, rebates, contests and sweepstakes, and trade promotions. The first four of these have been discussed earlier in Chapter 12 on pricing. The major non-price-related promotion techniques are described below. As might be expected, trade allowances made to retailers by manufacturers dominate their promotional expenditures. A huge portion of all items sold by supermarkets are discounted.

- **Sampling** has become increasingly important as marketers have found more efficient ways to get samples to their target markets. Today's sampling promotions are cleverly designed so that shoppers who receive the samples use them right away. For example, Unilever handed out its personal hygiene products to students at the end of a sweaty fitness class, and Starbucks gave away free samples of its iced-coffee drink, Frappuccino, to commuters in Manhattan during a sweltering afternoon.[32]

- **Contests and sweepstakes** add interest to the sale of ordinary products. In a consumer contest, buyers compete for prizes on the basis of skill. Contests typically require proof of purchase to enter or the use of an entry form available only from a dealer. Popular formats for contests include naming new products or finding new uses for existing products as in the famous Pillsbury Bake-off in the United States. Sweepstakes, on the other hand, distribute prizes on the basis of chance and in many countries cannot require proof of purchase as a condition of entry. But they do little to enhance the brand's image and often overshadow the product involved.

- **Trade promotions** are used by manufacturers to stimulate resellers to improve their performance in a variety of ways, including contests and incentives for sales personnel, training a distributor's salesforce, and cooperative advertising and promotional allowances including in store promotions. The latter are the most important. We discussed the role of trade promotions as incentives for distribution channel members in Chapter 12.

As is the case for advertising, designing a sales promotion program and budget involves choosing particular types of sales promotion and using past experience to predict what the response rates are likely to be. Unlike advertising, for

which considerable monies can be spent with little assurance that significant revenues will follow, many kinds of sales promotion require the customer to buy as the incentive is redeemed. This self-liquidating feature is true for coupons and rebates, for example, and for trade discounts to retailers who stock or display a new product. In this sense, sales promotion is less risky than advertising. Marketers also like it because its performance is usually easily measurable. As a result, and due also to scarce resources in small companies and to pressures on management in large public companies to deliver consistent short-term earnings, sales promotion is garnering an increasing share of many firms' total promotional budgets.

There's a downside to sales promotion, however. Empirical evidence in the automotive industry suggests that while sales promotions may increase demand in the short term, they can diminish financial performance and shareholder value over the long term. This may be due to habit formation, whereby customers learn to wait for the next promotion, rather than buying at full price.[33] From a managerial perspective, reliance on sales promotions to meet sales targets is somewhat akin to drug addiction: once started, it's difficult to stop the promoting for fear of a top-line sales slump.

## Making Public Relations Decisions

**Public relations** has many uses. One that is sometimes overlooked is its potential for marketing new products, whether goods or services. Many of today's most creative entrepreneurs use PR this way. When it catches the media's fancy, it can make a new company or a new brand (see Exhibit 13.13).

Public relations has several unique advantages (see Exhibit 13.4). It is credible; most people feel that the mass media have no reason to carry favorable information about a

---

### Exhibit 13.13    JONES SODA'S ICKY FLAVORS CREATE BUZZ

Brussels Sprout soda? Broccoli Casserole soda? Turkey and Gravy soda? "Repulsive. Awful. Tastes like gasoline," said the taste testers at *Inc.* magazine. But to Peter Van Stolk, Jones Soda's founder, cringing writers and gagging television commentators were music to his ears. Van Stolk's company caters to hip urban youth in their teens and twenties. He figured his customers—not to mention the media—would notice the wacky flavors and therefore notice his brand, for which public relations was the only affordable promotion strategy in the hotly competitive soft drink industry. His instincts were right. Thanks in part to a wacky press release and his icky flavors' appearances on the likes of Good Morning America and the Jay Leno Show, his company's sales jumped 18 per cent in the first nine months of 2005 over the prior year. "People went crazy for it," said Van Stolk. One customer even made money on it, selling a bottle of Turkey and Gravy soda on eBay for $100! Halloween flavors like Candy Corn and Caramel Apple followed, and Love Potion No. 6 made its debut for Valentine's Day in February 2006. While most of his revenue still comes from normal flavors like root beer and cream soda, the media attention garnered by the icky stuff surely helps them sell!

*Source:* Ellen Neuborne, "Gag Marketing," *Inc.* February 2006, p. 35. For more on offbeat promotional strategies, see Christopher Locke, *Gonzo Marketing: Winning through Worst Practices* (Cambridge, MA: Perseus Publishing, 2001). For more on Jones Soda and its wacky flavors; see *www.jonessoda.com*.

product unless it is true. Thus, public relations reinforces the firm's advertising campaign by increasing awareness and the believability of product claims. Favorable publicity also makes it easier for the salesforce to present a case for the product. Also, it is low cost, in that there are few media costs. The major disadvantage is that publicity is beyond the company's control, not only as to whether the release will be run, but also what is finally said about the company and/or the brand.

Of course, the media are not in business to provide free publicity to marketers. They do so only when they believe something is newsworthy because it is new, different, or tells an interesting story about a local person or organization. Because there is no cost entailed in having publicity picked up by the media, budgeting for public relations can be easy—simply staff time to manage the effort—although many firms choose to use specialized public relations agencies to handle the media contacts. Fees for such activities, once negotiated, are easily budgeted, but whether a given public relations effort will actually attain the desired results is another story. Unfortunately, most public relations firms are unwilling to accept assignments in which they are paid based on performance.

Through public relations, firms communicate with a variety of publics, including the consumer (information about new products), the financial community and stockholders (improvement in the company's profitability), the community (the firm's being a good citizen), prospective employees (a good place to work), current employees (developing pride in the company), and suppliers (a good company with which to build an enduring relationship). This listing of audiences suggests that publicity can be used to accomplish different objectives among different groups. Such objectives range from simply increasing awareness of a company or its products to stimulating an actual response, such as sending for a free bulletin. Thus, public relations can play an important role in the development of an integrated marketing communication program.

## . . . And All the Rest

Because marketers are inherently creative, there is a never-ending array of promotional tactics some of which don't fall neatly into any of the four traditional categories that we've discussed so far: advertising, personal selling, sales promotion, and public relations. Is a campaign based on SMS messages, or various web-based activities, really advertising? Some would say yes, others no. There is an entire cottage industry of companies that, for a fee, will seek placements of products—a can of Coke, a Mercedes convertible, or whatever—in the latest Hollywood or Bollywood movies. The movie producers like the extra revenue such placements generate, and the beverage or automakers like the cachet.

The most astute marketers use a blend of these less clearly defined tactics and the more traditional elements in the promotion mix as mutually reinforcing tools that can blur the distinction of which activities are taking the lead. Dove, with its long-running Real People, Real Beauty campaign, used a mix of TV advertising, social media including Facebook, outdoor (including bus-stop shelters in major cities), and public relations to portray baby boomer women in an authentic way. The results surpassed Dove's wildest dreams, with sales of Dove's firming products jumping nearly eightfold in Europe and sevenfold in the United States.[34] As the Dove story shows, a truly *integrated* marketing communications effort can deliver terrific performance when planned and executed effectively.

# TAKE-AWAYS

1. Marketing managers in most companies face fundamental strategic decisions about whether to emphasize advertising or personal selling in their promotion mix. Identifying the strategic circumstances (see Exhibit 13.3) provides direction for these decisions.

2. Getting marketing communications messages—of any kind, in any medium—noticed and understood is no easy task. Many ads and other communication attempts simply don't meet their objectives. Following the guidelines in this chapter will mitigate this risk.

3. A clear understanding of one's target market is essential for planning and implementing an effective promotional program. Without such an understanding, money is likely to be wasted.

4. Many marketing communications efforts are not easy to evaluate. Setting clear and measurable objectives up front facilitates doing so.

5. New media, including the internet, e-mail, and mobile telephones, are predicted to revolutionize ad spending, because their results—like those for direct marketing programs—can often be better targeted and directly measured.

6. In companies of all sizes, technology will play an increasingly meaningful role in managing sales and customer service efficiency and effectiveness. Caution must be exercised, however, to avoid sacrificing effectiveness for efficiency.

7. For new product launches on limited budgets, sales promotion alone can deliver substantial impact at a fraction of the cost of conventional approaches.

**Self-diagnostic questions to test your ability to apply the analytical tools and concepts in this chapter to marketing decision making may be found at this book's website at www.mhhe.com/mullins8e.**

# ENDNOTES

1. This material is drawn from Knowledge@Wharton, "No No No to Nano," March 12, 2011; *RushLane*, "Tata Nano Sales in Indian Car Market for May 2011," at *http://www.rushlane.com/tata-nano-sales-in-indian-car-market-for-may-2011-1214886.html*, June 2, 2011. "Electric Beat: GM Tries Again…", *Hindustan Times*, June 24, 2011; Shally Seth Mohile, "Suzuki Cuts Maruti Forecast," *Mint*, June 24, 2011, p. 8.

2. William F Arens, *Contemporary Advertising*, 10th ed. (New York: McGraw-Hill/Irwin, 2006), p. 245.

3. Michael White, "Super Swagonomics," *Bloomberg Businessweek* European Edition, February 21–27, 2011, pp. 80–81.

4. *Marketing News*, "2010 Marketing Fact Book," July 2010, p. 24. This fact book provides detailed marketing spending data broken down by region, by medium, and in other ways.

5. OurBeginning.com press release at *www.ourbeginning.com/home/nsf/*

6. Jon Fine, "Why General Mills' Marketing Pays Off," *BusinessWeek* European Edition, July 27, 2009, pp. 67–68.

7. Jonathan Birchall, "Best Deal on the Block," *Financial Times Boldness in Business*, March 17, 2011, pp. 36–39.

8. Tim Bradshaw, "Behavioural Advertising: An Answer to the Oldest Problem in Advertising," *Financial Times*, April 15, 2009, p. 11.

9. *Marketing News 2010 Marketing Factbook*, p. 24.

10. "The Box Rocks," *The Economist*, October 2, 2010, p. 73.

11. Ibid.

12. Jon Fine, "Don't Touch That Dial," *BusinessWeek* European Edition, June 2, 2008, p. 90.

13. Knowledge @ Wharton, "Saatchi & Saatchi's Kevin Roberts: 'It's All about Getting to the Future First,'" April 2, 2008, *http://knowlege.wharton.upenn.edu/article.cfm?articelid-1935*.

14. Esmé E. Deprez, "Time to Think beyond the Infomercial," *Bloomberg Businessweek* European Edition, November 22–28, 2010, pp. 72–74.

15. J. William Gurley, "How the Web Will Warp Advertising," *Fortune*, November 9, 1998, pp. 119–20.

16. Josh Quittner and Jessi Hempel, "The Battle for Your Social Circle," *Fortune* European Edition, November 26, 2007, pp. 11–13.

17. Ibid.

18. Brad Stone and Barrett Sheridan, "The Retailer's Clever Little Helper," *Bloomberg BusinessWeek* European Edition, August 30–September 5, 2010, pp. 31–32; Foursquare, *Fortune*, May 23, 2011, p. 84.

19. Seth Godin, *Permission Marketing* (New York: Simon and Schuster, 1999).

20. David Gelles and Allan Rappeport, "Domino's Eats Slice of Humble Pie in Push to Boost Sales," *Financial Times*, May 7–8, 2011, p. 18.

21. Knowledge @ Wharton, "Saatchi & Saatchi's Kevin Roberts: 'It's All about Getting to the Future First,'" April 2, 2008, *http://knowlege.wharton.upenn.edu/article.cfm?articelid-1935*.

22. Bruce Einhorn, "What Sold China on Amway," *Bloomberg Businessweek* European Edition, April 19, 2010, p. 64.

23. See, for example, Mark W. Johnston and Greg W. Marshall, *Churchill/Ford/Walker's Sales force Management*, 8th ed. (New York: McGraw-Hill/Irwin, 2010).

24. Ibid.

25. For a special section on companies that have developed real excellence in customer service (and conversely), see Jena McGregor et al., "When Service Means Survival," *Businessweek* European Edition, March 2, 2009, pp. 26–40.

26. "Financial Express—WNS to Expand Ops, Plans to Open a Call Centre Down South," *Financial Express*, January 7, 2003; Jim O'Rourke, "News–IT Jobs Go Overseas for Lower Pay Rates," *Sun Herald*, December 29, 2002.

27. Reena Jana, "Building a Social Network That Pays," *BusinessWeek* European Edition, July 13 & 20, 2009, p. 66.

28. Brian Smale, "Expertise to Make the Sale," *BusinessWeek* European Edition, June 15, 2009, p. 46.

29. For more on CRM, see Martha Rogers, "Customer Strategy: Observations from the Trenches," *Journal of Marketing*, October 2005, pp. 262–63; and Don Peppers and Martha Rogers, *Return on Customer: Creating Maximum Value from Your Scarcest Resource* (New York: Currency Doubleday, 2005).

30. See, for example, Johnston and Marshall, *Sales ForceManagement*.

31. Peter Crush, "Reebok Builds Email and SMS Database," *Brand Republic,* January 15, 2003.

32. Geoggrey A. Fowler, "Points of Sweat, Point of Thirst Marketing Offers Freebies When They Are Most Needed," *The Wall Street Journal,* August 12, 2001, p. B1.

33. Koen Pauwels, Jorge Silva-Russo, Shuba Srinivasan, and Dominique M. Hanssens, "New Products, Sales Promotions, and Firm Value: The Case of the Automobile Industry," *Journal of Marketing,* October 2004, pp. 142–56.

34. Marti Barletta, "The Real Story behind the Success of Dove's Campaign for Real Beauty," *MarketingProfs,* February 20, 2007, at *http://www .marketingprofs.com/articles/2007/2259/the-real-story-behind-the-success-of-doves-campaign-for-real-beauty#ixzz1QDnMhss8.*

# Section Four

# Strategic Marketing Programs for Selected Situations

# CHAPTER FOURTEEN

# Marketing Strategies for a Digitally Networked World

## Opportunities in the App Economy[1]

*(i)* IN THE EARLY DAYS OF digital time, software was something that one bought in a shrink-wrapped package with a disk inside, typically for a pricey sum. No more. These days, one of the hottest software markets is the market for apps: often bite-sized software programs that run on a mobile phone or within social networks like Facebook. It is growing at mind-boggling speed.

Apple's Apps Store, launched in the summer of 2009, was offering more than 100,000 apps for its hot-selling iPhone by year-end. Amazon, hoping to consolidate the fragmented market for apps for Android-based mobile phones and tablets, launched its Android Appstore with some 4,000 apps in March 2011. Dozens of rivals have also sprung up.

But it's not just the number of apps and stores that sell them that is growing. It's also the volumes of revenue— and profit—that some apps enjoy. Zynga, with its hits like FarmVille, an app that runs inside the Facebook community, surpassed the $100 million mark in revenue in just two years. Analysts expect apps to generate some $4 billion in revenue by 2012, not a bad figure for a market that did not even exist just a few years ago!

### Games as Apps

While it is not entirely clear to me why tens of millions of people want to be online farmers—and pay real money for digital cattle, seeds, tractors, and more—there's clearly something powerful happening here. And it's profitable, too. When Zynga offered its new digital sweet potato seeds at $5 per packet, FarmVille players bought more than $400,000 worth of them in the first three days. Since the seeds are virtual, of course, they cost Zynga virtually nothing to produce, and the revenue drops directly to Zynga's bottom line. It's no wonder that London-based imitator Playfish and California-based Playdom have attracted both venture capital as well as players in droves.

### More than Games

The hot app economy isn't just about games, however. Far from it. FedEx offers a mobile app for the iPhone that tracks shipments' status and provides updates of when the package arrives. Salesforce.com offers an app on a variety of platforms that lets salespeople monitor leads and account information while on the go. Proongo lets business travelers log their travel expenses and photos of receipts, then e-mails the data back to their desktop. Increasingly, thanks to apps, work that used to be done in the office on a PC can now be done on a tablet or mobile phone.

There's also a growing number of apps to suit just about anyone's lifestyle. With Flixster—a free app that works on your iPhone, Android device, BlackBerry, or Palm you can check movie show times, read reviews, and even watch trailers so you can decide where to go with the hot date you have lined up for next weekend.

With CNN Mobile—a $2 app for your iPhone—you can keep up-to-date with live video coverage of breaking news. With ESPN ScoreCenter on your iPhone, you can follow the play-by-play action and grab schedules and stats for your favorite team.

## Business Models

But how—other than selling digital sweet potato seeds and tractors—you might ask, can the proliferation of app providers make any money? The reality is that most of them don't. But one way, aside from selling virtual goods, is to charge a small fee for downloading the app, such as the $2 that CNN charges for CNN Mobile. The $2.99 "I am T-Pain" app, which lets fans of the performer mimic his robot like voice, pulled in downloads worth a seven figure sum. Another way to make money is by placing ads inside your app. AdMob, since its start-up in early 2006, has placed more than 200 billion ads—including ads for blue-chip clients like Ford and Coca-Cola—in websites appearing on mobile phones and in apps on iPhones and Android devices. Some researchers expect mobile advertising to grow into a $10 billion business by 2014.

## Is It Real, or Is It a Bubble?

All the phenomena we're discussing are rooted in today's reality that people are now digitally networked practically everywhere they go. They use LinkedIn to connect with business associates, Facebook to stay connected with family and friends, and their mobile phones to stay connected while on the go. Observers and investors wonder, however, whether there are enduring businesses here, or whether it's all just another internet bubble. As columnist Jessi Hempel noted in early 2009, "Twitter has no business model." Google paid $1.65 billion for YouTube but Hempel notes that Google "Still hasn't figured out how to make much money off it."

As the social networking phenomenon approaches market saturation, its double-digit growth in users is slowing down. Two-thirds of the online population will use a social network on some device at least monthly in 2013, according to a study by eMarketer, up from 52 percent in 2009. Noted investor Warren Buffett warns that valuations of social networking companies have become overvalued, and that investors should be wary as some of these companies prepare to sell their shares to the public in IPOs.

Whatever the valuations, though, it appears that digitally enabled social networks of many kinds and the apps that are developed to serve them are here to stay. Some will become real companies, making real money. Others, undoubtedly, will disappear as quickly as the morning dew on a warm summer day. For marketers of all kinds, however, the ubiquity and reach of the social networking phenomenon and the proliferation of apps means that these phenomena demand their full attention.

## Marketing Challenges Addressed in Chapter 14

As the vibrant market for apps shows, the quest for new, marketable ideas on the web in today's digitally networked world hasn't run out of fuel. The rapid pace of change on the web, in mobile telephony, and in related technologies offers an abundance of opportunities to create new companies, and it can help transform stone-age companies and provide attractive opportunities for growth. But, for most companies, the optimal path through the digital maze is far from clear.

Thus, in Chapter 14, we address several timely and important questions that marketing managers in today's companies and entrepreneurs must ask. Does the company need a social media strategy? Do recent technological advances represent threats or opportunities? Most important, how should marketers address the development of strategies to take advantage of—or defend against— the rapid pace of change inherent in today's digitally networked world? What marketing roles can the internet, social networking, and other recent and future technological developments play, and which of these should be pursued?

We begin by reviewing several trends that highlight the growing importance of social networking and other related digital developments. We then identify the key advantages and disadvantages inherent in recent developments in today's digital landscape, all of which every marketer must clearly understand. Next, we identify the roles that digital networking technologies can plausibly play in marketing strategies, and we articulate a decision framework for managers to use to decide which of the growing array of such tools their firms should employ—from web-based marketing research to advertising on mobile phones to the delivery of digitized information, goods, and services over the web. Finally, we take a brief look into what the future may have in store.

# Does Every Company Need a Social Media Strategy?

Like it or not, despite the scepticism of some early observers, social networks like Facebook, LinkedIn, and some not yet conceived as we write in mid-2011, are here to stay. And it's not just teens and twenty-somethings who are getting on board. Though social networking penetration is highest among the 18-to-24 age group at 90 percent, more than half the online population aged 45 to 64 were expected to use social networks regularly in 2011, with further growth expected in future years (see Exhibit 14.1)[2]

## Exhibit 14.1

SOCIAL NETWORKING DEMOGRAPHY

U.S. Social Network User Penetration, by Age, 2009–2013 (Historical and Forecast)

| % OF INTERNET USERS IN EACH GROUP WHO USE SOCIAL NETWORKS | | | | | |
|---|---|---|---|---|---|
| Age | 2009 | 2010 | 2011 | 2012 | 2013 |
| 0–11 | 12 | 14 | 15 | 16 | 17 |
| 12–17 | 75 | 78 | 81 | 84 | 85 |
| 18–24 | 83 | 88 | 90 | 92 | 93 |
| 25–34 | 70 | 77 | 82 | 84 | 85 |
| 35–44 | 52 | 65 | 72 | 75 | 77 |
| 45–54 | 42 | 53 | 58 | 63 | 65 |
| 55–64 | 35 | 48 | 52 | 55 | 57 |
| 65+ | 20 | 28 | 31 | 34 | 36 |
| **Total** | **52** | **60** | **64** | **66** | **67** |

*Note:* Internet users who use social networks via any device at least once per month.

*Source: eMarketer,* February 2011, "Days of Double-Digit Growth in Social Network Use Are Over," at *www.emarketer.com/ Article.aspx?R=1008288.*

Ted Schadler, a Forrester analyst who surveyed 68,000 U.S. homes, says there are important implications in the rapidly changing digital world for marketers. "The rise of consumers' adoption of personal devices, home networking and broadband, combined with the increasing importance of the internet in media, retail, banking, and healthcare, means that every consumer-facing industry must better understand the intricacies of technology adoption and use. Missing from most marketers' tool boxes is an understanding that consumers' attitudes toward technology determine a lot about how they receive marketing messages, get service online, adopt new technologies, and spend their time."[3] Consumers having more than five years of online experience spend 24 percent less time reading newspapers and 23 percent less time in front of the TV, according to the Forrester report. And these marketing implications are confined neither to social media nor to the United States. The implications of these changes are equally dramatic virtually everywhere, even in China (see Exhibit 14.2).

What should marketers conclude from these developments? Notwithstanding the mind-boggling stock market valuations of social networking companies, notwithstanding the difficulties many companies have had in developing business models that actually make money, and notwithstanding the so-called digital divide, in which some segments of the population are still underrepresented in the internet population, the long-term prospects for jumping into the digitally networked world with both feet are still enormous. The growing market acceptance of the internet and various digitally networked technologies and the inherent advantages that they bring suggest that nearly every company needs to examine how it will be affected by and can take advantage of these developments.

The outcome of such an examination should be the development of one's own social media strategy. The fact that one's competitors will surely develop and deploy such strategies is a further argument for doing so. But marketers should take heart, for the good news is this: "In the end, e-consumers and e-businesses aren't so different from traditional buyers and sellers after all. Customers are, by and large, pragmatists—be they individuals looking for a new shirt, or a big automaker looking for a new source of steel. When the e-way is easier, faster, and cheaper, it can win."[4] Today's well-educated business students

## Exhibit 14.2    CHINA'S AD SPENDING MOVES ONLINE

In 2005, Motorola was set to launch a new line of mobile phones targeting the youth market in China. A key question it faced was how best to reach that market. Its answer: *not* business as usual. Instead of the usual TV, magazine, or newspaper campaign, Motorola hired a couple of hip college students from Guangzhou who had already created an internet reputation in China with their home-produced lip-synched renditions of popular Western songs. By combining the "Back Dorm Boyz" with a related competition in which participants could lip-synch and remix their own songs, Motorola generated more than 14 million page views. "This was a grassroots, guerrilla way to relate to the youth of China," says Ian Chapman-Banks, head of Motorola's marketing in North Asia.

Motorola is not the only company in China moving its yuan online. Procter & Gamble, General Motors, and Tiffany have all run significant online efforts. Though online ad spending only accounted for a 2.3 percent share of the total Chinese advertising market in 2005, it's been growing by 75 percent annually. Traditional media are feeling the crunch, with newspaper ad sales down 5.1 percent and magazines down 16.5 percent in 2004. There's little on the horizon to suggest anything but more of the same.

*Source:* Dexter Roberts, "China's Online Ad Boom," *BusinessWeek,* May 15, 2006, p. 46.

can bring these insights—as well as digital and social networking expertise—to the companies they join.

# Threats or Opportunities? The Inherent Advantages and Disadvantages of the Digitally Networked World for Marketers

What advantages do the new internet, telecommunication, and social networking technologies provide to marketers and their customers? Seven potentially attractive elements characterize what's new here: the syndication of information, the increasing returns to scale of network products, the ability to efficiently personalize and customize market offerings, the ability to disintermediate distribution, global reach, round-the-clock access, and the possibility of instantaneous delivery.

## The Syndication of Information[5]

**Syndication** involves the sale of the same good—typically an informational good—to many customers, who may then combine it with information from other sources and distribute it. The entertainment and publishing worlds have long employed syndication, producing comic strips, newspaper columns, and TV shows that appear in many places at once. Without syndication, today's mass media would not exist as we know them. Though internet marketers rarely use the word *syndication* to describe what they do, it lies at the heart of many e-commerce business models. Inktomi, an **originator** of syndicated content, provides its search engine technology to many branded search engine sites. YellowBrix, a **syndicator,** collects articles in electronic form and delivers relevant portions of this content to other sites, each of which appeals to a different target audience. E*Trade, a **distributor** of syndicated information, brings together from many sources content relevant to its investor clientele and packages it in ways useful to these clients. iMode, the mobile telephone operator in Japan, syndicates an enormous variety of information—even cartoons.

Why is syndication important? First, because syndication delivers informational goods (digitized text, audio, music, photos, CAD/CAM files, even digital sweet potato seeds), rather than tangible goods, a person or company can syndicate the same informational goods or services to an almost infinite number of customers with little incremental cost. Variable costs approach zero. Producers of tangible goods and most services (from chocolate bars to haircuts) must spend money on sugar and chocolate or labor for each additional chocolate bar or haircut sold. Not so for information producers, where sending a digital copy of a photo or an internet news feature to one more recipient, or a Facebook posting of where you had lunch today, is essentially free. Second, the syndication process can be automated and digitized, enabling syndicated networks to be created, expanded, and flexibly adapted far more quickly than would be possible in the physical world. By using technology called **Really Simple Syndication (RSS),** syndicated content can be fed to users having preferences for such content (see Exhibit 14.3).

Syndication via the internet—and via mobile phones or other mobile devices—opens up endless opportunities for marketers. It replaces scarcity with abundance. Information can be replicated an infinite number of times and combined and recombined in an infinite number of ways. It can be distributed everywhere, all at once, and be available all the time. At Praxis, a web 2.0–based language school founded in 2005

**Exhibit 14.3   RSS Lets Expedia Send Customized Alerts for Hot Travel Deals**

You're planning your spring break holiday, and you know what you want, but you're tired of searching countless websites for the best deal to the sunniest destination. Now, thanks to Really Simply Syndication (RSS) technology, Expedia.com lets customers select alerts for exactly the sort of travel they are planning. A sunny beach in Mexico? No problem. A luxury villa in Italy? Easy. Expedia's Sally McKenzie says, "This is just another example of how Expedia (gives) travelers the travel intelligence and tools they want, when, where, and how they want it."

The power of RSS is that it lets consumers with newsreader facilities in their browsers specify the kind of syndicated information they want to see. Follow your stock portfolio? Track your favorite football team? RSS makes it simple. Or, if it's travel info you want, tell Expedia where you want to go at *www.expedia.com/rss,* and they'll watch the best deals for you.

*Source:* PR Newswire, "Expedia.com Introduces Most Comprehensive Service Providing Real-Time Travel Deal Alerts Leveraging RSS Technology," May 2, 2006.

by Shanghai-based Irishman Ken Carroll, millions of students in more than 100 countries have downloaded free Chinese podcast language lessons, an example of the power of syndication. About 250,000 listen regularly, and some sign up for premium services, such as live conversations in Mandarin with a tutor in Shanghai, using Skype and their broadband connection. Carroll's 35 employees in Shanghai, including some of the city's best language teachers, serve customers from Alaska to the Vatican.[6]

Taking advantage of the full potential of syndication, however, requires new thinking. Companies need to identify and occupy the most important niches in syndication networks. These are the ones that maximize the number and strength of links to other companies and customers, though shifting market conditions inevitably mean that these links must change as markets evolve. Bloomberg, the provider of syndicated information to stock traders and analysts, is an example of a company that has positioned itself well; many of its clients now regard their Bloomberg terminals as indispensable. Thus, almost any company can think of itself as part of a larger, interconnected world and seek ways to occupy originator, syndicator, or distributor roles in an appropriate syndication network.

## Increasing Returns to Scale of Network Products[7]

Any undergraduate economics student knows that an increased supply of a good leads to lower value, hence lower prices. But that was before fax machines, operating systems, and other products used in networks, where the second fax machine, for example, makes the first one more valuable, and so on. This characteristic of informational networks—a product becomes more valuable as the number of users increases—is often called a **positive network effect,** or **network externality.** When combined with the syndication of informational products, this characteristic has led to the seemingly crazy strategy of giving one's product away for free, often a strategy of choice for marketers! Facebook and other social networks offer potential value for advertisers and others in the large network that they have created.

Are the various networks a thing of the future, or will their "closed worlds," each walled off from the others, make them dinosaurs in the end? David Ascher, of Thunderbird, an open-source e-mail provider, says "E-mail in the wider sense is the most important social network." Charlene Li, an analyst with Forrester Research and author of *Groundswell,* a book on the social technology phenomenon, shares Ascher's doubts about their staying power. "We will look back to 2008 and think it archaic and quaint that we had to go to a destination like Facebook or LinkedIn to be social," she says. Future social networks "will be like air. They will be everywhere and anywhere we want them to be."[8]

## The Ability to Efficiently Personalize and Customize Market Offerings

Amazon tracks the books I buy and, using a technology known as **collaborative filtering,** is able to compare my purchases with those of others and thereby recommend to me books they think I would like, personalized to my taste and reading habits, as Amazon understands them. If they do this well, my purchases go up, and I become a happier customer because Amazon helps me find books I want to read. While collaborative filtering technology has a long way to go (the book I bought for my daughter when she was studying for a semester in Ecuador does not make me a Latin American culture buff), the potential of this and other new-economy technologies offers the promise of creating sharply targeted market segments—ultimately, market segments of one.

Collaborative filtering is but one way of personalizing a market offering to each customer. When formal decision rules can be identified in the way customers behave (for example, reminding customers of, or making special offers for, upcoming birthdays or offering supplementary items based on past purchases), **rules-based personalization** can be done. The most predictive rules, however, may require customers to divulge information that they do not want to take the time, or are not willing, to divulge.

**Customization** techniques, which are user-driven instead of marketer-driven (as we have seen for personalization approaches), allow users to specify the nature of what is offered to them. Several office supply firms, for example, offer corporate users the ability to create customized office supply catalogs tailored to their company. Such catalogs simplify ordering procedures, save time and money in the purchasing department, and help control expense by offering to perhaps far-flung employees only what the purchasing department has approved in advance. Similarly, some online music sellers offer consumers the opportunity to order customized CDs consisting of only the songs the customer chooses. In today's highly competitive markets, personalization and customization can help build customer loyalty and make it less likely that customers may switch to other suppliers.

## Disintermediation and Restructuring of Distribution Channels

Many goods and services are sold through distribution channels. The internet makes it possible for marketers to reach customers directly, without the expense or complication of distribution channels, a phenomenon known as **disintermediation.** Burlington Industries, for example, makes dress socks I like, but they are harder and harder to find because of the demise of local apparel retailers and the growing reach of chain retailers marketing their own brands. The solution? Burlington now sells them directly to consumers at *www .burlingtonsocks.com.*

What's next in the disintermediation derby? The tangled supply chain of the jewelry industry is one good candidate, where a cut diamond can pass through five or more middlemen before reaching a retailer. Jewelry e-tailers such as Blue Nile, Diamond.com, and even Amazon can cut through the lengthy channel, eliminate costly retail locations, and save consumers thousands of dollars in the process. Pete Dignan figured he saved about $4,000 on the ring he bought for his fiancée, Kelly Gilmore. Investing some of his savings in a fancy limousine ride to a park overlooking Colorado's Rocky Mountains made for "a really romantic proposal, and that was more important," he says."[9]

Deciding to disintermediate or restructure one's channel, however, should not be done lightly. Levi Strauss, the jeans manufacturer, angered its existing retailers by offering custom-fit jeans direct to consumers via the web. Ultimately, the company withdrew the offering due in part to the howls of protest it heard from its regular retail channel members. Similar concerns have arisen in the travel industry, as airlines and others have disintermediated travel agents by selling airline tickets and other travel services directly to consumers via the web. Someone must perform the functions normally performed by channel members—taking orders, delivering products, collecting payment, and so on—so those who consider disintermediating their channels and selling direct must determine how they will perform these functions and must evaluate whether doing so is more effective and efficient than using intermediaries.

**STRATEGIC ISSUE**

*Deciding to disintermediate or restructure one's channel should not be done lightly.*

Somewhat paradoxically, however, as web-based disintermediation has grown, new kinds of intermedaries have appeared to fill new needs. The music industry is now rife with new kinds of intermediaries, from Apple's iTunes music store and Apps Store to subscription-based services such as Pandora Radio, where subscribers can create their own personalized stations, and Microsoft's Zune, where a small monthly fee allows access to 3 million songs. For one subscriber's take on why subscription-based music is more appealing than other distribution methods, see Exhibit 14.4.

Other new intermediaries include aggregators and affiliate schemes. Aggregators such as Kayak.com, a travel aggregator, are a more evolved version of price comparison sites. These sites assist the customer in finding the best deal from hundreds of sites. Travel agency and tour operator sites cooperate with Kayak because of the vast amount of traffic Kayak attracts, as well as the fact that their competitors are likely to be on Kayak as well. Affiliate schemes, of which Commission Junction (*www.cj.com*) is one of the largest,

## Exhibit 14.4   Is Music Ownership Overrated?

Peter Burrows recently made a startling discovery. "I was sick of my music," he says. After spending a few hundred dollars on iTunes and converting the contents of his 500 CDs to MP3 format, he got tired of his playlist. Now, Burrows, a subscriber to RealNetworks' Rhapsody service, can check out long-forgotten albums, discover new favorites, or find the perfect song for dancing with his kids. He doesn't own the songs he listens to, but who cares?

Though Rhapsody and a handful of other subscription-based services have only modest numbers of subscribers so far and suffer from clunky software and compatibility problems—some don't work with an iPod, for example—RealNetworks CEO Steve Glaser remains optimistic. "Some of the factors necessary to create the Great Jukebox in the Sky have taken longer than I thought," he admits. "But that doesn't tell me it will never take off." MTV appears to agree, having acquired a 49 percent stake in Rhapsody. Burrows, who spends $15 a month, $180 each year, to quench his musical appetite, is optimistic as well. "I'm sure others will emerge that are even better and cheaper than Rhapsody—probably from Apple itself. I hope so."

*Sources:* Peter Burrows, "Stars Are Aligning for Subscription Music," *BusinessWeek,* European Edition, December 17, 2007, pp. 66–67; and Peter Burrows, "Waxing Rhapsodic," *BusinessWeek,* European Edition, December 17, 2007, p. 67. For more on Rhapsody, see *www.rhapsody.com.*

are similar. CJ is an application service provider whose platform allows businesses with products to sell (advertisers) to interact with businesses (or individuals) with websites to populate (publishers). The publisher makes money from commissions from the advertiser when a purchase is made by a customer who was directed from the publisher's site. Why are aggregators and affiliate schemes growing? The aggregator sites can focus on improving the technologies that allow customers to find exactly what they want, and publishers can specialize in promotion and attracting customers, since they are not involved in managing the product that the customer is actually buying.

## Global Reach, 24/7 Access, and Instantaneous Delivery

With the internet and digitally networked technologies, typically there is no extra cost entailed in making information, digital goods, or services available anywhere one can gain access to the web—literally, **global reach,** making them available 24 hours per day, seven days per week, 52 weeks per year and, in some cases, providing instantaneous delivery. In our increasingly time-pressed world, access and service like this can be of great value to customers (see Exhibit 14.5). Air Asia, the rapidly growing low-priced airline based in Singapore, sells most of its tickets on its own website, many of them to international travelers who reserve flights from afar, even from another continent. Flight confirmations are delivered instantly. Software vendors, like those selling apps as we saw at the beginning of this chapter, whose products may be purchased and instantaneously downloaded from the web, provide similar responsiveness. As mobile telephony and GPS technologies develop, similar benefits are starting to be available to customers and marketers whose products are well suited to mobile media.

## Are These Digital World Attributes Opportunities or Threats?

Most marketers can choose to take advantage of one or more of the benefits offered by today's digital and social networking technologies, including those we have outlined previously. To that extent, these technologies constitute opportunities available to marketers

---

### Exhibit 14.5   A BAKER GOES GLOBAL

In 1997, Michael Nielsen, a baker in the small Danish town of Højbjerg, started a small business to indulge his hobby of tinkering with small computer systems. He initially targeted online game players, figuring that others would view them as expert sources of information when buying or upgrading PCs. "If the gamers liked you, they recommended you," he says. Ten years on, Nielsen's company, SHG, expected to sell $50 million worth of electronic hardware over the web in 2007, reaching customers that most small-town merchants wouldn't dream of reaching. His story illustrates two key principles of going global on the web. First, credibility is important.

His key staff are Microsoft certified. Second, bringing customers to your site in a low-cost manner is critical, something his viral marketing in the gaming community took care of. Nielsen claimed no special expertise to stand out from the competition, and his margins were razor-thin. So his business, now doing business as Proshop, evolved into an aggregator of sites selling hardware and more. It certainly beats arising at the crack of dawn to crank up the ovens!

*Source:* Alan Cain, "The Weapon That Makes You a Giant Killer," *Financial Times, FT Digital Business,* June 21, 2006, p. 2. For more on SHG and Proshop, see *www.proshop.dk.*

## ETHICAL PERSPECTIVE 14.1
### Are Web "Cookies" a Good Thing?

In 1993, early days in internet time, a cartoon in *The New Yorker* magazine showed two dogs using a computer. One of them said to the other, "On the internet, nobody knows you're a dog." These days, somebody probably does know you're a dog, who your master is, and whether you prefer Iams or Purina dog chow. So-called "cookies," digital codes placed on your computer to enable websites to remember who you are when you log on and to track the sites you visit, how long you linger, and other such data, are what makes such detailed customer knowledge possible.

Collection of online consumer data is a growing phenomenon, one some observers are concerned about. "When you start to get into the details, it's scarier than you might suspect," says Marc Rotenberg, executive director of the Electronic Privacy Information Center, a watchdog for privacy rights.

Companies that collect all this data argue that it's all in the consumer's interest because it makes the ads they see more relevant. Matt Simpson, chairman of the digital media group of the Institute of Practitioners in Advertising and digital media head at OMD, a UK-based media agency, says, "In a perfect world, you can deliver a more relevant message and spend less money."

In a study by research firm comScore, Yahoo! emerged as the cookie champion, collecting data 811 times each month for an average user. That doesn't count another 1,709 data collection instances on partner sites such as eBay and others, where Yahoo! places ads, bringing the total for Yahoo! users to more than 2,500 data collections each day.

Consumers have not been vocal about such practices, perhaps because such data collection is largely invisible. But just how much would you like Yahoo!, or any other internet company, to know about your shopping habits, what you view on the web, and so on? Web companies say their policies on such data collection and dissemination are clearly spelled out, and most say they have consumer protection policies in place.

But Rotenberg is not convinced that all this data collection is a good thing. Web companies are "recording preferences, hopes, worries, and fears," he says. Government authorities in the United States and Europe are joining the fray. The U.S. Federal Trade Commission has called for a "do not track" system that would enable consumers to avoid having their click-streams tracked online. Proposed new rules in the European Union would give users the right to tell websites to permanently delete existing personal data. Will the regulators and privacy advocates prevail? Most online marketers are hoping they won't. Will that remain the case? Who knows?

*Sources:* Louise Story, "Internet Firms Keeping Ever-Closer Tabs on You," *International Herald Tribune*, March 15, 2007, p. 15; and Maija Palmer, "A Deeper Peeper," *Financial Times*, April 15, 2009, p. 11, John W. Miller, "EU Floats More Rights for Online Privacy," *The Wall Street Journal* European Edition, November 5–7, 2010, p 19; and Julia Angwin and Jennifer Valentino-DeVries, "Web Privacy 'Inadequate'," *The Wall Street Journal* European Edition, December 2, 2010, p. B2.

---

who employ them. Viewed differently, however, they raise complex ethical issues (see Ethical Perspective 14.1), and they also present potentially significant threats.

First, the fact that the variable cost for syndicated goods approaches zero sounds like a good thing, until one realizes that for most products, price, over the long run, usually is not far from variable cost. If variable cost is zero, will prices drop to near zero, too? If so, such an outcome might represent disaster for information producers. Amazon's Kindle and its e-reader copycats are wreaking havoc in the book-publishing industry, driving down the prices of books and threatening the existence of the traditional hard-cover book as we know it. In February 2011, according to the Association of American Publishers, $90 million worth of e-books were sold, triple the figure for February 2010, far surpassing paperback and hardcover sales.[10]

Selling music on the internet also seemed like a good idea to music publishers and even to artists. Imagine getting $12 to $15 for the music on a CD, with no retailers or distributors to take cuts of the revenue and no costs to pay for fancy packaging! Disintermediation sounds good if you are a music publisher, but it's a threat if you're a music retailer, even a web-based one such as Amazon! If you were Apple's Steve Jobs a decade ago, however, disintermediation was music to your ears. The combination of Apple's iPod portable digital

**STRATEGIC ISSUE**

*The fact that the variable cost for syndicated goods approaches zero sounds like a good thing.*

music player and its iTunes online music store followed by its iPhone and iPad, has transformed the company, with these lines of business growing to more than 75 percent of total revenue for Apple's six months ended March 26, 2011.[11]

The fact that the variable cost of downloading digital content is now essentially zero will likely have a profound effect on the pricing of books and music. Internet distribution may also change how new bands are discovered and promoted (see Exhibit 14.6).

Another threat to technologies is that there are few barriers to entry, and many internet strategies are easily imitated. Apps of all kinds have proliferated, but few win traction with users and most get lost in the crowd.

Other threats include privacy and security issues, which can drive away customers rather than attract them if they are not handled with care. The most restrictive jurisdictions' privacy rules may eventually apply to internet marketers anywhere. Privacy laws in Europe, compared to the United States, are substantially more strict.

In the United States, internet privacy has been dealt with largely through market forces, whereby consumers are expected to avoid sites where privacy is not handled to their liking. As firms attempt to take advantage of the global reach afforded by the internet, will they run afoul of privacy laws in countries whose consumers they serve? In what jurisdictions will complaints be heard and dealt with? Will the most restrictive countries end up ruling the roost? These ethical and legal privacy questions are far from settled.

## First-Mover Advantage: Fact or Fiction?[12]

In the internet gold rush in the late 1990s, and again in the later rush to build social networking sites, the key to success was said to be **first-mover advantage.** The first firm to establish a significant presence in each market niche would be the one that succeeded. Thus, Amazon would win in books. eBay would win in auctions. Myspace would win in social networking, and so on. Later followers need not bother. But is first-mover advantage on the internet or elsewhere real?

---

### Exhibit 14.6    ARCTIC MONKEYS SAY "NO THANKS" TO THE A&R CROWD

In January 2006, the Arctic Monkeys sold more than 360,000 copies of their album, "Whatever People Say I Am, That's What I'm Not," in its first week of release, the United Kingdom's fastest-selling debut since records began. But who are they? The Arctic Monkeys, based in Sheffield in the United Kingdom, were one of the hottest new acts in years. Says a spokesman for music retailer HMV, "In terms of sheer impact . . . we haven't seen anything quite like this since The Beatles."

But the traditional route to musical success, being discovered by an A&R person, signing a contract, then going on tour, and so on, isn't the route the Arctic Monkeys followed. Instead, the quartet started gigging at small venues in 2003 and handed out demo CDs to the crowd, who in turn put the band's songs on the internet for others to hear. Despite alluring promises of fame and fortune, they resisted signing with a major record label, opting eventually for the independent Domino Records label.

The band members are quick to point out that they did not put the songs online themselves and were barely aware of what was happening at the time. "The only reason people have got into it [the music] is because they've listened to it and they like it, so it's something real," says Jarvis Cocker, another Sheffield-based singer.

*Sources:* BBC website, *http://news.bbc.co.uk/1/hi/entertainment/ 4644214.stm* and *http://news.bbc.co.uk/1/hi/entertainment/4660394 .stm.* For more on the Arctic Monkeys, see *www.arcticmonkeys.com.*

Being the first mover can bring some potential advantages, but not all first movers are able to capitalize on those advantages. Thus, many are surpassed over time by later entrants, just as late-comer Facebook left Myspace in the dust by 2008. One thing a pioneer must do to hold on to its early leadership position is to continue to innovate in order to maintain a differential advantage over the many imitators likely to arrive late to the party but eager to get in. Easy to say, not so easy to do.

Jim Collins, author of the best sellers *Good to Great* and *Built to Last,* is more blunt about the supposed rule that nothing is as important as being first to reach scale. "It's wrong," he says. "Best beats first."[13] As Collins points out, VisiCalc was the first major personal computer spreadsheet. Where is VisiCalc today? It lost the battle to Lotus 1-2-3, which in turn lost to Excel. What about the once-ubiquitous Palm Pilot? It came to market years after early leader Sharp and the Apple Newton. Palm's designers found a better way to design personal digital assistants—using one reliable script, instead of everyone's own script—and sold more than 6 million units.[14] But Palm was then leapfrogged by Blackberry, which has been further leapfrogged by Apple's iPhone and other smartphones based on Google's Android operating system.

In the bricks-and-mortar economy, Walmart didn't pioneer discount retailing. Nucor didn't pioneer the minimill for making steel from scrap. Starbucks didn't pioneer the high-end coffee shop. Yet all were winners, while the early leaders fell behind or disappeared. None of these entrants were first—they were *better*. Being first may help attract investors and may make some founders and venture capitalists rich, but it's hardly a recipe for building a great company.

## Developing a Strategy for a Digitally Networked World: A Decision Framework

Most companies of substantial size or scope, whatever their industry, will need to develop strategies to take advantage of new digital and social networking technologies, but doing so is easier said than done. While we recognize that nonmarketing applications of these technologies may be compelling for many companies, our focus remains on marketing, Thus, in this section we focus on how the latest such tools—and, for some applications, mobile telephony—can fruitfully be employed for marketing purposes.[15]

## Marketing Applications for a Digitally Networked World

Earlier in this book we pointed out that a number of activities have to be performed by somebody for an exchange transaction to occur between a selling firm and a potential customer. Retaining that customer for future transactions adds additional activities, such as providing effective and responsive customer service after the sale. From the customer's point of view, these necessary activities can be summarized in a six-stage **consumer experience process** that begins with communicating one's wants and needs to prospective sellers; moving through the awareness, purchase, and delivery processes; obtaining any necessary service or support after the purchase to support its use or consumption; and ultimately sometimes returning or disposing of the product (we identify the six stages in Exhibit 14.7).

Customers first provide information about their needs to sellers, whose **customer insight** permits them to develop goods or services intended to meet the customer's

## Exhibit 14.7

A CUSTOMER EXPERIENCE MODEL FOR MARKETING DECISION MAKING

| Stage in customer experience process | Direction of information flows | Direction of product flows (goods or services) | Direction of cash flows (revenue opportunities) |
|---|---|---|---|
| Customer insight | P ◄──── C | | |
| Product promotion and brand building | P ────► C | | |
| Transaction | P ◄───► C | | |
| Product delivery | | P ────► C | P ◄──── C |
| Customer support and service | P ◄───► C | P ────► C | P ◄──── C |
| Product return or disposal | | P ◄──── C | P ────► C |

P = Producer
C = Customer

needs. This stage in the process requires that information flow from customer to seller, as shown in Exhibit 14.7. While there may be several back-and-forth iterations in the insight stage, as new product developers invent and refine their product ideas, ultimately some good or service is developed, and information about the new product—**promotion and brand building**—then flows to customers to inform and encourage them to buy. If the customer likes what is offered, a **transaction** ensues, requiring that information about pricing, terms, delivery, and so on flows both ways. With a transaction consummated, **delivery** of the good or service is made, with the product flowing to the customer and money or other compensation flowing to the seller. But the seller's job is not yet done for the customer may need some kind of **customer support or service** during use, in which case additional information may flow in either direction or additional goods or services may flow to the customer, possibly in exchange for additional revenue. Finally, the customer may need to **return, dispose** of, or discontinue use of the good or service, at which point the product may be returned to the seller, cash may flow back to the customer (as a result of the product's return or some kind of trade-in, perhaps), and another transaction—with this or another seller—may ensue, thereby repeating much of the process.

Social networking, the internet, and to an increasing extent, mobile telephony offer applications at some or all of these stages. We now explore some of these applications, though in this fast-moving arena, new ones will undoubtedly arise before the ink is dry on this book. Then, in the next section, we set forth a decision framework to assist marketers in deciding for which of these stages, and with which applications, such tools should become part of their strategies.

### Applications for Customer Insight

In Chapter 6, we discussed the role of marketing research in understanding customers and developing products—whether goods or services—to meet their needs. Marketers rely on a flow of information from customers or prospective customers about their wants and needs, however latent these may sometimes be, to generate the insight essential to the development of compelling new products (see Exhibit 14.8). How might today's digital and social networking technologies facilitate this process?

First, consider the trove of data posted daily on Facebook and other social networking sites. Sifting through such data—and providing it in an organized manner to customers willing to pay for it—is becoming a big business (see Exhibit 14.8). In some industries, keeping track of what customers are saying about your business can be crucial. Take hotels, for instance. These days, everybody checks out TripAdvisor, Yelp, or another website before booking a vacation, because user reviews are seen as more objective sources of information than the property's own site. Entrepreneurs Mark Heyneker and Jay Ashton saw an opportunity here, to alert hotels to potentially damaging posts on such sites. "We monitor fire hoses of Twitter content, all public Facebook content, YouTube, everything on Flickr," declares Ashton, who says that their company, Revinate, has about 1,000 clients, including hotels from the most widely recognized brands like Peninsula, Radisson, Kimpton, Best Western, Hyatt, and Holiday Inn.

Managers not only get timely insight about how their hotels are really performing, but they have an opportunity to respond online and deal with their critics—and compliments, for that matter—in a positive manner. In one such instance, Paul Frechette, manager of the Shorebreak Hotel in California, posted a heartfelt response on TripAdvisor. "Since I was able to match his user name to his e-mail and last name, I was able to personalize my response to him by addressing him as an HB (Huntington Beach) local," he says. "I went on to explain how the people in the city of Huntington Beach are our most important clients and that it would mean the world to me if he contacted me in person." The customer did so, and Frechette was able to turn an angry guest into a happy customer who returns regularly.[16]

Pollsters and other marketing researchers are increasingly turning to the internet to conduct marketing research, due to its cost-cutting, time-saving advantages over traditional survey methods.[17] Why? Just as internet marketers see the potential for "easier, faster, and cheaper," so, too, do researchers when they consider the internet.

Among the new online research techniques is the use of instant messaging (IM) to gather consumer data. "Clients are using the (IM) tools and liking what they get out of them," reports Joel Benenson, CEO of iModerate, an online market research firm. In IM-based focus groups, for example, researchers can use IM to probe respondents' answers more deeply in follow-up conversations.[18]

Nonetheless, using the web for research is not without controversy. Traditional researchers debate the web's merits on a number of dimensions: in terms of representativeness of the current makeup of the web audience, somewhat whiter, richer, younger, and more educated than the population as a whole; in terms of self-selection biases, where people volunteer to participate in web-based polls; and in terms of the randomness, or lack thereof, of

**STRATEGIC ISSUE**

*Using the web for research is not without controversy.*

---

## Exhibit 14.8  WHY DO MEN WEAR STUBBLE?

Marketers have long wanted to be able to gather evidence of trends using data floating around on the web. NetBase, a social media analytics company, enables them to do just that. On one assignment, NetBase found 77,000 mentions of stubble online, in less than six seconds. Its analysts then sorted the positive comments into themes and built a chart in less than an hour, ranking the top reasons why men wear stubble. The top-ranked answer wasn't a surprise—men who wear stubble do so because they see it as sexy—and any hip urbanite could have told them that. But the ability to now quickly gather and mine the abundance of web data is.

*Source:* Ryann Flinn, "The Big Business of Sifting through Social Media Data," *Bloomberg Businessweek,* October 25–31, 2010, pp. 20–21.

web samples. Procter & Gamble, the world's largest user of marketing research, reported that two online surveys by the same provider, conducted two weeks apart, delivered diametrically opposite results.[19] But many of these problems are present in other forms of research, too, especially as more people refuse to answer mail or telephone surveys.

Regardless of its limitations, however, web-based research, for customer insight, both for qualitative studies and for large-scale quantitative studies, is here to stay and will undoubtedly grow.

**Applications for Product Promotion and Brand Building**    The basic tools for these activities have grown extensively over the past few years. The "if we build it they will come" mind-set that allowed companies to perceive their website as a mere marketing tool as opposed to a channel that required its own, specific marketing efforts has become obsolete. The tools that today's *au courant* web marketers use comprise not only time-tested tactics like banner ads, search, e-mail marketing, blogs, and promotional websites. The pace of innovation is so rapid that new applications are arising and sometimes growing explosively. Consider the daily deals marketer Groupon, for example. Groupon enables Thalia Spice, an Asian fusion restaurant in Chicago, to offer discounted meals to fill tables that would otherwise be empty during slow periods. Groupon junkies can find daily deals on everything from meals to massages from merchants in their city".[20]

From its modest presence in just 30 American cities in 2009, with 2 million subscribers, Groupon has exploded into a global phenomenon, serving 565 cities worldwide by early 2011 and expecting sales north of $3 billion for the year. Groupon's targeted location-based approach was getting even more precise with the testing of its new app for mobile phones. Simply tell its Groupon Now application, "I'm hungry," and it will tell you which nearby restaurants have deals right now.[21] Advertising on mobile phones is beginning to skyrocket with the increasing penetration of smartphones in North America and Europe. Analysts predict that mobile advertising will be a $10 billion business by 2014.[22]

Then there's the burgeoning number of so-called flash sales sites like Rue La La and Gilt Group. These sites enable apparel makers and others to offload unwanted inventory in a classy manner, without disturbing their normal distribution channels. "It's a huge period of innovation for consumer-facing commerce, unlike anything we've seen in the past 10 years," says Josh Goldman, of Norwest Venture Partners, which has invested in a number of e-commerce startups.[23]

Finally, there's the newest form of search, one that holds considerable potential to grow, video search (see Exhibit 14.9). Though its commercial potential has not yet been widely tapped, some observers believe that video search is a plausible candidate on the short list for the web's "next big thing."

All of these new wrinkles enable companies of various kinds to build their brands or promote product sales in a highly targeted manner. Most of these and other web-based marketing tools benefit from being highly measurable as well.

**Applications for Conducting Transactions**    If promotional activities do their jobs, the hoped-for consequence is that some customers will decide to buy. Can the internet or mobile telephony help transactions occur? Several web-based companies are in the business of enabling client websites to handle transactions. BroadVision Inc., for example, offers a wide range of software products that enable clients to conduct B2B or B2C commerce on their websites or via kiosks or mobile telephones. Such products typically provide back-end systems and inventory control, prepare warehouse and shipping documents,

## Exhibit 14.9   VIDEO SEARCH TAKES OFF ON THE WEB

When 9-year-old Tyler Kennedy of Alameda, California, had to gather information for a school report on the platypus, he began his search on the web, of course. But he didn't use Google or Yahoo!. YouTube was his search engine of choice.

In November 2008, Americans conducted nearly 2.8 billion video searches on YouTube, which slipped past Yahoo! to become number two in the internet search derby, though still a long way behind Google's number one position. With so much video content now online, video search is a natural development. According to Suranga Chandratillake, CEO of Blink, a video search engine, "An increasing number of people...are doing video searches to supplement and improve what they do in their offline lives."

Do you need to regrout the tile in your bathroom? There's an online video to show you how. Are you thinking about buying one of the new touch-screen phones? Check out videos on YouTube of the weirdest, best, or even the most expensive models. As YouTube's director of product management Hunter Walk notes, "Video is part of the discovery process. Depending on the user and the type of content, users may want to start with video or text."

Will YouTube be the next Google? Blogger Alex Iskold, founder of internet start-up adaptiveblue.com, says that the "shift toward video will continue, and that young internet users would only accelerate it."

*Source:* Miguel Helft, "Video Search Opens New Frontier on internet." *International Herald Tribune,* January 19, 2009, p. 14.

and bill the customer for the sale. Some such systems now allow companies to engage in **dynamic pricing,** a controversial system that gauges a customer's desire to buy, measures his means, and sets the price accordingly.[24] In this respect, target markets of one are now here, to the chagrin of some consumers!

Another arena where internet transactions are growing in number is internet banking, with or without the banks! From online bill payment to moving money from one account to another, online banking seems here to stay, with its lower costs to handle a transaction (the banks like that) and 24/7 convenience that means the end of "bankers' hours" for consumers. Several new companies are even using web technology to do what banks do, without the bank (see Exhibit 14.10), though most such companies have struggled to date.

## Exhibit 14.10   BORROWERS, LENDERS, AND SOCIAL CAPITAL

Elizabeth Omalla, a widow in Uganda, supports an extended family of 11 by selling fish. Thanks to a microloan from Kiva.com, which she already has repaid, Omalia has expanded the range of fish she offers. According to her blog on Kiva, she has been able to "buy two cows and five goats and open a savings account." In its first five months in business in 2006, Kiva.com enabled 450 entrepreneurs to raise $200,000 in loans.

In the United Kingdom Zopa.com brings together buyers and lenders in a similar online manner. Having raised two rounds of venture capital, Zopa believes its model of internet-based lending that brings

borrowers and lenders together without banks is not only more efficient, but also more satisfying to lenders, since they know what their money is being used for.

The next banking innovation on the horizon is the integration of online banking with mobile phones, making person-to-person payments possible from cell phone to cell phone. Who needs an ATM any more?

*Sources:* Jessi Hempel, "A Little Money Goes a Long Way," *BusinessWeek,* European Edition, July 31, 2006, p. 64; Amy Feldman, "Buddy, Can You E-Mail Me 100 Bucks?" *BusinessWeek* European Edition, November 23, 2009, p. 68. *www.kiva.com; www.zopa.com.*

In Africa, where internet connections are not widespread, but mobile phones are everywhere, the mobile is fast becoming the banking instrument of choice. In Kenya, nearly one-quarter of Safaricom's subscribers use its M-PESA banking service for services ranging from paying a taxi driver to sending money to friends or family. Vodaphone, Safaricom's parent company, has already launched M-PESA in Tanzania and Afghanistan, and other mobile operators offer similar services elsewhere in Africa and in the Philippines.[25] These mobile banking accounts provide Africans, many of whom work in the informal economy and probably have never had a bank account before, with a safe place to keep their money and to transfer it as simply as sending a text message. There's lots of potential for bringing Africa's unbanked into the twenty-first century, banking-wise, since more than $1 trillion in cash currently resides—not very safely—under the mattress or, quite literally, in holes in the ground.[26]

### Applications for Delivering Digital Products

Many companies probably don't give much thought to it, but an increasing array of goods and services can be digitized and thereby delivered to customers via any digital medium, including the internet, satellites, and mobile telephones. More than fifty years ago, the then-current technological miracle was the analog delivery of sounds and images to consumers via the newfangled invention called television. Today, as we have seen earlier in this chapter, books, music, language lessons, and more can be delivered digitally any time, at any digitally connected place. In 2, 5, or 10 years, what else will be digitally deliverable? Psychotherapy, with or without a live therapist, and legal advice are available online from numerous providers.[27] Online postage is available at several websites, including that of the United States Postal Service. And a fast-expanding array of telemedicine applications, some using two-way video, is bringing medical expertise to the most remote places, like oil rigs in the South China Sea. Telemedicine is already a $3.9 billion business that includes hundreds of monitoring applications for smartphones and monitoring devices in homes. It even saves taxpayers money and improves public safety by offering remote diagnosis in prisons.[28]

Audio books, such as Madonna's *Mr. Peabody's Apples* children's book—read by the author herself—and more than 6,000 other downloadable titles, are available from Audible .com and from other sources such as Apple's iTunes online music site.[29] A new joint venture in the publishing industry seeks to put books into customers' hands in audio or printed form, in whole or in part, even when the store is out of stock (see Exhibit 14.11). One new company is even rumored to be developing technology for delivering scents online. Who knows what's next?

### Applications for Customer Service and Support

An increasingly important application on the internet is for various sorts of customer service, replacing more costly—and sometimes more inconsistent and error prone—human support. Companies from Dell to the Denver Zoo use the web to provide answers to frequently asked questions, from technical ones in Dell's case to how to arrange a children's birthday party at the zoo. Savvy marketers know that, for all the hoopla about acquiring new customers, the real driver of the bottom line is the ability to profitably retain existing ones and that effective, responsive customer service is a key ingredient in doing so. They also know that **customer retention** is a competitive necessity. In nearly every industry, some company will soon figure out new ways to exploit the potential of the internet to create value for customers. Without the ability to retain those customers, however, even the best-conceived business model on the web will collapse.

The growing number of web-based customer service applications—from tracking a FedEx parcel online to chat functionality that can access a real person—offers the

## Exhibit 14.11   MULTICHANNEL DELIVERY MAY LET BOOK BUYERS HAVE BOOKS WHEN, WHERE, AND HOW THEY WANT THEM

Peter Osnos is on a mission. The publishing industry veteran thinks readers should be able to read books when and how they choose, whether that means hardcover, digital, audio, print-on-demand, or even a chapter at a time. Osnos has assembled six nonprofit publishers, a few independent booksellers, and the leading U.S. book wholesaler (Ingram) to participate in his Caravan Project. The goal was to publish books in all five formats simultaneously. "We don't have to be big," Osnos notes. "We just have to show that this model is irresistible to everyone in the chain—to authors, publishers, and booksellers."

Are the big publishers concerned? "They are terrified of being Napsterized," says Al Greco, a senior researcher for the Book Industry Study Group, a trade association. But Osnos argues that the book industry would see increased revenue from digital and audio versions, as well as increased efficiency driven by fewer returns of unsold books. In 2005, some 33 percent of adult hardcover books were returned by bookstores to the publishers. The rapidly growing used book market, in which no margins are paid to publishers and no royalties to authors, might be dampened by Osnos's plan. Will it work? "There is no reason for you to go into a store, ask for a book, and not leave with it," he says.

*Source:* Tom Lowry, "Getting Out of a Bind," *BusinessWeek,* April 10, 2006.

tantalizing combination of better service and significant cost savings. The trick is to focus on the customer service benefits first, rather than mere cost cutting. Customers are quick to discern when cost cutting takes precedence over genuine service responsiveness. Does anyone like the way call center software has changed the way consumers obtain phone numbers from directory assistance, or the fact that some banks won't provide bank-by-mail envelopes to those who prefer to do their banking the old-fashioned way?

One myth some companies have bought into is that the internet is a self-service medium. They assume that they can let customers do all the work, but most customers really don't want to do more. One solution is **coproduction,** in which companies carefully consider which burdens they can remove from the customer, using digital technologies, and which customers can perform, assessing costs and benefits to both parties. Doing so can provide insights into new ways to serve customers better, as Charles Schwab has long done when it e-mails customers to alert them to big moves in their stocks.[30]

**STRATEGIC ISSUE**

*One myth that some companies have bought into is that the internet is a self-service medium.*

**Applications for Product Return and Disposal**   Customers' experiences with goods and some services do not end until the products are consumed, returned, or disposed of. Some companies have found ways to use digital technologies to facilitate these processes. Dell, for example, provides an internet space where Dell customers can sell their old computers when they upgrade to a new one. Many companies can avail themselves of similar applications. In retailing, many retailers with both online and offline stores accept returns at any location.

# Developing Digital World Marketing Strategies: The Critical Questions

Knowing what marketing arrows are available in one's digital quiver is one thing. Deciding which of these applications will deliver the best return on investment is quite another. Our flow model of the customer experience process (see again Exhibit 14.7) facilitates such decision making by raising six important questions that should be asked about whether to employ new digital and social networking tools at any or all stages of the process. These six diagnostic questions are shown in Exhibit 14.12. We address each of them in this section.

### Can We Digitize Any or All of the Necessary Flows at Each Stage in the Consumer Experience Process?

At the heart of today's digitally networked world is the reliance on digital means of transmitting *information,* some of which is recomposed into *goods*—CDs, books, and more. In considering whether to employ new digital world technologies at any stage of the consumer experience process, a company should ask whether any of the flows—information, goods or services, or cash—can be digitized.

For cash, the answer is an automatic yes, via credit cards or other forms of electronic payment, except where currency issues pose problems, such as in some international settings. New forms of electronic payment are already enhancing the security of cash flows over the web, and social networks hold the potential to enhance trust in transactions.

For goods and services, the question is more difficult. Text, audio, and visual images (moving or still) can be digitized, as can books, music, photos, and, given enough bandwidth, movies and other videos. But what about the *soft hand* of a cashmere sweater? The *heft and balance* of a carpenter's hammer? The *taste* of fine European chocolate? The *fragrance* of a new cologne? The fit of a sweater offered by an online retailer? Today, these important informational attributes of goods cannot be readily digitized, though one new

## Exhibit 14.12

DIAGNOSTIC QUESTIONS FOR DIGITAL WORLD MARKETING DECISIONS

company is using robotics technology to address the "fit" problem (see Exhibit 14.13). At present, most tangible goods and many services cannot easily be transmitted digitally. For others, however, such as legal advice, therapy for mental health patients, and other goods or services that can adequately be represented in words, sounds, or images, the possibilities are endless. Will technology soon make possible the digital transmission of physical goods? Who knows? When it happens, the many sci-fi buffs around the world will not be surprised! Beam me up, Scotty?[31]

When any of the flows at any stage of the consumer experience process can be digitized, given sufficient information and ingenuity, the remaining questions in Exhibit 14.12 should then be considered to decide whether or not other such applications for a particular flow should be implemented.

### Can We Do So First and/or in a Proprietary Way?

 As we have seen, barriers to entry on the web are low, and most good ideas can be quickly imitated. A key question in deciding whether or not to employ a new digital application is whether one can do so in a proprietary way, thereby deterring imitation, or do so with a sufficient head start so that competitive advantage can be established before others follow. Amazon was early in the internet retailing game and enjoyed a helpful head start.

For bricks-and-mortar companies, using the internet for applications that do not reinvent the heart of the business—for brochureware or customer service, for example—speed to market may or may not be critical, depending on how quickly others in their industry have moved into similar applications. As always, competitor intelligence, some of which can be gleaned from competitors' websites, is essential.

### How Valuable and How Time-Critical Are What Kinds of Information to the Recipient?

For the informational flows in Exhibit 14.7, a key question in making resource deployments is the importance of various kinds of information to the recipient,

---

## Exhibit 14.13    BEER-BELLIED OR TONED: THIS SHIRT'S FOR YOU

Two-thirds of all books and half of all PCs are sold online. For clothing, however, the number is only 8 percent. Why? It's obvious, right? Will the shirt fit? Will I like the fabric? Heikke Haldre and his team at Fits.Me, an Estonian start-up that hopes to take the online apparel business by storm, wants to solve the fit problem once and for all. The customer uncertainty translates into a huge problem for the retailers. Not only must they contend with a return rate that can be 25 percent or more, but many customers simply don't buy if they aren't confident that the shirt will fit.

Haldre's solution? A robotic mannequin that shows the consumer what this particular garment will look like on *his/her* particular body. How? The robot can replicate 2,000 body shapes. When a retailer signs up with Fits.me, they first send in their clothes. Each size is placed on the robot, which then cycles through all the body shapes it knows, while

a camera takes pictures of each permutation. This photographic log is then stored in an online database. Once you go online and type your measurements into the retailer's site, it calls up the photo corresponding to your precise body type and clothing size. "It can be as beer-bellied or gym-toned as you are," says Haldre. "And we can show you how a small versus a medium fits on you, for example."

Getting the male mannequin right took persistence, says Haldre, more than three years of development. The women's version is more difficult, he says. But his engineers are undaunted. As Haldre tells it, "My engineers now have the best job in the world: Studying women's breasts."

*Source:* Cliff Kuang, "Fits.Me's Shape-Shifting Robot Lets You Try on Clothes, Online," *Fast Company Online,* September 27, 2010, *http://www.fastcodesign.com/1662372/fitsme.* For more on Fits.Me, see *http://fits.me/.*

either the company or the customer, depending on the direction of the flow. The more valuable and time-critical the information, the more sensible it may be to invest in digital applications to provide easy, timely, and 24/7 access to those who can benefit from the information. Walmart posts on the web password-protected, up-to-the-minute, store-by-store, SKU-by-SKU sales information that its key suppliers can access, thereby enabling them to better ensure that Walmart's stores remain in stock on their merchandise.

### Can Digital and Social Networking Tools Reach and Build Relationships with Customers in the Target Market?

Making information, goods, or services available on the web is of little use if the people to whom those flows are directed lack web access. As we have seen, some groups are underrepresented on the internet. For example, people and businesses in some parts of the developing world are underrepresented. Applications that make the most business sense will be those targeting groups for whom use of the web is relatively widespread.

Simply *reaching* customers with digital tools may not be enough, however, especially for marketers of commodity-like products. Going beyond reach to build mutually beneficial *relationships* may be what is needed. Facebook hopes to develop a significant role here. Amazon has built loyal relationships with its customer base by focusing its efforts on exceptional customer service. While book lovers can often find books for lower prices elsewhere, many of them simply return to Amazon's site, with its easy 1-Click® ordering, customer reviews, and other customer-friendly features. Using the latest tools for building customer relationships may be these tools' most important application in the long run.

### Are New Economy Tools Measurably Effective and Efficient Compared to Other Solutions?

Ultimately, given favorable answers to the first four questions in this section, deciding to invest in a particular digital or social networking strategy or application comes down to two final questions. Is the new solution effective, and is it more efficient than other solutions? UPS was able to sell e-tailer SmartHome on its shipping because it was not only effective in getting SmartHome's parcels to their destinations on time, but also because SmartHome was able to improve on and save money on customer service at the same time, thanks to UPS links on the SmartHome site that sharply reduced customer service calls.[32]

**STRATEGIC ISSUE**

*Deciding to invest in a particular digital marketing strategy or application comes down to two final questions. Is the new solution effective, and is it more efficient than other solutions?*

Marketers' concerns over the effectiveness and efficiency of their websites have led to the development of web analytics, software solutions that monitor and summarize website usage patterns (see Exhibit 14.14). Web analytics technology is the equivalent of having a team of marketing researchers follow customers through a bricks-and-mortar retail store. The technology can uncover a variety of problems that can plague websites: cumbersome navigation, content that can't be easily found, underperforming search engine strategies, and unprofitable online marketing partnerships. The results of these analyses can improve customer satisfaction and response to the website, strengthen the marketer's hand in negotiating terms of partnership deals, and even identify new market segments that might be best served with tailored sites. "There are a lot of data flowing through companies," says Kate Delhagen, retail research director at Forrester Research, "but a lot of it is minutiae."[33] Deciding what metrics are the most important—to assess customer behavior on the site, not just traffic—is key.

For companies transacting business on the web, a particularly important issue is what Saul Klein of Index Ventures calls "the leaky bucket" issue. In Klein's view, at the top of the funnel is somebody visiting your site, while out the bottom end comes a completed

**Exhibit 14.14   WEB OPTIMIZATION CREATES A UTAH-BASED HIGH FLYER**

"Where," you probably wouldn't bother to ask, "is the fastest-growing publicly traded software company based?" Orem, Utah, might not come to mind. Omniture's web optimization software, which sits on the computers of more than 2,000 of the world's largest corporations—including Microsoft, Walmart, and Toyota—is revolutionizing how companies measure their websites' performance. Take Harrah's Hotels & Resorts, for example, long a measurement disciple. Harrah's used to pay an ad agency to manage the more than 70,000 keywords that it bids on every day from Yahoo!, Google, and other search engines. It needed

several software programs to analyze the results. No more. Omniture shows Harrah's not only how many clicks each search ad generates, but also the conversion rate—the number of consumers who actually buy based on a search ad. "It has dramatically changed the funding for each of the keywords and categories we buy," says Greg Johnston, Harrah's e-commerce director. "We are saving hundreds of thousands of dollars."

*Source:* Spencer E. Ante, "A Radar Screen for E-biz," *Business-Week*, European Edition, April 30, 2007, pp. 68–70. For more on Omniture, see www.omniture.com/en/.

transaction. The trick is to systematically measure the points where potential customers drop off without making a purchase, and then find ways to keep more of them in the funnel until they buy and pay. Kevin Cornils, CEO of spectacles e-tailer Glasses Direct discovered an even bigger benefit of tracking customer activity in his company's funnel. "The initial role was to try to save some of those customers, but it is actually making the business a lot better at being customer-focused for the long term," he says.[34]

In the final analysis, setting SMART objectives that the latest tools or activities are intended to meet—specific, measurable, attainable, relevant, and timebound—and running cost-benefit analyses to assess their likely performance are necessary for making go/no-go decisions and for prioritizing which initiatives should be pursued first. Fortunately, the inherent measurability of many of these tools often provides clear and compelling feedback on whether they are meeting the objectives. In addition, attention must be given to a variety of business process issues that can get in the way of effective execution of even the best intentions for a digital world strategy in an old-economy company. Avoiding these errors is easier said than done, of course, but web analytics can help catch any errors that are made.

## Managing Digitally Networked Strategies: The Talent Gap

Setting out the opportunities that new digitally-networked technologies provide—for almost any company, of any size, in any industry, anywhere—is easy, relatively speaking, as is providing conceptual frameworks for thinking about the issues and trade-offs involved. A much more difficult challenge is finding the people to manage and lead the necessary efforts and initiatives in this complex and rapidly changing arena, especially when it comes to marketing, rather than purely technological issues. Observers note that the shelf life of chief marketing officers (CMOs) is short—a mere 26 months, on average, according to a recent study—much shorter on average than that for CEOs, CFOs, or CIOs.[35]

While marketers confronted with a bewildering array of new media possibilities and consumers—thanks to the digital revolution—are better informed than ever, Wall Street wants results, quarter after quarter. "It makes for a deadly cocktail of high expectations, resistance, and complexity," says Mark Jarvis, CMO at Dell since October 2007.[36] John Costello, now CEO at Zounds, a hearing aid manufacturer—and a former CMO at Home Depot, Sears, and Yahoo!—adds, "CMOs have almost everyone second-guessing (them) and looking over their shoulder."

As Sean Meehan, a marketing professor at IMD business school in Switzerland notes, "The marketing playbook is the same playbook it always was, it's just that there are new tools and they're very powerful tools in terms of reach. And if you use them well, you will learn more about your served community. But if you misuse it, you can blow it completely."[37]

Several years ago, the CMO's job was much more straightforward than it is today: develop the brand's positioning, hire an ad agency to create great ads, and manage the promotional budget. If the campaign hit the mark, it was bonus time. If not, out the door you went. But how does a typical senior marketing executive in his or her 40s or 50s know what do with today's dizzying array of new media and new tools, most of which didn't even exist when he or she was learning the business? Blogs, search engine optimization, social networking, mobile advertising, and more; and never mind figuring out what's cool in the mind of tomorrow's consumer, much less today's.

As Wharton marketing professor Patti Williams points out, "It's not clear how Crest should leverage search advertising. How many people are going online to search for toothpaste?"[38] Then there's the difficulty of reaching a wide audience with many of today's highly targeted tools as well as figuring out how to buy the new media efficiently. A marketing executive at a large advertiser such as Procter & Gamble, Diageo, or Toyota might, as Wharton's Dave Reibstein notes, think all this sounds like great stuff, "but I would have to deal with 10,000 of you. I would need a manager to manage this interface and that becomes an overwhelming task. It takes a village of these (focused audiences) before we can have impact."[39]

Finally, there's the fact that changing habits is never easy, for marketers or anyone else. "In many cases, institutionalized cultures, agency relationships, and media relationships are still limiting them," says Donovan Neale-May, executive director of the CMO council, a trade group for marketing executives.[40] Thus, perhaps it is not surprising that younger companies without long histories of traditional advertising, as well as web-based businesses, are adopting these new digital strategies much faster than larger and older firms. Chris Moloney, CMO of Scottrade, an internet stock brokerage, thinks part of the problem is generational. He thinks about half of today's CMOs are extremely knowledgeable about the internet and what it offers.[41] Half are not.

The good news in all of this is that today's web-savvy, well-educated marketing graduates have much to bring to the table in the companies they join. Getting a grasp of how the digitally networked world really works, along with some experience in an internship or other work setting, may be a great way to jump-start one's marketing career, and having grown up as a digital denizen surely doesn't hurt!

## Developing Strategies to Serve Digital and Social Networking Markets

This chapter has, for the most part, addressed how companies of any kind, size, industry, or age can use digital and social networking tools and technologies for marketing purposes. No doubt, however, there are readers who see bigger fish to fry in the digital skillet. They see this arena as offering the prospect for starting an entrepreneurial venture, in a new firm or within an existing one, to serve a market created by the advent of social networking, the internet, wireless telephony, or other new or still-emerging digital technologies. Thus, we close the chapter with a brief look at some of the issues involved in serving the new markets created by the digital networking revolution.

## Serving the Dot-Com Markets of Tomorrow

What might tomorrow's entrepreneurs do to craft marketing strategies to serve new markets—like the one for apps—in our increasingly digitally networked world? For one, would-be internet or social networking entrepreneurs should consider the various ways in which revenue can be generated on the web or in other settings such as mobile phones. Unless someone, a business or a consumer, is eventually willing to fork over money for what a new business offers, its chances for success lie somewhere between slim and none. The rush to create new social networking sites, following the success of Facebook and YouTube in the United States and Friends Reunited in the United Kingdom, Bebo in Europe, and others like them elsewhere, raises exactly this question. Thus, understanding one's **revenue model** and being willing to change it as market and technological conditions warrant are essential.

Next, such entrepreneurs must ask not what can I sell but what do today's and tomorrow's customers need, and how and where might they want to consume what I have to offer? From business-to-business (Grainger.com), to business-to-consumer (Amazon or LandsEnd.com), to consumer-to-consumer (eBay.com), to consumer-to-business-(Priceline.com) models, there's no limit to the ways in which companies can provide better, easier, faster, or cheaper solutions using these tools and technologies. If a particular business idea does not fill some real, though perhaps currently latent, need identified by these questions, however, there is no viable business.

Finally, would-be entrepreneurs must now realize that barriers to entry are incredibly low in this new world. For everyone who has the next latest and greatest web-based idea, there are dozens of other prospective entrepreneurs likely to be exploring similar ideas concurrently. It's not really the ideas that count. What matters is the team that will execute an idea to deliver the performance and value that customers, whether businesses or consumers, want and will pay for. Only then are most investors likely to part with their money.

Thus, execution is key, a truism we explore in greater depth in Chapters 17 and 18. As Intel's Andy Grove said at the turn of the 21st century about building the next wave of (it is hoped successful) internet businesses, "It's work. Very unglamorous work.... The heavy lifting is still ahead of us."[42] Much of this work is of the kind set forth in the earlier chapters of this book: understanding customers and the markets they make up, understanding industries and the competitors that daily do battle in them, and developing marketing programs that can establish and maintain sustainable competitive advantage.

But there's also the work of developing marketing strategies well suited to the market and competitive conditions that currently prevail in one's industry and implementing those strategies. In this chapter, we've explored the digitally networked world and how both existing and new firms can find ways—measured in terms of effectiveness and efficiency— to take advantage of the promise it offers. In the chapters that remain, we examine strategies for the various stages of the product life cycle and how best to organize for the effective implementation of, and monitor the results generated by, these strategies. "Give me 'A' execution of a 'B' plan over 'B' execution of an 'A' plan" is a common refrain heard from venture capitalists and other investors. Planning is important. But effective execution delivers the results, and results are what count.

# TAKE-AWAYS

1. Today's digitally networked world offers powerful new tools for marketers—not to mention opportunities for entrepreneurs—from social networks to apps plus many more. Their power and ubiquity demands that virtually every company needs a social media strategy today.

2. Seven potentially attractive elements characterize many technologies in today's digitally networked world: the syndication of information, the increasing returns to scale of network products, the ability to efficiently personalize and customize market offerings, the ability to disintermediate distribution, global reach, 24/7 access, and the possibility of instantaneous delivery.

3. First-mover advantage is simply wrong. Best beats first.

4. Most observers now believe that the internet is better suited for delivering measurable marketing results—as is direct marketing—than for brand building.

5. Web-based customer service applications offer the tantalizing combination of better service and significant cost savings. The trick, of course, is to focus on the customer service benefits first, rather than mere cost cutting, since customers are quick to discern when cost cutting takes precedence over genuine service responsiveness.

6. Keys to success in tomorrow's digital world ventures include clearly understanding one's business model (Exactly where will revenue come from: commerce, content, community, or infrastructure?), filling real (though perhaps latent) customer needs, and putting together the right management team that can deliver the performance and value that customers want and will pay for. Only then will investors part with their money.

**Self-diagnostic questions to test your ability to apply the analytical tools and concepts in this chapter to marketing decision making may be found at this book's website at www.mhhe.com/mullins8e.**

# ENDNOTES

1. This material is drawn from Joseph Menn, Richard Waters, and Alan Rappeport, "Amazon Launches Android App Store," *Financial Times,* March 23, 2011, p. 24; Douglas MacMillen, Peter Burrows, and Spencer E. Ante, "The App Economy," *BusinessWeek* European Edition, November 2, 2009, pp. 4–49; Peter Burrows, "Innovator: Omar Hamoui," *Bloomberg Businessweek* European Edition, May 3–9, 2010; Jessi Hempel, "Web 2.0 Is So Over. Welcome to Web 3.0," *Fortune* European Edition, January 19, 2009, p. 27; and Daya Baran, "Buffett Warns of Bubble in Social Networking IPOs," *www.webguild.org,* March 28, 2011.

2. "Days of Double Digit Growth in Social Network Users Are Over," *eMarketer Daily Newsletter,* March 18, 2011.

3. "Broadband Users," CMP TechWeb.

4. Joseph B. White, "What Works?" *The Wall Street Journal,* October 23, 2000, p. R4.

5. This section is based on Kevin Werbach, "Syndication: The Emerging Model for Business in the Internet Era," *Harvard Business Review,* May–June 2000, pp. 85–93.

6. "Mandarin 2.0: How Skype, Podcasts, and Broadband Are Transforming Language Teaching," *The Economist,* June 9, 2007, p. 75.

7. This section is based on Thomas Petzinger, Jr., "So Long, Supply and Demand," *The Wall Street Journal,* January 1, 2000; and W. Brian Arthur, *Increasing Returns and Path Dependence in the Economy* (Ann Arbor, MI: University of Michigan Press, 1994).

8. "Everywhere and Nowhere: Social Networking Will Become a Ubiquitous Feature of Online Life, That Does Not Mean It Is a Business," *The Economist,* March 22, 2008, pp. 81–82.

9. Timothy J. Mullaney, "Jewelry Heist," *BusinessWeek,* May 10, 2004, pp. 82–83.

10. Windsor Genova, "E-books Outsells Paperbacks, Hardcovers in February," *All Headline News,* April 18, 2011, *http://www.allheadlinenews.com/articles/90045414?E-books%20outsells%20paperbacks%2C%20hardcovers%20in%20February.*

11. Apple, Inc., Form 10-Q for the quarterly period ended March 26, 2011.

12. Much of this section is based on Jim Collins, "Best Beats First," *Inc.,* August 2000, pp. 48–51.

13. Ibid., p. 48.

14. Ibid., p. 49.

15. For a broader look at internet marketing, see Ward Hanson and Kirthi Kalyanam, *Internet Marketing and E-Commerce* (Cincinnati: South-Western College Publishing, 2006).

16. Chris Warren, "Damage Control," *American Way,* April 1, 2011.

17. Zoomerang.com is one commonly used provider, with over 2 million survey respondents in its database.

18. Deborah L. Vence, "In an Instant," *Marketing News,* March 1, 2006, p. 53.

19. Joel Rubinson, "Online Marketing Research: It Was the Best of Times, It Was the Worst of Times," *Fast Company,* October 8, 2009, at *http://www.fastcompany.com/blog/joel-rubinson/brave-new-marketing/online-marketing-research-it-was-best-times-it-was-worst-time.*

20. Brad Stone and Douglas MacMillan, "Are Four Words Worth $25 Billion?" *Bloomberg Businessweek* European Edition, March 21–27, 2011.

21. "Groupon Anxiety," *The Economist,* March 19, 2011, p. 64; Brad Stone and Douglas MacMillan, "Are Four Words Worth $25 Billion?" *Bloomberg Businessweek* European Edition, March 21–27, 2011.

22. Peter Burrows, "Innovator: Omar Hamoui," *Bloomberg Businessweek* European Edition, May 3–9, 2010.

**23.** David Gelles, "Innovation Brings a Touch of Class to Online Shopping," *Financial Times,* June 14, 2010.

**24.** David Streitfeld, "On the Web, Price Tags Blur," *The Washington Post Online,* www.washingtonpost.com/wp-dyn/articles/A 15159-2000Sep25.html.

**25.** "The Meek Shall Inherit the Web," *The Economist Technology Quarterly,* September 16, 2008, pp. 3–4.

**26.** Alex Halperin, "Mobile Money," *Fortune,* International Edition, January 21, 2008, p. 8.

**27.** Rochelle Sharpe, "The Virtual Couch," *BusinessWeek e.biz,* September 18, 2000, pp. EB 135–37; and Richard B. Schmitt, "Lawyers vs. the internet," *The Wall Street Journal,* July 17, 2000, p. B12.

**28.** Milt Freudenheim, "You Can't Get to a Doctor's Office? Now It's Only a Few Keystrokes Away," *International Herald Tribune,* May 31, 2010, p. 15.

**29.** Jeffrey A. Trachtenberg, "A New Chapter Online," *The Wall Street Journal Europe,* March 22, 2004, p. A11.

**30.** Youngme Moon and Frances X. Frei, "Exploding the Self-Service Myth," *Harvard Business Review,* May–June 2000, pp. 26–27.

**31.** From the science fiction movie *Star Trek,* in which it was routine to digitally transmit objects, including people, from place to place.

**32.** Charles Haddad, "Big Brown's Coup," *BusinessWeek e.biz,* September 18, 2000, pp. EB 76–77.

**33.** Michael Totty, "So Much Information …," *The Wall Street Journal Europe,* December 13–15, 2002, p. R3.

**34.** Jonathan Moules, "Observe, Measure, Respond: The Keys to Web Selling," *Financial Times FT Weekend,* June 26–27, 2010, pp. 30–31.

**35.** David Kiley and Burt Helm, "The Short Life of the Chief Marketing Officer," *BusinessWeek,* European Edition, December 10, 2007, pp. 63–65.

**36.** Ibid.

**37.** Beth Gardiner, "Business Schools Tackle Social Media," *The Wall Street Journal* European Edition, December 7, 2010, p. 27.

**38.** "If Online Marketing Is the Future, Why Are Some CMOs Stuck in the Past?" *Knowledge@Wharton,* February 26, 2008, *http://knowledge .wharton.upenn.edu/article.cfm?articleid=1892.*

**39.** Ibid.

**40.** Ibid.

**41.** Ibid.

**42.** Jerry Useem, "What Have We Learned?" *Fortune,* October 30, 2000, pp. 82–104.

# CHAPTER FIFTEEN

# Strategies for New and Growing Markets

## Canon, Inc.—Success That Is Hard to Copy[1]

EVEN BEFORE THE GLOBAL ECONOMIC slump of 2008 and the devastating earthquake and tsunami of 2011, Japan's economy had suffered through four recessions during the 1990s and the early years of this century. Consequently, many Japanese manufacturers—even some of the largest global competitors—struggled to remain profitable and survive. However, a few firms not only survived but grew and prospered in spite of the difficult domestic market environment. Canon, Inc., is one of those stellar performers. From 2000 on, the company delivered seven straight years of record annual sales and profits and averaged a 16 percent return on equity. Unfortunately, the worldwide recession of 2008 brought that string of performance records to an end, but Canon still managed to earn $4.4 billion on net sales of $42 billion in 2010.

How has Canon managed to wring so much money out of its copiers, printers, and cameras when other Japanese electronics firms have floundered? For one thing, Fujio Mitarai, the firm's CEO, has been willing to adopt some Western cost-cutting practices he learned during the 23 years he worked for Canon in America. First, he narrowed the company's strategic scope by concentrating on a few product markets where the firm had an established market presence and superior technological capabilities, while abandoning other businesses where it had a weaker competitive position, such as personal computers and liquid-crystal displays. Mr. Mitarai also scrapped the assembly lines

in all of Canon's Japanese plants, replacing them with small work teams—or "cells"—of about six employees who do the work of about 30 workers under the old system. These self-managed cells have not only reduced Canon's labor costs but enabled the firm to cut its inventory of component parts by 30 percent and to close 20 of its 34 warehouses.

But a sharper market focus and increased manufacturing efficiency are not sufficient to explain the firm's strong performance. Other Japanese electronics firms have copied such cost-cutting actions without duplicating Canon's results. A second important strategic thrust underlying Canon's success is a heavy emphasis on developing and marketing a stream of new products, product improvements, and line extensions in order to sustain a leading share position in its core businesses.

As a first step toward implementing this product development strategy, the company plows more than 8 percent of its total revenues back into product R&D. Some of that investment is targeted at continued improvement of Canon's offerings in businesses where it already holds a dominant market share. For instance, Canon's technical leadership has enabled it to maintain a 60 percent share of the global market for the core engines used to power laser printers, including printers developed through an alliance with Hewlett-Packard. In other cases, Canon's development efforts focus on innovative new-to-the-world products, like the development of a digital radiography system or an advanced diagmatic imaging technology, which the firm hopes will enable detection of metabolic changes in patients and thus facilitate early diagnosis of disease. And sometimes the firm simply modifies existing products or technologies to better serve new application segments, such as developing a wide-format bubble-jet printer for use in the commercial printing industry.

Of course, it is one thing to develop a bunch of new products on the cutting edge of technology, but making potential customers aware of those new products and their benefits—and actually generating sales revenues—requires effective and well-funded marketing and sales efforts as well. Consequently, Canon has restructured its global sales and marketing organization in recent years to decentralize decision making and make its marketing plans better adapted to local market conditions. This is particularly critical because the firm earns more than 80 percent of its sales revenues in markets outside of Japan. For example, the company established Canon Europe Ltd. in the United Kingdom to help coordinate regional marketing efforts and strengthen its sales network in the European Union, which is now the company's largest market in terms of revenue.

# Marketing Challenges Addressed in Chapter 15

Canon's success illustrates several important points about new product and market development. First, both sales growth and cost cutting can help improve profits. But while it is often easier to cut costs in the short term, revenue growth—particularly growth generated by the development of innovative new products—can have a bigger impact on a firm's profitability and shareholder value over the long haul. This point is confirmed by a study of 847 large corporations conducted by Mercer Management Consulting. The authors found that the compound annual growth rate in the market value of companies that achieved higher-than-average profit growth but lower revenue growth than their industry's average—companies that increased profits mostly by cutting costs, in other words—was 11.6 percent from 1989 to 1992. By contrast, companies that achieved higher-than-average profits as the result of higher-than-average revenue growth saw their market value jump at an annual rate double that—23.5 percent.[2]

Canon's history also illustrates that new product introductions can involve products that differ in their degree of newness from the perspective of the company and its customers. Some of the products developed by the firm, such as its first office copier, presented a new technical challenge to the company but did not seem very innovative to potential customers who viewed the copiers merely as simpler and cheaper versions of Xerox's machines. But some of the firm's new product introductions—such as its digital radiology system—were truly innovations that were new to potential customers and the company alike.

In Chapter 10 we focused on the problems and processes involved in developing and evaluating product offerings that are *new to the company*. The first part of this chapter examines marketing strategies and programs appropriate for developing markets for offerings that are *new to the target customers*. Our primary focus is on programs used by the pioneer firm—or first entrant—into a particular product-market. Being the pioneer gains a firm a number of potential competitive advantages, but it also involves some major risks. Some pioneers capitalize on their early advantage and maintain a leading market share of the product category, earning substantial revenues and profits, well into the later stages of the product's life cycle.

Other pioneers are less successful. While Canon has pioneered some new product categories, for instance, it has not always ended up as the share leader in those categories as they grew and matured. In some cases this was a consequence of Canon's strategy of withdrawing from markets where it could not sustain superior technical expertise, as in the case of liquid-crystal displays. But in other cases, followers have overtaken the pioneer by offering better products, superior customer service, or lower prices. This leads to an interesting strategic question: Is it usually better for a firm to bear the high costs and risks of being the pioneer in hopes of maintaining a profitable position as the market grows or to be a follower that watches for possible design or marketing mistakes by the pioneer before joining the fray with its own entry? We examine this question in the next section.

Not all pioneers are intent on remaining the overall share leader as the market grows. Some adopt a niche market strategy geared to making substantial profits from specialized market segments where they will face fewer large competitors. Others—like Canon—try to stay one jump ahead of the competition by introducing a constant stream of new products and withdrawing from older markets as they become more competitive. Which strategy is best? It depends on the firm's resources and competencies, the strength of likely future competitors, and characteristics of the product and its target market. Therefore, we will examine some alternative strategies that might be adopted by a pioneer and the situations where each makes the most sense.

Finally, we'll examine how marketing strategies change as the product moves from the introductory to the growth stage of its life cycle. How should the pioneer adjust its strategy to maintain its position as market leader when new competitors arrive on the scene? And what marketing programs might those late-arriving followers employ to successfully challenge an entrenched market leader? We'll examine the strategic alternatives available to both parties—and the market and competitive conditions that make some of those alternatives more viable than others—in the last part of the chapter.

## How New Is New?

A survey of the new product development practices of 700 U.S. corporations conducted by the consulting firm of Booz, Allen & Hamilton found that the products introduced by those firms over a five-year period were not all equally "new." The study identified six categories of new products based on their degree of newness as perceived by both the company and the target customers. These categories are discussed below and diagrammed in Exhibit 15.1, which also indicates the percentage of new entries falling in each category during the five-year study period. Notice that only 10 percent of all new product introductions fell into the new-to-the-world category.[3]

- *New-to-the-world products*—True innovations that are new to the firm and create an entirely new market (10 percent).
- *New product lines*—A product category that is new for the company introducing it, but not new to customers in the target market because of the existence of one or more competitive brands (20 percent).
- *Additions to existing product lines*—New items that supplement a firm's established product line. These items may be moderately new to both the firm and the customers in its established product-markets. They may also serve to expand the market segments appealed to by the line (26 percent).

# Exhibit 15.1

CATEGORIES OF NEW PRODUCTS DEFINED ACCORDING TO THEIR DEGREE OF NEWNESS TO THE COMPANY
AND CUSTOMERS IN THE TARGET MARKET

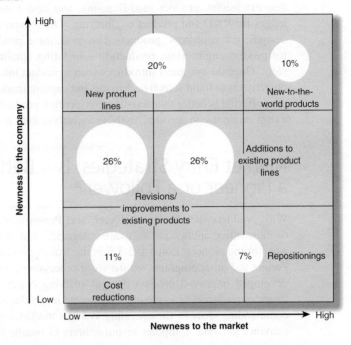

Source: *New Products Management for the 1980s* (New York: Booz, Allen & Hamilton, 1982). Used
by permission.

- *Improvements in or revisions of existing products*—Items providing improved performance
  or greater perceived value brought out to replace existing products. These items may present
  moderately new marketing and production challenges to the firm, but unless they represent a
  technologically new generation of products, customers are likely to perceive them as similar
  to the products they replace (26 percent).
- *Repositionings*—Existing products that are targeted at new applications and new market segments (7 percent).
- *Cost reductions*—Product modifications providing similar performance at lower cost (11 percent).

A product's degree of newness—to the company, its target customers, or both—helps
determine the amount of complexity and uncertainty involved in the engineering, operations, and marketing tasks necessary to make it a successful new entry. It also contributes
to the amount of risk inherent in those tasks.

Introducing a product that is new to both the firm and target customers requires the
greatest expenditure of effort and resources. It also involves the greatest amount of uncertainty and risk of failure because of the lack of information and experience with the technology and the target customers.

Products new to target customers but not new to the firm (such as line extensions or
modifications aimed at new customer segments or repositionings of existing products) are
often not very innovative in design or operations, but they may present a great deal of marketing uncertainty. The marketing challenge here—as with new-to-the-world products—is

to build **primary demand,** making target customers aware of the product and convincing them to adopt it.[4] We investigate this marketing problem in the first half of this chapter.

Finally, products new to the company but not to the market (such as new product lines, line extensions, product modifications, and cost reductions) often present fewer challenges for R&D and product engineering. The company can study and learn from earlier designs or competitors' products. However, these products can present major challenges for process engineering, production scheduling, quality control, and inventory management. Once the company introduces such a product into the market, its primary marketing objective is to build selective demand and capture market share, convincing customers the new offering is better than existing competitive products. We discuss marketing programs a firm might use to accomplish these objectives later in this chapter.

## Market Entry Strategies: Is it Better to Be a Pioneer or a Follower?

With products such as Word, Excel, and Powerpoint, Microsoft holds a leading share of most office application software categories. But in most of those categories, the firm was not the pioneer. Lotus 1-2-3 was the leading spreadsheet for many years, and Word-Perfect and other programs led the word processing category. But as a follower, Microsoft developed improved product designs offering better performance, and it had superior financial resources to aggressively promote its products. Microsoft's Windows also held a commanding share of the operating systems market, a position the firm could leverage to convince personal computer manufacturers to bundle its applications software with their machines.

On the other hand, some of the software industry's pioneers have not fared so well in the marketplace. Lotus, for example, experienced financial difficulties and was ultimately acquired by IBM. While we have stressed the competitive importance of growth via the introduction of new products, the important strategic question is whether it always makes sense to go first. Or do *both* pioneer and follower market entry strategies have some particular advantages under different conditions?

## Pioneer Strategy

Conventional wisdom holds that although they take the greatest risks and probably experience more failures than their more conservative competitors, successful pioneers are handsomely rewarded. It is assumed competitive advantages inherent in being the first to enter a new product-market can be sustained through the growth stage and into the maturity stage of the product life cycle, resulting in a strong share position and substantial returns.

Some of the potential sources of competitive advantage available to pioneers are briefly summarized in Exhibit 15.2 and discussed below.[5]

1. *First choice of market segments and positions.* The pioneer has the opportunity to develop a product offering with attributes most important to the largest segment of customers or to promote the importance of attributes that favor its brand. Thus, the pioneer's brand can become the standard of reference customers use to evaluate other brands. This can make it more difficult for followers with me-too products to convince existing customers that their new brands are superior to the older and more familiar pioneer. If the pioneer has successfully tied its offering to the choice criteria of the largest group of customers, it also becomes more difficult for followers to differentiate their offerings in ways that are attractive to the mass-market segment. They may have to target a smaller peripheral segment or niche instead.

# Exhibit 15.2

POTENTIAL ADVANTAGES OF PIONEER AND FOLLOWER STRATEGIES

**Pioneer**

- First choice of segments and positions; influence on customer choice criteria
- Pioneer defines the rules of the game
- Distribution advantages
- Economies of scale and experience
- High switching costs for early adopters
- Possibility of positive network effects
- Possibility of preempting scarce resources

**Follower**

- Ability to take advantage of pioneer's positioning mistakes
- Ability to take advantage of pioneer's product mistakes
- Ability to take advantage of pioneer's marketing mistakes
- Ability to take advantage of the latest technology
- Ability to take advantage of pioneer's limited resources

2. *The pioneer defines the rules of the game.* The pioneer's actions on such variables as product quality, price, distribution, warranties, postsale service, and promotional appeals and budgets set standards that subsequent competitors must meet or beat. If the pioneer sets those standards high enough, it can raise the costs of entry and perhaps preempt some potential competitors.[6]

3. *Distribution advantages.* The pioneer has the most options in designing a distribution channel to bring the new product to market. This is particularly important for industrial goods where, if the pioneer exercises its options well and with dispatch, it should end up with a network of the best distributors. This can exclude later entrants from some markets. Distributors are often reluctant to take on second or third brands. This is especially true when the product is technically complex and the distributor must carry large inventories of the product and spare parts or invest in specialized training and service.

   For consumer package goods, it is more difficult to slow the entry of later competitors by preempting distribution alternatives. Nevertheless, the pioneer can often attain more shelf-facings in retail stores than followers. And as many retailers are reducing the number of brands they carry in a given product category to speed inventory turnover and reduce costs, it is becoming more difficult for followers with unfamiliar brands and small market shares to gain extensive distribution.[7]

4. *Economies of scale and experience.* Being first means the pioneer can gain accumulated volume and experience and thereby lower per unit costs at a faster rate than followers. This advantage is particularly pronounced when the product is technically sophisticated and involves high development costs or when its life cycle is likely to be short, with sales increasing rapidly during the introduction and early growth stages.

   As we shall see later, the pioneer can deploy these cost advantages in a number of ways to protect its early lead against followers. One strategy is to lower price, which can discourage followers from entering the market because it raises the volume necessary for them to break even. Or the pioneer might invest its savings in additional marketing efforts to expand its penetration of the market, such as heavier advertising, a larger salesforce, or continuing product improvements or line extensions.

5. *High switching costs for early adopters.* Customers who are early to adopt a pioneer's new product may be reluctant to change suppliers when competitive products appear. This is particularly true for industrial goods where the costs of switching suppliers can be high. Compatible equipment and spare parts, investments in employee training, and the risks of lower product quality or customer service make it easier for the pioneer to retain its early customers over time.

   In some cases, however, switching costs can work against the pioneer and in favor of followers. A pioneer may have trouble converting customers to a new technology if they must bear high switching costs to abandon their old way of doing things. Pioneers in the development of music CDs, for instance, faced the formidable task of convincing potential buyers to abandon their substantial investments in turntables and LP record libraries and to start all over again with the new technology. Once the pioneers had begun to convince consumers that the superior convenience, sound quality, and durability of CDs justified those high switching costs, however, demand for CDs and CD players began to grow rapidly and it was easier for followers to attract customers.

6. *Possibility of positive network effects.* The value of some kinds of goods and services to an individual customer increases as greater numbers of other people adopt the product and the network of users grows larger. Economists say that such products exhibit **network externalities** or **positive network effects.** Information and communications technologies, such as wireless phones, fax machines, computer software, e-mail, and many internet sites, are particularly likely to benefit from network effects.[8] For instance, the value of eBay as an auction site increases as the number of potential buyers and sellers who visit and trade on the site increase.

If the pioneer in such a product or service category can gain and maintain a substantial customer base before competing technologies or providers appear on the market, the positive network effects generated by that customer base will enhance the benefits of the pioneer's offering and make it more difficult for followers to match its perceived value. And recent research suggests that the positive impacts of such network effects on pioneer survival and economic success are enhanced when the new products involved are relatively radical and technologically advanced.[9]

On the other hand, for the digital new products and services most likely to benefit from positive network effects, some of the other potential first-mover advantages may not be as relevant. For instance, because of the relatively modest fixed costs and low marginal costs of producing digitized information products like software and music, pioneers are unlikely to benefit from substantial economies of scale.[10]

7. *Possibility of preempting scarce resources and suppliers.* The pioneer may be able to negotiate favorable deals with suppliers who are eager for new business or who do not appreciate the size of the opportunity for their raw materials or component parts. If later entrants subsequently find those materials and components in short supply, they may be constrained from expanding as fast as they might like or be forced to pay premium prices. For example, Apple computer was able to absorb more than half the entire production of Toshiba's innovative 1.8-inch hard disk; a crucial component of its iPod digital music player. As a result, competitors had difficulty matching the small size and simplicity of Apple's product for several years until Toshiba was able to expand production capacity and other producers—like Hitachi—developed similar hard drives.[11]

# Not All Pioneers Capitalize on Their Potential Advantages

There is some evidence to suggest that the above advantages can help pioneers gain and maintain a competitive edge in new markets. For instance, some research has found that surviving pioneers hold a significantly larger average market share when their industries reach maturity than firms that were either fast followers or late entrants in the product category.[12]

On the other hand, some pioneers fail. They either abandon the product category, go out of business, or get acquired before their industry matures. One study, which took these failed pioneers into account and averaged their performance together with that of the more successful survivors, found that pioneers overall did not perform as well over the long haul as followers.[13] However, a more recent study suggests that—in industrial goods industries, at least—pioneers have substantially better 10-year survival rates than followers.[14]

Of course, volume and market share are not the only dimensions on which success can be measured. Unfortunately, there is little evidence concerning the effect of the timing of a firm's entry into a new market on its ultimate profitability in that market or the value generated for shareholders.[15]

In view of the mixed research evidence, then, it seems reasonable to conclude that while a pioneer may have some *potential* competitive advantages, not all pioneers are successful at capitalizing on them. Some fail during the introductory or shakeout stages of their industries' life cycles. And those that survive may lack the resources to keep up with rapid growth or the competencies needed to maintain their early lead in the face of onslaughts by strong followers.

## Follower Strategy

In many cases a firm becomes a follower by default. It is simply beaten to a new product-market by a quicker competitor. But even when a company has the capability of being the first mover, the above observations suggest there may be some advantages to letting other firms go first into a product-market.[16] Let the pioneer shoulder the initial risks while the followers observe their shortcomings and mistakes. Possible advantages of such a follower strategy are briefly summarized in Exhibit 15.2 and discussed below.

1. *Ability to take advantage of the pioneer's positioning mistakes.* If the pioneer misjudges the preferences and purchase criteria of the mass-market segment or attempts to satisfy two or more segments at once, it is vulnerable to the introduction of more precisely positioned products by a follower. By tailoring its offerings to each distinct segment, the follower(s) can successfully encircle the pioneer.

2. *Ability to take advantage of the pioneer's product mistakes.* If the pioneer's initial product has technical limitations or design flaws, the follower can benefit by overcoming these weaknesses. Even when the pioneering product is technically satisfactory, a follower may gain an advantage through product enhancements. For example, the iPhone's sleek design, innovative software, and functionality enabled Apple to capture a substantial share of the global mobile phone market from well-established competitors like Nokia and Motorola.

3. *Ability to take advantage of the pioneer's marketing mistakes.* If the pioneer makes any marketing mistakes in introducing a new entry, it opens opportunities for later entrants. This observation is closely related to the first two points, yet goes beyond product positioning and design to the actual execution of the pioneer's marketing program. For example, the pioneer may fail to attain adequate distribution, spend too little on introductory advertising, or use ineffective promotional appeals to communicate the product's benefits. A follower can observe these mistakes, design a marketing program to overcome them, and successfully compete head-to-head with the pioneer.

   Marketing mistakes can leave a pioneer vulnerable to challenges from later entrants even in product categories with substantial positive network effects. For example, Microsoft's Windows operating system was not the first user-friendly system on the market. However, Microsoft promoted and priced Windows very aggressively, it formed alliances with original equipment manufacturers (OEMs) in the personal computer industry to encourage them to install Windows on their machines, and it engaged in extensive licensing and cooperative agreements with other software developers. All these actions helped Windows capture a commanding share of the operating systems market, which in turn generated tremendous positive network effects for Windows and made it difficult for alternative systems to compete (perhaps *too* difficult, from the U.S. Justice Department's and European Union antitrust officials' perspectives).

4. *Ability to take advantage of the latest technology.* In industries characterized by rapid technological advances, followers can possibly introduce products based on a superior, second-generation

technology and thereby gain an advantage over the pioneer. And the pioneer may have difficulty reacting quickly to such advances if it is heavily committed to an earlier technology. Thus, Canon expects its new diagmatic imaging technology to give it an advantage in the medical imaging market that major competitors like General Electric will have trouble matching.

5. *Ability to take advantage of the pioneer's limited resources.* If the pioneer has limited resources for production facilities or marketing programs, or fails to commit sufficient resources to its new entry, followers willing and able to outspend the pioneer experience few enduring constraints.

# Determinants of Success for Pioneers and Followers

Our discussion suggests that a pioneering firm stands the best chance for long-term success in market-share leadership and profitability when (1) the new product-market is insulated from the entry of competitors, at least for a while, by strong patent protection, proprietary technology, substantial investment requirements, or positive network effects; or (2) the firm has sufficient size, resources, and competencies to take full advantage of its pioneering position and preserve it in the face of later competitive entries. Evidence suggests that organizational competencies, such as R&D and marketing skills, not only affect a firm's success as a pioneer, but may also influence the company's decision about whether or not to be a pioneer in the first place. Firms that perceive they lack the competencies necessary to sustain a first-mover advantage may be more likely to wait for another company to take the lead and to enter the market later.[17]

McDonald's is an example of a pioneer that has succeeded by aggressively building on the foundations of its early advantage. Although the firm started small as a single hamburger restaurant, it used the franchise system of distribution to rapidly expand the number of McDonald's outlets with a minimum cash investment. That expansion plus stringent quality and cost controls, relatively low prices made possible by experience-curve effects, heavy advertising expenditures, and product line expansion aimed at specific market segments (such as Egg McMuffin for the breakfast crowd) have all enabled the firm to maintain a commanding share of the fast-food hamburger industry.

On the other hand, a follower will most likely succeed when there are few legal, technological, or financial barriers to inhibit entry and when it has sufficient resources or competencies to overwhelm the pioneer's early advantage. For example, given Procter & Gamble's well-established brand name and superior advertising and promotional resources, the company was able to quickly take the market share lead away from pioneer Minnetonka, Inc., in the plaque-fighting toothpaste market with a reformulated version of Crest.

A study conducted across a broad range of industries in the PIMS database supports these observations.[18] The author's findings are briefly summarized in Exhibit 15.3 and discussed below. The author found that, regardless of the industry involved, pioneers able to maintain their preeminent position well into the market's growth stage had supported their early entry with the following marketing strategy elements:

- *Large entry scale*—Successful pioneers had sufficient capacity, or could expand quickly enough, to pursue a mass-market targeting strategy, usually on a national rather than a local or regional basis. Thus, they could expand their volume quickly and achieve the benefits of experience-curve effects before major competitors could confront them.

- *Broad product line*—Successful pioneers also quickly add line extensions or modifications to their initial product to tailor their offerings to specific market segments. This helps reduce their vulnerability to later entrants who might differentiate themselves by targeting one or more peripheral markets. This point gains further support from a recent study of over

# Exhibit 15.3

MARKETING STRATEGY ELEMENTS PURSUED BY SUCCESSFUL PIONEERS, FAST FOLLOWERS, AND LATE ENTRANTS

| These marketers . . . | are characterized by one or more of these strategy elements: |
|---|---|
| Successful pioneers | • Large entry scale |
| | • Broad product line |
| | • High product quality |
| | • Heavy promotional expenditures |
| Successful fast followers | • Larger entry scale than the pioneer |
| | • Leapfrogging the pioneer with superior: |
| |     product technology |
| |     product quality |
| |     customer service |
| Successful late entrants | • Focus on peripheral target markets or niches |

2,000 manufacturing businesses that found that market pioneers have a higher probability of engaging in further product development than either fast followers or late entrants, but that they tend to emphasize product improvements and line extensions rather than radical innovations.[19]

- *High product quality*—Successful pioneers also offer a high-quality, well-designed product from the beginning, thus removing one potential differential advantage for later followers. Competent engineering, thorough product and market testing before commercialization, and good quality control during the production process are all important to the continued success of pioneers.

- *Heavy promotional expenditures*—Successful pioneers had marketing programs characterized by relatively high advertising and promotional expenditures as a percentage of sales. Initially the promotion helps to stimulate awareness and primary demand for the new product category, build volume, and reduce unit costs. Later, this promotion focuses on building selective demand for the pioneer's brand and reinforcing loyalty as new competitors enter.

The same study found that the most successful fast followers had the resources to enter the new market on a larger scale than the pioneer. Consequently they could quickly reduce their unit costs, offer lower prices than incumbent competitors, and enjoy any positive network effects. Some fast followers achieved success, however, by leapfrogging earlier entrants. These followers won customers away from the pioneer by offering a product with more sophisticated technology, better quality, or superior service. Indeed, a recent study of competitors in high-tech markets indicates that market-share leadership in such markets tends to accrue to the firm with the highest-quality product regardless of whether it was a pioneer or a follower, even when there are substantial network effects.[20]

Finally, some late entrants also achieved substantial profits by avoiding direct confrontations with more established competitors and by pursuing peripheral target markets. They often offer tailor-made products to smaller market niches and support them with high levels of service.[21]

Followers typically enter a market after it is in the growth phase of its life cycle, and they start with low market shares relative to the established pioneer. Consequently, our discussion later in this chapter of marketing strategies for low-share competitors in growth markets is germane to both fast followers and later entrants. Before focusing on strategies for followers, however, we should first examine strategies that might be successfully employed by the first entrant in a new product-market.

# Strategic Marketing Programs for Pioneers

The preceding discussion suggests that the ultimate success of a pioneering strategy depends on the nature of the demand and competitive situation the pioneer encounters in the market and on the pioneer's ability to design and support an effective marketing pro-

gram. It also depends on how the pioneer defines *success*—in other words, the objectives it seeks to achieve. Thus, a pioneer might choose from one of three different types of marketing strategies: mass-market penetration, niche penetration, or skimming and early withdrawal. Exhibit 15.4 summarizes the primary objectives of each strategy and the circumstances favoring their use. But, while specific conditions may favor a given strategy, they do not guarantee its success. Much still depends on how effectively a firm implements the strategy. Also, it is highly unlikely that all the listed conditions will exist simultaneously in any single product-market.

## Mass-Market Penetration

The ultimate objective of a mass-market penetration strategy is to capture and maintain a commanding share of the total market for the new product. Thus, the critical marketing task is to convince as many potential customers as possible to adopt the pioneer's product quickly to drive down unit costs and build a large contingent of loyal customers before competitors enter the market.

Mass-market penetration tends to be most successful when entry barriers inhibit or delay the appearance of competitors, thus allowing the pioneer more time to build volume, lower costs, and create loyal customers, or when the pioneer has competencies or resources that most potential competitors cannot match, as in the case of Canon's technical and R&D expertise in the copier industry. Other relevant competencies include product engineering, promotional and channel management skills, and the financial and organizational resources necessary to expand capacity in advance of demand. In some cases, though, a smaller firm with limited resources can successfully employ a mass-market penetration strategy if the market has a protracted adoption process and slow initial growth. Slow growth can delay competitive entry because fewer competitors are attracted to a market with questionable future growth. This allows the pioneer more time to expand capacity.

Mass-market penetration is also an appropriate strategy when the product category is likely to experience positive network effects. Since the value of such products increases as the number of users grows, it makes sense for the pioneer to quickly capture and maintain as large a customer base as possible.

## Niche Penetration

Even when a new product-market expands quickly, however, it may still be possible for a small firm with limited resources to be a successful pioneer. In such cases, though, the firm must define success in a more limited way. Instead of pursuing the objective of capturing and sustaining a leading share of the entire market, it may make more sense for such firms to focus their efforts on a single market segment. This kind of **niche penetration** strategy can help the smaller pioneer gain the biggest bang for its limited bucks and avoid direct confrontations with bigger competitors.

A niche penetration strategy is most appropriate when the new market is expected to grow quickly and there are a number of different benefit or applications segments to appeal to. It is particularly attractive when there are few barriers to the entry of major competitors

# Exhibit 15.4

MARKETING OBJECTIVES AND STRATEGIES FOR NEW PRODUCT PIONEERS

| | ALTERNATIVE MARKETING STRATEGIES | | |
|---|---|---|---|
| Situational variables | Mass-market penetration | Niche penetration | Skimming: early withdrawal |
| Primary objective | • Maximize number of triers and adopters in *total market*. <br><br> • Maintain leading share position in *total market*. | • Maximize number of triers and adopters in *target segment*. <br><br> • Maintain leading share position in *target segment*. | • Recoup development and commercialization costs as soon as possible. <br><br> • Withdraw from market when increasing competition puts pressure on margins. |
| Market characteristics | • Large potential demand. <br><br> • Relatively homogeneous customer needs. <br><br> • Customers likely to adopt product relatively quickly; short diffusion process. | • Large potential demand. <br><br> • Fragmented market; many different applications and benefit segments. <br><br> • Customers likely to adopt product relatively quickly; short adoption process. | • Limited potential demand. <br><br> • Customers likely to adopt product relatively slowly; long adoption process. <br><br> • Early adopters willing to pay high price; demand is price inelastic. |
| Product characteristics | • Product technology patentable or difficult to copy. <br><br> • Substantial network effects; value increases with growth of installed customer base. <br><br> • Components or materials difficult to obtain; limited sources of supply. <br><br> • Complex production process; substantial development and/or investment required. | • Product technology offers little patent protection; easily copied or adapted. <br><br> • Limited or no network effects. <br><br> • Components or materials easy to obtain; many sources of supply. <br><br> • Relatively simple production process; little development or additional investment required. | • Product technology offers little patent protection; easily copied or adapted. <br><br> • Limited or no network effects. <br><br> • Components or materials easy to obtain; many sources of supply. <br><br> • Relatively simple production process; little development or additional investment required. |
| Competitor characteristics | • Few potential competitors. <br><br> • Most potential competitors have limited resources and competencies; few sources of differential advantage. | • Many potential competitors. <br><br> • Some potential competitors have substantial resources and competencies; possible sources of differential advantage. | • Many potential competitors. <br><br> • Some potential competitors have substantial resources and competencies; possible sources of differential advantage. |
| Firm characteristics | • Strong product engineering skills; able to quickly develop product modifications and line extensions for multiple market segments. <br><br> • Strong marketing skills and resources; ability to identify and develop marketing programs for multiple segments; ability to shift from stimulation of primary demand to stimulation of selective demand as competitors enter. <br><br> • Sufficient financial and organizational resources to build capacity in advance of growth in demand. | • Limited product engineering skills and resources. <br><br> • Limited marketing skills and resources. <br><br> • Insufficient financial or organizational resources to build capacity in advance of growing demand. | • Strong basic R&D and new product development skills; a prospector with good capability for continued new product innovation. <br><br> • Good sales and promotional skills; able to quickly build primary demand in target market; perhaps has limited marketing resources for long-term market maintenance. <br><br> • Limited financial or organizational resources to commit to building capacity in advance of growth in demand. |

and when the pioneer has only limited resources and competencies to defend any advantage it gains through early entry.

Some pioneers may intend to pursue a mass-market penetration strategy when introducing a new product or service, but they end up implementing a niche penetration strategy instead. This is particularly likely when the new market grows faster or is more fragmented than the pioneer expects. Facing such a situation, a pioneer with limited resources may decide to concentrate on holding its leading position in one or a few segments, rather than spreading itself too thin developing unique line extensions and marketing programs for many different markets or going deep into debt to finance rapid expansion.

## Skimming and Early Withdrawal

Even when a firm has the resources to sustain a leading position in a new product-market, it may choose not to. Competition is usually inevitable, and prices and margins tend to drop dramatically after followers enter the market. Therefore, some pioneers opt to pursue a **skimming** strategy while planning an early withdrawal from the market. This involves setting a high price and engaging in only limited advertising and promotion to maximize per-unit profits and recover the product's development costs as quickly as possible. At the same time, the firm may work to develop new applications for its technology or the next generation of more advanced technology. Then when competitors enter the market and margins fall, the firm is ready to cannibalize its own product with one based on new technology or to move into new segments of the market.

The 3M Company is a master of the skimming strategy. According to one 3M manager, "We hit fast, price high (full economic value of the product to the user), and get the heck out when the me-too products pour in." The new markets pioneered by the company are often smaller ones of $50 million to $100 million, and the firm may dominate them for only a few years. By then, it is ready to launch the next generation of new technology or to move the old technology into new applications. For instance, within two years of 3M's introduction of the first water-activated casting tape for setting broken bones, eight other firms had introduced similar products. But since the company's R&D people had been working on a replacement version all along, it was able to drop the old product and introduce a technically superior tape that was stronger, easier to use, and commanded a premium price.[22]

As Exhibit 15.4 indicates, either small or large firms can use strategies of skimming and early withdrawal. But it is critical that the company have good R&D and product development skills so it can produce a constant stream of new products or new applications to replace older ones as they attract heavy competition. Also, since a firm pursuing this kind of strategy plans to remain in a market only short term, it is most appropriate when there are few barriers to entry, the product is expected to diffuse rapidly, and the pioneer lacks the capacity or other resources necessary to defend a leading share position over the long haul.

## Marketing Program Components for a Mass-Market Penetration Strategy

As mentioned, the crucial marketing task in a mass-market penetration strategy is to maximize the number of customers adopting the firm's new product as quickly as possible. This requires a marketing program focused on (1) *aggressively building product awareness and motivation to buy* among a broad cross-section of potential customers and (2) *making it as easy as possible for those customers to try the new product,* on the assumption that they will try it, like it, develop loyalty, and make repeat purchases.

Exhibit 15.5 outlines a number of marketing activities that might help increase customers' awareness and willingness to buy or improve their ability to try the product. This is by

## Exhibit 15.5

COMPONENTS OF STRATEGIC MARKETING PROGRAMS FOR PIONEERS

| Strategic objectives and tasks | ALTERNATIVE STRATEGIC MARKETING PROGRAMS | | |
|---|---|---|---|
| | Mass-market penetration | Niche penetration | Skimming: early withdrawal |
| Increase customers' awareness and willingness to buy | • Heavy advertising to generate awareness among customers in mass market; broad use of mass media. | • Heavy advertising directed at target segment to generate awareness; use selective media relevant to target. | • Limited advertising to generate awareness; particularly among least price-sensitive early adopters. |
| | • Extensive salesforce efforts to win new adopters; possible use of incentives to encourage new product sales. | • Extensive salesforce efforts focused on potential customers in target segment; possible use of incentives to encourage new product sales to target accounts. | • Extensive salesforce efforts, particularly focused on largest potential adopters; possible use of volume-based incentives to encourage new product sales. |
| | • Advertising and sales appeals stress generic benefits of new product type. | • Advertising and sales appeals stress generic benefits of new product type. | • Advertising and sales appeals stress generic benefits of new product type. |
| | • Extensive introductory sales promotions to induce trial (sampling, couponing, quantity discounts). | • Extensive introductory sales promotions to induce trial, but focused on target segment. | • Limited use, if any, of introductory sales promotions; if used, they should be volume-based quantity discounts. |
| | • Move relatively quickly to expand offerings (line extensions, multiple package sizes) to appeal to multiple segments. | • Additional product development limited to improvements or modifications to increase appeal to target segment. | • Little, if any, additional development within the product category. |
| | • Offer free trial, liberal return, or extended warranty policies to reduce customers' perceived risk of adopting the new product. | • Offer free trial, liberal return, or extended warranty policies to reduce target customers' perceived risk of adopting the new product. | • Offer free trial, liberal return, or extended warranty policies to reduce target customers' perceived risk of adopting the new product. |
| Increase customers' ability to buy | • Penetration pricing; or start with high price but bring out lower-priced versions in anticipation of competitive entries. | • Penetration pricing; or start with high price but bring out lower-priced versions in anticipation of competitive entries. | • Skimming pricing; attempt to maintain margins at level consistent with value of product to early adopters. |
| | • Extended credit terms to encourage initial purchases. | • Extended credit terms to encourage initial purchases. | • Extended credit terms to encourage initial purchases. |
| | • Heavy use of trade promotions aimed at gaining extensive distribution. | • Trade promotions aimed at gaining solid distribution among retailers or distributors pertinent for reaching target segment. | • Limited use of trade promotions; only as necessary to gain adequate distribution. |
| | • Offer engineering, installation, and training services to increase new product's compatibility with customers' current operations to reduce switching costs. | • Offer engineering, installation, and training services to increase new product's compatibility with customers' current operations to reduce switching costs. | • Offer limited engineering, installation, and training services as necessary to overcome customers' objections. |

no means an exhaustive list; nor do we mean to imply that a successful pioneer must necessarily engage in all of the listed activities. Marketing managers must develop programs combining activities that fit both the objectives of a mass-market penetration strategy and the specific market and potential competitive conditions the new product faces.

**Increasing Customers' Awareness and Willingness to Buy**   Obviously, heavy expenditures on advertising, introductory promotions such as sampling and couponing, and personal selling efforts can all increase awareness of a new product or service among potential customers. This is the critical first step in the adoption process for a new entry. The relative importance of these promotional tools varies, however, depending on the nature of the product and the number of potential customers. For instance, personal selling efforts are often the most critical component of the promotional mix for highly technical industrial products with a limited potential customer base, such as Canon's new wide-format bubble jet printer. Media advertising and sales promotion are usually more useful for building awareness and primary demand for a new consumer good among customers in the mass market. In either case, when designing a mass-market penetration marketing program, firms should broadly focus promotional efforts to expose and attract as many potential customers as possible before competitors show up.

Firms might also attempt to increase customers' willingness to buy their products by reducing the risk associated with buying something new. This can be done by letting customers try the product without obligation, as when car dealers allow potential customers to test-drive a new model, or when software developers allow customers to download a trial version and use it free for 30 days. Liberal return policies and extended warranties can serve the same purpose.

Finally, a firm committed to mass-market penetration might also broaden its product offerings to increase its appeal to as many market segments as possible. This helps reduce its vulnerability to later entrants who could focus on specific market niches. Firms can accomplish such market expansion through the rapid introduction of line extensions, additional package sizes, or product modifications targeted at new applications and market segments.

**Increasing Customers' Ability to Buy**   For customers to adopt a new product and develop loyalty toward it, they must be aware of the item and be motivated to buy. But they must also have the wherewithal to purchase it. Thus, to capture as many customers in as short a time as possible, it usually makes sense for a firm pursuing mass-market penetration to keep prices low (penetration pricing) and perhaps offer liberal financing arrangements or easy credit terms during the introductory period.

Pioneers introducing new information or communications technologies tend to be particularly aggressive in pricing their offerings for two reasons. First, as we have seen, such products can often benefit from positive network effects if enough customers can be induced to adopt them quickly. Second, the variable costs of producing and distributing additional units of such products is usually very low, perhaps even approaching zero. For instance, the costs of developing a new software product are high, but once it is developed copies can be made and distributed over the internet for next to nothing. These two factors mean that it often makes sense for pioneers in such product categories to set their price very low to initial customers—perhaps even to give away trial copies—in hopes of quickly building a large installed base, capturing more value from later customers with higher prices, and maximizing the lifetime value of their customers by selling them upgrades and enhanced versions of the product in the future.[23]

Another factor that can inhibit customers' ability to buy is a lack of product availability. Thus, extensive personal selling and trade promotions aimed at gaining adequate distribution are usually a critical part of a mass-market penetration marketing program. Such efforts should take place before the start of promotional campaigns to ensure that the product is available as soon as customers are motivated to buy it.

A highly technical new product's incompatibility with other related products or systems currently used can also inhibit customers' purchases. It can result in high switching costs for a potential adopter. The pioneer might reduce those costs by designing the product to be as compatible as possible with related equipment. It might also offer engineering services to help make the new product more compatible with existing operations, provide free installation assistance, and conduct training programs for the customer's employees.

The above actions are suited not just to the marketing of products; most are essential elements of mass-market penetration strategies for new service, retail, and even e-commerce websites as well. The marketing actions of an e-tailer such as Amazon, discussed in Exhibit 15.6, provide a textbook example of the elements of, as well as some of the risks inherent in, a mass-market penetration strategy.

### Additional Considerations When Pioneering Global Markets
Whether the product-market a pioneer is trying to penetrate is domestic or foreign, many of the marketing tasks appropriate for increasing potential customers' awareness, willingness, and ability to buy the new product or service are largely the same. Of course, some of the tactical aspects of the pioneer's strategic marketing program—such as specific product features, promotional appeals, or distribution channels—may have to be adjusted to fit different cultural, legal, or economic circumstances across national borders. For Bausch & Lomb to develop the Chinese market for contact lenses, for instance, it first had to develop an extensive training program for the country's opticians and build a network of retail outlets, actions that were unnecessary in more developed markets.

Unless the firm already has an economic presence in a country via the manufacture or marketing of other products or services, however, a potential global pioneer faces at least one additional question to answer. What mode of entry is most appropriate? As we saw in Chapter 12 there are three basic mechanisms for entering a foreign market—exporting through agent middlemen (using local manufacturers reps or distributors), contractual agreements such as licensing or franchise arrangements with local firms, or direct investment.

Exporting lowers the financial risk involved for the pioneer when entering an unfamiliar foreign market. Unfortunately, such arrangements also afford the pioneer relatively little control over the marketing and distribution of its product or service, activities that are critical for winning customer awareness and loyalty in a new market. At the other extreme, investing in a wholly owned subsidiary typically makes little sense until it becomes clear whether the pioneering product will win customer acceptance. Consequently, intermediate modes of entry, such as licensing or forming a joint venture with a local firm in the host country, tend to be the preferred means of developing global markets for new products. Joint ventures are particularly appropriate in this regard because they avoid quotas and import restrictions or taxes, and they allow the pioneer to share financial risks while gaining local marketing expertise.[24] Thus, Bausch & Lomb established a joint venture with Beijing Optical as a basis for building contact lens factories in China and for gaining access to Chinese opticians. Consequently, the firm was able to develop a leading market share in the world's most heavily populated country with a modest investment of only about $20 million.

## Marketing Program Components for a Niche Penetration Strategy

Because the objectives of a niche penetration strategy are similar to but more narrowly focused than those of a mass-market strategy, the marketing program elements are also likely to be similar under the two strategies. Obviously, however, the niche penetrator

## Exhibit 15.6    AMAZON'S MASS-MARKET PENETRATION STRATEGY

Founded in 1994 by Jeff Bezos as the first online bookstore, Amazon (*www.amazon.com*) has employed many of the marketing tactics we have listed as possible components of a mass-market penetration strategy. In the early days, the firm spent heavily on various promotional tools to attract buyers and build a base of loyal customers. In the late 1990s, the firm was spending an average of more than $50 for each new customer it attracted. The money was spent on banner advertising and alliances with other sites and web portals, traditional media advertising, special consumer promotions, and an "associates" program through which sites that offered a link to Amazon got a cut of any sales they referred. As Amazon has built its customer base and increased public awareness, its acquisition costs per customer have declined substantially.

In the early years, many of Amazon's inventory-storage and order-fulfillment functions were outsourced, its fixed costs were low, and it had huge amounts of capital to play with. Consequently, it was able to attract customers from bricks-and-mortar bookstores by offering very low prices and a wide selection of titles.

To gain the loyalty of new customers it attracted, Amazon worked hard to constantly improve its customer service. It collected information from customers concerning their preferences, desires, and complaints, then launched a series of customer service innovations, such as one-click ordering and a popular bestseller list ranking sales on the site. More recently, it has invested hundreds of millions of dollars to build a network of automated distribution centers around the world to better control order fulfillment, ensure quick and reliable delivery, and lower fulfillment costs.

Finally, Amazon has greatly expanded its product lines over the years to include CDs, toys, electronics, tools, and a variety of other things. In part, this was accomplished by inviting independent suppliers to sell their wares through the Amazon website on a commission basis. This move was motivated by the company's desire to become a one-stop shopping venue and to increase average annual revenues per customer.

Amazon's mass-market strategy has been very successful so far. The firm made $1.2 billion in net income on $34.2 billion of global sales in 2010. However, the future remains somewhat unsettled due to ongoing changes in the firm's competitive and technical environments. New challengers in internet retailing include both established bricks-and-mortar firms, like Walmart and Tesco, and other web portals, like Germany's Otto. To stay one step ahead of such rivals, Amazon has been investing heavily in new technology—particularly software development—to further personalize its website and improve the customer's shopping experience.

The company is also leveraging those investments in technical infrastructure by selling internet services to other firms who want a sophisticated internet presence but don't have the resources to develop it in-house.

Some analysts and investors were concerned that Amazon might never be able to recoup the heavy investments inherent in its pursuit of the mass market. Consequently, Amazon's stock price fell from more than $50 a share to as low as $26. Recently, however, Amazon has emerged as the undisputed e-commerce champ. In spite of a technical glitch that shut down part of its server network for a couple of days, its internet services are winning acceptance among both start-up firms and major corporations. As a result, the firm's stock price was flirting with $200 a share in the summer of 2011.

*Sources:* Fred Vogelstein, "Mighty Amazon," *Fortune*, May 26, 2003, pp. 60–74; Robert Hof, "Amazon's Costly Bells and Whistles," *BusinessWeek Online*, February 3, 2006; Peter Burrows, "Bezos: How Frugality Drives Innovation," *BusinessWeek*, April 28, 2008, pp. 64–66; and Amazon's 2010 annual report, archived at *www.amazon.com*.

should keep its marketing efforts clearly focused on the target segment to gain as much impact as possible from its limited resources. This point is evident in the outline of program components in Exhibit 15.5. For example, while a niche strategy calls for the same advertising, sales promotion, personal selling, and trade promotion activities as a mass-market program, the former should use more selective media, call schedules, and channel designs to precisely direct those activities toward the target segment.

 Luckily, the internet provides firms with a number of promotional tools that can reach specific segments at relatively low cost. For example, companies like Nantucket Nectars in the United States and Innocent Drinks in the United Kingdom have relied on quirky public relations efforts, internet ads, word-of-mouth on social networking sites like Facebook, and blogs to build their brands' identities among niche segments of younger consumers and build distribution in specialty health-food retail outlets. Such efforts generated sufficient customer demand over time that some big retail chains began carrying their products.[25]

# Marketing Program Components for a Skimming Strategy

As Exhibit 15.5 suggests, one major difference between a skimming strategy and a mass-market penetration strategy involves pricing policies. A relatively high price is appropriate for a skimming strategy to increase margins and revenues, even though some price-sensitive customers may be reluctant to adopt the product at that price.[26] This also suggests that introductory promotional programs might best focus on customer groups who are least sensitive to price and most likely to be early adopters of the new product. This can help hold down promotion costs and avoid wasting marketing efforts on less profitable market segments. Thus, in many consumer goods businesses, skimming strategies focus on relatively upscale customers, since they are often more likely to be early adopters and less sensitive to price.

Another critical element of a skimming strategy is the nature of the firm's continuing product-development efforts. A pioneer that plans to leave a market when competitors enter should not devote much effort to expanding its product line through line extensions or multiple package sizes. Instead, it should concentrate on the next generation of technology or on identifying new application segments, in other words, preparing its avenue of escape from the market.

Now that we have examined some strategies a pioneer might follow in entering a new market, we are left with two important strategic questions. The pioneer is by definition the early share leader in the new market; hence the first question is, What adjustments in strategy might be necessary for the pioneer to *maintain its leading share position* after competitors arrive on the scene? The second is, What strategies might followers adopt *to take business away from the early leader and increase their relative share position* as the market grows? We examine these two issues next.

# Growth-Market Strategies for Market Leaders

As a product-market enters the growth stage of its life cycle, the competitor with the leading market share is usually the pioneer or at least one of the first entrants. Often, that firm's strategic objective is to maintain its leading share position in the face of increasing competition as the market expands. Share maintenance may not seem like a very aggressive objective, because it implies the business is merely trying to stay even rather than forge ahead. But two important facts must be kept in mind.

First, the dynamics of a growth market—including the increasing number of competitors, the fragmentation of market segments, and the threat of product innovation from within and outside the industry—make maintaining an early lead in relative market share very difficult. The continuing need for investment to finance growth, the likely negative cash flows that result, and the threat of governmental antitrust action can make it even more difficult. For example, 31 percent of the 877 market-share leaders in the PIMS database experienced losses

## STRATEGIC ISSUE

*The dynamics of a growth market—including the increasing number of competitors, the fragmentation of market segments, and the threat of product innovation from within and outside the industry—make maintaining an early lead in relative market share very difficult.*

in relative share, and leaders were especially likely to suffer this fate when their market shares were very large.[27]

Second, a firm can maintain its current share position in a growth market only if its sales volume continues to grow at a rate equal to that of the overall market, enabling the firm to stay even in *absolute* market share. It may, however, be able to maintain a relative share lead even if its volume growth is less than the industry's.

## Marketing Objectives for Share Leaders

Share maintenance for a market leader involves two important marketing objectives. First, the firm must *retain its current customers,* ensuring that those customers remain brand loyal when making repeat or replacement purchases. This is particularly critical for firms in consumer nondurable, service, and industrial materials and components industries where a substantial portion of total sales volume consists of repeat purchases. Second, the firm must *stimulate selective demand among later adopters* to ensure that it captures a large share of the continuing growth in industry sales.

In some cases the market leader might pursue a third objective: stimulating primary demand to help speed up overall market growth. This can be particularly important in product-markets where the adoption process is protracted because of the technical sophistication of the new product, high switching costs for potential customers, or positive network effects.

The market leader is the logical one to stimulate market growth in such situations; it has the most to gain from increased volume, assuming it can maintain its relative share of that volume. However, expanding total demand—by promoting new uses for the product or stimulating existing customers' usage and repeat purchase rates—is often more critical near the end of the growth stage and early in the maturity stage of a product's life cycle. Consequently, we discuss marketing actions appropriate to this objective in Chapter 16.

## Marketing Actions and Strategies to Achieve Share-Maintenance Objectives

A business might take a variety of marketing actions to maintain a leading share position in a growing market. Exhibit 15.7 outlines a lengthy, though not exhaustive, list of such actions and their specific marketing objectives. Because share maintenance involves multiple objectives, and different marketing actions may be needed to achieve each one, a strategic marketing program usually integrates a mix of the actions outlined in the exhibit.

Not all the actions summarized in Exhibit 15.7 are consistent with one another. It would be unusual, for instance, for a business to invest heavily in new product improvements and promotion to enhance its product's high-quality image and simultaneously slash prices, unless it was trying to drive out weaker competitors in the short run with an eye on higher profits in the future. Thus, the activities outlined cluster into five internally consistent strategies that a market leader might employ, singly or in combination, to maintain its leading share position: a **fortress,** or **position defense, strategy;** a **flanker strategy;** a **confrontation strategy;** a **market expansion strategy;** and a **contraction,** or **strategic withdrawal, strategy.**

Exhibit 15.8 diagrams this set of strategies. It is consistent with what a number of military strategists and some marketing authorities have identified as common defensive strategies.[28] To think of them as strictly defensive, though, can be misleading. Companies can use some of these strategies offensively to preempt expected future actions by potential competitors. Or they can use them to capture an even larger share of future new customers.

## Exhibit 15.7

MARKETING ACTIONS TO ACHIEVE SHARE-MAINTENANCE OBJECTIVES

| Marketing objectives | Possible marketing actions |
|---|---|
| *Retain current customers by:* | |
| • Maintaining/improving satisfaction and loyalty. | • Increase attention to quality control as output expands.<br>• Continue product modification and improvement efforts to increase customer benefits and/or reduce costs.<br>• Focus advertising on stimulation of selective demand; stress product's superior features and benefits; reminder advertising.<br>• Increase salesforce's servicing of current accounts; consider formation of national or key account representatives to major customers; consider replacing independent manufacturer's reps with company salespeople where appropriate.<br>• Expand postsale service capabilities; develop or expand company's own service force, or develop training programs for distributors' and dealers' service people; expand parts inventory; develop customer service hotline or website. |
| • Encouraging/simplifying repeat purchase. | • Expand production capacity in advance of increasing demand to avoid stockouts.<br>• Improve inventory control and logistics systems to reduce delivery times.<br>• Continue to build distribution channels; use periodic trade promotions to gain more extensive retail coverage and maintain shelf-facings; strengthen relationships with strongest distributors/dealers.<br>• Consider negotiating long-term requirements contracts with major customers.<br>• Consider developing automatic reorder systems or logistical alliances. |
| • Reducing attractiveness of switching. | • Develop a second brand or product line with features or price more appealing to a specific segment of current customers (*flanker strategy*—see Exhibit 15.8 and Exhibit 15.9).<br>• Develop multiple-line extensions or brand offerings targeted to the needs of several user segments within the market (*market expansion*).<br>• Meet or beat lower prices or heavier promotional efforts by competitors—or try to preempt such efforts by potential competitors—when necessary to retain customers and when lower unit costs allow (*confrontation strategy*). |
| *Stimulate selective demand among later adopters by:* | |
| • Head-to-head positioning against competitive offerings or potential offerings. | • Develop a second brand or product line with features or price more appealing to a specific segment of potential customers (*flanker strategy*).<br>• Make product modifications or improvements to match or beat superior competitive offerings (*confrontation strategy*).<br>• Meet or beat lower prices or heavier promotional efforts by competitors when necessary to retain customers and when lower unit costs allow (*confrontation strategy*).<br>• When resources are limited relative to a competitor's, consider withdrawing from smaller or slower-growing segments to focus product development and promotional efforts on higher potential segments threatened by competitor (*contraction or strategic withdrawal strategy).* |
| • Differentiated positioning against competitive offerings or potential offerings. | • Develop multiple-line extensions or brand offerings targeted to the needs of various potential user applications or geographical segments within the market (*market expansion*).<br>• Build unique distribution channels to more effectively reach specific segments of potential customers (*market expansion strategy*).<br>• Design multiple advertising and/or sales promotion campaigns targeted at specific segments of potential customers (*market expansion strategy*). |

# Exhibit 15.8

STRATEGIC CHOICES FOR SHARE LEADERS IN GROWTH MARKETS

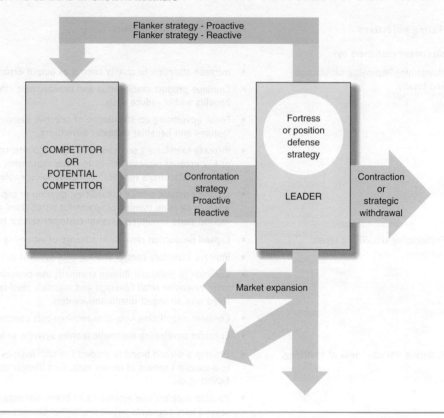

Which, or what combination, of these five strategies is most appropriate for a particular product-market depends on (1) the market's size and its customers' characteristics, (2) the number and relative strengths of the competitors or potential competitors in that market, and (3) the leader's own resources and competencies. Exhibit 15.9 outlines the situations in which each strategy is most appropriate and the primary objectives for which they are best suited.

## Fortress, or Position Defense, Strategy

The most basic defensive strategy is to continually strengthen a strongly held current position—to build an impregnable fortress capable of repelling attacks by current or future competitors. This strategy is nearly always part of a leader's share-maintenance efforts. By shoring up an already strong position, the firm can improve the satisfaction of current customers while increasing the attractiveness of its offering to new customers with needs and characteristics similar to those of earlier adopters.

**STRATEGIC ISSUE**

*The most basic defensive strategy is to continually strengthen a strongly held current position.*

# Exhibit 15.9

## MARKETING OBJECTIVES AND STRATEGIES FOR SHARE LEADERS IN GROWTH MARKETS

| Situational variables | SHARE MAINTENANCE STRATEGIES | | | | |
|---|---|---|---|---|---|
| | Fortress or position defense | Flanker | Confrontation | Market expansion | Contraction or strategic withdrawal |
| Primary objective | Increase satisfaction, loyalty, and repeat purchase among current customers by building on existing strengths; appeal to late adopters with same attributes and benefits offered to early adopters. | Protect against loss of specific segments of current customers by developing a second entry that covers a weakness in original offering; improve ability to attract new customers with specific needs or purchase criteria different from those of early adopters. | Protect against loss of of share among current customers by meeting or beating a head-to-head competitive offering; improve ability to win new customers who might otherwise be attracted to competitor's offering. | Increase ability to attract new customers by developing new product offerings or line extensions aimed at a variety of new applications and user segments; improve ability to retain current customers as market fragments. | Increase ability to attract new customers in selected high-growth segments by focusing offerings and resources on those segments; withdraw from smaller or slower growing segments to conserve resources. |
| Market characteristics | Relatively homogeneous market with respect to customer needs and purchase criteria; strong preference for leader's product among largest segment of customers. | Two or more major market segments with distinct needs or purchase criteria. | Relatively homogeneous market with respect to customers' needs and purchase criteria; little preference for, or loyalty toward, leader's product among largest segment of customers. | Relatively heterogeneous market with respect to customers' needs and purchase criteria; multiple product uses requiring different product or service attributes. | Relatively heterogeneous market with respect to customers' needs, purchase criteria, and growth potential; multiple product uses requiring different product or service attributes. |
| Competitors' characteristics | Current and potential competitors have relatively limited resources and competencies. | One or more current or potential competitors with sufficient resources and competencies to effectively implement a differentiation strategy. | One or more current or potential competitors with sufficient resources and competencies to effectively implement a head-to-head strategy. | Current and potential competitors have relatively limited resources and competencies, particularly with respect to R&D and marketing. | One or more current or potential competitors with sufficient resources and competencies to present a strong challenge in one or more growth segments. |
| Firm's characteristics | Current product offering enjoys high awareness and preference among major segment of current and potential customers; firm has marketing and R&D resources and competencies equal to or greater than any current or potential competitor. | Current product offering perceived as weak on at least one attribute by a major segment of current or potential customers; firm has sufficient R&D and marketing resources to introduce and support a second offering aimed at the disaffected segment. | Current product offering suffers low awareness, preference, and/or loyalty among major segment of current or potential customers; firm has R&D and marketing resources and competencies equal to or greater than any current or potential competitor. | No current offerings in one or more potential applications segments; firm has marketing and R&D resources and competencies equal to or greater than any current or potential competitor. | Current product offering suffers low awareness, preference, and/or loyalty among current or potential customers in one or more major growth segments; firm's R&D and marketing resources and competencies are limited relative to those of one or more competitors. |

Strengthening the firm's position makes particularly good sense when current and potential customers have relatively homogeneous needs and desires and the firm's offering already enjoys a high level of awareness and preference in the mass market. In some homogeneous markets, a well-implemented position defense strategy may be all that is needed for share maintenance.

Most of the marketing actions listed in Exhibit 15.7 as being relevant for retaining current customers might be incorporated into a position defense strategy. Anything the business can do to improve customer satisfaction and loyalty and encourage and simplify repeat purchasing should help the firm protect its current customer base and make its offering more attractive to new customers. Some of the specific actions appropriate for accomplishing these two objectives are discussed in more detail below.

### Actions to Improve Customer Satisfaction and Loyalty

The rapid expansion of output necessary to keep up with a growth market can often lead to quality control problems for the market leader. As new plants, equipment, and personnel are quickly brought on line, bugs can suddenly appear in the production process. Thus, the leader must pay particular attention to quality control during this phase. Most customers have only limited, if any, positive past experiences with the new brand to offset their disappointment when a purchase does not live up to expectations.

Perhaps the most obvious way a leader can strengthen its position is to continue to modify and improve its product. This can reduce the opportunities for competitors to differentiate their products by designing in features or performance levels the leader does not offer. The leader might also try to reduce unit costs to discourage low-price competition.

The leader should take steps to improve not only the physical product but customers' perceptions of it as well. As competitors enter or prepare to enter the market, the leader's advertising and sales promotion emphasis should shift from stimulating primary demand to building selective demand for the company's brand. This usually involves creating appeals that emphasize the brand's superior features and benefits. While the leader may continue sales promotion efforts aimed at stimulating trial among later adopters, some of those efforts might be shifted toward encouraging repeat purchases among existing customers. For instance, it might include cents-off coupons inside the package to give customers a price break on their next purchases of the brand.

For industrial goods, some salesforce efforts should shift from prospecting for new accounts to servicing existing customers. Firms that relied on independent manufacturer's reps to introduce their new product might consider replacing them with company salespeople to increase the customer service orientation of their sales efforts. Firms whose own salespeople introduced the product might reorganize their salesforces into specialized groups focused on major industries or user segments. Or they might assign key account representatives, or cross-functional account teams, to service their largest customers.

Finally, a leader can strengthen its position as the market grows by giving increased attention to postsale service. Rapid growth in demand can not only outstrip a firm's ability to produce a high-quality product, but it can also overload the firm's ability to service customers. This can lead to a loss of existing customers as well as negative word of mouth that might inhibit the firm's ability to attract new users. Thus, the growth phase often requires increased investments to expand the firm's parts inventory, hire and train service personnel and dealers, improve the information content on the firm's website, and closely monitor and respond to any problems or complaints reported to the company's call center or on customer blogs.[29]

**Actions to Encourage and Simplify Repeat Purchasing** One of the most critical actions a leader must take to ensure that customers continue buying its product is to maximize its availability. It must reduce stockouts on retail store shelves or shorten delivery times for industrial goods. To do this, the firm must invest in plant and equipment to expand capacity in advance of demand, and it must implement adequate inventory control and logistics systems to provide a steady flow of goods through the distribution system. The firm should also continue to build its distribution channels. In some cases, a firm might even vertically integrate parts of its distribution system—such as building its own warehouses, as Amazon and several other e-tailers have done—to gain better control over order fulfillment activities and ensure quick and reliable deliveries.

Some market leaders, particularly in industrial goods markets, can take more proactive steps to turn their major customers into captives and help guarantee future purchases. For example, a firm might negotiate requirements contracts or guaranteed price agreements with its customers to ensure future purchases, or it might tie them into a computerized reorder system or logistical alliance.

## Flanker Strategy

One shortcoming of a fortress strategy is that a challenger might simply choose to bypass the leader's fortress and try to capture territory where the leader has not yet established a strong presence. This can represent a particular threat when the market is fragmented into major segments with different needs and preferences and the leader's current brand does not meet the needs of one or more of those segments. A competitor with sufficient resources and competencies can develop a differentiated product offering to appeal to the segment where the leader is weak and thereby capture a substantial share of the overall market.

To defend against an attack directed at a weakness in its current offering (its exposed flank), a leader might develop a second brand (a **flanker** or **fighting brand**) to compete directly against the challenger's offering. This might involve trading up, where the leader develops a high-quality brand offered at a higher price to appeal to the prestige segment of the market. This was Toyota's rationale for introducing its Lexus brand of luxury automobiles, for instance.

More commonly, though, a flanker brand is a lower-quality product designed to appeal to a low-price segment to protect the leader's primary brand from direct price competition. Thus, Toyota introduced the Scion brand in the U.S. market in 2003, a line of cars that appeals to young car buyers looking for good quality, funky design, low prices, and no-hassle shopping. The Scion brand is an attempt to insulate Toyota cars from low-price competitors and to establish a presence among young, first-time buyers who might "trade up" to more expensive Toyota models in the future.

A flanker strategy is always used in conjunction with a position defense strategy. The leader simultaneously strengthens its primary brand while introducing a flanker to compete in segments where the primary brand is vulnerable. This suggests that a flanker strategy is appropriate only when the firm has sufficient resources to develop and fully support two or more entries. After all, a flanker is of little value if it is so lightly supported that a competitor can easily wipe it out.

## Confrontation Strategy

Suppose a competitor chooses to attack the leader head to head and attempts to steal customers in the leader's main target market. If the leader has established a strong position and attained a high level of preference and loyalty among customers and the trade, it may be able to sit back and wait for the competitor to fail. In many cases, though, the leader's brand is not strong enough to withstand a frontal assault from a well-funded, competent competitor. For example, Nokia introduced the first mobile phone with full personal digital assistant (PDA) capabilities—the 9000 Communicator—in 1996 and it quickly captured the leading global market share among PDA devices. But PDA phones with greater functionality (e.g., RIM's BlackBerry), more versatile Smartphones (e.g., Apple's iPhone), and cheaper Android-based phones from Asia have all substantially reduced Nokia's share of the market.

In such situations, the leader may have no choice but to confront the competitive threat directly. If the leader's competitive intelligence is good, it may decide to move proactively and change its marketing program before a suspected competitive challenge occurs. A confrontational strategy, though, is more commonly reactive. The leader usually decides to meet or beat the attractive features of a competitor's offering—by making product improvements, increasing promotional efforts, or lowering prices—only after the challenger's success has become obvious.

## STRATEGIC ISSUE

*Simply meeting the improved features or lower price of a challenger, however, does nothing to reestablish a sustainable competitive advantage for the leader.*

Simply meeting the improved features or lower price of a challenger, however, does nothing to reestablish a sustainable competitive advantage for the leader. And a confrontation based largely on lowering prices creates an additional problem of shrinking margins for all concerned.[30]

Unless decreased prices generate substantial new industry volume and the leader's production costs fall with that increasing volume, the leader may be better off responding to price threats with increased promotion or product improvements while trying to maintain its profit margins. Evidence also suggests that in product-markets with high repeat-purchase rates or a protracted diffusion process, the leader may be wise to adopt a penetration pricing policy in the first place. This would strengthen its share position and might preempt low-price competitors from entering.[31]

The leader can avoid the problems of a confrontation strategy by reestablishing the competitive advantage eroded by challengers' frontal attacks. But this typically requires additional investments in process improvements aimed at reducing unit costs, improvements in product quality or customer service, or even the development of the next generation of improved products to offer customers greater value for their dollars.

## Market Expansion

A market expansion strategy is a more aggressive and proactive version of the flanker strategy. Here the leader defends its relative market share by expanding into a number of market segments. This strategy's primary objective is to capture a large share of new customer groups who may prefer something different from the firm's initial offering, protecting the firm from future competitive threats from a number of directions. Such a strategy is particularly appropriate in fragmented markets if the leader has the resources to undertake multiple product development and marketing efforts.

The most obvious way a leader can implement a market expansion strategy is to develop line extensions, new brands, or even alternative product forms utilizing similar technologies to appeal to multiple market segments. For instance, Nokia has become the leading seller of cellular phones in both India and China by developing phones with unique features tailored to those developing nations' customers, such as phones with dust covers and a slip-free grip for use in scorching summer weather, software in seven regional languages for non-Hindi speakers, phones that respond to Chinese characters written with a stylus, and phones that retail for as little as $30.[32]

A less-expensive way to appeal to a variety of customer segments is to retain the basic product but vary other elements of the marketing program to make it relatively more attractive to specific users. Thus, a leader might create specialized salesforces to deal with the unique concerns of different user groups. Or it might offer different ancillary services to different types of customers or tailor sales promotion efforts to different segments. Thus, performing arts groups often promote reduced ticket prices, transportation services, and other inducements to attract senior citizens and students to matinee performances.

## Contraction or Strategic Withdrawal

In some highly fragmented markets, a leader may be unable to defend itself adequately in all segments. This is particularly likely when newly emerging competitors have more resources than the leader. The firm may then have to reduce or abandon its efforts in some segments to focus on areas where it enjoys the greatest relative advantages or that have the greatest potential for future growth. Even some very large firms may decide that certain segments are not profitable enough to continue pursuing. As we saw in Chapter 1, for instance, Samsung has withdrawn from the most price-sensitive consumer electronics segments to concentrate on higher-margin products emphasizing cutting-edge technology and hip design.

# Share-Growth Strategies for Followers

## Marketing Objectives for Followers

Not all late entrants to a growing product-market have illusions about eventually surpassing the leader and capturing a dominant market share. Some competitors, particularly those with limited resources and competencies, may simply seek to build a small but profitable business within a specialized segment of the larger market that earlier entrants have overlooked. As we have seen, this kind of *niche strategy* is one of the few entry options that small, late entrants can pursue with a reasonable degree of success. If a firm can successfully build a profitable business in a small segment while avoiding direct competition with larger competitors, it can often survive the shakeout period near the end of the growth stage and remain profitable throughout the maturity stage.

Many followers, particularly larger firms entering a product-market shortly after the pioneer, have more grandiose objectives. They often seek to displace the leader or at least to become a powerful competitor within the total market. Thus, their major marketing objective is to attain *share growth*, and the size of the increased relative share such challengers seek is usually substantial. For instance, when Haier, the Chinese appliance manufacturer, started making refrigerators just two decades ago, it set its sights on becoming a global share leader even though the category was dominated by large international brands like Whirlpool, Electrolux, and General Electric. Today, Haier is the leader in its home market with a 29 percent share, and is number two worldwide behind Whirlpool.[33]

## Marketing Actions and Strategies to Achieve Share Growth

A challenger with visions of taking over the leading share position in an industry has two basic strategic options, each involving somewhat different marketing objectives and actions. Where the share leader and perhaps some other early followers have already penetrated a large portion of the potential market, a challenger may have no choice but to *steal away some of the repeat purchase or replacement demand from the competitors' current customers.* As Exhibit 15.10 indicates, the challenger can attempt this through marketing activities that give it an advantage in a head-to-head confrontation with a target competitor. Or it can attempt to leapfrog over the leader by developing a new generation of products with enough benefits to induce customers to trade in their existing brand for a new one. Secondarily, such actions may also help the challenger attract a larger share of late adopters in the mass market.

If the market is relatively early in the growth phase and no previous entrant has captured a commanding share of potential customers, the challenger can focus on *attracting a larger share of potential new customers* who enter the market for the first time. This may also be a viable option when the overall market is heterogeneous and fragmented and the current share leader has established a strong position in only one or a few segments. In either case, the primary marketing activities for increasing share via this approach should aim at *differentiating* the challenger's offering from those of existing competitors by making it more appealing to new customers in untapped or underdeveloped market segments.

Once again, Exhibit 15.10's list of possible marketing actions for challengers is not exhaustive, and it contains actions that do not always fit well together. The activities that do fit tend to cluster into four major strategies that a challenger might use singly or in combination to secure growth in its relative market share. As Exhibit 15.11 indicates, these four share-growth strategies are *frontal attack, leapfrog strategy, flanking attack, and encirclement.*[34] These strategies are basically mirror images of the share-maintenance strategies discussed earlier.

Which, or what combination, of these four strategies is best for a particular challenger depends on market characteristics, the existing competitors' current positions and strengths, and the challenger's own resources and competencies. The situations in which each strategy is likely to work best are briefly outlined in Exhibit 15.12 and discussed in the following sections.

# Frontal Attack Strategy

Where the market for a product category is relatively homogeneous, with few untapped segments and at least one well-established competitor, a follower wanting to capture an increased market share may have little choice but to tackle a major competitor head-on. Such an approach is most likely to succeed when most existing customers do not have strong brand preferences or loyalties, the target competitor's product does not benefit from positive network effects, and when the challenger's resources and competencies—particularly in marketing—are greater than the target competitor's. But even superior resources are no guarantee of success if the challenger's assault merely imitates the target competitor's offering.

To successfully implement a frontal attack, a challenger should seek one or more ways to achieve a sustainable advantage over the target competitor. As discussed earlier, such an advantage is usually based on attaining lower costs or a differentiated position in the market. If the challenger has a cost advantage, it can cut prices to lure away the target competitor's customers—as Ryanair has done in the European air travel market—or it can maintain a similar price but engage in more extensive promotion.

Challenging a leader solely on the basis of low price is a highway to disaster, however, unless the challenger really does have a sustainable cost advantage. Otherwise, the leader might simply match the lower prices until the challenger is driven from the market. The problem is that initially a challenger is often at a cost *disadvantage* because of the experience-curve effects established competitors have accumulated. The challenger must have offsetting advantages like superior production technology, established relations with low-cost suppliers, the

# Exhibit 15.10

MARKETING ACTIONS TO ACHIEVE SHARE-GROWTH OBJECTIVES

| Marketing objectives | Possible marketing actions |
|---|---|
| *Capture repeat/replacement purchases from current customers of the leader or other target competitor by:* | |
| • Head-to-head positioning against competitor's offering in primary target market | • Develop products with features and/or performance levels superior to those of the target competitor. |
| | • Draw on superior product design, process engineering, and supplier relationships to achieve lower unit costs. |
| | • Set prices below target competitor's for comparable level of quality or performance, but only if low-cost position is achieved. |
| | • Outspend the target competitor on promotion aimed at stimulating selective demand: |
| |    Comparative advertising appeals directed at gaining a more favorable positioning than the target competitor's brand enjoys among customers in the mass market. |
| |    Sales promotions to encourage trial if offering's quality or performance is perceptively better than target competitor's, or induce brand switching. |
| |    Build more extensive and/or better-trained salesforce than target competitor's. |
| | • Outspend the target competitor on trade promotion to attain more extensive retail coverage, better shelf space, and/or representation by the best distributors/dealers. |
| | • Outperform the target competitor on customer service: |
| |    Develop superior production scheduling, inventory control, and logistics systems to minimize delivery times and stockouts. |
| |    Develop superior postsale service capabilities; build a more extensive company service force, or provide better training programs for distributor/dealer service people than those of target competitor. |
| • Technological differentiation from target competitor's offering in its primary target market. | • Develop a new generation of products based on different technology that offers superior performance or additional benefits desired by current and potential customers in the mass market (*leapfrog strategy*). |
| | • Build awareness, preference, and replacement demand through heavy introductory promotion: |
| |    Comparative advertising stressing product's superiority. |
| |    Sales promotions to stimulate trial or encourage switching. |
| |    Extensive, well-trained salesforce; heavy use of product demonstrations in sales presentations. |
| | • Build adequate distribution through trade promotions and dealer training programs. |
| *Stimulate selective demand among later adopters by:* | |
| • Head-to-head positioning against target competitor's offering in established market segments. | • See preceding actions. |
| • Differentiated positioning focused on untapped or underdeveloped segments. | • Develop a differentiated brand or product line with unique features or prices that is more appealing to a major segment of potential customers whose needs are not met by existing offerings (*flanking strategy*). |
| | or |
| | • Develop multiple line extensions or brand offerings with features or prices targeted to the unique needs and preferences of several smaller potential applications or regional segments (*encirclement strategy*). |
| | • Design advertising, personal selling, and/or sales promotion campaigns that address specific interests and concerns of potential customers in one or multiple underdeveloped segments to stimulate selective demand. |
| | • Build unique distribution channels to more effectively reach potential customers in one or multiple underdeveloped segments. |
| | • Design service programs to reduce the perceived risks of trial and/or solve the unique problems faced by potential customers in one or multiple underdeveloped segments (e.g., systems engineering, installation, operator training, extended warranties, service hotline, or website). |

## Exhibit 15.11

STRATEGIC CHOICES FOR CHALLENGERS IN GROWTH MARKETS

*Source:* Adapted from Kotler, P., and Singh, R. (1981). "Marketing Warfare in the 1980s," *Journal of Business Strategy,* Winter, pp. 30–41. Copyright 1981 by Emerald Group Publishing Limited. Reproduced with permission of Emerald Group Publishing Limited in the format textbook via copyright clearance center.

ability to share production facilities or marketing efforts across multiple SBUs, or other sources of synergy before a low-price assault makes sense.

A similar caveat applies to frontal assaults based solely on heftier promotional budgets. Unless the target competitor's resources are substantially more limited than the challenger's, it can retaliate against any attempt to win away customers through more extensive advertising or attractive sales and trade promotions.

One possible exception to this limitation of greater promotional effort is the use of a more extensive and better-trained salesforce to gain a competitive advantage. A knowledgeable salesperson's technical advice and problem-solving abilities can give additional value to a firm's product offering, particularly in newly developing high-tech industries.

In general, the best way for a challenger to effectively implement a frontal attack is to differentiate its product or associated services in ways that better meet the needs and preferences of many customers in the mass market. If the challenger can support those meaningful product differences with strong promotion or an attractive price, so much the better, but usually the unique features or services offered are the foundation for a sustainable advantage. For example, until recently, Dell succeeded as a follower in the PC market by offering *both* superior customer service and low prices. Customers could design their own computers on the company's website, get exactly the features they wanted, and have

## Exhibit 15.12

MARKETING OBJECTIVES AND STRATEGIES FOR CHALLENGERS IN GROWTH MARKETS

SHARE-GROWTH STRATEGIES

| Situational variables | Frontal attack | Leapfrog | Flank attack | Encirclement |
|---|---|---|---|---|
| Primary objective | Capture substantial repeat/replacement purchases from target competitor's current customers; attract new customers among later adopters by offering lower price or more attractive features. | Induce current customers in mass market to replace their current brand with superior new offering; attract new customers by providing enhanced benefits. | Attract substantial share of new customers in one or more major segments where customers' needs are different from those of early adopters in the mass market. | Attract a substantial share of new customers in a variety of smaller, specialized segments where customers' needs or preferences differ from those of early adopters in the mass market. |
| Market characteristics | Relatively homogeneous market with respect to customers' needs and purchase criteria; relatively little preference or loyalty for existing brands; no positive network effects. | Relatively homogeneous market with respect to customers' needs and purchase criteria, but some needs or criteria not currently met by existing brands. | Two or more major segments with distinct needs and purchase criteria; needs of customers in at least one segment not currently met by existing brands. | Relatively heterogeneous market with a number of small, specialized segments; needs and preferences of customers in some segments not currently satisfied by competing brands. |
| Competitor's characteristics | Target competitor has relatively limited resources and competencies, particularly in marketing and R&D; would probably be vulnerable to direct attack. | One or more current competitors have relatively strong resources and competencies in marketing, but relatively unsophisticated technology and limited R&D competencies. | Target competitor has relatively strong resources and competencies, particularly in marketing and R&D; would probably be able to withstand direct attack. | One or more competitors have relatively strong marketing, R&D resources and competencies, and/or lower costs; could probably withstand a direct attack. |
| Firm's characteristics | Firm has stronger resources and competencies in R&D and marketing and/or lower operating costs than target competitor. | Firm has proprietary technology superior to that of competitors; firm has necessary marketing and production resources to stimulate and meet primary demand for new generation of products. | Firm's resources and competencies are limited, but sufficient to effectively penetrate and serve at least one major market segment. | Firm has marketing, R&D, and production resources and competencies necessary to serve multiple smaller segments; firm has decentralized and adaptable management structure. |

the equipment delivered to their doors in two or three days. Such excellent service was possible, in large part, due to the close coordination between Dell and its suppliers. Dell's competitive advantage proved to be sustainable, too, because its alliances with suppliers took years to develop and were hard for its competitors to match.

In recent years, however, Dell's aggressive cost-cutting in order to pursue share growth via ever-lower prices caused the firm to reduce its investments in things like R&D and technical training for customer support personnel. Subsequent shortcomings in Dell's new-product development and customer service opened the door for competitors like Hewlett-Packard, Lenovo, and Acer to challenge its lead.[35] The lesson once again is that low price alone is not a good way to capture or hold a leading share position unless customers also perceive they are receiving good value for that price.

Variables that might limit the competitor's willingness or ability to retaliate can also improve the chances for successful frontal attack. For instance, a target competitor with a reputation for high product quality may be loath to cut prices in response to a lower-priced challenger for fear of cheapening its brand's image. And a competitor pursuing high ROI or cash-flow objectives may be reluctant to increase its promotion or R&D expenditures in the short run to fend off an attack.[36]

## Leapfrog Strategy

A challenger stands the best chance of attracting repeat or replacement purchases from a competitor's current customers when it can offer a product that is attractively differentiated from the competitor's offerings. The odds of success might be even greater if the challenger can offer a far superior product based on advanced technology or a more sophisticated design. This is the essence of a leapfrog strategy. It is an attempt to gain a significant advantage over the existing competition by introducing a new generation of products that significantly outperform or offer more desirable customer benefits than do existing brands. For example, the introduction of reasonably priced video cameras by Sony and other Japanese electronics manufacturers largely took over the market for home movie equipment and a large share of the market for Polaroid's self-developing photography equipment as well. And then digital cameras did the same thing to the video market.

In addition, such a strategy often inhibits quick retaliation by established competitors. Firms that have achieved some success with one technology—or that have committed substantial resources to plant and equipment dedicated to a current product—are often reluctant to switch to a new one because of the large investments involved or a fear of disrupting current customers.

A leapfrog strategy is not viable for all challengers. To be successful, the challenger must have technology superior to that of established competitors as well as the product and process engineering capabilities to turn that technology into an appealing product. Also, the challenger must have the marketing resources to effectively promote its new products and convince customers already committed to an earlier technology that the new product offers sufficient benefits to justify the costs of switching.

## Flanking and Encirclement Strategies

The military historian B. H. Liddell-Hart, after analyzing battles ranging from the Greek Wars to World War I, determined that only 6 out of 280 victories were the result of a frontal attack.[37] He concluded that it is usually wiser to avoid attacking an established adversary's point of strength and to focus instead on an area of weakness in his defenses. This is the basic premise behind flanking and encirclement strategies. They both seek to avoid direct confrontations by focusing on market segments whose needs are not being satisfied by existing brands and where no current competitor has a strongly held position.

**Flank Attack**   A flank attack is appropriate when the market can be broken into two or more large segments, when the leader and/or other major competitors hold a strong position in the primary segment, and when no existing brand fully satisfies the needs of customers in at least one other segment. A challenger may be able to capture a significant share of the total market by concentrating primarily on one large untapped segment. This usually involves developing product features or services tailored to the needs and preferences of the targeted customers, together with appropriate promotional and pricing policies to quickly build selective demand. Japanese auto companies, for instance, penetrated the U.S. car market by focusing on the low-price segment, where domestic manufacturers' offerings were limited. Domestic car manufacturers were relatively unconcerned by this flanking action at first. They failed to retaliate very aggressively because the Japanese were pursuing a segment they considered to be small and unprofitable. History proved them wrong.

In some cases, a successful flank attack need not involve unique product features. Instead, a challenger can sometimes meet the special needs of an untapped segment by providing specially designed customer services or distribution channels. For instance, Apple's iTunes music store captured a substantial share of the global recorded music market by offering a convenient (and legal) way for web-savvy consumers to locate and download songs for their personal music libraries.

**Encirclement** An encirclement strategy involves targeting several smaller untapped or underdeveloped segments in the market simultaneously. The idea is to surround the leader's brand with a variety of offerings aimed at several peripheral segments. This strategy makes most sense when the market is fragmented into many different applications segments or geographical regions with somewhat unique needs or tastes.

Once again, this strategy usually involves developing a varied line of products with features tailored to the needs of different segments. Rather than try to compete with Coke and Pepsi in the soft drink market, for example, Cadbury-Schweppes offers a wide variety of flavors such as cream soda, root beer, and ginger ale—almost anything but cola—to appeal to small groups of customers with unique tastes.

# Supporting Evidence

Several studies conducted with the PIMS database provide empirical support for many of the managerial prescriptions we have discussed.[38] These studies compare businesses that achieved high market shares during the growth stage of the product life cycle, or that increased their market shares over time, with low-share businesses. As shown in Exhibit 15.13, the marketing programs and activities of businesses that successfully achieved increased market share differed from their less-successful counterparts in the following ways:

- Businesses that increased the quality of their products relative to those of competitors achieved greater share increases than businesses whose product quality remained constant or declined.
- Share-gaining businesses typically developed and added more new products, line extensions, or product modifications to their line than share-losing businesses.
- Share-gaining businesses tended to increase their marketing expenditures faster than the rate of market growth. Increases in both salesforce and sales promotion expenditures were effective for producing share gains in both consumer and industrial goods businesses. Increased advertising expenditures were effective for producing share gains primarily in consumer goods businesses.
- Surprisingly, there was little difference in the relative prices charged between firms that gained and those that lost market share.

These findings are consistent with many of our earlier observations. For instance, they underline the folly of launching a frontal attack solely on the basis of lower price. Unless the challenger has substantially lower unit costs or the leader is inhibited from cutting its own prices for some reason, the challenger's price cuts are likely to be retaliated against and will generate few new customers. On the other hand, frontal, leapfrog, flanking, or encirclement attacks based on product improvements tailored to specific segments are more likely to succeed, particularly when the challenger supports those attacks with substantial promotional efforts.

# Exhibit 15.13

STRATEGIC CHANGES MADE BY CHALLENGERS THAT GAINED VERSUS LOST MARKET SHARE

| Strategic changes | Share-gaining challengers | Share-losing challengers |
| --- | --- | --- |
| Relative product quality scores | +1.8 | −0.6 |
| New products as a percent of sales | +0.1 | −0.5 |
| Relative price | +0.3 | +0.2 |
| Marketing expenditures (adjusted for market growth): | | |
| Salesforce | +9.0% | −8.0% |
| Advertising: | | |
| Consumer products | +13.0% | −9.0% |
| Industrial products | −1.0 | −14.0 |
| Promotion: | | |
| Consumer products | +13.0% | −5.0% |
| Industrial products | +7.0 | −10.0 |

Source: Adapted with the permission of The Free Press, a Division of Simon & Schuster, Inc., from *The PIMS Principles: Linking Strategy to Performance,* by Robert D. Buzzell and Bradley T. Gale. Copyright © 1987 by The Free Press. All rights reserved.

Regardless of the strategies pursued by market leaders and challengers during a product-market's growth stage, the competitive situation often changes as the market matures and its growth rate slows. In the next chapter, we examine the environmental changes that occur as a market matures and the marketing strategies that firms might use to adapt to those changes.

# TAKE-AWAYS

1. Being the pioneer in a new product or service category gains a firm a number of potential advantages. But not all pioneers are able to sustain a leading position in the market as it grows. A pioneering firm stands the best chance for long-term share leadership and profitability when the market can be insulated from the rapid entry of competitors by patent protection or other means and when the firm has the necessary resources and competencies to capitalize on its first-mover advantages.

2. Some pioneers attempt to penetrate the mass market and remain the share leader as that market grows. Others adopt a strategy geared to making profits from specialized niche markets where they will face fewer direct competitors. Still others try to stay one jump ahead of competitors by introducing a stream of new products and withdrawing from older markets as they become more competitive. The appropriate strategy to adopt depends on the firm's resources and competencies, the strength of likely competitors, and the characteristics of the product and its target market.

3. If a market leader wishes to maintain its number one share position as the product category moves through rapid growth, it must focus on two important objectives: (1) retaining its current customers, and (2) stimulating selective demand among later adopters. Marketing strategies a leader might adopt to achieve these objectives are position defense, flanker, confrontation, market expansion, and contraction. The best one to choose depends on the homogeneity of the market and the firm's resources and competencies relative to potential competitors.

4. For a challenger to increase its market share relative to the leader, it must differentiate its offering by delivering superior product benefits, better service, or a lower price than the leader. Challenging a leader solely on the basis of price is a highway to disaster, however, unless the challenger has a sustainable cost advantage.

**Self-diagnostic questions to test your ability to apply the analytical tools and concepts in this chapter to marketing decision making may be found at this book's website at www.mhhe.com/mullins8e**

# ENDNOTES

1. This example is based on information found in Irene M. Kunii, "Quick Studies," *BusinessWeek,* November 18, 2002, pp. 48–49; "Hard To Copy," *The Economist,* November 2, 2002, pp. 63–64; Clay Chandler, "Canon's Big Gun," *Fortune,* February 6, 2006, pp. 92–98; and Canon's 2010 Annual Report available at the company's website, *www.canon.com.*

2. These results are reported in Myron Magnet, "Let's Go for Growth," *Fortune,* March 7, 1994, pp. 60–72.

3. *New Products Management for the 1980s* (New York: Booz, Allen & Hamilton, 1982). More recent studies, though focusing on smaller samples of new products, suggest that the relative proportions of new-to-the-world versus less innovative product introductions have not changed substantially over the years. For example, see Eric M. Olson, Orville C. Walker, Jr., and Robert W. Ruekert, "Organizing for Effective New Product Development: The Moderating Role of Product Innovativeness," *Journal of Marketing* 59 (January 1995), pp. 48–62.

4. Katrijn Gielens and Jan-Benedict E. M. Steenkamp, "Drivers of Consumer Acceptance of New Packaged Goods: An Investigation across Products and Countries," *International Journal of Research in Marketing* 24 (June 2007), pp. 97–111.

5. For a more extensive review of the potential competitive advantages of being a first mover, and the controllable and uncontrollable forces that influence a firm's ability to capitalize on those potential advantages, see Roger A. Kerin, P. Rajan Varadarajan, and Robert A. Peterson, "First-Mover Advantage: A Synthesis, Conceptual Framework, and Research Propositions," *Journal of Marketing* 56 (October 1992), pp. 33–52; and David M. Szymanski, Lisa M. Troy, and Sundar J. Bharadwaj, "Order-of Entry and Business Performance: An Empirical Synthesis and Reexamination," *Journal of Marketing,* 59 (October 1995), pp. 17–33.

6. Thomas S. Gruca and D. Sudharshan, "A Framework for Entry Deterrence Strategy: The Competitive Environment, Choices, and Consequences," *Journal of Marketing* 59 (July 1995), pp. 44–55.

7. Robert Berner, "There Goes The Rainbow Nut Crunch," *BusinessWeek,* July 19, 2004, p. 38.

8. Carl Shapiro and Hal R. Varian, *Information Rules* (Boston: Harvard Business School Press, 1999), chap. 7.

9. Raji Srinivasan, Gary L. Lilien, and Arvid Rangaswamy, "First In, First Out? The Effects of Network Externalities on Pioneer Survival," *Journal of Marketing* 68 (January 2004), pp. 41–58.

10. Rajan Varadarajan, Manjit S. Yadav, and Venkatesh Shankar, "First-Mover Advantage on the internet: Real or Virtual?" *MSI Report* #05–100 (Cambridge, MA: The Marketing Science Institute, 2005).

11. Rob Walker, "The Guts of a New Machine," *The New York Times Magazine,* November 30, 2003, pp. 78–84.

12. For example, see William T. Robinson, "Market Pioneering and Sustainable Market Share Advantages in Industrial Goods Manufacturing Industries," working paper, Purdue University, 1984; and Robert D. Buzzell and Bradley T. Gale, *The PIMS Principles: Linking Strategy to Performance* (New York: Free Press, 1987), p. 183.

13. Peter N. Golder and Gerard J. Tellis, "Pioneer Advantage: Marketing Logic or Marketing Legend," *Journal of Marketing Research* 30 (May 1993), pp. 158–70.

14. William T. Robinson and Sungwook Min, "Is the First to Market the First to Fail? Empirical Evidence for Industrial Goods Businesses," *Journal of Marketing Research* 39 (February 2002), pp. 120–28.

15. Marvin B. Lieberman and David B. Montgomery, "First-Mover Advantages," *Strategic Management Journal* 9 (1988), pp. 41–59; and Michael J. Moore, William Boulding, and Ronald C. Goodstein, "Pioneering and Market Share: Is Entry Time Endogenous and Does It Matter?" *Journal of Marketing* 28 (February 1991), pp. 97–104.

16. Venkatesh Shankar, Gregory S. Carpenter, and Lakshman Krishnamukthi, "Late Mover Advantages: How Innovative Late Entrants Outsell Pioneers," *Journal of Marketing Research* 35 (February 1998), pp. 54–70.

17. Szymanski, Troy, and Bharadwaj, "Order-of-Entry and Business Performance."

18. Mary L. Coyle, "Competition in Developing Markets: The Impact of Order of Entry," unpublished doctoral dissertation, University of Toronto, 1986. Also see Kerin, Varadarajan, and Peterson, "First-Mover Advantage."

19. William T. Robinson and Jeongwen Chiang, "Product Development Strategies for Established Market Pioneers, Early Followers, and Late Entrants," *Strategic Management Journal* 23 (September 2002), pp. 855–66.

20. Gerard J. Tellis, Eden Yin, and Rakesh Hiraj, "Does Quality Win? Network Effects versus Quality in High-Tech Markets," *Journal of Marketing Research* 46 (April 2009), pp. 135–149.

21. Shankar, Carpenter, and Krishnamukthi, "Late Mover Advantages."

22. George S. Day, *Analysis for Strategic Marketing Decisions* (St. Paul, MN: West, 1986), pp. 103–4; Michael Arndt, "3M's Rising Star," *BusinessWeek,* April 12, 2004, pp. 62–74, and Brian Hindo, "At 3M, a struggle between Efficiency and Creativity," *BusinessWeek—Indepth,* June 2007, pp. in8–in14.

23. Shapiro and Varian, *Information Rules,* chap. 2.

24. Franklin R. Root, *Entry Strategy for International Markets* (Lexington, MA: D. C. Heath, 1987). Also see Jeremy Main, "Making Global Alliances Work," *Fortune,* December 17, 1990, pp. 121–26.

25. For additional examples, see Dan Macsai, "Marketing to Milennials," *www.businessweek.com/smallbiz,* August 22, 2008.

26. This assumes that demand is relatively price inelastic. In markets where price elasticity is high, a skimming price strategy may lead to lower total revenues due to its dampening effect on total demand.

27. Buzzell and Gale, *The PIMS Principles,* pp. 188–90.

28. For a detailed discussion of these strategies in a military context, see Carl von Clausewitz, *On War* (London: Routledge and Kegan Paul, 1908); and B. H. Liddell-Hart, *Strategy* (New York: Praeger, 1967). For a related discussion of the application of such strategies in a business setting, see Philip Kotler and Ravi Singh Achrol, "Marketing Warfare in the 1980s," *Journal of Business Strategy,* Winter 1981, pp. 30–41.

29. Jeff Jarvis, "Love the Customers Who Hate You," *BusinessWeek,* March 3, 2008, p. 58.

30. Thomas T. Nagle, "Managing Price Competition," *Marketing Management* 2 (Spring 1993), pp. 36–45; and Akshay R. Rao, Mark E. Bergen, and Scott Davis, "How To Fight a Price War," *Harvard Business Review,* March–April 2000, pp. 107–16.

31. Robert J. Dolan and Abel P. Jewland, "Experience Curves and Dynamic Demand Models: Implications for Optimal Pricing Strategy," *Journal of Marketing,* Winter 1981, p. 52.

32. Bruce Einhorn and Nandini Lakshman, "Nokia Connects," *BusinessWeek* March 27, 2006, pp. 44–45; and Mehul Srivastava, "Giving Indians the Phones They Want," *Bloomberg Businessweek,* August 16, 2010, pp. 36–38.

33. "Haier Group Ranks Second in Global Fridge Markets," *People's Daily Online,* January 13, 2002, archived at *www.english.peopledaily.com.cn.,* and "Haier's Purpose," *The Economist,* March 20, 2004, p. 72.

34. There are some more specialized strategies that challengers may pursue under specific circumstances that are beyond the scope of this discussion. For a more detailed examination of such strategies see Orville C. Walker, Jr., and John W. Mullins, *Marketing Strategy: A Decision-Focused Approach,* 7th ed., (Burr Ridge, IL: McGraw-Hill/Irwin, 2006), chap. 9.

**35.** Nanette Byrnes, Peter Burrows, and Louise Lee, "Dark Days at Dell," *BusinessWeek,* September 4, 2006, pp. 26–29; and Aaron Ricadela, "Dell: Scant Signs of Recovery," *www.businessweek.com/technology*, July 14, 2009.

**36.** For a more extensive discussion of factors that can limit a leader's willingness or ability to retaliate against a direct attack, see Michael E. Porter, *Competitive Advantage* (New York: Free Press, 1985), chap. 15.

**37.** Liddell-Hart, *Strategy,* p. 163.

**38.** Robert D. Buzzell and Federik D. Wiersema, "Successful Share-Building Strategies," *Harvard Business Review,* January–February 1981, pp. 135–43; Carl R. Anderson and Carl P. Zeithaml, "Stages in the Product Life Cycle, Business Strategy, and Business Performance," *Academy of Management Journal,* March 1984, pp. 5–25; and Buzzell and Gale, *The PIMS Principles,* chap. 9.

# CHAPTER SIXTEEN

# Strategies for Mature and Declining Markets

## Johnson Controls—Making Money in Mature Markets[1]

AT FIRST GLANCE, Johnson Controls Inc., in Glendale, Wisconsin, appears to be the epitome of a staid, slow-growing, "old-economy" company. The firm's success and survival depend on several product and service categories that have not experienced much growth in the domestic market in recent years. Johnson's major businesses include batteries, seats, and other internal components for automobiles; heating and cooling equipment for large commercial buildings and schools; and facilities management services.

But first glances can be deceiving. The firm's managers have developed a four-pronged strategy for making money in such mature markets. First, Johnson has acquired a number of weaker competitors in each of its product categories over the years in order to gain market share and remove excess capacity. Second, the firm has expanded sales volume by moving aggressively into global markets. The firm now operates in 500 locations around the world.

Most important, the firm has nurtured close relationships with established customers such as General Motors, Chrysler, BMW, and Toyota. Those relationships have enabled Johnson to maintain solid profit margins by improving customer retention and gaining operating efficiencies via logistical alliances, just-in-time delivery systems, and other process improvements. Finally, the firm's close customer relationships have provided it with market intelligence and facilitated joint development projects, both of which have helped the firm gain additional revenue from the introduction of new product and service offerings targeted at those customers.

A strong balance sheet and a long-term perspective have helped Johnson build market share—and expand into other countries—through the acquisition of competitors. In some cases, the firm has snapped up firms with product or service offerings that complement and extend Johnson's own product line in one of its established target markets. For instance, the firm spent $167 million to acquire Pan Am's World Services division, a facility management operation that does everything from mow the lawn to run the cafeteria. That acquisition, when combined with Johnson's existing heating and cooling systems business and some new products and services developed internally, turned the company into a full-service facilities operator. Johnson can now manage a client's entire building while offering highly customized heating and cooling systems and controls that minimize energy use. This combination of customized products and full service has both expanded the company's share of the commercial real estate market and enabled it to maintain relatively high margins in a highly competitive business.

In other businesses, Johnson has combined the economies of scale generated through savvy acquisitions with the knowledge gained from close customer relationships to both develop new products and drive down operating costs. For example, Johnson has become the leading worldwide supplier of automotive seating and interior systems, such as floor consoles and instrument panels, by assisting manufacturers with the design and development, as well as the manufacture, of such components. As one engineer at Chrysler pointed out, "Johnson is able to completely integrate the design, development, and manufacture of [our] seats," and do it for less than the auto companies could. On the design side, Johnson Controls has maintained its own industrial design department for many years. The firm's European design center in Cologne, Germany, alone has 70 staff members, more than the interior design teams of many car makers. The center includes an in-house market research department to help identify trends in consumer tastes in European markets, and pre-test consumer reactions to possible design innovations.

On the manufacturing side, by closely coordinating inventories and production schedules, Johnson has reduced costs even further for both its customers and itself. For instance, by locating its plants close to a customer's production facility, Johnson is able to assemble seats to order, load them on a truck in a sequence that matches the cars coming down the assembly line, and deliver them to the customer all in as little as 90 minutes.

Despite the maturity of its markets, Johnson's strategy is paying off, both in terms of revenue growth and profits. While the firm's sales and profits took a hit during the global financial crisis of 2008–2009, they rebounded quickly. In the 2010 fiscal year, the company's revenues hit a record $34.3 billion and produced $1.49 billion in net income and a 16 percent return on shareholders' equity.

## Marketing Challenges Addressed in Chapter 16

Many managers, particularly those in marketing, seem obsessed with growth. Their objectives tend to emphasize annual increases in sales volume, market share, or both. But the biggest challenge for many managers in developed nations in future years will be making money in markets that grow slowly, if at all. The majority of product-markets in those nations are in the mature or decline stages of their life cycles. And as accelerating rates of technological and social change continue to shorten such life cycles, today's innovations will move from growth to maturity—and ultimately to decline—ever faster.

A period of competitive turbulence almost always accompanies the transition from market growth to maturity in an industry. This period often begins after approximately half the potential customers have adopted the product and the rate of sales growth starts to decline. As the growth rate slows, many competitors tend to overestimate future sales volume and consequently end up developing too much production capacity. Competition becomes more intense as firms battle to increase sales volume to cover their high fixed costs and maintain profitability. As a result, such transition periods are commonly accompanied by a **shakeout** during which weaker businesses fail, withdraw from the industry, or are acquired by other firms, as has happened to some of Johnson Controls' competitors in the United States and European automotive seat and battery industries.

# Challenges in Mature Markets

Businesses that survive the shakeout face new challenges as market growth stagnates. As a market matures, total volume stabilizes; replacement purchases rather than first-time buyers account for the vast majority of that volume. A primary market-

ing objective of all competitors in mature markets, therefore, is simply to hold their existing customers—to sustain a meaningful competitive advantage that will help ensure the continued satisfaction and loyalty of those customers. Thus, a product's financial success during the mature life-cycle stage depends heavily on the firm's ability to achieve and sustain a lower delivered cost or some perceived product quality or customer-service superiority.

Some firms tend to passively defend mature products while using the bulk of the revenues produced by those items to develop and aggressively market new products with more growth potential. This can be shortsighted, however. All segments of a market and all brands in an industry do not necessarily reach maturity at the same time. Aging brands such as Adidas, Johnson's baby shampoo, and Arm & Hammer baking soda experienced sales revivals in recent years because of creative marketing strategies. Thus, a share leader in a mature industry might build on a cost or product differentiation advantage and pursue a marketing strategy aimed at increasing volume by promoting new uses for an old product or by encouraging current customers to buy and use the product more often. Therefore, in this chapter we examine basic business strategies necessary for survival in mature markets and marketing strategies a firm might use to extend a brand's sales and profits, including the strategies that have been so successful for Johnson Controls.

# Challenges in Declining Markets

Eventually, technological advances, changing customer demographics, tastes, or life-styles, and development of substitutes result in declining demand for most product forms and brands. As a product starts to decline, managers face the critical question of whether to divest or liquidate the business. Unfortunately, firms sometimes support dying products too long at the expense of current profitability and the aggressive pursuit of future breadwinners.

An appropriate marketing strategy can, however, produce substantial sales and profits even in a declining market. If few exit barriers exist, an industry leader might attempt to increase market share via aggressive pricing or promotion policies aimed at driving out weaker competitors. Or it might try to consolidate the industry, as Johnson Controls has done in its automotive components businesses, by acquiring weaker brands and reducing overhead by eliminating both excess capacity and duplicate marketing programs. Alternatively, a firm might decide to harvest a mature product by maximizing cash flow and profit over the product's remaining life. The last section of this chapter examines specific marketing strategies for gaining the greatest possible returns from products approaching the end of their life cycle.

# Strategic Choices in Mature Markets

The maturity phase of an industry's life cycle is often depicted as one of stability characterized by few changes in the market shares of leading competitors and steady prices. The industry leaders, because of their low per unit costs and little need to make any further investments, enjoy high profits and positive cash flows. These cash flows are harvested and diverted to other SBUs or products in the firm's portfolio that promise greater future growth.

Unfortunately, this conventional scenario provides an overly simplistic description of the situation businesses face in most mature markets. For one thing, it is not always easy to tell when a market has reached maturity. Variations in brands, marketing programs, and customer groups can mean that different brands and market segments reach maturity at different times.

Further, as the maturity stage progresses, a variety of threats and opportunities can disrupt an industry's stability. Shifts in customer needs or preferences, product substitutes, increased raw material costs, changes in government regulations, or factors such as the entry of low-cost producers or mergers and acquisitions can threaten individual competitors and even throw the entire industry into early decline. Consider, for instance, Kodak, a brand that dominated the world market for photographic film for decades. First the appearance of high-quality foreign competitors like Fuji film, and then the development and consumer acceptance of digital cameras, quickly eroded the size of the photographic film market and Kodak's share of that market.

On the positive side, such changes can also open new growth opportunities in mature industries. Product improvements (such as the development of high-fiber nutritional cereals), advances in process technology (the creation of minimills for steel production), falling raw materials costs, increased prices for close substitutes, or environmental changes can all provide opportunities for a firm to dramatically increase its sales and profits. An entire industry can even experience a period of renewed growth.

Discontinuities during industry maturity suggest that it is dangerously shortsighted for a firm to simply milk its cash cows. Even industry followers can substantially improve volume, share, and profitability during industry maturity if they can adjust their marketing objectives and programs to fit the new opportunities that arise.[2] Thus, success in mature markets requires two sets of strategic actions: (1) the development of a well-implemented business strategy to sustain a competitive advantage, customer satisfaction, and loyalty; and (2) flexible and creative marketing programs geared to pursue growth or profit opportunities as conditions change in specific product-markets.

# Strategies for Maintaining Competitive Advantage

As discussed in Chapter 9, both *analyzer* and *defender strategies* may be appropriate for units with a leading, or at least a profitable, share of one or more major segments in a mature industry. Analyzers and defenders are both concerned with maintaining a strong share position in established product-markets. But analyzers also do some product and market development to avoid being leapfrogged by competitors with more advanced products or being left behind in new applications segments. On the other hand, defenders may initiate some product improvements or line extensions to protect and strengthen their position in existing markets, but they spend relatively little on new product R&D. Thus, an analyzer strategy is most appropriate for developed industries that are still experiencing some technological change and may have opportunities for continued growth, such as the computer and commercial aircraft industries. The defender strategy works best in industries where the basic technology is not very complex or is unlikely to change dramatically in the short run, as in the food industry.

Both analyzers and defenders can attempt to sustain a competitive advantage in established product-markets through *differentiation* of their product offering (either on the basis of superior quality or service) or by maintaining a low-cost position. Evidence suggests the ability to maintain either a strongly differentiated or a low-cost position continues to be a critical determinant of success throughout both the transition and the maturity stage. One study examined the competitive strategies pursued by the two leading firms (in terms of return on investment) in eight mature industries characterized by slow growth and intense competition. In each industry, the two leading firms offered either the lowest relative delivered cost or high relative product differentiation.[3] Similarly, as we saw in Chapter 2, observations by Treacy and Wiersema found that market leaders tend to pursue one of three strategic disciplines. They either stress operational excellence, which typically translates into lower costs, or differentiate themselves through product leadership or customer intimacy and superior service.[4]

Generally, it is difficult for a single business to pursue both low-cost and differentiation strategies at the same time. For instance, businesses taking the low-cost approach typically compete primarily by offering the lowest prices in the industry. Such prices allow little room for the firm to make the investments or cover the costs inherent in maintaining superior product quality, performance, or service over time.

Of course, improvements in quality—especially the reduction of product defects via improved production and procurement processes—can also reduce a product's cost, as advocates of "six sigma" programs point out. There is some evidence, however, that efforts aimed at improving quality in order to increase the benefits customers associate with the product, and thereby produce increased sales and market share, generate greater financial returns for a firm than quality improvement efforts focused mainly on cost reduction.[5] Therefore, in the following sections we discuss quality improvement efforts aimed at differentiating a firm's offering and making it more appealing to customers separately from methods for reducing an offering's cost.

It is important to keep in mind, however, that pursuit of a low-cost strategy does not mean that a business can ignore the delivery of desirable benefits to the customer. Similarly, customers will not pay an unlimited price premium for superior quality or service, no matter how superior it is. In both consumer and commercial markets customers seek good *value* for the money; either a solid, no-frills product or service at an outstanding price or an offering whose higher price is justified by the superior benefits it delivers on one or more dimensions.[6] Thus, even low-cost producers should continually seek ways to improve the quality and performance of their offerings within the financial constraints of their competitive strategy. And even differentiated defenders should continually work to improve efficiency without sacrificing product quality or performance. This point is clearly illustrated in the diagram of the customer value management process in Exhibit 16.1, which shows that actions to improve customers' perceptions of quality (whether of goods or service) and to reduce costs both impact customer value. The critical strategic questions facing the marketing manager, then, are, How can a business continue to differentiate its offerings and justify a premium price as its market matures and becomes more competitive? and, How can businesses, particularly those pursuing low-cost strategies, continue to reduce their costs and improve their efficiency as their markets mature?

# Methods of Differentiation

At the most basic level, a business can attempt to differentiate its offering from competitors' by offering either superior product quality, superior service, or both. The problem is that *quality* and *service* may be defined in a variety of different ways by customers.

**Dimensions of Product Quality[7]**    To maintain a competitive advantage in product quality, a firm must understand what *dimensions customers perceive to underlie differences*

# Exhibit 16.1

THE PROCESS OF CUSTOMER VALUE MANAGEMENT

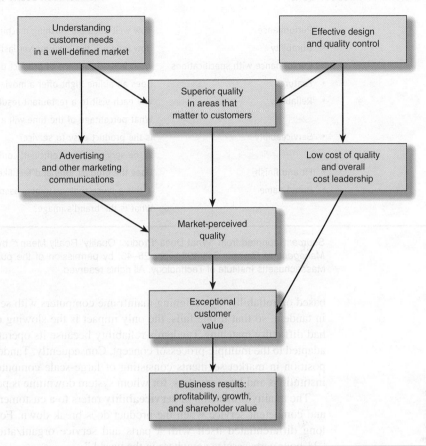

*across products* within a given category. One authority has identified eight such dimensions of product quality. These are summarized in Exhibit 16.2 and discussed below.

European manufacturers of prestige automobiles, such as Mercedes-Benz and Porsche, have emphasized the first dimension of product quality—**functional performance.** These automakers have designed cars that provide excellent performance on such attributes as handling, acceleration, and comfort. Volvo, on the other hand, has emphasized and aggressively promoted a different quality dimension—**durability** (and the related attribute of safety). A third quality dimension, **conformance to specifications,** or the absence of defects, has been a major focus of the Japanese automakers. Until recent years, American carmakers relied heavily on broad product lines and a wide **variety of features,** both standard and optional, to offset their shortcomings on some of the other quality dimensions.

The **reliability** quality dimension can refer to the consistency of performance from purchase to purchase or to a product's uptime, the percentage of time that it can perform satisfactorily over its life. Tandem Computers has maintained a competitive advantage

## Exhibit 16.2

DIMENSIONS OF PRODUCT QUALITY

| | |
|---|---|
| • Performance | How well does the washing machine wash clothes? |
| • Durability | How long will the lawn mower last? |
| • Conformance with specifications | What is the incidence of product defects? |
| • Features | Does an airline flight offer a movie and dinner? |
| • Reliability | Will each visit to a restaurant result in consistent quality? |
| | What percentage of the time will a product perform satisfactorily? |
| • Serviceability | Is the product easy to service? |
| | Is the service system efficient, competent, and convenient? |
| • Fit and finish | Does the product look and feel like a quality product? |
| • Brand name | Is this a name that customers associate with quality? |
| | What is the brand's image? |

*Source:* Reprinted from "What Does 'Product Quality' Really Mean?" by David A. Garvin, MIT, *Sloan Management Review*, Fall 1984, pp. 25–43, by permission of the publisher. Copyright © 1984 by Massachusetts Institute of Technology. All rights reserved.

based on reliability by designing mainframe computers with several processors that work in tandem, so that if one fails, the only impact is the slowing of low-priority tasks. IBM had difficulty matching Tandem's reliability because its operating system was not easily adapted to the multiple-processor concept. Consequently, Tandem has maintained a strong position in market segments consisting of large-scale computer users, such as financial institutions and large retailers, for whom system downtime is particularly undesirable.

The quality dimension of **serviceability** refers to a customer's ability to obtain prompt and competent service when the product does break down. For example, Caterpillar has long differentiated itself with a parts and service organization dedicated to providing "24-hour parts service anywhere in the world."

Many of these quality dimensions can be difficult for customers to evaluate, particularly for consumer products. As a result, consumers often generalize from quality dimensions that are more visual or qualitative. Thus, the **fit and finish** dimension can help convince consumers that a product is of high quality. They tend to perceive attractive and well-designed products as generally high in quality, as witnessed by the success of Samsung's consumer electronics products. Similarly, the **quality reputation of the brand name,** and the promotional activities that sustain that reputation, can strongly influence consumers' perceptions of a product's quality.[8] A brand's quality reputation together with psychological factors such as name recognition and loyalty substantially determine a brand's **equity**—the perceived value customers associate with a particular brand name and its logo or symbol.[9] To successfully pursue a differentiation strategy based on quality, then, a business must understand what dimensions or cues its potential customers use to judge quality, and it should pay particular attention to some of the less-concrete but more visible and symbolic attributes of the product.

### Dimensions of Service Quality

Customers also judge the quality of the service they receive on multiple dimensions. A number of such dimensions of perceived service quality have been identified by a series of studies conducted across diverse industries such as retail banking and appliance repair, and five of those dimensions are listed and briefly defined in Exhibit 16.3.[10]

## Exhibit 16.3

DIMENSIONS OF SERVICE QUALITY

| | |
|---|---|
| • Tangibles | Appearance of physical facilities, equipment, personnel, and communications materials. |
| • Reliability | Ability to perform the promised service dependably and accurately. |
| • Responsiveness | Willingness to help customers and provide prompt service. |
| • Assurance | Knowledge and courtesy of employees and their ability to convey trust and confidence. |
| • Empathy | Caring, individualized attention the firm provides its customers. |

*Source:* Adapted with the permission of The Free Press, a Division of Simon & Schuster, Inc., from *Delivering Quality Service: Balancing Customer Perceptions and Expectations* by Valarie A. Zeithaml, A. Parasuraman, and Leonard L. Berry. Copyright © 1990 by The Free Press. All rights reserved.

The quality dimensions listed in Exhibit 16.3 apply specifically to service businesses, but most of them are also relevant for judging the service component of a product offering. This pertains to both the objective performance dimensions of the service delivery system, such as its **reliability** and **responsiveness,** as well as to elements of the performance of service personnel, such as their **empathy** and level of **assurance.**

The results of a number of surveys suggest that customers perceive all five dimensions of service quality to be very important regardless of the kind of service being evaluated. Customers of four different kinds of services gave reliability, responsiveness, assurance, and empathy mean importance ratings of more than 9 on a 10-point rating scale. And though the mean ratings for tangibles were somewhat lower in comparison, they still fell toward the upper end of the scale.

The same respondents were also asked which of the five dimensions they would choose as being the most critical in their assessment of service quality. Their responses suggest that reliability is the most important aspect of service quality to the greatest number of customers.

## Are the Dimensions the Same for Service Quality on the Internet?

Some of the researchers who identified the dimensions of service quality listed in Exhibit 16.3 have also studied whether service quality on the internet has the same or different underlying dimensions. They defined online service quality as the extent to which a website facilitates efficient and effective shopping, purchasing, and delivery. They identified 11 dimensions of perceived e-service quality: access, ease of navigation, efficiency, flexibility, reliability, personalization, security/privacy, responsiveness, assurance/trust, site aesthetics, and price knowledge.[11]

While e-service quality obviously has more underlying dimensions, some of the most important of those dimensions are the same online as offline, such as reliability and responsiveness. This helps explain why e-tailers like Amazon have spent millions building distribution centers geared toward improving the reliability of their order fulfillment activities.

On the other hand, some dimensions that are important offline are not as crucial on the internet. Empathy, for example, doesn't appear to be a major concern for online customers, unless they are having problems on some of the other service dimensions.

The key to a differentiation strategy based on providing superior service is to meet or exceed target customers' service quality expectations and to do it more consistently than competitors. The problem is that sometimes managers underestimate the level of those customer expectations, and sometimes those expectations can be unrealistically high. Therefore, a firm needs to clearly identify target customers' desires with respect to service quality and to clearly define and communicate what level of service they intend to deliver. When this is done, customers have a more realistic idea of what to expect and are less likely to be disappointed with the service they receive.

**Improving Customer Perceptions of Service Quality**    The major factors that determine a customer's expectations and perceptions concerning service quality—and five gaps that can lead to dissatisfaction with service delivery—are outlined in Exhibit 16.4 and discussed next.

# Exhibit 16.4

DETERMINANTS OF PERCEIVED SERVICE QUALITY

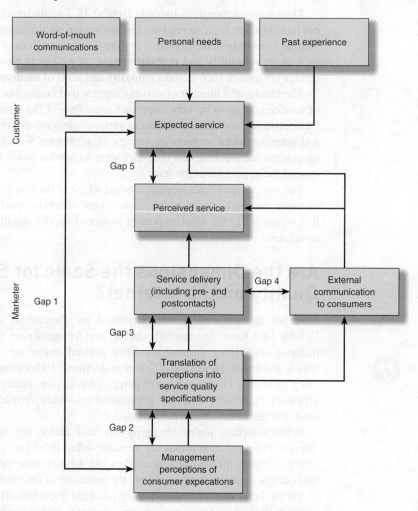

*Source:* Reprinted from A. Parasuraman, Valarie A. Zeithaml, and Leonard L. Berry, "A Conceptual Model of Service Quality and Its Implications for Future Research," *Journal of Marketing,* Fall 1985, p. 44. Used by permission of the American Marketing Association.

1. **Gap between the customer's expectations and the marketer's perceptions.** Managers do not always have an accurate understanding of what customers want or how they will evaluate a firm's service efforts. The first step in providing good service is to collect information—through customer surveys, evaluations of customer complaints, or other methods—to determine what service attributes customers consider important.

2. **Gap between management perceptions and service quality specifications.** Even when management has a clear understanding of what customers want, that understanding might not get translated into effective operating standards. A firm's policies concerning customer service may be unclear, poorly communicated to employees, or haphazardly enforced. Unless a firm's employees know what the company's service policies are and believe that management is seriously committed to those standards, their performance is likely to fall short of desired levels.

3. **Gap between service quality specifications and service delivery.** Lip service by management is not enough to produce high-quality service. High standards must be backed by the programs, resources, and rewards necessary to enable and encourage employees to deliver good service. Employees must be provided with the training, equipment, and time necessary to deliver good service. Their service performance must be measured and evaluated. And good performance must be rewarded by making it part of the criteria for pay raises or promotions, or by other more direct inducements, in order to motivate the additional effort good service requires.

4. **Gap between service delivery and external communications.** Even good service performance may disappoint some customers if the firm's marketing communications cause them to have unrealistically high expectations. If the photographs in a vacation resort's advertising and brochures make the rooms look more spacious and luxurious than they really are, for instance, first-time customers are likely to be disappointed no matter how clean or well-tended those rooms are kept by the resort's staff.

5. **Gap between perceived service and expected service.** This results when management fails to close one or more of the other four gaps. It is this difference between a customer's expectations and his or her actual experience with the firm that leads to dissatisfaction.

The above discussion suggests a number of actions management can take to close the possible gaps and improve customer satisfaction with a company's service.[12] Achieving and sustaining high levels of service quality can present difficult implementation problems, however, because it usually involves the coordination of efforts of many employees from different functional departments and organizational levels. Some of these coordination problems are examined in Chapter 17.

# Methods of Maintaining a Low-Cost Position

Moving down the experience curve is the most commonly discussed method of achieving and sustaining a low-cost position in an industry. But a firm does not necessarily need a large relative market share to implement a low-cost strategy. For instance, Johnson Controls relies on close alliances with customers, as well as economies of scale, to hold down its inventory and distribution costs. And Michael Dell, as a small follower in the personal computer industry, managed to achieve costs below those of much larger competitors by developing logistical alliances with suppliers and an innovative, internet-based direct distribution channel.

Some other means for obtaining a sustainable cost advantage include producing a no-frills product, creating an innovative product design, finding cheaper raw materials, automating or outsourcing production, developing low-cost distribution channels, and reducing overhead.[13]

**A No-Frills Product**  A direct approach to obtaining a low-cost position involves simply removing all frills and extras from the basic product or service. Thus, Ryanair's flights from secondary airports on the outskirts of major cities, warehouse furniture stores, legal services clinics, and grocery stores selling canned goods out of crates all offer lower costs and prices than their competitors. This lower production cost is often sustainable because established differentiated competitors find it difficult to stop offering features and services their customers have come to expect. However, those established firms may lower their own prices in the short run—even to the point of suffering losses—in an attempt to drive out a no-frills competitor that poses a serious threat. Thus, a firm considering a no-frills strategy needs the resources to withstand a possible price war.[14]

**Innovative Product Design**    A simplified product design and standardized component parts can also lead to cost advantages. In the office copier industry, for instance, Japanese firms overcame substantial entry barriers by designing extremely simple copiers, with a fraction of the number of parts in the design used by market-leading Xerox.

**Cheaper Raw Materials**    A firm with the foresight to acquire or the creativity to find a way to use relatively cheap raw materials can also gain a sustainable cost advantage. For example, Fort Howard Paper achieved an advantage by being the first major papermaker to rely exclusively on recycled pulp. While the finished product was not so high in quality as paper from virgin wood, Fort Howard's lower cost gave it a competitive edge in the price-sensitive commercial market for toilet paper and other such products used in hotels, restaurants, and office buildings.

**Innovative Production Processes**    Although low-cost defender businesses typically spend little on *product R&D,* they often continue to devote substantial sums to *process R&D.* Innovations in the production process, including the development of automated or computer-controlled processes, can help them sustain cost advantages over competitors.

In some labor-intensive industries, a business can achieve a cost advantage, at least in the short term, by gaining access to inexpensive labor. This is usually achieved by moving all or part of the production process to countries with low wage rates, such as China or Mexico. Because such moves are relatively easy to emulate, however this kind of cost advantage may not be sustainable.[15] Also, as developing nations become increasingly successful economically, wages and other operating costs tend to rise, thereby reducing the cost advantages of outsourcing to those countries.[16]

**Low-Cost Distribution**    When distribution accounts for a relatively high proportion of a product's total delivered cost, a firm might gain a substantial advantage by developing lower-cost alternative channels. Typically, this involves eliminating, or shifting to the customer, some of the functions performed by traditional channels in return for a lower price. In the consumer banking industry, for example, automated teller machines helped reduce labor costs and investment in bricks-and-mortar branch banks. But they also reduced the amount of personalized service banks provided to their customers, which contributed to a decline in customer satisfaction.

And that, in turn, helps to explain why Barclays Bank, Bank of America, and many other European and North American banks are developing and analyzing customer databases to identify the needs and preferences of different market segments, redesigning branches to make them more welcoming, and adding personal services—everything from free museum tickets to customer lounges and free coffee—to strengthen customer satisfaction and loyalty.[17]

**Reductions in Overhead**    Successfully sustaining a low-cost strategy requires that the firm pare and control its major overhead costs as quickly as possible as its industry matures. With increasing globalization in recent years, many companies have learned this lesson the hard way as the high costs of old plants, labor, outmoded administrative processes, and large inventories have left them vulnerable to more efficient foreign competitors and to corporate raiders.

# Customers' Satisfaction and Loyalty Are Crucial for Maximizing Their Lifetime Value

Analyzer, and particularly defender, businesses are mostly concerned with protecting their existing positions in one or more mature market segments and maximizing profitability over the remaining life of those product-markets. Thus, financial dimensions of performance, such as return on investment and cash flow, are usually of greater interest to such businesses than are more growth-oriented dimensions, like volume increases or new product success. Businesses can achieve such financial objectives by either successfully differentiating their offerings or by maintaining a low-cost position.

While the primary emphasis in many businesses during the early years of the 21st century was on improving efficiency through downsizing and reengineering, there is substantial evidence that firms with superior quality goods and services also obtain higher returns on investment than do businesses with average or below-average offerings.[18] The lesson to be learned, then, is that the choice between a differentiation or a low-cost strategy is probably not the critical determinant of success in mature markets. What is critical is that a business *continually work to improve the value* of its offerings—either by improving product or service quality, reducing costs, or some combination—as a basis for maintaining its customer base as its markets mature and become increasingly competitive.

**Measuring Customer Satisfaction**   To gain the knowledge necessary to continually improve the value of their offerings to customers, firms must understand how satisfied existing and potential customers are with their current offerings. This focus on customer satisfaction has become increasingly important as more firms question whether all attempts to improve *absolute* quality of their products and services generate sufficient additional sales and profits to justify their cost. This growing concern with the economic "return on quality" has motivated firms to ask which dimensions of product or service quality are most important to customers and which dimensions customers might be willing to sacrifice. For instance, Amazon discovered that many customers would like to receive their purchases more quickly than they usually arrive via the firm's standard delivery process. Consequently, the firm created Amazon Prime, a service that guarantees delivery of products within two days for an annual fee of $79. While a relatively small segment of customers have signed up so far, Prime has been very successful at encouraging those buyers to concentrate more of their purchases with Amazon. Analysts estimate that Prime members increase their purchases by about 150 percent after signing up and may now be responsible for as much as 20 percent of Amazon's volume in the United States. Amazon has expanded Prime to Britain, France, Germany, and Japan, and is considering a move to guaranteed delivery within 24 hours.[19]

Because lengthy questionnaires often suffer from low response rates and can be subject to varying interpretations by different managers, some companies employ simple overall measures of customer satisfaction. Perhaps the most popular of these is the single question measure proposed by Fred Reichheld:[20] "On a scale of zero to 10, how likely is it that you would recommend us to your friends or colleagues?" While such measures are simple for customers to answer and make it easy for managers to identify trends in satisfaction overtime, they don't provide any information about *why* customers are either happy or disappointed with a firm's product or service. Indeed, if a substantial portion of respondents turn out to be "detractors" who would advise their friends against purchasing the product, the firm would need to conduct a second, more detailed survey to find the source of their dissatisfaction and how it might be dealt with. For example, General Electric Healthcare's European services business, which maintains hospital imaging equipment, had to ask managers to follow up with dissatisfied customers in order to discover that a chief source of irritation was slow response times from GE engineers. Once the firm overhauled its call center and put more specialist engineers in the field, its satisfaction score on the "would you recommend us?" measure jumped by 10 to 15 points.

To be useful analytical tools, then, measures of customer satisfaction should examine both (1) customers' *expectations and preferences* concerning the various dimensions of product and service quality (such as product performance, features, reliability, on-time delivery, competence of service personnel, and so on) and (2) their *perceptions* concerning how well the firm is meeting those expectations. Any gaps where customer expectations exceed their recent experiences may indicate fruitful areas for the firm to work at improving customer value and satisfaction. Of course, such measurements must be made periodically to determine whether the actions taken have been effective.[21]

**Improving Customer Retention and Loyalty**   As we discussed in Chapter 1, maintaining the loyalty of existing customers is crucial for a business's profitability. This is especially true as markets mature because loyal customers become more profitable over time. The firm not only avoids the high costs associated with trying to acquire replacement customers in an increasingly competitive market, but it also benefits because loyal customers (1) tend to concentrate their purchases, thus leading to larger volumes and lower selling and distribution costs; (2) provide positive word-of-mouth and customer referrals; and (3) may be willing to pay premium prices for the value they receive.[22]

Periodic measurement of customer satisfaction is important because a dissatisfied customer is unlikely to remain loyal over time. Unfortunately, the reverse is not always true: Customers who describe themselves as satisfied are not necessarily loyal. Indeed, one author estimates that 60 to 80 percent of customer defectors in most businesses said they were "satisfied" or "very satisfied" on the last customer survey before their defection.[23] In the interim, perhaps competitors improved their offerings, the customer's requirements changed, or other environmental factors shifted. Companies that measure customer satisfaction should be commended—but urged not to stop there. Satisfaction measures need to be supplemented with examinations of customer *behavior,* such as measures of the annual retention rate, frequency of purchases, and the percentage of a customer's total purchases captured by the firm.

Most important, any problems or complaints reported to the company's call center or on customer blogs should be closely monitored and responded to.[24] Indeed, recently developed software enables managers to engage in a continuous, real-time analysis of customers' perceptions about a brand and its various attributes by analyzing comments—both positive and negative—from millions of sites on the web, including personal blogs, Twitter tweets, and Facebook pages. This kind of **sentiment analysis** examines peoples' comments about the brand using statistical analysis and "natural language processing," a software system designed to interpret written communications even when they include slang and abbreviations.[25]

Defecting customers should also be studied in detail to discover why the firm failed to provide sufficient value to retain their loyalty. Such failures often provide more valuable information than satisfaction measures because they stand out as a clear, understandable message telling the organization exactly where improvements are needed.

**Are All Customers Equally Valuable?**[26]   While improving customer loyalty is crucial for maintaining market share and profitability as markets mature, an increasing number of companies are asking whether every customer's loyalty is worthy of the same level of effort and expense. In these firms, technology is creating a new business model that alters the level of service and benefits provided to a customer based on projections of that customer's value to the firm. With the development of extensive customer databases it is possible for companies to measure what different levels of customer service cost on an individual level. They can also know how much business a particular customer has generated in the past, estimate what she is likely to buy in the future, and calculate a rate of return for that individual for different levels of service.

The ability of firms to tailor different levels of service and benefits to different customers based on each person's potential to produce a profit has been facilitated by the internet. The web has made it easier to track and measure individual transactions across businesses. It has also provided firms with new, low-cost service options; people can now serve themselves at their own convenience, but they have to accept little or no human contact in return.

The end result of this trend toward individually tailored service levels could be an increased stratification of consumer society. The top tier may enjoy unprecedented levels of personal attention. But those who fall below a certain level of profitability for too long may face increased service fees or receive reduced levels of service and benefits. For example, some credit-card companies charge higher annual fees to customers who do not rack up some minimum level of interest charges during the year. In other firms, call center personnel route customers to different queues. Big spenders are turned over to high-level problem solvers while less profitable customers may never speak to a live person. Finally, choice customers may get fees waived or receive promotional discounts based on the value of their business, while less valuable customers may never know the promotions exist.[27]

The segmentation of customers based on projections of their value, and the tailoring of different service levels and benefits to those segments, raises both ethical and strategic questions, some of which are explored in Ethical Perspective 16.1. One possible way for a firm to resolve some of the dilemmas involved in dealing with less profitable customers is to find ways to increase their lifetime value by increasing the frequency and/or volume of their purchases. This is one strategy examined in detail in the following section.

# Marketing Strategies for Mature Markets

## Strategies for Maintaining Current Market Share

Since markets can remain in the maturity stage for decades, milking or harvesting mature product-markets by maximizing short-run profits makes little sense. Pursuing such an objective typically involves substantial cuts in marketing and R&D expenses, which can lead to premature losses of volume and market share and lower profits in the longer term. The business should strive during the early years of market maturity to *maximize the flow of profits over the remaining life of the product-market.* Thus, the most critical marketing objective is to *maintain and protect the business's market share.* In a mature market where few new customers buy the product for the first time, the business must continue to win its share of repeat purchases from existing customers.

In Chapter 15 we discussed a number of marketing strategies that businesses might use to maintain their market share in growth markets. Many of those same strategies continue to be relevant for holding on to customers as markets mature, particularly for those firms

## ETHICAL PERSPECTIVE 16.1
### Pros and Cons of Varying Service Levels According to Customers' Profitability

From a purely economic viewpoint, tailoring different levels of service and benefits to different customer segments depending on their profitability makes sense, at least in the short run. In an era when labor costs are increasing while many markets, especially mature ones, are getting more competitive, many firms argue they cannot afford to provide extensive hands-on service to everyone. Companies also point out that they're often delivering a wider range of products and services than ever before, including more ways for customers to handle transactions. Thanks to the internet, for example, consumers have better tools to conveniently serve themselves. And finally, service segmentation may actually produce some positive benefits for customers—more personalized service for the best customers and, in many cases, lower overall costs and prices for everyone else. For instance, Fidelity Investments gets more than 700,000 daily phone calls, three-quarters of which go to automated systems that cost the company less than a dollar each, including research and development costs. The rest are handled by human operators, at a cost of about $13 per call.

From an ethical standpoint, however, many people question the inherent fairness and potential invasion of privacy involved in using a wealth of personal information about individual consumers as a basis for withholding services or benefits from some of them, especially when such practices are largely invisible to the consumer. You don't know when you're being shuttled to a different telephone queue or sales promotion. You don't know what benefits you're missing or what additional fees you're being charged. Some argue that this lack of transparency is unfair because it deprives consumers of the opportunity to take actions,

such as concentrating their purchases with a single supplier, switching companies, or paying a service fee that would enable them to acquire the additional services and benefits they are currently denied.

From a strategic view, there are also some potential dangers in cutting services and benefits to customers who have not generated profits in the past. For one thing, past behavior is not necessarily an accurate indicator of a customer's future lifetime value. The life situations and spending habits of some customer groups—college students, for instance—can change dramatically over time. In addition, looking only at a customer's purchases may overlook some indirect ways that the customer affects the firm's revenues, such as positive word-of-mouth recommendations and referrals to other potential buyers. And some customers may not be spending much with a company precisely because of the lousy service they have received as a result of not spending very much with that company. Instead of simply writing off low-volume customers it may make more strategic sense to first attempt to convert them into high-volume customers by targeting them for additional promotions, by trying to sell complementary goods and services, or by instituting loyalty programs (e.g., the airlines' frequent-flier programs).

Finally, by debasing the satisfaction and loyalty of low-volume customers, firms risk losing those customers to competitors. In a mature industry, particularly one with substantial economies of scale, such a loss of market share can increase unit costs and reduce the profitability of those high-volume customers that do remain loyal. And, a creative competitor may find ways to make other firms' cast-off customers very profitable after all.

*Sources:* Diane Brady, "Why Service Stinks," *BusinessWeek*, October 23, 2000; and Christian Homburg, Mathias Daoll, and Dirk Totzek, "Customer Prioritization; Does it Pay Off, and How Should it Be Implemented?" *Journal of Marketing* 72, September 2008, pp. 110–30.

that survived the shakeout period with a relatively strong share position. The most obvious strategy for such share leaders is simply to continue strengthening their position through a *fortress defense.* Recall that such a strategy involves two sets of marketing actions: those aimed at improving customer satisfaction and loyalty, and those intended to encourage and simplify repeat purchasing. Actions like those discussed earlier for improving the quality of a firm's offering and for reducing costs suggest ways to increase customer satisfaction and loyalty. Similarly, improvements to service quality, such as just-in-time delivery arrangements or computerized reordering systems, can help encourage repeat purchases.

Since markets often become more fragmented as they grow and mature, share leaders may also have to expand their product lines, or add one or more *flanker* brands, to protect their position against competitive inroads. Thus, Johnson Controls has strengthened its position in the commercial facilities management arena by expanding its array of services through a combination of acquisitions and continued internal development. Many of those new services were developed in response to changing customer desires or emerging environmental trends, such as the growing demand for "greener" commercial buildings with more sustainable energy requirements and a smaller impact on the natural environment.

Small-share competitors can also earn substantial profits in a mature market. To do so, however, it is often wise for them to focus on strategies that avoid prolonged direct confrontations with larger share leaders. A *niche strategy* can be particularly effective when the target segment is too small to appeal to larger competitors or when the smaller firm can establish a strong differential advantage or brand preference in the segment. For instance, with fewer than 50 hotels worldwide, the Four Seasons chain is a small player in the lodging industry. But by focusing on the high end of the business travel market, the chain has grown and prospered. The chain's hotels differentiate themselves by offering a wide range of amenities, such as free overnight shoeshines, that are important to business travelers. Thus, while they charge relatively high prices, they are also seen as delivering good value.

# Strategies for Extending Volume Growth

Market maturity is defined by a flattening of the growth rate. In some instances growth slows for structural reasons, such as the emergence of substitute products or a shift in customer preferences. Marketers can do little to revitalize the market under such conditions. But in some cases a market only *appears* to be mature because of the limitations of current marketing programs, such as target segments that are too narrowly defined or limited product offerings. Here, more innovative or aggressive marketing strategies might successfully extend the market's life cycle into a period of renewed growth. Thus, *stimulating additional volume* growth can be an important secondary objective under such circumstances, particularly for industry share leaders because they often can capture a relatively large share of any additional volume generated.

A firm might pursue several different marketing strategies—either singly or in combination—to squeeze additional volume from a mature market. These include an *increased penetration strategy,* an *extended use strategy,* and a *market expansion strategy.* Exhibit 16.5 summarizes the environmental situations where each of these strategies is most appropriate and the objectives each is best suited for accomplishing. Exhibit 16.6 then outlines specific marketing actions a firm might employ to implement each of the strategies, as discussed in more detail in the following paragraphs.

**Increased Penetration Strategy**   The total sales volume produced by a target segment of customers is a function of (1) the number of potential customers in the segment; (2) the product's penetration of that segment, that is, the proportion of potential customers who actually use the product; and (3) the average frequency with which customers consume the product and make another purchase. Where usage frequency is quite high among current customers but only a relatively small portion of all potential users actually buy the product, a firm might aim at increasing market penetration. It is an appropriate strategy for an industry's share leader because such firms can more likely gain and retain a substantial share of new customers than smaller firms with less-well-known brands.

The secret to a successful increased-penetration strategy lies in discovering why nonusers are uninterested in the product. Very often the product does not offer sufficient value from the potential customer's view to justify the effort or expense involved in buying

# Exhibit 16.5

SITUATIONAL DETERMINANTS OF APPROPRIATE MARKETING OBJECTIVES AND STRATEGIES
FOR EXTENDING GROWTH IN MATURE MARKETS

| Situation Variables | GROWTH EXTENSION STRATEGIES | | |
| --- | --- | --- | --- |
| | Increased penetration | Extended use | Market expansion |
| Primary objective | Increase the proportion of users by converting current nonusers in one or more major market segments. | Increase the amount of product used by the average customer by increasing frequency of use or developing new and more varied ways to use the product. | Expand the number of potential customers by targeting under-developed geographic areas or applications segments. |
| Market characteristics | Relatively low penetration in one or more segments (i.e., low percentage of potential users have adopted the product); relatively homogeneous market with only a few large segments. | Relatively high penetration but low frequency of use in one or more major segments; product used in only limited ways or for special occasions; relatively homogeneous market with only a few large segments. | Relatively heterogeneous market with a variety of segments; some geographic areas, including foreign countries, with low penetra-tion; some product applica-tions underdeveloped. |
| Competitors' characteristics | Competitors hold relatively small market shares; comparatively limited resources or competen-cies make it unlikely they will steal a significant portion of converted nonusers. | Competitors hold relatively small market shares; comparatively limited resources or compe-tencies make it unlikely their brands will be purchased for newly developed uses. | Competitors hold relatively small market shares; have insufficient resources or com-petencies to preempt under-developed geographic areas or applications segments. |
| Firm's characteristics | A market-share leader in the industry; has R&D and marketing competencies to produce prod-uct modifications or line exten-sions; has promotional resources to stimulate primary demand among current nonusers. | A market-share leader in the industry; has marketing competencies and resources to develop and promote new uses. | A market-share leader in the industry; has marketing and distribution competencies and resources to develop new global markets or applications segments. |

and using it. One obvious solution to such a problem is to enhance the product's value to potential customers by adding features or benefits, usually via line extensions.

Another way to add value to a product is to develop and sell integrated systems that help improve the basic product's performance or ease of use. For instance, instead of sim-ply selling control mechanisms for heating and cooling systems, Johnson Controls offers integrated facilities management programs designed to lower the total costs of operating a commercial building.

A firm may also enhance a product's value by offering services that improve its per-formance or ease of use for the potential customer. Since it is unlikely that people who do not know how to knit will ever buy yarn or knitting needles, for example, most yarn shops offer free knitting lessons.

Product modifications or line extensions will not, however, attract nonusers unless the enhanced benefits are effectively promoted. For industrial goods, this may mean redirect-ing some sales efforts toward nonusers. The firm may offer additional incentives for new account sales or assign specific salespeople to call on targeted nonusers and convert them into new customers. For consumer goods, some combination of advertising to stimulate primary demand in the target segment and sales promotions to encourage trial, such as free samples or tie-in promotions with complementary products that nonusers currently buy, can be effective.

# Exhibit 16.6

POSSIBLE MARKETING ACTIONS FOR ACCOMPLISHING GROWTH EXTENSION OBJECTIVES

| Marketing strategy and objectives | Possible marketing actions |
|---|---|

**Increased penetration**

| | |
|---|---|
| Convert current nonusers in target segment into users | • Enhance product's value by adding features, benefits, or services.<br>• Enhance product's value by including it in the design of integrated systems.<br>• Stimulate additional primary demand through promotional efforts stressing new features or benefits:<br>   Advertising through selective media aimed at the target segment.<br>   Sales promotions directed at stimulating trial among current nonusers (e.g., tie-ins with other products).<br>   Some sales efforts redirected toward new account generation, perhaps by assigning some sales personnel as account development reps or by offering incentives for new account sales.<br>   Improve product's availability by developing innovative distribution systems. |

**Extended use**

| | |
|---|---|
| Increase frequency of use among current users | • Move storage of the product closer to the point of end use by offering additional package sizes or designs.<br>• Encourage larger volume purchases (for nonperishable products):<br>   Offer quantity discounts.<br>   Offer consumer promotions to stimulate volume purchases or more frequent use (e.g., multipack deals, frequent flier programs).<br>• Reminder advertising stressing basic product benefits for a variety of usage occasions. |
| Encourage a wider variety of uses among current users | • Develop line extensions suitable for additional uses or applications.<br>• Develop and promote new uses, applications, or recipes for the basic product.<br>   Include information about new applications/recipes on package.<br>   Develop extended use advertising campaign, particularly with print media.<br>   Communicate new application ideas through sales presentations to current customers.<br>• Encourage new uses through sales promotions (e.g., tie-ins with complementary products). |

**Market expansion**

| | |
|---|---|
| Develop differentiated positioning focused on untapped or underdeveloped segments | • Develop a differentiated flanker brand or product line with unique features or price that is more appealing to a segment of potential customers whose needs are not met by existing offerings.<br>or<br>• Develop multiple line extensions or brand offerings with features or prices targeted to the unique needs and preferences of several smaller potential applications or regional segments.<br>• Consider producing for private labels.<br>• Design advertising, personal selling, and/or sales promotion campaigns that address specific interests and concerns of potential customers in one or multiple underdeveloped segments to stimulate selective demand.<br>• Build unique distribution channels to more effectively reach potential customers in one or multiple underdeveloped segments.<br>• Design service programs to reduce the perceived risks of trial and/or solve the unique problems faced by potential customers in one or multiple underdeveloped segments (e.g., systems engineering, installation, operator training, extended warranties).<br>• Enter global markets where product category is in an earlier stage of its life cycle. |

Finally, some potential customers may be having trouble finding the product due to limited distribution, or the product's benefits may simply be too modest to justify much purchasing effort. In such cases, expanding distribution or developing more convenient and accessible channels may help expand market penetration. For example, few travelers are so leery of flying that they would go through the effort of calling an insurance agent to buy an accident policy for a single flight. But the sales of such policies are greatly increased by making them conveniently available as an optional purchase through the credit-card companies travelers use to pay for their flights.

**Extended Use Strategy**    Some years ago, the manager of General Foods' Cool Whip frozen dessert topping discovered through marketing research that nearly three-fourths of all U.S. households used the product, but the average consumer used it only four times per year and served it on only 7 percent of all toppable desserts. In situations of good market penetration but low frequency of use, an extended use strategy may increase volume. This was particularly true in the Cool Whip case; the relatively large and homogeneous target market consisted for the most part of a single mass-market segment. Also, General Foods held nearly a two-thirds share of the frozen topping market, and it had the marketing resources and competencies to capture most of the additional volume that an extended use strategy might generate.

One effective approach for stimulating increased frequency of use is to move product inventories closer to the point of use. This approach works particularly well with low-involvement consumer goods. Marketers know that most consumers are unlikely to expend any additional time or effort to obtain such products when they are ready to use them. If there is no Cool Whip in the refrigerator when the consumer is preparing dessert, for instance, he or she is unlikely to run to the store immediately and will probably serve the dessert without topping.

One obvious way to move inventory closer to the point of consumption is to offer larger package sizes. The more customers buy at one time, the less likely they are to be out of stock when a usage opportunity arises. This approach can backfire, though, for a perishable product or one that consumers perceive to be an impulse indulgence. Thus, most superpremium ice creams, such as Häagen-Dazs, are sold in small pint containers; most consumers want to avoid the temptation of having large quantities of such a high-calorie indulgence too readily available.

The design of a package can also help increase use frequency by making the product more convenient or easy to use. Examples include single-serving packages of pudding or salad to pack in lunches, packages of paper cups that include a convenient dispenser, and frozen-food packages that can go directly into a microwave oven.

Various sales promotion programs also help move inventories of a product closer to the point of use by encouraging larger volume purchases. Marketers commonly offer quantity discounts for this purpose in selling industrial goods. For consumer products, multi-item discounts or two-for-one deals serve the same purpose. Promotional programs also encourage greater frequency of use and increase customer loyalty in many service industries. Consider, for instance, the frequent-flier programs offered by major airlines or the "rewards" programs offered by credit-card providers.

Sometimes the product's characteristics inhibit customers from using it more frequently. If marketers can change those characteristics, such as difficulty of preparation or high calories, a new line extension might encourage customers to use more of the product or to use it more often. Microwave waffles and low-calorie salad dressings are examples of such line extensions. For industrial goods, however, firms may have to develop new technology to overcome a product's limitations for some applications. For instance, Johnson

Controls recently acquired Prince Automotive to gain the expertise necessary to develop instrument panels and consoles incorporating the sophisticated electronics desired by top-end manufacturers such as BMW and Mercedes-Benz.

Finally, advertising can sometimes effectively increase use frequency by simply reminding customers to use the product more often. For instance, General Foods conducted a reminder campaign for Jell-O pudding that featured Bill Cosby asking, "When was the last time you served pudding, Mom?"

Another approach for extending use among current customers involves finding and promoting new functional uses for the product. Jell-O gelatin is a classic example, having generated substantial new sales volume over the years by promoting the use of Jell-O as an ingredient in salads, pie fillings, and other dishes.

Firms promote new ways to use a product through a variety of methods. For industrial products, firms send technical advisories about new applications to the salesforce to present to their customers during regular sales calls. For consumer products, new use suggestions or recipes may be included on the package, in an advertising campaign, or on the firm's website. Sales promotions, such as including cents-off coupons in ads featuring a new recipe, encourage customers to try a new application.

In some cases, slightly modified line extensions might encourage customers to use more of the product or use it in different ways. For example, Australian, French, Chilean, and even a few large U.S. winemakers have attempted to attract more young consumers and broaden the variety of occasions at which they drink wine rather than beer or other beverages. They have pursued these objectives by blending fruitier, less tannic wines, designing whimsical labels and logos—such as the Yellow Tail wallaby from Australia and Fat Bastard from France—and lowering prices to between $3 and $9 a bottle. Consequently, U.S. consumers drank a record 278 million cases of wine in 2005, and consumption has been growing at a brisk 3 percent annual rate.[28]

### Market Expansion Strategy

In a mature industry with a fragmented and heterogeneous market where some segments are less well developed than others, a market expansion strategy may generate substantial additional volume growth. Such a strategy aims at gaining new customers by targeting new or underdeveloped geographic markets (either regional or foreign) or new customer segments. Once again, share leaders tend to be best suited for implementing this strategy. But even smaller competitors can employ such a strategy successfully if they focus on relatively small or specialized market niches.

**STRATEGIC ISSUE**

*In a fragmented and heterogeneous market where some segments are less well developed than others, a market expansion strategy may generate substantial additional volume growth.*

Pursuing market expansion by strengthening a firm's position in new or underdeveloped **domestic geographic markets** can lead to experience-curve benefits and operating synergies. The firm can rely on largely the same expertise and technology, and perhaps even the same production and distribution facilities, it has already developed. Unfortunately, domestic geographic expansion is often not viable in a mature industry because the share leaders usually have attained national market coverage. Smaller regional competitors, on the other hand, might consider domestic geographic expansion a means for improving their volume and share position. However, such a move risks retaliation from the large national brands as well as from entrenched regional competitors in the prospective new territory.

To get around the retaliation problem, a regional producer might try to expand through the acquisition of small producers in other regions. This can be a viable option when (1) the low profitability of some regional producers enables the acquiring firm to buy their assets for less than the replacement cost of the capacity involved and (2) synergies gained by combining regional operations and the infusion of resources from the acquiring firm can improve the effectiveness and profitability of the acquired producers. For example, Clear Channel Worldwide, got its start in 1972 when the founders Lowry Mays and Billy Joe McCombs acquired an unprofitable country music radio station in San Antonio, Texas. It then grew, first by buying out other radio stations in a variety of U.S. states, and then by acquiring small, struggling TV stations and outdoor advertising companies. Clear Channel's strategy was to buy radio, TV, and outdoor advertising properties with operations in many of the same local markets; share facilities and staff to cut costs; improve programming; and sell advertising to customers in packages incorporating all three media. As a result, the company achieved significant cost savings, boosted profit margins, and grew to become the fourth-largest media company in the world by 2003.

In a different approach to domestic market expansion, the firm identifies and develops entirely **new customer** or **application segments.** Sometimes the firm can effectively reach new customer segments by simply expanding the distribution system without changing the product's characteristics or the other marketing-mix elements. For example, General Mills, Procter & Gamble, Verizon, and other consumer goods and services companies have targeted America's 46 million Hispanics by shifting substantial portions of their promotional budgets into ads on Spanish-language TV. Even though Hispanic households were hit hard by the economic crisis of 2008, they continue to spend heavily on the basics—like packaged foods and wireless phone services—they like to buy brands advertised on TV, and viewership of the major Hispanic TV networks was up 22 percent in 2008 compared to the stagnant audiences of the English-language networks. Consequently, the Hispanic segment offered a growth opportunity that did not require any major product modifications.[29] In most instances, though, developing new market segments requires modifying the product to make it more suitable for the application or to provide more of the benefits desired by customers in the new segment.

One final possibility for domestic market expansion is to produce **private-label brands** for large retailers. Firms whose own brands hold relatively weak positions and who have excess production capacity find this a particularly attractive option. Private labeling allows such firms to gain access to established customer segments without making substantial marketing expenditures, thus increasing the firm's volume and lowering its per unit costs. However, since private labels typically compete with low prices and their sponsors usually have strong bargaining power, producing private labels is often not a very profitable option unless a manufacturer already has a relatively low-cost position in the industry. It can also be a risky strategy, particularly for the smaller firm, because reliance on one or a few large private-label customers can result in drastic volume reductions and unit-cost increases should those customers decide to switch suppliers.[30]

## Global Market Expansion—Sequential Strategies

For firms with leading positions in mature domestic markets, less-developed markets in foreign countries often present the most viable opportunities for geographic expansion. As discussed in previous chapters, firms can enter foreign markets in a variety of ways, from simply relying on import agents to developing joint ventures to establishing wholly owned subsidiaries— as Johnson Controls has done by acquiring automotive seat and battery manufacturers in Europe.

Regardless of which mode of entry a firm chooses, it can follow a number of different routes when pursuing global expansion.[31] By *route* we mean the sequence or order in which the firm enters global markets. Japanese companies provide illustrations of different global expansion paths. The most common expansion route involves moving from Japan to developing countries to developed countries. They used this path, for example, with automobiles (Toyota); consumer electronics (National); watches (Seiko); cameras (Minolta);

and home appliances, steel, and petrochemicals. This routing reduced manufacturing costs and enabled them to gain marketing experience. In penetrating the U.S. market, the Japanese obtained further economies of scale and gained recognition for their products, which made penetration of European markets easier.

A second type of *expansion path* has been used primarily for high-tech products such as computers and semiconductors. For the Japanese it consists of first securing their home market and then targeting developed countries. Japan largely ignored developing countries in this strategy because of their small demand for high-tech products. When demand increased to a point where developing countries became "interesting," Japanese producers quickly entered and established strong market positions using price cuts of up to 50 percent.

A home market—developed markets—developing markets sequence is also usually appropriate for discretionary goods such as soft drinks, convenience foods, or cosmetics. For instance, firms such as the French cosmetics giant L'Oreal have positioned a number of different "world brands"—including Ralph Lauren perfumes, L'Oreal hair products, and Maybelline and Helena Rubinstein cosmetics—to convey the allure of different cultures to developing markets around the world.[32]

## Strategies for Declining Markets

Most products eventually enter a decline phase in their life cycles. As sales decline, excess capacity once again develops. As the remaining competitors fight to hold volume in the

STRATEGIC ISSUE

*The relative attractiveness of the declining product-market and the business's competitive position within it should dictate the appropriate strategy.*

face of falling sales, industry profits erode. Consequently, conventional wisdom suggests that firms should either divest declining products quickly or harvest them to maximize short-term profits. Not all markets decline in the same way or at the same speed, however; nor do all firms have the same competitive strengths and weaknesses within those markets. Therefore, as in most other situations, the relative attractiveness of the declining product-market and the business's competitive position within it should dictate the appropriate strategy.

## Relative Attractiveness of Declining Markets

Although U.S. high school enrollment declined by about 2 million students from 1976 through the early 1990s, Jostens, Inc., the leading manufacturer of class rings and other school merchandise, achieved annual increases in revenues and profits every year during that period. One reason for the firm's success was that it saw the market decline coming and prepared for it by improving the efficiency of its operations and developing marketing programs that were effective at persuading a larger proportion of students to buy class rings.

Jostens' experience shows that some declining product-markets can offer attractive opportunities well into the future, at least for one or a few strong competitors. In other product-markets, particularly those where decline is the result of customers switching to a new technology (e.g., students buying personal computers instead of portable typewriters), the potential for continued profits during the decline stage is more bleak.

Three sets of factors help determine the strategic attractiveness of declining product-markets: *conditions of demand,* including the rate and certainty of future declines in volume; *exit barriers,* or the ease with which weaker competitors can leave the market; and factors affecting the *intensity of future competitive rivalry* within the market.[33] The impact of these variables on the attractiveness of declining market environments is summarized in Exhibit 16.7 and discussed below.

## Exhibit 16.7

FACTORS AFFECTING THE ATTRACTIVENESS OF DECLINING MARKET ENVIRONMENTS

| | ENVIRONMENTAL ATTRACTIVENESS | |
|---|---|---|
| **Conditions of demand** | **Hospitable** | **Inhospitable** |
| Speed of decline | Very slow | Rapid or erratic |
| Certainty of decline | 100% certain, predictable patterns | Great uncertainty, erratic patterns |
| Pockets of enduring demand | Several or major ones | No niches |
| Product differentiation | Brand loyalty | Commodity-like products |
| Price stability | Stable, price premiums attainable | Very unstable, pricing below costs |
| **Exit barriers** | | |
| Reinvestment requirements | None | High, often mandatory and involving capital assets |
| Excess capacity | Little | Substantial |
| Asset age | Mostly old assets | Sizable new assets and old ones not retired |
| Resale markets for assets | Easy to convert or sell | No markets available, substantial costs to retire |
| Shared facilities | Few, freestanding plants | Substantial and interconnected with important businesses |
| Vertical integration | Little | Substantial |
| Single-product competitors | None | Several large companies |
| **Rivalry determinants** | | |
| Customer industries | Fragmented, weak | Strong bargaining power |
| Customer switching costs | High | Minimal |
| Diseconomies of scale | None | Substantial penalty |
| Dissimilar strategic groups | Few | Several in same target markets |

*Source:* Reprinted by permission of *Harvard Business Review.* From "End-Game Strategies for Declining Industries," by Kathryn Rudie Harrigan and Michael E. Porter, July–August 1983. Copyright © 1983 by the Harvard Business School Publishing Corporation, all rights reserved.

**Conditions of Demand**    Demand in a product-market declines for a number of reasons. Technological advances produce substitute products (such as electronic calculators for slide rules), often with higher quality or lower cost. Demographic shifts lead to a shrinking target market (baby foods). Customers' needs, tastes, or lifestyles change (the falling consumption of lard). Finally, the cost of inputs or complementary products rises and shrinks demand (the effects of rising gasoline prices on sales of recreational vehicles).

The cause of a decline in demand can affect both the rate and the predictability of that decline. A fall in sales due to a demographic shift, for instance, is likely to be gradual, whereas the switch to a technically superior substitute can be abrupt. Similarly, the fall in demand as customers switch to a better substitute is predictable, while a decline in sales due to a change in tastes is not.

As Exhibit 16.8 indicates, both the rate and certainty of sales decline are demand characteristics that affect a market's attractiveness. A slow and gradual decline allows an orderly withdrawal of weaker competitors. Overcapacity does not become excessive and lead to predatory competitive behavior, and the competitors who remain are more likely to make profits than in a quick or erratic decline. Also, when most industry managers believe market decline is

# Exhibit 16.8

SITUATIONAL DETERMINANTS OF APPROPRIATE MARKETING OBJECTIVES AND STRATEGIES FOR DECLINING MARKETS

| Situational variables | STRATEGIES FOR DECLINING MARKETS | | | |
| --- | --- | --- | --- | --- |
| | Harvesting | Maintenance | Profitable survivor | Niche |
| Primary objective | Maximize short-term cash flow; maintain or increase margins even at the expense of a slow decline in market share. | Maintain share in short term as market declines, even if margins must be sacrificed. | Increase share of the declining market with an eye to future profits; encourage weaker competitors to exit. | Focus on strengthening position in one or a few relatively substantial segments with potential for future profits. |
| Market characteristics | Future market decline is certain, but likely to occur at a slow and steady rate. | Market has experienced recent declines, but future direction and attractiveness are currently hard to predict. | Future market decline is certain, but likely to occur at a slow and steady rate; substantial pockets of demand will continue to exist. | Overall market may decline quickly, but one or more segments will remain as demand pockets or decay slowly. |
| Competitors' characteristics | Few strong competitors; low exit barriers; future rivalry not likely to be intense. | Few strong competitors; but intensity of future rivalry is hard to predict. | Few strong competitors; exit barriers are low or can be reduced by firm's intervention. | One or more stronger competitors in mass market, but not in the target segment. |
| Firm's characteristics | Has a leading share position; has a substantial proportion of loyal customers who are likely to continue buying brand even if marketing support is reduced. | Has a leading share of the market and a relatively strong competitive position. | Has a leading share of the market and a strong competitive position; has superior resources or competencies necessary to encourage competitors to exit or to acquire them. | Has a sustainable competitive advantage in target segment, but overall resources may be limited. |

predictable and certain, reduction of capacity is more likely to be orderly than when they feel substantial uncertainty about whether demand might level off or even become revitalized.

Not all segments of a market decline at the same time or at the same rate. The number and size of enduring niches or pockets of demand and the customer purchase behavior within them also influence the continuing attractiveness of the market. When the demand pockets are large or numerous and the customers in those niches are brand loyal and relatively insensitive to price, competitors with large shares and differentiated products can continue to make substantial profits. For example, even though the market for cigars shrank for years, there continued to be a sizable number of smokers who bought premium-quality cigars. Those firms with well-established positions at the premium end of the cigar industry have continued to earn above-average returns.

**Exit Barriers**    The higher the exit barriers, the less hospitable a product-market will be during the decline phase of its life cycle. When weaker competitors find it hard to leave a product-market as demand falls, excess capacity develops and firms engage in aggressive pricing or promotional efforts to try to prop up their volume and hold down unit costs. Thus, exit barriers lead to competitive volatility.

Once again, Exhibit 16.8 indicates that a variety of factors influence the ease with which businesses can exit an industry. One critical consideration involves the amount of highly specialized assets. Assets unique to a given business are difficult to divest because of their low liquidation value. The only potential buyers for such assets are other firms who would use them for a similar purpose, which is unlikely in a declining industry. Thus, the firm may have little choice but to remain in the business or to sell the assets for their scrap value. This option is particularly unattractive when the assets are relatively new and not fully depreciated.

Another major exit barrier occurs when the assets or resources of the declining business intertwine with the firm's other business units, either through shared facilities and programs or through vertical integration. Exit from the declining business might shut down shared production facilities, lower salesforce commissions, damage customer relations, and increase unit costs in the firm's other businesses to a point that damages their profitability. Emotional factors can also act as exit barriers. Managers often feel reluctant to admit failure by divesting a business even though it no longer produces acceptable returns. This is especially true when the business played an important role in the firm's history and it houses a large number of senior managers.

### Intensity of Future Competitive Rivalry
Even when substantial pockets of continuing demand remain within a declining business, it may not be wise for a firm to pursue them in the face of future intense competitive rivalry. In addition to exit barriers, other factors also affect the ability of the remaining firms to avoid intense price competition and maintain reasonable margins: size and bargaining power of the customers who continue to buy the product; customers' ability to switch to substitute products or to alternative suppliers; and any potential diseconomies of scale involved in capturing an increased share of the remaining volume.

## Divestment or Liquidation

When the market environment in a declining industry is unattractive or a business has a relatively weak competitive position, the firm may recover more of its investment by selling the business in the early stages of decline rather than later. The earlier the business is sold, the more uncertain potential buyers are likely to be about the future direction of demand in the industry and thus the more likely that a willing buyer can be found. Thus, Raytheon sold its vacuum-tube business in the early 1960s even though transistors had just begun replacing tubes in radios and TV sets and there was still a strong replacement demand for tubes. By moving early, the firm achieved a much higher liquidation value than companies that tried to unload their tube-making facilities in the 70s when the industry was clearly in its twilight years.[34]

Of course, the firm that divests early runs the risk that its forecast of the industry's future may be wrong. Also, quick divestment may not be possible if the firm faces high exit barriers, such as interdependencies across business units or customer expectations of continued product availability. By planning early for departure, however, the firm may be able to reduce some of those barriers before the liquidation is necessary.

## Marketing Strategies for Remaining Competitors

Conventional wisdom suggests that a business remaining in a declining product-market should pursue a harvesting strategy aimed at maximizing its cash flow in the short run. But such businesses also have other strategic options. They might attempt to maintain their position as the market declines, improve their position to become the profitable survivor, or focus efforts on one or more remaining demand pockets or market niches. Once again, the appropriateness of these strategies depends on factors affecting the attractiveness of the declining market and on the business's competitive strengths and weaknesses. Exhibit 16.8 summarizes the situational determinants of the appropriateness of each strategy. Some of the marketing actions a firm might take to implement them are discussed below and listed in Exhibit 16.9.

# Exhibit 16.9

POSSIBLE MARKETING ACTIONS APPROPRIATE FOR DIFFERENT STRATEGIES IN DECLINING MARKETS

| Marketing strategy and objectives | Possible marketing actions |
|---|---|

**Harvesting strategy**

Maximize short-term cash flow; maintain or increase margins even at the expense of market share decline.

- Eliminate R&D expenditures and capital investments related to the business.
- Reduce marketing and sales budgets.
  - Greatly reduce or eliminate advertising and sales promotion expenditures, with the possible exception of periodic reminder advertising targeted at current customers.
  - Reduce trade promotions to the minimum level necessary to prevent rapid loss of distribution coverage.
  - Focus salesforce efforts on attaining repeat purchases from current customers.
- Seek ways to reduce production costs, even at the expense of slow erosion in product quality.
- Raise price if necessary to maintain margins.

**Maintenance strategy**

Maintain market share for the short term, even at the expense of margins.

- Continue product and process R&D expenditures in short term aimed at maintaining or improving product quality.
- Continue maintenance levels of advertising and sales promotion targeted at current users.
- Continue trade promotion at levels sufficient to avoid any reduction in distribution coverage.
- Focus salesforce efforts on attaining repeat purchases from current users.
- Lower prices if necessary to maintain share, even at the expense of reduced margins.

**Profitable survivor strategy**

Increase share of the declining market; encourage weaker competitors to exit.

- Signal competitors that firm intends to remain in industry and pursue an increased share.
  - Maintain or increase advertising and sales promotion budgets.
  - Maintain or increase distribution coverage through aggressive trade promotion.
  - Focus some salesforce effort on winning away competitors' customers.
  - Continue product and process R&D to seek product improvements or cost reductions.
- Consider introducing line extensions to appeal to remaining demand segments.
- Lower prices if necessary to increase share, even at the expense of short-term margins.
- Consider agreements to produce replacement parts or private labels for smaller competitors considering getting out of production.

**Niche strategy**

Strengthen share position in one or a few segments with potential for continued profit.

- Continued product and process R&D aimed at product improvements or modifications that will appeal to target segment(s).
- Consider producing for private labels in order to maintain volume and hold down unit costs.
- Focus advertising, sales promotion, and personal selling campaigns on customers in target segment(s); stress appeals of greatest importance to those customers.
- Maintain distribution channels appropriate for reaching target segment; seek unique channel arrangements to more effectively reach customers in target segment(s).
- Design service programs that address unique concerns/problems of customers in the target segment(s).

**Harvesting Strategy**   The objective of a harvesting or milking strategy is to generate cash quickly by maximizing cash flow over a relatively short term. This typically involves avoiding any additional investment in the business, greatly reducing operating (including marketing) expenses, and perhaps raising prices. Since the firm usually expects to ultimately divest or abandon the business, some loss of sales and market share during the pursuit of this strategy is likely. The trick is to hold the business's volume and share declines to a relatively slow and steady rate. A precipitous and premature loss of share would limit the total amount of cash the business could generate during the market's decline.

A harvesting strategy is most appropriate for a firm holding a relatively strong competitive position in the market at the start of the decline and a cadre of current customers likely to continue buying the brand even after marketing support is reduced. Such a strategy also works best when the market's decline is inevitable but likely to occur at a relatively slow and steady rate and when rivalry among remaining competitors is not likely to be very intense. Such conditions enable the business to maintain adequate price levels and profit margins as volume gradually falls.

Implementing a harvesting strategy means avoiding any additional long-term investments in plant, equipment, or R&D. It also necessitates substantial cuts in operating expenditures for marketing activities. This often means that the firm should greatly reduce the number of models or package sizes in its product line to reduce inventory and manufacturing costs.

The business should improve the efficiency of sales and distribution. For instance, an industrial-goods manufacturer might service its smaller accounts through telemarketing or a website rather than a field salesforce or assign its smaller customers to agent middlemen. For consumer goods, the business might move to more selective distribution by concentrating its efforts on the larger retail chains.

The firm would likely reduce advertising and promotion expenditures, usually to the minimum level necessary to retain adequate distribution. Finally, the business should attempt to maintain or perhaps even increase its price levels to increase margins.

**Maintenance Strategy**   In markets where future volume trends are highly uncertain, a business with a leading share position might consider pursuing a strategy aimed at maintaining its market share, at least until the market's future becomes more predictable. In such a maintenance strategy, the business continues to pursue the same strategy that brought it success during the market's mature stage. This approach often results in reduced margins and profits in the short term, though, because firms usually must reduce prices or increase marketing expenditures to hold share in the face of declining industry volume. Thus, a firm should consider share maintenance an interim strategy. Once it becomes clear that the market will continue to decline, the business should switch to a different strategy that will provide better cash flows and return on investment over the market's remaining life.

**Profitable Survivor Strategy**   An aggressive alternative for a business with a strong share position and a sustainable competitive advantage in a declining product-market is to invest enough to increase its share position and establish itself as the industry leader for the remainder of the market's decline. This kind of strategy makes most sense when the firm expects a gradual decline in market demand or when substantial pockets of continuing demand are likely well into the future. It is also an attractive strategy when a firm's declining business is closely intertwined with other SBUs through shared facilities and programs or common customer segments.

A strong competitor can often improve its share position in a declining market at relatively low cost because other competitors may be harvesting their businesses or preparing to exit. The key to the success of such a strategy is to encourage other competitors to leave the market early. Once the firm has achieved a strong and unchallenged position, it can switch to a harvesting strategy and reap substantial profits over the remaining life of the product-market.

A firm might encourage smaller competitors to abandon the industry by being visible and explicit about its commitment to become the leading survivor. It should aggressively seek increased market share, either by cutting prices or by increasing advertising and promotion expenditures. It might also introduce line extensions aimed at remaining pockets of demand to make it more difficult for smaller competitors to find profitable niches. Finally, the firm might act to reduce its competitors' exit barriers, making it easier for them to leave the industry. This could involve taking over competitors' long-term contracts, agreeing to supply spare parts or to service their products in the field, or providing them with components or private-label products. For instance, large regional bakeries have encouraged grocery chains to abandon their own bakery operations by supplying them with private-label baked goods.

The ultimate way to remove competitors' exit barriers is to purchase their operations and either improve their efficiency or remove them from the industry to avoid excess capacity. With continued decline in industry sales a certainty, smaller competitors may be forced to sell their assets at a book value price low enough for the survivor to reap high returns on its investment.

**Niche Strategy**    Even when most segments of an industry are expected to decline rapidly, a niche strategy may still be viable if one or more substantial segments will either remain as stable pockets of demand or decay slowly. The business pursuing such a strategy should have a strong competitive position in the target segment or be able to build a sustainable competitive advantage relatively quickly to preempt competitors. This is one strategy that even smaller competitors can sometimes successfully pursue, because they can focus the required assets and resources on a limited portion of the total market. The marketing actions a business might take to strengthen and preserve its position in a target niche are similar to those discussed earlier concerning niche strategies in mature markets.

# TAKE-AWAYS

1. Strategic choices in mature, or even declining, markets are by no means always bleak. Many of the world's most profitable companies operate largely in such markets.

2. A critical marketing objective for all competitors in a mature market is to maintain the loyalty of existing customers. To accomplish that goal, firms must pursue improvements in the perceived value those customers receive from their offerings—either by differentiating themselves on the basis of superior quality or service, by lowering costs and prices, or both.

3. An important secondary objective for some firms, particularly share leaders, in mature markets is to stimulate further volume growth by taking actions to

convert nonusers into users, to increase use frequency among current users, or to expand into untapped or underdeveloped markets.

4. Declining markets can still offer attractive opportunities for sales revenues and profits. Their attractiveness—and the appropriate marketing strategy to follow—depends on, among other things, the pace and certainty of market decline, the presence of exit barriers, the firm's competitive strengths, and the likely intensity of future competition.

**Self-diagnostic questions to test your ability to apply the analytical tools and concepts in this chapter to marketing decision making may be found at this book's website at www.mhhe.com/mullins8e.**

# ENDNOTES

**1.** This example is based on material found in Rick Tetzeli, "Mining Money in Mature Markets," *Fortune,* March 22, 1993, pp. 77–80; Edmund Chew, "Johnson Controls Inc. Displays Interior Concepts at Frankfurt Auto Show," *Automotive News,* October 29, 2001, p. 18; Thomas Content, "Johnson Controls Completes Two European Acquisitions," *www.jsonline.com,* June 20, 2011; and *Johnson Controls' 2010 Annual 10K Report,* found on the company's website at *www.jci.com.*

**2.** Cathy Anterasian and Lynn W. Phillips, "Discontinuities, Value Delivery, and the Share-Returns Association: A Re-Examination of the 'Share-Causes-Profits' Controversy," distributed working paper (Cambridge, MA: Marketing Science Institute, April 1988). Also see Robert Jacobson, "Distinguishing among Competing Theories of the Market Share Effect," *Journal of Marketing,* October 1988, pp. 68–80.

**3.** William K. Hall, "Survival Strategies in a Hostile Environment," *Harvard Business Review,* September–October 1980, pp. 75–85.

**4.** Michael Treacy and Fred Wiersema, *The Discipline of Market Leaders* (Reading, MA: Addison-Wesley Publishing, 1995).

**5.** Roland T. Rust, Christine Moorman, and Peter R. Dickson, "Getting Return on Quality: Revenue Expansion, Cost Reduction, or Both?" *Journal of Marketing* 66, October 2002, pp. 7–24.

**6.** Rahul Jacob, "Beyond Quality and Value," *Fortune,* Special Issue, Autumn–Winter 1993, pp. 8–11.

**7.** The following discussion is based on material found in David A. Garvin, "What Does 'Product Quality' Really Mean?" *Sloan Management Review,* Fall 1984, pp. 25–43; and David A. Aaker, *Strategic Market Management,* 5th ed. (New York: John Wiley & Sons, 1998), chap. 9.

**8.** Kathleen Kerwin, "When Flawless Isn't Enough," *BusinessWeek,* December 8, 2003, pp. 80–82.

**9.** For a more extensive discussion of brand equity see David A. Aaker, *Brand Equity* (New York: Free Press, 1991).

**10.** Valarie A. Zeithaml, A. Parasuraman, and Leonard L. Berry, *Delivering Quality Service: Balancing Customer Perceptions and Expectations* (New York: Free Press, 1990).

**11.** Valarie A. Zeithaml, A. Parasuraman, and Arvind Malhotra, "A Conceptual Framework for Understanding E-Service Quality: Implications for Future Research and Managerial Practice," *Report* No. 00-115 (Cambridge, MA: Marketing Science Institute, 2000). Also see Mary Wolfinbarger and Mary C. Gilly, "E-TailQ: Dimensionalizing, Measuring, and Predicting E-Tail Quality," *Journal of Retailing* 79 (Fall 2003), pp. 183–98.

**12.** For a case example of how an employee training program might be designed to improve performance on the five service quality dimensions, see Andrew J. Czaplewski, Eric M. Olson, and Stanley F. Slater, "Applying the RATER Model for Service Success," *Marketing Management,* January/February 2002, pp. 14–17. For a broader review of academic research on service, see Roland T. Rust and Tuck Siong Chung, "Marketing Models of Service and Relationships," *Marketing Science* 25 (November–December 2006), pp. 560–80.

**13.** For a more detailed discussion of these and other approaches for lowering costs, see Aaker, *Strategic Market Management,* chap. 10.

**14.** Akshay R. Rao, Mark E. Bergen, and Scott Davis, "How to Fight a Price War," *Harvard Business Review,* March–April 2000, pp. 107–16.

**15.** Pete Engardio, "The Future of Outsourcing," *BusinessWeek,* January 30, 2006, pp. 50–64.

**16.** Pete Engardio, "Can the U.S. Bring Jobs Back from China?" *BusinessWeek,* June 30, 2008, pp. 39–43; and Kevin Brown, "Rising Chinese Wages Pose Relocation Risk," *Financial Times online* (*www.ft/asia-pacific.com*), February 15, 2011.

**17.** Mara Der Hovanesian, "Coffee, Tea, Or Mortgage," *BusinessWeek,* April 3, 2006, pp. 48–49.

**18.** Robert Jacobson and David A. Aaker, "The Strategic Role of Product Quality," *Journal of Marketing,* October 1987, pp. 31–44; and Rust, Moorman, and Dickson, "Getting Return on Quality"; and Gerard J. Tellis, Eden Yin, and Rakesh Niraj, "Does Quality Win? Network Effects versus Quality in High-Tech Markets," *Journal of Marketing Research* 46 (April 2009), pp. 135–49.

**19.** Brad Stone, "What's in the Box? Instant Gratification," *Bloomberg BusinessWeek,* November 29, 2010, pp. 39–40.

**20.** Frederick F. Reichheld, *The Ultimate Question: Driving Good Profits and True Growth* (Toronto: The University of Toronto Press, 2006). See also Jena McGregor, "Would You Recommend Us?" *BusinessWeek,* January 30, 2006, pp. 94–95.

**21.** For a discussion of various approaches to measuring customer satisfaction, see J. Joseph Cronin and Steven A. Taylor, "Measuring Service Quality: A Reexamination and Extension," *Journal of Marketing,* July 1992, pp. 55–68; Susan J. Devlin and H. K. Dong, "Service Quality from the Customer's Perspective," *Marketing Research* 6 (1994), pp. 5–13; and Paul W. Farris, Neil T. Bendle, Phillip E. Pfeifer, and David J. Reibstein, *Marketing Metrics* 2nd ed. (Upper Saddle River, NJ: Pearson Education, Inc., 2010), pp. 56–62.

**22.** Frederick F. Reichheld, "Loyalty and the Renaissance of Marketing," *Marketing Management* 2 (1994), pp. 10–21. Also see Rahul Jacob, "Why Some Customers Are More Equal Than Others," *Fortune,* September 19, 1994, pp. 215–24.

**23.** Reichheld, "Loyalty and the Renaissance of Marketing." See also Thomas O. Jones and W. Earl Sasser, Jr., "Why Satisfied Customers Defect," *Harvard Business Review,* November–December 1995, pp. 88–99; and Murali Chandrashekaran, Kristin Rotte, Stephen S. Tax, and Rajdeep Grewal, "Satisfaction Strength and Customer Loyalty," *Journal of Marketing Research* 44 (February 2007), pp. 153–63.

**24.** Jeff Jarvis, "Love the Customers Who Hate You," *BusinessWeek,* March 3, 2008, p. 58; and Jena McGregor, "Consumer Vigilantes," *BusinessWeek,* March 3, 2008, pp. 38–42.

**25.** Rachael King, "Sentiment Analysis Gives Companies Insight into Consumer Opinion," *www.businessweek.com,* March 1, 2011.

**26.** The following discussion is based, in part, on Diane Brady, "Why Service Stinks," *BusinessWeek,* October 23, 2000, pp. 118–28.

**27.** Emily Thornton, "Fees! Fees! Fees!" *BusinessWeek,* September 29, 2003, pp. 99–104.

**28.** Julia Flynn, "In Napa Valley, Winemaker's Brands Divide an Industry," *The Wall Street Journal,* February 22, 2005, pp. A1 & A8; and David Kiley, "Winning Back Joe Corkscrew," *BusinessWeek,* April 24, 2006, pp. 82–83.

**29.** Ronald Grover, "The Payoff from Targeting Hispanics," *BusinessWeek,* April 20, 2009, p. 76.

**30.** For a more detailed discussion of private-label strategy, see Nirmalya Kumar and Jan-Benedict E. M. Steenkamp, *Private Label Strategy: How to Meet the Store-Brand Challenge* (Boston: Harvard Business School Press, 2007); and Jan-Benedict E. M. Steenkamp, Harald J. Van Heerde, and Inge Geyskens, "What Makes Consumers Willing to Pay a Price Premium for National Brands over Private Labels?" *Journal of Marketing Research* 47 (December 2010), pp. 1011–24.

**31.** The following discussion of sequential strategies is based largely on material found in Somkid Jatusripitak, Liam Fahey, and Philip Kotler, "Strategic Global Marketing: Lessons from the Japanese," *Columbia Journal of World Business,* Spring 1985, pp. 47–53.

**32.** Gail Edmonson, "The Beauty of Global Branding," *BusinessWeek,* June 28, 1999, pp. 70–75.

**33.** Kathryn Rudie Harrigan and Michael E. Porter, "End-Game Strategies for Declining Industries," *Harvard Business Review,* July–August 1983, pp. 111–20. Also see Kathryn Rudie Harrigan, *Managing Maturing Businesses* (New York: Lexington Books, 1988).

**34.** Harrigan and Porter, "End-Game Strategies," p. 114.

# SECTION FIVE

# IMPLEMENTING AND CONTROLLING MARKETING PROGRAMS

| CHAPTER 17 | Organizing and Planning for Effective Implementation | CHAPTER 18 | Measuring and Delivering Marketing Performance |
|---|---|---|---|

# CHAPTER SEVENTEEN

# Organizing and Planning for Effective Implementation

## Electrolux—Organizing to Rule the World of Household Appliances[1]

ELECTROLUX, the Swedish household appliances giant, began selling Lux vacuum cleaners in a few European countries in 1919. The company soon undertook an aggressive growth strategy, largely via mergers and acquisitions. It grew by both acquiring other kinds of appliance lines—refrigerators in 1925, washing machines in 1951, dishwashers in 1959, food service equipment in 1962, and so on—and by buying established local brands in many countries around the world, such as Frigidaire in North America, Zanussi and AEG in Europe, and Simpson in Australia. This strategy made Electrolux the world's number one household appliance company by the early years of this century, until a merger between Whirlpool and Maytag in 2006 bumped it to number two.

Electrolux's aggressive acquisition strategy not only increased the firm's revenues, it also established its presence in more countries than many of its competitors. As Keith McLoughlin, the firm's CEO, points out, "We're the only one that has the distribution and local market presence in over 150 countries. You have to know the local consumer, and we do that globally more than anyone." Indeed, less than a third of the firm's revenues come from the Scandinavian countries and Europe. North America accounts for 32 percent of sales, Latin America for 18 percent, and the Asia-Pacific region for another 8 percent.

## Too Many Brands, Too Little Coordination

During Electrolux's decades of rapid growth, many of the firm's newly acquired brands retained a substantial amount of operational autonomy. While the parent company imposed financial goals and cost controls, the various brands were essentially managed as separate business units, each with its own R&D, manufacturing, and marketing departments. This gave the different brands substantial freedom to grow and compete in their regional markets as they saw fit.

Eventually, though, the proliferation of brands—more than 50 in all—and the lack of coordination among them, became a major problem. For one thing, different brands were targeted at different ends of the market—from superpremium to discount—and had different levels of awareness and acceptance in different geographic regions. Thus, Electrolux did not have a strong, coherent brand image around the world, and it was wasting marketing dollars on many unrelated, and sometimes competing, product development projects and marketing campaigns. Similarly, the large number of autonomous brands and product lines limited the opportunities for synergy and economies of scale in purchasing and manufacturing. These inefficiencies became especially critical when low-cost Asian manufacturers, like LG and Haier emerged as major players in the global market. Electrolux's managers realized that without strong brands with a reputation for high quality and innovation, the company would have no defense against lower-priced competitors, and no way to differentiate themselves from other high-end manufacturers like Bosch-Siemens, General Electric, or Samsung. Summarizing the firm's new competitive strategy, the CEO said, "Our aim is to become a reliable and trusted partner with our customers and retailers. That means we need a few strong brands. We can't support too many."

Consequently, the firm pulled the plug on some of its weaker brands and licensed other regional brands to local manufacturers. While it continues to support a few strong regional brands like Frigidaire and AEG, its marketing efforts are currently concentrated on a single premium global brand—Electrolux. Strangely, in order to implement its new strategy, it first had to buy back the rights to the Electrolux name in North America, which it had sold in the 1960s to raise money for its global acquisition spree.

## A New Structure to Implement the New Strategy

In order to coordinate its more focused brand strategy across countries around the world, the old company structure with its semiautonomous brands obviously had to change. The new structure is a matrix organization (a form we will examine later in this chapter) with both product-market and functional components. First, the company's various product lines and remaining brands were collapsed into three main product sectors: (1) Major Appliances, (2) Small Appliances and Floor Care, and (3) Professional Products (equipment for restaurants and dry cleaners). The Major Appliances sector was further subdivided into four geographic regions—(a) Europe, Middle East, & Africa, (b) North America, (c) Latin America, and (d) Asia-Pacific—in order to respond to the differing consumer desires, distribution channels, and competitive environments across countries.

All seven of the product-market sectors are serviced by five group-level staff units: (1) Finance, (2) Human Resources, (3) Legal Affairs, (4) Corporate Communications, and (5) Branding (responsible for licensing activities). Finally, in order to gain economies of scale and synergy across the firm's product lines, three group-level global operations units are responsible for all (a) technical R&D, (b) purchasing, and (c) manufacturing activities.

Marketing decisions—including the design and introduction of new products, advertising and promotional campaigns, budgeting, internet utilization, and website design—are decentralized and largely left to the individual product/market sectors. Such decisions are the responsibility of sector boards made up of the top functional managers within the sector plus the company president and the chief financial officer. However, oversight and coordination of those sector decisions is provided by regular meetings of a group management committee consisting of the CEO, the sector heads, and top executives of the staff and global operations departments.

## Preliminary Results

The global economic crisis of 2008–2009 has made it difficult to fully evaluate the performance of Electrolux's new corporate structure. But judging from the firm's financial performance in 2010, it is working quite well. The company earned an operating income of $835 million on global revenues of $16.3 billion, for a return on equity of over 20 percent.

# Marketing Challenges Addressed in Chapter 17

Electrolux's recent history illustrates that a business's success is determined by two aspects of strategic fit. First, its competitive and marketing strategies must fit the needs and desires of its target customers and the competitive and technological realities of the marketplace. Thus, the entry of low-cost Asian manufacturers into the global major appliances market helped force Electrolux to adopt a new strategy aimed at building a widely recognized global brand with a reputation for premium quality and innovative design.

But even if a firm's competitive strategy is appropriate for the circumstances it faces, it must be capable of implementing that strategy effectively. This is where the second aspect of strategic fit enters the picture. A business's orga-

## STRATEGIC ISSUE

*A business's organizational structure, internal policies, procedures, and resources must fit its chosen strategy or else implementation will fall short.*

nizational structure, internal policies, procedures, and resources must fit its chosen strategy or else implementation will fall short. For instance, the old structure with multiple brands organized into largely autonomous business units would obviously not be effective for implementing the new strategy focusing on the Electrolux brand and strengthening its global image.

Therefore, in the next section we examine several questions related to the issue of **organizational fit**—the fit between a business's competitive and marketing strategies and the organizational structures, policies, processes, and plans necessary to effectively implement those strategies.

- For companies with multiple business units or product lines, what is the appropriate administrative relationship between corporate headquarters and the individual SBUs? How much autonomy should business unit managers be given to make their own strategic decisions, how much control should they have over the SBU's resources and programs, and how should they be evaluated and rewarded?

- Within a given business unit, whether it's part of a larger corporation or a one-product entrepreneurial start-up, what organizational structures and coordination mechanisms are most appropriate for implementing different competitive strategies? Answering this question involves decisions about variables such as the desired level of technical competence of the various functional departments within the business, the manner in which resources are allocated across those functions, and the mechanisms used to coordinate and resolve conflicts among the departments.

- How should organizational structures and policies be adjusted, if at all, as an organization moves into international markets?

However, even if a business has crafted brilliant competitive and marketing strategies, and it has the necessary organizational arrangements and wherewithal to implement them, implementation is unlikely to be very effective unless all of the business's people are following the same plan. This fact underlines the importance of developing formal, written marketing plans to document all the decisions made in formulating the intended strategy for a given good or service so it can be clearly communicated to everyone responsible for its implementation and to firmly establish who is responsible for doing what and when. And as we'll see in the next chapter, formal plans also establish the timetables and objectives that are the benchmarks for management's evaluation and control of the firm's marketing strategies. Thus, good planning is important.

Given the importance of formal plans as tools to aid implementation and control, we will return in the last part of this chapter to the planning framework we introduced briefly in Chapter 1. We will examine the content of effective marketing plans in more detail and review the many strategic decisions involved in formulating that content. The purpose of these planning decisions is to lay a well-conceived foundation that permits effective implementation of the marketing strategy. While good planning is important, effective implementation is crucial.

# Designing Appropriate Administrative Relationships for the Implementation of Different Competitive Strategies

In Chapter 9 we pointed out that businesses, whether small independent firms or units within a larger corporation, compete in different ways depending on their intended rate of new product-market development (i.e., prospectors versus analyzers versus defenders) and whether they seek an advantage by differentiating themselves via superior product or service quality or by being the low-cost producer.

The chosen competitive strategy tends to influence the marketing strategies pursued by individual product offerings within the business unit, at least in the short term. The differentiated analyzer strategy of Electrolux's major appliances sector, for example, dictates an aggressive new product development program, as well as extensive advertising and social media campaigns to build awareness of the Electrolux brand and the stream of new products.

Because different competitive strategies seek to satisfy customers and gain a sustainable advantage in varying ways, different organizational structures, policies, and resources are necessary to effectively implement them.[2] For one thing, the administrative relationships between the unit and corporate headquarters influence the ability of SBU managers, including its marketing personnel, to implement specific competitive and marketing strategies successfully. This section examines three aspects of the corporate–business unit relationship that can affect the SBU's success in implementing a particular competitive strategy:

1. The degree of autonomy provided each business-unit manager.
2. The degree to which the business unit shares functional programs and facilities with other units.
3. The manner in which the corporation evaluates and rewards the performance of its SBU managers.

Exhibit 17.1 summarizes how these variables relate to the successful implementation of different business strategies. Analyzer strategies are not included because they incorporate some elements of both prospector and defender strategies. The administrative arrangements appropriate for implementing an analyzer strategy typically fall somewhere between those best suited for the other two types. To simplify the following discussion we focus only on the polar types—prospector, differentiated defender, and low-cost defender strategies.

## Business-Unit Autonomy

Prospector business units are likely to perform better on the critical dimensions of new product success and increased volume and market share when organizational decision making is relatively decentralized and the SBU's managers have substantial autonomy to make their own decisions. There are several reasons for this. First, decentralized decision making allows the managers closest to the market to make more major decisions on their own. Greater autonomy also enables the SBU's managers to be more flexible and adaptable. It frees them from the restrictions of standard procedures imposed from above,

## Exhibit 17.1

ADMINISTRATIVE FACTORS RELATED TO THE SUCCESSFUL IMPLEMENTATION OF BUSINESS STRATEGIES

| | TYPES OF BUSINESS STRATEGY | | |
| --- | --- | --- | --- |
| Administrative factor | Prospector | Differentiated defender | Low-cost defender |
| SBU autonomy | Relatively high level | Moderate level | Relatively low level |
| Shared programs and synergy | Relatively little synergy—few shared programs | Little synergy in areas central to differentiation—shared programs elsewhere | High level of synergy and shared programs |
| Evaluation and reward systems | High incentives based on sales and share growth | High incentives based on profits or ROI | Incentives based on profits or ROI |

allows them to make decisions with fewer consultations and participants, and disperses power. All of these help produce quicker and more innovative responses to environmental opportunities.

One caveat must be attached to the above generalization, however. High levels of autonomy and independence can lead to coordination problems across business units. This can have a negative effect on market performance in situations where a firm's business units are narrowly defined and focused on a single product category or technology but the firm's customers want to buy integrated systems incorporating products or services from different units. This was the problem encountered by IBM, Hewlett-Packard, and other computer hardware manufacturers as the growing popularity of the internet caused customers to attach greater importance to system integration. One possible solution to this coordination problem is to redefine SBUs with a focus on customer or application segments rather than on narrowly defined product categories, as we discussed in Chapter 2. An alternative approach is to reduce the SBUs' autonomy somewhat by installing an additional level of managers responsible for coordinating the efforts of related business units. The risk inherent in this approach is that the essential flexibility and creativity of the individual business units may be compromised.

On the other hand, low-cost defender SBUs perform better on ROI and cash flow by giving their managers relatively little autonomy. For a low-cost strategy to succeed, managers must relentlessly pursue cost economies and productivity improvements. Such efficiencies are more likely to be attained when decision making and control are relatively centralized, or at least closely monitored.

The relationship between autonomy and the ROI performance of differentiated defenders is more difficult to predict. On the one hand, such businesses defend existing positions in established markets and their primary objective is ROI rather than volume growth. Thus, the increased efficiency and tighter control associated with relatively low autonomy should lead to better performance. On the other hand, such businesses can maintain profitability only if they continue to differentiate themselves by offering superior products and services. As customers' wants change and new competitive threats emerge, the greater flexibility and market focus associated with greater autonomy may allow these businesses to more successfully maintain their differentiated positions and higher levels of ROI over time. These arguments suggest that the relationship between autonomy and performance for differentiated defenders (and probably for differentiated analyzers as well) may be mediated by the level of stability in their environments and by the proportion of offensive or proactive marketing strategies they employ. Units operating in relatively unstable environments and pursuing more proactive marketing programs (such as extended-use or market-expansion strategies) are likely to perform better when they have relatively greater autonomy.

## Shared Programs and Facilities

Firms face a trade-off when designing strategic business units. An SBU should be large enough to afford critical resources and to operate on an efficient scale, but it should not be so large that its market scope is too broad or that it is inflexible and therefore cannot respond to its unique market opportunities. Some firms attempt to avoid this trade-off between efficiency and adaptability by designing relatively small, narrowly focused business units but then having two or more units share functional programs or facilities, such as common manufacturing plants, R&D programs, or a single salesforce.

Sharing resources can pose a problem for prospector business units.[3] Suppose, for instance, a business wants to introduce a new product but shares a manufacturing plant and salesforce with other SBUs. The business would have to negotiate a production schedule for the new product, and it may not be able to produce adequate quantities as quickly as needed if other units sharing the plant are trying to maintain sufficient volumes of their own products. It may also be difficult to train salespeople on the new product or to motivate them to reduce the time spent on established products to push the new item. When Frito-Lay introduced Grandma's soft cookies, for instance, it relied on its 10,000 salty-snack route salespeople to attain supermarket shelf space for the new line. But because those salespeople were paid a commission based on their total sales revenue, they were reluctant to take time away from their profitable salty-snack lines to sell the new cookies. The resulting lack of strong sales support contributed to Grandma's failure to capture a sustainable share of the packaged cookie market.

One exception to this generalization, though, may be sharing sales and distribution programs across consumer package goods SBUs. In such cases, a prospector's new product may have an easier time obtaining retailer support and shelf space if it is represented by salespeople who also sell established brands to the same retail outlets. Similarly, sharing, or at least coordinating, sales, distribution, and customer service functions may be a good idea for business units that produce complementary goods or services that customers want to purchase as integrated systems rather than stand-alone offerings. In general, however, functional independence usually facilitates good performance for prospector businesses.

On the other hand, the increased efficiencies gained through sharing functional programs and facilities often boost the ROI performance of low-cost defender SBUs. Also, the inflexibility inherent in sharing is usually not a major problem for such businesses because their markets and technologies tend to be mature and relatively stable. Thus, Heinz, the cost leader in a number of food categories, uses a single salesforce to represent a wide variety of products from different business units when calling on supermarkets.

The impact of shared programs on the performance of differentiated defenders is more difficult to predict because they must often modify their products and marketing programs in response to changing market conditions to maintain their competitive advantage over time. Thus, greater functional independence in areas directly related to the SBU's differential advantage—such as R&D, sales, and marketing—tends to be positively associated with the long-run ROI performance of such businesses. But greater sharing of facilities and programs in less-crucial functional areas, such as manufacturing or distribution, may also help improve their efficiency and short-run ROI levels.

# Evaluation and Reward Systems

Increasingly, U.S. firms are adopting some form of pay-for-performance compensation scheme. Some do it for individuals who meet specific goals (e.g., bonuses for salespeople who exceed their quotas), others on the basis of the performance of the SBU or the company as a whole (e.g., stock options). In either case, SBU managers are often motivated to achieve their objectives by bonuses or other financial incentives tied to one or more dimensions of their unit's performance. The question is, which dimensions of performance should be rewarded?

For defender businesses in relatively mature markets, particularly those competing as low-cost defenders, operating efficiency and profitability tend to be the most important objectives, for reasons discussed in Chapter 9. Consequently, tying a relatively large portion of managers' incentive compensation to short-term profits seems sensible. This can be done either through bonuses based on last year's profit performance or economic value added (EVA) or through options keyed to increases in the firm's stock price. However, recent research suggests that such bonus systems are most effective at motivating good performance when they are made available to all employees, not just top managers.[4]

In prospector businesses, on the other hand, basing too large a portion of managers' rewards on current profitability may cause problems. Such rewards may motivate managers to avoid innovative but risky actions or investments that may not pay off for some years into the future.[5] Even successful new product introductions can dramatically increase costs and drain profits early in the product's life cycle. By the time the new product starts contributing to the unit's profits, the manager who deserves the credit may have been transferred to a different business. Therefore, evaluation and reward systems that place relatively more emphasis on sales volume or market share objectives, or on the percentage of volume generated by new products, may be more appropriate for businesses pursuing prospector strategies.

# Designing Appropriate Organizational Structures and Processes for Implementing Different Strategies

Different strategies emphasize varying ways to gain a competitive advantage. Thus, a given functional area may be key to the success of one type of strategy but less critical for others. For instance, competence in new product R&D is critical for the success of a prospector business but less so for a low-cost defender.

Successful implementation of a given strategy is more likely when the business has the **functional competencies** demanded by its strategy and supports them with substantial **resources** relative to competitors; is **organized** suitably for its technical, market, and competitive environment; and has developed appropriate **mechanisms** for coordinating efforts and resolving conflicts across functional departments. Exhibit 17.2 summarizes the relationships between these organizational structure and process variables and the performance of different business strategies.

## Functional Competencies and Resource Allocation

Competence in marketing, sales, product R&D, and engineering are critical to the success of prospector businesses because those functions play pivotal roles in new product and market development and thus must be supported with budgets set at a larger percentage

## Exhibit 17.2

ORGANIZATIONAL AND INTERFUNCTIONAL FACTORS RELATED TO THE SUCCESSFUL IMPLEMENTATION OF BUSINESS STRATEGIES

| Organizational factor | TYPE OF BUSINESS STRATEGY | | |
| --- | --- | --- | --- |
| | Prospector | Differentiated defender | Low-cost defender |
| Functional competencies of the SBU | SBU will perform best on critical volume and share-growth dimensions when its functional strengths include marketing, sales, product R&D, and engineering. | SBU will perform best on critical ROI dimensions when its functional strengths include sales, financial management and control, and those functions related to its differential advantage (e.g., marketing, product R&D). | SBU will perform best on critical ROI and cash flow dimensions when its functional strengths include process engineering, production, distribution, and financial management and control. |
| Resource allocation across functions | SBU will perform best on volume and share-growth dimension when percentage of sales spent on marketing, sales, and product R&D are high and when gross fixed assets per employee and percent of capacity utilization are low relative to competitors'. | SBU will perform best on the ROI dimension when percentage of sales spent on the salesforce, gross fixed assets per employee, percent of capacity utilization, and percentage of sales devoted to other functions related to the SBU's differential advantage are high relative to competitors'. | SBU will perform best on ROI and cash flow dimensions when marketing, sales, and product R&D expenses are low, but process R&D, fixed assets per employee, and percentage of capacity utilization are high relative to competitors'. |
| Decision-making influence and participation | SBU will perform best on volume and share-growth dimensions when managers from marketing, sales, product R&D, and engineering have substantial influence on unit's business and marketing strategy decisions. | SBU will perform best on ROI dimension when financial managers, controller, and managers of functions related to unit's differential advantage have substantial influence on business and marketing strategy decisions. | SBU will perform best on ROI and cash flow when controller, financial, and production managers have substantial influence on business and marketing strategy decisions. |
| SBU's organization structure | SBU will perform best on volume and share-growth dimension when structure has low levels of formalization and centralization, but high level of specialization. | SBU will perform best on ROI dimensions when structure has moderate levels of formalization, centralization, and specialization. | SBU will perform best on ROI and cash flow dimensions when structure has high levels of formalization and centralization, but low level of specialization. |
| Functional coordination and conflict resolution | SBU will experience high levels of interfunctional conflict; SBU will perform best on volume and share-growth dimensions when participative resolution mechanisms are used (e.g., product teams). | SBU will experience moderate levels of interfunctional conflict; SBU will perform best on ROI dimension when resolution is participative for issues related to differential advantage, but hierarchical for others (e.g., product managers, product improvement teams). | SBU will experience low levels of interfunctional conflict; SBU will perform best on ROI and cash flow dimensions when conflict resolution mechanisms are hierarchical (e.g., functional organization). |

*Source:* Adapted from Orville C. Walker, Jr., and Robert W. Ruekert, "Marketing's Role in the Implementation of Business Strategies," *Journal of Marketing,* July 1987, p. 31. Used by permission of the American Marketing Association.

of sales than their competitors. Because marketing, sales, and R&D managers are closest to the changes occurring in a business's market, competitive, and technological environments, they should be given considerable authority in making strategic decisions. This argues that bottom-up strategic planning systems are particularly well-suited to prospector businesses operating in unstable environments. Success here is positively affected by the extent to which customer orientation is an integral part of the unit's corporate culture.

In low-cost defender businesses, on the other hand, the functional areas most directly related to operating efficiency, such as financial management and control, production, process R&D, and distribution or logistics, play the most crucial roles in enabling the SBU to attain good ROI performance. Because differentiated defenders need to attain high returns on their established products, functional areas related to efficiency are also critical for their success. Similarly, such units also seek to improve efficiency by investing in process R&D, making needed capital investments, and maintaining a high level of capacity utilization. But because they must also maintain their differential advantage over time, functional departments related to the source of that advantage—the salesforce and product R&D for SBUs with a technical product advantage or sales, marketing, and distribution for SBUs with a customer service advantage—are also critical for the unit's continued success. As we have seen, for example, in an attempt to defend its leading share position, cement the loyalty of its growing customer base, and generate greater revenues from repeat purchases, Amazon has invested millions in software and distribution centers to improve the speed and reliability of its order fulfillment.

## Additional Considerations for Service Organizations

Given that service organizations pursue the same kinds of business-level competitive strategies as goods producers, they must meet the same functional and resource requirements to implement those strategies effectively. However, service organizations—and manufacturers that provide high levels of customer service as part of their product offering—often need some additional functional competencies because of the unique problems involved in delivering quality service.

This is particularly true for services involving high customer contact. Because the sale, production, and delivery of such services occur almost simultaneously, close coordination between operations, sales, and marketing is crucial. Also, because many different employees may be involved in producing and delivering the service—as when thousands of different cooks prepare Big Macs at McDonald's outlets around the world—production planning and standardization are needed to reduce variations in quality from one transaction to the next. Similarly, detailed policies, procedures, and perhaps facilitating technologies—such as touch-screen kiosks and interactive voice-response units—for dealing with customers are necessary to reduce variability in customer treatment across employees. All of this suggests that personnel management—particularly the activities of employee selection, training, motivation, and evaluation—is an important adjunct to the production and marketing efforts of high-contact service organizations.[6] A good example of how well-trained service personnel can help improve sales and customer retention in even the most mundane businesses is provided by Wawa convenience stores, as discussed in Exhibit 17.3.

Competence in human resource development is more crucial for service businesses pursuing prospector strategies—and perhaps also for defenders and analyzers who differentiate

**STRATEGIC ISSUE**

*Personnel management—particularly the activities of employee selection, training, motivation, and evaluation—is an important adjunct to the production and marketing efforts of high-contact service organizations.*

**Exhibit 17.3   GOOD SERVICE PERSONNEL CAN TURN CUSTOMERS INTO FANS**

Wawa is a chain of convenience stores with 550 locations in five states on the East Coast of the United States. Convenience stores, where employee turnover is often high and transactions impersonal, might seem like the perfect venue for indifferent service. But many Wawa customers are enthusiastic fans. The "I Love Wawa" group on MySpace.com grew to more than 5,000 members, and one couple even had their wedding at the Wawa store where they first met.

Wawa has been successful at making loyal fans among its clientele by focusing on repeat customers—some of whom stop by every day—and trying to provide satisfying customer–employee interactions via careful hiring and training practices. While Wawa wages are about the same as those of its competitors, the firm does a better job of investing in the development of the people it hires: training them at its Wawa Corporate University, providing them with benefits that facilitate self-improvement—such as reimbursing tuition for college courses—and the like. Consequently, employee turnover rates are low and the firm receives hundreds of applicants for each job opening. If a lowly convenience store chain can turn customers into fans, perhaps many other service companies could benefit from increased investments in employee recruitment, training, and rewards.

*Source:* Rob Walker, "Convenience Cult?" *New York Times Magazine,* July 30, 2006, p. 15.

their offerings on the basis of good service—than for those focused primarily on efficiency and low cost. In prospector service organizations, employees often play a critical role in identifying potential new service offerings and in introducing them to potential customers. Consequently, the effective implementation of such a strategy requires employees with superior communication and social skills and necessitates frequent employee retraining and performance feedback. For instance, banks pursuing a prospector strategy not only have more branches and engage in more market scanning, advertising, and new service development than those with other types of competitive strategies, but also devote more effort to screening potential employees and providing training and support after they are hired.[7]

## Organizational Structures

Three structural variables—formalization, centralization, and specialization—are important in shaping both an SBU's and its marketing department's performance within the context of a given competitive strategy. **Formalization** is the degree to which formal rules and standard policies and procedures govern decisions and working relationships. **Centralization** refers to the location of decision authority and control within an organization's hierarchy. In highly centralized SBUs or marketing departments, only one or a few top managers hold most decision-making authority. In more decentralized units, middle- and lower-level managers have more autonomy and participate in a wider range of decisions. Finally, **specialization** refers to the division of tasks and activities across positions within the organizational unit. A highly specialized marketing department, for instance, has a large number of specialists, such as market researchers, advertising managers, and sales promotion managers, who perform a narrowly defined set of activities often as consultants to product managers.

Highly structured business units and marketing departments are unlikely to be very innovative or quick to adapt to a changing environmental circumstance. Adaptiveness and innovativeness are enhanced when (1) decision-making authority is decentralized, (2) managerial discretion and informal coordination mechanisms replace rigid rules and policies, and (3) more specialists are present. Thus, prospector business units and their marketing departments are likely to perform better when they are decentralized, have little formalization, and are highly specialized.[8]

Differentiated defenders perform best when their organization structures incorporate moderate levels of formalization, centralization, and specialization. Those departments most directly related to the source of a differentiated defender's competitive advantage (sales, marketing, and R&D), however, should be less highly structured than those more crucial for the efficiency of the unit's operations (production and logistics).

Several common organizational designs incorporate differences in both the structural variables (formalization, centralization, and specialization) and in the mechanisms for resolving interfunctional conflicts. These include (1) functional, (2) product management, (3) market management, and (4) various types of matrix organizational designs.

**Functional Organizations**    The functional form of organization is the simplest and most bureaucratic design. At the SBU level, managers of each functional department, such as production or marketing, report to the general manager. Within the marketing department, managers of specific marketing activity areas, such as sales, advertising, or marketing research, report to the marketing vice president or director, as shown in Exhibit 17.4. At each level the top manager coordinates the activities of all the functional areas reporting to him or her, often with heavy reliance on standard rules and operating procedures. This is the most centralized and formalized organization form and relies primarily on hierarchical mechanisms for resolving conflicts across functional areas. Also, because top managers perform their coordination activities across all product-markets in the SBU, there is little specialization by product or customer type.

These characteristics make the functional form simple, efficient, and particularly suitable for companies operating in stable and slow-growth industries where the environments are predictable. Thus, the form is appropriate for low-cost defender SBUs attempting to maximize their efficiency and profitability in mature or declining industries. For example, Ingersoll-Rand, a low-cost manufacturer of low-tech air compressors and air-driven tools such as jackhammers, uses a functional structure.

## Exhibit 17.4

FUNCTIONAL ORGANIZATION OF AN SBU AND ITS MARKETING DEPARTMENT

The simplicity of the functional organization also makes it the most common organizational form among entrepreneurial start-ups. Even though the functional form is very hierarchical, such firms can still be nimble and innovative provided that (1) the company remains small enough that the entrepreneur can personally supervise and coordinate the various functions, (2) the firm is focused on a single product or product line targeted at one customer segment, and (3) the entrepreneur's personal vision is an adequate source of innovation to differentiate the entire company. As the start-up grows, its product offerings expand, and its markets fragment, however, it is usually wise to adopt a more decentralized and specialized organizational form. Unfortunately, some entrepreneurs find it difficult to delegate decision-making authority to their subordinates.

**Product Management Organizations**   When a company or SBU has many product-market entries, the simple functional form of organization is inadequate. A single manager finds it difficult to stay abreast of functional activities across a variety of different product-markets or to coordinate them efficiently. One common means of dealing with this problem is to adopt a product management organization structure. As Exhibit 17.5 illustrates, this form adds an additional layer of managers to the marketing department, usually called product managers, brand managers, or marketing managers, each of whom has the responsibility to plan and manage the marketing programs and to coordinate the activities of other functional departments for a specific product or product line.

A product management structure decentralizes decision making while increasing the amount of product specialization within the SBU. If the product managers are also given substantial autonomy to develop their own marketing plans and programs, this structure can also decrease the formalization within the business. Finally, although the product managers are responsible for obtaining cooperation from other functional areas both within and outside the marketing department, they have no formal authority over these areas. They must rely on persuasion and compromise—in other words, more participative methods—to overcome conflicts and objections when coordinating functional activities. These factors make the product management form of organization less bureaucratic than the functional structure. It is more appropriate, then, for businesses pursuing differentiated defender and analyzer strategies, particularly when they operate in industries with complex and

## Exhibit 17.5

A MARKETING DEPARTMENT WITH A PRODUCT MANAGEMENT ORGANIZATION relatively unstable market and competitive environments. Thus, many large consumer packaged-goods companies with multiple brands competing in diverse segments—such as Nestlé, Unilever, and Procter & Gamble—incorporate a product management structure.

When large firms target a number of brands at different market segments, a product management organization typically also includes one or more "group" or "category" marketing managers, on the level immediately above the product managers, who allocate resources across brands. Category management also provides an opportunity for the involvement of more experienced managers in brand management, particularly those concerned with coordinating pricing and other marketing efforts.[9]

Product management organizations have a number of advantages, including the ability to identify and react more quickly to the threats and opportunities individual product-market entries face, improved coordination of functional activities within and across product-markets, and increased attention to smaller product-market entries that might be neglected in a functional organization. Consequently, about 85 percent of all consumer goods manufacturers use some form of product management organization.

Despite its advantages, a product management organization has shortcomings. The major one is the difficulty of obtaining the cooperation necessary to develop and implement effective programs for a particular product given that a product manager has little direct authority. Also, the environment facing product managers is changing drastically. They increasingly must face the fact that customers can quickly compare products and prices—and even suggest their own price—over the internet; that customers are becoming more price sensitive and less brand loyal; that competition is becoming more global; that rapidly changing technologies are providing new ways to improve production and distribution efficiency, but also shortening product life cycles; and that the power of large retailers and distributors has increased due in part to their ability to collect and control information about the marketplace. These environmental trends have led to an increase in the sales of private-label brands and more aggressive bargaining by distributors.[10] As a result of these trends and the inherent weakness of the product manager type of organization, many companies have undertaken two major types of modifications—market management and matrix organization—discussed next.

### Market Management Organizations

In some industries an SBU may market a single product to a large number of markets where customers have very different requirements and preferences. Pepsi-Cola, for example, is sold through restaurants, fast-food outlets, and supermarkets. The syrup needed to make Pepsi is sold directly to institutions such as Kentucky Fried Chicken and Taco Bell. But marketing Pepsi to consumers for home consumption involves the use of franchised bottlers who process and package the product and distribute it to a variety of retail outlets. The intermediaries and marketing activities involved in selling to the two markets are so different that it makes sense to have a separate market manager in charge of each. Such a company or SBU might organize itself along the lines shown in Exhibit 17.6. Some SBUs have adopted a combination of product and regional market management organization structures. A product manager has overall responsibility for planning and implementing a national marketing program for the product, but several market managers are also given some authority and an independent budget to work with salespeople and develop promotion programs geared to a particular user segment or geographic market. This kind of decentralization or regionalization has become popular with consumer goods companies in their efforts to increase geographic segmentation and cope with the growing power of regional retail chains.

### Matrix Organizations

A business facing an extremely complex and uncertain environment may find a matrix organization appropriate. The matrix form is the least bureaucratic

## Exhibit 17.6

A MARKETING DEPARTMENT WITH A MARKET MANAGEMENT ORGANIZATION

or centralized and the most specialized type of organization. It brings together two or more different types of specialists within a participative coordination structure. One example is the product team, which consists of representatives from a number of functional areas assembled for each product or product line. As a group, the team must agree on a business plan for the product and ensure the necessary resources and cooperation from each functional area. This kind of participative decision making can be very inefficient; it requires a good deal of time and effort for the team to reach mutually acceptable decisions and gain approval from all the affected functional areas. But once reached, those decisions are more likely to reflect the expertise of a variety of functional specialists, to be innovative, and to be quickly and effectively implemented. Thus, the matrix form of organization particularly suits prospector businesses and the management of new product development projects within analyzer or differentiated defender businesses. Some examples are discussed in Exhibit 17.7.

Another form of matrix structure involves the creation of an additional organizational unit or managerial position responsible for coordinating the actions of other units within the firm. For example, nearly every business school has an MBA program director responsible for coordinating the courses offered by the functional departments in hopes of creating a tightly integrated and coherent curriculum.

## Exhibit 17.7    USING TEAMS TO GET THE JOB DONE

Pillsbury, which has merged with General Mills, replaced its traditional marketing department with multiple discipline teams centered around a product group (pizza snacks). Each involves managers from marketing, sales, and production. Lever Brothers restructured in a similar fashion. It reorganized its marketing and sales departments into a series of business groups and set up a separate customer development team responsible for retailer relations across all the various SBU brands. And large companies are increasingly relying on small interdisciplinary teams to launch new product or service initiatives in their attempts to improve innovativeness and reduce time to market.

*Source:* "Death of the Brand Manager," *The Economist,* April 9, 1994, p. 67; and Steve Hamm, "Speed Demons," *BusinessWeek,* March 27, 2006, pp. 68–76.

Electrolux's new structure incorporates both of the above matrix types taken up to the corporate level. First, product specialists and market specialists were combined in the four regional major appliances sectors (e.g., Major Appliances North America, Latin America, etc.). The ongoing operations of the various product/market sectors are managed by boards made up of the sector's functional managers plus representatives of the corporate staff departments. Finally, common activities with substantial potential for cross-country synergies and economies of scale, such as purchasing and manufacturing, are coordinated across the product/market sectors by global operations units.

## Recent Trends in Organizational Design

As we have stressed throughout this book, the dynamics of the marketplace are forcing companies to respond more quickly to their opportunities and threats if they hope to survive and prosper. This has spurred a search for organizational structures that are flexible, responsive, able to learn, and market oriented.[11] While we are only just beginning to gain insights into organizational structures of the future, certain aspects seem reasonably clear. We briefly discuss the more important of these.

Organizations will increasingly emphasize the **managing of business processes** in contrast to functional areas.[12] Every business has about six basic or core processes, such as, for example, new product development and supply chain management. The former would be staffed by individuals from marketing, R&D, manufacturing, and finance. The latter would contain people with expertise in purchasing, manufacturing, order delivery, and billing.

Managing processes will make the organization essentially horizontal—flat and lean versus a vertical or hierarchical model. Thus, executive positions will no longer be defined in terms of managing a group of functionally oriented people; instead, executives will be concerned with a process that strongly emphasizes the importance of customer satisfaction.[13] Process management is quite different from the management of a function because, first, it uses external objectives, such as customer satisfaction versus simple revenues. Second, people with different skills are grouped to undertake a complete piece of work; their work is done simultaneously, not in sequence. Third, information flows directly to where it is used. Thus, if you have an upstream problem, you deal with people involved directly rather than via your boss.

Next, the use of **self-managing teams** is increasing. Regardless of the form of worker self-management, all are based on the concept of *empowerment*—the theory that those doing the work should have the means to do what it takes to please the customer. In turn, this requires that performance objectives and evaluation of activities be linked to customer satisfaction. Successful teams can dramatically improve productivity; for example, Boeing used empowered teams to reduce the number of hang-ups by half when developing its 777 jet.[14] But many teams have failed because management was not serious about their empowerment, team members were poorly selected, or the team was launched in isolation with little training or support.[15]

In the future many companies will use teams as the basis for collaborative networks that link thousands of people together with the help of a variety of new technologies. Such networks enable businesses to form and dissolve relations quickly and to bring to bear on an opportunity or a threat the needed resources regardless of who owns them.[16] For example, XM Satellite Radio formed an alliance with Samsung Electronics to develop the first portable satellite radio combined with a digital music player. The two companies created a virtual product development team jointly headed by one manager from each company. Samsung engineers focused on industrial design and manufacturing, while XM dealt with the user interface, the antenna, and performance features—such as the ability to "bookmark" a song playing on the radio and purchase it later online. Samsung and XM were able to introduce their cobranded Helix radio just nine months after forming their alliance.[17]

But not all such collaborative networks are successful, especially those involving **joint ventures.** Partnering is at best a difficult and demanding undertaking requiring considerable managerial skills as well as a great deal of trust.[18] A major difficulty, especially for those involving companies from different parts of the world, is that "they cannot be controlled by formal systems, but require a dense web of interpersonal connections and internal infrastructures that enhance learning."[19]

## Organizational Adjustments as Firms Grow and Markets Change

Managers often think of the design of their organization as stable and not subject to change. In rapidly growing entrepreneurial companies and in changing markets, however, such thinking can be dangerous. As the number of customers and the range of product lines grow, the best way to organize the marketing and sales functions should be subject to change.

An entrepreneurial start-up may begin with a simple functional structure, perhaps even simpler than that diagrammed in Exhibit 17.4. As it grows and its product offerings become broader and more complex, it may assign specialized product managers to coordinate the marketing efforts for the various products or product lines. Eventually, the firm might even split into several product divisions, each with its own sales and marketing departments. Or the firm's customers might fragment into a number of diverse segments with unique needs and requirements, favoring the adoption of a market management or matrix structure.

With each of these adjustments to a company's organization structure, however, comes added complexity and potential disadvantages. For instance, what if the new structure results in multiple salespeople, representing the company's different product lines, competing with each other for a customer's business? Such competition may be contrary to the company's self-interest as well as confusing and inconvenient for the customer. More importantly, such a lack of coordination would make it difficult to sell comprehensive solutions that cut cross the firm's product or divisional boundaries.

How should managers decide when the time has come to restructure an organization, and what new structure should replace the old one? There are five key drivers of such decisions: (1) customer needs, (2) informational requirements of the sales and marketing personnel charged with meeting those needs, (3) ability of a given structure to motivate and coordinate the kinds of activities that market conditions require, (4) available competencies and resources, and (5) costs.

When customers all tend to use a narrow range of goods or services to satisfy similar needs, a simple functional structure may be sufficient. When customer segments use goods or services in different ways, either a product-focused or market-focused structure is likely to work well. If individual customers buy a broad range of the firm's goods or services, however, having multiple salespeople calling on those customers, unless they are organized into teams, is probably a bad idea. When a company's offerings are relatively simple and easy to understand, a single salesforce may be able to handle the entire line. But when products are technically complex or open to customization, each line may require its own specialized sales and marketing organization. When the firm is not well established or needs to educate potential buyers about the advantages of an innovative offering, it may need heavy incentives to encourage salespeople to expend the effort necessary to win new business. Under such circumstances, team-oriented selling arrangements are likely to be ineffectual. Finally, the fact that more highly specialized structures also tend to increase personnel and administrative costs should not be overlooked.

Thus, growing firms or those serving rapidly changing markets are likely to need to rethink—and perhaps change—the structure of their sales and marketing organizations frequently. Such changes can be disruptive to both internal and customer relationships, but failure to adjust in the face of changing market conditions can make it hard for the firm to implement its marketing strategy and maintain a leading position in its industry.

## Organizational Designs for Selling in Global Markets[20]

An organization's complexity increases, often quite dramatically, as it "goes international" and especially so as overseas sales as a percentage of total sales increase. The issue is essentially one of deciding what organizational design is best for developing and implementing worldwide strategies while simultaneously maintaining flexibility with regard to individual markets. In evaluating the several types of international organizational structures discussed in this section, keep in mind two things: "first, that innovation is the key to success. An organization which relies on one culture for its ideas and treats foreign subsidiaries as dumb production-colonies might as well hire subcontractors."[21] Second, technology is making the world smaller.

**Little or No Formal Organization**    Early on in a firm's international involvement, the structure typically ranges between the domestic organization handling international transactions and a separate export department. The latter may be tied to the marketing department or may be a freestanding functional department.

**An International Division**    To avoid discriminating against international customers in comparison with domestic customers, an international division is often established to house all international activities, most of which relate to marketing. Manufacturing, engineering, finance, and R&D typically remain in their previous form to take advantage of scale effects. This type of organization serves best with a limited number of products that lack cultural sensitivity—for example, basic commodity types such as chemicals, metals, and industrial machinery.

Many Japanese firms historically emphasized low-cost manufacturing coupled with quality assurance as the essence of their international competitive strategy. Both of these require strong centralized control and, thus, the use of an export-based organizational structure. In recent years, though, Japanese firms have become more interested in global structures based on products or geographic areas.[22]

**Global Structures**    There are a variety of global types, of which the simplest replicates the firm's basic functional departments. A global company using the functional type of organization would have vice presidents (worldwide) for such areas as manufacturing, marketing, and finance—all reporting to the president.

By far the most common global structure is one based on products, which translates into giving SBUs worldwide control over their product lines. The main advantages of this type of structure are the economies derived from centralizing manufacturing activities and the ability to respond quickly to product-related problems originating in overseas markets. Marketing is usually localized at the country or regional level. This is essentially the structure that evolved at Electrolux during the decades of its merger and acquisitions spree. As the number of product lines and brands proliferated, however, this structure lead to a lack of coordination and substantial duplication of effort.

The *area structure* is another popular global organizational type and is especially appropriate when there is considerable variance across markets regarding product acceptance and marketing activities. Firms typically organize on a regional basis (North America, Europe, Latin America, Far East, Middle East, and Africa) using a central staff that coordinates worldwide planning and control activities. In some cases this kind of geographic structure is taken all the way down to individual countries. As we saw in Chapter 12, for example, Procter & Gamble has established a nearly autonomous operation in China with the authority to develop new products and line extensions suited to the Chinese market (such as Morning Lotus Blossom Crest), an extensive network of wholesale subdistributors who service small retailers, and a substantial budget for market development within the country.[23]

Some companies use a hybrid organization that typically is some combination of the functional, product, or area types of structure. The global matrix is one such attempt. It has individual business managers reporting to both area and functional groups, or—as in the case of Electrolux—area managers responsible for marketing and product development strategies, but report to global functional mangers for manufacturing and purchasing decisions. Such dual reporting can lead to conflicts and slow down decision making. Therefore, the firm created sector and group management boards to deal with such issues.

**Decision Making and Organizational Structure**   Global organization structures can be centralized or decentralized in terms of decision making. In the case of the latter, controls are relatively simple and relations between subsidiaries and headquarters mainly financial. The logic here is that local management is closest to the market and can respond quickly to change. But multinationals faced with strong global competition require more centralization, which calls for headquarters to provide the overall strategy that subsidiaries (country units) implement within a range agreed upon with headquarters.[24]

## Marketing Plans: The Foundation for Implementing Marketing Actions

As we pointed out in Chapter 1, preparation of a written plan is a key step in ensuring the effective execution of a strategic marketing program because it spells out what actions are to be taken, when, and by whom. Written plans are particularly crucial in larger organizations because a marketing manager's proposals must usually be reviewed and approved by higher levels of management, and because the approved plan then provides the benchmark against which the manager's and the marketing program's performances will be evaluated. Preparing formal, written marketing plans, however brief, is a useful exercise even in small firms because the discipline involved helps ensure that the proposed objectives, strategy, and marketing actions are based on rigorous analysis of the 4 Cs and sound reasoning. Marketing plans can vary a good deal in content and organization, but they generally follow a format similar to the one outlined in Exhibit 1.6 and reproduced in Exhibit 17.8.[25] To illustrate the kinds of information that might be included in each section of the plan, the contents of a marketing plan for a disguised Pillsbury refrigerated dough product in the U.S. market are summarized in Exhibit 17.9.

Much of this book has focused on the planning process, the decisions that must be made when formulating a marketing strategy and its various components, the development of strategic marketing plans, and the analytical tools managers can use in reaching those decisions. Consequently, we will say little here about the processes or procedures involved

# Exhibit 17.8

CONTENTS OF AN ANNUAL MARKETING PLAN

| Section | Content |
|---|---|
| I. Executive summary | Presents a short overview of the issues, objectives, strategy, and actions incorporated in the plan and their expected outcomes for quick management review. |
| II. Current situation and trends | Summarizes relevant background information on the market, competition and the macroenvironment, and trends therein, including size and growth rates for the overall market and key segments. |
| III. Performance review (for an existing product or service only) | Examines the past performance of the product and the elements of its marketing program (e.g., distribution, promotion, etc.). |
| IV. Key issues | Identifies the main opportunities and threats to the product that the plan must deal with in the coming year, and the relative strengths and weaknesses of the product and business unit that must be taken into account in facing those issues. |
| V. Objectives | Specifies the goals to be accomplished in terms of sales volume, market share, and profit. |
| VI. Marketing strategy | Summarizes the overall strategic approach that will be used to meet the plan's objectives. |
| VII. Action plans | This is the most critical section of the annual plan for helping to ensure effective implementation and coordination of activities across functional departments. It specifies<br>• The target market to be pursued.<br>• What specific actions are to be taken with respect to each of the 4 Ps.<br>• Who is responsible for each action.<br>• When the action will be engaged in.<br>• How much will be budgeted for each action. |
| VIII. Projected profit-and-loss statement | Presents the expected financial payoff from the plan. |
| IX. Controls | Discusses how the plan's progress will be monitored: may present contingency plans to be used if performance falls below expectations or the situation changes. |
| X. Contingency plans | Describes actions to be taken if specific threats or opportunities materialize during the planning period. |

in putting together a marketing plan. Instead, our purpose is to summarize how the topics we've covered can be integrated within a coherent marketing plan, and how the plan's content should be organized and presented to best ensure that the strategy will be effectively carried out.

The success of a marketing plan depends on effective communication with other parts of the organizations (such as production, engineering, and R&D) and a variety of marketing units, especially those concerned with sales, advertising, promotions, and marketing research. By using the experience of others (as consultants) in preparing the action programs (for instance, in-store promotions), the planner not only benefits from the expertise of specialists, but also increases their buy-in to the overall marketing plan, thereby increasing the likelihood of its success.

The action programs should reflect agreements made with other departments and marketing units as to their responsibilities over the planning period concerning the product. For example, if a special sale is to occur in a given month, the production department must

## Exhibit 17.9

I. Analysis of current situation

A. Market situation
- The total U.S. market for dinner breadstuffs is enormous, amounting to about 10.5 billion servings per year.
- Specialty breads, such as whole-grain breads, are growing in popularity, largely at the expense of traditional white breads.
- Pillsbury's share of the total dinner breadstuffs market, accounted for by several brands including Crescent rolls as well as refrigerated bread dough, is small, amounting to only about 2 percent of the total dollar volume.
- Since its introduction several years ago, refrigerated bread dough (RBD) has been able to achieve only low levels of penetration (only about 15 percent of all households have used the product) and use frequency (nearly two-thirds of the product's volume comes from light users who buy only one or two cans per year).
- RBD consumption is concentrated in the northern states and during the fall and winter months (about 75 percent of volume is achieved from September through February).
- Marketing research results suggest consumers believe RBD is relatively expensive in terms of price/value compared to alternative forms of dinner breadstuffs.

B. Competitive situation
- RBD's share of the total dinner breadstuffs category is likely to remain low because of the wide variety of competing choices available to consumers.
- The largest proportion of volume within the category is captured by ready-to-eat breads and rolls produced by super-market chains and regional bakeries and distributed through retail grocery stores.
- RBD's major competition within the refrigerated dough category comes from other Pillsbury products, such as Crescent rolls and Soft Breadsticks.
- There are currently no other national competitors in the refrigerated bread dough category; but Merico, a small regional producer, was recently acquired by a major national food manufacturer. Evidence suggests Merico may be preparing to introduce a competing product line into national distribution at a price about 10 percent lower than Pillsbury's.

C. Macroenvironmental situation
- Changes in American eating habits may pose future problems for dinner breadstuffs in general, and for RBD in particular:
  
  More meals are being eaten away from home, and this trend is likely to continue.
  
  People are eating fewer starch foods.
  
  While total volume of dinner breadstuffs has not fallen over the past decade, neither has it kept pace with popula-tion growth.
- Increasing numbers of women working outside of the home, and the resulting desire for convenience, may reduce consumers' willingness to wait 30 minutes while RBD bakes, even though the dough is already prepared.
- Because RBD does not use yeast as a leavening agent, Food and Drug Administration regulations prohibit the company from referring to it as "bread" in advertising or package copy, even though the finished product looks, smells, and tastes like bread.

D. Past product performance
- While sales volume in units increased only slightly during the past year, dollar volume increased by 24 percent due to a price increase taken early in the year.
- The improvement to gross margin was even greater than the price increase due to an improvement in manufacturing costs.
- The improvement to gross margin, however, was not sufficient to produce a positive net margin due to high advertis-ing and sales promotion expenditures aimed at stimulating primary demand and increasing market penetration of RBD.
- Consequently, while RBD showed improvement over the last year, it was still unable to make a positive contribution to overhead and profit.

II. Key issues

A. Threats
- Lack of growth in the dinner breadstuff category suggests the market is mature and may decline in the future.
- The large variety of alternatives available to consumers suggest it may be impossible for RBD to substantially increase its share of the total market.
- Potential entry of a new, lower-priced competitor poses a threat to RBD's existing share and may result in lower margins if RBD responds by reducing its price.

(CONTINUED)

# Exhibit 17.9

(CONTINUED)

   B. Opportunities
- The largest percentage of RBD volume accounted for by light users suggests an opportunity of increasing volume among current users by stimulating frequency of use.
- Trends toward increased consumption of specialty breads suggests possible line extensions, such as whole wheat or other whole grain flavors.

   C. Strengths
- RBD has a strong distribution base, with shelf-facings in nearly 90 percent of available retail outlets.
- RBD sales have proved responsive to sales promotion efforts (e.g., cents-off coupons), primarily by increasing volume among existing users.
- The fact that most consumers who try RBD make repeat purchases indicates a high level of customer satisfaction.

   D. Weaknesses
- RBD sales have proved unresponsive to advertising. Attempts to stimulate primary demand have not been able to increase market penetration.
- Consumer concerns about RBD's price/value place limits on ability to take future price increases.

III. Objectives

   A. Financial objectives
- Achieve a positive contribution to overhead and profit of $4 million in current year.
- Reach the target level of an average of 20 percent return on investment over the next five years.

   B. Marketing objectives
- Maintain market share and net sales revenues at previous year's levels.
- Maintain current levels of retail distribution coverage.
- Reduce marketing expenditures sufficiently to achieve profit contribution objective.
- Identify viable opportunities for future volume and profit expansion.

IV. Marketing strategy
- Pursue a maintenance strategy aimed at holding or slightly increasing RBD volume and market share primarily by stimulating increased frequency of use among current users.
- Reduce advertising aimed at stimulation of primary demand/penetration and reduce manufacturing costs in order to achieve profit contribution objective.
- Initiate development and test marketing of possible line extensions to identify opportunities for future volume expansion.

V. Marketing action plans
- Improve the perceived price/value of RBD by maintaining current suggested retail price at least through the peak selling season (February). Review the competitive situation and the brand's profit performance in March to assess the desirability of a price increase at that time.
- Work with production to identify and implement cost savings opportunities that will reduce manufacturing costs by 5 percent without compromising product quality.
- Maintain retail distribution coverage with two trade promotion discount offers totaling $855,000; one offered in October–November to support peak season inventories, and another offered in February–March to maintain inventories as volume slows.
- Reduce advertising to maintenance level of 1,100 gross ratings points during the peak sales period of September to March. Focus copy on maintaining awareness among current users.
- Encourage greater frequency of use among current users through three sales promotion events, with a total budget of $748,000, that will stimulate immediate purchase:
- One freestanding insert (FSI) coupon for 15 cents off next purchase to appear in newspaper on September 19.
- One tear-off refund offer (buy three, get one free) placed on the retailer's shelves during November.
- A $1 refund with proof of purchase offer placed in women's service books (i.e., women's magazines like Good Housekeeping) during March.

VI. Contingency plans
- Maintain the above marketing strategy and action plans without change during the planning period even if Merico (see item I.B) enters the market.
- If Merico enters, carefully monitor its pricing and promotion actions, sales results, consumer perceptions, and so on, and prepare recommendations for next year's plan.

commit to making sufficient product available and to the use of a special package; the promotion group must agree to develop and have available for use by the salesforce in-store displays; the salesforce must allocate the time necessary to do the in-store work; and so on. Thus, the annual plan serves as a means of allocating the firm's resources as well as a way of assigning responsibility for the plan's implementation.[26]

# The Situational Analysis[27]

While many marketing plans start with a brief executive summary of their contents, this is typically the first substantive section in which the marketing manager details his or her assessment of the current situation. It is the "homework" portion of the plan where the manager summarizes an analysis of current and potential customers, the competitive environment and the company's relative strengths and weaknesses, trends in the broader macroenvironment that may impact the product, and past performance outcomes for existing products. This section also typically includes estimates of sales potential, forecasts, and other assumptions underlying the plan. Chapters 2 through 7 provide the principal tools and analytical frameworks for completing this section. Based on these analyses, the manager may then call attention to one or more key issues, major opportunities or threats that should be dealt with during the planning period.

**Market Situation**    Here data are presented on the target market. Total market size and growth trends should be discussed, along with any variations across geographic regions or other market segments. Marketing research information might also be presented concerning customer perceptions (say, awareness of the brand) and buying-behavior trends (market penetration, repeat purchase rate, heavy versus light users). As Exhibit 17.9 indicates, for instance, information about the market situation presented in the plan for Pillsbury's refrigerated bread dough (RBD) not only includes data about the size of the total market for dinner breadstuffs and Pillsbury's market share, but also points out the low penetration and use frequency of RBD among potential users. Most of the kinds of customer analysis, market segmentation and targeting information discussed in Chapters 4, 5, and 7 would be relevant here.

**Competitive Situation**    This section identifies and describes the product's major competitors in terms of their size, market share, product quality, marketing strategies, and other relevant factors, as discussed in Chapter 3. It should also discuss the likelihood that other potential competitors will enter the market in the near future and the possible impact of such entry on the product's competitive position. Note, for instance, that while other Pillsbury brands are the primary competitors for RBD in the refrigerated dough category, the potential entry of a new low-cost competitor could dramatically change the competitive situation.

**Macroenvironmental Situation**    This section describes broad environmental occurrences or trends that may have a bearing on the product's future. The issues mentioned here include any relevant economic, technological, political/legal, or social/cultural changes, as outlined in Chapter 3. As Exhibit 17.9 indicates, for example, lifestyle trends leading to more meals being eaten away from home and increased desires for convenience pose a threat to future demand for Pillsbury's RBD.

**Past Product Performance**    If the plan is for an existing product, this part of the situation analysis discusses the product's performance on such dimensions as sales volume, margins, marketing expenditures, and profit contribution for several recent years. This information is usually presented in the form of a table, such as the one for RBD shown in Exhibit 17.10. As the table indicates, even though RBD showed an improvement in gross margin due in part to reduced manufacturing costs, high advertising and sales expenditures prevented the product from making a positive contribution to overhead and profit.

The data contained in Exhibit 17.10 do not answer the question of whether the company's RBD prices and costs are competitive. Such information is critical since if a product's costs are not in line, then the product's market position is in jeopardy. This is especially true with commodity-type products, although even when products are differentiated it is essential that costs be maintained at competitive levels and any price premium charged provide a corresponding benefit to buyers. Some methods for measuring and monitoring costs and profitability are examined in the next chapter.[28]

**Sales Forecast and Other Key Assumptions**    Finally, the assessment of the current situation also typically includes estimates of sales potential, sales forecasts, and other evidence or assumptions underlying the plan. As we discussed in Chapter 6, such market measurements are particularly critical as the foundation for marketing plans for new goods or services were there is no past history to draw on. While the RBD plan does not explicitly report an estimate of total market potential, a sales forecast underlies the expected volume for next year reported in the fourth column of Exhibit 17.10.

# Key Issues

After analyzing the current situation, the product manager must identify the most important issues facing the product in the coming year. These issues typically represent either threats to the future market or financial performance of the product or opportunities to improve those performances. This section should also highlight any special strengths of the product or weaknesses that must be overcome in responding to future threats and opportunities. Some of the key threats and opportunities faced by Pillsbury's RBD, together with the product's major strengths and weaknesses, are summarized in section II of Exhibit 17.9.

## Exhibit 17.10

HISTORICAL AND PROJECTED FINANCIAL PERFORMANCE OF REFRIGERATED BREAD DOUGH PRODUCT

| Variable | Last year | This year | Percent change | Next year | Percent change |
|---|---|---|---|---|---|
| Sales volume (cases) | 2,290M | 2,350M | 3% | 2,300M | (2%) |
| Net sales ($) | 17,078M | 21,165M | 24 | 21,182M | 0 |
| Gross margin ($) | 6,522M | 10,787M | 65 | 11,430 | 5 |
| Gross margin/net sales | 38% | 51% | — | 54% | — |
| Advertising and sales promotion ($) | 11,609M | 12,492M | 6 | 6,100M | (51) |
| Advertising & sales promotion/gross margin | 178% | 116% | — | 53% | — |
| Net margin ($) | (5,087M) | (1,725M) | — | 5,330M | — |
| Net margin/net sales | — | — | — | 25% | — |
| Product contribution ($) | (6,342M) | (3,740M) | — | 4,017M | — |

## Objectives

Information about the current situation, the product's recent performance, and the key issues to be addressed now serve as the basis for setting specific objectives for the coming year. Two types of objectives need to be specified. **Financial objectives** provide goals for the overall performance of the brand and should reflect the objectives for the SBU as a whole and its competitive strategy. Those financial goals must then be converted into **marketing objectives** that specify the changes in customer behavior and levels of performance of various marketing program elements necessary to reach the product's financial objectives.

The major financial and marketing objectives for Pillsbury's RBD are summarized in section III of Exhibit 17.9. Sales volume and market share are not expected to increase, but the product is expected to make a $4 million contribution to overhead and profit through additional cost reductions.

## Marketing Strategy

Because there may be a number of ways to achieve the objectives specified in the preceding section, the manager must now specify the overall marketing strategy to be pursued. It is likely to be one, or a combination of several, of the strategies discussed earlier in Chapters 14, 15, and 16. The chosen strategy should fit the market and competitive conditions faced by the product and its strategic objectives. It should also incorporate all of the necessary decisions concerning the 4 Ps, as we have discussed in Chapters 10 through 13.

The RBD product manager recommends that a **maintenance strategy** be pursued. The intense competitive situation, uncertainty over the possible entry of Merico, and the past inability of primary-demand advertising to increase market penetration all suggest that it would be difficult to expand RBD's market by simply doing more of the same. Consequently, the recommended strategy seeks to maintain or slightly increase RBD volume and share primarily by stimulating repeat purchases among current customers. Reductions in advertising expenditures and continued improvements in manufacturing costs will be relied on to help the brand achieve its profit contribution objective. In addition, it is recommended that development and test marketing of several line extensions (for example, whole wheat and a French-style loaf) be initiated in an attempt to identify viable opportunities for future volume expansion.

## Action Plans

The action plan is the most crucial part of the annual marketing plan for ensuring proper execution. Here the specific actions necessary to implement the strategy for the product are listed, together with a clear statement of who is responsible for each action, when it will be done, and how much is to be spent on each activity. Of course, actions requiring the cooperation of other functional departments should be included, but only after the product manager has contacted the departments involved, worked out any potential conflicts, and received assurances of support.

Here is where specific timelines and milestones are set forth. A variety of planning and project management tools—such at Gantt charts, stage-gate development processes, and others—may be used to illustrate and orchestrate the action steps entailed in the plan. Some of the action programs specified for RBD are outlined in section V of Exhibit 17.9.

## Projected Profit-and-Loss Statement

The action plan includes a supporting budget that is essentially a projected profit-and-loss statement. On the revenue side, it forecasts next year's sales volume in units and dollars. On the expense side, it reflects manufacturing, distribution, and marketing costs associated with the planned actions. This budget is then presented to higher levels of management for review and possible modification. Once approved, the product's budget serves as a basis for the plans and resource allocation decisions of other functional departments within the SBU, such as manufacturing and purchasing, as well as other marketing units (e.g., marketing research). The projected financial results of RBD's annual plan are summarized in the second-to-last column of Exhibit 17.10.

## Contingency Plans

Finally, the manager might also detail contingency plans to be implemented if specific threats or opportunities should occur during the planning period. The RBD product manager, for instance, recommended that no changes should be made in the product's overall marketing strategy nor in its pricing or promotion tactics in the event that Merico entered the national market. The rationale was that time should be taken to carefully analyze Merico's market impact and the magnitude of its competitive threat before crafting a response.

## TAKE-AWAYS

1. While much of this book has covered the various analytical tools and frameworks necessary to develop effective marketing strategies, such strategies are worthless without good implementation. Therefore, marketing managers, and general managers concerned about marketplace issues, must attend to organizational design issues. A business's structure, policies, procedures, and resources must fit its chosen strategy or else implementation will fall short.

2. For firms with multiple businesses or product lines, different administrative relationships between the business unit and corporate headquarters are appropriate for different competitive strategies. Prospector businesses perform better with high levels of autonomy, fewer shared resources, and more top-line focused reward systems than defender businesses.

3. Within a given business—whether it's part of a larger organization or a one-product entrepreneurial start-up—different functional competencies, levels of specialization, amounts of employee participation in decision making, and mechanisms for the resolution of

internal conflicts are needed to effectively implement varying competitive strategies.

4. Several different organizational designs incorporate differences in both structural variables (formalization, centralization, and specialization) and mechanisms for resolving interfunctional conflicts. These include functional, product management, market management, and various types of matrix organizational designs.

5. Writing a formal marketing action plan is a key step toward ensuring the effective execution of a strategic marketing program because it spells out what actions need to be taken, when, and by whom. Written plans also provide the benchmarks by which the marketing strategy can be evaluated and controlled, as discussed in the next chapter.

**Self-diagnostic questions to test your ability to apply the analytical tools and concepts in this chapter to marketing decision making may be found at this book's website at www.mhhe.com/mullins8e.**

## ENDNOTES

1. This opening case is based on material found in "Electrolux: Brand Challenge," *The Economist,* April 4, 2002, archived at *www.economist.com;* Ola Kinnander and Kim McLaughlin, "Electrolux Wants to Rule the Appliance World," *Bloomberg Businessweek,* March 28, 2011, pp. 33–34; and the *Electrolux Group's 2010 Annual Report* and supporting documents found at the company's website *www.electrolux.com.*

2. Eric M. Olson, Stanley F. Slater, and G. Thomas M. Hult, "The Performance Implications of Fit among Business Strategy, Marketing Organization Structure, and Strategic Behavior," *Journal of Marketing* 69, (July 2005), pp. 49–65.

3. Robert W. Ruekert and Orville C. Walker, Jr., "The Sharing of Marketing Resources across Strategic Business Units: The Effect of Strategy on Performance," in *Review of Marketing 1990* (Chicago: American Marketing Association, 1990).

**4.** Vivek Wadhwa, "How to Fix Oversize Executive Compensation," *www.businessweek.com,* March 25, 2011.

**5.** Bernard J. Jaworski, "Toward a Theory of Marketing Control: Environmental Context, Control Types, and Consequences," *Journal of Marketing,* July 1988, pp. 23–39.

**6.** For a more detailed discussion, see Jeffery F. Rayport and Bernard J. Jaworski, *Best Face Forward* (Boston: Harvard Business School Press, 2005).

**7.** Daryl O. McKee, P. Rajan Varadarajan, and William M. Pride, "Strategic Adaptability and Firm Performance: A Market-Contingent Perspective," *Journal of Marketing,* July 1989, p. 19. For an interesting discussion of developments in the implementation of strategies for service organizations, see James L. Heskett, W. Earl Sasser, Jr., and Christopher W. L. Hart, *Implementing Strategy: Service Breakthroughs: Changing the Rules of the Game* (Cambridge, MA: The Mac Group, n.d.).

**8.** For empirical evidence, see Douglas W. Vorhies and Neil M. Morgan, "A Configuration Theory Assessment of Marketing Organization Fit with Business Strategy and Its Relationship with Marketing Performance," *Journal of Marketing* 67 (January 2003), pp. 100–15; and Stanley F. Slater, Eric M. Olson, and Tomas M. Hult, "Worried about Strategy Implementation? Don't Overlook Marketing's Role," *Business Horizons* 53 (2010), pp. 469–9.

**9.** Michael J. Zenor, "The Profit Benefits of Category Management," *Journal of Marketing Research,* May 1994, p. 202.

**10.** Allen D. Shocker, Rajendra K. Srivastava, and Robert W. Ruekert, "Challenges and Opportunities Facing Brand Management," *Journal of Marketing Research,* May 1994, p. 149.

**11.** For a discussion of firms as learning organizations and hence better able to cope with change, see "The Knowledge Firm," *The Economist,* November 11, 1995, p. 63; Stanley F. Slater and John C. Narver, " Market Organization and the Learning Organization," *Journal of Marketing,* July 1995, p. 63; and Jena McGregor, "The World's Most Innovative Companies," *BusinessWeek,* April 24, 2006, pp. 62–76.

**12.** Some analysts believe this may lead to a strategic advantage. See David A. Garvin, "Leveraging Processes for Strategic Advantage," *Harvard Business Review,* September–October 1995, p. 77.

**13.** Rahul Jacob, "The Struggle to Create an Organization for the 21st Century," *Fortune,* April 3, 1995, p. 90; Thomas A. Stewart, "Planning a Career in a World without Managers," *Fortune,* March 20, 1995, p. 72; John A. Byrne, "Management by Web," *BusinessWeek,* August 21, 2000,

pp. 84–96; and Frederick E. Webster, "Marketing Management in Changing Times," *Marketing Management,* January–February 2002, pp. 18–23.

**14.** Brian Dumaine, "The Trouble with Teams," *Fortune,* September 5, 1994, p.86.

**15.** Ibid.

**16.** Samuel E. Blucker, "The Virtual Organization," *The Futurist,* March–April 1994, p. 9. and Peter Coy, "The Creative Economy," *BusinessWeek,* August 21, 2000, pp. 76–82.

**17.** Steve Hamm, "Speed Demons," *BusinessWeek,* March 27, 2006, p. 74.

**18.** Rosabeth Moss Kanter, "Collaborative Advantage: The Art of Alliance," *Harvard Business Review,* July–August 1994, p. 97.

**19.** Ibid.

**20.** The discussion that follows draws heavily from Michael R. Czinkota, Pietra Rivali, and Idkka A. Ronkausen, *International Business* (New York: Dryden Press, 1992), pp. 536–45.

**21.** "The Discreet Charm of the Multicultural Multinational," *The Economist,* July 30, 1994, p. 57.

**22.** Christopher A. Bartlett and Sumantra Ghoshal, *Transnational Management* (Burr Ridge, IL: Richard D. Irwin, 1992), p. 520.

**23.** Dexter Roberts, "Scrambling to Bring Crest to the Masses," *BusinessWeek,* June 25, 2007, pp. 72–73; For additional examples, see Lauren Coleman-Lochner, "Procter & Gamble Needs to Shave More Indians," *Bloomberg Businessweek,* June 13, 2011, pp. 21–22.

**24.** Czinkota et al., *International Business,* p. 545.

**25.** For a more in-depth discussion of the contents and ways of organizing marketing plans, see Marian Burk Wood, *The Marketing Plan: A Handbook* (Upper Saddle River, NJ: Prentice Hall, 2003).

**26.** Donald R. Lehmann and Russell S. Winer, *Product Management* (Burr Ridge, IL: Richard D. Irwin, 1994), pp. 28–29.

**27.** While this example is based on the material contained in an actual marketing plan for a Pillsbury product, the name of the brand and some of the specific numbers included in this example have been disguised in order to protect proprietary information.

**28.** Robin Cooper and Robert S. Kaplan, "Measure Costs Right: Make the Right Decisions," *Harvard Business Review,* September–October 1988, pp. 96–103; and Paul W. Farris, Neil T. Bendle, Phillip E. Pfeifer, and David J. Reibstein, *Marketing Metrics,* 2nd ed. (Upper Saddle River, NJ: Pearson Education, Inc., 2010), chaps. 3 and 10.

# CHAPTER EIGHTEEN

# Measuring and Delivering Marketing Performance

## Metrics Pay for Walmart[1]

WALMART, the discount general merchandise and grocery retailer, generated sales of $419 billion and after-tax income of over $16 billion in fiscal 2010–2011. It is America's largest, most profitable, and, in some circles but not others, one of its most admired companies.

As of January 2011, the company operated over 8,900 stores, of which more than 8,500 were in 14 countries outside the United States (in the Americas, Europe, and Asia). In the United States, Walmart operates stores in several different formats apart from its original stores—some are supercenters (a combination supermarket and general merchandise store), some are Sam's Clubs (a members-only warehouse store, selling high volumes, but at very low individual profit margins), and some are a smaller format, Neighborhood Markets, with a focus on groceries, in carefully chosen urban locations. Walmart stores serve more than 200 million customers per week, and the company employs more than 2 million people.

A major reason for Walmart's success is its ability to control costs. In 2010–2011, it was able to hold its operating, selling, and general administrative costs to 19.3 percent of sales. This was substantially below its closest competitors in the United States, Kmart and Target, and explains, in part, the company's excellent profitability record.

In the 1960s when he had only 10 stores, Walmart founder Sam Walton realized he couldn't expand successfully unless he could capture the information needed to control his operations. He became, according to one competitor, the best utilizer of management information in the industry. By the late 1970s, Walmart was using a company-wide computer-driven information system that linked stores, distribution centers, and suppliers. Kmart started using a similar system only in the early 1990s. In the late 1980s, Sam Walton tapped David Glass to take over as CEO. Glass, more than anyone, successfully engineered the development of Walmart's advanced distribution and merchandise-tracking systems, which were needed to handle the enormous sales increases as the company's stores spread throughout the United States and internationally. "Walmart's incomparable systems are a secret of its success—the unadvertised contributor to the stock's 46.8 percent average annual return during the decade before Sam's death."

Today, the company can convert information into action almost immediately. To do so required a massive investment (over $700 million) in computer and satellite systems, which collectively generate the largest civilian database of its kind in the world. In addition to automated replenishment, the system provides up-to-the-minute sales of any item by region, district, and store. By looking at the computer screens in the satellite room, a manager can see systemwide data on the day's sales as they happen, the number of stolen bank cards retrieved that day, whether the seven-second credit card approval system is working properly, the number of customer transactions completed that day, and more.

## Changing Metrics for a Changing Strategy

The combination of its nearly fanatical focus on keeping costs low and the availability of sophisticated and timely management information, which has enabled Walmart management at all levels to respond quickly to new opportunities as well as to performance problems, has served Walmart well. But in recent years, Walmart has struggled.

As the purchasing power of Walmart's mostly low-income core U.S. customers has been squeezed by a combination of low hourly wages and rising housing and energy costs, the company has sought to trade up in an effort to attract more selective middle-income shoppers. For these customers, quality, style, and store ambience are as important as—maybe more important than—price. New kinds of management tools and new metrics for the new merchandise mix may be in order.

But trading up has not been smooth sailing for Walmart, and by the end of the important Christmas selling season in 2010, U.S. sales had dropped for seven consecutive quarters, the company's longest such streak ever. And its stock price languished, up a meagre 5.8 percent over the last decade, compared to 53 percent for archrival Target and 83 percent for Costco.

## Can Walmart's Overseas Stores Plug the Gap?

Fortunately for Walmart, its expansion into international markets—which now deliver nearly one-quarter of the company's sales—has begun to pay dividends. In spite of the global economic downturn, Walmart's Brazilian business has delivered nearly double-digit sales increases, outpacing the overall 6 percent growth in Brazilian retailing overall. And Walmart's Todo Dia convenience store concept in Brazil has been translated in China as Smart Choice, where Walmart now has more than 250 stores, across multiple formats. As further evidence of Walmart's commitment to fast-growing emerging markets, a joint venture in India with the Bharti group is underway.

Will Walmart bounce back and return to its former glory? New CEO Michael T. Duke, who took the leadership reins in 2009 after 15 years with the company, is bullish about Walmart's future. "We live at a time and in a world that I believe truly calls out for Walmart and the work that our 2 million associates do every day. We strongly believe that Walmart is the best-positioned global retailer and that we can continue to build on our momentum." Time will tell.

## Marketing Challenges Addressed in Chapter 18

In Chapter 17, we said that planning is important and that effective implementation is crucial. The Walmart example demonstrates how effective planning and implementation can play out in the performance of a company. Together, these two activities constitute the heart of most business endeavors. In the end, however, it is neither planning nor implementation that really counts. What really counts? Results. Results are what managers and entrepreneurs are paid to deliver. Results are what attract investment capital to permit a company—whether a large public company such as Walmart or an emerging start-up—to grow. Just watch what happens to a public company's stock price when the results are not what Wall Street expects. The share price plummets and, sometimes, heads roll. Weak sales and profit performance at Gap Inc. beginning in late 1999 cut Gap's stock price by half by 2002 and led to a series of middle- and upper-management changes at the once high-flying retailer.[2] Gap's revolving door at the top has continued to spin. The focus on results is not restricted to for-profit organizations either. Exhibit 18.1 shows how some nonprofit organizations are adapting measurement methodologies to their own environments.

In Chapter 18, we address several critical questions that provide the link between a company's efforts to plan and implement marketing strategies and the actual results that those strategies produce. How can we design **strategic monitoring systems** to make sure our strategies remain in sync with the changing market and competitive environment in which we operate? How can we design systems of **marketing metrics** to ensure that the marketing results we plan for are the results we deliver? In other words, if the ship gets off course during the journey, either strategically or in terms of execution of the marketing strategy, how can we make sure that we know quickly of the deviation so that midcourse corrections can be made in a timely manner? In today's rapidly changing markets, even the best-laid plans are likely to require changes as their implementation unfolds.

We begin by developing a five-step process for monitoring and evaluating marketing performance on a continuous basis. We then apply the process to the issue of **strategic control:** How can we monitor and evaluate our overall marketing strategy to ensure that it remains viable in the face of changing market and competitive realities? Next, we apply the process to tracking the performance of a particular product-market entry and to the marketing actions taken to implement its marketing plan, or **marketing performance measurement.** Are we meeting sales and margin targets in the aggregate and for various products and market segments? Is each element of the marketing mix doing its job: Which items in the product line are selling best, are the ads producing enough sales leads, is the

## Exhibit 18.1    MEASURING RESULTS AT NONPROFIT ORGANIZATIONS

The mission of the Nature Conservancy, the world's largest conservation organization, is to preserve biodiversity by protecting the lands and waters that rare species need to survive. Historically, the Conservancy used a measure dubbed "bucks and acres" to gauge progress achieved every year. The "bucks" referred to charitable contributions raised and the "acres" to the number of acres under their control. During the 1990s, the Conservancy's total revenue grew at a rate of 18 percent compounded annually, and over the same period, acres protected in the United States grew from 5 million to more than 10 million. Despite this stellar progress as measured by this scale, the Conservancy realized that their mission of conserving biodiversity was becoming exponentially harder to achieve. According to Harvard biologist E. O. Wilson, the species extinction rate today parallels that of the great epidemic of extinction that wiped out the dinosaurs 65 million years ago.

In their quest to develop more meaningful performance metrics that track progress toward their stated mission, the group researched issues that a host of other nonprofit groups were grappling with. Some had found means (with varying degrees of success) for measuring their own progress toward their stated missions. The result, following a period of experimentation with new performance measures, was a system built around three themes: *impact, activity,* and *capacity.* The experience of the Nature Conservancy with developing its own metrics taught it that the important factors in achieving success in performance measurement are to derive measures aligned to its mission statements and to ensure that they are not too cumbersome to implement. While there is no one magic "profitability" measure that spans the broad spectrum of nonprofits, the Nature Conservancy has shown that measurement is indeed possible and more importantly, very desirable.

*Source:* John C. Sawhill, David Williamson, "Mission Impossible? Measuring Success in Nonprofit Organizations," *Nonprofit Management and Leadership,* April 1, 2001, Vol. 11, Issue 3.

salesforce generating enough new accounts, and so on? Finally, we show how **marketing audits** can be used periodically to link the overall process—that for both strategic control and for measuring current marketing performance—with marketing planning.

## Designing Marketing Metrics Step by Step

As the Walmart example and a recent empirical study demonstrate, a well-functioning performance measurement system is critical to the success of a business.[3] To be successful, it should be well integrated with the other steps in the marketing management process—setting objectives, formulating strategies, and implementing a plan of action. The performance measurement system monitors the extent to which the firm is achieving its objectives. When it is not, the firm determines whether the reason lies in the environment, the strategies employed, the action plans, the way the plans are being implemented, or some combination thereof. Thus, reappraisal is diagnostic, serving to start the marketing management process anew.

Performance measurement processes differ at each organizational level. Thus, in a large diversified company, corporate management is concerned with how well its various SBUs are performing relative to the opportunities and threats each faces and the resources given them, a strategic issue. At the SBU level, or in smaller companies, concern is primarily with the unit's own strategy, especially as it pertains to its individual product-market entries. We will concentrate mainly on this latter organizational level since it constitutes the bulk of any performance measurement system.

Regardless of the organizational level involved, the performance measurement process is essentially the same. It consists of five steps: setting performance standards, specifying feedback, obtaining data, evaluating it, and taking corrective action (see Exhibit 18.2). Although the staff organization is typically responsible for reporting the performance data, the line organization administers the process. Certainly, this is the case with Walmart, as seen in the involvement of regional vice presidents, district managers, store managers, and

## Exhibit 18.2

THE PERFORMANCE MEASUREMENT PROCESS

department heads in obtaining and processing performance data as well as taking corrective action. More importantly, line managers need to be closely involved with the development of the performance measurement system, so that they can be assured of getting the performance data they need, on a timely basis and in a format they can easily use to support their long-term and day-to-day decision-making.

## Setting Standards of Performance

Performance standards derive largely from the objectives and strategies set forth at the SBU and individual product-market entry level. They generate a series of performance expectations for profitability (return on equity, return on assets managed, gross margins, or operating margins), market share, and sales. At the product-market level, standards of performance also include sales and market-share determinants such as percent effective distribution, relative shelf-facings, awareness, consumers' attitude change toward a given product attribute, customer satisfaction, and the extent of price parity.

Similarly, for every line item in a marketing budget—product development costs, advertising and promotional expenses, costs for salespeople, and so on—specific and measurable standards of performance must be set so that each of these elements of marketing performance can be evaluated. We address the development of these standards later in this chapter. Without a reasonable set of performance standards, managers cannot know what results are being obtained, the extent to which they are satisfactory, or why they are or are not satisfactory. Performance-based measures are often tied to the compensation of those individuals responsible for attaining the specified goals. Such a system can cause actions to be taken that in the short term may help attain the desired goals but in the longer term may be detrimental to the firm (see Exhibit 18.3).

Recent years have witnessed a shift from primarily using financially based performance measures to treating them as simply part of a broader array of marketing metrics. The now widely used balanced scorecard is one such approach.[4] While the use of nonfinancial measures is not new, giving them equal or greater status is. Thus, more and more companies are turning to metrics they feel better reflect how their managers and customers think about issues that drive the firm's success, such as customer satisfaction, product quality, market share, and new product development. For Walmart store managers, no longer is

**STRATEGIC ISSUE**

*For every line item in a marketing budget—product development costs, advertising and promotional expenses, costs for salespeople, and so on—specific and measurable standards of performance must be set.*

---

## Exhibit 18.3    ARE DRUG MANUFACTURES ADDICTED TO SHOWING PROFITS?

In 2002, Bristol-Meyers Squibb faced the problem of two of its blockbuster products, the breast-cancer drug Taxol and the antianxiety medication BuSpar, coming off patent and losing market share to generics in the U.S. marketplace. When the drugs that the company had depended on to replace these were delayed, the company resorted to "stuffing the channel," that is, forcing its distributors to stock up on 56 weeks worth of stock for these drugs. Such overselling into the channel is commonplace in this industry and normally goes unnoticed. However, when news of a SEC enquiry reached the marketplace, several top executives were forced to resign, and the stock price dropped by 37 percent. Schering-Plough ran into a similar issue when its antiallergy drug Claritin came off patent.

Other industry giants such as Merck and Johnson & Johnson reported that they monitor inventory levels. Johnson & Johnson said that it had put in place programs to reduce the volatility of inventories and that it was working closely with its largest distributors to forecast demand and restocking plans.

*Source:* Amy Tsao, "Drugmakers Struggle with an Addiction," *BusinessWeek,* April 22, 2002.

profit the only thing that matters at bonus time. Scores on customer surveys now matter. To make managers more accessible to customers, their offices have been moved to the front of the store.[5]

To be of any value, performance standards must be measurable; further, they must be tied to specific time periods, particularly when they concern a management compensation system. The SMART acronym (specific, measurable, attainable, relevant, and timebound) is a useful framework for setting performance standards. In recent years, the trend has been for performance measurement systems to operate over shorter periods (weekly and even daily) and for performance data to be more readily available. Walmart's inventory control system, for example, provides instantaneous up-to-date data. Strategic control tends to operate over longer periods.

Of particular importance is whether a business or business unit as a whole and its individual product-market entries have set forth milestone achievement measures based on the strategies that were originally developed. For example, in a venture capital backed start-up, a short-term **dashboard** will be set up to track such metrics as the cost of acquiring a customer, sales and gross margin by product or product line, and repeat purchase rates. Given the rampant uncertainty entailed in most early-stage ventures, disciplined attention to such metrics will assist the entrepreneurial team in determining whether the original plan is on track or whether midcourse pivots are called for.[6]

In recent years, major multinationals such as Tata, DuPont, Roche, IBM, and others have used another performance measure—benchmarking. What this means is that the firm's performance in a given area is compared against the performance of other companies. Thus, Walmart regularly compares itself with its competitors on merchandise assortments, service quality, and out of stocks. The comparison does not have to be with companies in the same industry. For example, Xerox benchmarked its order filling/shipping performance against L. L. Bean (a mail-order retailer catering to the outdoor set), which has a well-deserved reputation for fulfilling orders both quickly and accurately.[7] Small companies also use benchmarking to find out how they can better serve their customers and thereby increase sales.

### Return on Marketing Investment
Increasingly these days, investors, boards, CFOs, and others are insisting that marketing managers do a better job of measuring the return their marketing programs deliver on the investment therein. Doing so is important for a variety of reasons, including demonstrating the overall and program-by-program effectiveness of marketing expenditures, choosing among various marketing tactics or media, and obtaining the financial resources necessary to support top-line sales growth.

Fortunately, as we saw in Chapter 14, the growing use of online promotional strategies, most of which are eminently measurable, is making this task more doable than it used to be. But for many kinds of marketing spending, including many brand-building efforts, it can be difficult to make clear connections between an advertising campaign, for example, and the short-term and long-term impact it has on revenue and brand equity, because a host of other variables—from the weather to competitor actions and more—can also play significant roles. In short, ensuring the accountability of marketing managers and their spending is a good idea. But turning that good idea into practice and doing so without incurring adverse consequences is a lot harder than it looks, as shown in Exhibit 18.4.

### Profitability Analysis
In brief, **profitability analysis** requires that analysts determine the costs associated with specific marketing activities to find out the profitability of different market segments, products, customer accounts, and distribution channels. Walmart does this at the department and individual store levels as well as for individual

## Exhibit 18.4    DOES ROI ADD UP?

These days, there's lots of interest in measuring ROI as a means of holding marketing accountable for its performance. A good idea, right? Not so fast, argues Tim Ambler, author of *Marketing and the Bottom Line*. Ambler agrees that accountability is essential. But "this focus on ROI is misguided for five reasons," he says. "First, very few can calculate ROI with any accuracy. Second, ROI ignores the longer term. Third, it is inconsistent with corporate financial goals. Fourth, marketers do not really mean 'ROI' anyway. Fifth, zealous application of ROI will bankrupt the business."

Like the old tale about improving a donkey's ROI by cutting its food rations and increasing its loads until what results is a dead donkey, Ambler argues that much of the talk about ROI for marketing is fashion rather than substance. Nonetheless, he argues that it does constitute a step "toward increasing accountability and the understanding of marketing by top management."

*Sources:* Tim Ambler, "Why ROI Doesn't Add Up," *Financial Times,* FT Creative Business, October 14, 2003, p. 15; and Tim Ambler, *Marketing and the Bottom Line: The Marketing Metrics to Pump Up Cash Flow,* 2nd ed. (Upper Saddle River, NJ: Prentice Hall, 2003).

lines of goods within a department. More and more managers are attempting to obtain profitability measures for individual products by market segments.

Profitability is probably the single most important measure of performance, but it has limitations. These are that (1) many objectives can best be measured in nonfinancial terms (e.g., customer satisfaction); (2) profit is a short-term measure and can be manipulated by taking actions that may prove dysfunctional in the longer term (reducing R&D expenses); and (3) profits can be affected by factors over which management has no control (the weather). Sometimes, a managerial obsession with profitability can prove counterproductive, leading to decisions that sap customer loyalty and can, over the long term, erode profits rather than enhance them. For one view of how obsession with profit targets leads to customer abuse, see Exhibit 18.5.

**STRATEGIC ISSUE**

*Profitability is probably the single most important measure of performance, but it has limitations.*

## Exhibit 18.5    GOOD PROFITS OR BAD PROFITS?

Some retail banks have found a new and lucrative source of earnings—nuisance fees, as customers call them. Charges for bouncing a check are a whopping $25 or $30 at many banks. As if that were not bad enough, some banks process the largest checks first each day, potentially hitting customers with bad check fees for the greater number of small checks that follow and may bounce. Is this any way to earn long-term customer loyalty?

But it's not just banks that engage in customer-abusive behavior such as this. Cell phone operators offer such a confusing array of rate plans that it's nearly impossible for customers to know which plan is best for their pattern of calls. Putting customers on the plan that's best for them would cut profits by as much as 40 percent, according to one operator.

A book by Fred Reichheld, *The Ultimate Question: Driving Good Profits and True Growth,* argues

that accounting systems and incentive plans often fail to distinguish between profits that result from customer-abusive policies and those that arise from activities that enhance customer loyalty. Thus, as we'll see later in this chapter, in some companies measures of customer satisfaction are taking their place alongside measures of profitability. Reichheld and his co-author James Allen argue that there's an undeclared war on customers raging in many companies, a war that companies cannot afford and cannot win. Thinking differently about performance metrics may offer an olive branch to end the fighting.

*Sources:* Fred Reichheld and James Allen, "How Companies Can End the Cycle of Customer Abuse," *Financial Times,* March 23, 2006, p. 43; and Fred Reichheld, *The Ultimate Question: Driving Good Profits and True Growth* (Cambridge, MA: Harvard Business School Press, 2006).

Analysts can use direct or full costing in determining the profitability of a product or market segment. In **full costing,** analysts assign both direct, or variable, and indirect costs to the unit of analysis. **Indirect costs** involve certain fixed joint costs that cannot be linked directly to a single unit of analysis. For example, the costs of occupancy, general management, and the management of the salesforce are all indirect costs for a multiproduct company. Those who use full costing argue that only by allocating all costs to a product or a market can they obtain an accurate picture of its value.

**Direct costing** involves the use of **contribution accounting.** Those favoring the direct costing approach argue there is really no accurate way to assign indirect costs. Further, because indirect costs are mostly fixed, a product or market may make a contribution to profits even if it shows a loss. Thus, even though the company must eventually absorb its overhead costs, the contribution method clearly indicates what is gained by adding or dropping a product or a customer. Exhibit 18.6 shows an example of full and direct costing. The difference in the results obtained is substantial—$370,000 using full costing versus $650,000 with the contribution method.

Contribution analysis is helpful in determining the yield derived from the application of additional resources (for instance, to certain sales territories). Using the data in Exhibit 18.7 we can answer the question: "How much additional profit would result from a marginal increase in sales of $300,000—assuming the gross margin remains at 29.62 percent and the only cost is $35,000 more in sales commissions and expenses?" As Exhibit 18.7 shows, the answer is a profit increase before taxes of $53,000.

# Exhibit 18.6

FINDING PRODUCT OR MARKET PROFITABILITY WITH FULL COSTING AND MARGINAL CONTRIBUTION METHODS ($000)

| | Full Costing | Marginal Contribution |
|---|---|---|
| **Net sales** | $5,400 | $5,400 |
| Less: Cost of goods sold—includes direct costs (labor, material, and production overhead)* | 3,800 | 3,800 |
| Gross margin | $1,600 | $1,600 |
| **Expenses** | | |
| Salesforce—includes direct costs (commissions) plus indirect costs (sales expenses, sales management overhead)† | 510 | 450 |
| Advertising—includes direct costs (media, production) plus indirect costs (management overhead) | 215 | 185 |
| Physical logistics—includes direct costs (transportation) plus indirect costs (order processing, warehousing costs) | 225 | 190 |
| Occupancy—includes direct costs (telephone) plus indirect costs (heat/air, insurance, taxes, building maintenance) | 100 | 25 |
| Management overhead—includes direct costs (product/brand manager and staff) plus indirect costs (salaries, expenses, occupancy costs of SBU's general management group) | 180 | 100 |
| Total | $1,230 | $ 950 |
| Profit before taxes | $ 370 | |
| Contribution to fixed costs and profits | | $ 650 |

*Production facilities dedicated to a single product.
†Multiproduct salesforce.

## Exhibit 18.7

EFFECT OF $300,000 INCREASE IN SALES RESULTING FROM INCREASED SALES COMMISSIONS AND EXPENSES OF $35,000 (SAME DATA AS IN EXHIBIT 18.6) ($000)

| | |
|---|---:|
| Net sales | $5,700 |
| Less: direct costs (70.38%) | 4,012 |
| | $1,688 |
| **Expenses** | |
| Sales commissions and expenses | 485 |
| Advertising | 185 |
| Physical logistics | 190 |
| Occupancy | 25 |
| Management | 100 |
| | $ 985 |
| Contribution to overhead and profits | $ 703 |
| Increase in profit (before tax) = $703 – $650 = | $ 53 |

Companies are increasingly turning from traditional accounting methods, which identify costs according to various expense categories, to activity-based costing (ABC), which bases costs on the different tasks involved in performing a given activity. ABC advocates have used it to improve product costing, thereby improving pricing parameters, providing better service, trimming waste, and evaluating quality initiatives.[8]

**Customer Satisfaction**   So far, we have been discussing performance measures in essentially financial terms. But financial terms are insufficient since they fail to recognize the importance of customer satisfaction, which is an important driving force of the firm's future market share and profitability. As products and services become more alike in an already highly competitive marketplace, the ability to satisfy the customer across a variety of activities (of which the product is only one) will become an even greater success determinant. Thus, measures relating to customer preferences and satisfaction are essential as an early warning of impending problems and opportunities.

Developing meaningful measures of customer satisfaction can be done in various ways. One way involves understanding and measuring the criteria used by customers to evaluate the quality of the firm's relationship with them. Knowing the product/service attributes that constitute the customer's choice criteria as well as the relative importance of each should facilitate this task. Once these attributes are identified, they serve as the basis for developing expectation measures. Then, measures are taken of how well the firm is meeting the customer's expectations on an individual attribute as well as an overall basis. For example, if the choice criteria of a cruise line's target market included such attributes as food, exercise facilities, and entertainment, then a performance measure would be developed for each. By weighting these by the relative importance of each, an overall performance measure can be obtained. These two measures collectively serve as the basis for evaluating the company's performance on customer satisfaction.

Another approach favored by some companies is far simpler. General Electric, Enterprise Car Rental, and others ask customers one simple question: How likely is it that you would recommend us to a friend or a colleague? Such a simple approach has some significant benefits.

It gets high response rates—as much as 70 percent in some cases—and can be conducted often enough and inexpensively enough to give timely and granular information by product, by car rental branch, or whatever. GE adds the percentages of customers who are happiest (scores of 9 or 10 out of 10) and subtracts the percentage who are clearly unhappy (those scoring 6 or lower). The net score provides a clear and compelling—and actionable—indicator of customer satisfaction. At Enterprise, employees working at branches scoring below the company mean are ineligible for promotion. Not surprisingly, employees seeking to boost their branches' scores have developed many customer-friendly innovations at Enterprise.[9]

Face-to-face approaches to assessing customer satisfaction are also used, adding depth to the more cursory quantitative approaches. In recent years, more top-level executives are visiting their major accounts (whether they be end-use customers or intermediaries) to learn firsthand how to better serve them. Such visits frequently result in joint projects designed to reduce the costs incurred by both parties in the sale of a given set of products.

Finally, some companies are using the growing availability of customer relationship management (CRM) data to measure the lifetime value of customers. Doing so enables them to more effectively allocate marketing resources.[10]

## Specifying and Obtaining Feedback Data

Once a company has established its performance standards, its next step is to develop a system that provides usable and timely feedback data on actual performance. In most cases, someone must gather and process considerable data to obtain the performance measures, especially at the product-market level. Analysts obtain feedback data from a variety of sources, including company accounting records and syndicated marketing information services such as Nielsen.

The sales invoice or other transaction records, such as those produced by retailers' point-of-sale systems, are the basic internal source of data because they provide a detailed record of each transaction. Invoices are the basis for measuring profitability, sales, and various budget items. They also provide data for the analysis of the geographic distribution of sales and customer accounts by type and size. Exhibit 18.8 gives an example of how Tesco, the British supermarket chain, used customer purchasing data to strengthen its low-price image.

 Tesco's ClubCard data has informed numerous strategic decisions, including the company's move into smaller store formats, the launch of its internet shopping business, the development of its up-market Finest food assortment, and others. "ClubCard has brought about a step-change in the size of the company," says Tim Mason, who heads Tesco's nascent business in the United States. In Mason's view, ClubCard has been the driver of Tesco's recent success. Retail analyst Mike Tattersall of Cazenove agrees. "Contrary to popular belief, Tesco's most significant competitive advantage in the UK is not its scale," he says. "We believe that ClubCard, which conveys an array of material benefits across virtually every discipline in its business, is Tesco's most potent weapon in the ongoing battle for market share."[11]

Another source, and typically the most expensive and time-consuming, involves undertaking one or more marketing research projects to obtain needed information. In-house research projects are apt to take longer and be more expensive than using an outside syndicated service. But there may be no alternative, for example, in determining awareness and attitude changes and obtaining data on customer service.

## Evaluating Feedback Data

Management evaluates feedback data to find out whether there is any deviation from the plan and, if so, why. Walmart does this in a variety of ways, including sending its regional vice presidents into the field on a regular basis to learn what's going on and why.

## Exhibit 18.8     IT'S NOT ABOUT THE BANANAS

Tesco, the largest and most profitable supermarket chain in the United Kingdom, has pioneered the use of loyalty card information to better manage its pricing, product assortment, and store location decisions, along with a host of other crucial management issues. Tesco wanted to beat Asda's image for having the lowest prices. The question was how. The obvious first step was to cut the price of bananas, since nearly everyone buys bananas. But Tesco's targeted marketing director, Laura Wade-Gery, wouldn't buy it. Instead, she used Tesco's loyalty card data to carefully examine the segment of Tesco customers that was its most price-sensitive, as revealed by their shopping habits recorded on their Tesco ClubCard accounts.

She found cutting the price of a bunch of bananas is emphatically not the place to start because you are giving a discount to everyone, including lots of people who are not really looking for low prices. The solution? Tesco Value Brand Margarine, along with a carefully targeted group of similar products bought largely by price-conscious shoppers. By cutting prices on these items, Tesco was able to buy a low-price image with the customers to whom such an image mattered most, for a lower net cost overall. Its ability to use customer data insightfully has been a powerful source of competitive advantage. According to Edwina Dunn, whose company Dunnhumby works with Tesco on its ClubCard program, "They obviously have to get the basics of grocery retailing right, and we are only part of the equation. But if you asked them how it would affect them, they'd say it is fundamental to their business."

*Sources:* Clive Humby, Terry Hunt, with Tim Phillips, *Scoring Points: How Tesco Is Winning Customer Loyalty* (London: Kogan Page, 2003), pp. 146–47; and "Marketing—Clubbing Together," *Retail Week*, November 8, 2002. For more on Tesco or Dunnhumby, see www.tesco.com or www.dunnhumby.com.

Typically, managers use a variety of information to determine what the company's performance *should* have been under the actual market conditions that existed when the plan was executed. In some cases, this information can be obtained in measured form; examples include a shift in personal disposable income (available from government sources), a change in the demand for a given product type (obtained when measuring market share), the impact of a new brand on market share (reported by a commercial source), or a change in price by a major competitor. Often, however, the explanation rests on inferences drawn from generalized data, as would be the case in attributing poor sales performance to an improvement in a competitor's salesforce.

At the line-item level, whether for revenue or expenses, results are compared with the standards set in step one of the control process. A merchandise manager or buyer at an apparel retailer such as Gap, for example, would track sales results of each style or merchandise category in terms of its selling rate (how many weeks' supply is on hand overall and in which stores) and its gross margin performance. For a district sales team of an industrial goods manufacturer, salespeople might be measured on the number of sales calls they make per week, the number of new accounts they generate, their sales volume in revenue and units, their travel expenses, and a variety of other metrics. A stylist in a beauty salon might be measured in terms of the number of haircuts or the sales revenue she produces per day or per hour.

## Taking Corrective Action

The last step in the control process concerns prescribing the needed action to correct the situation. At Walmart, this is partly accomplished at its various congresses held every Friday and Saturday when managers decide what actions to take to solve selected problems. Success here depends on how well managers carry out the evaluation step. When linkages between inputs and outputs are clear, managers can presume a causal relationship and specify appropriate action. For example, assume that input consisted of an advertising schedule that specified the frequency of a given TV message. The objective was to change attitudes about a given product attribute (the output). If the attitude change did not occur, remedial action would start with an evaluation of the firm's advertising effort, particularly the advertising message and how frequently it ran.

But in many cases it is difficult to identify the cause of the problem. Almost always, an interactive effect exists among the input variables as well as the environment. There is also the problem of delayed responses and carryover effects. For example, advertisers can rarely separate the effects of the message, media, frequency of exposure, and competitive responses in an attempt to determine advertising effects. Even if the company could determine the cause of a problem, it faces the difficulty of prescribing the appropriate action to take. The result of these difficulties is that marketers continue to struggle with quantifying the value of marketing efforts and with creating a culture of accountability for marketing performance.[12]

## Design Decisions for Strategic Monitoring Systems

While it's difficult to argue that managers can actually "control" anything they are asked to monitor, strategic monitoring is concerned with evaluating a firm's SBU-level strategies (see Exhibit 18.9 for the kinds of questions this type of system is designed to answer). Such a system is difficult to implement because there is usually a substantial amount of time between strategy formulation and when a strategy takes hold and results are evident. Since both the external and internal environments are constantly evolving, strategic monitoring must provide some way of changing the firm's thrust if new information about the environment and/or the firm's performance so dictates. Inevitably, much of this intermediate assessment is based on information about the marketplace and the results obtained from the firm's marketing plan.

**STRATEGIC ISSUE**

*Strategic monitoring must provide some way of changing the firm's thrust if new information about the environment and/or the firm's performance so dictates.*

## Identifying Key Variables

To implement strategic monitoring, a company must identify the key variables to monitor, which are usually the major assumptions made in formulating the strategy. The key variables to monitor are of two types:

- Those concerned with external forces.
- Those concerned with the effects of certain actions taken by the firm to implement the strategy.

## Exhibit 18.9

EXAMPLES OF QUESTIONS A STRATEGIC MONITORING SYSTEM SHOULD BE ABLE TO ANSWER

1. What changes in the environment have negatively affected the current strategy (e.g., demographic or social trends, interest rates, government controls, or price changes in substitute products)?

2. What changes have major competitors made in their objectives and strategies?

3. What changes have occurred in the industry in such attributes as capacity, entry barriers, and substitute products?

4. What new opportunities or threats have derived from changes in the environment, competitors' strategies, or the nature of the industry?

5. What changes have occurred in the industry's key success factors?

6. To what extent is the firm's current strategy consistent with the preceding changes?

Examples of the former include changes in the external environment such as changes in long-term demand, the advent of new technology, a change in governmental legislation, and actions by a competitor. Examples of the latter types (actions by the firm) include the firm's advertising efforts to change attitudes and in-store merchandising activities designed to improve product availability.

The frameworks and analytical tools for market and competitive analysis that we discussed in Chapter 3 are useful in determining what variables to monitor in a strategic monitoring system. Deciding exactly which variables to monitor is a company-specific decision; in general, it should focus on those variables most likely to affect the company's future position within its industry group.

## Tracking and Monitoring

The next step is to specify what information or measures are needed on each of the key variables to determine whether the implementation of the strategic plan is on schedule—and if not, why not. The firm can use the plan as an early-warning system as well as a diagnostic tool. If, for example, the firm has made certain assumptions about the rate at which market demand will increase, it should monitor industry sales regularly. If it has made assumptions about advertising and its effect on attitudes, it would be likely to use measures of awareness, trial, and repeat buying. In any event, the firm must closely examine the relevance, accuracy, and cost of obtaining the needed measures.

The advent of e-mail, intranets, and other digital tools for disseminating information has made it easier for sometimes far-flung managers to monitor strategic developments. Critical strategic information can now be monitored on a real-time basis anywhere in the world.

## Strategy Reassessment

This can take place at periodic intervals—for example, quarterly or annually, when the firm evaluates its performance to date along with major changes in the external environment. A strategic monitoring system can also alert management of a significant change in its external/internal environments. This involves setting triggers to signal the need to reassess the viability of the firm's strategy. It requires a specification of both the level at which an alert will be called and the combination of events that must occur before the firm reacts. For example, total industry sales of 10 percent less than expected for a single month would not be likely to trigger a response, whereas a 25 percent drop would. Or a firm might decide that triggering will occur only after three successive months in which a difference of 10 percent occurred in each month.

In today's fast-changing world, strategy reassessment may happen much more quickly, as competitive and technological developments cause firms to quickly change their entire strategies and business models. Such developments enabled Amazon to grow from an online bookseller into a veritable online global shopping mall, with a huge assortment of merchandise categories and a local presence in several countries across the globe.

## Design Decisions for Marketing Metrics

Designing systems to measure marketing performance at the product-market and line-item levels involves answering four essential questions:

- Who needs what information?
- When and how often is the information needed?

- In what media and in what format(s) or levels of aggregation should the information be provided?
- What contingencies should be planned for?

In essence, designing a marketing performance measurement system is like designing the dashboard of a car. Such a system needs to include the most critical metrics to assess whether the car or the business is progressing toward its objectives. Thus, for a

car, the dashboard includes a speed gauge and odometer to measure progress toward the destination, a fuel gauge, warning lights for engine and braking system malfunction, and so on, but it typically does not indicate how much windshield wiper fluid remains, how much weight the car is

carrying, or other relatively nonessential indicators. The same holds true for a business: The "drivers" who are managing the business need to know certain essential information while the "car"—or strategy—is running, whereas other less crucial indicators can be omitted or provided only when requested. Designing such an information dashboard for the top management team is a good place to start, since it provides a clear signal about the kinds of data to which the rest of the organization should attend. We now address the four key questions, or **design parameters,** of marketing performance measurement systems.[13]

# Who Needs What Information?

Marketing performance measurement systems are designed to ensure that the company achieves the customer image, sales, profits, and other objectives set forth in its marketing and strategic plans. In the aggregate, these plans reflect the outcomes of the company's or the SBU's planning efforts, which have specified how resources are to be allocated across markets, products, and marketing-mix activities. These plans, as we noted in Chapter 17, include line-item budgets and typically specify the actions expected of each organizational unit—whether inside or outside the marketing function or department—and deemed necessary to attain the company's customer, financial, and competitive positioning objectives. The first and foremost objective for marketing is often the level of sales the company or the product-market entry achieves.

Who needs sales information? Top management needs it. Functional managers in other parts of the organization—manufacturing, procurement, finance, and so on—need it. Marketing managers responsible for the various marketing-mix activities, from product design to pricing to channel management to selling and other promotional activities, need it. Even the ad agency needs it.

**Sales Analysis**   A sales analysis involves breaking down aggregate sales data into such categories as products, end-user customers, channel intermediaries, sales territories, and order size. The objective of such an analysis is to find areas of strength and weakness; for example, products producing the greatest and least volume, customers accounting for the bulk of the revenues, and salespersons and territories performing the best and the worst.

Sales analysis recognizes that aggregate sales and cost data often mask the real situation. Sales analysis not only helps to evaluate and control marketing efforts, but also helps management to better formulate objectives and strategies and administer such nonmarketing activities as production planning, inventory management, and facilities planning.

An important decision in designing the firm's sales analysis system concerns which units of analysis to use. Most companies analyze data in the following groupings:

- Geographical areas—regions, counties, and sales territories.
- Product, package size, and grade.

- Customer—by type and size.
- Channel intermediary—such as type and/or size of retailer.
- Method of sale—mail, phone, channel, internet, or direct.
- Size of order—less than $10, $10–100, and so on.

These breakdowns are not mutually exclusive. Most firms perform sales analyses hierarchically, for example, by county within a sales territory within a sales region. Further, they usually combine product and account breakdowns with a geographical one, for example, the purchase of product X by large accounts located in sales territory Y, which is part of region A. Only by conducting sales analysis on a hierarchical basis using a combination of breakdowns can analysts be at all sure that they have made every reasonable attempt to locate the opportunities and problems facing their firms.

### Sales Analysis by Territory

The first step in a sales territory analysis is to decide which geographical control unit to use. In the United States, the county is the typical choice since it can be combined into larger units such as sales territories, and it is also a geographical area for which many kinds of data are available, such as population, employment, income, and retail sales. Analysts can compare actual sales (derived from company invoices) by county against a standard such as a sales quota that takes into account such factors as market potential and last year's sales adjusted for inflation. They can then single out territories that fall below standard for special attention. Is competition unusually strong? Has less selling effort been expended here? Is the salesforce weak? Studies dealing with such questions as these help a company improve its weak areas and exploit its stronger ones. Category and brand development indices, such as those described in Chapter 6, (see Exhibit 6.5) are often used in assessing sales performance by territory.

Exhibit 18.10 illustrates a sales territory analysis. It shows that only one territory out of seven shown exceeded its 2011 quota, or standard of performance, and by just $18,112.

**STRATEGIC ISSUE**

*Category and brand development indices are often used in assessing sales performance by territory.*

The other six territories accounted for a total of $394,685 under quota. Territory 3 alone accounted for 55 percent of the total shortfall. The sales and the size of the quota in this territory suggest the need for further breakdowns, especially by accounts and products. Such breakdowns may reveal that the firm needs to allocate more selling resources to this territory. The company needs to improve its sales primarily in territories 3 and 5. If it can reach its potential in these two territories, overall sales would increase by $301,911, assuming that the quotas set are valid.

## Exhibit 18.10

SALES ANALYSIS BASED ON SELECTED SALES TERRITORIES

| Sales Territory | Salesperson | (1) Company Sales 2011 | (2) Sales Quota 2011 | (3) Overage, Underage | (4) Percent of Potential Performance |
|---|---|---|---|---|---|
| 1 | Barlow | $552,630 | $585,206 | –$32,576 | 94% |
| 2 | Burrows | 470,912 | 452,800 | +18,112 | 104 |
| 3 | White | 763,215 | 981,441 | –218,226 | 77 |
| 4 | Finch | 287,184 | 297,000 | –9,816 | 96 |
| 5 | Brown | 380,747 | 464,432 | –83,685 | 82 |
| 6 | Roberts | 494,120 | 531,311 | –37,191 | 93 |
| 7 | Macini | 316,592 | 329,783 | –13,191 | 96 |

Without a standard against which to compare results, the conclusions would be much different. Thus, if only company sales were considered (column 1), White would be the best salesperson and Finch the worst. By using sales quotas as a performance standard, White was not the best but the worst salesperson, with a 77 percent rating.

### Sales Analysis by Product

Over time, a company's product line tends to become overcrowded and less profitable unless management takes strong and continuous action to eliminate no-longer-profitable items. By eliminating weak products and concentrating on strong ones, a company can sometimes increase its profits substantially. An important element in Procter & Gamble's strong performance under former CEO A. G. Lafley was the company's renewed emphasis on its 17 billion-dollar brands, for which sales volume was up an average of 7 percent in 2006 alone.[14] Before deciding which products to abandon, management must study such variables as market-share trends, contribution margins, scale effects, and the extent to which a product is complementary with other items in the line.[15]

A product sales analysis is particularly helpful when combined with account size and sales territory data. Using such an analysis, managers can often pinpoint substantial opportunities and develop specific tactics to take advantage of them. For example, one firm's analysis revealed that sales of one of its highest-margin products were down in all the Scandinavian sales territories. Further investigation showed that a regional producer was aggressively promoting a recently modified product with reduced prices. An analysis of the competing product revealed questionable reliability under certain operating conditions. The salesforce used this information to turn around the sales problem.

### Sales Analysis by Order Size

Sales analysis by order size may identify which orders, in monetary size, are not profitable. For example, if some customers frequently place small orders that require salesforce attention and need to be processed, picked, and shipped, a problem of some importance may exist.

Analysis by order size locates products, sales territories, and customer types and sizes where small orders prevail. Such an analysis may lead to setting a minimum order size, charging extra for small orders, training sales reps to develop larger orders, and dropping some accounts. An example of such an analysis involved a nationwide needlework product distributor, which found that 28 percent of all its orders were $10 and under. A study revealed that the average cost of servicing such orders was $12.82. The analysis also showed that the company did not break even until the order size reached $20. Based on these findings, the company installed a $35 minimum order, charged a special handling fee of $7.50 on all orders below $35, and alerted its field sales reps and telephone salespeople to the problem. As a result, the company increased its profits substantially.

### Sales Analysis by Customer

Analysts use procedures similar to those described earlier to analyze sales by customers. Such analyses typically show that a relatively small percentage of customers account for a large percentage of sales. For example, the needlework products distributor cited previously found that 13 percent of its accounts represented 67 percent of its total sales. Frequently, a study of sales calls shows that the salesforce spends a disproportionate amount of its time with the small accounts as compared with the larger ones. Shifting some of this effort to the larger accounts may well increase sales.

Tesco, using its ClubCard data, now categorizes its customers into various buckets, or market segments, based on the premise that "you are what you eat." It then tailors quarterly coupon mailings based on the customer's own shopping behavior. The "Loyal Low Spenders" get different coupons than the "High Spending Superstore Families," for example. Within these still broad segments, the quarterly offers are further tailored. Tesco mails more than 400,000 variations each quarter.[16]

The key to sales analysis by customer is to find useful decompositions of the sales data that are meaningful in a behavioral way. Three useful variables in doing so are recency (how recently did the customer last buy), frequency (how often), and monetary value (how much did the customer spend). These variables can lead to the development of metrics that can aid the marketer in defining market segments and in understanding the dynamics that underlie changes in sales.[17]

**Line-Item Margin and Expense Analysis**    Sales data are not the only marketing performance information needed. Gross and net margins must be tracked, and the effectiveness and efficiency of all line-item marketing expenses must be measured. The designers of marketing performance measurement systems must develop appropriate metrics to track the critical performance indicators for margins and expenses so that timely midcourse corrections can be made. Thus, the weeks-on-hand metric, which tells a Benetton sweater buyer how quickly each style is selling, tells her whether to buy more of a particular style if it is selling well or mark it down if it is not moving. Making such decisions on a timely basis can have a profound effect on gross margins. A not-so-pretty sweater may be more salable at 25 percent off before Christmas than at 60 percent off after December 26. The same idea holds for swimsuits in summer, as shown in Exhibit 18.11.

Because budgets project revenues and expenses for a given time period, they are a vital part of the firm's planning and control activities. They provide the basis for a continuous evaluation and comparison of what was planned with what actually happened. In this sense, budgeted revenues and profits serve as objectives against which to measure performance in sales, profits, and actual costs.

Budget analysis requires that managers continuously monitor marketing expense ratios to make certain the company does not overspend in its effort to reach its objectives. Managers also evaluate the magnitude and pattern of deviations from the target ratios. Managers of the various marketing units often have their own control measures. For example, advertising managers track advertising costs per 1,000 target audience, buyers per media vehicle, print ad readership, size and composition of TV audiences, and attitude change. Sales managers typically track number of calls per salesperson, costs per call, sales per call, and new accounts.

---

**Exhibit 18.11    WEB-BASED PRICING METRICS FATTEN SWIMSUIT MARGINS**

Steven Schwartz, senior vice president of planning at Casual Male, the 410-store U.S. clothing chain selling big and tall sizes, knew that swimsuit prices had to fall after the Fourth of July holiday in the United States. But was the optimal timing the same in the lake country in Minnesota as at the beaches of Florida or New Jersey or California? Guesswork wasn't good enough, so Schwartz and his team loaded boatloads of the prior year's swimsuit sales data into a web-based pricing system to get some answers. Northeasterners stopped dead in their tracks in July. Midwesterners kept buying into August. Sun Belt shoppers never stopped at all.

By making smarter pricing decisions, Casual Male improved its swimsuit gross margins by 25 percent over the prior year. Dillard's, the department store chain, saw 5 percent to 6 percent increases in gross margin across 17 departments using similar tools. Best of all, sales rose, too. Swimsuits may be getting skimpier, but their margins are moving the other way!

*Source:* Faith Keenan, "The Price Is Really Right," *BusinessWeek,* March 31, 2003, pp. 62–67. For more on Casual Male, see *www .casualmale.com.*

Recent advances in data gathering and analytics have led to a new breed of integrated marketing software such as Aprimo (*www.aprimo.com*). Such tools enable marketing managers to keep track of the varied kinds of activities that comprise any integrated marketing communications effort. They bring together data on all kinds of marketing projects and campaigns into a coherent and integrated platform, so that various elements of the marketing program—from e-mail marketing, to a new branding campaign still under development, to your media spend by region or by channel—can be tracked in a common manner.

# SEO and SEM Analysis

In today's online world, where for many companies online traffic to the website is an important generator of leads, sales transactions, and more, the inherent measurability of the online world means that metrics to examine the effectiveness and efficiency of websites are essential.

**Search engine optimization** (SEO) refers to a set of techniques that helps ensure that a company's web pages are ranked highly when consumers search for information using Google, China's Baidu, or any other search engine. The search engines' **organic search,** as it is called, is driven by proprietary algorithms which vary from one search engine to another and are programmed to look for certain things. SEO's job is to figure out what these things are, despite that fact that this is a moving target, and optimize the company's web pages by, for example, ensuring that commonly searched-for keywords appear where the search engines are programmed to look for them. The results of a company's effective use of SEO are that a company's web pages rank higher in the results returned from consumers' searches—the left-hand side of a page on Google's search results, for example— than they would otherwise.

The Villa Poggiale, a lovely place for a family vacation in the heart of the Chianti region in Tuscany, would love it if its page would come up near the top of the listings when vacationers search for Tuscany or Chianti hotels, and might be tempted to use SEO to accomplish that goal. Because the Villa Poggiale is a small property, however, it is unlikely to rank nearly as high on the search engines as more widely visited sites offering more properties, such as TripAdvisor. Thus it might decide that **search engine marketing** (SEM) is a better way to go.

SEM is a related but fundamentally different activity from SEO. It involves buying keywords—AdWords, in Google-speak—for which consumers are likely to search so that one's **paid links,** on the right-hand side of a page of Google search results, come up at or near the top of the **paid search** listings. Villa Poggiale may choose to buy AdWords such as "Chianti hotels" or "Tuscany hotels" so that it ranks near the top of the paid search listings when consumers type either of those phrases into Google. Optimizing SEM means bidding a high enough price for your site to be highly ranked, but not so high that the cost of buying the AdWords is higher than their value as leads. AdWords are a main source of revenue for search engines like Google.

For marketers whose websites are intended to deliver completed transactions—booking a week's stay on the Villa Poggiale site, for example—there is a host of other metrics that the villa's **webmaster** should track to measure how effective each of its web pages is. The goal, of course, is that the consumer's journey from the Villa Poggiale **landing page** to its various other pages ultimately ends up on the booking page with an inquiry at least, or a completed booking, at best. The attractiveness of the photos, the way copy is worded, and the design and

**STRATEGIC ISSUE**

*"There's nothing more wasteful than doing a great job on SEO or SEM and having users visit a set of pages that just don't work."*

mechanics of the overall website—Do pages load slowly or quickly, for example?—all play important roles in determining whether the consumer follows though and makes a booking, or whether she goes elsewhere. Savvy online marketers run experiments—Which photo works best, or what copy keeps the visitor hooked?—and use information on the dropout rates from page to page, in order to improve the productivity of the traffic that visits the site as a result of effective SEO or SEM efforts. There's nothing more wasteful than doing a great job on SEO or SEM and having users visit a set of pages that just don't work.

In the paragraphs above, we've only scratched the surface of a few of the analytical techniques that separate the best online marketers from the also-rans. The use of these and other kinds of **web analytics,** which take advantage of the inherent measurability of the web, opens a wide array of possibilities in an exciting new world in which marketing results can be clearly linked to marketing actions.

## When and How Often Is the Information Needed?

Timeliness is a key criterion for the development of a marketing performance measurement system. As we have seen, Walmart's systems provide sales information at the store and item level on an up-to-the-minute basis. More commonly, managers attend to performance information—whether for sales, margins, or expenses—on a periodic basis, since they don't have time or the need to assess the performance of every item at every minute of every day. Buyers and merchandise managers in retailing firms typically assess item and category sales performance on a weekly basis. In fashion categories, such as women's apparel, where timeliness is especially important, having sales information a couple of days, or even hours, ahead of competitors can make the difference between obtaining more of a hot-selling item and being left in a faster-moving competitor's dust. For global retailers such as Mango, fast data is a crucial driver of the company's fast-fashion strategy (see Exhibit 18.12).

Store payroll expense, another key performance criterion for retailers that impacts both customer service and profitability, is typically measured on a weekly basis, though store managers may be encouraged to send employees home if business is unexpectedly slow on a given day or call in extra help when more is needed. The performance of industrial salespeople—in terms of number of sales calls, sales volume, expense control, and other indicators—is typically done on a monthly basis, though some firms may do so more or less frequently as they see fit. Strategic control indicators, such as changes in market share, macro trends, and so

---

### Exhibit 18.12   MANGO BREAKS THE FASHION RULES

Fashion retailers know that having the right goods in the right stores at the right time is the name of the fashion game. But doing so isn't easy, what with fickle consumers and their changing tastes in everything from hemlines to colors to silhouettes. David Egea, merchandising director at Mango, the Barcelona-based fast-fashion chain with more than 1200 boutiques in 91 countries, says, "To react and have what people want, we have to break some rules."

Breaking the rules, in Mango's case, means that designs for new items can move from sketchpad to stores in as little as four weeks. By sourcing its styles close to home—instead of making big commitments to Asian suppliers with longer lead times—Mango can drop what's not selling and move quickly into what's hot, as it did in February 2004, when its collection of leather-trimmed black styles inspired by the movie *Matrix* weren't selling. Out went the black, and in came softer, more feminine styles.

Mango's fast-fashion system demands flexibility and speed, as well as up-to-the-minute sales data from the stores, all of which have paid big dividends for the young company, less than 30 years old. With fast data and fast fashion, "We know how to improvise," says Egan.

*Sources:* Erin White, "Speeding Up Fast Fashion," *The Wall Street Journal Europe,* May 28–30, 2004, p. A5; Mango.com website at *http://www.mango.com/web/pv/servicios/IN/franquicias/mangoMundo.htm.* For more on Mango, see *www.mango.com.*

on, are likely to be measured and reported less frequently because these kinds of longer-term issues may not be readily apparent or may give false alarms at more frequent intervals.

## In What Media and in What Format(s) or Levels of Aggregation Should the Information Be Provided?

Advances in information technology have made possible the measurement and reporting of marketing performance information with previously unheard-of case of access and timeliness, without even printing the data! As we have seen, Walmart's sales information is available on its intranet on an up-to-the-minute basis. In other companies, salespeople around the world now log on to company intranets to see the latest order status of a customer before they walk in the door on a sales call. But *having* good and timely information and *reporting* it in such a manner that it is easy and quick to use are different things. Imagine a Mango buyer having to manually add up the performance of various styles to determine how the category or a particular vendor is performing. Reports should provide such aggregation, of course, but someone must decide what sort of aggregation is most useful for each information user.

**STRATEGIC ISSUE**

*Having good and timely information and reporting it in such a manner that it is easy and quick to use are different things.*

The format or medium in which performance information is presented can make a big difference to the manager using the data. Weekly weeks-on-hand sales reports that retail buyers and merchandise managers depend on are most usefully reported in order of how fast the styles are selling, rather than alphabetically or some other way. The styles at the top of the report (those with little stock on hand, as measured by their weeks-on-hand sales rate) are candidates for reorders. Styles at the bottom of the report (the ugly wool sweater in mid-November with 25 weeks of inventory on hand) are candidates for markdowns. The ones in between may need little attention. Once a season ends, a different report, aggregating styles by vendor, perhaps, might be useful to determine which suppliers have performed well and which have performed poorly across the assortment of styles they provide. Thoughtful attention to the format in which marketing performance information is reported, to the levels at which it is aggregated, for different kinds of decision purposes, and for different users can provide a company with a significant competitive advantage. As we noted earlier in this chapter, it took Kmart many years to come close to Walmart's system of tracking and reporting store and item sales performance.

## Does Your System of Marketing Metrics Measure Up?

A key issue in developing a set of marketing metrics as part of an overall performance measurement system is getting the metrics aligned with the strategy. Just as professional athletes measure their performance in order to raise the bar, so too must marketing managers quantify and measure what they accomplish against what was planned. Doing so is particularly difficult if there's no explicit strategy or no culture of measurement that goes beyond summary financial performance.

As we've seen in this chapter, marketing metrics involve far more than simple analysis of the variances reported by the company's accounting system. So where should one start? A good first step is to identify the elements in an informational dashboard that the top management team can use to track marketing performance from period to period. Doing so will help gain top management involvement in marketing issues, and it will identify some of the data to which the rest of the organization should attend. Exhibit 18.13 lists 10 questions for assessing any firm's system of marketing metrics and for identifying some of the elements that its dashboard might report. For many companies, these questions provide a useful wake-up call.

## Exhibit 18.13

DO YOUR MARKETING METRICS MEASURE UP?

Ten questions for your company's top executive team

1. Does the exec regularly and formally assess marketing performance?
   (a) Yearly (b) Six-monthly (c) Quarterly (d) More often (e) Rarely (f) Never

2. What does it understand by "customer value"?
   (a) Don't know. We are not clear about this (b) Value of the customer to the business (as in 'customer lifetime value') (c) Value of what the company provides from the customer's point of view (d) Sometimes one, sometimes the other

3. How much time does the exec give to marketing issues?
   —%

4. Does the business/marketing plan show the nonfinancial corporate goals and link them to market goals?
   (a) No/no plan (b) Corporate no, market yes (c) Yes to both

5. Does the plan show the comparison of your marketing performance with competitors or the market as a whole?
   (a) No/no plan (b) Yes, clearly (c) In between

6. What is your main marketing asset called?
   (a) Brand equity (b) Reputation (c) Other term (d) We have no term

7. Does the exec's performance review involve a quantified review of the main marketing asset and how it has changed?
   (a) Yes to both (b) Yes but only financially (brand valuation) (c) Not really

8. Has the exec quantified what "success" would look like 5 or 10 years from now?
   (a) No (b) Yes (c) Don't know

9. Does your strategy have quantified milestones to indicate progress toward that success?
   (a) No (b) Yes (c) What strategy?

10. Are the marketing performance indicators seen by the exec aligned with these milestones?
    (a) No (b) Yes, external (customers and competitors) (c) Yes, internal (employees and innovativeness) (d) Yes, both

*Source:* Tim Ambler, *Marketing and the Bottom Line. The Marketing Metrics to Pump Up Cash Flow,* 2nd edition. (Copyright © 2003. Pearson Education Limited)

# What Contingencies Should Be Planned For?

Because all strategies and the action plans designed to implement them are based on assumptions about the future, they are subject to considerable risk. Too often, assumptions are regarded as facts; and little attention is paid to what action or actions can be taken if any or all of the assumptions turn out to be wrong.

Managers, therefore, often follow a contingency planning process that includes the elements shown in Exhibit 18.14: identifying critical assumptions, assigning probabilities of being right about the assumptions, ranking the importance of each assumption, tracking and monitoring the action plan, setting the "triggers" that will activate the contingency plan, and specifying alternative response options. We discuss these steps briefly as follows.

**Identifying Critical Assumptions**    Because there are simply too many assumptions to track them all, contingency plans must cover only the more important ones. Assumptions about events beyond the control of the individual firm but that strongly affect the entry's strategic objectives are particularly important. For example, assumptions about the rate of market growth coupled with the entry's market share will strongly affect the entry's profitability objectives. The effect of a wrong assumption here can be either good or bad, and the contingency plan must be prepared to handle both. If the market grows at a rate

## Exhibit 18.14

THE CONTINGENCY PLANNING PROCESS

Identifying critical assumptions about the future

Determining probability of each critical assumption's being right

Rank ordering of critical assumptions

Tracking/monitoring of action plan

Setting triggers to activate contingency plan

Specifying alternative response options

faster then expected, then the question of how to respond needs to be considered. Too often contingency plans focus only on the downside.

Another type of uncontrollable event that can strongly affect sales and profits is competitive actions. This is particularly true with a new entry (when a competitor responds with its own new product), although it can apply with more mature products (competitor's advertising is increased). Assumptions about industry price levels must be examined in depth because any price deterioration can quickly erode margins and profits.

Assumptions about the effects of certain actions taken by the firm to attain its strategic objectives also need to be considered in depth. Examples include the firm's advertising objectives, which are based on assumptions about an improvement or maintenance of consumer attitudes toward the product's characteristics compared with competing brands, or the monies allocated to merchandising to improve the product's availability. Further, once the targeted levels of the various primary objectives are reached, there are assumptions about what will happen to sales and share.

**Determining Probabilities**   This step consists of assigning to the critical assumptions probabilities of being right. These probabilities must be considered in terms of the consequences of being wrong. Thus, assumptions that have a low probability of being wrong but could affect the firm strongly need to be considered in depth (for automakers, for instance, political turmoil in oil-producing countries in the middle east.

**Rank Ordering the Critical Assumptions**   If assumptions are categorized on the basis of their importance, the extent to which they are controllable, and the confidence management has in them, then the basis for rank ordering the assumptions and drafting the contingency plan has been set forth. Ordinarily, these criteria will have screened out those assumptions that need not be included—those with a low impact and those about which there is a high confidence they will not occur. Assumptions that relate to uncontrollable events should, however, be monitored if they strongly affect the entry's strategic objectives since the firm can react to them. For example, if the assumption about the rate of market growth is wrong, then the firm can either slow or increase its investments in plant construction.

**Tracking and Monitoring**    The next step is to specify what information or measures are needed to determine whether the implementation of the action plan is on schedule—and if not, why not. The contingency plan is, therefore, an early warning system as well as a diagnostic tool. If, for example, the firm has made certain assumptions about the rate of market demand increase, then it would monitor industry sales on a regular basis. If assumptions were made about advertising and its effect on attitudes, then measures of awareness, trial, and repeat buying would be likely to be used. Relevance, accuracy, and cost of obtaining the needed measures must be examined in depth. Some of the information needed in the contingency plan might have been specified in the control plan, in which case it is already available.

**Activating the Contingency Plan**    This step involves setting the "triggers" to activate the contingency plan. It requires a specification of both the level at which an alert will be called and the combination of events that must occur before the firm reacts. If, for example, total industry sales were 10 percent less than expected for a single month, this might not be likely to trigger a response, whereas a 25 percent drop would. Or a firm may decide the triggering would occur only after three successive months in which a difference of 10 percent occurred. Triggers must be defined precisely and responsibility assigned for putting the contingency plan into operation.

**Specifying Response Options**    Actually, the term *contingency plan* is somewhat misleading. It implies that the firm knows in advance exactly how it will respond if one or more of its assumptions go awry. This implication is unrealistic because there are a great many ways for critical assumptions to turn out wrong. To compound the problem, the firm's preplanned specific responses can be difficult to implement, depending on the situation and how it develops. This can lead to a set of responses that build in intensity. Thus, most firms develop a set of optional responses that are not detailed to any great extent in an effort to provide flexibility and ensure further study of the forces that caused the alert.

# Global Marketing Monitoring

Measuring the performance of global marketing activities is more difficult than with domestic marketing, primarily because of the number of countries involved, each presenting a unique set of opportunities and threats. This makes it difficult to monitor simultaneously a variety of environments and to prescribe corrective action on an individual country basis where appropriate. Differences in language and customs, accentuated by distance, further compound the control problem.

Nonetheless, global companies typically use essentially the same format for both their domestic and foreign operations, though report frequency and extent of detail can vary by the subsidiary's size and environmental uncertainties. The great advantage of using a single system is that it facilitates comparisons between operating units and communications between home office and local managers. If Mango didn't have uniform systems across its 1200-plus stores in 91 countries, it simply would not have been able to grow as it has.

On the surface, the use of **electronic data interchange** and the internet should simplify performance evaluation across countries. While this is true in terms of budget control, it leaves much to be desired in terms of understanding the reasons for any deviations.

# A Tool for Periodic Assessment of Marketing Performance: The Marketing Audit

While marketing performance measurement systems are essential for tracking day-to-day, week-to-week, and month-to-month performance to see that planned results are actually delivered, it is sometimes useful to step back and take a longer view of the marketing performance of an SBU or of the entire company. Marketing audits are growing in popularity, especially for firms with a variety of SBUs that differ in their market orientation. They are both a control and planning activity that involves a comprehensive review of the firm's or SBU's total marketing efforts cutting across all products and business units. Thus, they are broader in scope and cover longer time horizons than sales and profitability analyses.

**STRATEGIC ISSUE**

*While marketing performance measurement systems are essential, it is sometimes useful to step back and take a longer view of the marketing performance of a SBU or of the entire company by using marketing audits.*

Our concern here is at the individual SBU level or the entire company, for smaller or single-business firms. Such an audit covers both the SBU's objectives and strategy and its plan of action for each product-market entry. It provides an assessment of each SBU's current overall competitive position as well as that of its individual product-market entries. It requires an analysis of each of the marketing-mix elements and how well they are being implemented in support of each entry. The audit must take into account any environmental changes that can affect the SBU's strategy and product-market action programs.

## Types of Audits

Audits are normally conducted for such areas as the SBU's marketing environment, objectives and strategy, planning and control systems, organization, productivity, and individual marketing activities such as sales and advertising. These areas are shown in Exhibit 18.15 with examples of the kinds of data needed and serve as the basis for the discussion that follows.

- The **marketing environment audit** requires an analysis of the firm's present and future environment with respect to its macro components, as discussed in Chapter 3. The intent is to identify the more significant trends to see how they affect the firm's customers, competitors, channel intermediaries, and suppliers.

- The **objectives and strategy audit** calls for an assessment of how appropriate these internal factors are, given current major environmental trends and any changes in the firm's resources.

- The unit's **planning and control system audit** evaluates the adequacy of the systems that develop the firm's product-market entry action plans and the control and reappraisal process. The audit also evaluates the firm's new product development procedures.

- The **organization audit** deals with the firm's overall structure (can it meet the changing needs of the marketplace), how the marketing department is organized (can it accommodate the planning requirements of the firm's assortment of brands), and the extent of synergy between the various marketing units (are there good relations between sales and merchandising).

- The **marketing productivity audit** evaluates the profitability of the company's individual products, markets (including sales territories), and key accounts. It also studies the cost-effectiveness of the various marketing activities.

- The **marketing functions audit** examines, in depth, how adequately the firm handles each of the marketing-mix elements. Questions relating to the *product* concern the attainability of the

## Exhibit 18.15

SOME MAJOR AREAS COVERED IN A MARKETING AUDIT AND QUESTIONS CONCERNING EACH
FOR A CONSUMER GOODS COMPANY

| Audit area | Examples of Questions to Be Answered |
| --- | --- |
| Marketing environment | What opportunities and/or threats derive from the firm's present and future environment; that is, what demographic, social, technological, political, economic, and natural, trends are significant? How will these trends affect the firm's target markets, competitors, suppliers, and channel intermediaries? Which opportunities/threats emerge from within the firm? |
| Objectives and strategy | How logical are the company's objectives, given the more significant opportunities/threats and its relative resources? How valid is the firm's strategy, given the anticipated environment, including the actions of competitors? |
| Planning and control system | Does the firm have adequate and timely information about consumers' satisfaction with its products? With the actions of competitors? With the services of intermediaries? Is the new product development process effective and efficient? |
| Organization | Does the organizational structure fit the evolving needs of the marketplace? Can it handle the planning needed at the individual product/brand level? |
| Marketing productivity | How profitable is each of the firm's products/brands? How effective and efficient is each of its major marketing activities? |
| Marketing functions | How well does the product line meet the line's objectives? How well do the products/brands meet the needs of the target markets? Does pricing reflect cross-elasticities, experience effects, and relative costs? Is the product readily available? What is the level of retail stockouts? What percentage of large stores carries the firm's in-store displays? Is the salesforce large enough? Is the firm spending enough on advertising? |

present product-line objective, the extent to which individual products fit the needs of the target markets, and whether the product line should be expanded or contracted. *Price* questions have to do with price elasticity; experience effects, relative costs, and the actions of major competitors; and consumers' perceptions of the relationship between a product's price and its value. *Distribution* questions center on coverage, functions performed, and cost-effectiveness. Questions about *advertising* focus on advertising objectives and strategies, media schedules, and the procedures used to develop advertising messages. The audit of the salesforce covers its objectives, role, size, coverage, organization, and duties plus the quality of its selection, training, motivation, compensation, and control activities.

- The company's **ethical audit** evaluates the extent to which the company engages in ethical and socially responsible marketing. Clearly this audit goes well beyond monitoring to make sure the firm is well within the law in its market behavior. If the company has a written code of ethics, then the main purpose of this audit is to make certain that it is disseminated, understood, and practiced.

- The **product manager audit,** especially in consumer goods companies, seeks to determine whether product managers are channeling their efforts in the best ways possible. They are queried on what they're doing versus what they *ought* to be doing. They are also asked to rate the extent to which various support units were helpful.

# Measuring and Delivering Marketing Performance

As we've seen in this final chapter, the challenges entailed in measuring expenditures in marketing programs in relation to marketing performance in such a manner as to produce information that is timely, relevant, easy to use, cost-effective, useful to managers,

## Exhibit 18.16    DASHBOARDS: THE CEO'S KILLER APP?

ⓘ Jerry Driggs, COO of Little Earth Productions, a marketer of funky, eco-fashion clothing and accessories such as handbags made out of recycled license plates, used to run his business by the seat of his pants. It showed. Without a good system to keep track of the amount of raw materials his Chinese suppliers needed, it used to take Little Earth six weeks to make and ship a handbag. Too much cash was tied up in trim pieces and closures that weren't really needed. To solve his problems, Driggs spent four months installing a dashboard from NetSuite, a fast-growing software company that specializes in this arena. Now he gets critical information displayed in easy-to-read graphics whenever and wherever he needs it.

Little Earth and many much larger companies including Verizon, Home Depot, and Microsoft swear by their dashboards, which some observers now regard as the CEO's killer app, making details that used to be buried deep inside the business available at a moment's notice. "The dashboard puts me and more and more of our executives in real-time touch with the business," says CEO Ivan Seidenberg of Verizon. While some critics worry that executives will spend too much time glued to their PCs and that the instant availability of data can add to the pressures that line managers already face, Driggs is a convert. As he puts it, "All of those things that used to drive us crazy are literally at our fingertips. Once you see it is so intuitive, you wonder how we ran the business before."

*Source:* Spencer E. Ante, "Giving the Boss the Big Picture," *BusinessWeek,* European Edition, February 13, 2006, pp. 48–51. For more on Little Earth or NetSuite, see *http://shop.littlearth.com or www.netsuite.com.*

and credible across the organization are daunting. But tackling these challenges head-on can make the difference when it comes to the sort of superior returns on investment that companies such as Walmart—at least in their glory days—deliver year after year. While marketing audits and various kinds of decision support systems do not guarantee strong performance, they help responsible, committed managers make decisions on the basis of current and valid information instead of hunches or uninformed guesses. It is for this reason that companies are paying increased attention to the development of information dashboards that provide people at all levels—from board members to top execs to line managers who deal with customers every day—the information they need to make timely, well-informed decisions about marketing, operational, and a host of other crucial decisions (see Exhibit 18.16). Whether Walmart's strengths in gathering and putting to use management information will enable the company to recover its mojo remains to be seen.

Even in entrepreneurial start-ups, the rampant uncertainty about consumers' needs, their responses to a new offering, competitor responses, and a host of other issues means that the best-laid strategies outlined in the company's business plan rarely pan out. For this reason, many early stage companies are avoiding the straight jacket that a business plan can be and turning to dashboards as their key tool for planning their entrepreneurial journey and tracking their progress. A dashboard can identify the life-or-death metrics that can signal whether the company's "Plan A" is working and alert it to the need for mid-course pivots before it's too late.[18]

In companies of any size or stage, as the saying goes, what gets measured gets done. Measuring marketing performance and doing so effectively is the all-important icing on the marketing manager's cake. Measure well—and in a timely and easy-to-use fashion—and performance is likely to follow.

# TAKE-AWAYS

1. Most managers and entrepreneurs are evaluated primarily on the results they deliver. Effective design of control systems, whether for strategic control or for marketing performance measurement, helps ensure the delivery of planned results. A step-by-step process for doing so is provided in this chapter.

2. Control systems that deliver the right information—in a timely manner and in media, formats, and levels of aggregation that users need and can easily use—can be important elements for establishing competitive advantage. Four key questions that designers of such systems should address are discussed in this chapter.

3. Building a dashboard to track the crucially important metrics in your business makes good sense, for companies large and small.

4. From time to time, it is useful to step back from day-to-day results and take a longer view of marketing performance for a company or an SBU. A marketing audit, as outlined in this chapter, is a useful tool for conducting such an assessment.

**Self-diagnostic questions to test your ability to apply the analytical tools and concepts in this chapter to marketing decision making may be found at this book's website at www.mhhe.com/mullins8e.**

# ENDNOTES

1. Based on Sam Walton, *Sam Walton: Made in America* (New York: Doubleday, 1992), pp. 85–86, 118, 212–27; Bill Saporito, "What Sam Walton Taught America," *Fortune,* May 4, 1992, p. 104; "Remove Control," *The Economist,* May 29, 1993, p. 90; Patricia Sellers, "Can Walmart Get Back the Magic?" *Fortune,* April 29, 1996, p. 132; Anthony Blanco, "Walmart's Midlife Crisis," *BusinessWeek* European Edition, April 30, 2007, pp. 46–56; Miguel Bustillo, "Walmart Thinks Outside the Big Box," *The Wall Street Journal* European Edition, August 14–16, 2009, p. 1; Miguel Bustillo, "Walmart Tries to Recapture Mr. Sam's Winning Formula," *The Wall Street Journal* European Edition, February 23, 2011, p. 14; and Walmart 2010 Annual Report and information from the company's website at *www.walmartstores.com.*

2. Calmetta Coleman, "Gap Inc. Stumbles as Respected CEO Loosens Reins," *The Wall Street Journal,* September 7, 2000, p. B4; and Heesun Wee, "The Challenge in Store for Gap," *BusinessWeek Online,* October 9, 2002.

3. Don O'Sullivan and Andrew V. Abela, "Marketing Performance Measurement Ability and Firm Performance," *Journal of Marketing* 71 (April 2007), pp. 79–93.

4. Robert S. Kaplan and David P. Norton, "Putting the Balanced Scorecard to Work," *Harvard Business Review,* September–October 1993.

5. Matthew Boyle, "Walmart's Magic Moment," *BusinessWeek* European Edition, June 15, 2009, pp. 51–52.

6. John Mullins and Randy Komisar, *Getting to Plan B: Breaking Through to a Better Business Model* (Boston: Harvard Business Press, 2009).

7. Jeremy Mann, "How to Steal the Best Ideas Around," *Fortune,* October 19, 1992, p. 102.

8. For more on activity-based costing, see any current textbook in managerial accounting, such as Ray H. Garrison, Eric Noreen, and Peter C. Brewer, *Managerial Accounting* (Burr Ridge, IL: McGraw-Hill, 2007).

9. Fred Reichheld and James Allen, "How Companies Can End the Cycle of Customer Abuse," *Financial Times,* March 23, 2006, p. 43.

10. See Rajkumar Venkatesan and V. Kumar, "A Customer Lifetime Value Framework for Customer Selection and Resource Allocation Strategy," *Journal of Marketing,* October 2004, pp. 106–25.

11. Elizabeth Rigby, "Eyes in the Till," *Financial Times FT Magazine,* November 11–12, 2006, pp. 16–22.

12. Deborah L. Vence, "Return on Investment," *Marketing News,* October 15, 2005, pp. 14–18.

13. For two overviews of recent thinking about measuring marketing performance, see Donald R. Lehmann, "Metrics for Making Marketing Matter," *Journal of Marketing,* October 2004, pp. 73–75; and Roland T. Rust, Tim Ambler, Gregory S. Carpenter, V. Kumar, and Rajendra Srivastava, "Measuring Marketing Productivity: Current Knowledge and Future Directions," *Journal of Marketing,* October 2004, pp. 76–89.

14. From the *Procter & Gamble 2006 Annual Report.*

15. Activity-based costing is particularly helpful to managers in determining product profitability since it allocates costs to products more accurately than traditional methods by breaking down overhead costs more precisely.

16. Clive Humby, Terry Hunt, with Tim Phillips, *Scoring Points: How Tesco Is Winning Customer Loyalty* (London: Kogan-Page, 2003), pp. 148–49.

17. Bruce Hardie, "Metrics for Customer Base Analysis," presentation to a conference of the Marketing Science Institute, *Does Marketing Measure Up?* London, June 21–22, 2004.

18. John Mullins and Randy Komisar, *Getting to Plan B: Breaking Through to a Better Business Model* (Boston: Harvard Business Press, 2009).

# Index